WHO'S WHO
IN
BRITISH SPORT

EDITED BY IAN PATEN

First published in Great Britain in 1994 by
Virgin Books
an imprint of Virgin Publishing Ltd
332 Ladbroke Grove
London W10 5AH

A catalogue record for this book is available
from the British Library

ISBN 0 86369 711 9

Book design by Roger Kohn
Typeset by
Phoenix Photosetting, Chatham, Kent
Printed and bound in Great Britain by
Mackays of Chatham PLC, Chatham, Kent

Acknowledgements
Particular thanks to Teresa Chris, Sally
Holloway, Paul Forty, Mal Peachey, and to
all those who completed and returned a
questionnaire.

— CONTENTS —

The entries in the body of the text include information supplied by competitors, and details of major honours reported elsewhere up to the end of February 1994. For subsequent developments (Cup wins, overseas tours, inter-club transfers, and retirements) readers are referred to the **Stop Press** section beginning on page 302

LIST OF ABBREVIATIONS

AAA	Amateur Athletics Association
ABA	Amateur Boxing Association
ACU	Auto-Cycle Union
AEWHA	All England Women's Hockey Association
AFA	Amateur Fencing Association
AIMS	Association of International Marathons and Road Races
ARA	Amateur Rowing Association
ARLFC	Amateur Rugby League Football Club
ASA	Amateur Swimming Association
Assoc.	Association
Aus.	Australia(n)
b.	born
BBC	British Broadcasting Corporation
BC	Boat Club
Beds.	Bedfordshire
Berks.	Berkshire
BHB	British Horseracing Board
BMBF	British Mountain Bike Federation
Brit.	British
Bucks.	Buckinghamshire
BUSF	British University Sporting Federation
C1	single Canadian canoe (similarly C2, etc.)
Cambs.	Cambridgeshire
capt.	captain
CBE	Commander, Order of the British Empire
CCC	County Cricket Club
ch.	children
champ.	champion
Champs.	championship(s)
CIS	Commonwealth of Independent States (former USSR)
Co.	County
CPE	College of Physical Education
CVO	Commander, Royal Victorian Order
d	died
d.	daughter
Derbys.	Derbyshire
Div.	Division
E.	East
ed(s)	editor(s)
F1	Formula One (similarly F2, etc.)
FA	Football Association
FC	Football Club
Fed.	Federation
FIM	Fédération Internationale Motocycliste
FITASC	Fédération Internationale de Tir aux Armes Sportives de Chasse (clay pigeon shooting)
FP	Former Pupils
GB	Great Britain

GBI	Great Britain and Ireland
Glos.	Gloucestershire
GP	Grand Prix
Gt	Great
Hants.	Hampshire
HC	Hockey Club
Herts.	Hertfordshire
IAAF	International Amateur Athletics Federation
IBF	International Boxing Federation
individ.	individual
int(s).	international(s)
IoM	Isle of Man
ISDE	International Six Days Enduro (motorcycling)
jnr(s)	junior(s)
K1	single kayak (similarly K2, etc.)
kg	kilograms
km	kilometre
Lancs.	Lancashire
LCC	Ladies' Cricket Club
Leics.	Leicestershire
LTA	Lawn Tennis Association
Ltd	Limited
m	metre(s)
m.	married
MBE	Member, Order of the British Empire
MCC	Marylebone Cricket Club
mem.	member
Middx	Middlesex
N.	North(ern)
nat.	national
NCA	National Cricket Association
N.E.	North-East
NH	National Hunt
NI	Northern Ireland
n.o.	not out
no.	number
Northants.	Northamptonshire
Notts.	Nottinghamshire
N.W.	North-West
NY	New York
NZ	New Zealand
OBE	Officer, Order of the British Empire
Oxon	Oxfordshire
PFA	Professional Footballers Association
PGA	Professional Golfers' Association
Pres.	President
Prof.	professional
qv	*quod vide* – see
RC	Rowing Club
rep.	represented

RFC	Rugby Football Club		**UEFA**	Union of European Football Associations
RLFC	Rugby League Football Club		**UK**	United Kingdom
RTTC	Road Time Trials Council (cycling)		**Univ.**	University (ies)
RU	Rugby Union		**US(A)**	United States (of America)
RYA	Royal Yachting Association		**USSR**	Union of Soviet Socialist Republics
s.	son		**Utd**	United
S.	South(ern)		**v.**	versus
SA	South Africa(n)		**W.**	West
S.E.	South-East		**Warks.**	Warwickshire
snr	senior		**WBC**	World Boxing Council
Soc.	Society		**WBO**	World Boxing Organization
SRA	Squash Rackets Association		**WCC**	Women's Cricket Club
Staffs.	Staffordshire		**WDC**	World Darts Council
sub.	substitute		**WFA**	Women's Football Association
S.W.	South-West		**Wilts.**	Wiltshire
TT	Tourist Trophy (motorcycling)		**WI**	West Indies
U-18	Under-18 (similarly U-21, etc.)		**Worcs.**	Worcestershire
UAE	United Arab Emirates		**YC**	Young Cricketers
UAU	Universities Athletic Union		**Yorks.**	Yorkshire

WHO'S WHO IN BRITISH SPORT is intended to provide a comprehensive and up-to-date profile of those currently competing in British sport. Unlike other directories of its type, it has no international or historical dimension, thus enabling it to cover as wide a range of sports as possible, including those pursuits that are less widely covered in the media and which have no dedicated directories of their own, and similarly to embrace up-and-coming participants as well as established names. Indoor 'sports', such as chess and bridge, are, however, excluded. One or two disciplines, among them angling and wrestling, have been omitted from this first edition owing to the lack of a significant response from competitors and/or their representative organizations.

Except for the team sports specified below, entrants will have achieved at least national championship status and/or international representation. In only a few sports (such as Formula 1 motor racing, for example) can entrants be said not to meet these criteria, in which case they are featured because they are the best British participants in their field.

Each entrant was sent, either directly or through their club, team or association, a detailed questionnaire. Not all responded, of course, in which case material has been researched from other sources where available. My thanks are due to the many clubs and associations that supplied statistical and biographical material.

Entrants are British nationals or, in the case of, for example, some footballers, cricketers, and jockeys, overseas nationals whose sporting career is currently based in Britain. Only active competitors are included, although football managers and horseracing trainers, while arguably not (or no longer) actively participating in their respective sports, are featured on the grounds that they receive as much press coverage as their charges, and readers will therefore find their career histories useful. Coverage in future editions may expand to include leading administrators, coaches, journalists, and disabled competitors.

Entries are in alphabetical order by surname. Where two or more entrants share exactly the same name, they appear in the order of their birth dates. Competitors whose names begin with Mac/Mc have their own section before M (no alphabetical distinction is made between Mac and Mc); those whose names begin with O' come at the beginning of the O section.

The entries are not intended to give every fact pertaining to a competitor's career but rather to concentrate on career highlights. They vary in format between sports, but the following basic patterns are followed:

For team-based sports:
Surname/Christian names (*full names where known; any nickname other than obvious contractions – e.g. Bob, Tony – given in brackets*)**/date of birth/name of husband or wife and year of marriage/number of sons and daughters/clubs played for, in order, with dates where known/international career** (*may include year of representational debut, number of caps, overseas tours*)**/other sporting achievements, awards/publications/leisure interests** (*besides principal sport*)**/contact address.**

For individual-based sports, the body of the entry is amended as follows:

Amateur championships (*junior, regional, national, international*)**/professional championships** (*regional, national, international*)**/international representation in ascending order of 'significance': Commonwealth Games, European championships, World championships, Olympic Games/tournaments won/records held/other sporting achievements, etc.**

Thus the progression is from junior or regional achievements to international achievements, and championship/tournament wins will therefore not necessarily be in chronological order.

The length of entry does not imply any judgement on my part of the entrant's relative significance – some 'names' have entries that are skeleton in comparison to less well-known competitors who have supplied full career details.

Given the frequent changes in sponsorship in British sport, details of cup/tournaments by and large omit the sponsor's name, unless doing so leads to ambiguity. In the case of winter sports where a season spans two years, dates given for championship wins cite both years (e.g. 1993/94), while those for cup wins are the year of the second half of the season, even though finals may in some cases be played at the end of the preceding year.

Readers should be aware of the following points in relation to specific sports:

BOWLS
All entrants are Association flat green bowlers unless indicated otherwise.

BOXING
Title-wins are listed together with the year in which the title was won; the boxer does not necessarily still hold any or all of the titles credited to him.

CRICKET
Selection is based on first-class county status. Dates given for county debuts relate to first-team appearances. A player's tally of international caps is specified only if further representation is unlikely. Members of England's World Cup-winning women's team are also included.

FOOTBALL
Those featured are players with international caps and those who have played in the English Premiership and First Division and the Scottish Premier Division in the last two years, although within these criteria coverage is not totally comprehensive. The first year given represents, where possible, the year of signature of the player's contract, irrespective of the actual date of their debut.

The terms League Cup (and Scottish League Cup) are used generically to embrace their variously sponsored derivatives. The years given for Scottish League Cup honours refer to the second half of the season (see above).

No account has knowingly been taken of loan periods, nor of periods under contract to clubs for which no first-team appearance was made.

Individual honours, where available, concentrate on cup-winners' medals and international caps. In order to avoid rapid dating, current international players have their tally of caps expressed as, for example, 'over 25'.

HORSERACING
Career details generally concentrate on English and Irish Classic wins, although Prix de l'Arc de Triomphe, King George VI and Queen Elizabeth Diamond Stakes, and Hennessy, Whitbread and Mackeson Gold Cup wins are also regularly noted.

RUGBY
For both Union and League, entrants have been selected on the basis of international and/or first-division representation (English, Scottish and Welsh in the case of Rugby Union) over the last two years. Again, coverage is not entirely comprehensive.

SWIMMING
Achievements are long-course unless indicated otherwise.

Any mistakes, other than those inadvertently made by entrants, are my own, and will be willingly corrected in future editions if notified to me care of the publishers.

Ian Paten
London
June 1994

A Selection of High Achievers

BBC SPORTS PERSONALITY OF THE YEAR 1993
★ Linford CHRISTIE

ATHLETICS
World Championships medal-winners 1993
★ Linford CHRISTIE
(100m gold and 4 x 100m relay silver)
★ Jonathan EDWARDS
(triple jump bronze)
★ Sally GUNNELL
(400m hurdles gold and world record, 4 x 400m relay bronze)
★ Mick HILL
(javelin bronze)
★ Colin JACKSON
(110m hurdles gold and world record, 4 x 100m relay silver)
★ Tony JARRETT
(110m hurdles and 4 x 100m relay silver)
★ Linda KEOUGH
(4 x 400m relay bronze medal)
★ John REGIS
(200m silver and UK record, 4 x 100m relay silver)
★ Steve SMITH
(high jump bronze)

BADMINTON
World Championships medal-winners 1993
★ Gillian CLARK
(mixed doubles bronze)
★ Nicholas PONTING
(mixed doubles bronze)

BOWLS
World Indoor Championships medal-winners 1993
★ Gary SMITH
(pairs gold)
★ Andrew THOMSON
(pairs gold)

BOXING
Title-winners 1993/94
★ Henry AKINWANDE
(Commonwealth heavyweight)
★ Francis AMPOFO
(Commonwealth flyweight)
★ Neville BROWN
(British middleweight)
★ Paul BURKE
(British and Commonwealth lightweight)
★ Darren FIFIELD
(Commonwealth flyweight)
★ Herbie HIDE
(British heavyweight, WBO heavyweight)
★ Gary JACOBS
(European welterweight)
★ Eamonn LOUGHRAN
(WBO welterweight)
★ Robert McCRACKEN
(British light-middleweight)
★ Duke McKENZIE
(British featherweight)
★ Johnny NELSON
(IBF cruiserweight)
★ Christopher PYATT
(WBO middleweight)
★ Steve ROBINSON
(WBO featherweight)
★ Billy SCHWER
(British and Commonwealth lightweight)
★ John WEIR
(WBO mini-flyweight)

CANOEING
World Championships medal-winners 1993
★ Richard FOX
(K1 slalom individual and team gold)
★ Melvyn JONES
(K1 slalom individual bronze and team gold)
★ Gareth MARRIOTT
(C2 slalom team silver)
★ Shaun PEARCE
(K1 slalom team gold)
★ Lynn SIMPSON
(women's K1 slalom team bronze)
★ Andrew TRAIN
(C2 10,000m silver)

CRICKET
Derbyshire CCC, Benson and Hedges Cup winners 1993
★ Christopher ADAMS
★ Kim BARNETT
★ Peter BOWLER
★ Dominic CORK
★ Frank GRIFFITH
★ Karl KRIKKEN
★ Devon MALCOLM
★ John MORRIS
★ Ole MORTENSEN
★ Timothy O'GORMAN
★ Allan WARNER

Glamorgan CCC, Sunday League champions 1993
★ Stephen BARWICK
★ Phillip COTTEY
★ Robert CROFT
★ Adrian DALE
★ Stephen JAMES
★ Roland LEFEBVRE
★ Matthew MAYNARD
★ Colin METSON
★ Hugh MORRIS
★ Vivian RICHARDS
★ Steven WATKIN

Middlesex CCC, county champions 1993
★ Keith BROWN
★ John CARR
★ Norman COWANS
★ John EMBUREY
★ Mark FELTHAM
★ Angus FRASER
★ Michael GATTING
★ Desmond HAYNES
★ Richard JOHNSON
★ Matthew KEECH
★ Jason POOLEY
★ Mark RAMPRAKASH
★ Michael ROSEBERRY
★ Robin SIMS
★ Charles TAYLOR
★ Philip TUFNELL
★ Paul WEEKES
★ Neil WILLIAMS

Warwickshire CCC, NatWest Trophy winners 1993
★ Asif DIN
★ Andrew MOLES
★ Timothy MUNTON
★ Dominic OSTLER
★ Keith PIPER
★ Jason RATCLIFFE
★ Dermot REEVE
★ Gladstone SMALL
★ Neil SMITH
★ Paul SMITH
★ Roger TWOSE

England Test/tour squad 1993/94
★ Michael ATHERTON
★ Martin BICKNELL
★ Andrew CADDICK
★ John EMBUREY
★ Angus FRASER
★ Michael GATTING
★ Graham GOOCH
★ Graeme HICK
★ Nasser HUSSAIN
★ Alan IGGLESDEN
★ Mark ILOTT
★ Mark LATHWELL
★ Christopher LEWIS
★ Martin MCCAGUE
★ Devon MALCOLM
★ Matthew MAYNARD
★ Mark RAMPRAKASH
★ Jack RUSSELL
★ Ian SALISBURY
★ Robin SMITH
★ Alec STEWART
★ Peter SUCH
★ Graham THORPE
★ Philip TUFNELL
★ Steven WATKIN

CYCLING
World Track Championships medal-winners 1993
★ Christopher BOARDMAN
(4000m individual pursuit bronze medal)
★ Graeme OBREE
(4000m individual pursuit gold medal and world record)

FOOTBALL

England squad 1993/94

★ Anthony ADAMS
★ Darren ANDERTON
★ David BATTY
★ Peter BEARDSLEY
★ Stephen BOULD
★ Lee DIXON
★ Anthony DORIGO
★ Leslie FERDINAND
★ Timothy FLOWERS
★ Paul GASCOIGNE
★ Paul INCE
★ Robert JONES
★ Graeme LE SAUX
★ Matthew LE TISSIER
★ Paul MERSON
★ Gary PALLISTER
★ Carlton PALMER
★ Stuart PEARCE
★ David PLATT
★ Kevin RICHARDSON
★ Stuart RIPLEY
★ David SEAMAN
★ Lee SHARPE
★ Alan SHEARER
★ Andrew SINTON
★ Desmond WALKER
★ Dennis WISE
★ Ian WRIGHT

Scotland squad 1993/94

★ Scott BOOTH
★ David BOWMAN
★ Thomas BOYD
★ Stephen CLARKE
★ John COLLINS
★ Gordon DURIE
★ Iain DURRANT
★ Ian FERGUSON
★ Kevin GALLACHER
★ Andrew GORAM
★ Bryan GUNN
★ Colin HENDRY
★ Brian IRVINE
★ Eoin JESS
★ James LEIGHTON
★ Craig LEVEIN
★ Gary McALLISTER

★ Stuart McCALL
★ Stuart McKIMMIE
★ William McKINLAY
★ Rob McKINNON
★ Alan McLAREN
★ Paul McSTAY
★ Patrick NEVIN
★ Phillip O'DONNELL
★ David ROBERTSON
★ Duncan SHEARER

Ireland squad 1993/94

★ John ALDRIDGE
★ Philip BABB
★ Pat BONNER
★ Anthony CASCARINO
★ Owen COYLE
★ Thomas COYNE
★ Raymond HOUGHTON
★ Dennis IRWIN
★ Roy KEANE
★ Alan KELLY
★ David KELLY
★ Garry KELLY
★ Alan KERNAGHAN
★ Jason McATEER
★ Edward McGOLDRICK
★ Paul McGRATH
★ Alan McLOUGHLIN
★ Kevin MORAN
★ William O'BRIEN
★ Terence PHELAN
★ Niall QUINN
★ John SHERIDAN
★ Stephen STAUNTON
★ Andrew TOWNSEND
★ Ronald WHELAN

Northern Ireland squad 1993/94

★ Kingsley BLACK
★ Mal DONAGHY
★ Iain DOWIE
★ Alan FETTIS
★ Gary FLEMING
★ Philip GRAY
★ Michael HUGHES
★ Alan McDONALD
★ James MAGILTON
★ Stephen MORROW

★ Michael O'NEILL
★ James QUINN
★ Keith ROWLAND
★ Gerald TAGGART
★ Kevin WILSON
★ Nigel WORTHINGTON
★ Thomas WRIGHT

Wales squad 1993/94
★ Mark AIZLEWOOD
★ Malcolm ALLEN
★ Clayton BLACKMORE
★ Nathan BLAKE
★ Paul BODIN
★ Mark BOWEN
★ Christopher COLEMAN
★ Ryan GIGGS
★ Jeremy GOSS
★ Barry HORNE
★ Ceri HUGHES
★ Mark HUGHES
★ Andrew MELVILLE
★ Alan NEILSON
★ Mark PEMBRIDGE
★ Jason PERRY
★ David PHILLIPS
★ Anthony ROBERTS
★ Ian RUSH
★ Dean SAUNDERS
★ Neville SOUTHALL
★ Gary SPEED
★ Christopher SYMONS
★ Eric YOUNG

GOLF
Ryder Cup team 1993 (with 1993 tournament wins)
★ Peter BAKER
(winner British Masters, Scandinavian Masters)
★ Nick FALDO
(winner Asian Classic, Irish Open)
★ Bernard GALLACHER
(non-playing captain)
★ Mark JAMES
★ Barry LANE
(winner European Masters)
★ Colin MONTGOMERIE
(winner Dutch Open, Volvo Masters)

★ Sam TORRANCE
(winner Catalan Open, Hamburg Open)
★ Ian WOOSNAM
(winner English Open)

Other tournament-winners
★ Laura DAVIES
(Thailand Ladies' Open 1993, 94, English Open, Australian Ladies' Masters 1993, LPGA champ. 1994)
★ Helen DOBSON
(European Masters 1993)
★ David GILFORD
(Tenerife Open 1994)

HORSERACING
Winners of the Classics 1993/94
★ Peter BEAUMONT
(trainer of Jodami, winner Cheltenham Gold Cup 1993)
★ Clive BRITTAIN
(trainer of Sayyedati, winner 1000 Guineas 1993)
★ William CARSON
(winner Irish 1000 Guineas (Mehthaaf) 1994)
★ Henry CECIL
(trainer of Commander In Chief, winner Derby, Irish Derby 1993)
★ Peter CHAPPLE-HYAM
(trainer of Turtle Island, winner Irish 2000 Guineas 1994)
★ John DUNLOP
(trainer of Mehthaaf, winner Irish 1000 Guineas 1994)
★ Richard DUNWOODY
(champion National Hunt jockey 1992/93, winner Grand National (Miinnehoma) 1994)
★ Mark DWYER
(Winner Cheltenham Gold Cup (Jodami) 1993, Champion Hurdle (Flakey Dove) 1994)
★ Pat EDDERY
(winner Irish Derby (Commander In Chief), 2000 Guineas (Zafonic), Irish Oaks (Wemyss Bight) 1993)
★ Joshua GIFFORD
(trainer of Bradbury Star, winner Mackeson Gold Cup 1993)

★ Barrington HILLS
(trainer of Nicer, winner Irish 1000 Guineas 1993)
★ Michael HILLS
(winner Irish 1000 Guineas (Nicer) 1993)
★ Michael KINANE
(winner Derby (Commander In Chief) 1993)
★ Martin PIPE
(trainer of Miinnehoma, winner Grand National 1994)
★ John REID
(winner 1000 Guineas (Las Meninas), Irish 2000 Guineas (Turtle Island) 1994)
★ Michael ROBERTS
(winner Oaks (Intrepidity), King George VI and Queen Elizabeth Diamond Stakes (Opera House) 1993)
★ Charles SWAN
(winner Whitbread Gold Cup (Ushers Island) 1994)
★ Walter SWINBURN
(winner 1000 Guineas (Sayyedati) 1993)
★ Andrew TURNELL
(trainer of Cogent, winner Hennessy Gold Cup 1993)

MODERN PENTATHLON
★ Richard PHELPS
(world champion 1993)

ROWING
World Championships medal-winners 1993
★ Alison BROWNLESS
(lightweight women's coxless fours gold)
★ Anna Marie DRYDEN
(lightweight women's coxless fours gold)
★ Jane HALL
(lightweight women's coxless fours gold)
★ Matthew PINSENT
(coxless pairs gold)
★ Steve REDGRAVE
(coxless pairs gold)
★ Greg SEARLE
(coxed pairs gold)
★ Johnny SEARLE
(coxed pairs gold)

RUGBY LEAGUE
Great Britain squad 1993/94
★ John BENTLEY
★ Philip CLARKE
★ Gary CONNOLLY
★ Jonathan DAVIES
★ Martin DERMOTT
★ John DEVEREUX
★ Shaun EDWARDS
★ St John ELLIS
★ Richard EYRES
★ Karl FAIRBANK
★ Andrew FARRELL
★ Deryck FOX
★ Karl HARRISON
★ Lee JACKSON
★ Michael JACKSON
★ Christopher JOYNT
★ Steve McNAMARA
★ Barrie-Jon MATHER
★ Stephen MOLLOY
★ Paul MORIARTY
★ Paul NEWLOVE
★ Sonny NICKLE
★ Martin OFFIAH
★ Daryl POWELL
★ Jason ROBINSON
★ Garry SCHOFIELD
★ Kelvin SKERRETT
★ Graham STEADMAN
★ Alan TAIT

RUGBY UNION
England squad 1993/94
★ Christopher (Rob) ANDREW
★ Neil BACK
★ Stuart BARNES
★ Martin BAYFIELD
★ Kyran BRACKEN
★ Jonathan CALLARD
★ William CARLING
★ Benjamin CLARKE
★ Richard DAWE
★ Philip DE GLANVILLE
★ Jeremy GUSCOTT
★ Jonathan HALL
★ Ian HUNTER
★ Martin JOHNSON

★ Jason LEONARD
★ Brian MOORE
★ Colin MORRIS
★ Stephen OJOMOH
★ Christopher OLVER
★ David PEARS
★ Nigel REDMAN
★ Dean RICHARDS
★ Timothy RODBER
★ Graham ROWNTREE
★ Victor UBOGU
★ Rory UNDERWOOD
★ Tony UNDERWOOD

Scotland squad 1993/94
★ Gary ARMSTRONG
★ Paul BURNELL
★ Craig CHALMERS
★ Damian CRONIN
★ Michael DODS
★ Neil EDWARDS
★ Gavin HASTINGS
★ Scott HASTINGS
★ Carl HOGG
★ Ian JARDINE
★ Kenneth LOGAN
★ Andrew MacDONALD
★ David McIVOR
★ Robert MacNAUGHTON
★ Kenneth MILNE
★ Iain MORRISON
★ Donald (Shade) MUNRO
★ Andrew NICOL
★ Bryan REDPATH
★ Andrew REED
★ Alan SHARP
★ Graham SHIEL
★ Ian SMITH
★ Anthony STANGER
★ Gregor TOWNSEND
★ Derek TURNBULL
★ Robert WAINWRIGHT
★ Peter WALTON
★ Alan WATT
★ George (Doddie) WEIR
★ Peter WRIGHT
★ Douglas WYLLIE

Wales squad 1993/94
★ Anthony CLEMENT
★ Anthony COPSEY
★ Adrian DAVIES
★ John DAVIES
★ Nigel DAVIES
★ Philip DAVIES
★ Stuart DAVIES
★ Ieuan EVANS
★ Richard EVANS
★ Ian GIBBS
★ Michael GRIFFITHS
★ Michael HALL
★ Garin JENKINS
★ Neil JENKINS
★ Richard JONES
★ Robert JONES
★ Andrew LAMERTON
★ Emyr LEWIS
★ Gareth LLEWELLYN
★ Rupert MOON
★ Mark PEREGO
★ Wayne PROCTOR
★ Scott QUINNELL
★ Michael RAYER
★ Nigel WALKER
★ Hugh WILLIAMS-JONES
★ Huw WOODLAND

SNOOKER
Tournament winners 1993/94 season
★ Steve DAVIS
(Welsh Open, Irish Masters)
★ Stephen HENDRY
(Dubai Classic, World Championship)
★ Alan MCMANUS
(Masters)
★ Ronnie O'SULLIVAN
(Benson and Hedges Championship, UK Championship, British Open)
★ John PARROTT
(International Open)

SWIMMING
European Championships medal-winners 1993
★ Mark FOSTER
(4 x 100m medley relay bronze)

★ Nick GILLINGHAM
(200m breaststroke bronze, 100m breaststroke silver, 4 x 100m medley relay bronze)
★ Sarah HARDCASTLE
(4 x 200m freestyle relay bronze)
★ Marie HARDIMAN
(200m breaststroke bronze)
★ Martin HARRIS
(100m backstroke and 4 x 100m medley relay bronze)
★ Robert MORGAN
(highboard silver)
★ Paul PALMER
(400m freestyle silver)
★ Karen PICKERING
(200m freestyle and 4 x 200m freestyle relay bronze)
★ Laila VAKIL
(synchronized duet bronze)

**World Short-Course Championships
medal-winners 1993**
★ Mark FOSTER
(50m freestyle gold and 4 x 100m medley relay bronze)
★ Nick GILLINGHAM
(200m breaststroke gold and 4 x 100m medley relay bronze)

★ Martin HARRIS
(100m backstroke silver and 4 x 100m medley relay bronze)
★ Karen PICKERING
(200m freestyle gold and 100m freestyle bronze)
★ Fraser WALKER
(200m individ. medley silver)

WHO EARNED WHAT?
The best-paid British sportsman is believed to be Lennox Lewis, with an estimated income in 1993 of approximately £10.5 million, followed at some distance by Nick Faldo with £3.5 million. A successful Premiership football manager might expect to earn £250,000 annually, while his charges will receive upwards of £50,000 (considerably more in some cases, of course). In the lower reaches of the Football League, players might well have to content themselves with a salary of between £15,000 and £20,000. Towards the bottom of the professional scale, a first-year capped county cricket players earns a miserly £11,000.

Many of those appearing in the following pages, of course, earn nothing from their sport but personal satisfaction and, in many cases, glory.

A-Z OF COMPETITORS

ABBOTT, Julien: powerboat racer (navigator); b. 21 February 1965, Taplow; GB offshore circuit racing B class champ. 1991, 93, world champ. 1993. *Leisure interests:* meeting people, weight training, mountain biking, motorcycling, watching other sports, night-clubbing, horseriding, cinema, raising money for charity. *Address:* 3 Thornbury Close, Crowthorne, Berks. RG11 6PE.

ABLETT, Gary: footballer; b. 19 November 1965, Liverpool; player Liverpool 1983–92, Everton 92–   ; with Liverpool: winners FA Cup 1989, League champs. 1987/88, 89/90; 1 England U-21 cap. *Address:* Everton FC, Goodison Park, Liverpool L4 4EL.

ACKLAND, Dorothy Janet: flat green bowler; b. 19 December 1938, Ystrad Mynach, Mid Glamorgan; m. Robert William Ackland 1960; 2 s.; rep. Glamorgan; GB fours champ. 1989, 90; Wales int. debut (outdoor) 1973, (indoor) 1980; Commonwealth Games squad 1982, 86, 90; World Champs. women's pairs and fours bronze medals 1977, singles gold 1988. *Leisure interests:* organizing open bowls tournaments. *Address:* 62 Dochdwy Rd, Llandough, Penarth, S. Glamorgan CF64 2PD.

ADAM, Marcus: athlete; b. 28 February 1968, London; AAA 200m champ. 1989; UK 100m champ. 1989, 200m champ. 1989, 92; European Jnr Champs. 200m gold medal 1987; Commonwealth Games 200m gold medal 1990; European Champs. 4 x 100m relay silver medal 1990; European Cup 4 x 100m relay gold medal 1989; World Cup 4 x 100m relay silver medal 1989. *Address:* c/o Brit. Athletic Fed., 225A Bristol Rd, Edgbaston, Birmingham B5 7UB.

ADAMS, Anthony Alexander: footballer; b. 10 October 1966, Romford, Essex; m. Jane Margaret Adams 1992; 1 s., 1 d.; player Arsenal 1984–   , winners League Cup 1987, 93, FA Cup 1993, League champs. 1988/89, 90/91; 5 England U-21 caps, 1 England B cap, over 26 full England caps. *Leisure interests:* snooker, golf, reading, walking the dog. *Address:* Arsenal FC, Arsenal Stadium, Highbury, London N5 1BU.

ADAMS, Christopher John: cricketer; b. 6 May 1970, Whitwell; m. Samantha Adams 1992; player Derbys. 1988–   , winners Benson and Hedges Cup 1993, Sunday League champs. 1990; rep. Young England 1989. *Address:* Derbys. CCC, County Cricket Ground, Nottingham Rd, Derby DE2 6DA.

ADAMS, Michael: footballer; b. 8 November 1961, Sheffield; player Gillingham 1979–83, Coventry City 83–87, Leeds Utd 87–89, Southampton 89–   . *Address:* Southampton FC, The Dell, Milton Rd, Southampton SO9 4XX.

ADAMS, Neil: footballer; b. 23 November 1965, Stoke; player Stoke City 1985–86, Everton 86–89, Oldham Athletic 89–94, Norwich City 94–   ; with Everton: League champs. 1986/87; 1 England U-21 cap. *Address:* Norwich City FC, Carrow Rd, Norwich NR1 1JE.

ADAMSON, Lee: Rugby Union footballer; b. 17 June 1958, Newcastle-upon-Tyne; player Metropolitan Police, Wasps, Saracens 1986–   (capt. 1987/88); rep. Middx. *Address:* Saracens FC, Bramley Rd Sports Ground, Chaseside, Southgate, London N14 4AB.

ADCOCK, Anthony: footballer; b. 27 February 1963, Bethnal Green; player Colchester Utd 1981–87, Manchester City 87–88, Northampton Town 88–89, Bradford City 89–91, Northampton Town 1991, Peterborough Utd 1991–   . *Address:* Peterborough Utd FC, London Rd Ground, Peterborough, Cambs. PE2 8AL.

ADEBAYO, Adedayo Adeyemi: Rugby Union footballer; b. 30 November 1970; player Bath; rep. S.W. Div.; England U-21 debut v. Belgium 1991, England B debut v. Spain 1991, winning squad World Cup Sevens 1993, England A tour Canada 1993. *Address*: Bath RFC, Recreation Ground, Bath BA2 6PW.

AFFORD, John Andrew: cricketer; b. 12 May 1964, Peterborough; m. Lynn Afford 1988; 1 d.; player Notts. 1984–ꞏ, county champs. 1987, Sunday League champs. 1991; England A tour Kenya/Zimbabwe 1989/90. *Address*: Notts. CCC, Trent Bridge, Nottingham NG2 6AG.

AGANA, Anthony: footballer; b. 2 October 1963, Bromley; player Watford 1987–88, Sheffield Utd 88–91, Notts County 91–ꞏ. *Address*: Notts County FC, Meadow Lane Ground, Nottingham NG2 3HJ.

AGNEW, Paul: footballer; b. 15 August 1965, Lisburn, NI; player Grimsby Town 1984–ꞏ; 1 NI U-21 cap. *Address*: Grimsby Town FC, Blundell Park, Cleethorpes, S. Humberside DN35 7PY.

AINSCOUGH, Gerry Christopher: Rugby Union footballer; b. 7 August 1964, Wigan; m. Karen Ainscough; player Leicester, Orrell; rep. Lancs., county champs. 1992/93, N. Div.; England B debut v. Spain 1989. *Address*: Orrell RUFC, Edgehall Rd, Orrell, Wigan WN5 8TL.

AITKEN, Robert (Roy): footballer; b. 24 November 1958, Irvine; player Celtic 1975–90, Newcastle Utd 90–91, Aberdeen 91–ꞏ; with Celtic: winners Scottish Cup 1977, 80, 85, 88, 89, Scottish League Cup 1983, Scottish League champs. 1985/86; 16 Scotland U-21 caps, 57 full Scotland caps. *Address*: Aberdeen FC, Pittodrie Stadium, Pittodrie St, Aberdeen AB2 1QH.

AITKEN, Scott Alexander: Rugby Union footballer; b. 13 July 1970, Leith; player Melrose 1988–91, Watsonians 91–ꞏ; rep. Scottish Schools 1987/88, tour NZ 1988, Scottish Colleges 1989/90; Scotland U-21 squad 1990/91. *Leisure interests*: squash, badminton, shooting, cricket. *Address*: Watsonians RFC, Myreside, Myreside Rd, Edinburgh EH10 5DB.

AIZLEWOOD, Mark: footballer; b. 1 October 1959, Newport; player Newport County 1975–78, Luton Town 78–82, Charlton Athletic 82–87, Leeds Utd 87–89, Bradford City 89–90, Bristol City 90–93, Cardiff City 93–ꞏ; with Luton Town: 2nd Div. champs. 1981/82; 1 Wales U-21 cap, over 36 full Wales caps. *Address*: Cardiff City FC, Ninian Park, Sloper Rd, Cardiff CF1 8SX.

AKERS, Stephen George: swimmer; b. 16 May 1971, Shoreham-by-Sea; England youth and intermediate debut 1987, Commonwealth Games squad 1990 (1500m freestyle), snr debut 1991; GB youth debut 1987, Olympic squad 1992 (400m, 1500m freestyle and 4 x 200m freestyle relay). *Leisure interests*: cooking, golf. *Address*: c/o ASA, Harold Fern House, Derby Square, Loughborough, Leics. LE11 0AL.

AKINWANDE, Henry: boxer; b. 12 October 1965; ABA heavyweight champ. 1988, 89; England debut 1986; Olympic squad 1988; prof. debut 1989; titles won: European heavyweight 1992, Common-wealth heavy-weight 1993; over 19 prof. wins. *Address*: Nat. Promotions, Nat. House, 60–66 Wardour St, London W1V 3HP.

ALLCOCK, Anthony, MBE: flat green bowler; b. 11 June 1955, Thurmaston, Leics.; English singles champ. (outdoor) 1990, 91, triples champ. (outdoor) 1990; GB singles champ. (outdoor) 1992; England debut (outdoor) 1978, (indoor) 1976; World Champs. singles gold medal 1992, pairs silver 1984, 88, triples gold 1980, fours gold 1984, bronze 1988, team gold 1980, 88; World Indoor Champs. singles gold medals 1986, 87, pairs gold 1986, 87, 89–92. *Address*: c/o English Indoor Bowling Assoc., 290A Barking Rd, London E6 3BA.

ALLCOCK, Christopher: cyclist; b. 17 June 1972, Sutton-in-Ashfield; rep. Raleigh 1992– ; RTTC jnr 10-mile time trial champ. 1990, snr 100km team time trial champ. 1992; GB jnr debut 1990, World Jnr Champs. squad 1990 (GB 70km team time trial record-holders); stage-winner Tour of Malta 1992. *Leisure interests*: cars, music. *Address*: c/o Special Products Div., Raleigh Cycles, Triumph Rd, Notts. NG7 2DD.

ALDRIDGE, John William: footballer; b. 18 September 1958, Liverpool; m. Joan Margaret Aldridge 1980; 1 s., 1 d.; player Newport County 1979–84, Oxford Utd 84–87, Liverpool 87–89, Real Sociedad (Spain) 89–91, Tranmere Rovers 91– ; with Oxford Utd: winners League Cup 1986, 2nd Div. champs. 1984/85; with Liverpool: League champs. 1987/88; over 54 Ireland caps. *Publications: Inside Anfield*, 1988. *Leisure interests*: fishing, golf, snooker, pool. *Address*: Tranmere Rovers FC, Prenton Park, Prenton Rd W., Birkenhead, Merseyside L42 9PN.

ALLEN, Bradley: footballer; b. 13 September 1971, Romford; player Queens Park Rangers 1988– ; 4 England U-21 caps. *Address*: Queens Park Rangers FC, Rangers Stadium, S. Africa Rd, London W12 7PA.

ALLEN, Christopher: footballer; b. 18 November 1972, Oxford; player Oxford Utd 1991– . *Address*: Oxford Utd FC, Manor Ground, London Rd, Headington, Oxford OX3 7RS.

ALLEN, Clive: footballer; b. 20 May 1961, Stepney; player Queens Park Rangers 1978–80, Crystal Palace 80–81, Queens Park Rangers 81–84, Tottenham Hotspur 84–88, Bordeaux (France) 88–89, Manchester City 89–91, Chelsea 91–92, W. Ham Utd 92– ; with Queens Park Rangers: 2nd Div.

champs. 1982/83; 3 England U-21 caps, 5 full England caps. *Address*: W. Ham Utd FC, Boleyn Ground, Green St, Upton Park, London E13 9AZ.

ALLEN, Hayley: diver; b. 25 June 1975, Pembury; GB women's jnr highboard champ. 1992, 93, jnr 3m springboard champ. 1993, snr highboard champ. 1991, 93; GB debut 1989, Olympic squad 1992 (1st Brit. woman finalist for 30 years). *Leisure interests*: trampolining (nat. competitor), writing for local newspaper, coaching, playing the violin. *Address*: 17 Bounds Oak Way, Southborough, Tunbridge Wells, Kent TN4 0TX.

ALLEN, Katrina Margaret: real tennis player; b. 11 May 1955, London; GB ladies' open champ. 1983–86, doubles champ. 1985; French ladies' open champ. 1986, 92, doubles champ. 1986; Aus. ladies' open singles and doubles champ. 1988; US ladies' open doubles champ. 1984; world ladies' doubles champ. 1987; ranked world no. 1 1988; rep. Middx, Sussex jnr lawn tennis. *Leisure interests*: all racket sports, languages, travel, chess, anything gastronomic. *Address*: Frame, Set and Match, 113 Notting Hill Gate, London W11 3LB.

ALLEN, Kevin: Rugby Union footballer; b. 17 August 1971; player Aberavon; Wales U-21 debut v. Scotland U-21 1992. *Address*: Aberavon RFC, Manor St, Port Talbot, W. Glamorgan.

ALLEN, Malcolm: footballer; b. 21 March 1967, Deiniolen, Gwynedd; player Watford 1985–88, Norwich City 88–90, Millwall 90–93, Newcastle Utd 93– ; over 13 Wales caps. *Address*: Newcastle Utd FC, St James' Park, Newcastle-upon-Tyne, Tyne & Wear NE1 4ST.

ALLEN, Mark: squash player; b. 3 September 1971, Grays; player N. Walsham 1989–92, Lingfield 1992, OSC Munich (Germany) 1992–93; rep. Essex 1988– ;

Essex U-19 champ. 1988, 89; SA U-21 open champ. 1992; England U-16 debut 1987, U-19 debut 1989; World Jnr Champs. team gold medal 1990 (capt.). *Leisure interests*: rock music, travel, socializing, reading. *Address*: 1 Bryanstone Mews, Lexden, Colchester, Essex CO2 5XZ.

ALLEN, Martin: footballer; b. 14 August 1965, Reading; player Queens Park Rangers 1983–89, W. Ham Utd 89– ; 2 England U-21 caps. *Address*: W. Ham Utd FC, Boleyn Ground, Green St, Upton Park, London E13 9AZ.

ALLEN, Paul: footballer; b. 28 August 1962, Aveley, Essex; player W. Ham Utd 1979–85, Tottenham Hotspur 85–93, Southampton 93– ; with W. Ham Utd: winners FA Cup 1980 (youngest-ever finalist); with Tottenham Hotspur: winners FA Cup 1991; 3 England U-21 caps. *Address*: Southampton FC, The Dell, Milton Rd, Southampton SO9 4XX.

ALLENBY, David Malcolm: powerboat racer; b. 10 October 1954, Chandler's Ford; GB offshore circuit racing class III 4-litre champ. 1986, 87, class I and class II champ. 1993; winner Cowes–Torquay Offshore Race 1993 (1st Brit. winner since 1977); Bournemouth class II speed record-holder 1993. *Address*: 40 Randall Rd, Chandler's Ford, Hants. SO5 1AL.

ALLEYNE, Mark Wayne: cricketer; b. 23 May 1968, Tottenham; player Glos. 1986– ; England YC tours Sri Lanka 1987, Aus. 1988; youngest player to score 100 for Glos. *Address*: Glos. CCC, Phoenix County Ground, Nevil Rd, Bristol BS6 9EJ.

ALLON, Joseph: footballer; b. 12 November 1966, Gateshead; player Newcastle Utd 1984–87, Swansea City 87–88, Hartlepool Utd 88–91, Chelsea 91–92, Brentford 92– ; 1 England Youth cap. *Leisure interests*: socializing. *Address*: Brentford FC, Griffin Park, Braemar Rd, Brentford, Middx TW8 0NT.

AMBROSE, Curtly Elconn Lynwall: cricketer; b. 21 September 1963, Antigua; m. Bridgette Ambrose 1991; 1 d.; player Northants. 1989– , winners NatWest Trophy 1992; Test debut 1987, WI tours England 1988, Aus. 1988/89, India 1989/90, Pakistan 1990/91, England 1991, Pakistan 1991/92, Aus. (World Cup) 1991/92, Aus./SA 1992/93. *Address*: Northants. CCC, County Cricket Ground, Wantage Rd, Northampton NN1 4TJ.

AMOS, John Peter: Rugby Union footballer; b. 25 January 1968, Bergen, Norway; player Gala; rep. S. of Scotland; Scotland tour N. America 1991. *Address*: Gala RUFC, Netherdale, Nether Rd, Galashiels TD1 3HE.

AMPADU, Kwame: footballer; b. 20 December 1970, Bradford; player Arsenal 1988–91, W. Bromwich Albion 91– ; 2 Ireland U-21 caps. *Address*: W. Bromwich Albion FC, The Hawthorns, W. Bromwich B71 4LF.

AMPOFO, Francis: boxer; b. 5 June 1967; prof. debut 1990; titles won: GB flyweight 1991, 92, Commonwealth flyweight 1993; over 8 prof. wins. *Address*: Matchroom Ltd, 10 Western Rd, Romford, Essex RM1 3JT.

ANDERSON, Grant: Rugby League footballer; b. 21 February 1969, Castleford; player Castleford 1987– , winners Regal Trophy 1994; GB U-21 debut v. France 1989. *Address*: Castleford RLFC, Wheldon Rd, Castleford WF10 2SD.

ANDERSON, Julian Alexander: windsurfer; b. 2 April 1969, Haverfordwest; Irish champ. 1984, 85, Mistral champ. 1985, 88; UK Mistral champ. 1987, 88, funboard champ. 1990, 91; European Champs. Mistral gold medals (heavyweight) 1986, 89, silver 1988; World Champs. Mistral gold medals 1986, 89, 91, production board silver 1991. *Leisure interests*: sailing, water skiing, golf, basketball, weight training, cricket, rugby, hockey, tennis, TV. *Address*: Surf Marketing Ltd, Southbrook Lodge, Southbrook Rd, W. Ashling, Chichester PO18 8DN.

ANDERSON, Paul: Rugby League footballer; b. 25 October 1971; player Redhill ARLFC, Leeds 1991– ; GB U-21 debut v. France 1992. *Address*: Leeds RLFC, Bass Headingley, St Michael's Lane, Leeds LS6 3BR.

ANDERSON, Robert Charles: darts player; b. 7 November 1947, Winchester; m. Mary Anderson 1970; 1 s., 1 d.; GB pairs champ. 1986, 88; world pairs champ. 1986, prof. champ. 1988; England debut 1980 (capt. 1992); winner World Masters 1986–88, Danish Open, Swedish Open 1986, Brit. Open, World Matchplay 1987, Pacific Masters 1987–89, Brit. Matchplay 1988, 89, Canadian Open 1990, 92, N. American Open 1993. *Leisure interests*: golf, fly fishing, shooting. *Address*: c/o Dick Allix, McLeod Holden Enterprises Ltd, Priory House, 1133 Hessle High Rd, Hull HU4 6SB.

ANDERSON, Tony: Rugby League footballer; b. 23 July 1961; player Oldham, Bradford Northern 1991–93, Huddersfield 93– . *Address*: Huddersfield RLFC, The New Office, Fartown, Huddersfield HD2 2SD.

ANDERSON, Vivian: footballer; b. 29 August 1956, Nottingham; player Nottingham Forest 1974–84, Arsenal 84–87, Manchester Utd 87–91, Sheffield Wednesday 91–93, player/manager Barnsley 93– ; with Nottingham Forest: winners European Cup 1979, 80, League Cup 1978, League champs. 1977/78; with Sheffield Wednesday: winners League Cup 1991; 1 England U-21 cap, 30 full England caps; 1st black player to win England cap. *Address*: Barnsley FC, Oakwell Ground, Grove St, Barnsley, Yorks. S71 1ET.

ANDERTON, Darren: footballer; b. 3 March 1972, Southampton; player Portsmouth 1990–92, Tottenham Hotspur 92– ; England U-21 int. *Address*: Tottenham Hotspur FC, 748 High Rd, Tottenham, London N17 0AP.

ANDREW, Christopher Robert: Rugby Union footballer; b. 18 February 1963, Richmond, Yorks.; m. Sara Andrew; 1 d.; player Middlesbrough, Cambridge Univ. (Blue 1982–84), Nottingham, Gordon (Aus.), Wasps, Toulouse (France), Wasps; with Wasps: League champs. 1989/90; rep. N. Div. 1985–86, London Div.; with London Div.: Div. champs. 1990; England debut v. Romania 1985, Five Nations debut v. France 1985, Grand Slam champs. 1991; Brit. Lions tours Aus. 1989, NZ 1993. *Address*: Wasps FC, Wasps Football Ground, Repton Ave, Sudbury, nr Wembley, Middx HA0 3DW.

ANDREW, Stephen Jon Walter: cricketer; b. 27 January 1966, London; player Hants. 1984–89, Essex 90– ; with Hants.: Sunday League champs. 1986; with Essex: county champs. 1991, 92; Young England tour WI 1985. *Address*: Essex CCC, County Cricket Ground, New Writtle St, Chelmsford DM2 0PG.

ANDREWS, Ian: footballer; b. 1 December 1964, Nottingham; player Leicester City 1982–88, Celtic 88–89, Southampton 89– ; 1 England U-21 cap. *Address*: Southampton FC, The Dell, Milton Rd, Southampton SO9 4XX.

ANDREWS, Richard Neil: Rugby Union footballer; b. 25 March 1964, Stevenage; m. Diana Mary Andrews 1988; player Bacavians 1981–84, Saracens 86– ; with Saracens: 2nd Div. champs. 1988/89; rep. Herts. U-21 1983–85, London Div. B 1992– . *Leisure interests*: weight training, motor racing. *Address*: Saracens FC, Bramley Rd Sports Ground, Chaseside, Southgate, London N14 4AB.

ANGELL, Brett: footballer; b. 20 August 1968, Marlborough; player Stockport County 1988–90, Southend Utd 90– . *Address*: Southend Utd FC, Roots Hall, Victoria Ave, Southend-on-Sea, Essex SS2 6NQ.

ANGUS, Ian: footballer; b. 19 November 1961, Glasgow; player Aberdeen 1979–86, Dundee 86–90, Motherwell 90– ; with Motherwell: winners Scottish Cup 1991. *Address*: Motherwell FC, Fir Park, Fir Park St, Motherwell ML1 2QN.

ANSAH, Andrew: footballer; b. 19 March 1969, Lewisham; player Brentford 1989–90, Southend Utd 90– . *Address*: Southend Utd FC, Roots Hall, Victoria Ave, Southend-on-Sea, Essex SS2 6NQ.

ANTHROBUS, Stephen: footballer; b. 10 November 1968, Lewisham; player Millwall 1986–90, Wimbledon 90– . *Address*: Wimbledon FC, Selhurst Park, London SE25 6PY.

APPLEBY, Matthew: footballer; b. 16 April 1972, Middlesbrough; player Newcastle Utd 1990– . *Address*: Newcastle Utd FC, St James' Park, Newcastle-upon-Tyne, Tyne & Wear NE1 4ST.

APPLETON, David Robertson: croquet player; b. 30 September 1944, Kilmarnock; Scotland debut 1991; winner Scottish Masters 1992. *Leisure interests*: crossword puzzles, music. *Address*: c/o Scottish Croquet Assoc., 13 Park Place, Dunfermline KY12 7QL.

ARCHER, Graeme Francis: cricketer; b. 26 September 1970, Carlisle; player Staffs. 1990–91, Notts. 92– . *Address*: Notts. CCC, Trent Bridge, Nottingham NG2 6AG.

ARCHER, Simon David: badminton player; b. 27 June 1973, Leamington Spa; rep. Worcs.; Welsh doubles champ. 1993; English doubles champ. 1994; England debut 1991, Thomas Cup team 1992; winner Icelandic Open doubles 1992, Austrian Open doubles and mixed doubles 1993, Hants. Open doubles 1994; Worcs. Sports Personality of the Year 1992. *Leisure interests*: tennis, food. *Address*: Martin Cottage, Church Lane, Martin Hassingtree, Worcester, Worcs.

ARDILES, Osvaldo César: football manager; b. 3 August 1952, Córdoba, Argentina; player Huracán (Argentina) 1975–78, Tottenham Hotspur 78–88, Queens Park Rangers 88–89; with Tottenham Hotspur: winners FA Cup 1981, UEFA Cup 1984; 42 Argentina caps, winners World Cup 1978; manager Swindon Town 1989–91, Newcastle Utd 91–92, W. Bromwich Albion 92–93, Tottenham Hotspur 93– . *Address*: Tottenham Hotspur FC, 748 High Rd, Tottenham, London N17 0AP.

ARMOUR, John: boxer; b. 26 October 1968; ABA flyweight champ. 1990; England debut 1987; prof. debut 1990; titles won: Commonwealth bantamweight 1992; over 11 prof. wins. *Address*: Nat. Promotions, Nat. House, 60–66 Wardour St, London W1V 3HP.

ARMSTRONG, Christopher: footballer; b. 19 June 1971, Newcastle; player Wrexham 1988–91, Millwall 91–92, Crystal Palace 92– . *Address*: Crystal Palace FC, Selhurst Park Stadium, London SE25 6PU.

ARMSTRONG, Gary: Rugby Union footballer; b. 30 September 1966, Edinburgh; m. Shona Armstrong; 1 s.; player Jed Thistle, Jed-Forest; Scotland B debut v. Italy 1987, snr debut v. Aus. 1988, Five Nations debut v. Wales 1989, Grand Slam champs. 1990; Brit. Lions tour Aus. 1989. *Address*: Jed-Forest RUFC, Riverside Park, Jedburgh.

ARMSTRONG, Gordon: footballer; b. 15 July 1967, Newcastle; player Sunderland 1985– , 3rd Div. champs. 1987/88. *Address*: Sunderland FC, Roker Park Ground, Sunderland, Tyne and Wear SR6 9SW.

ARMSTRONG, Mark: equestrianist (show jumping); b. 23 June 1961, Leicester; European Champs. team silver medal 1993 (Corella). *Leisure interests*: fly fishing, skiing. *Address*: Frensham Manor, Frensham, Farnham, Surrey GU10 3ED.

ARNOLD, Paul: Rugby Union footballer; b. 28 April 1968, Swansea; player Swansea; Wales U-21 debut v. Scotland 1990, snr debut v. Namibia 1990, Five Nations debut v. England 1991, tours Namibia 1990, Aus. 1991, Zimbabwe/Namibia 1993. *Leisure interests*: weight training, squash, running, swimming, music, cinema. *Address*: Swansea RFC, St Helens, Swansea SA2 0AR.

ARNOTT, Doug: footballer; b. 5 August 1964, Lanark; player Motherwell 1986– , winners Scottish Cup 1991. *Address*: Motherwell FC, Fir Park, Fir Park St, Motherwell ML1 2QN.

ARTHUR, Gordon: footballer; b. 30 May 1958, Kirkcaldy; player Stirling Albion 1977–84, Dumbarton 84–88, Raith Rovers 88– . *Address*: Raith Rovers FC, Stark's Park, Pratt St, Kirkcaldy, Fife KY1 1SA.

ASHBY, Barry: footballer; b. 21 November 1970, Brent; player Watford 1988– . *Address*: Watford FC, Vicarage Rd Stadium, Watford, Herts. WD1 8ER.

ASHCROFT, Christopher John: hockey player; b. 20 July 1960, Bebington; player Neston 1979– (capt. 86–), winners League Cup 1984, club champs. 1983; rep. Cheshire 1979– (capt. 1990/91), Cheshire indoor 1988–90; Wales debut 1980, over 60 caps; rep. GB Univ. 1983–84, European Students Champs. silver medallist 1984; GB debut 1982, Olympic reserve 1984. *Publications*: contributor to *Hockey Digest*. *Leisure interests*: golf, cricket, Kennedy assassination literature, music, walking, driving. *Address*: Neston HC, Station Rd, Parkgate, S. Wirral.

ASHCROFT, Lee: footballer; b. 7 September 1972, Preston; player Preston N. End 1991–93, W. Bromwich Albion 93– ; England U-21 int. *Address*: W. Bromwich Albion FC, The Hawthorns, Halfords Lane, W. Bromwich B71 4LF.

ASHLEY, Kevin: footballer; b. 31 December 1968, Birmingham; player Birmingham City 1986–90, Wolverhampton Wanderers 90– . *Address*: Wolverhampton Wanderers FC, Molineux Stadium, Waterloo Rd, Wolverhampton WV1 4QR.

ASHMEAD, Paul: Rugby Union footballer; b. 3 January 1966; player Longlevens, Gloucester. *Address*: Gloucester RUFC, Kingsholm, Worcester St, Gloucester GL3 3AX.

ASIF DIN, Mohamed: cricketer; b. 21 September 1960, Kampala, Uganda; m. Ahmerin Asif Din 1987; 1 d.; player Warks. 1981– , winners NatWest Trophy 1993 (Man of the Match). *Address*: Warks. CCC, County Ground, Edgbaston, Birmingham B5 7QU.

ASKEW, Philip Thawley: ice dancer; b. 4 October 1973, Sutton in Ashfield; with Marie James: GB northern champ. 1992. *Leisure interests*: swimming, gym, cycling, dancing, skiing, music, ballet. *Address*: Nottingham Ice Dance and Figure Skating Club, Nottingham Ice Stadium, Nottingham.

ASPINALL, Simon James: fencer (épée); b. 29 December 1967, Maldon, Essex; rep. Oxford Univ. 1988–91 (Blue 1991), S.E. England 1989– ; with Oxford: Brit. univ. champs. 1990, 91; England and GB debuts 1992, European Champs. squad 1992, World Champs. squad 1993; winner Leicester City Open 1992, Bristol Open 1993. *Leisure interests*: skiing, tennis, squash, travel. *Address*: c/o AFA, 1 Barons Gate, 33–35 Rothschild Rd, London W4 5HT.

ASPINALL, Warren: footballer; b. 13
September 1967, Wigan; player Wigan
Athletic 1985–86, Everton 86–87, Aston
Villa 87–88, Portsmouth 88– . *Address*:
Portsmouth FC, Fratton Park, Frogmore
Rd, Portsmouth PO4 8RA.

ASTON, Mark Richard: Rugby League
footballer; b. 27 September 1967, Allerton
Bywater; player Selby ARLFC, Sheffield
Eagles 1986– ; GB debut v. France 1991.
Address: Sheffield Eagles RLFC, Stadium
Corner, 824 Attercliffe Rd, Sheffield S9 3RS.

ATCHESON, Paul: Rugby League footballer; b. 17 May 1973; player Widnes, Wigan
1992– ; with Widnes: winners Regal
Trophy 1992. *Address*: Wigan RLFC, The
Pavilion, Central Park, Wigan WN1 1XF.

ATHERTON, Michael Andrew: cricketer;
b. 23 March 1968, Manchester; player
Cambridge Univ. 1987–89 (capt. 88–89),
Lancs. 87– (vice-capt. 92–); Test debut
1989, tours Aus./NZ 1990/91, India
1992/93, WI 1994; England capt. 1993– .
Address: Lancs. CCC, Old Trafford,
Manchester M16 0PX.

ATHERTON, Peter: footballer; b. 6 April
1970, Orrell; player Wigan Athletic
1988–91, Coventry City 91– ; 1 England
U-21 cap. *Address*: Coventry City FC,
Highfield Rd Stadium, King Richard St,
Coventry CV2 4FW.

ATHEY, Charles William Jeffrey (Bill):
cricketer; b. 27 September 1957,
Middlesbrough; m. Janet Linda Athey
1982; player Yorks. 1976–83, Glos. 84–92
(capt. 1989), Sussex 93– ; England U-19
tour WI 1976, 23 Tests, debut 1980, 31 1-
day ints, tours WI 1980/81, Aus. 1986/87,
Pakistan/Aus./NZ (World Cup) 1987/88,
Sri Lanka (England B) 1985/86; MCC tour
Kenya 1993. *Leisure interests*: most sport,
history, gardening, travel. *Address*: Sussex
CCC, County Ground, Eaton Rd, Hove, E.
Sussex BN3 3AN.

ATKINS, Jill: hockey player; b. 30 May
1963; player Bradford Swithenbank;
England U-21 debut 1982, snr debut 1985,
European Champs. silver medallist 1987,
gold 1991, World Cup squad 1986, 90; GB
debut 1986, Olympic bronze medallist
1992. *Address*: c/o All England Women's
Hockey Assoc., 51 High St, Shrewsbury
SY1 1ST.

ATKINS, Mark: footballer; b. 14 August
1968, Doncaster; player Scunthorpe Utd
1986–88, Blackburn Rovers 88– . *Address*:
Blackburn Rovers FC, Ewood Park,
Blackburn, Lancs. BB2 4JF.

ATKINSON, Brian: footballer; b. 19
January 1971, Darlington; player
Sunderland 1989– ; 6 England U-21 caps.
Address: Sunderland FC, Roker Park
Ground, Sunderland, Tyne and Wear
SR6 9SW.

ATKINSON, Dalian: footballer; b. 21
March 1968, Shrewsbury; player Ipswich
Town 1985–89, Sheffield Wednesday 89–90,
Real Sociedad (Spain) 90–91, Aston Villa
91– . *Address*: Aston Villa FC, Villa Park,
Trinity Rd, Birmingham B6 6HE.

ATKINSON, Ronald: football manager; b.
18 March 1939, Liverpool; player Oxford
Utd 1962–72, 3rd Div. champs. 1967/68;
manager Kettering Town, Cambridge Utd
1974–78, W. Bromwich Albion 78–81,
Manchester Utd 81–86, W. Bromwich
Albion 87–88, Atletico Madrid, Sheffield
Wednesday 1989–91, Aston Villa 1991– ;
with Manchester Utd: winners FA Cup
1983, 85; with Sheffield Wednesday:
winners League Cup 1991. *Address*: Aston
Villa FC, Villa Park, Trinity Rd,
Birmingham B6 6HE.

AUGER, Christian: powerboat racer; b. 26
February 1968, Upney, Essex; GB offshore
circuit racing C class champ. 1988, 93;
winner Duckhams Trophy 1993;
Windermere C class speed record-holder

1988, 93. *Leisure interests*: football, golf. *Address*: 13 Dunmow Drive, Rainham, Essex RM13 7UD.

AUSTIN, Andrew Peter: clay pigeon shooter (Olympic skeet); b. 31 January 1956, Sawbridgeworth; English champ. 1986–88, 91, 92; GB champ. 1988, 89, 91, 92; Commonwealth Games team silver, individ. bronze medals 1990; GB debut 1976, Olympic reserve 1988, squad 1992. *Leisure interests*: golf, other forms of shooting. *Address*: Inglewood, High St, Thurleigh, Beds. MK44 2DS.

AUSTIN, Dean: footballer; b. 26 April 1970, Hemel Hempstead; player Southend Utd 1990–92, Tottenham Hotspur 92– . *Address*: Tottenham Hotspur FC, 748 High Rd, Tottenham, London N17 0AP.

AUSTIN, Ian David: cricketer; b. 30 May 1966, Haslingden; player Lancs. 1986– , tours Jamaica 1987, 88, Zimbabwe 1989, Tasmania/W. Aus. 1990, 91; England U-19 tour Bermuda 1985. *Address*: Lancs. CCC, Old Trafford, Manchester M16 0PX.

AWFORD, Andrew: footballer; b. 14 July 1972, Worcester; player Portsmouth 1989– . *Address*: Portsmouth FC, Fratton Park, Frogmore Rd, Portsmouth PO4 8RA.

AYERS, Michael: boxer; b. 26 January 1965; ABA lightweight champ. 1987; England debut 1987; prof. debut 1989; titles won: WBC int. lightweight 1992; over 11 prof. wins. *Address*: Matchroom Ltd, 10 Western Rd, Romford, Essex RM1 3JT.

AYLING, Jonathan Richard: cricketer; b. 13 June 1967, Portsmouth; player Hants. 1988– . *Address*: Hants. CCC, County Cricket Ground, Northlands Rd, Southampton SO9 2TY.

AYMES, Adrian Nigel: cricketer; b. 4 June 1964, Southampton; m. Marie Aymes 1992; player Hants. 1987– . *Address*: Hants. CCC, County Cricket Ground, Northlands Rd, Southampton SO9 2TY.

BABB, Philip: footballer; b. 30 November 1970, Lambeth; player Bradford City 1990–92, Coventry City 92– . *Address*: Coventry City FC, Highfield Rd Stadium, King Richard St, Coventry CV2 4FW.

BACK, Neil Antony: Rugby Union footballer; b. 16 January 1969, Coventry; player Nottingham, Leicester; with Leicester: winners Pilkington Cup 1993; rep. Midland Div.; England U-21 debut v. Romania 1989, England B debut v. Emerging Aus. 1990, England A tour Canada 1993, snr and Five Nations debut v. Scotland 1994. *Address*: Leicester FC, Welford Rd, Leicester LE2 7LF.

BACKLEY, Steven James: athlete (javelin); b. 12 February 1969, Sidcup, Kent; AAA champ. 1989, 92; UK champ. 1988–92; European Jnr Champs. gold medal 1987; World Jnr Champs. silver medal 1988; Commonwealth Games gold medal 1990; European Cup gold medal 1989; European Champs. gold medal 1990; World Cup gold medal 1989; Olympic bronze medal 1992; UK and Commonwealth record-holder; Brit. Sports Writers' Sportsman of the Year and IAAF Athlete of the Year 1990. *Leisure interests*: golf. *Address*: c/o Brit. Athletic Fed., 225A Bristol Rd, Edgbaston, Birmingham B5 7UB.

BAGNALL, Geoff: Rugby League footballer; b. 4 November 1965; player Wakefield Trinity 1992– . *Address*: Wakefield Trinity RLFC, 171 Doncaster Rd, Belle Vue, Wakefield WF1 5EZ.

BAILEY, Christopher: tennis player; b. 29 April 1968; rep. Norfolk; GB U-12 grass court champ. 1980; GB debut 1989, Davis Cup team 1989, 90, 92, 93, European Cup team 1989, 90, 92; winner Central African Satellite 1988, French Satellite 1992, Bristol Challenger 1993. *Leisure interests*: Norwich City FC, golf. *Address*: c/o LTA, The Queen's Club, W. Kensington, London W14 9EG.

BAILEY, Dennis: footballer; b. 13 November 1965, Lambeth; player Crystal Palace 1987–89, Birmingham City 89–91, Queens Park Rangers 91– . *Address*: Queens Park Rangers FC, Rangers Stadium, S. Africa Rd, London W12 7PA.

BAILEY, Mark: Rugby League footballer; b. 5 May 1968, Leigh; player St Helens, Halifax 1992– ; GB colt. *Address*: Halifax RLFC, The Pavilion, Thrum Hall, Gibbet St, Halifax, W. Yorks. HX1 4TL.

BAILEY, Robert John: cricketer; b. 28 October 1963, Biddulph; m. Rachel Bailey 1987; 1 s.; player Northants. 1982– , tours Durban (SA) 1992, Cape Town (SA) 1993; England tours Sharjah (UAE) 1985, 87, Test debut 1988; scored 1000 runs in season 1993. *Address*: Northants. CCC, County Cricket Ground, Wantage Rd, Northampton NN1 4TJ.

BAILY, James Nathan Roger: tennis player; b. 1 February 1975, Portsmouth; rep. Hants.; GB U-12 grass court champ. 1987, U-14 hard court champ. 1988, 89, grass court champ. 1988; Chinese U-18 singles and doubles champ. 1992; Aus. U-18 singles champ. 1993 (1st Brit. Grand Slam tournament-winner since 1965). *Leisure interests*: music, languages, driving, water sports. *Address*: c/o LTA, The Queen's Club, W. Kensington, London W14 9EG.

BAIN, Kevin: footballer; b. 19 September 1972, Kirkcaldy; player Dundee 1989– ; Scotland U-21 int. *Address*: Dundee FC, Dens Park, Dundee DD3 7JY.

BAINBRIDGE, Philip: cricketer; b. 16 April 1958, Stoke on Trent; m. Barbara Bainbridge 1979; 1 s., 1 d.; player Glos. 1977–91, Durham 92– (capt. 94–); rep. Young England v. Aus. 1977; England Counties tour Zimbabwe 1985. *Address*: Durham CCC, County Ground, Riverside, Chester-le-Street, Co. Durham DH3 3QR.

BAIRD, Ian: footballer; b. 1 April 1964, Rotherham; player Southampton 1982–85, Leeds Utd 85–87, Portsmouth 87–88, Leeds Utd 88–90, Middlesbrough 90–91, Heart of Midlothian 91–93, Bristol City 93– . *Address*: Bristol City FC, Ashton Gate, Bristol BS3 2EJ.

BAIRD, Roger: Rugby Union footballer; b. 12 April 1960, Kelso; m. Louise J. Baird 1986; 1 s., 1 d.; player Kelso 1978–91, Watsonians 91– ; with Kelso: Scottish League champs. 1987/88, 88/89; rep. S. of Scotland 1978–89; Scotland debut v. Aus. 1981, 27 caps; Brit. Lions tour NZ 1983. *Leisure interests*: golf, tennis, cricket, socializing. *Address*: Watsonians RFC, Myreside, Myreside Rd, Edinburgh EH10 5DB.

BAKER, David: cyclist; b. 30 December 1965, Sheffield; m. Grace Baker 1993; rep. Peugeot, Raleigh 1991– ; prof. debut 1988; GB jnr cyclo-cross champ. 1983, snr open champ. 1990, 92, mountain bike point series champ. 1991–93, cross-country champ. 1992, 93; World Mountain Bike Champs. cross-country bronze medal 1992; winner Nat. Trophy (cyclo-cross) 1988–91, Tour of Derbys. 1991. *Leisure interests*: wine-making, DIY, travel. *Address*: Raleigh Industries, Triumph Rd, Nottingham NG1 2DD.

BAKER, Nik: windsurfer; b. 11 May 1971, Brighton; UK slalom champ., U-19 champ. 1989, wave champ. 1990, 91; prof. debut 1989; World Cup expression gold medal 1991; leading UK prof. sailor. *Leisure interests*: surfing, mountain biking, weight training. *Address*: SSM Ltd, Chelsea Reach, 79–89 Lots Rd, London SW10 0RN.

BAKER, Peter Alan: golfer; b. 7 October 1967, Shifnal, Shropshire; m. Helen Jane Baker 1990; 1 d.; joint English open amateur strokeplay champ. and Walker Cup debut 1985; prof. debut 1986; European U-25 open champ. 1990; Ryder and Dunhill Cup teams 1993; winner Benson and Hedges Int. Open

1988, Brit. Masters, Scandinavian Masters 1993. *Leisure interests*: Wolverhampton Wanderers FC, all sport, music, cars. *Address*: Int. Management Group, Pier House, Strand on the Green, London W4 3NN.

BAKER, Ronald Iverton: basketball player; b. 28 July 1969, Montserrat, WI; 1 d.; player Brixton Topcats 1987–90, Worthing Bears 90–92, London Towers 92–93, Guildford Kings 93–   ; England debut 1988, Commonwealth Champs. gold medallist 1991. *Leisure interests*: watching movies, playing the drums, eating out. *Address*: 32A W. Bank, Stamford Hill, London N16.

BAKKER, Paul-Jan: cricketer; b. 19 August 1957, Vlaardingen, The Netherlands; player Hants. 1986–93; MCC tours USA 1989/90, Namibia 1990/91; Holland int., 1st Dutch prof. *Address*: Hants. CCC, County Cricket Ground, Northlands Rd, Southampton SO9 2TY.

BALDING, Ian Anthony: racehorse trainer; b. 7 November 1938; 1st trainer's licence 1964; winner Derby, Prix de l'Arc de Triomphe 1971 (Mill Reef), Irish 1000 Guineas 1987 (Forest Flower). *Address*: c/o BHB, 42 Portman Square, London W1H 0EN.

BALDWIN, Gavin Paul: Rugby Union footballer; b. 6 December 1968, Hereford; player Worcester, Nottingham, Northampton; rep. Midland Div.; England U-21 debut v. The Netherlands 1990, England B debut v. Spain 1992, tour NZ 1992. *Address*: Northampton FC, Franklins Gardens, Weedon Rd, Northampton NN5 5BG.

BALDWIN, Simon: Rugby League footballer; b. 31 March 1975; player Leigh 1992– . *Address*: Leigh RLFC, Hilton Park, Kirkhall Lane, Leigh WN7 1RN.

BALL, Alan James: football manager; b. 12 May 1945, Farnworth; player Blackpool 1962–66, Everton 66–71, Arsenal 71–76, Southampton 76–79, Vancouver (Canada), Blackpool (player/manager) 1980–81, Southampton 81–82, Hong Kong, Bristol Rovers 1983; with Everton: League champs. 1969/70; 8 England U-23 caps, 72 full England caps, winners World Cup 1966 (youngest English player); manager Portsmouth 1984–89, Stoke City 89–91, Exeter City 91–94, Southampton 94– . *Address*: Southampton FC, The Dell, Milton Rd, Southampton SO9 4XX.

BALL, Kevin: footballer; b. 12 November 1964, Hastings; player Portsmouth 1982–90, Sunderland 90– . *Address*: Sunderland FC, Roker Park Ground, Sunderland, Tyne and Wear SR6 9SW.

BALL, Martyn Charles John: cricketer; b. 26 April 1970, Bristol; m. Mona Ball 1991; 1 d.; player Glos. 1988– , tours Namibia 1989, Kenya 1990; rep. Young England v. NZ 1989. *Address*: Glos. CCC, Phoenix County Ground, Nevil Rd, Bristol BS6 9EJ.

BALMER, Stuart: footballer; b. 20 September 1969, Falkirk; player Charlton Athletic 1990– . *Address*: Charlton Athletic FC, The Valley, Floyd Rd, London SE7 8BL.

BAMFORD, Reginald Lewis: croquet player; b. 11 October 1967, Cape Town, SA; SA champ. 1986–89, 91, 92, doubles champ. 1982, 84, 86, 87, 89, 91, 92; GB men's champ., open champ. 1993; winner San Francisco Open 1993; SA debut 1982. *Leisure interests*: golf, bridge. *Address*: Flat 3, 22 Leathwaite Rd, London SW11 1XQ.

BANGER, Nicholas: footballer; b. 25 February 1971, Southampton; player Southampton 1989– . *Address*: Southampton FC, The Dell, Milton Rd, Southampton SO9 4XX.

BANNISTER, Gary: footballer; b. 22 July 1960, Warrington; player Coventry City 1978–81, Sheffield Wednesday 81–84, Queens Park Rangers 84–88, Coventry City 88–90, W. Bromwich Albion 90–92, Nottingham Forest 92–93, Stoke City 93– ; 1 England U-21 cap. *Address:* Stoke City FC, Victoria Ground, Stoke on Trent, Staffs. ST4 4EG.

BARBER, Frederick: footballer; b. 26 August 1963, Ferryhill; player Darlington 1981–86, Walsall 86–91, Peterborough Utd 91– . *Address:* Peterborough Utd FC, London Rd Ground, Peterborough, Cambs. PE2 8AL.

BARBER, Philip: footballer; b. 10 June 1965, Tring; player Crystal Palace 1984–91, Millwall 91– . *Address:* Millwall FC, The Den, Zampa Rd, Bermondsey, London SE16 3LH.

BARCLAY, Stephen Lewis: Rugby Union footballer; b. 17 October 1969, Wakefield; player Oxford Univ. 1988–92 (Blue 1990, 91), Neath 91–92, Swansea 93– ; Welsh Schools debut 1988, Welsh Students debut 1991, Wales U-21 squad 1990. *Leisure interests:* geology, photography, skiing, reading, cinema, travel. *Address:* Swansea RFC, St Helens, Swansea SA2 0AR.

BARDSLEY, David: footballer; b. 11 September 1964, Manchester; player Blackpool 1982–83, Watford 83–87, Oxford Utd 87–89, Queens Park Rangers 89– ; 2 full England caps. *Address:* Queens Park Rangers FC, Rangers Stadium, S. Africa Rd, London W12 7PA.

BARKER, Simon: footballer; b. 4 November 1964, Farnworth; player Blackburn Rovers 1982–88, Queens Park Rangers 88– ; 4 England U-21 caps. *Address:* Queens Park Rangers FC, Rangers Stadium, S. Africa Rd, London W12 7PA.

BARKWORTH, Julian: Rugby League footballer; b. 10 April 1969; player Ionians

(RU), Hull Kingston Rovers 1991– . *Address:* Hull Kingston Rovers RLFC, Craven Park, Preston Rd, Hull HU9 5HE.

BARLOW, Andrew: footballer; b. 24 November 1965, Oldham; player Oldham Athletic 1984– , 2nd Div. champs. 1990/91. *Address:* Oldham Athletic FC, Boundary Park, Oldham, Lancs. OL1 2PA.

BARLOW, Stuart: footballer; b. 16 July 1968, Liverpool; player Everton 1990– . *Address:* Everton FC, Goodison Park, Liverpool L4 4EL.

BARMBY, Nicholas: footballer; b. 11 February 1974, Hull; player Tottenham Hotspur 1991– ; England U-21 int. *Address:* Tottenham Hotspur FC, 748 High Rd, Tottenham, London N17 0AP.

BARNES, Colette Elizabeth: practical pistol shooter; b. 30 November 1965, Saltburn; GB ladies' champ. 1991–93; French ladies' champ. 1992, 93; UK debut 1992 (ladies' capt. 1992–); European Champs. gold medal 1992; World Champs. gold medal 1991, silver 1993. *Leisure interests:* martial arts, fitness training, parachuting, bungie jumping, hot-air ballooning, travel, art, music. *Address:* 66 Strauss Rd, S. Bank, Middlesbrough, Cleveland TS6 6QG.

BARNES, David: footballer; b. 16 November 1961, Paddington; player Coventry City 1979–82, Ipswich Town 82–84, Wolverhampton Wanderers 84–87, Aldershot 87–89, Sheffield Utd 89– . *Address:* Sheffield Utd FC, Bramall Lane, Sheffield, S. Yorks S2 4SU.

BARNES, David (Bobby): footballer; b. 17 December 1962, Kingston; player W. Ham Utd 1980–86, Aldershot 86–87, Swindon Town 87–89, Bournemouth 1989, Northampton Town 1989–92, Peterborough Utd 92– . *Address:* Peterborough Utd FC, London Rd Ground, Peterborough, Cambs. PE2 8AL.

BARNES, John: footballer; b. 7 November 1963, Jamaica; player Watford 1981–87, Liverpool 87– (capt.); with Liverpool: winners FA Cup 1989, League champs. 1987/88, 89/90; 2 England U-21 caps, over 72 full England caps; PFA Player of the Year and Football Writers' Assoc. Player of the Year 1988. *Address*: Liverpool FC, Anfield Rd, Liverpool L4 0TH.

BARNES, Stuart: Rugby Union footballer; b. 22 November 1962, Grays, Essex; m. Lesley Barnes 1989; 1 s., 1 d.; player Bristol, Bath 1985– (capt. 1988–91); with Bath: winners Pilkington Cup 1990, 92, League champs. 1990/91, 91/92, 92/93; Wales debut 1981, England B debut 1983, tour NZ 1992, snr debut v. Aus. 1984, Five Nations debut v. Scotland 1986; Brit. Lions tour NZ 1993; most-capped Welsh Schools player. *Leisure interests*: literature, music, wine, gourmet food, drinking with Gareth Chilcott. *Address*: Bath RFC, Recreation Ground, Bath BA2 6PW.

BARNESS, Anthony: footballer; b. 25 March 1973, Lewisham; player Charlton Athletic 1991–92, Chelsea 92– . *Address*: Chelsea FC, Stamford Bridge, Fulham Rd, London SW6 1HS.

BARNETT, Alex Anthony: cricketer; b. 11 September 1970, Malaga, Spain; player Middx 1991, Lancs. 1992– ; England U-19 tour Aus. 1989/90. *Address*: Lancs. CCC, Old Trafford, Manchester M16 0PX.

BARNETT, Glyn Cawley Daer: full-bore rifle shooter; b. 1 December 1970, Bradford; Norfolk champ. 1986–88, 90, 92; BUSF champ. 1990–93, small-bore champ. 1993; UAU small-bore champ. 1993; GB U-25 debut 1986, snr debut 1990, Palma Match team (winners) 1992, Kolapore Match team (winners) 1993; winner Grand Aggregate, Bisley 1993 (youngest ever). *Leisure interests*: running, weight training, skiing, water skiing, horseriding, cricket, travel. *Address*: 116 Barons Keep, Gliddon Rd, London W14 9AX.

BARNETT, Kim John: cricketer; b. 17 July 1960, Stoke on Trent; 1 s.; player Derbys. 1979– (capt.), winners Benson and Hedges Cup 1993, Sunday League champs. 1990; England Schools tour India 1977, Young England tour Aus. 1978/79, England B tour Sri Lanka 1986 (vice-capt.), Test debut 1988. *Address*: Derbys. CCC, County Cricket Ground, Nottingham Rd, Derby DE2 6DA.

BARONS, David Hawken: racehorse trainer (NH); b. 6 December 1936; m. Jennifer Rose Barons 1961; 3 s.; 1st licence 1963; winner Hennessy Gold Cup 1987 (Playschool), Grand National 1991 (Seagram), Whitbread Gold Cup 1992, 93 (Topsham Bay). *Address*: c/o BHB, 42 Portman Square, London, W1H 0EN.

BARRETT, Christopher: canoeist; b. 9 September 1976, Sheffield; GB U-16 and U-18 C1 slalom champ. 1992; GB jnr debut and World Jnr Champs. squad 1992. *Leisure interests*: squash, tennis, athletics, mountain biking. *Address*: 2 Meadow Rise, Ashgate, Chesterfield, Derbys. S42 7PX.

BARRETT, Earl: footballer; b. 28 April 1967, Rochdale; player Manchester City 1985–87, Oldham Athletic 87–91, Aston Villa 91– ; 4 England U-21 caps, snr debut v. NZ 1991. *Address*: Aston Villa FC, Villa Park, Trinity Rd, Birmingham B6 6HE.

BARROW, Jason: hockey player; b. 19 March 1970, Manchester; player Macclesfield 1983–85, Alderley Edge 85–88, Indian Gymkhana 88–91, Hounslow 91– ; with Hounslow: European Cup Winners' Cup silver medallist 1992, 93, club champs. 1992, 93, League champs. 1993; rep. Cheshire and Berks. U-21 1986–92, Middx snr 1992; England U-16 and U-18 debuts 1986, U-21 debut 1989 (U-21 indoor debut 1986), snr debut 1993; North-West jnr open-weight judo champ. 1983–84, GB triallist 1984. *Leisure interests*: keeping fit, socializing, travel. *Address*: Hounslow HC, Chiswick Boat House, Dukes Meadows, London W4 2SH.

BARSCH, Nicholas Paul: powerboat racer; b. 8 May 1950, Salcombe; m. Jeanne Barsch 1983; 1 s., 1 d.; GB offshore circuit racing 1.8-litre champ. 1987–89, A class champ. 1990–93; winner Dunoon Powerboat Champs., World Cup 1993; winner Duckhams Trophy 1987, 88, 90–92; holds GB record for highest number of consecutive champs. wins. *Leisure interests*: recreational boating, water skiing, motor sport, cycling. *Address*: 'Barn Coombe', Penwartha Coombe, Perranporth, Cornwall TR6 0AZ.

BART-WILLIAMS, Christopher: footballer; b. 16 June 1974, Sierra Leone; player Leyton Orient 1991, Sheffield Wednesday 1991– . *Address*: Sheffield Wednesday FC, Hillsborough, Sheffield, S. Yorks. S6 1SW.

BARTLETT, Kevin: footballer; b. 12 October 1962, Portsmouth; player Cardiff City 1986–89, W. Bromwich Albion 89–90, Notts County 90– . *Address*: Notts County FC, Meadow Lane Ground, Nottingham NG2 3HJ.

BARTON, Warren: footballer; b. 19 March 1969, Stoke Newington; player Maidstone Utd 1989–90, Wimbledon 90– . *Address*: Wimbledon FC, Selhurst Park, London SE25 6PY.

BARWICK, Stephen Royston: cricketer; b. 6 September 1960, Neath; m. Margaret Barwick 1987; 1 s.; player Glamorgan 1981– , Sunday League champs. 1993. *Address*: Glamorgan CCC, Sophia Gardens, Cardiff CF1 9XR.

BASSETT, David: football manager; b. 4 September 1944, Hendon; player Wimbledon 1974–78; manager Wimbledon 1981–87, Watford 87–88, Sheffield Utd 88– ; with Wimbledon: 4th Div. champs. 1982/83. *Address*: Sheffield Utd FC, Bramall Lane, Sheffield, S. Yorks S2 4SU.

BASTIEN, Steven: cricketer; b. 13 March 1963, Stepney; 1 s.; player Glamorgan 1988– , tours Barbados 1989, Zimbabwe 1991, SA 1993. *Leisure interests*: music, travel. *Address*: Glamorgan CCC, Sophia Gardens, Cardiff CF1 9XR.

BATEMAN, Allan Glen: Rugby League footballer; b. 6 March 1965, Caerau, S. Wales; player Neath (RU), Warrington 1990– ; with Warrington: winners Regal Trophy 1991; Wales RU int.; Wales RL debut v. Papua New Guinea 1991; GB debut v. France 1992. *Address*: Warrington RLFC, Wilderspool Stadium, Wilderspool Causeway, Warrington WA4 6PY.

BATES, Jamie Alan: footballer; b. 24 February 1968, Croydon; m. Sharron Bates; player Brentford 1986– , 3rd Div. champs. 1991/92. *Leisure interests*: swimming, golf. *Address*: Brentford FC, Griffin Park, Braemar Rd, Brentford, Middx TW8 0NT.

BATES, Jeremy: tennis player; b. 19 June 1962; m. Ruth Leech 1992; rep. Surrey; GB U-18 covered court and grass court champ. 1979, snr champ. 1985, 88, 90, 92, 93, doubles champ. 1986, 87, 89, 90, 91, 93; GB debut 1981, European Cup team 1981, 83–91, Davis Cup team 1985– , Olympic squad 1988; winner Wimbledon mixed doubles 1987, Aus. Champs. mixed doubles 1991, Brit. Indoor Satellite singles and doubles, Nagoya Challenger doubles 1992. *Address*: c/o LTA, The Queen's Club, W. Kensington, London W14 9EG.

BATES, Steven Michael: Rugby Union footballer; b. 4 March 1963, Merthyr Tydfil; m. Sarah Bates; 1 d.; player Welwyn, Wasps 1981– ; with Wasps: League champs. 1989/90; rep. London Div. 1986– ; England B debut v. USSR 1989, snr debut v. Romania 1989, tours Argentina 1990, Canada 1993. *Address*: Wasps FC, Wasps Football Ground, Repton Ave, Sudbury, nr Wembley, Middx HA0 3DW.

BATTEN, Guin: oarswoman; b. 27 September 1967, Cuckfield; rep. Leeds Univ. RC 1988–91, Thames RC 87– ; GB women's eights champ. 1992, single sculls champ. 1993. *Leisure interests*: mountaineering, sailing. *Address*: Thames RC, The Embankment, Putney, London SW15 1LB.

BATTEN, Miriam: oarswoman; b. 4 November 1964, Dartford; rep. Southampton Univ. 1984–87, Thames RC 87– ; GB women's eights champ. 1989; GB debut 1990, World Champs. women's coxless pairs bronze medal 1991 (1st Brit. women's rowing medal), Olympic squad 1992. *Leisure interests*: music, climbing, sailing, container gardening. *Address*: 25 Castell House, Deptford Church St, London SE8 4SD.

BATTY, David: footballer; b. 2 December 1968, Leeds; player Leeds Utd 1987–93, Blackburn Rovers 93– ; with Leeds Utd: 2nd Div. champs. 1989/90, League champs. 1991/92; 7 England U-21 caps, over 13 full England caps. *Address*: Blackburn Rovers FC, Ewood Park, Blackburn, Lancs. BB2 4JF.

BATTY, Jeremy David: cricketer; b. 15 May 1971, Bradford; player Yorks. 1989– ; England YC tour Aus. 1989/90. *Address*: Yorks. CCC, Headingley Cricket Ground, Leeds LS6 3BU.

BAXTER, Alain: Alpine skier; b. 26 December 1973, Edinburgh; GB jnr giant slalom, super giant slalom champ. 1992, snr giant slalom, combined champ. 1994; Scotland debut 1990; GB debut 1992. *Leisure interests*: ice hockey, tennis, squash, cycling, golf. *Address*: c/o Brit. Ski Fed., 258 Main St, E. Calder, Livingston, W. Lothian EH53 0EE.

BAYFIELD, Martin Christopher: Rugby Union footballer; b. 21 December 1966, Bedford; player Bedford, Northampton; England B debut v. Emerging Aus. 1991, tour NZ 1992, snr debut v. Fiji 1991, Five Nations debut v. Scotland 1992, Grand Slam champs. 1991, 92, tour Aus./Fiji 1991. *Address*: Northampton FC, Franklins Gardens, Weedon Rd, Northampton NN5 5BG.

BAYLISS, Lisa: hockey player; b. 27 November 1966; player Sutton Coldfield; England U-21 debut 1985, snr debut 1987, European Champs. gold medallist 1991; GB debut 1990, Olympic bronze medallist 1992. *Address*: First Personnel Sutton Coldfield HC, Rectory Park, Sutton Coldfield, W. Midlands.

BAZELEY, Darren: footballer; b. 5 October 1972, Northampton; player Watford 1991– ; England U-21 int. *Address*: Watford FC, Vicarage Rd Stadium, Watford, Herts. WD1 8ER.

BEADLE, Peter: footballer; b. 13 May 1972, Lambeth; player Gillingham 1990–92, Tottenham Hotspur 92– . *Address*: Tottenham Hotspur FC, 748 High Rd, Tottenham, London N17 0AP.

BEAGRIE, Peter: footballer; b. 29 November 1965, Middlesbrough; player Middlesbrough 1984–86, Sheffield Utd 86–88, Stoke City 88–89, Everton 89– ; 2 England U-21 caps. *Address*: Everton FC, Goodison Park, Liverpool L4 4EL.

BEARDSLEY, Peter: footballer; b. 18 January 1961, Newcastle; player Carlisle Utd 1979–82, Manchester Utd 82–83, Newcastle Utd 83–87, Liverpool 87–91, Everton 91–93, Newcastle Utd 93– (capt. 94–); with Liverpool: winners FA Cup 1989, League champs. 1987/88, 89/90; England debut v. Egypt (sub.) 1986, over 49 caps. *Address*: Newcastle Utd FC, St James' Park, Newcastle-upon-Tyne, Tyne & Wear NE1 4ST.

BEASANT, David: footballer; b. 20 March 1959, Willesden; player Wimbledon 1979–88, Newcastle Utd 88–89, Chelsea 89–93, Southampton 93– ; with Wimbledon: winners FA Cup 1988, 4th Div. champs. 1982/83; with Chelsea: 2nd Div. champs. 1988/89; 7 England B caps, 2 full England caps; only goalkeeper to have saved a penalty in an FA Cup Final. *Address*: Southampton FC, The Dell, Milton Rd, Southampton SO9 4XX.

BEATON, Stephen: darts player; b. 5 April 1964, Coventry; m. Nanette Beaton 1993; England debut 1991, World Cup team 1993; winner Belgian Open, Danish Open, Brit. Matchplay, World Masters 1993. *Leisure interests*: golf, swimming, tennis. *Address*: Southam, Leamington Spa, Warks.

BEAUCHAMP, Joseph: footballer; b. 13 March 1971, Oxford; player Oxford Utd 1989– . *Address*: Oxford Utd FC, Manor Ground, London Rd, Headington, Oxford OX3 7RS.

BEAUMONT, David: footballer; b. 10 December 1963, Edinburgh; player Dundee Utd 1980–89, Luton Town 89–91, Hibernian 91– ; 1 Scotland U-21 cap. *Address*: Hibernian FC, Easter Rd Stadium, 64 Albion Rd, Edinburgh EH7 5QG.

BEAUMONT, Peter: racehorse trainer; b. 2 August 1934; m. Margaret Beaumont; 1 s., 1 d.; 1st licence 1986; winner Cheltenham Gold Cup 1993 (Jodami). *Address*: c/o BHB, 42 Portman Square, London W1H 0EN.

BECK, Laurie: Rugby Union footballer; b. 2 January 1971; player Gloucester; England U-21 int. *Address*: Gloucester RUFC, Kingsholm, Worcester St, Gloucester GL3 3AX.

BECKFORD, Darren: footballer; b. 12 May 1967, Manchester; player Manchester City 1984–87, Port Vale 87–91, Norwich City 91–92, Oldham Athletic 92– . *Address*: Oldham Athletic FC, Boundary Park, Oldham, Lancs. OL1 2PA.

BEECH, Paul: Rugby Union footballer; b. 4 April 1972; player Lydney, Gloucester; England U-21 int. *Address*: Gloucester RUFC, Kingsholm, Worcester St, Gloucester GL3 3AX.

BEEDIE, Stuart: footballer; b. 16 August 1960, Aberdeen; player Montrose 1978–81, St Johnstone 81–84, Dundee Utd 84–86, Hibernian 86–87, Dunfermline Athletic 87–89, Dundee 89– . *Address*: Dundee FC, Dens Park, Dundee DD3 7JY.

BEENEY, Mark: footballer; b. 30 December 1967, Tunbridge Wells; player Gillingham 1986–87, Maidstone Utd 87–91, Brighton and Hove Albion 91–93, Leeds Utd 93– . *Address*: Leeds Utd FC, Elland Rd, Leeds, W. Yorks. LS11 0ES.

BEESLEY, Paul: footballer; b. 21 July 1965, Liverpool; player Wigan Athletic 1984–89, Leyton Orient 89–90, Sheffield Utd 90– . *Address*: Sheffield Utd FC, Bramall Lane, Sheffield, S. Yorks S2 4SU.

BEESON, Bryan Douglas: squash player; b. 26 July 1960, Gateshead; 1 s.; Northumbrian champ. 1980–88, 90–92; English champ. 1986; England debut 1985; European champ. of champs. 1987, 88; European Champs. team gold medals 1987–91. *Leisure interests*: golf, DIY, reading. *Address*: 22 Danby Close, Rickleton, Washington NE38 9JB.

BEHRENS, James Henry John: oarsman; b. 23 September 1969, Bradford; rep. Reading Univ. 1990–91, Cambridge Univ. BC 91–93 (Pres. 1992/93); with Cambridge: winners Univ. Boat Race 1993 (1st Cambridge Pres. to row in winning boat since 1973); GB coxless pairs champ. 1992; World Student Games eights silver medal 1993. *Leisure interests*: tennis, wildlife. *Address*: Park Green, Littlethorpe, Ripon, N. Yorks. HG4 3LX.

BELL, Eileen: flat green bowler; 4 ch.; Ireland debut 1967; Commonwealth Games squad 1982, 86, 90; World Champs. women's pairs gold medal 1981. *Leisure interests*: keep-fit, sewing and dressmaking, cooking, travel, charity work. *Address*: 78 Crossgar Rd, Ballynahinch, Co. Down BT24 8XS.

BELL, Graham: Alpine skier; b. 4 January 1966, Akrotiri, Cyprus; m. Sarah Bell 1991; GB downhill, super giant slalom and overall champ. 1993; GB debut 1982; World Jnr Champs. downhill silver medal 1984; Olympic squad (downhill) 1984, 88, 92, 94. *Leisure interests*: rowing, water skiing, windsurfing, tennis, playing the guitar. *Address*: 40 Gravel Hill, Henley-on-Thames, Oxon RG9 2EE.

BELL, John Nicholson: flat green bowler; b. 14 December 1947, Aspatria, Cumbria; m. Jeanette Wynn Bell 1979; 1 s., 1 d.; rep. Lancs. 1967–69, Cumbria 70– ; English singles champ. (outdoor) 1983, pairs champ. (outdoor) 1991, triples champ. (outdoor) 1976, 91, (indoor) 1991, fours champ. (indoor) 1992; GB singles champ. (outdoor) 1984, pairs and triples champ. (outdoor) 1992, fours champ. (indoor) 1993; England debut (outdoor) 1978, (indoor) 1983; World Champs. team gold medals 1980, 88, fours gold 1984, bronze 1988, triples bronze 1988; 1st English bowler to win indoor and outdoor nat. triples titles in same year (1991). *Leisure interests*: music, quizzes, watching rugby. *Address*: Bangla, Cross Lane, Wigton, Cumbria CA7 9DB.

BELL, Martin Neil: Alpine skier; b. 6 December 1964, Akrotiri, Cyprus; GB jnr debut 1978, snr debut 1980, World Champs. squad 1985, 87, 89, 91, 93, World Cup squad 1981– , Olympic squad (downhill) 1984, 88, 92, 94; achieved best-ever Brit. men's result (8th) in Olympic downhill 1988. *Publications: Let's Go Skiing*, 1990 (also video), contributor to *Ski Survey*

magazine, 1987– . *Leisure interests*: tennis, squash, football. *Address*: Int. Management Group, Pier House, Strand on the Green, London W4 3NN.

BELL, Michael Anthony Vincent: cricketer; b. 19 December 1967, Birmingham; player Warks. 1992– . *Address*: Warks. CCC, County Ground, Edgbaston, Birmingham B5 7QU.

BELL, Nigel: Rugby League footballer; b. 4 November 1962, Wakefield; player Eastmoor ARLFC, Wakefield Trinity 1983– . *Address*: Wakefield Trinity RLFC, 171 Doncaster Rd, Belle Vue, Wakefield WF1 5EZ.

BELL, Stuart Christian: figure skater; b. 21 March 1975, Solihull; Welsh primary champ. 1990; GB debut and World Jnr Champs. squad 1991. *Leisure interests*: music, reading, sport. *Address*: Solihull Ice Rink, Hobs Moat Rd, Solihull.

BELLAMY, Gary: footballer; b. 4 July 1962, Worksop; player Chesterfield 1980–87, Wolverhampton Wanderers 87– ; with Chesterfield: 4th Div. champs. 1984/85; with Wolverhampton Wanderers: 4th Div. champs. 1987/88, 3rd Div. champs. 1988/89. *Address*: Wolverhampton Wanderers FC, Molineux Stadium, Waterloo Rd, Wolverhampton WV1 4QR.

BENALI, Francis: footballer; b. 30 December 1968, Southampton; player Southampton 1986– . *Address*: Southampton FC, The Dell, Milton Rd, Southampton SO9 4XX.

BENJAMIN, Ian: footballer; b. 11 December 1961, Nottingham; player Sheffield Utd 1979, W. Bromwich Albion 79–82, Peterborough Utd 82–84, Northampton Town 84–87, Cambridge Utd 87–88, Chester City 88–89, Exeter City 89–90, Southend Utd 90– ; with Northampton Town: 4th Div. champs.

1986/87. *Address*: Southend Utd FC, Roots Hall, Victoria Ave, Southend-on-Sea, Essex SS2 6NQ.

BENJAMIN, Joseph Emmanuel (Joey): cricketer; b. 2 February 1961, Christchurch, St Kitts; player Warks. 1988–91, Surrey 92– . *Address*: Surrey CCC, The Oval, Kennington, London SE11 5SS.

BENJAMIN, Winston Keithroy Matthew: cricketer; b. 31 December 1964, St John's, Antigua; player Leics. 1986–93, Hants. 94– ; Test debut 1987, WI tours Aus./Pakistan 1986/87, India 1987/88, England 1988, Aus. 1988/89. *Address*: Hants. CCC, County Cricket Ground, Northlands Rd, Southampton SO9 2TY.

BENN, Nigel: boxer; b. 22 January 1964; ABA middleweight champ. 1986; prof. debut 1987; titles won: Commonwealth middleweight 1988, WBO middleweight 1990, WBC super-middleweight 1992; over 36 prof. wins. *Address*: Matchroom Ltd, 10 Western Rd, Romford, Essex RM1 3JT.

BENNETT, Alexandra Joanne: swimmer; b. 22 February 1977, Peterborough; rep. Cheshire 1988–89, Notts. 90– ; England youth debut 1991, snr debut 1994; GB jnr debut 1991, snr debut 1992; European Jnr Champs. women's 100m backstroke, 4 x 100m freestyle relay, 4 x 100m medley relay bronze medals 1992; GB jnr women's 50m and 100m backstroke record-holder. *Leisure interests*: reading, writing letters, cooking chocolate cookies, volleyball, dancing, shopping. *Address*: c/o ASA, Harold Fern House, Derby Square, Loughborough, Leics. LE11 0AL.

BENNETT, David: footballer; b. 11 July 1959, Manchester; player Manchester City 1977–81, Cardiff City 81–83, Coventry City 83–89, Sheffield Wednesday 89–90, Swindon Town 90– ; with Coventry City: winners FA Cup 1987. *Address*: Swindon Town FC, The County Ground, Swindon, Wilts. SN1 2ED.

BENNETT, Gary: footballer; b. 4 December 1961, Manchester; player Cardiff City 1981–84, Sunderland 84– ; with Sunderland: 3rd Div. champs. 1987/88. *Address*: Sunderland FC, Roker Park Ground, Sunderland, Tyne and Wear SR6 9SW.

BENNETT, Ian: footballer; b. 10 October 1970, Worksop; player Peterborough Utd 1991–93, Birmingham City 93– . *Address*: Birmingham City FC, St Andrews Ground, Birmingham B9 4NH.

BENNETT, Michael: footballer; b. 27 July 1969, Camberwell; player Charlton Athletic 1987–90, Wimbledon 90– . *Address*: Wimbledon FC, Selhurst Park, London SE25 6PY.

BENNETT, Stephen: golfer; b. 23 April 1959, Cleethorpes; m. Diane Bennett 1992; rep. Lincs. 1975–79, Lincs. amateur champ. 1977, 78, Lincs. open champ. 1979; England youth debut 1977, snr debut 1978; prof. debut 1980; winner Tunisian Open 1985, Zimbabwe Open 1986. *Leisure interests*: Grimsby Town FC, snooker, squash, relaxing at home. *Address*: 92 Louth Rd, Grimsby, S. Humberside DN33 2HX.

BENNETT, Thomas: footballer; b. 12 December 1969, Falkirk; player Wolverhampton Wanderers 1988– . *Address*: Wolverhampton Wanderers FC, Molineux Stadium, Waterloo Rd, Wolverhampton WV1 4QR.

BENNETT, Tracy Margaret: oarswoman; b. 10 April 1968, Cambridge, Mass., USA; rep. Oxford Univ. Women's BC 1986–91, Thames RC 91–92, Thames Tradesmen's RC 91– ; with Oxford: winners women's Univ. Boat Race 1988 (record time), 1991; GB lightweight and open women's coxless fours champ. 1991, 92; GB lightweight women's squad 1991– . *Leisure interests*: swimming, hockey, bridge. *Address*: 12 Roseland House, Weimar St, Putney, London SW15 1SY.

BENSON, Justin David Ramsay: cricketer; b. 1 March 1967, Dublin, Ireland; player Leics. 1988–93. *Address*: Leics. CCC, County Ground, Grace Rd, Leicester LE2 8AD.

BENSON, Mark Richard: cricketer; b. 6 July 1958, Shoreham; m. Sarah Benson 1986; 2 s.; player Kent 1980–   (capt.); 1 Test (1986), 1 1-day int. *Address*: Kent CCC, St Lawrence Ground, Canterbury CT1 3NZ.

BENTLEY, John: Rugby League footballer; b. 5 September 1966, Dewsbury; player Leeds, Halifax 1992– ; England RU int. *Address*: Halifax RLFC, The Pavilion, Thrum Hall, Gibbet St, Halifax, W. Yorks. HX1 4TL.

BERESFORD, John: footballer; b. 4 September 1966, Sheffield; player Barnsley 1986–89, Portsmouth 89–92, Newcastle Utd 92– . *Address*: Newcastle Utd FC, St James' Park, Newcastle-upon-Tyne, Tyne & Wear NE1 4ST.

BERGSSON, Gudni: footballer; b. 21 July 1965, Reykjavik, Iceland; player Valur (Iceland), Tottenham Hotspur 1988– ; with Tottenham Hotspur: winners FA Cup 1991; Iceland int. *Address*: Tottenham Hotspur FC, 748 High Rd, Tottenham, London N17 0AP.

BERNARD, Paul: footballer; b. 30 December 1972, Edinburgh; player Oldham Athletic 1991– ; 4 Scotland U-21 caps. *Address*: Oldham Athletic FC, Boundary Park, Oldham, Lancs. OL1 2PA.

BERRY, Jack: racehorse trainer (Flat); b. 7 October 1937, Leeds; m. Josephine Mary Thames 1962; 2 s.; NH jockey 1953–69; 1st trainer's licence 1969; winner Ayr Gold Cup 1988 (So Careful); leading Northern trainer 1989–92; trained 132 winners in season 1993; winner Golden Spurs Award 1988. *Publications*: It's Tougher at the Bottom, 1991, A Year in Red Shirts, 1993. *Leisure interests*: boxing, greyhound racing, dog-coursing, football. *Address*: Moss Side Racing Stables, Crimbles Lane, Cockerham, nr Lancaster LA2 0ES.

BERRY, Neil: footballer; b. 6 April 1963, Edinburgh; player Bolton Wanderers 1981–84, Heart of Midlothian 84– . *Address*: Heart of Midlothian FC, Tynecastle Park, Gorgie Rd, Edinburgh EH11 2NL.

BERRY, Philip John: cricketer; b. 28 December 1966, Saltburn; m. Judith Berry; player Yorks. 1986–91, Durham 92– . *Address*: Durham CCC, County Ground, Riverside, Chester-le-Street, Co. Durham DH3 3QR.

BESSELL, Edna: flat green bowler; b. 26 June 1946, Chipping Sodbury; m. Roderick Bessell 1967; 1 s., 2 d.; rep. Somerset 1984– ; England debut (indoor) 1989, (outdoor) 1991; World Indoor Champs. women's singles silver medal 1988; World Champs. women's triples and fours bronze medals 1992; *Daily Telegraph*/Henselite Bowler of the Year 1991/92. *Leisure interests*: swimming, caravanning, embroidery. *Address*: Yeovil Bowling Club, Higher Kingston, Yeovil, Somerset.

BETT, Jim: footballer; b. 25 November 1959, Hamilton; player Airdrieonians 1976–78, Rangers 80–83, Aberdeen 85– ; with Rangers: winners Scottish Cup 1981, Scottish League Cup 1982; with Aberdeen: winners Scottish Cup 1986, 90, Scottish League Cup 1990; 25 Scotland caps. *Address*: Aberdeen FC, Pittodrie Stadium, Pittodrie St, Aberdeen AB2 1QH.

BETTS, Denis: Rugby League footballer; b. 14 September 1969, Salford; player Leigh Rangers ARLFC, Wigan 1986– ; with Wigan: winners Challenge Cup 1989–93, Regal Trophy 1989, 90, 93, Premiership 1992; GB debut v. France 1990, Brit. Lions tours NZ/Papua New Guinea 1990, Aus./NZ/Papua New Guinea 1992. *Address*: Wigan RLFC, The Pavilion, Central Park, Wigan WN1 1XF.

BICKNELL, Darren John: cricketer; b. 24 June 1967, Guildford; m. Rebecca Bicknell 1992; player Surrey 1987– , tours Sharjah (UAE) 1988, 89, Dubai 1990; England A tours Zimbabwe/Kenya 1989/90, Pakistan 1990/91, WI 1991/92. *Address*: Surrey CCC, The Oval, Kennington, London SE11 5SS.

BICKNELL, Martin Paul: cricketer; b. 14 January 1969, Guildford; player Surrey 1986– ; England YC tours Sri Lanka 1986/87, Aus. 1987/88, England A tours Zimbabwe/Kenya 1989/90, WI 1991/92, SA 1993/94 (aborted), snr tour Aus. 1990/91, Test debut v. Aus. 1993. *Address*: Surrey CCC, The Oval, Kennington, London SE11 5SS.

BIDGOOD, Roger Anthony: Rugby Union footballer; b. 15 September 1965, Caerphilly; m. Deborah Bidgood; player Pontypridd, Pontypool, Cardiff, Newport 1990– ; Wales B debut v. France B 1986, snr and Five Nations debut v. Scotland 1992, tour Zimbabwe/Namibia 1993. *Address*: Newport RFC, Rodney Parade, Newport, Gwent.

BIDNER, Todd: ice hockey player; b. 5 July 1961; player Fife Flyers 1985–86, Peterborough Pirates 86–89, Telford Tigers 89–90, Nottingham Panthers 90–91, Bracknell Bees 91–92, Humberside Seahawks 92– ; with Peterborough Pirates: Div. 1 champs. 1986/87. *Address*: The Ice Arena, Kingston St, Hull.

BIGGINS, Wayne: footballer; b. 20 November 1961, Sheffield; player Lincoln City 1980–81, Burnley 83–85, Norwich City 85–88, Manchester City 88–89, Stoke City 89–92, Barnsley 92– ; with Norwich City: 2nd Div. champs. 1985/86. *Address*: Barnsley FC, Oakwell Ground, Barnsley, S. Yorks. S71 1ET.

BIGHAM, David Bryce: decathlete; b. 4 July 1971, Walthamstow; UK youth javelin and 60m hurdles champ. 1987, jnr octathlon champ. 1988, jnr indoor octathlon champ. and jnr decathlon champ. 1990. *Publications*: contributor to *Athletics Weekly*, *Athletics Today*. *Leisure interests*: water skiing, windsurfing, pop music, Tottenham Hotspur FC. *Address*: c/o Brit. Athletic Fed., 225A Bristol Rd, Edgbaston, Birmingham B5 7UB.

BILLING, Peter: footballer; b. 24 October 1964, Liverpool; player Everton 1986, Crewe Alexandra 86–89, Coventry City 89–93, Port Vale 93– . *Address*: Port Vale FC, Vale Park, Burslem, Stoke on Trent, Staffs. ST6 1AW.

BIRCH, Jason: motorcyclist; b. 28 December 1970, Wythenshawe; ACU Brit. clubman's 125cc champ. 1992. *Leisure interests*: camping, canoeing, mountain biking, badminton, snooker, keep-fit, photography. *Address*: 1 Bath Close, Hazel Grove, Stockport, Cheshire SK7 4RX.

BIRCH, John Philip: basketball player; b. 4 April 1970, Bishopton; player Paisley 1984– ; Scotland U-19 debut 1986, snr debut 1992, Commonwealth Champs. silver medallist 1991. *Leisure interests*: weight training, swimming, watching football. *Address*: 59 Kingswood Rd, Bishopton PA7 5LG.

BIRCH, Paul: footballer; b. 20 November 1962, Birmingham; player Aston Villa 1980–91, Wolverhampton Wanderers 91– . *Address*: Wolverhampton Wanderers FC, Molineux Stadium, Waterloo Rd, Wolverhampton WV1 4QR.

BIRCH, Ryan Alexander: judo player (U-78kg); b. 14 April 1969, Hull; GB U-18 champ. 1986, U-21 champ. 1987, French and German U-21 open champ. 1989; GB open champ. 1990, 91, 93, US open champ. 1991, Belgian open champ. 1992; GB U-21 debut 1987, European Jnr Champs. bronze medal 1988, snr debut and European Champs. team bronze medal 1988; World

Champs. squad 1993; Olympic squad 1992. *Leisure interests*: golf, cinema, eating out, walking and climbing in the Lake District. *Address*: `Berndale', Hull Rd, Keyingham HU12 9ST.

BIRKETT, Martin: Rugby League footballer; b. 16 September 1965, Frizington; player Harlequins (RU), Frizington ARLFC, Salford 1989– . *Address*: Salford RLFC, The Willows, Willows Rd, Weaste, Salford M5 2ST.

BIRMINGHAM, Jeremy: water polo player; b. 10 June 1960, London; m. Sarah Birmingham 1992; player Beckenham 1976–80, London Polytechnic 80– ; with London Polytechnic: GB, League champs. 1985–88, 90–92, winners Knockout Cup 1981, 82, 86–88, 90, 91; rep. Kent; England capt. 1984– ; GB jnr debut 1979, snr debut 1981 (capt. 1984–), European Champs. squad 1981, 85, 87, 89, 91, 93; World Masters bronze medal 1992. *Leisure interests*: family, cycling, good restaurants. *Address*: 119 New Crane Wharf, Wapping, London E1 9TU.

BIRT, Michael John: windsurfer; b. 19 March 1973, Durham; UK youth champ. 1990, nat. series raceboard champ. (lightweight) 1991; World Youth Champs. raceboard silver medal 1990; European Champs. raceboard gold medal (lightweight) 1990; World Champs. raceboard silver medal (lightweight) 1990. *Leisure interests*: squash, frisbee, music. *Address*: Bishopton Lake, Bishopton, Stockton, Cleveland TS21 1EY.

BISHOP, Ian: footballer; b. 29 May 1965, Liverpool; player Everton 1983–84, Carlisle Utd 84–88, Bournemouth 88–89, Manchester City 1989, W. Ham Utd 1989– . *Address*: W. Ham Utd FC, Boleyn Ground, Green St, Upton Park, London E13 9AZ.

BISHOP, Ian Raphael: cricketer; b. 24 October 1967, Port of Spain, Trinidad;

player Derbys. 1989–93, Sunday League champs. 1990; Test debut 1988, WI tours England 1988, Aus. 1988/89, India 1989/90, Pakistan 1990/91, Pakistan/Aus. 1991/92, Aus./SA 1992/93. *Address*: Derbys. CCC, County Cricket Ground, Nottingham Rd, Derby DE2 6DA.

BISHOP, Paul: Rugby League footballer; b. 5 July 1967, Leeds; player Warrington, St Helens, Halifax; GB U-21 int. *Address*: Halifax RLFC, The Pavilion, Thrum Hall, Gibbet St, Halifax, W. Yorks. HX1 4TL.

BLACK, Kingsley: footballer; b. 22 June 1968, Luton; player Luton Town 1986–91, Nottingham Forest 91– ; with Luton Town: winners League Cup 1988; 1 NI U-23 cap, over 27 full NI caps. *Address*: Nottingham Forest FC, City Ground, Nottingham NG2 5FJ.

BLACK, Roger Anthony: athlete; b. 31 March 1966, Portsmouth; European Jnr Champs. 400m and 4 x 400m relay gold medals 1985; 400m GP champ. 1991; Commonwealth Games 400m and 4 x 400m relay gold medals 1986; European Cup 400m gold medal 1991; European Champs. 400m and 4 x 400m relay gold medals 1986, 90; World Champs. 4 x 400m relay silver medal 1987, 4 x 400m relay gold, 400m silver 1991; Olympic 4 x 400m relay bronze medal 1992. *Leisure interests*: music, film, art. *Address*: Direction Sportive, Rhodens, The Green, Sands, Farnham, Surrey.

BLACK, Tom: footballer; b. 11 October 1962, Lanark; player Airdrieonians 1980–89, St Mirren 89–92, Kilmarnock 92– . *Address*: Kilmarnock FC, Rugby Park, Kilmarnock KA1 2DP.

BLACKMORE, Andrew George: Rugby Union footballer; b. 1 November 1965, Bristol; player Bristol; rep. S.W. Div., Div. champs. 1993/94; England A debut v. SA 1992, tour Canada 1993. *Address*: Bristol FC, Memorial Ground, Filton Ave, Horfield, Bristol BS7 0AQ.

BLACKMORE, Clayton: footballer; b. 23 September 1964, Neath; player Manchester Utd 1982– , winners FA Cup 1990, European Cup Winners' Cup 1991, League champs. 1992/93; 3 Wales U-21 caps, over 36 full Wales caps. *Address:* Manchester Utd FC, Old Trafford, Manchester M16 0RA.

BLACKMORE, Richard: Rugby League footballer; b. 2 July 1969; player Castleford 1991– , winners Regal Trophy 1994; NZ debut v. France 1991. *Address:* Castleford RLFC, Wheldon Rd, Castleford WF10 2SD.

BLACKWELL, Dean: footballer; b. 5 December 1969, Camden; player Wimbledon 1988– ; 6 England U-21 caps. *Address:* Wimbledon FC, Selhurst Park, London SE25 6PY.

BLACKWELL, Kevin: footballer; b. 21 December 1958, Luton; player Barnet, Scarborough 1987–89, Notts County 89– . *Address:* Notts County FC, Meadow Lane Ground, Nottingham NG2 3HJ.

BLADES, Paul: footballer; b. 5 January 1965, Peterborough; m. Fiona Kay Blades 1985; 2 s., 1 d.; player Derby County 1982–90, Norwich City 90–92, Wolverhampton Wanderers 92– ; with Derby County: 2nd Div. champs. 1986/87. *Leisure interests:* golf, all sport. *Address:* Wolverhampton Wanderers FC, Molineux Stadium, Waterloo Rd, Wolverhampton WV1 4QR.

BLAKE, Mark: footballer; b. 16 December 1970, Nottingham; player Aston Villa 1989–93, Portsmouth 93– ; 8 England U-21 caps. *Address:* Portsmouth FC, Fratton Park, Frogmore Rd, Portsmouth PO4 8RA.

BLAKE, Nathan: footballer; b. 27 January 1972, Cardiff; player Cardiff City 1990–94, Sheffield Utd 94– ; Wales U-21 int., snr debut v. Norway 1994. *Address:* Sheffield Utd FC, Bramall Lane, Sheffield, S. Yorks. S2 4SU.

BLAKELEY, Steve: Rugby League footballer; b. 17 October 1972, Leigh; player Leigh Rangers ARLFC, Wigan, Salford 1992– . *Address:* Salford RLFC, The Willows, Willows Rd, Weaste, Salford M5 2ST.

BLAKEY, Richard John: cricketer; b. 15 January 1967, Huddersfield; m. Michelle Blakey 1991; player Yorks. 1985– , tours Barbados 1987, Cape Town (SA) 1991; Young England tour WI 1985, England A tours Zimbabwe/Kenya 1989/90, Pakistan 1990/91, snr tour India/Sri Lanka 1992/93, Test debut v. India 1993. *Address:* Yorks. CCC, Headingley Cricket Ground, Leeds LS6 3BU.

BLISSETT, Gary: footballer; b. 29 June 1964, Manchester; player Crewe Alexandra 1983–87, Brentford 87–93, Wimbledon 93– ; with Brentford: 3rd Div. champs. 1991/92. *Address:* Wimbledon FC, Selhurst Park, London SE25 6PY.

BLUNDELL, Mark: F1 driver; b. 8 April 1966, Barnet; 1 s.; F3000 debut 1987; F1 debut 1991, rep. Brabham 1991, Ligier 1993, Tyrrell 1994– ; world sportscar debut 1989, rep. Nissan 1989–90, Peugeot 1992, winner Le Mans 24-hour race 1992. *Leisure interests:* squash, golf, music, go-karting. *Address:* Mill Studio Business Centre, Crane Mead, Ware, Herts. SG12 9PY.

BLYTH, David: Rugby Union footballer; b. 14 March 1971, Liverpool; player W. Hartlepool 1992– ; rep. England colts. *Address:* W. Hartlepool RFC, Brierton Lane, Hartlepool, Cleveland TS25 5DR.

BOARDMAN, Christopher Miles, MBE: cyclist; b. 26 August 1968, Clatterbridge; m. Sally Boardman; rep. GAN 1993– ; RTTC 25-mile time trial champ. 1989–93, 25-mile team champ. 1986, 89–92, 50-mile individ. and team champ. 1991, 92, individ. hill-climb champ. 1988–91, team champ.

1987–91, 100km team champ. 1988, 89, 91; GB 4000m individ. pursuit champ. 1989, 91, 92, team pursuit champ. 1993; Commonwealth Games 4000m team pursuit bronze medal 1986; World Champs. 4000m individ. pursuit bronze medal 1993; Olympic squad 1988, 4000m individ. pursuit gold medal 1992; prof. debut 1993; winner Eddy Merckx GP time trial 1993. *Address*: c/o Brit. Cycling Fed., 36 Rockingham Rd, Kettering, Northants. NN16 8HG.

BODEN, Peter: clay pigeon shooter; b. 18 September 1947, Newcastle under Lyme; m. Marilyne Christine Boden 1972; 1 d.; English GP Olympic trap champ. 1980, auto trap champ. 1982; Welsh GP Olympic trap champ. 1979, 80; GB GP Olympic trap champ. 1975, 80, auto trap champ. 1978, universal trap champ. 1980; England debut 1982; Commonwealth Games Olympic trap individ. gold, pairs silver medals 1982, individ. silver, pairs gold 1986; GB debut 1975; World Champs. 5-trap silver medal 1982, double-trap individ. and pairs gold 1991; Olympic squad 1976, 80, 84. *Leisure interests*: tennis, fishing. *Address*: 14 Millais Close, Bedworth, Warks. CV12 8TH.

BODIN, Paul: footballer; b. 13 September 1964, Cardiff; player Cardiff City 1982–84, Newport County 1988, Swindon Town 1988–91, Crystal Palace 91–92, Swindon Town 92– ; 1 Wales U-21 cap, over 19 full Wales caps. *Address*: Swindon Town FC, The County Ground, Swindon, Wilts. SN1 2ED.

BODLEY, Michael: footballer; b. 14 September 1967, Hayes; player Chelsea 1985–89, Northampton Town 1989, Barnet 1989–93, Southend Utd 93– . *Address*: Southend Utd FC, Roots Hall, Victoria Ave, Southend-on-Sea, Essex SS2 6NQ.

BOGIE, Ian: footballer; b. 6 December 1967, Newcastle; player Newcastle Utd 1985–89, Preston N. End 89–91, Millwall 91– . *Address*: Millwall FC, The Den, Zampa Rd, Bermondsey, London SE16 3LH.

BOILING, James: cricketer; b. 8 April 1968, New Delhi, India; player Surrey 1988– ; England YC tour Aus. (Youth World Cup) 1988, England A tour Aus. 1992/93. *Address*: Surrey CCC, The Oval, Kennington, London SE11 5SS.

BOLLAN, Gary: footballer; b. 24 March 1973, Dundee; player Dundee Utd 1990– ; Scotland U-21 int. *Address*: Dundee Utd FC, Tannadice Park, Dundee DD3 7JW.

BONAR, Kirsty Margaret: hockey player; b. 20 April 1972, Ballymena, NI; player Mid Antrim Ladies 1988–90, Randalstown Ladies 90– ; with Randalstown: All-Ireland League champs. 1993; Ulster U-21 debut 1990, snr debut 1992; Ireland U-21 debut 1991. *Leisure interests*: reading, cycling, swimming, music. *Address*: 64 Portglenone Rd, Randalstown, Co. Antrim BT41 3EG.

BONDS, Billy, MBE: football manager; b. 17 September 1946, Woolwich, London; player Charlton Athletic 1964–67, W. Ham Utd 67–88; with W. Ham Utd: winners FA Cup 1975, 80, 2nd Div. champs. 1980/81; 2 England U-23 caps; manager W. Ham Utd 1990– . *Address*: W. Ham Utd FC, Boleyn Ground, Green St, Upton Park, London E13 9AZ.

BONINGTON, Christian John Storey: mountaineer; b. 1934, London; m. Muriel Wendy Marchant 1962; 2 s.; 1st ascents: Annapurna II 1960, Nuptse and Central Pillar of Freney, Mont Blanc 1961, Central Tower of Paine, Patagonia 1963, Old Man of Hoy 1966, Brammah, Kashmir 1973, Changabang, Garhwal Himalaya 1974, Ogre 1977, Mount Kongur 1981, W. Summit of Shivling 1983; 1st Brit. ascents: N. Wall of the Eiger 1962, Mount Vinson 1983; leader Annapurna S. face expedition

1970, Brit. Everest expedition 1972, Brit. K2 expedition 1978, Brit. S.W. face and N.E. ridge of Everest expeditions 1982, Norwegian/Brit. Menlungtse expedition 1987, Tibet expedition 1988; joint leader Indian/Brit. Kumaon expedition 1992; climbing leader Brit. Mount Kongur expedition 1981, 'Greenland the Hard Way' expedition 1991; mem. Norwegian Everest expedition 1985. *Publications: I Chose to Climb*, 1966, *Annapurna South Face*, 1971, *The Next Horizon*, 1973, *Everest South West Face*, 1973, *Changabang* (joint author), 1975, *Everest the Hard Way*, 1976, *Quest for Adventure*, 1981, *Kongur:* China's Elusive Summit, 1982, *Everest:* The Unclimbed Ridge (with Dr Charles Clarke), 1983, *The Everest Years*, 1986, *Mountaineer – Thirty Years of Climbing on the World's Great Peaks*, 1991, *The Climbers*, 1992, *Sea, Ice and Rock* (with Robin Knox-Johnston), 1992. *Leisure interests*: skiing, orienteering, war games. *Address*: Badger Hill, Nether Row, Hesket Newmarket, Wigton, Cumbria CA7 8LA.

BONNER, Pat: footballer; b. 25 May 1960, Donegal, Ireland; player Celtic 1978– , winners Scottish League Cup 1983, Scottish Cup 1985, 89; over 70 Ireland caps. *Address*: Celtic FC, Celtic Park, 95 Kerrydale St, Glasgow G40 3RE.

BOOBYER, Neil: Rugby Union footballer; b. 11 June 1972, Bridgend; player Llanelli, Welsh League champs. 1992/93; Wales U-21 debut v. Scotland 1992, snr debut v. Zimbabwe, tour Zimbabwe/Namibia 1993. *Address*: Llanelli RFC, Stradey Park, Llanelli, Dyfed.

BOOKER, Robert: footballer; b. 25 January 1958, Watford; m. Christine Booker 1991; player Brentford 1978–88, Sheffield Utd 88–91, Brentford 91– ; with Brentford: 3rd Div. champs. 1991/92. *Leisure interests*: birdwatching, wildlife, walking and training the dog. *Address*: Brentford FC, Griffin Park, Braemar Rd, Brentford, Middx TW8 0NT.

BOON, Timothy James: cricketer; b. 1 November 1961, Doncaster; player Leics. 1980– , tour Zimbabwe 1980/81; England YC tour WI 1980 (capt.). *Address*: Leics. CCC, County Ground, Grace Rd, Leicester LE2 8AD.

BOONE, William Robin: rackets player; b. 12 July 1950, Norwich; m. Alison Victoria Boone 1983; 1 s., 1 d.; public schools jnr doubles champ. 1966, snr doubles champ. 1968; GB amateur champ. 1976, 78, 81, 84, 85, 87, 89, 90, 94, doubles champ. 1975–77, 80–84, 86, 92, open champ. 1979, 84, 86, open doubles champ. 1981–85, over-40 singles and doubles champ. 1993; Canadian open champ. 1994; world champ. 1984–86; rep. Norfolk squash 1978–84, county champ. 1980, Cambs. tennis 1983–89. *Leisure interests*: golf, gardening. *Address*: Globe Place, Hellingly, E. Sussex BN27 4EY.

BOOTH, Neil: flat green bowler; b. 19 February 1968, Antrim, NI; Irish U-25 singles champ. 1990, 92, 93, open singles champ. 1993; Ireland debut (indoor) 1990, (outdoor) 1991. *Leisure interests*: golf, horseracing. *Address*: 55 Ash Green, Greystone Rd, Antrim, Co. Antrim BT41 1HL.

BOOTH, Scott: footballer; b. 16 December 1971, Aberdeen; player Aberdeen 1988– ; over 3 Scotland caps. *Address*: Aberdeen FC, Pittodrie Stadium, Pittodrie St, Aberdeen AB2 1QH.

BOOTH, Simon: Rugby League footballer; b. 9 December 1971, Leigh; player Leigh Miners ARLFC, Leigh 1990– . *Address*: Leigh RLFC, Hilton Park, Kirkhall Lane, Leigh WN7 1RN.

BORROWS, Brian: footballer; b. 20 December 1960, Liverpool; player Everton 1981–83, Bolton Wanderers 83–85, Coventry City 85– (capt. 93–). *Address*: Coventry City FC, Highfield Rd Stadium, King Richard St, Coventry CV2 4FW.

BOSNICH, Mark: footballer; b. 13 January 1972, Sydney, Aus.; m. Lisa Bosnich 1992; player Manchester Utd 1989–90, Sydney Croatia (Aus.) 90–92, Aston Villa 92– ; Aus. int. *Leisure interests*: cricket, basketball. *Address*: Aston Villa FC, Villa Park, Trinity Rd, Birmingham B6 6HE.

BOTICA, Frano: Rugby League footballer; b. 3 August 1963, Mangakino, NZ; player Wigan, winners Challenge Cup 1991–93, Premiership 1992, Regal Trophy 1993; NZ RU int.; NZ RL debut v. France 1991. *Address*: Wigan RLFC, The Pavilion, Central Park, Wigan WN1 1XF.

BOTTERMAN, Gregg Richard: Rugby Union footballer; b. 3 March 1968, Welwyn Garden City; m. Cindy Susan Botterman 1992; player Saracens 1988– ; rep. Herts. U-21, London Div. 1992– ; N. Herts. schools cross-country champ. 1984. *Leisure interests*: tennis, squash, martial arts, my wife. *Address*: Saracens FC, Bramley Rd Sports Ground, Chaseside, Southgate, London N14 4AB.

BOULD, Stephen: footballer; b. 16 November 1962, Stoke; player Stoke City 1981–88, Arsenal 88– ; with Arsenal: League champs. 1988/89, 90/91, winners League Cup 1993. *Address*: Arsenal FC, Arsenal Stadium, Highbury, London N5 1BU.

BOURNE, Grayson Hugh: canoeist; b. 30 May 1959, Blaine; GB jnr debut 1975, snr debut 1977; World Champs. K2 10,000m silver medal 1989, gold 1990; Olympic squad 1980, 84, 88, 92; GB K1 500m record-holder. *Leisure interests*: movies, sculpture, travel. *Address*: c/o Brit. Canoe Union, John Dudderidge House, Adbolton Lane, W. Bridgford, Nottingham NG2 5AS.

BOWEN, Mark: footballer; b. 7 December 1963, Neath; player Tottenham Hotspur 1981–87, Norwich City 87– ; 3 Wales U-21 caps, over 23 full Wales caps. *Address*: Norwich City FC, Carrow Rd, Norwich NR1 1JE.

BOWEN, Mark Nicholas: cricketer; b. 6 December 1967, Redcar; player Northants. 1992– , tour SA 1991/92. *Address*: Northants. CCC, County Cricket Ground, Wantage Rd, Northampton NN1 4TJ.

BOWIE, Alison: squash player; b. 14 April 1963, Dundee; m. George Fergus Bowie 1989; player Edinburgh Sports Club 1989– , Scottish club champs. 1991–93; rep. Lothian 1986– ; Scottish girls' U-16 champ. 1978, U-19 champ. 1978, 79, 81, U-21 open champ. 1981, ladies' champ. 1990, 91, champ. of champs. 89–92; Scotland jnr debut 1977, snr debut 1982; most-capped Scottish woman player. *Leisure interests*: golf, mountain biking, tennis, running. *Address*: 5B London St, New Town, Edinburgh EH3 6LZ.

BOWLER, Paul Martin: gymnast; b. 13 October 1967; m. Ann Bowler 1990; GB pommel horse champ. 1991, horizontal bar, rings, horse vault champ. 1991, 93, floor, parallel bars champ. 1993; GB debut 1989, Olympic squad 1992. *Leisure interests*: cars, water skiing, gardening, go-karting. *Address*: 12 Duffield Rd, Alkrington, Middleton, Manchester M24 1WQ.

BOWLER, Peter Duncan: cricketer; b. 30 July 1963, Plymouth; m. Joanne Bowler 1992; player Leics. 1986–88, Derbys. 88– ; with Derbys.: winners Benson and Hedges Cup 1993, Sunday League champs. 1990. *Address*: Derbys. CCC, County Cricket Ground, Nottingham Rd, Derby DE2 6DA.

BOWMAN, David: footballer; b. 10 March 1960, Tunbridge Wells; player Heart of Midlothian 1980–84, Coventry City 84–86, Dundee Utd 86– ; 1 Scotland U-21 cap, over 4 full Scotland caps. *Address*: Dundee Utd FC, Tannadice Park, Dundee DD3 7JW.

BOWMAN, George: equestrianist (carriage driving); b. 14 October 1934, Penrith; m. Eileen Bowman 1962; 2 s., 1 d.; GB champ.

16 times; World Champs. team gold medals 1974, 80. *Leisure interests*: horses. *Address*: Nine Chimneys, Redhills, Penrith, Cumbria CA11 0DR.

BOX, Toby: athlete; b. 9 September 1972, Stockport; GB U-21 debut 1991, snr debut and World Champs. squad (4 x 100m relay) 1993. *Leisure interests*: classic cars, cooking, films, music. *Address*: Wolverhampton and Bilston Athletics Club, Aldersley Stadium, Aldersley, Wolverhampton.

BOYD, Thomas: footballer; b. 24 November 1965, Glasgow; player Motherwell 1983–91, Chelsea 91–92, Celtic 92– ; with Motherwell: winners Scottish Cup 1991; 5 Scotland U-21 caps, over 17 full Scotland caps. *Address*: Celtic FC, Celtic Park, 95 Kerrydale St, Glasgow G40 3RE.

BRACEWELL, Julia Helen: fencer (foil); b. 26 April 1964, Rochford, Essex; rep. Bristol Univ. 1982–85, UAU 83–85; UAU ladies' champ. 1983, 84; Scottish open champ. 1990; Scotland debut 1986; Commonwealth Champs. team bronze medals 1986, 90; GB debut and World Champs. squad 1990, Olympic squad 1992. *Leisure interests*: skiing, sailing, walking, tennis, dance. *Address*: Gouldens, 22 Tudor St, London EC4Y 0JJ.

BRACEWELL, Paul: footballer; b. 19 July 1962, Stoke; player Stoke City 1980–83, Sunderland 83–84, Everton 84–89, Sunderland 89–92, Newcastle Utd 92– ; with Everton: winners European Cup Winners' Cup 1985, League champs. 1984/85; 13 England U-21 caps, 3 full England caps. *Address*: Newcastle Utd FC, St James' Park, Newcastle-upon-Tyne, Tyne & Wear NE1 4ST.

BRACKEN, Kyran Paul Patrick: Rugby Union footballer; b. 22 November 1972, Dublin, Ireland; player Bristol Univ.,

Bristol; rep. S.W. Div. 1993– ; England U-21 debut 1992, snr debut v. NZ 1993, England A tour Canada 1993. *Leisure interests*: most ball sports, all water sports, music, socializing, travel. *Address*: Bristol FC, Memorial Ground, Filton Ave, Horfield, Bristol BS7 0AQ.

BRADBURY, Julie Jane: badminton player; b. 12 February 1967, Chalgrove; rep. Oxon 1984– ; English ladies' champ. 1991, ladies' doubles champ. 1992, Welsh ladies' doubles champ. 1993; England debut 1992; European Champs. team bronze medal 1992; Olympic squad 1992; winner Spanish Open ladies' doubles 1991. *Leisure interests*: watching and participating in all sports, Indian food. *Address*: 45 Wensum Drive, The Poplars, Didcot, Oxon OX11 7RJ.

BRADLEY, Alison Sarah: equestrianist (show jumping); b. 28 July 1970, Louth; European Jnr Champs. team silver medal 1988; GB ladies' show jumping champ., Horse of the Year Show 1993. *Leisure interests*: night-clubbing, parties, shopping. *Address*: 3 Drift Rd, Lakenheath, Brandon, Suffolk IP27 9JL.

BRADLEY, Darren: footballer; b. 24 November 1965, Birmingham; player Aston Villa 1983–86, W. Bromwich Albion 86– . *Address*: W. Bromwich Albion FC, The Hawthorns, W. Bromwich B71 4LF.

BRADSHAW, Carl: footballer; b. 2 October 1968, Sheffield; player Sheffield Wednesday 1986–88, Manchester City 88–89, Sheffield Utd 89– . *Address*: Sheffield Utd FC, Bramall Lane, Sheffield, S. Yorks S2 4SU.

BRADY, Kieron: footballer; b. 17 September 1971, Glasgow; player Sunderland 1989– ; 1 Ireland U-21 cap. *Address*: Sunderland FC, Roker Park Ground, Sunderland, Tyne and Wear SR6 9SW.

BRADY, William (Liam): football manager; b. 13 February 1956, Dublin, Ireland; player Arsenal 1973–80, Juventus, Sampdoria, Internazionale, Ascoli (all Italy), W. Ham Utd 1987–90; with Arsenal: winners FA Cup 1979; 72 Ireland caps; Football Writers' Assoc. Player of the Year 1979; manager Celtic 1991–-93, Brighton and Hove Albion 93– . *Address*: Brighton and Hove Albion FC, Goldstone Ground, Newtown Rd, Hove, E. Sussex BN3 7DE.

BRANAGAN, Keith: footballer; b. 10 July 1966, Fulham; player Cambridge Utd 1983–88, Millwall 88–92, Bolton Wanderers 92– . *Address*: Bolton Wanderers FC, Burnden Park, Manchester Rd, Bolton, Lancs. BL3 2QR.

BRAND, Gordon, Jnr: golfer; b. 19 August 1958, Burntisland, Fife; Glos. amateur champ. 1977; English open amateur stroke-play champ. 1978, Scottish open amateur strokeplay champ. 1980, Swedish open amateur strokeplay champ. 1979, Portuguese amateur champ. 1981; Scotland debut 1978; GB debut 1978, Walker Cup team 1979; prof. debut 1981; Dunhill Cup team (Scotland) 1985–89, 91– ; Ryder Cup team 1987 (winners), 89; winner European Open 1984, 93, Dutch Open 1987, S. Aus. Open 1988, Benson and Hedges Int. Open 1989. *Address*: c/o PGA European Tour, Wentworth Club, Wentworth Drive, Virginia Water, Surrey GU25 4LS.

BRANNAN, Gerard (Ged): footballer; b. 15 January 1972, Prescot; player Tranmere Rovers 1990– . *Address*: Tranmere Rovers FC, Prenton Park, Prenton Rd W., Birkenhead, Merseyside L42 9PN.

BREACKER, Timothy: footballer; b. 2 July 1965, Bicester; player Luton Town 1983–90, W. Ham Utd 90– ; with Luton Town: winners League Cup 1988; 2 England U-21 caps. *Address*: W. Ham Utd FC, Boleyn Ground, Green St, Upton Park, London E13 9AZ.

BREBANT, Rick: ice hockey player; b. 21 February 1964; player Durham Wasps 1987–93, Cardiff Devils 93– ; with Durham Wasps: winners Autumn Cup 1989, 91, GB champs. 1987/88, 90/91, 91/92, League champs. 1988/89, 90/91, 91/92. *Address*: Wales Nat. Ice Rink, Hayes Bridge Rd, Cardiff CF1 2GH.

BREITKREUTZ, Matthias: footballer; b. 12 May 1971, Berlin, Germany; player Bergman Bosnig (Germany), Aston Villa 1991– . *Address*: Aston Villa FC, Villa Park, Trinity Rd, Birmingham B6 6HE.

BRESSINGTON, Graham: footballer; b. 8 July 1966, Eton; player Lincoln City 1987–93, Southend Utd 93– . *Address*: Southend Utd FC, Roots Hall, Victoria Ave, Southend-on-Sea, Essex SS2 6NQ.

BREVETT, Rufus: footballer; b. 24 September 1969, Derby; player Doncaster Rovers 1988–91, Queens Park Rangers 91– . *Address*: Queens Park Rangers FC, Rangers Stadium, S. Africa Rd, London W12 7PA.

BREW, Robin: triathlete; b. 28 June 1962; m. Lynn Brew; 1 s., 1 d; European Champs. team gold medal 1991, bronze 1987; GB Olympic swimming squad 1984. *Address*: c/o Brit. Triathlon Assoc., 4 Tynemouth Terrace, Tynemouth NE30 4BH.

BREWSTER, Craig: footballer; b. 13 December 1966, Dundee; player Forfar Athletic 1985–91, Raith Rovers 91–93, Dundee Utd 93– . *Address*: Dundee Utd FC, Tannadice Park, Dundee DD3 7JW.

BRIDGE, Peter Alan John: oarsman; b. 3 June 1972, Pembury, Kent; rep. Eton College 1989–90, Oxford Univ. BC 90– , Leander Club 91– ; with Eton: Nat. Schools Regatta eights champ. 1989, eights, coxed fours and coxless pairs champ. 1990; with Oxford: winners Univ. Boat Race 1991, 92; GB jnr debut and World Jnr

Champs. coxless fours gold medal 1990, U-23 debut 1991, World U-23 Champs. eights gold medal 1991, coxless pairs silver 1992, snr debut 1991. *Leisure interests*: sailing, photography, travel, juggling, music, French 19th- and 20th-century literature and art. *Address*: Leander Club, Henley-on-Thames, Oxon.

BRIDGES, Christopher Jeffrey: Rugby Union footballer; b. 31 August 1968, Pontypridd; m. Sarah Bridges; 1 s.; player Beddau, Neath; Wales debut v. Namibia, tour 1990. *Address*: Neath RFC, The Gnoll, Gnoll Park Rd, Neath, W. Glamorgan.

BRIERS, Nigel Edwin: cricketer; b. 15 January 1955, Leicester; m. Suzanne Mary Tudor 1977; 2 s.; player Leics. 1971– ; MCC tours Far East 1981, Virgin and Leeward Islands 1991/92. *Address*: Leics. CCC, County Ground, Grace Rd, Leicester LE2 8AD.

BRIGGS, Karen Valerie, MBE: judo player (U-48kg); b. 11 April 1963, Hull; GB women's open champ. 1981, 82, 86, 87, 89, 90, 92; Dutch women's open champ. 1981, 82; German women's open champ. 1982, 83, 85; Austrian women's open champ. 1982, 83, 85, 86, 89, 92; Japanese women's open champ. 1983–86, 88; Swiss women's open champ. 1984; Belgian women's open champ. 1984, 89; Norwegian women's open champ. 1990; US women's open champ. 1991; Commonwealth Games gold medal 1990; GB jnr debut 1979, snr debut 1981; European Champs. gold medals 1982–84, 86, 87; World Champs. gold medals 1982, 84, 86, 89; Olympic squad 1992. *Leisure interests*: all sport, embroidery, shopping. *Address*: c/o Brit. Judo Assoc., 7A Rutland St, Leicester LE1 1RB.

BRIGHTWELL, David: footballer; b. 7 January 1971, Lutterworth; player Manchester City 1988– . *Address*: Manchester City FC, Maine Rd, Moss Side, Manchester M14 7WN.

BRIGHTWELL, Ian: footballer; b. 9 April 1968, Lutterworth; player Manchester City 1986– ; 4 England U-21 caps. *Address*: Manchester City FC, Maine Rd, Moss Side, Manchester M14 7WN.

BRIMBLE, Sue: hockey player; b. 14 May 1965; player Clifton; England U-21 debut 1983, snr debut 1985. *Address*: Clifton HC, Bristol University Astroturf, Coombe Dingle, Stoke Bishop, Bristol.

BRISTOW, Andrew Deryck Jason: athlete (cross-country); b. 2 September 1961, Brighton; m. Jane Bristow 1988; English schools 5000m champ. 1979; World Champs. team bronze medal 1992, squad 1988, 90, 91, 93. *Leisure interests*: skiing, biking, travel. *Address*: 8 Meadow View, Marlow, Bucks. SL7 3PA.

BRISTOW, Eric John, MBE: darts player; b. 25 April 1957, Stoke Newington; GB prof. champ. 1982, 85; world prof. champ. 1980, 81, 84–86, pairs champ. 1987; England debut 1975, winners World Cup 1979–91, Nations Cup 1979, 80, 82–84, 86–88; winner World Masters 1977, 79, 81, 83, 84, Brit. Open 1978, 81, 83, 85, 86, Brit. Matchplay 1982, 83, 86, *News of the World* Champs. 1983, 84, World Cup singles 1983, 85, 87, 89, World Matchplay 1985, 88. *Address*: c/o World Prof. Darts Players Assoc., 5 Hayfield Close, Wingerworth, Chesterfield, Derbys. S42 6QF.

BRITTAIN, Clive Edward: racehorse trainer (Flat); b. 15 December 1933, Calne; m. Maureen Helen Brittain 1957; 1st licence 1972; winner St Leger 1978 (Julio Mariner), 1992 (User Friendly), 1000 Guineas 1984 (Pebbles), 1993 (Sayyedati), 2000 Guineas 1991 (Mystiko), Oaks, Irish Oaks 1992 (User Friendly). *Leisure interests*: shooting. *Address*: Carlburg, 49 Bury Rd, Newmarket, Suffolk CB8 7BY.

BRITTIN, Janette Ann: cricketer; b. 4 July 1959, Kingston; player Tadking LCC 1970–76, Chelsea CPE 77–79, Gunnersbury LCC 80–88, Redoubtables WCC 90– ; rep. Surrey jnr 1973–76, snr 80– ; England jnr debut 1975; Test debut 1979, tours NZ (World Cup) 1982, Aus./NZ 1984/85, Aus. (World Cup) 1988, NZ 1992 (vice-capt.), winners World Cup 1993; highest run-scorer in int. women's cricket; rep. England indoor hockey 1986–87; Sports Writers' Assoc. Team of the Year award-winner 1993. *Leisure interests*: golf, hockey, swimming, gardening, DIY, discovering new restaurants. *Address*: c/o Women's Cricket Assoc., 41 St Michael's Lane, Headingley, Leeds LS6 3BR.

BRITTON, Gerard: footballer; b. 20 October 1970, Glasgow; m. Clare McAuley 1993; player Celtic 1987–92, Partick Thistle 92– . *Leisure interests*: coaching, studying for degree in social sciences. *Address*: Partick Thistle FC, Firhill Stadium, 80 Firhill Rd, Glasgow G20 7BA.

BROAD, Brian Christopher: cricketer; b. 29 September 1957, Bristol; 1 s., 1 d.; player Glos. 1979–83, Notts. 84–92, Glos. 93– ; 25 Tests, debut 1984, 34 1-day ints, tours Aus. 1986/87, Pakistan/Aus./NZ 1987/88. *Publications*: *Home Thoughts from Abroad*, 1987. *Address*: Glos. CCC, Phoenix County Ground, Nevil Rd, Bristol BS6 9EJ.

BROADHURST, Paul: golfer; b. 14 August 1965; England debut 1986; GB debut 1988; prof. debut 1988; Ryder Cup team 1991; winner Cannes Open 1989, Benson and Hedges Int. Open 1993. *Address*: c/o PGA European Tour, Wentworth Club, Wentworth Drive, Virginia Water, Surrey GU25 4LS.

BROCK, Kevin: footballer; b. 9 September 1962, Middleton Stoney; player Oxford Utd 1979–87, Queens Park Rangers 87–88, Newcastle Utd 88– ; with Oxford Utd: winners League Cup 1986, 3rd Div.

champs. 1983/84, 2nd Div. champs. 1984/85; 4 England U-21 caps. *Address*: Newcastle Utd FC, St James' Park, Newcastle-upon-Tyne, Tyne & Wear NE1 4ST.

BRODDLE, Julian: footballer; b. 1 November 1964, Laughton-en-le-Morthen; m. Janet Lea Broddle 1986; 2 s.; player Sheffield Utd 1982–83, Scunthorpe Utd 83–87, Barnsley 87–90, Plymouth Argyle 1990, St Mirren 1990–93, Partick Thistle 93– . *Leisure interests*: golf, film, driving, family life. *Address*: Partick Thistle FC, Firhill Stadium, 80 Firhill Rd, Glasgow G20 7BA.

BROOME, David McPherson, OBE: equestrianist (show jumping); b. 1 March 1940, Cardiff; m. Liz Broome; European Champs. individ. gold medals 1961 (Sunsalve), 1967, 69 (Mister Softee); World Champs. individ. gold medal 1970 (Beethoven), team gold 1978; Olympic individ. bronze medals 1960 (Sunsalve), 68 (Mister Softee), squad 1964, 72, 88, 92; winner Derby 1966 (Mister Softee), King George V Gold Cup 1960 (Sunsalve), 1966 (Mister Softee), 1972 (Sportsman), 1977 (Philco), 1981 (Mr Ross), 1991 (Lannegan). *Address*: c/o Brit. Horse Soc., Brit. Equestrian Centre, Stoneleigh Park, Kenilworth, Warks. CV8 2LR.

BROTHERTON, Paul: yachtsman (470 class); b. 11 July 1966, Oldham; UK youth debut 1981, snr debut 1988; UK champ., Spanish champ. 1991; French open champ. 1990; World Champs. bronze medal 1991; Olympic squad 1992. *Leisure interests*: cycling, running, windsurfing, good food. *Address*: Hyde Sails, 263 Church Rd, Benfleet, Essex SS7 4QR.

BROWN, Alan: Rugby Union footballer; b. 20 September 1967, Stockton; player W. Hartlepool 1990– ; rep. Durham U-19 and snr, N. Div. *Address*: W. Hartlepool RFC, Brierton Lane, Hartlepool, Cleveland TS25 5DR.

BROWN, Alistair Duncan: cricketer; b. 11 February 1970, Beckenham; player Surrey 1992– . *Address*: Surrey CCC, The Oval, Kennington, London SE11 5SS.

BROWN, Barrie: Rugby Union footballer; b. 21 July 1961, Edinburgh; m. Carmel Brown 1989; 1 s., 1 d.; player Edinburgh Academicals 1979–86, Boroughmuir 86– ; rep. Edinburgh District 1985–   ; Scotland tour Zimbabwe 1988; Scotland U-21 javelin champ. 1978, 79. *Leisure interests*: golf, family. *Address*: Boroughmuir RFC, Meggetland, Colinton Rd, Edinburgh EH14 1AS.

BROWN, Carolyn Frances: race walker; b. 24 May 1974, Douglas, IoM; Manx women's 10km road race champ. 1992; GB jnr debut 1991; top-ranked Brit. U-20 female race walker 1992, 93. *Leisure interests*: cycling, swimming, aerobics, reading. *Address*: 5 Laureston Close, Douglas, IoM.

BROWN, David: Nordic skier; b. 2 September 1969; m. Nadia Brown 1993; 2 s., 2 d.; GB debut 1992, World Champs. squad (10km classical, 15km freestyle cross-country) 1993. *Leisure interests*: athletics. *Address*: 9 Eliot Drive, Marlow, Bucks. SL7 1TT.

BROWN, Emma-Jane: equestrianist (show jumping); b. 17 March 1964; GB ladies' champ. 1984; GB debut 1988; winner Foxhunter Champs., Horse of the Year Show 1987 (Oyster), Queen Elizabeth II Cup 1990 (Oyster). *Address*: c/o Brit. Horse Soc., Brit. Equestrian Centre, Stoneleigh Park, Kenilworth, Warks. CV8 2LR.

BROWN, John: footballer; b. 26 January 1962, Stirling; player Hamilton Academical 1979–84, Dundee 84–88, Rangers 88– ; with Rangers: winners Scottish League Cup 1989, 91, Scottish Cup 1992, 93. *Address*: Glasgow Rangers FC, Ibrox Stadium, 150 Edmiston Drive, Glasgow G51 2XD.

BROWN, Jonathan Michael: athlete; b. 27 February 1971, Kenfig Hill, Mid Glamorgan; rep. Yorks. 1984– ; English schools 3000m champ. 1987, youth cross-country champ. 1988; US nat. collegiate 5000m indoor champ. 1992; AAA and UK 5000m champ. 1993; World Student Games squad 1991, World Champs. and World Cross-Country Champs. squads 1993; UK 5000m jnr record-holder. *Leisure interests*: music, cinema, cycling. *Address*: 11 Sandstone Drive, Sheffield S9 1DU.

BROWN, Keith Robert: cricketer; b. 18 March 1963, Edmonton; m. Marie Brown 1984; 2 s., 1 d.; player Middx 1984– , county champs. 1985, 90, 93, Sunday League champs. 1992. *Leisure interests*: family, DIY, most sports. *Address*: Middx CCC, Lord's Cricket Ground, London NW8 8QN.

BROWN, Kenneth: footballer; b. 11 July 1967, Upminster; player Norwich City 1985–88, Plymouth Argyle 88–91, W. Ham Utd 91– . *Address*: W. Ham Utd FC, Boleyn Ground, Green St, Upton Park, London E13 9AZ.

BROWN, Michael (Mickey): footballer; b. 8 February 1968, Birmingham; player Shrewsbury Town 1986–91, Bolton Wanderers 91– . *Address*: Bolton Wanderers FC, Burnden Park, Manchester Rd, Bolton, Lancs. BL3 2QR.

BROWN, Neville: boxer; b. 26 February 1966; ABA jnr champ. 1981, 82; ABA light-middleweight champ. 1987, 89; England debut 1986; European Champs. light-middleweight bronze medal 1987; prof. debut 1989; titles won: GB middleweight 1993; over 20 prof. wins. *Address*: Nat. Promotions, Nat. House, 60–66 Wardour St, London W1V 3HP.

BROWN, Philip: footballer; b. 30 May 1959, S. Shields; player Hartlepool Utd 1978–85, Halifax Town 85–88, Bolton Wanderers 88– (capt.). *Address*: Bolton Wanderers FC, Burnden Park, Manchester Rd, Bolton, Lancs. BL3 2QR.

BROWN, Shaun: Rugby League footballer; b. 19 October 1969; player Leigh E. ARLFC, Salford 1989– . *Address*: Salford RLFC, The Willows, Willows Rd, Weaste, Salford M5 2ST.

BROWN, Shirley: squash player; b. Edinburgh; player Edinburgh Sports Club; rep. Lothian; Scottish girls' U-16 open champ. 1980, U-19 open champ. 1982, 83, U-21 open champ. 1984, ladies' champ. 1987–89, open champ. 1989; Scotland jnr debut 1980, snr debut 1982. *Leisure interests*: skiing, photography, golf. *Address*: 6 Moorgate, Lancaster LA1 3QF.

BROWN, Simon John Emmerson: cricketer; b. 29 June 1969, Sunderland; player Northants. 1987–91, Durham 92– ; England YC tours Sri Lanka 1987, Aus. (Youth World Cup) 1988. *Address*: Durham CCC, County Ground, Riverside, Chester-le-Street, Co. Durham DH3 3QR.

BROWN, Timothy Royce: boxer; b. 27 November 1973; Welsh light-heavyweight champ. 1993. *Leisure interests*: banger racing, cars. *Address*: Glyn Malden Lodge, Tywyn Rd, Dolgellau, Gwynedd LL40 1YA.

BROWNLEE, Craig: basketball player; b. 26 March 1971, Glasgow; player Glasgow City 1986– ; Scotland debut 1989. *Leisure interests*: swimming. *Address*: c/o Scottish Basketball Assoc., Caledonia House, S. Gyle, Edinburgh EH12 9DQ.

BROWNLESS, Alison Ruth: oarswoman; b. 27 August 1962, Bury; rep. Reading Univ. Women's BC 1982–86 (Pres. 1984/85), Staines BC 87–88, Thames RC 88– ; GB lightweight women's coxless fours champ. 1988, lightweight women's

double sculls champ. 1990; GB debut 1991, World Champs. lightweight women's coxless fours silver medals 1991, 92, gold 1993. *Leisure interests*: cycling, cinema, travel and languages, ice-cream, wine, art and literature. *Address*: 20 Schubert Rd, Putney, London SW15 2QS.

BROWNLOW, Katharine Charlotte Deirdre: oarswoman; b. 16 August 1964, Altrincham; GB debut 1988, World Champs. lightweight women's coxless fours silver medals 1989, 91, Olympic squad 1992. *Leisure interests*: reading, clubbing, music, fast cars, motorbikes, running, swimming, hippy culture. *Address*: c/o 330 Cowley Mansions, Mortlake High St, London SW14 8SL.

BRUCE, Ian Stanley: flat green bowler; b. 2 January 1952, Kincardine O'Neil; m. Diana Mae Bruce 1975; 2 s.; Scottish pairs champ. 1985; Scotland debut (outdoor) 1984, (indoor) 1986; Commonwealth Games fours gold medal 1990. *Leisure interests*: watching football. *Address*: 57A High St, Banchory, Kincardineshire AB31 3TJ.

BRUCE, Stephen: footballer; b. 31 December 1960, Corbridge; player Gillingham 1978–84, Norwich City 84–87, Manchester Utd 87– (capt.); with Norwich City: winners League Cup 1985, 2nd Div. champs. 1985/86; with Manchester Utd: winners FA Cup 1990, European Cup Winners' Cup 1991, League champs. 1992/93. *Address*: Manchester Utd FC, Old Trafford, Manchester M16 0RA.

BRUNDLE, Martin John: F1 driver; b. 1 June 1959, Norfolk; m. Elizabeth Brundle 1981; 1 s., 1 d.; F3 debut 1982; F1 debut 1984, rep. Tyrell 1984–86, Zakspeed 1987, Brabham 1989, 91, Benetton 1992, Ligier 1993, 2nd place US GP 1984, Italian GP 1992, 3rd place San Marino GP 1993; world sportscar debut 1985, rep. Jaguar 1985–91, world champ. 1988, winner Daytona 24-hour race 1988, Le Mans 24-hour race 1990. *Leisure interests*: flying helicopters, golf, cars. *Address*: c/o 26 Chapel St, Titchmarsh, Northants. NN14 3DA.

BRUNO, Frank, MBE: boxer; b. 16 November 1961, Hammersmith; m. Laura Mooney; 2 d.; ABA heavyweight champ. 1980; prof. debut 1982; titles won: European heavyweight 1985; over 35 prof. wins. *Publications: Know What I Mean?*, 1987, *Eye of the Tiger*, 1992. *Address*: c/o Equity, 8 Harley St, London W1.

BRYANT, David John, CBE: flat green bowler; b. 27 October 1931, Clevedon; m. Ruth Georgina Bryant 1960; 2 d.; rep. Somerset (outdoor) 1952– , (indoor) 1974– ; English singles champ. (outdoor) 1960, 66, 71–73, 75, (indoor) 1964, 65, 67, 69, 71, 72, 77, 79, 83, pairs champ. (outdoor) 1965, 69, 74, (indoor) 1982, triples champ. (outdoor) 1966, 77, 85, fours champ. (outdoor) 1957, 68, 69, 71; GB singles champ. (outdoor) 1960, 71–73, (indoor) 1967, 69, 77, 79, pairs champ. (outdoor) 1965, 74, (indoor) 1983, triples champ. (outdoor) 1986, fours champ. (outdoor) 1957, 69, 71; England debut (outdoor) 1958, (indoor) 1965; Commonwealth Games singles gold medals 1962, 70, 74, 78, fours gold 1962; World Champs. singles gold medals 1966, 80, 88, bronze 1976, 84, pairs silver 1984, 88, bronze 1966, triples gold 1980, silver 1976, team gold 1980, 88; World Indoor Champs. singles gold medals 1979–81, pairs gold 1986, 87, 89–92; winner Kodak Masters singles 1978, 79, 82, Gateway Masters singles 1984, 85, 86, 87, Woolwich Masters singles 1988, 89, John Player Classic singles 1981, Triple Crown Classic singles 1982, Welsh Classic singles 1986; life mem. English Bowling Assoc. and English Indoor Bowling Assoc. *Publications: Bryant on Bowls*, 1966 (revised 1985), *Bowl with Bryant*, 1984, *The Game of Bowls*, 1990, *Bowls with Bryant* (video), 1992. *Leisure interests*: angling, gardening, cricket. *Address*: Clevedon Bowling Club, Chapel Hill, Clevedon, Somerset.

BRYCE, Steven: footballer; b. 30 June 1969, Shotts; player Motherwell 1987– . *Address*: Motherwell FC, Fir Park, Fir Park St, Motherwell ML1 2QN.

BRYSON, Ian: footballer; b. 26 November 1962, Kilmarnock; player Sheffield Utd 1988–93, Barnsley 93– . *Address*: Barnsley FC, Oakwell Ground, Barnsley, S. Yorks. S71 1ET.

BUCKETT, Ian: Rugby Union footballer; b. 23 December 1967, Holywell; player Oxford Univ., Swansea; Wales A debut v. The Netherlands 1990, snr tours Namibia 1990, Zimbabwe/Namibia 1993. *Address*: Swansea RFC, St Helen's, Swansea SA2 0AR.

BUCKLEY, Alan: football manager; b. 20 April 1951, Eastwood; player Nottingham Forest 1968–73, Walsall 73–78, Birmingham City 1978, Walsall 79–85; manager Walsall, Kettering, Grimsby Town 1988– . *Address*: Grimsby Town FC, Blundell Park, Cleethorpes, S. Humberside DN35 7PY.

BUCKTON, John Richard: Rugby Union footballer; b. 22 December 1961, Hull; m. Carol Buckton; player Hull, E. Riding, Saracens 1985– (capt. 1990–92); rep. Yorks., county champs. 1986/87; England debut v. Aus. 1988, tour Argentina 1990. *Address*: Saracens FC, Bramley Rd Sports Ground, Chaseside, Southgate, London N14 4AB.

BUDD, Danny: water skier; b. 8 December 1971, Colchester; GB dauphin slalom, jump and overall champ. 1987, jnr slalom, jump and overall champ. 1988, U-21 tricks champ. 1989, jump champ. 1992, open men's jump champ. 1992; Irish jump champ. 1991; European jnr overall champ. 1988; GB debut 1984; European Youth Cup silver medal 1987. *Leisure interests*: cycling, weight training, tennis. *Address*: 5 Point Clear Rd, St Osyth, Clacton, Essex CO16 8EP.

BUDWORTH, Marion Elaine: archer (crossbow); b. 25 May 1952, Holbeach, Lincs.; m. Philip John Budworth 1972; 2 d.; GB ladies' outdoor champ. 1991, 92, indoor champ. 1991–93; GB debut 1989, World Champs. squad 1990. *Leisure interests*: bowling, eating out. *Address*: 19 Welby Drive, Gosberton, Spalding PE11 4HU.

BULL, Stephen: footballer; b. 28 March 1965, W. Bromwich; m. Julie Bull 1991; 1 s.; player W. Bromwich Albion 1985–86, Wolverhampton Wanderers 86– ; with Wolverhampton Wanderers: 4th Div. champs. 1987/88, 3rd Div. champs. 1988/89; 5 England U-21 caps, 13 full England caps. *Leisure interests*: golf, swimming, TV. *Address*: Wolverhampton Wanderers FC, Molineux Stadium, Waterloo Rd, Wolverhampton WV1 4QR.

BUNN, Frank: footballer; b. 6 November 1962, Birmingham; player Luton Town 1980–85, Hull City 85–87, Oldham Athletic 87– . *Address*: Oldham Athletic FC, Boundary Park, Oldham, Lancs. OL1 2PA.

BURBERRY, Eden: surfer; b. 7 April 1965, Hanworth; English ladies' champ. 1983, 84, 86, 88, 89, 92; GB ladies' champ. 1985, 87–89, 93; European ladies' champ. 1989; England debut 1983; GB debut 1989. *Leisure interests*: cycling, sailing, swimming, sub-aqua. *Address*: 56 Edgcombe Ave, Newquay, Cornwall TR7 2NJ.

BURGESS, Andy: Rugby League footballer; b. 1 April 1970, Salford; player Irlam ARLFC, Salford 1987– ; GB U-21 debut v. France 1991. *Address*: Salford RLFC, The Willows, Willows Rd, Weaste, Salford M5 2ST.

BURGESS, Daryl: footballer; b. 24 January 1971, Birmingham; player W. Bromwich Albion 1989– . *Address*: W. Bromwich Albion FC, The Hawthorns, W. Bromwich B71 4LF.

BURKE, David: footballer; b. 6 August 1960, Liverpool; player Bolton Wanderers 1977–81, Huddersfield Town 81–87, Crystal Palace 87–90, Bolton Wanderers 90– . *Address*: Bolton Wanderers FC, Burnden Park, Manchester Rd, Bolton, Lancs. BL3 2QR.

BURKE, Mark: footballer; b. 12 February 1969, Solihull; player Aston Villa 1987, Middlesbrough 1987–91, Wolverhampton Wanderers 91– . *Address*: Wolverhampton Wanderers FC, Molineux Stadium, Waterloo Rd, Wolverhampton WV1 4QR.

BURKE, Paul: boxer; b. 2 July 1966, Preston; prof. debut 1987; titles won: GB and Commonwealth lightweight 1993; over 17 prof. wins. *Address*: c/o Phil Martin, 79 Buckingham Rd, Chorlton, Manchester M21 1QT.

BURKINSHAW, Keith: football manager; b. 23 June 1935, Barnsley; player Liverpool 1953–57, Workington 57–65, Scunthorpe Utd 65–67; manager W. Bromwich Albion 1993– . *Address*: W. Bromwich Albion FC, The Hawthorns, Halfords Lane, W. Bromwich B71 4LF.

BURNELL, Andrew Paul: Rugby Union footballer; b. 29 September 1965, Edinburgh; player Marlow, Harlequins, Leicester, London Scottish; Scotland B debut v. Italy 1989, snr and Five Nations debut v. England 1989, Grand Slam champs. 1990, tours Zimbabwe 1988, NZ 1990. *Address*: London Scottish FC, Richmond Athletic Ground, Kew Foot Rd, Richmond, Surrey TW9 2SS.

BURNS, Charlotte Sara: lacrosse player; b. 27 March 1968, Edinburgh; player Edinburgh Thistle (capt.); Scotland debut 1991, tours USA 1992, 93. *Leisure interests*: golf, tennis. *Address*: 108/10 St Stephen St, Stockbridge, Edinburgh EH3 5AQ.

BURNS, Christopher: footballer; b. 9 November 1967, Manchester; player Portsmouth 1991– . *Address*: Portsmouth FC, Fratton Park, Frogmore Rd, Portsmouth PO4 8RA.

BURNS, Hugh: footballer; b. 13 December 1965, Lanark; player Rangers 1982–86, Hamilton Academical 86–87, Heart of Midlothian 87–88, Dunfermline Athletic 88–90, Hamilton Academical 90–91, Kilmarnock 91– ; with Rangers: winners Scottish League Cup 1984. *Address*: Kilmarnock FC, Rugby Park, Kilmarnock KA1 2DP.

BURNS, Michael: cricketer; b. 6 February 1969, Barrow-in-Furness; player Cumberland 1989–90, Warks. 91– . *Address*: Warks. CCC, County Ground, Edgbaston, Birmingham B5 7QU.

BURNS, Neil David: cricketer; b. 19 September 1965, Chelmsford; m. Susan Burns 1987; player Essex 1986, Somerset 1987– ; with Essex: tour Barbados 1986; Christians in Sport tour India 1990; England YC tour WI 1985; established 1-day record of 4 stumpings in innings v. Kent 1991. *Address*: Somerset CCC, The County Ground, Taunton, Somerset TA1 1JT.

BURNS, Richard: rally driver; b. 17 January 1971, Reading; rep. Peugeot 1991, Subaru 1992– ; GB N3 champ. 1991, overall champ. 1992, 93; winner Peugeot Challenge 1990, 91, Manx Int. Rally 1993. *Leisure interests*: swimming, cycling. *Address*: Prodrive Ltd, Acorn Way, Banbury, Oxon OX16 7XS.

BURNS, Tommy: footballer; b. 16 February 1956, Glasgow; player Celtic 1974–89, Kilmarnock 89– , player/manager 92– ; 8 Scotland caps. *Address*: Kilmarnock FC, Rugby Park, Kilmarnock KA1 2DP.

BURRIDGE, John: footballer; b. 3 December 1951, Workington; player Workington 1969–71, Blackpool 71–75, Aston Villa 75–78, Crystal Palace 78–80, Queens Park Rangers 80–82, Wolverhampton Wanderers 82–84, Sheffield Utd 84–87, Southampton 87–89, Newcastle Utd 89–91, Hibernian 91– ; with Hibernian: winners Scottish League Cup 1992. *Address*: Hibernian FC, Easter Rd Stadium, 64 Albion Rd, Edinburgh EH7 5QG.

BURROW, Mark: Rugby Union footballer; b. 9 July 1969, Chelmsford; player Ilford Wanderers, Saracens 1990– ; rep. E. Counties. *Address*: Saracens FC, Bramley Rd Sports Ground, Chaseside, Southgate, London N14 4AB.

BURROWS, David: footballer; b. 25 October 1968, Dudley; player W. Bromwich Albion 1985–88, Liverpool 88–93, W. Ham Utd 93– ; with Liverpool: winners FA Cup 1992, League champs. 1989/90; 7 England U-21 caps. *Address*: W. Ham Utd FC, Boleyn Ground, Green St, Upton Park, London E13 9AZ.

BURROWS, Noel: crown green bowler; b. 18 January 1944, Manchester; m. Susan Burrows; 1 s., 1 d.; rep. Lancs. 1970–79, Greater Manchester 80–86, Derbys. 88– ; Lancs. champ. 1968, 76; GB champ. 1976; winner Waterloo Handicap 1972, Champion of Champions 1978, 80, Top Crown pairs 1980, 87, Bass Masters 1982, Crown King 1984, Bass Olympia 1991; flat green: winner Granada Superbowl 1985 (1st crown green bowler to win major flat green tournament), English Bowls Players' Assoc. singles champ. 1993; UK target bowls champ. 1983. *Leisure interests*: golf, snooker, watching sport on TV. *Address*: The Lamb Inn, Hayfield Rd, Chinley, Derbys. SK12 6AL.

BURTON, Louise Helen: hockey player; b. 15 April 1971, Edinburgh; player Merchants School FP 1989–90, Royal High Gymnasts 90– ; Scotland U-21 debut 1990, snr debut 1992; Scotland U-21 Player of the Year 1991. *Leisure interests*: skiing, water skiing, windsurfing, socializing. *Address*: 34 Elliot Park, Colinton, Edinburgh EH14 1DX.

BUSBY, Dean: Rugby League footballer; b. 1 February 1973, Hull; player Hull 1990– , winners Premiership 1991; rep. Humberside, Yorks. *Address*: Hull RLFC, The Boulevard Ground, Airlie St, Hull HU3 3JD.

BUTCHER, Mark Alan: cricketer; b. 23 August 1972, Croydon; player Surrey 1991– ; England U-19 tour NZ 1990/91. *Address*: Surrey CCC, The Oval, Kennington, London SE11 5SS.

BUTLER, Felicity Maria Margarete: rock climber; b. 1 December 1958, Weybridge; GB women's open champ. 1990, 92; GB debut 1990, World Cup squad 1990– ; 1st ascents by Brit. woman: 'Headhunter', 'Fitzcarraldo', 'Get Some In', 'Just Another Day', 'Ships that Pass in the Night' (all grade E5) 1990, 'Barbarella Direct' (E5) 1991, 'Fireball XL5', 'Right Wall', 'Warpath' (all E5), 'Bastille' (E6) 1991, 'Hunger' (E5) 1992. *Leisure interests*: running, swimming, walking, cooking, music. *Address*: 1 Church View, Beeley, Matlock, Derbys. DE4 2NT.

BUTLER, Peter: footballer; b. 27 August 1966, Halifax; player Huddersfield Town 1984–86, Bury 1986, Cambridge Utd 1986–88, Southend Utd 88–92, W. Ham Utd 92– . *Address*: W. Ham Utd FC, Boleyn Ground, Green St, Upton Park, London E13 9AZ.

BUTLER, Stephen: footballer; b. 27 January 1962, Birmingham; player Brentford 1984–89, Maidstone Utd 89–91, Watford 91–92, Cambridge Utd 92– . *Address*: Cambridge Utd FC, Abbey Stadium, Newmarket Rd, Cambridge CB5 8LL.

BUTT, Ikram: Rugby League footballer; b. 25 October 1968, Leeds; player Leeds, Featherstone Rovers 1990– . *Address*: Featherstone Rovers RLFC, The Croft, Batley Rd, W. Ardsley, Wakefield WF3 1DX.

BUTTERS, Guy: footballer; b. 30 October 1969, Hillingdon; player Tottenham Hotspur 1988–90, Portsmouth 90– ; 3 England U-21 caps. *Address*: Portsmouth FC, Fratton Park, Frogmore Rd, Portsmouth PO4 8RA.

BUTTERWORTH, Ian Stuart: footballer; b. 25 January 1964, Crewe; m. Kathryn Ann Butterworth 1986; 1 s., 1 d.; player Coventry City 1981–85, Nottingham Forest 85–86, Norwich City 86– (capt.); 8 England U-21 caps. *Leisure interests*: most sports, gardening, listening to music. *Address*: Norwich City FC, Carrow Rd, Norwich NR1 1JE.

BUTTLE, Michael Alan: motorcyclist (off-road); b. 27 January 1966, London; ACU expert +350cc 4-stroke solo enduro champ. 1992; ISDE team bronze medal 1990 (Sweden). *Leisure interests*: cycling, mountain biking, off-road driving, skiing, reading. *Address*: 2 Hurst Cottages, Root Hill Lane, Betchworth, Surrey RH3 7AS.

BUXTON, Nikki Louise: golfer; b. 9 March 1973, Huddersfield; rep. Yorks. 1989– ; Yorks. ladies' champ. 1990–93; English girls' champ. 1991, ladies' amateur champ. 1991, 93; England debut 1991; Curtis Cup team (winners) 1992. *Leisure interests*: music, Chinese food, Rugby League. *Address*: Woodsome Hall Golf Club, Fenay Bridge, Huddersfield, Yorks.

BUZZA, Alan Jan: Rugby Union footballer; b. 3 March 1966, Beverley; player Wasps; England A debut v. France A 1990, tour Canada 1993. *Address*: Wasps FC, Wasps Football Ground, Repton Ave, Sudbury, Wembley, Middx HA0 3DW.

BYAS, David: cricketer; b. 26 August 1963, Kilham; m. Rachael Elizabeth Byas 1990; 1 d.; player Yorks. 1986– . *Address*: Yorks. CCC, Headingley Cricket Ground, Leeds LS6 3BU.

BYRD, Joseph Alton: basketball player; b. 3 November 1957, San Francisco, USA; m. Joni Angella Byrd 1983; 1 s., 1 d.; player Crystal Palace 1979–82, Murray Int. Metals (Livingston) 82–86, Manchester Utd 87–88 (capt.), Kingston 89– ; with Crystal Palace: winners Nat. Cup 1980, 81, Federation Cup 1980, League champs. 1979/80, 81/82; with Livingston: winners Scottish Cup 1983, 86, Scottish League champs. 1982/83, 83/84, 84/85, 85/86; with Kingston: winners Nat. Cup 1990, 92, League Cup 1990, 91, 92, League champs. 1989/90, 90/91, 91/92, world invitational club champs. 1989/90; England debut and Commonwealth Champs. gold medallist 1991; Olympic squad 1992. *Leisure interests*: travel, classic cars. *Address*: 5 The Spinney, Bedford Hill, Streatham, London SW16 1LA.

BYRNE, David: footballer; b. 5 March 1961, Hammersmith; player Gillingham 1985–86, Millwall 86–89, Plymouth Argyle 89–90, Watford 90– ; with Millwall: 2nd Div. champs. 1987/88. *Address*: Watford FC, Vicarage Rd Stadium, Watford, Herts. WD1 8ER.

BYRNE, John: footballer; b. 1 February 1961, Manchester; player York City 1979–84, Queens Park Rangers 84–87, Le Havre (France), Brighton and Hove Albion 1990–91, Sunderland 91–92, Millwall 92– ; with York City: 4th Div. champs. 1983/84; 23 Ireland caps. *Address*: Millwall FC, The Den, Zampa Rd, Bermondsey, London SE16 3LH.

CADDICK, Andrew Richard: cricketer; b. 21 November 1968, Christchurch, NZ; player Somerset 1991– ; NZ U-19 tour Aus. (Youth World Cup) 1987/88, England 1988; England A tour Aus. 1992/93, Test debut v. Aus. 1993, tour WI 1994. *Address*: Somerset CCC, The County Ground, Taunton, Somerset TA1 1JT.

CADOGAN, Gary Anthony: athlete; b. 8 October 1966, London; Middx, Inter-Counties, AAA and UK 400m hurdles champ. 1993; GB debut 1990, European Indoor Champs. squad 1990, 92, World Champs. squad 1993. *Leisure interests*: Liverpool FC, basketball, music, fashion. *Address*: c/o Brit. Athletic Fed., 225A Bristol Rd, Edgbaston, Birmingham B5 7UB.

CAIRNS, Christopher Lance: cricketer; b. 13 June 1970, Picton, NZ; player Notts. 1988–93, Sunday League champs. 1991; NZ tour Aus. 1989/90, Test debut 1990. *Address*: Notts. CCC, Trent Bridge, Nottingham NG2 6AG.

CALDERWOOD, Colin: footballer; b. 20 January 1965, Glasgow; m. Karen Ann Calderwood 1989; 1 d.; player Mansfield Town 1982–85, Swindon Town 85–93, Tottenham Hotspur 93– ; with Swindon Town: 4th Div. champs. 1985/86. *Leisure interests*: golf. *Address*: Tottenham Hotspur FC, 748 High Rd, Tottenham, London N17 0AP.

CALDWELL, Carole: golfer; b. 23 April 1949, Kingston-upon-Thames; Kent ladies' champ. 1970, 75, 77, 86, Berks. ladies' champ. 1982; Portuguese ladies' open amateur champ. 1980; England debut 1973; Curtis Cup team 1978, 80. *Address*: c/o Ladies' Golf Union, The Scores, St Andrews, Fife KY16 9AT.

CALLAND, Matt: Rugby League footballer; b. 20 August 1971; player Rochdale Hornets 1990–93, Featherstone Rovers 93– . *Address*: Featherstone Rovers RLFC, The Croft, Batley Rd, W. Ardsley, Wakefield WF3 1DX.

CALLARD, Jonathan Edward Brooks:
Rugby Union footballer; b. 1 January 1966,
Leicester; m. Gail Callard 1992; player
Newport 1985–89, Bath 89– ; with Bath:
winners Pilkington Cup 1990; rep. S.W.
Div., Div. champs. 1992/93, 93/94;
England B debut v. Spain 1989, England A
and snr debuts v. NZ 1993. *Leisure interests*:
watching most sports, golf, music, reading.
Address: Bath RFC, Recreation Ground,
Bath BA2 6PW.

CALZAGHE, Joseph: boxer; b. 23 March
1972, Hammersmith; Welsh ABA welterweight champ. 1991, light-middleweight
champ. 1992, middleweight champ. 1993;
ABA welterweight champ. 1991, light-middleweight champ. 1992, middleweight
champ. 1993; prof. debut 1993; only 2nd
boxer in history to win 3 ABA titles in suc-
cession at different weights. *Leisure interests*: football, music, cinema. *Address*: Nat.
Promotions, Nat. House, 60–66 Wardour
St, London W1V 3HP.

CAME, Mark: footballer; b. 14 September
1961, Exeter; player Bolton Wanderers
1984–92, Chester City 92– . *Address*:
Chester City FC, The Deva Stadium,
Bumpers Lane, Chester CH1 4LT.

CAMERON, Ian: footballer; b. 24 August
1966, Glasgow; player St Mirren 1983–89,
Aberdeen 89–92, Partick Thistle 92– ;
with St Mirren: winners Scottish Cup 1987.
Address: Partick Thistle FC, Firhill Stadium,
80 Firhill Rd, Glasgow G20 7BA.

CAMMISH, Ian Scott: cyclist; b. 1 October
1956, S. Cerney, Glos.; m. Jayne Anne
Cammish 1991; rep. Raleigh 1990–93,
Cyman/Maxim 93– ; RTTC 50-mile time
trial champ. 1980, 82–84, 100-mile individ.
champ. 1980–83, 85–89, team champ. 1981,
83, 86–89; GB debut 1981; prof. debut 1990.
Leisure interests: TV, rugby, athletics,
music. *Address*: c/o Brit. Cycling Fed., 36
Rockingham Rd, Kettering, Northants.
NN16 8HG.

CAMPBELL, Calum: footballer; b. 7
November 1965, Erskine; player
Airdrieonians 1987–89, Partick Thistle
89–90, Kilmarnock 90– . *Address*:
Kilmarnock FC, Rugby Park, Kilmarnock
KA1 2DP.

CAMPBELL, Colin Mackay: Rugby Union
footballer; b. 25 July 1967, Edinburgh;
player Watsonians 1985– ; rep. Edinburgh
U-21 1986–88; Scotland U-19 debut v. Italy
U-19 1986. *Leisure interests*: swimming,
five-a-side football. *Address*: Watsonians
RFC, Myreside, Myreside Rd, Edinburgh
EH10 5DB.

CAMPBELL, Darren: athlete; b. 12
September 1973, Manchester; European Jnr
Champs. 100m and 200m gold medals
1991; European U-23 Champs. 100m and
200m gold medals 1992; World Jnr
Champs. 100m and 200m silver medals
1992. *Address*: c/o Brit. Athletic Fed., 225A
Bristol Rd, Edgbaston, Birmingham
B5 7UB.

CAMPBELL, Duncan: footballer; b. 11
September 1970, Paisley; player Dundee
1988– . *Address*: Dundee FC, Dens Park,
Dundee DD3 7JY.

CAMPBELL, Kevin: footballer; b. 4
February 1970, Lambeth; player Arsenal
1988– , winners League Cup, FA Cup
1993; 4 England U-21 caps. *Address*:
Arsenal FC, Arsenal Stadium, Highbury,
London N5 1BU.

CAMPBELL, Marvin: gymnast (artistic);
b. 14 July 1971, Manchester; GB U-18
champ. 1988; N.W. open champ. 1993;
English champ. 1993; GB high bar champ.
1990, combined champ. 1993 (1st black
champ.); GB debut 1988, World Champs.
squad 1991, 93, Olympic squad 1992.
Leisure interests: cars, music, computer
games. *Address*: Flat 15, Lancaster House,
71 Whitworth St, Manchester M1 6LQ.

CAMPBELL, Stephen: footballer; b. 20 November 1967, Dundee; player Dundee 1985– ; Scotland U-21 int. *Address*: Dundee FC, Dens Park, Dundee DD3 7JY.

CAMPBELL, Sulzeer Jeremiah (Sol): footballer; b. 18 September 1974, Newham; player Tottenham Hotspur 1992– . *Address*: Tottenham Hotspur FC, 748 High Rd, Tottenham, London N17 0AP.

CANTONA, Eric: footballer; b. 24 May 1966, Paris, France; player Auxerre, Bordeaux, Montpellier, Marseilles, Nimes (all France), Leeds Utd 1992, Manchester Utd 1992– ; with Leeds: League champs. 1991/92; with Manchester Utd: League champs. 1992/93; France int. *Address*: Manchester Utd FC, Old Trafford, Manchester M16 0RA.

CAPEL, David John: cricketer; b. 6 July 1963, Northampton; m. Debbie Capel 1985; 1 d.; player Northants. 1981– ; England tour Sharjah (UAE) 1986, Test debut 1987, tours Pakistan/NZ/Aus. 1987/88, India/WI 1989/90, Aus. (England A) 1992/93. *Address*: Northants. CCC, County Cricket Ground, Wantage Rd, Northampton NN1 4TJ.

CARL, Martin: swimmer; b. 5 April 1975, Orsett, Essex; rep. Essex 1985– ; England youth debut 1990, snr debut 1993; GB youth debut and European Jnr Champs. 100m freestyle gold medal 1992. *Leisure interests*: music, socializing. *Address*: c/o ASA, Harold Fern House, Derby Square, Loughborough, Leics. LE11 0AL.

CARLING, William David Charles, OBE: Rugby Union footballer; b. 12 December 1965, Bradford-on-Avon; player Durham Univ., Harlequins; England B debut v. France 1987, snr and Five Nations debut v. France 1988, capt. 1988– , Grand Slam champs. 1991, 92; Brit. Lions tour NZ 1993; most-capped England centre; holds world record for int. appearances as capt. *Address*: Harlequins FC, Stoop Memorial Ground, Craneford Way, Twickenham, Middx.

CARLSEN, Adäle: synchronized swimmer; b. 12 November 1975, Aldershot; GB figures and solo jnr champ. 1991; England and GB youth debuts 1990, snr debuts 1993. *Leisure interests*: photography. *Address*: c/o ASA, Harold Fern House, Derby Square, Loughborough, Leics. LE11 0AL.

CARPENTER, Dean John: water skier (barefoot); b. 21 February 1966, Bexley; 1 d.; GB tricks, slalom champ. 1991, 92; European tricks champ. 1987, tricks, slalom and overall tour champ. 1989; GB debut 1987 (capt. 1990–91); World Champs. squad 1988, 90, 92. *Leisure interests*: karate, shooting, motocross, cycling. *Address*: 243 Burnt Ash Lane, Bromley, Kent BR1 5DL.

CARR, Franz: footballer; b. 24 September 1966, Preston; player Nottingham Forest 1984–91, Newcastle Utd 91– ; with Nottingham Forest: winners League Cup 1990; 9 England U-21 caps. *Address*: Newcastle Utd FC, St James' Park, Newcastle-upon-Tyne, Tyne & Wear NE1 4ST.

CARR, John Donald: cricketer; b. 15 June 1963, St John's Wood; m. Vicky Carr 1990; player Middx 1983–90, Herts. 1991, Middx 1992– ; with Middx: county champs. 1985, 90, 93, Sunday League champs. 1992. *Address*: Middx CCC, Lord's Cricket Ground, London NW8 8QN.

CARR, Paul: Rugby League footballer; b. 13 May 1967; player Hunslet, Sheffield Eagles 1992– . *Address*: Sheffield Eagles RLFC, Stadium Corner, 824 Attercliffe Rd, Sheffield S9 3RS.

CARRICK, Phillip: cricketer; b. 16 July 1952, Leeds; m. Elspeth Carrick 1977; 2 d.; player Yorks. 1970–93 (capt. 87–89), winners Benson and Hedges Cup 1987; MCC tour Namibia 1991. *Address*: Yorks. CCC, Headingley Cricket Ground, Leeds LS6 3BU.

CARRICK-ANDERSON, Emma: Alpine skier; b. 17 June 1975, Stirling; GB women's slalom champ. 1993, 94; Olympic squad 1992 (youngest Brit. team member), 94. *Leisure interests*: squash, windsurfing, tennis, mountain biking. *Address*: Pine Crest, Glen Rd, Dunblane, Perthshire FK15 0DS.

CARRUTHERS, Martin: footballer; b. 7 August 1972, Nottingham; player Aston Villa 1991–93, Stoke City 93– . *Address*: Stoke City FC, Victoria Ground, Stoke on Trent, Staffs. ST4 4EG.

CARSON, Thomas: footballer; b. 26 March 1959, Dumbarton; player Dumbarton 1978–84, Dundee 84–92, Raith Rovers 92– . *Address*: Raith Rovers FC, Stark's Park, Pratt St, Kirkcaldy, Fife KY1 1SA.

CARSON, William Hunter Fisher, OBE; jockey (Flat); b. 16 November 1942, Stirling; m. Elaine Carson 1982; 3 s.; winner 2000 Guineas 1972 (High Top), 1980 (Known Fact), 1987 (Don't Forget Me), 1989 (Nashwan), Oaks 1977 (Dunfermline), 1980 (Bireme), 1983 (Sun Princess), 1990 (Salsabil), St Leger 1977 (Dunfermline), 1983 (Sun Princess), 1988 (Minster Son), Derby 1979 (Troy), 1980 (Henbit), 1989 (Nashwan), Irish Derby 1979 (Troy), 1990 (Salsabil), Irish Oaks 1982 (Swiftfoot), 1985 (Helen Street), Irish 2000 Guineas 1987 (Don't Forget Me), 1000 Guineas 1990 (Salsabil), 1991 (Shadayid); champ. jockey 1972, 73, 78, 80, 83; rode 187 winners in season 1990. *Address:* c/o BHB, 42 Portman Square, London W1H 0EN.

CARTER, James William Charles: footballer; b. 9 November 1965, Hammersmith, London; m. Ann-Marie Carter 1984; 1 s.; player Millwall 1987–91, Liverpool 91–92, Arsenal 92– ; with Millwall: 2nd Div. champs. 1987/88; with Arsenal: winners League Cup 1993. *Leisure interests*: swimming, running, sunbathing. *Address*: Arsenal FC, Arsenal Stadium, Highbury, London N5 1BU.

CARTER, Richard Andrew: paraglider pilot; b. 30 October 1963, Nottingham; GB champ. 1992; World Champs. team silver medal 1991, team bronze 1993. *Leisure interests*: climbing, skiing. *Address*: 16 Lime Tree Ave, Kiverton Park, Sheffield S31 8NY.

CARTER, Timothy: footballer; b. 5 October 1967, Bristol; player Bristol Rovers 1985–87, Sunderland 87–93, Hartlepool Utd 93– . *Address*: Hartlepool Utd FC, Victoria Ground, Clarence Rd, Hartlepool, Cleveland TS24 8BZ.

CARTWRIGHT, Neil: footballer; b. 20 February 1971, Stourbridge; player W. Bromwich Albion 1989– . *Address*: W. Bromwich Albion FC, The Hawthorns, W. Bromwich B71 4LF.

CASCARINO, Anthony: footballer; b. 1 September 1962, Orpington; player Gillingham 1982–87, Millwall 87–90, Aston Villa 90–91, Celtic 91–92, Chelsea 92– ; with Millwall: 2nd Div. champs. 1987/88; over 43 Ireland caps. *Address*: Chelsea FC, Stamford Bridge, Fulham Rd, London SW6 1HS.

CASEY, Leo: Rugby League footballer; b. 17 September 1965, Co. Antrim, NI; player Oldham, Featherstone Rovers 1990– . *Address*: Featherstone Rovers RLFC, The Croft, Batley Rd, W. Ardsley, Wakefield WF3 1DX.

CASKIE, Don: Rugby Union footballer; b. 12 December 1966; player London Scottish, Gloucester; Scotland A and B int. *Address*: Gloucester RUFC, Kingsholm, Worcester St, Gloucester GL3 3AX.

CASS, Martin Roger: Rugby Union footballer; b. 20 May 1967, Dorking; player Harlequins 1986–90, Saracens 91– ; rep. London Div. U-21 1987, Sussex U-21 1986–87, Surrey 1990– ; player Lavinia Duchess of York XI (cricket) 1990– .

Leisure interests: golf, skiing. *Address*: Saracens FC, Bramley Rd Sports Ground, Chaseside, Southgate, London N14 4AB.

CASSELL, Justyn Paul Sheldon: Rugby Union footballer; b. 25 May 1967, Reading; m. Melissa Cassell; player Marlow 1985–88, Saracens 88–93, Harlequins 93– ; England B debut v. France 1992, tour NZ 1992, winning squad World Cup Sevens and tour NZ 1993. *Address*: Harlequins FC, Stoop Memorial Ground, Craneford Way, Twickenham, Middx.

CASSON, Rachel: water skier (racing); b. 11 March 1971, Evesham; GB ladies' F1 inland champ. 1993; European Champs. bronze medals 1988, 89, 91, gold 1990; European Cup bronze medal 1988, gold 1989. *Leisure interests*: skiing, weight training, running, swimming, cycling, aerobics, coaching. *Address*: 28 Hollywood Lane, Hollywood, Birmingham B47 5PX.

CAW, Lorraine: netball player; b. 22 April 1963, Glasgow; player Scotstoun 1981– ; rep. Glasgow District; Scotland debut 1981, World Tournament squad 1983, 91, World Games squad 1985, 89, World Champs. squad and tour Aus. 1987. *Leisure interests*: football, driving, children. *Address*: c/o Scottish Netball Assoc., Kelvin Hall, Argyle St, Glasgow G3 8AW.

CAWTHORNE, Helen Margaret: triathlete; b. 9 July 1961, Hatfield; E. Midlands duathlon and triathlon champ. 1992, 93; GB women's Olympic-distance champ., sprint champ. 1993. *Leisure interests*: walking, mountaineering, canoeing, reading, films. *Address*: 28 Lynmouth Drive, Ilkeston, Derbys. DE7 9HN.

CECIL, Henry Richard Amherst: racehorse trainer (Flat); b. 11 January 1943; m. Natalie Cecil 1991; 1st licence 1969; winner 2000 Guineas 1975 (Bolkonski), 1976 (Wollow), 1000 Guineas 1979 (One in a Million), 1981 (Fairy Footsteps), 1985 (Oh So Sharp), St Leger 1980 (Light Cavalry), 1985 (Oh So Sharp), 1987 (Reference Point), 1989 (Michelozzo), Derby 1985 (Slip Anchor), 1987 (Reference Point), 1993 (Commander In Chief), Oaks 1985 (Oh So Sharp), 1988 (Diminuendo), 1989 (Snow Bride), Irish Oaks 1988 (Diminuendo), 1989 (Alydaress), Irish Derby 1989 (Old Vic), 1993 (Commander In Chief); leading trainer 1976, 78, 79, 82, 84, 85, 87, 88, 90, 93; 1st Brit. trainer to train winners of races worth over £1 million 1985. *Address*: c/o BHB, 42 Portman Square, London W1H 0EN.

CHALLINOR, Andrew Paul: Rugby Union footballer; b. 5 December 1969, Wolverhampton; player Harlequins; rep. Midland Div.; England A debut v. France A 1992, tour Canada 1993. *Address*: Harlequins FC, Stoop Memorial Ground, Craneford Way, Twickenham, Middx.

CHALMERS, Craig Minto: Rugby Union footballer; b. 15 October 1968, Galashiels; player Melrose, Scottish League champs. 1989/90, 91/92; rep. S. of Scotland; Scotland B debut v. France B 1988 (youngest-ever player), snr and Five Nations debut v. Wales 1989, Grand Slam champs. 1990, tours NZ 1990, N. America 1991, Aus. 1992; Brit. Lions tour Aus. 1989. *Address*: Melrose RFC, The Greenyards, Melrose TD6 9SA.

CHAMBERLAIN, Alec: footballer; b. 20 June 1964, March; player Colchester Utd 1982–87, Luton Town 88–93, Sunderland 93– . *Address*: Sunderland FC, Roker Park Ground, Sunderland, Tyne and Wear SR6 9SW.

CHAMBERLAIN, Joanna Michelle: cricketer; b. 25 April 1969, Oadby, Leics.; player Leicester WCC 1985–87, Newark and Sherwood WCC 88– ; rep. E. Midlands Ladies 1985– , county champs. 1989–91; England jnr debut 1984; Test debut 1987, tours Aus. (World Cup) 1988,

NZ 1992, winners World Cup 1993; youngest woman to win Test cap; holds women's world record for 7th-wicket partnership with Karen Smithies (110); Sports Writers' Team of the Year award-winner 1993. *Leisure interests*: all sport, socializing, touring, family. *Address*: c/o Women's Cricket Assoc., 41 St Michael's Lane, Headingley, Leeds LS6 3BR.

CHAMBERLAIN, Mark: footballer; b. 19 November 1961, Stoke; player Port Vale 1979–82, Stoke City 82–85, Sheffield Wednesday 85–88, Portsmouth 88–   ; 4 England U-21 caps, 8 full England caps. *Address*: Portsmouth FC, Fratton Park, Frogmore Rd, Portsmouth PO4 8RA.

CHAMBERLAIN, Richard: Rugby League footballer; b. 1 April 1973; player Greatfield ARLFC, Hull Kingston Rovers 1991– . *Address*: Hull Kingston Rovers RLFC, Craven Park, Preston Rd, Hull HU9 5HE.

CHAMBERS, Gary: Rugby League footballer; b. 5 January 1970, Whitehaven; player Kells ARLFC, Warrington 1989– ; with Warrington: winners Regal Trophy 1991; GB U-21 debut v. France 1991. *Address*: Warrington RLFC, Wilderspool Stadium, Wilderspool Causeway, Warrington WA4 6PY.

CHAMBERS, Melanie Jane: water skier; b. 24 November 1956, Edinburgh; Scottish women's slalom, tricks, jump and overall champ. 1979–86, 88–92; Scotland debut 1979; GB debut 1991; European Champs. ladies' overall silver medal 1991. *Leisure interests*: skiing, swimming. *Address*: 23 Bell Place, Edinburgh EH3 5HT.

CHANNING, Justin: footballer; b. 19 November 1968, Reading; player Queens Park Rangers 1986– . *Address*: Queens Park Rangers FC, Rangers Stadium, S. Africa Rd, London W12 7PA.

CHANNON, Michael: racehorse trainer; b. 28 November 1948, Salisbury; as footballer: player Southampton 1965–77, Manchester City 77–79, Southampton 79–82, Newcastle Utd 1982, Bristol Rovers 1982, Norwich City 1982–85, Portsmouth 85–86; 9 England U-23 caps, 46 full England caps; as trainer: 1st licence 1990. *Address*: c/o BHB, 42 Portman Square, London W1H 0EN.

CHAPMAN, Lee: footballer; b. 5 December 1959, Lincoln; m. Leslie Chapman; player Stoke City 1978–82, Arsenal 82–83, Sunderland 83–84, Sheffield Wednesday 84–88, Niort (France) 1988, Nottingham Forest 88–90, Leeds Utd 90–93, Portsmouth 1993, W. Ham Utd 93– ; with Nottingham Forest: winners League Cup 1989; with Leeds Utd: 2nd Div. champs. 1989/90, League champs. 1991/92; 1 England U-21 cap. *Publications*: *More than a Match*: A Player's Story, 1992. *Address*: W. Ham Utd FC, Boleyn Ground, Green St, Upton Park, London E13 9AZ.

CHAPMAN, Roger: golfer; b. 1 May 1959, Nakuru, Kenya; English amateur champ. 1979; England and GB debut 1980, Walker Cup team 1981; prof. debut 1981; winner Zimbabwe Open 1988. *Address*: c/o PGA European Tour, Wentworth Club, Wentworth Drive, Virginia Water, Surrey GU25 4LS.

CHAPPLE, Glen: cricketer; b. 23 January 1974, Skipton; player Lancs. 1992– ; England U-18 tour Canada 1991, U-19 tours NZ 1991, Pakistan 1992. *Address*: Lancs. CCC, Old Trafford, Manchester M16 0PX.

CHAPPLE, Philip: footballer; b. 26 November 1966, Norwich; player Cambridge Utd 1988–93, Charlton Athletic 93– . *Address*: Charlton Athletic FC, The Valley, Floyd Rd, London SE7 8BL.

CHAPPLE-HYAM, Peter William: racehorse trainer (Flat); b. 2 April 1963, Leamington Spa; m. Jane Fiona Chapple-Hyam 1990; 1st licence 1991; winner 2000 Guineas, Irish 2000 Guineas 1992 (Rodrigo de Triano), Derby 1992 (Dr Devious). *Leisure interests*: cricket, W. Bromwich Albion FC, golf. *Address*: Swettenham Stud, Manton House, Manton House Estate, Marlborough, Wilts. SN8 1PN.

CHARLERY, Kenneth: footballer; b. 28 November 1964, Stepney; player Maidstone Utd 1989–91, Peterborough Utd 91–92, Watford 92–93, Peterborough Utd 93– . *Address*: Peterborough Utd FC, London Rd Ground, Peterborough, Cambs. PE2 8AL.

CHARLES, Gary: footballer; b. 13 April 1970, Newham; player Nottingham Forest 1986–93, Derby County 93– ; 4 England U-21 caps, 2 full England caps. *Address*: Derby County FC, The Baseball Ground, Shaftesbury Crescent, Derby DE3 8NB.

CHARLES, Glyn Roderick: yachtsman; b. 4 September 1965, Winchester; UK open Laser champ. (youngest-ever winner) 1985, Soling champ. 1987, 91, champ. of champs. 1989; Swedish open Laser champ. 1985; European Champs. Laser bronze medal 1986, CHS gold 1993; Olympic squad 1988; Admiral's Cup team (The Netherlands) 1989, (GB) 1993 (skipper *GBE International*). *Leisure interests*: skiing, running, cycling, gym, furniture-building. *Address*: 17 Avocet Quay, Emsworth Yacht Harbour, Emsworth, Hants. PO10 8BY.

CHARLTON, Roger John: racehorse trainer (Flat); b. 18 January 1950; m. Clare Charlton 1981; 1 s., 1 d.; 1st licence 1990; winner Derby 1990 (Quest for Fame). *Address*: c/o BHB, 42 Portman Square, London W1H 0EN.

CHARLTON, Simon: footballer; b. 25 October 1971, Huddersfield; player Huddersfield Town 1989–93, Southampton 93– . *Address*: Southampton FC, The Dell, Milton Rd, Southampton SO9 4XX.

CHARMAN, Linda Jayne: squash player; b. 21 November 1971, Eastbourne; player Lee-on-Solent; Middx ladies' open champ. 1991, 92; Sussex ladies' champ. 1987–91; England U-16 debut 1985, U-19 debut 1989; winner Swiss Open 1993. *Leisure interests*: cycling, pottery, drawing. painting, cinema. *Address*: `Simla', Old Ghyll Rd, Sandy Cross, Heathfield, E. Sussex TN21 8BP.

CHATFIELD, Gary: Rugby League footballer; b. 26 July 1967, Hull; player Eureka ARLFC, Hull Kingston Rovers 1990– . *Address*: Hull Kingston Rovers RLFC, Craven Park, Preston Rd, Hull HU9 5HE.

CHEN, Xinhua: table tennis player; b. 30 January 1960; m. Jeanette Wood 1989; Chinese champ. 1981; English champ. 1992; World Champs. mixed doubles silver medals 1981, 83, team gold 1985, 87 (China); winner World Cup 1985; England debut 1990. *Address*: c/o English Table Tennis Assoc., 3rd Floor, Queensbury House, Havelock Rd, Hastings, E. Sussex TN34 1HF.

CHERRY, Steven: footballer; b. 5 August 1960, Nottingham; player Derby County 1978–84, Walsall 84–86, Plymouth Argyle 86–89, Notts County 89– . *Address*: Notts County FC, Meadow Lane Ground, Nottingham NG2 3HJ.

CHESHIRE, Colin Charles Chance, OBE: full-bore rifle shooter; b. 23 August 1941, Warmsworth, Yorks.; m. Angela Mary Cheshire 1976; 1 s., 1 d., 2 step-d.; Army closed champ. 1978, target rifle club champ. 1988, 90; Hants. open champ. 1989, 93; England debut 1978; GB debut 1971, Palma Match team 1971, 76, 82 (vice-capt.),

88, 92 (capt.), winners 1992, Kolapore Match team 1981 (winners), Empire Match team 1988, 92 (capt. 1992); winner Corporation Cup, Bisley 1970 (record score); 1st rifle shooter to be awarded OBE. *Publications*: *The History of the Palma Match*, 1992. *Leisure interests*: golf, opera. *Address*: c/o Nat. Rifle Assoc., Bisley Camp, Brookwood, Woking, Surrey GU24 0PB.

CHETTLE, Stephen: footballer; b. 27 September 1968, Nottingham; player Nottingham Forest 1986– , winners League Cup 1990; 12 England U-21 caps. *Address*: Nottingham Forest FC, City Ground, Nottingham NG2 5FJ.

CHILDERLEY, Stuart: yachtsman; b. 17 February 1966, Lowestoft; UK 6m champ. 1990; European Champs. Finn gold medals 1987, 92; Olympic squad (Finn class) 1992; Admiral's Cup team 1989 (*Indulgence*), 1991 (skipper *Wings of Oracle*), 1993 (skipper *Provezza*). *Leisure interests*: golf, cycling, fitness, relaxing from time to time. *Address*: 95 Firs Drive, Highwood Park, Hedge End, Southampton SO3 4AY.

CHILDS, Gary: footballer; b. 19 April 1964, Birmingham; player W. Bromwich Albion 1982–83, Walsall 83–87, Birmingham City 87–89, Grimsby Town 89– . *Address*: Grimsby Town FC, Blundell Park, Cleethorpes, S. Humberside DN35 7PY.

CHILDS, Graham Christopher: Rugby Union footballer; b. 3 April 1968; player Wasps; tours Argentina 1990, NZ (England B) 1992, Canada (England A) 1993. *Address*: Wasps FC, Wasps Football Ground, Repton Ave, Sudbury, nr Wembley, Middx HA0 3DW.

CHILDS, John Henry: cricketer; b. 15 August 1951, Plymouth; m. Jane Anne Childs 1978; 2 s.; player Glos. 1977–84, Essex 85– ; with Essex: county champs.

1991, 92; 2 Tests, debut 1988. *Address*: Essex CCC, County Cricket Ground, New Writtle St, Chelmsford DM2 0PG.

CHINN, Nicky: ice hockey player; b. 14 September 1972; player Cardiff Devils 1988– , Div. 1 champs. 1988/89, GB champs., League champs. 1989/90, 92/93. *Address*: Wales Nat. Ice Rink, Hayes Bridge Rd, Cardiff CF1 2GH.

CHISHOLM, Gordon: footballer; b. 8 April 1960, Glasgow; player Sunderland 1978–85, Hibernian 85–87, Dundee 87–92, Partick Thistle 1992– . *Address*: Partick Thistle FC, Firhill Stadium, 80 Firhill Rd, Glasgow G20 7BA.

CHITTENDEN, John Slingsby: yachtsman (ocean racing); b. 23 June 1940, Nottingham; m. Catherine Mary Chittenden 1964 (d 1992); 1 s., 1 d.; skipper *Creightons Naturally*, winners Whitbread Round the World Race (cruising class) 1989/90, *Nuclear Electric*, winners Brit. Steel Challenge 1992/93; RYA cruising secretary 1985–88. *Address*: c/o 21 Ambleside Rd, Lymington, Hants.

CHRISTENSEN, Jayne, MBE (née Torvill): ice dancer; b. 7 October 1957, Nottingham; m. Philip Lee Christensen 1990; with Michael Hutchinson: GB jnr figure skating pairs champ. 1970, snr champ. 1971; with Christopher Dean (qv): GB ice dance champ. 1978–83, 94; GB debut 1976; European Champs. gold medals 1981, 82, 84, 94; World Champs. gold medals 1981–84; Olympic gold medal 1984, bronze 1994; world prof. champ. 1984, 85, 90; winner Vandervell Trophy 1981–84, European Trophy 1981, 82, 84, Jacques Favart Trophy 1986; Sports Writers' Sportswoman of the Year 1981, BBC Sports Personality of the Year 1984. *Leisure interests*: theatre, cinema, ballet, contemporary dance. *Address*: c/o Debbie Turner, 59 Goodwin Ave, Swalecliffe, Kent CT5 2RA.

CHRISTIE, Gary: Rugby League footballer; b. 23 January 1972; player Widnes Tigers ARLFC, Oldham 1991–93, Wakefield Trinity 93– . *Address*: Wakefield Trinity RLFC, 171 Doncaster Rd, Belle Vue, Wakefield WF1 5EZ.

CHRISTIE, Linford, MBE: athlete; b. 2 April 1960, St Andrews, Jamaica; Commonwealth Games 100m gold medal 1990; European Champs. 100m gold medals 1986, 90; European Cup 100m gold medals 1989, 91, 93, 4 x 100m relay gold 1993; World Cup 100m gold and 4 x 100m relay silver medals 1989, 100m gold 1992; World Champs. 100m gold and 4 x 100m relay silver medals 1993; Olympic 100m and 4 x 100m relay silver medals 1988, 100m gold 1992; UK 100m record-holder; Sports Writers' Sportsman of the Year 1992, 93, BBC Sports Personality of the Year 1993. *Address*: 'Nuff' Respect, Rosedale House, Rosedale Rd, Richmond, Surrey TW9 2SZ.

CHRISTIE, Max: footballer; b. 7 November 1971, Edinburgh; player Heart of Midlothian 1988–91, Meadowbank Thistle 91–92, Dundee 92– ; Scotland U-21 int. *Address*: Dundee FC, Dens Park, Dundee DD3 7JY.

CLAPPER, Alexander Joel: swimmer; b. 27 June 1974, Ilford; rep. Essex 1989–90; GB jnr 100m and 200m breaststroke champ. 1990; England youth debut 1991, intermediate debut 1992, snr debut 1993; GB youth debut and European Jnr Champs. squad 1991 (100m and 200m breaststroke), Olympic triallist 1992. *Leisure interests*: softball, golf, fitness training, volleyball, science fiction, food. *Address*: c/o ASA, Harold Fern House, Derby Square, Loughborough, Leics. LE11 0AL.

CLARIDGE, Stephen: footballer; b. 10 April 1966, Portsmouth; player Bournemouth 1984–85, Aldershot 88–90, Cambridge Utd 90–94, Birmingham City 94– ; with Cambridge Utd: 3rd Div. champs. 1990/91.

Address: Birmingham City FC, St Andrews Ground, Birmingham B9 4NH.

CLARK, Frank: football manager; b. 9 September 1943, Rowlands Gill; player Newcastle Utd 1962–75, Nottingham Forest 75–78; manager Leyton Orient 1982–91, Nottingham Forest 93– . *Address*: Nottingham Forest FC, City Ground, Nottingham NG2 5FJ.

CLARK, Gary: Rugby Union footballer; b. 3 May 1965, Coventry; player Old Elizabethans, Saracens 1988– . *Address*: Saracens FC, Bramley Rd Sports Ground, Chaseside, Southgate, London N14 4AB.

CLARK, Gillian Margaret: badminton player; b. 2 September 1961, Baghdad, Iraq; rep. Surrey; England debut 1981 (over 120 caps); Commonwealth Games team gold medals 1982, 86, 90, ladies' doubles silver 1982, 90, gold 1986, ladies' singles bronze 1982, 86, mixed doubles bronze 1990; European Champs. ladies' doubles gold medals 1982, 84, 86, silver 1988, bronze 1990, mixed doubles bronze 1984, gold 1988; World Champs. ladies' doubles bronze medal 1983, mixed doubles bronze 1993; winner Taiwan Open ladies' doubles 1983, 85, 90, mixed doubles 1987, Japan Open ladies' doubles 1983, 89, 91, Swedish Open ladies' doubles 1991, mixed doubles 1982, Finnish Open ladies' doubles 1991, Malaysian Open ladies' doubles 1985, mixed doubles 1987, Indonesian Open ladies' doubles 1982, mixed doubles 1986, Singapore Open ladies' doubles 1990, 92, Canadian Open ladies' doubles 1982, Dutch Open ladies' doubles 1982, 83, 85, 88, German Open mixed doubles 1988, Danish Open ladies' doubles 1986, Thailand Open mixed doubles 1988, Scottish Open ladies' doubles 1982, 88, 89, Indian Open ladies' doubles 1982, Swiss Open ladies' doubles 1993. *Leisure interests*: golf, squash, art history. *Address*: Wimbledon Squash and Badminton Club, Cranbrook Rd, Wimbledon, London SW19 4HD.

CLARK, Howard: golfer; b. 26 August 1954, Leeds; Yorks. amateur champ. 1973; England debut 1973; Walker Cup team 1973; prof. debut 1973; Dunhill Cup team 1985–87, 89, 90 (winners 1987); Ryder Cup team 1977, 81, 85–89 (winners 1985, 87); winner Portuguese Open 1978, Madrid Open 1978, 84, 86, Jersey Open 1985, Spanish Open 1986, Moroccan Open 1987, English Open 1988. *Address:* c/o PGA European Tour, Wentworth Club, Wentworth Drive, Virginia Water, Surrey GU25 4LS.

CLARK, John: footballer; b. 22 September 1964, Edinburgh; player Dundee Utd 1981–94, Stoke City 94– . *Address:* Stoke City FC, Victoria Ground, Stoke on Trent, Staffs. ST4 4EG.

CLARK, Lee: footballer; b. 27 October 1972, Wallsend; player Newcastle Utd 1989– ; 2 England U-21 caps. *Address:* Newcastle Utd FC, St James' Park, Newcastle-upon-Tyne, Tyne & Wear NE1 4ST.

CLARK, Martin: footballer; b. 13 October 1968, Holytown; player Clyde 1987–89, Nottingham Forest 89–90, Mansfield Town 90–92, Partick Thistle 92– . *Address:* Partick Thistle FC, Firhill Stadium, 80 Firhill Rd, Glasgow G20 7BA.

CLARK, Trevor: Rugby League footballer; b. 28 May 1962, Rotarua, NZ; player Otaru (NZ), Leeds, Featherstone Rovers, Bradford Northern 1992– ; NZ int. *Address:* Bradford Northern RLFC, Odsal Stadium, Bradford BD6 1BS.

CLARKE, Andrew: footballer; b. 22 July 1967, Islington; player Wimbledon 1991– . *Address:* Wimbledon FC, Selhurst Park, London SE25 6PY.

CLARKE, Arthur Eric: full-bore rifle shooter; b. 3 December 1922, Greenock; m. Phyllis Florence Emily Clarke 1944; 1 s., 1 d.; rep. Hants. 1973– ; Army small-bore champ. 1959, sub-machine champ. 1961, 62;

Kenyan champ. 1971, 77, 79; Scottish champ. 1984; GB match rifle champ. 1991; Scotland debut 1977, Elcho Shield team 1979, 80, 89–93; Commonwealth Games gold medal 1982, squad 1986, 90; GB debut 1959, Palma Match team 1982, 85, 88, 92 (winners 1992), Kolapore Match team 1979, 85, 87, 88, 89, 92 (capt. 1992); winner Grand Aggregate, Bisley 1979, 80. *Leisure interests:* golf. *Address:* Peska, Pinehill Rise, Sandhurst, Camberley, Surrey GU17 8BA.

CLARKE, Benjamin Bevan: Rugby Union footballer; b. 15 April 1968, Bishop's Stortford; player Bishop's Stortford, Saracens, Bath; with Bath: winners Pilkington Cup 1992, League champs. 1992/93; rep. S.W. Div.; England B debut v. Spain 1990, tour NZ 1992, snr debut v. SA 1992, Five Nations debut v. France 1993; Brit. Lions tour NZ 1993. *Address:* Bath RFC, Recreation Ground, Bath BA2 6PW.

CLARKE, Colin: footballer; b. 30 October 1962, Newry, NI; player Peterborough Utd 1981–84, Tranmere Rovers 84–85, Bournemouth 85–86, Southampton 86–89, Queens Park Rangers 89–90, Portsmouth 90– ; 35 NI caps. *Address:* Portsmouth FC, Fratton Park, Frogmore Rd, Portsmouth PO4 8RA.

CLARKE, Philip: Rugby League footballer; b. 16 May 1971, Blackrod; player Wigan St Pats ARLFC, Wigan 1987– ; with Wigan: winners Challenge Cup 1991–93, Premiership 1992, Regal Trophy 1993; GB debut v. Papua New Guinea 1990, Brit. Lions tours NZ/Papua New Guinea 1990, Aus/NZ/Papua New Guinea 1992. *Address:* Wigan RLFC, The Pavilion, Central Park, Wigan WN1 1XF.

CLARKE, Stephen: footballer; b. 29 August 1963, Saltcoats; player St Mirren 1981–87, Chelsea 87– ; with Chelsea: 2nd Div. champs. 1988/89; 8 Scotland U-21 caps, over 5 full Scotland caps. *Address:* Chelsea FC, Stamford Bridge, Fulham Rd, London SW6 1HS.

CLARKE, Stuart Michael: clay pigeon shooter; b. 24 April 1959, Epping; rep. Essex; English FITASC sporting champ. 1992, 93, open sporting champ. 1993; GB all-round champ. 1988, FITASC sporting champ. 1990, 92, open sporting champ. 1993; UK FITASC sporting champ. 1992; England debut 1988; GB debut 1989; European FITASC Sporting Champs. bronze medal 1992; World FITASC Sporting Champs. silver medal 1991; World Beretta Sporting Champs. gold medal 1992. *Leisure interests*: game-keeping. *Address*: 94 Markwell Wood, Harlow, Essex CM19 5QZ.

CLARKE, Troy: Rugby League footballer; b. 19 April 1967; player Carlisle, Leigh 1993– . *Address*: Leigh RLFC, Hilton Park, Kirkhall Lane, Leigh WN7 1RN.

CLAXTON, Aileen: hockey player; b. 22 August 1968; player Balsam Leicester; England U-21 debut 1987, snr debut 1989. *Address*: c/o All England Women's Hockey Assoc., 51 High St, Shrewsbury SY1 1ST.

CLAYDON, Russell: golfer; b. 19 November 1965; Cambridge champ. 1987, 88; English amateur champ. 1988; England debut 1988; Walker Cup team (winners) 1989; prof. debut 1989; leading amateur in Open 1989. *Address*: c/o PGA European Tour, Wentworth Club, Wentworth Drive, Virginia Water, Surrey GU25 4LS.

CLAYTON, Andrew James: swimmer; b. 10 April 1973, Bradford; GB 200m and 400m freestyle jnr champ. 1990; England youth debut 1990, intermediate and snr debuts 1991; GB jnr debut 1990, snr debut 1991, European Champs. squad 1991, 93. *Leisure interests*: snooker, music, photography. *Address*: c/o ASA, Harold Fern House, Derby Square, Loughborough, Leics. LE11 0AL.

CLAYTON, Gary: footballer; b. 2 February 1963, Sheffield; m. Deborah Clayton 1990; player Doncaster Rovers 1986–87, Cambridge Utd 1987– ; with Cambridge Utd: 3rd Div. champs. 1990/91; Yorks. U-12 golf champ. 1974. *Leisure interests*: golf, socializing. *Address*: Cambridge Utd FC, Abbey Stadium, Newmarket Rd, Cambridge CB5 8LL.

CLELAND, Alec: footballer; b. 10 December 1970, Glasgow; player Dundee Utd 1987– ; Scotland U-21 int. *Address*: Dundee Utd FC, Tannadice Park, Dundee DD3 7JW.

CLEMENT, Anthony: Rugby Union footballer; b. 8 February 1967, Swansea; m. Debra Clement; player Swansea 1985– , Welsh League champs. 1991/92; Wales debut v. US Eagles 1987, Five Nations debut v. England 1988, tour Aus. 1991; Brit. Lions tours Aus. 1989, NZ 1993. *Address*: Swansea RFC, St Helens, Swansea SA2 0AR.

CLINTON, Patrick: boxer; b. 4 April 1964, Glasgow; 1 s.; ABA flyweight champ. 1984, 85; Scotland debut 1981; Commonwealth Federation Champs. flyweight gold medal 1983; GB debut 1983, Olympic squad 1984; prof. debut 1985; titles won: GB flyweight 1988, European flyweight 1990, WBO flyweight 1992; over 19 prof. wins. *Leisure interests*: golf, horseriding, football. *Address*: St Andrew's Sporting Club, Forte Crest Hotel, Bothwell St, Glasgow G2 7EN.

CLOSE, Shaun: footballer; b. 8 September 1966, Islington; player Tottenham Hotspur 1984–88, Bournemouth 88–89, Swindon Town 89– . *Address*: Swindon Town FC, The County Ground, Swindon, Wilts. SN1 2ED.

CLOUGH, Nigel: footballer; b. 19 March 1966, Sunderland; player Nottingham Forest 1985–93, Liverpool 93– ; with Nottingham Forest: winners League Cup 1989, 90; 15 England U-21 caps, over 13 full England caps. *Address*: Liverpool FC, Anfield Rd, Liverpool L4 0TH.

COBBING, Richard Geoffrey: freestyle skier; b. 15 October 1957; GB aerials champ. 1990, 92; World Freestyle Champs. aerials silver medal 1993; Olympic squad 1992, 94; top-ranked Brit. trampolinist 1987–91. *Address:* c/o Brit. Ski Fed., 258 Main St, E. Calder, Livingston, W. Lothian EH53 0EE.

COCHRANE, Raymond: jockey (Flat); b. 18 June 1957; m. Anne Cochrane 1978; winner Oaks, 1000 Guineas 1986 (Midway Lady), Derby, Irish Derby 1988 (Kahyasi). *Address:* c/o BHB, 42 Portman Square, London W1H 0EN.

COCKERILL, Glenn: footballer; b. 25 August 1959, Grimsby; player Lincoln City 1976–79, Swindon Town 79–81, Lincoln City 81–84, Sheffield Utd 84–85, Southampton 85– . *Address:* Southampton FC, The Dell, Milton Rd, Southampton SO9 4XX.

COCKERILL, Richard: Rugby Union footballer; b. 16 December 1970; player Coventry, Leicester; with Leicester: winners Pilkington Cup 1993; rep. Midland Div.; England U-21 debut v. The Netherlands 1991. *Address:* Leicester FC, Welford Rd, Leicester LE2 7LF.

COCKROFT, Timothy Bruce: rackets player; b. 23 June 1967, Eton; GB U-24 champ. 1991, U-24 doubles champ. 1989–91, amateur doubles champ. 1992; Canadian amateur doubles champ. 1992, open doubles champ. 1994; rep. Berks. U-15 and U-19 cricket, U-19 hockey. *Leisure interests:* golf, cricket, tennis. *Address:* 46 Upcerne Rd, London SW10 0SQ.

COLE, Andrew: footballer; b. 15 October 1971, Nottingham; player Arsenal 1989–92, Bristol City 92–93, Newcastle Utd 93– ; 3 England U-21 caps. *Address:* Newcastle Utd FC, St James' Park, Newcastle-upon-Tyne, Tyne & Wear NE1 4ST.

COLE, Paul Frederick Irvine: racehorse trainer (Flat); b. 11 September 1941; m. Vanessa Cole 1976; 3 s.; 1st licence 1968; winner St Leger 1990 (Snurge), Irish Oaks 1990 (Knight's Baroness), Irish St Leger 1990 (Ibn Bey), Derby 1991 (Generous); leading trainer 1991. *Address:* c/o BHB, 42 Portman Square, London W1H 0EN.

COLE, Sean: tennis player; b. 2 June 1966; rep. Surrey; GB U-18 hard court champ. 1984; winner Caribbean Satellite 1992. *Address:* c/o LTA, The Queen's Club, W. Kensington, London W14 9EG.

COLEMAN, Christopher: footballer; b. 10 June 1970, Swansea; player Swansea City 1987–91, Crystal Palace 91– ; 3 Wales U-21 caps, 2 full Wales caps. *Address:* Crystal Palace FC, Selhurst Park Stadium, London SE25 6PU.

COLLIER, Andrew: Rugby League footballer; b. 6 March 1968, Leigh; player Leigh Miners ARLFC, Leigh 1991– . *Address:* Leigh RLFC, Hilton Park, Kirkhall Lane, Leigh WN7 1RN.

COLLINGS, John Stuart: full-bore rifle shooter; b. 13 March 1953, Croydon; m. Nicola Dilger 1981; 2 s.; rep. London Univ. 1971–74, Essex 73–80, Berks. 81–83, Bucks. 85– ; Welsh open champ. 1988; GB match rifle champ. 1990, 92, 93; England debut 1987, Elcho Shield team 1990–93, Empire Match team 1992; GB debut 1984. *Leisure interests:* cycling, golf. *Address:* 22 Lock Rd, Marlow, Bucks. SL7 1QW.

COLLINS, John: footballer; b. 31 January 1968, Galashiels; player Hibernian 1984–90, Celtic 90– ; over 13 Scotland caps. *Address:* Celtic FC, Celtic Park, 95 Kerrydale St, Glasgow G40 3RE.

COLLYMORE, Stanley: footballer; b. 22 January 1971, Stone; player Crystal Palace 1990–92, Southend Utd 92–93, Nottingham Forest 93– . *Address:* Nottingham Forest FC, City Ground, Nottingham NG2 5FJ.

COLQUHOUN, John: footballer; b. 14 July 1963, Stirling; player Stirling Albion 1980–83, Celtic 83–85, Heart of Midlothian 85–91, Millwall 91–92, Sunderland 92–93, Heart of Midlothian 93– . *Address:* Heart of Midlothian FC, Tynecastle Park, Gorgie Rd, Edinburgh EH11 2NL.

COLTMAN, Gary: cyclist; b. 29 June 1965, Leicester; m. Theresa Coltman 1987; 1 d.; rep. Ammaco, Raleigh; GB madison champ. 1989–91, prof. omnium champ. 1989–93, mountain bike downhill champ. 1991; Commonwealth Games team pursuit bronze medal 1986. *Leisure interests:* inland water- way boating, golf. *Address:* 4 Greensward, E. Goscote, Leicester LE7 3QW.

CONNOLLY, Gary: Rugby League foot- baller; b. 22 June 1971, St Helens; player Blackbrook ARLFC, St Helens 1988–93, Wigan 93– ; with St Helens: winners Premiership 1993; GB debut v. Papua New Guinea 1991, tour Aus./NZ/Papua New Guinea 1992. *Address:* Wigan RLFC, The Pavilion, Central Park, Wigan WN1 1XF.

CONNOLLY, Patrick: footballer; b. 25 June 1970, Glasgow; player Dundee Utd 1986– ; Scotland U-21 int. *Address:* Dundee Utd FC, Tannadice Park, Dundee DD3 7JW.

CONNOR, Cardigan Adolphus: cricketer; b. 24 March 1961, Anguilla; player Hants. 1984– , Sunday League champs. 1986. *Address:* Hants. CCC, County Cricket Ground, Northlands Rd, Southampton SO9 2TY.

CONNOR, Robert James: footballer; b. 4 August 1960, Kilmarnock; m. Anne Connor 1984; 1 s., 1 d.; player Ayr Utd 1978–84, Dundee 84–86, Aberdeen 86– ; with Aberdeen: winners Scottish League Cup, Scottish Cup 1990; 4 Scotland caps; former Scotland U-15 basketball player. *Leisure interests:* golf, snooker, relaxing with family. *Address:* Aberdeen FC, Pittodrie Stadium, Pittodrie St, Aberdeen AB2 1QH.

CONWAY, Billy: Rugby League footballer; b. 31 January 1967, Wakefield; player Wakefield Trinity 1984– . *Address:* Wakefield Trinity RLFC, 171 Doncaster Rd, Belle Vue, Wakefield WF1 5EZ.

CONWAY, Kevin: ice hockey player; b. 13 July 1963; player Ayr Raiders 1985–86, Durham Wasps 86–87, Telford Tigers 87–89, Cleveland Bombers 89–91, Basingstoke Beavers 91– ; with Durham Wasps: GB champs. 1986/87; with Telford Tigers: Div. 1 champs. 1987/88. *Address:* The Playground, W. Ham Park, W. Ham, Basingstoke, Hants.

COOK, Christine: hockey player; b. 22 June 1970; player Hightown Ladies; England U-21 debut 1988, snr debut 1992; GB debut and Champions Trophy squad 1993. *Address:* Hightown Ladies HC, Thirlmere Rd, Hightown, Merseyside.

COOK, Glenn: triathlete; b. 23 January 1963; European Champs. middle-distance individ. gold medals 1987, 92, team gold 1992, Olympic-distance individ. bronze 1992, team gold 1991, 92; World Champs. silver medal 1989. *Address:* c/o Brit. Triathlon Assoc., 4 Tynemouth Terrace, Tynemouth NE30 4BH.

COOK, James: boxer; b. 17 May 1959; prof. debut 1982; titles won: S. middleweight 1984, GB super-middleweight 1990, European super-middleweight 1991; over 20 prof. wins. *Address:* Nat. Promotions, Nat. House, 60–66 Wardour St, London W1V 3HP.

COOK, Nicholas Grant Billson: cricketer; b. 17 June 1956, Leicester; m. Shan Cook 1991; player Leics. 1978–85, Northants. 86– ; Test debut 1983, tours NZ/Pakistan 1983/84, Sri Lanka (England B) 1985/86, Pakistan 1987/88, India 1989/90. *Address:* Northants. CCC, County Cricket Ground, Wantage Rd, Northampton NN1 4TJ.

COOK, Paul: footballer; b. 22 February 1967, Liverpool; m. Susanne Cook 1989; 1 s.; player Wigan Athletic 1984–88, Norwich City 88–89, Wolverhampton Wanderers 89– . *Leisure interests*: running, golf, squash, badminton, watching football. *Address*: Wolverhampton Wanderers FC, Molineux Stadium, Waterloo Rd, Wolverhampton WV1 4QR.

COOKE, Alan: table tennis player; b. 23 March 1966, Holmegate; m. Susan Jane Cooke 1990; rep. Derbys. 1979– ; English champ. 1988, 89, doubles champ. 1990, 92; Commonwealth champ. 1989, team champ. 1985, 89, 94; England debut 1983; European Champs. team bronze medal 1990; World Champs. team bronze medal 1990; Olympic squad 1988, 92; Hungarian Open team winner 1990. *Leisure interests*: golf, soccer, tennis, water skiing. *Address*: 23 Elvaston Rd, N. Wingfield, Chesterfield, Derbys. S42 5HH.

COOKE, David: Rugby Union footballer; b. 7 August 1959, Otley; player Billingham, Stockton, Middlesbrough, W. Hartlepool 1988– ; rep. Durham and N. Div. *Address*: W. Hartlepool RFC, Brierton Lane, Hartlepool, Cleveland TS25 5DR.

COOPER, Colin: footballer; b. 28 February 1967, Sedgefield; player Middlesbrough 1984–91, Millwall 91–93, Nottingham Forest 93– ; 8 England U-21 caps. *Address*: Nottingham Forest FC, City Ground, Nottingham NG2 5FJ.

COOPER, David: Rugby League footballer; b. 29 March 1964, Leeds; player Bramley RUFC, Bradford Northern, Halifax 1992– . *Address*: Halifax RLFC, The Pavilion, Thrum Hall, Gibbet St, Halifax, W. Yorks HX1 4TL.

COOPER, Davie: footballer; b. 25 February 1956, Hamilton; player Clydebank 1974–77, Rangers 77–89, Motherwell 89–93, Clydebank 93– ; with Rangers: winners Scottish Cup 1978, 79, 81, Scottish League Cup 1978, 79, 82, 84, 85, 87, 88; with Motherwell: winners Scottish Cup 1991; 22 Scotland caps. *Address*: Clydebank FC, Kilbowie Park, Arran Place, Clydebank G81 2PT.

COOPER, Gary: footballer; b. 20 November 1965, Hammersmith; player Maidstone Utd 1989–91, Peterborough Utd 91–93, Birmingham City 93– . *Address*: Birmingham City FC, St Andrews Ground, Birmingham B9 4NH.

COOPER, Gavin: motorcyclist (off-road); b. 21 May 1968, Maidstone; S.E. trials champ. 1990–92; ACU solo clubman's trials champ. 1992; winner Guernsey Masters 2 days trial 1990, 91. *Leisure interests*: motor racing, golf, weight training, jet and snow skiing, driving fast cars, night-clubbing. *Address*: WLA Specialist Cars, 736 London Rd, Larkfield, Kent ME20 6BG.

COOPER, Ian: ice hockey player; b. 29 November 1968, Peterlee; player Durham Jnrs 1976–84, Durham Wasps 84–88, Cardiff Devils 88–90, Durham Wasps 90–92, Cardiff Devils 92– ; with Durham Wasps: winners Autumn Cup 1985, 88, 91, League champs. 1984/85, 85/86, 90/91, 91/92, GB champs. 1986/87, 87/88, 90/91, 91/92; with Cardiff Devils: winners Autumn Cup 1993, Div. 1 champs. 1988/89, GB champs., League champs. 1989/90, 92/93; England debut 1990; GB U-19 debut 1984, U-21 debut 1985, snr debut 1989, World Champs. gold medal (Pool C) 1992; Young Brit. Player of the Year 1987/88. *Leisure interests*: jet skiing, cinema, golf, squash, fitness, tennis, eating. *Address*: Cardiff Devils, Harlech Court, Bute Terrace, Cardiff CF1 2FE.

COOPER, Malcolm Douglas, MBE: small-bore rifle shooter; b. 20 December 1947, Camberley; m. Sarah Jane Cooper 1974; rep. Hants. 1966– ; England debut 1974; Commonwealth Games prone pairs gold medal 1982, 3 positions individ. gold 1986, pairs gold 1982, 86; GB debut 1970; Olympic squad 1972, 76, 3 positions gold medals 1984 (1st Brit. winner since 1908), 88; winner of 168 medals in int. competition, including 2 Olympic, 8 World Champs., 14 European Champs. and 4 Commonwealth Games gold. *Leisure interests*: reading, walking, scuba diving, sporting clay shooting. *Address*: P.O. Box 81, Portsmouth, Hants. PO3 5SJ.

COOPER, Shane: Rugby League footballer; b. 26 May 1960, Auckland, NZ; player Mangere E. (NZ), St Helens 1987– (capt.); with St Helens: winners John Player Special Trophy 1988, Premiership 1993; NZ int. *Address*: St Helens RLFC, Dunriding Lane, St Helens, Merseyside WA10 4AD.

COOPER, Stephen: footballer; b. 22 June 1964, Birmingham; player Newport County 1984–85, Plymouth Argyle 85–88, Barnsley 88–90, Tranmere Rovers 90–93, York City 93– . *Address*: York City FC, Bootham Crescent, York YO3 7AQ.

COOPER, Stephen: ice hockey player; b. 11 November 1966, Horden, Co. Durham; player Durham Wasps 1983–88, Cardiff Devils 88–90, Durham Wasps 90–92, Cardiff Devils 92– ; with Durham Wasps: winners Autumn Cup 1985, 88, 91, League champs. 1984/85, 85/86, 90/91, 91/92, GB champs. 1986/87, 87/88, 90/91, 91/92; with Cardiff Devils: winners Autumn Cup 1993, Div. 1 champs. 1988/89, League champs., GB champs. 1989/90, 92/93; GB U-21 debut 1983, snr debut 1988, World Champs. gold medal (Pool B) 1993. *Leisure interests*: golf, football, weight training, squash, tennis. *Address*: Wales Nat. Ice Rink, Hayes Bridge Rd, Cardiff CF1 2GH.

COPE, Lucy: hockey player; b. 13 March 1975; player Balsam Leicester; England U-21 debut 1992, European U-21 Indoor Champs. silver medallist 1994, snr debut 1993.

Address: c/o All England Women's Hockey Assoc., 51 High St, Shrewsbury SY1 1ST.

COPSEY, Anthony Hugh: Rugby Union footballer; b. 25 January 1965, Romford; m. Amanda Copsey; player Llanelli 1989– , winners Welsh Cup 1991, 92, 93, Welsh League champs. 1992/93; Wales and Five Nations debut v. Ireland 1992, tour Zimbabwe/Namibia 1993. *Address*: Llanelli RFC, Stradey Park, Llanelli, Dyfed.

CORCORAN, Ian: Rugby Union footballer; b. 11 May 1963, Edinburgh; player Gala; Scotland B debut v. France 1990, snr tours Aus. 1992, Fiji/Tonga/W. Samoa 1993. *Address*: Gala RFC, Netherdale, Nether Rd, Galashiels TD1 3HE.

CORDLE, Gerald: Rugby League footballer; b. 29 September 1960, Cardiff; player Cardiff (RU), Bradford Northern 1989– ; Wales debut v. Papua New Guinea 1991; GB debut v. France 1990. *Address*: Bradford Northern RLFC, Odsal Stadium, Bradford BD6 1BS.

CORE, Maurice: boxer; b. 22 June 1965; prof. debut 1990; titles won: GB light-heavyweight 1992; over 11 prof. wins. *Address*: c/o Phil Martin, 79 Buckingham Rd, Chorlton, Manchester M21 1QT.

CORK, Alan: footballer; b. 4 March 1959, Derby; player Wimbledon 1978–92, Sheffield Utd 92– ; with Wimbledon: winners FA Cup 1988. *Address*: Sheffield Utd FC, Bramall Lane, Sheffield, S. Yorks S2 4SU.

CORK, Dominic Gerald: cricketer; b. 7 August 1971, Newcastle-under-Lyme; player Derbys. 1990– , winners Benson and Hedges Cup 1993, Sunday League champs. 1990; England YC tour Aus. 1989/90, England A tours Bermuda/WI 1991/92, Aus. 1992/93, SA 1993/94 (aborted), snr 1-day int. debut v. Pakistan 1992. *Address*: Derbys. CCC, County Cricket Ground, Nottingham Rd, Derby DE2 6DA.

CORLESS, Patricia Anne (Trish):
oarswoman; b. 18 September 1966,
Addlestone; rep. Staines BC 1987– ; GB
women's quadruple sculls champ. 1987,
women's lightweight and open double
sculls champ. 1992; GB U-23 debut 1987,
snr debut 1992, World Champs. squad
(women's lightweight double sculls) 1992,
93. *Leisure interests*: squash, cycling, swimming. *Address*: `Mildura', 136 Kingston Rd,
Staines, Middx TW18 1BL.

CORNWALLIS, Charlotte Louise:
real tennis player; b. 3 September 1972,
Tenterden; GB ladies' open champ. 1992;
US ladies' open champ. 1991; world ladies'
doubles champ. 1993; rep. England U-18
hockey. *Leisure interests*: all sport, go-
karting, concerts, socializing, films.
Address: 15 Mablethorpe Rd, London
SW6 6AQ.

CORNWELL, John: footballer; b. 13
October 1964, Bethnal Green; player
Leyton Orient 1982–87, Newcastle Utd
87–88, Swindon Town 88–90, Southend Utd
90– . *Address*: Southend Utd FC, Roots
Hall, Victoria Ave, Southend-on-Sea, Essex
SS2 6NQ.

CORSIE, Richard: flat green bowler; b. 27
November 1966, Edinburgh; m. Suzanne
Joyce 1988; 1 s.; Scottish junior champ.
(outdoor) 1983, (indoor) 1985, 88, Scottish
pairs champ. 1992; Scottish int. debut
(outdoor) 1984, (indoor) 1989; GB junior
champ. (outdoor) 1984, (indoor) 1989;
Commonwealth Games singles bronze
medals 1986, 90; World Champs. pairs and
team gold medals, singles silver 1992;
World Indoor Champs. singles gold
medals 1989, 91, 93; winner Hong Kong
Classic pairs 1987, singles 1988, Aus.
World Classic singles 1988, Jersey Int.
singles 1990, Mazda Jack High singles
1993; youngest-ever world singles champ.
Leisure interests: golf. *Address*: 14 Ferguson
Green, Musselburgh EH21 6XB.

COSTELLO, John: Rugby League foot-
baller; b. 10 March 1970; player Leigh
Miners ARLFC, Leigh 1991– . *Address*:
Leigh RLFC, Hilton Park, Kirkhall Lane,
Leigh WN7 1RN.

COSTELLO, Peter: footballer; b. 31
October 1969, Halifax; player Bradford
City 1988–90, Rochdale 90–91,
Peterborough Utd 91– . *Address*:
Peterborough Utd FC, London Rd Ground,
Peterborough, Cambs. PE2 8AL.

COTON, Anthony: footballer; b. 19 May
1961, Tamworth; player Birmingham City
1978–84, Watford 84–90, Manchester City
90– . *Address*: Manchester City FC, Maine
Rd, Moss Side, Manchester M14 7WN.

COTTAM, Andrew Colin: cricketer; b. 14
July 1973, Northampton; player Somerset
1992–93, Northants. 94– ; England U-19
tour Pakistan 1992. *Leisure interests*:
Tottenham Hotspur FC, playing football,
relaxing in sauna after work-out. *Address*:
Northants. CCC, County Cricket Ground,
Wantage Rd, Northampton NN1 4TJ.

COTTEE, Anthony: footballer; b. 11 July
1965, W. Ham; player W. Ham Utd
1982–88, Everton 88– ; 8 England U-21
caps, 7 full England caps. *Address*: Everton
FC, Goodison Park, Liverpool L4 4EL.

COTTERILL, Stephen: footballer; b. 20
July 1964, Cheltenham; player Wimbledon
1989–93, Bournemouth 93– . *Address*:
Bournemouth FC, Dean Court,
Bournemouth, Dorset BH7 7AF.

COTTEY, Phillip Anthony: cricketer; b. 2
June 1966, Swansea; player Glamorgan
1986– , Sunday League champs. 1993;
player Swansea City FC 1982–85. *Address*:
Glamorgan CCC, Sophia Gardens, Cardiff
CF1 9XR.

COWAN, Jonathan: table tennis player; b. 16 November 1975, Belfast, NI; Ulster U-12 open champ. 1988, U-14 open champ. 1990, U-17 open champ., closed champ. 1991; Irish U-14 open champ. 1990, U-17 open champ. 1991, snr open champ. 1992, closed champ. 1993; Ulster U-14 debut 1989, U-17 debut 1990; Ireland U-14 debut 1989, snr debut 1991; rep. NI U-18 football. *Leisure interests*: golf. *Address*: 54 Ravenhill Gardens, Ravenhill Rd, Belfast BT6 8GQ.

COWAN, Richard Gordon Lockhart: Rugby Union footballer; b. 14 October 1969, Edinburgh; player Napier Univ., Watsonians 1989– . *Leisure interests*: golf, tennis, water skiing, squash, fives, football. *Address*: Watsonians RFC, Myreside, Myreside Rd, Edinburgh EH10 5DB.

COWAN, Thomas: footballer; b. 28 August 1969, Bellshill; player Clyde 1988–89, Rangers 89–91, Sheffield Utd 91– . *Address*: Sheffield Utd FC, Bramall Lane, Sheffield, S. Yorks S2 4SU.

COWANS, Gordon: footballer; b. 27 October 1958, Cornforth, Durham; player Aston Villa 1975–85, Bari (Italy) 85–88, Aston Villa 88–91, Blackburn Rovers 91–93, Aston Villa 93– ; 5 England U-21 caps, 10 full England caps. *Address*: Aston Villa FC, Villa Park, Trinity Rd, Birmingham B6 6HE.

COWANS, Norman George: cricketer; b. 17 April 1961, Enfield St Mary, Jamaica; 1 d.; player Middx 1980–93, Hants. 94– ; with Middx: county champs. 1985, 90, 93, Sunday League champs. 1992; 19 Tests, debut 1982, 23 1-day ints, tours Aus./NZ 1982/83, NZ/Pakistan 1983/84, India/Aus. 1984/85, Sri Lanka (England B) 1985/86. *Address*: Hants. CCC, County Cricket Ground, Northlands Rd, Southampton SO9 2TY.

COWDREY, Graham Robert: cricketer; b. 27 June 1964, Farnborough; m. Maxine Juster 1993; player Kent 1984– ; MCC tour WI 1992. *Address*: Kent CCC, St Lawrence Ground, Canterbury CT1 3NZ.

COWIE, Neil: Rugby League footballer; b. 16 January 1967, Hebden Bridge; player Todmorden ARLFC, Rochdale Hornets, Wigan 1991– ; with Wigan: winners Challenge Cup, Premiership 1992, Regal Trophy 1993; Brit. Lions tour Aus./Papua New Guinea 1992. *Address*: Wigan RLFC, The Pavilion, Central Park, Wigan WN1 1XF.

COX, Ailsa: lacrosse player; b. 1 June 1967, Cardiff; rep. Manchester Univ. 1985–88 (capt. 86–88), Middx 88–89, Staffs. and Warks. 89– ; Wales debut 1987, World Cup squad 1989, 93, tours USA 1991, 92, 93. *Leisure interests*: squash, swimming, horseriding, cinema, eating chocolate. *Address*: 73 Harrow Rd, Selly Oak, Birmingham B29 7DW.

COX, James Anderson: hockey player; b. 14 January 1965, Dundee; player Menzieshill, winners Scottish Cup 1987, 89, Scottish Indoor Cup 1985, 86, 90, 92, 93, Glenfiddich Int. Tournament 1985, 88, 91, club champs. 1986, 89, indoor champs. 1986, 90, 91–93; Scotland U-21 debut 1984, snr debut 1985, European Champs. indoor bronze medallist 1991; GB U-21 debut 1986, Olympic training squad 1990, 91. *Leisure interests*: golf, martial arts, running. *Address*: 49 Whitfield Gardens, Dundee DD4 0AW.

COX, Neil: footballer; b. 8 October 1971, Scunthorpe; player Scunthorpe Utd 1990–91, Aston Villa 91– . *Address*: Aston Villa FC, Villa Park, Trinity Rd, Birmingham B6 6HE.

COX, Rupert Michael Fiennes: cricketer; b. 20 August 1967, Guildford; player Hants. 1990– . *Address*: Hants. CCC, County Cricket Ground, Northlands Rd, Southampton SO9 2TY.

COYLE, Owen: footballer; b. 14 July 1966, Glasgow; player Dumbarton 1985–88, Clydebank 88–90, Airdrieonians 90–93, Bolton Wanderers 93– ; Ireland U-21 int. *Address*: Bolton Wanderers FC, Burnden Park, Manchester Rd, Bolton, Lancs. BL3 2QR.

COYLE, Ronald: footballer; b. 19 August 1961, Glasgow; player Celtic 1983–86, Middlesbrough 86–87, Rochdale 87–88, Raith Rovers 88– . *Address*: Raith Rovers FC, Stark's Park, Pratt St, Kirkcaldy, Fife KY1 1SA.

COYNE, Peter: Rugby League footballer; b. 28 October 1964; player Castleford 1992– . *Address*: Castleford RLFC, Wheldon Rd, Castleford WF10 2SD.

COYNE, Thomas: footballer; b. 14 November 1962, Glasgow; player Clydebank 1981–83, Dundee Utd 83–86, Dundee 86–89, Celtic 89–93, Tranmere Rovers 1993, Motherwell 1993– ; 8 Ireland caps. *Address*: Motherwell FC, Fir Park, Fir Park St, Motherwell ML1 2QN.

CRABBE, Scott: footballer; b. 12 August 1968, Edinburgh; player Heart of Midlothian 1986–92, Dundee Utd 92– ; Scotland U-21 int. *Address*: Dundee Utd FC, Tannadice Park, Dundee DD3 7JW.

CRAM, Stephen: athlete; b. 14 October 1960, Gateshead; AAA 1500m champ. 1981–83, 800m champ. 1984, 86, 88; UK 5000m champ. 1989; European Jnr Champs. 3000m gold medal 1979; Commonwealth Games 1500m gold medal 1982, 800m and 1500m gold 1986; European Champs. 1500m gold medals 1982, 86, 800m bronze 1986; European Cup 1500m bronze medal 1981, gold 1983, 85, silver 1987; World Champs. 1500m gold medal 1983; Olympic squad 1980, 1500m silver medal 1984; UK 1500m record-holder; BBC Sports Personality of the Year 1983, Sports Writers' Sportsman of the Year 1983, 85.

Address: c/o Brit. Athletic Fed., 225A Bristol Rd, Edgbaston, Birmingham B5 7UB.

CRAMB, Valerie Anne: fencer; b. 2 December 1970, St Andrews; rep. Glasgow Univ. 1988–92; Scottish univ. ladies' foil champ. 1988–90, épée champ. 1992, GB univ. ladies' foil champ. 1990; Scottish ladies' open épée champ. 1993; GB ladies' U-18 foil champ. 1989; Scotland debut 1989; Commonwealth Champs. ladies' épée team silver medal, foil team bronze 1990; GB U-20 debut 1990, snr debut and World Student Games squad 1991. *Leisure interests*: skiing, aerobics. *Address*: 31 Westwood Court, Middleton, Leeds LS10 4PA.

CRANSTON, Tim: ice hockey player; b. 13 December 1962; player Fife Flyers 1988–89, Cleveland Bombers 89–91, Durham Wasps 91–92, Sheffield Steelers 92– ; with Durham Wasps: League champs., GB champs. 1991/92. *Address*: Sheffield Arena, Broughton Lane, Sheffield S9 2DF.

CRAWFORD, Stephen: footballer; b. 9 January 1974, Dunfermline; player Raith Rovers 1992– . *Address*: Raith Rovers FC, Stark's Park, Pratt St, Kirkcaldy, Fife KY1 1SA.

CRAWLEY, Barry: Rugby Union footballer; b. 24 November 1964, Southend; player Southend, Rochford, Warwick Univ., Saracens 1991– ; rep. E. Counties. *Address*: Saracens FC, Bramley Rd Sports Ground, Chaseside, Southgate, London N14 4AB.

CRAWLEY, John Paul: cricketer; b. 21 September 1971, Malden; player Cambridge Univ., Lancs. 1990– ; England U-19 tours Aus. 1989/90, NZ 1990/91 (capt.), England A tour SA 1993/94. *Address*: Lancs. CCC, Old Trafford, Manchester M16 0PX.

CRAWLEY, Mark Andrew: cricketer; b. 16 December 1967, Newton-le-Willows; m. Natasha Crawley 1991; player Lancs. 1990, Notts. 1991– ; Young England tour Sri Lanka 1987. *Address*: Notts. CCC, Trent Bridge, Nottingham NG2 6AG.

CREANEY, Gerard: footballer; b. 13 April 1970, Coatbridge; player Celtic 1987–94, Portsmouth 94– ; Scotland U-21 int. *Address*: Portsmouth FC, Fratton Park, Frogmore Rd, Portsmouth PO4 8RA.

CRIBB, Guy Diomedes Hatfield: wind-surfer; b. 3 April 1970, Bournemouth; UK youth champ. 1988, snr champ. 1993, nat. series champ. 1990, 91; European Champs. raceboard silver medal 1991. *Publications*: contributor to *Boards* magazine. *Leisure interests*: sailing, chess, music, art, reading. *Address*: 11 Bingham Ave, Lilliput, Poole, Dorset BH14 8ND.

CRICHTON, Paul: footballer; b. 3 October 1965, Pontefract; player Peterborough Utd 1988–90, Doncaster Rovers 90–93, Grimsby Town 93– . *Address*: Grimsby Town FC, Blundell Park, Cleethorpes, S. Humberside DN35 7PY.

CRITCHLEY, Jason: Rugby League foot-baller; b. 7 December 1970, St Helens; player Blackbrook ARLFC, Townsville (Aus.), Widnes, Salford 1992– . *Address*: Salford RLFC, The Willows, Willows Rd, Weaste, Salford M5 2ST.

CROCKER, Emily Louise: gymnast (sports acrobatics); b. 31 January 1981, Kingston-upon-Thames; English women's pairs champ. 1990; GB jnr women's pairs champ. 1992; GB jnr debut 1991, World Jnr Champs. tempo gold medal, balance and combined gold (joint) 1993. *Address*: 161 Fleetside, W. Molesey, Surrey KT8 2NH.

CROFT, Robert Damien Bale: cricketer; b. 25 May 1970, Swansea; player Glamorgan 1989– , Sunday League champs. 1993; England A tours WI 1991/92, SA 1993/94. *Address*: Glamorgan CCC, Sophia Gardens, Cardiff CF1 9XR.

CROMPTON, Martin: Rugby League footballer; b. 29 September 1969; player Warrington, Wigan 1992–93, Oldham 93– . *Address*: Oldham RLFC, The Pavilion, Watersheddings, Oldham OL4 2PB.

CRONIN, Damian Francis: Rugby Union footballer; b. 17 April 1963, Wegberg, Germany; m. Annie Cronin; player Bath, London Scottish; Scotland B debut 1987, snr and Five Nations debut v. Ireland 1988, Grand Slam champs. 1990, tours Zimbabwe 1988, NZ 1990, Aus. 1992; Brit. Lions tour NZ 1993. *Address*: London Scottish FC, Richmond Athletic Ground, Kew Foot Rd, Richmond, Surrey TW9 2SS.

CROOK, Carl: boxer; b. 10 November 1963; England debut 1984; prof. debut 1985; titles won: GB and Commonwealth lightweight 1990; over 25 prof. wins. *Address*: Matchroom Ltd, 10 Western Rd, Romford, Essex RM1 3JT.

CROOK, Ian: footballer; b. 18 January 1963, Romford; player Tottenham Hotspur 1980–86, Norwich City 86– . *Address*: Norwich City FC, Carrow Rd, Norwich NR1 1JE.

CROOKS, Lee: Rugby League footballer; b. 18 September 1963, Castleford; player Hull 1980–87, W. Suburbs (Aus.), Balmain (Aus.), Leeds, Castleford 1990– ; with Hull: winners Challenge Cup 1982; with Castleford: winners Regal Trophy 1994; GB colts tour Aus. 1982 (capt.), snr debut v. Aus. 1982, Brit. Lions tours Aus./NZ/Papua New Guinea 1984, 88, 92. *Address*: Castleford RLFC, Wheldon Rd, Castleford WF10 2SD.

CROSBY, Dean John: hang glider/
paraglider pilot; b. 10 December 1963,
Sheffield; GB paragliding champ. 1993.
Leisure interests: climbing, caving, moun-
tain biking. *Address*: Active Edge,
Watershed Mill, Langcliffe Rd, Settle
BD24 9LY.

CROSBY, Gary: footballer; b. 8 May 1964,
Sleaford; player Lincoln City 1986–87,
Grantham Town, Nottingham Forest
1987– ; with Nottingham Forest: winners
League Cup 1990. *Address*: Nottingham
Forest FC, City Ground, Nottingham
NG2 5FJ.

CROSBY, Kevin: swimmer; b. 27
September 1973, Widnes; rep. Cheshire
1983– ; GB 200m butterfly champ. 1991,
93; England youth debut 1988, intermediate debut 1991, snr debut 1992; GB jnr
debut 1989, World Student Games squad
1993. *Leisure interests*: Widnes RLFC, golf,
computer games. *Address*: 30 Duncansby
Crescent, Gt Sankey, Warrington
WA5 3PD.

CROSS, Karen Marie: tennis player; b. 19
February 1974, Exeter; rep. Devon, county
ladies' champ. 1988; GB debut 1993. *Leisure
interests*: cinema, reading. *Address*: c/o
LTA, The Queen's Club, W. Kensington,
London W14 9EG.

CROSSLEY, Mark: footballer; b. 16 June
1969, Barnsley; player Nottingham Forest
1988– ; 3 England U-21 caps. *Address*:
Nottingham Forest FC, City Ground,
Nottingham NG2 5FJ.

CROW, Alastair Henry: point-to-point
rider; b. 12 May 1968, Shrewsbury; GB
champ. 1993. *Address*: Hardwicke Hall,
Hadnall, Shrewsbury, Shropshire SY4 3DL.

CRUTCHLEY, Robert: hockey player; b. 24
May 1970, Bebington; player Neston
1983–92, Hounslow 92– ; with Hounslow:
European Cup Winners' Cup silver medal-
list, club and League champs. 1993;
England U-16 debut 1986, U-18 debut 1987,
U-21 debut and World Cup squad 1989,
snr debut 1993; World Student Games gold
medal 1991; GB snr debut 1994. *Leisure
interests*: visiting Guernsey. *Address*:
Bodyline Sportswear, Unit 1, Hillside
Court, Barbot Hall Industrial Estate,
Rotherham SE1 4RJ.

CUDDY, Tom: motorcyclist; b. 1967,
London; Irish endurance race champ. 1989;
GB 1300cc production-class club racing
champ. 1990; ACU Brit. clubman's F1
champ. 1992. *Leisure interests*: keep-fit,
mountain biking, socializing. *Address*: 1
Petworth Gardens, Raynes Park, London
SW20 0UH.

CULLEN, Christina Louise: hockey player;
b. 1 March 1970; player Moss Side Ladies
1981–86, Didsbury Greys 86–88, Hightown
Ladies 88– ; with Hightown: club
champs. 1992, indoor club champs.
1991–93, European Indoor Cup bronze
medallist 1993; rep. Greater Manchester U-
18 1987–88, Lancs. U-21 88–90, snr 89–92;
with Lancs.: county champs. 1989–92;
England U-18 debut 1988, U-21 debut 1989,
snr debut 1992. *Leisure interests*: all sport,
theatre, cinema, travelling. *Address*:
Hightown Ladies HC, Thirlmere Rd,
Hightown, Merseyside.

CULLEN, Paul: Rugby League footballer;
b. 4 March 1963, Warrington; player
Crosfields ARLFC, Warrington 1980– ;
with Warrington: winners Regal Trophy
1991; rep. Lancs. *Address*: Warrington
RLFC, Wilderspool Stadium, Wilderspool
Causeway, Warrington WA4 6PY.

CULVERHOUSE, Ian: footballer; b. 22
September 1964, Bishops Stortford; player
Tottenham Hotspur 1982–85, Norwich City
85– ; with Norwich City: 2nd Div.
champs. 1985/86. *Address*: Norwich City
FC, Carrow Rd, Norwich NR1 1JE.

CUMMINS, Anderson Cleophas:
cricketer; b. 7 April 1966; player Durham
1993– ; WI tours Aus./NZ (World Cup)
1991/92, Aus./SA 1992/93. *Address*:
Durham CCC, County Ground, Riverside,
Chester-le-Street, Co. Durham DH3 3QR.

CUMMINS, Damian George: Rugby
Union footballer; b. 8 December 1964,
Tenby; m. Susan Caroline Cummins 1989; 1
s.; player Exeter Univ., Gloucester 1987– ;
rep. Middx CCC 2nd XI 1983–86. *Leisure
interests*: cricket, golf, surfing, sailboard-
ing. *Address*: Gloucester RUFC, Kingsholm,
Worcester St, Gloucester GL3 3AX.

CUNDY, Jason: footballer; b. 12 November
1969, Wandsworth; player Chelsea
1988–92, Tottenham Hotspur 92– ; 3
England U-21 caps. *Address*: Tottenham
Hotspur FC, 748 High Rd, Tottenham,
London N17 0AP.

CUNLIFFE, Derek John: hockey player;
b. 5 December 1972, Liss; player Havant
1990– , winners League Cup 1990,
European Cup silver medallist 1991, club
champs. 1990, League champs. 1991, 92;
rep. Hants. U-18, county U-18 champs.
1990 (capt.); Scotland U-21 and snr debuts
1991; GB U-21 debut and tour Pakistan
1992. *Address*: Havant HC, Havant Park,
Havant, Hants.

CUNNINGHAM, Kenneth: footballer;
b. 28 June 1971, Dublin, Ireland; player
Millwall 1989– ; 4 Ireland U-21 caps.
Address: Millwall FC, The Den, Zampa Rd,
Bermondsey, London SE16 3LH.

CUNNINGTON, Shaun: footballer;
b. 4 January 1966, Bournemouth; player
Wrexham 1984–88, Grimsby Town 88–92,
Sunderland 92– . *Address*: Sunderland FC,
Roker Park Ground, Sunderland, Tyne and
Wear SR6 9SW.

CURBISHLEY, Llewellyn (Alan): football
manager; b. 8 November 1957, Forest Gate;
player W. Ham Utd 1974–79, Birmingham
City 79–83, Aston Villa 83–84, Charlton
Athletic 84–87, Brighton and Hove Albion
87–90, Charlton Athletic 90–91; 1 England
U-21 cap; joint player/manager Charlton
Athletic 1991– . *Address*: Charlton
Athletic FC, The Valley, Floyd Rd, London
SE7 8BL.

CURLE, Keith: footballer; b. 14 November
1963, Bristol; player Bristol Rovers
1981–83, Torquay Utd 83–84, Bristol City
84–87, Reading 87–88, Wimbledon 88–91,
Manchester City 91– (capt.); 3 England
caps. *Address*: Manchester City FC, Maine
Rd, Moss Side, Manchester M14 7WN.

CURRAN, Henry: footballer; b. 9 October
1966, Glasgow; player Dumbarton 1984–87,
Dundee Utd 87–89, St Johnstone 89– .
Address: St Johnstone FC, McDiarmid Park,
Crieff Rd, Perth PH1 2SJ.

CURRAN, Kevin Malcolm: cricketer; b. 7
September 1959, Rusape, Rhodesia; player
Glos. 1985–90, Northants. 91– ;
Zimbabwe tours Sri Lanka 1982, England
1982, 83 (World Cup), Sri Lanka 1984,
Pakistan/India (World Cup) 1987; 1st
player to achieve Sunday League double of
hat-trick and 50 runs in same match, Glos.
v. Warks. 1989; achieved 1st-class double
of 1000 runs and 50 wickets in season 1990.
Address: Northants. CCC, County Cricket
Ground, Wantage Rd, Northampton
NN1 4TJ.

CURRIER, Andrew: Rugby League
footballer; b. 8 April 1966, Widnes; player
Widnes 1983–93, Featherstone Rovers
93– ; GB debut v. NZ 1989. *Address*:
Featherstone Rovers RLFC, The Croft,
Batley Rd, W. Ardsley, Wakefield
WF3 1DX.

CURRY, Jilliain Mary: freestyle skier; b. 29 November 1962, Cobham; m. Robin John Wallace 1990; GB debut 1984; European Champs. combined bronze medal 1987, silver 1990; World Cup aerials silver medal 1991, bronze 1992, 94; Olympic squad 1992, 94. *Leisure interests*: tennis, squash, riding, trampolining, water skiing, European history, French literature, sports physiology, palm trees. *Address*: Garden Flat, 61 Inverness Terrace, London W2 3JT.

CURTIS, Timothy Stephen: cricketer; b. 15 January 1960, Chislehurst; m. Philippa Curtis 1985; 1 d.; player Durham Univ., Worcs. 1979– (capt. 92–), county champs. 1988, 89, Sunday League champs. 1987, 88; NCA U-19 tour Canada 1979; Test debut 1988. *Address*: Worcs. CCC, County Ground, New Rd, Worcester WR2 4QQ.

CUSACK, Loretta Margaret: judo player (U-48–U-56kg); b. 12 July 1963, London; m. William Scott Cusack (qv); 1 d.; Commonwealth Games silver medal (England) 1986, gold (Scotland) 1990; European Champs. bronze medals 1980, 84, silver 1981, 82, 91, gold 1983, 92, team gold 1985, silver 1986, 91, bronze 1987; World Champs. bronze medal 1980, gold 1982. *Leisure interests*: swimming, tenpin bowling, working with children, cooking. *Address*: The Edinburgh Club, 2 Hillside Crescent, Edinburgh EH23 4TY.

CUSACK, William Scott: judo player (U-78kg); b. 23 May 1966, Glasgow; m. Loretta Margaret Cusack (qv); 1 d.; New York open champ., US open champ. 1991, Scottish open champ. 1992; GB champ. 1993; Commonwealth Games squad 1986, bronze medal 1990; European Champs. squad 1991, 92, World Champs. squad 1991, Olympic squad 1992. *Leisure interests*: football, swimming, working with children. *Address*: The Edinburgh Club, 2 Hillside Crescent, Edinburgh EH23 4TY.

DA CRUZ, Natalia: gymnast (sports acrobatics); b. 19 May 1975, Canterbury; English women's pairs champ. 1990; GB jnr women's pairs champ. 1992; GB jnr debut 1991, World Jnr Champs. tempo gold medal, balance and combined gold (joint) 1993. *Address*: 39 Kenton Ave, Sunbury, Middx TW16 5AS.

DAILLY, Christian: footballer; b. 23 October 1973, Dundee; player Dundee Utd 1990– ; Scotland U-21 debut 1990, snr debut v. Estonia 1993. *Address*: Dundee Utd FC, Tannadice Park, Dundee DD3 7JW.

DAIR, Jason: footballer; b. 15 June 1974, Dunfermline; player Raith Rovers 1991– ; Scotland U-21 int. *Address*: Raith Rovers FC, Stark's Park, Pratt St, Kirkcaldy, Fife KY1 1SA.

DALE, Adrian: cricketer; b. 24 October 1968, Germiston, SA; player Glamorgan 1989– , Sunday League champs. 1993, tours Trinidad 1990, Zimbabwe 1991; England A tour SA 1993/94. *Address*: Glamorgan CCC, Sophia Gardens, Cardiff CF1 9XR.

DALEY, James Arthur: cricketer; b. 24 September 1973, Sunderland; player Durham 1992– , tour Zimbabwe 1991/92. *Address*: Durham CCC, County Ground, Riverside, Chester-le-Street, Co. Durham DH3 3QR.

DALGLISH, Kenneth Mathieson, MBE: football manager; b. 4 March 1951, Glasgow; player Celtic 1970–77, Liverpool 77–89; manager Liverpool 1985–91, Blackburn Rovers 91– ; as player: winner Scottish Cup 1972, 74, 75, 77, Scottish League Cup 1975, Scottish League champs. 1971/72, 72/73, 73/74, 76/77 (Celtic), FA Cup 1986, League Cup 1981–84, European Cup 1978, 81, 84, League champs. 1978/79, 79/80, 81/82, 82/83, 83/84, 85/86 (Liverpool), 4 Scotland U-23 caps, 102 full

Scotland caps; only player to have scored 100 goals in both the English and Scottish leagues; as manager: winner FA Cup 1986, 89, League champs. 1985/86, 87/88, 89/90 (Liverpool). *Address*: Blackburn Rovers FC, Ewood Park, Blackburn, Lancs. BB2 4JF.

DALLAGLIO, Laurence Bruno: Rugby Union footballer; b. 10 August 1972; player Wasps; England U-21 debut v. The Netherlands 1992, tour Aus. 1993, snr squad, winners World Cup Sevens 1993. *Address*: Wasps FC, Wasps Football Ground, Repton Ave, Sudbury, nr Wembley, Middx HA0 3DW.

DALLAS, Victor Noel: flat green bowler; b. 7 October 1959, Coleraine, NI; m. Sheena Dallas 1984; 2 s.; Ireland debut 1988, World Champs. squad 1992; winner Jersey Int. Classic triples 1993. *Leisure interests*: football, golf, cricket. *Address*: 4 Tullybeg Ave, Coleraine, Co. Londonderry BT51 3NG.

DALZIEL, Gordon: footballer; b. 16 March 1962, Motherwell; player Rangers 1978–83, Manchester City 83–84, Partick Thistle 84–86, E. Stirling 86–87, Raith Rovers 87– ; with Rangers: winners Scottish League Cup 1982. *Address*: Raith Rovers FC, Stark's Park, Pratt St, Kirkcaldy, Fife KY1 1SA.

DANBY, Rob: Rugby League footballer; b. 30 August 1974; player Hull 1991– . *Address*: Hull RLFC, The Boulevard Ground, Airlie St, Hull HU3 3JD.

DANGERFIELD, Stuart John: cyclist; b. 17 September 1971, Walsall; RTTC hill-climb champ. 1992, 93; GB jnr debut 1988, snr debut 1990. *Address*: 42 Kewstoke Rd, Willenhall, W. Midlands WV12 5DL.

DANIEL, Alan: Rugby League footballer; b. 1 February 1969, Leeds; player Hunslet 1991–93, Castleford 93– . *Address*: Castleford RLFC, Wheldon Rd, Castleford WF10 2SD.

DANIEL, Raymond: footballer; b. 10 December 1964, Luton; player Luton Town 1982–86, Hull City 86–89, Cardiff City 89–90, Portsmouth 90– . *Address*: Portsmouth FC, Fratton Park, Frogmore Rd, Portsmouth PO4 8RA.

DANIELS, Barbara Ann: cricketer; b. 17 December 1964, Ditton Priors, Shropshire; player Edgbaston 1981–84, Wolverhampton 84–90, Invicta 91– ; rep. W. Midlands 1981– (capt. 89–), county champs. 1983; England jnr debut 1982 (capt. 1984), Young England tour Ireland 1984, snr debut and World Cup team (winners) 1993; scored 1000 runs in season 1992; Sports Writers' Assoc. Team of the Year award-winner 1993. *Leisure interests*: hockey, reading, theatre, cooking. *Address*: c/o Women's Cricket Assoc., 41 St Michael's Lane, Headingley, Leeds LS6 3BR.

DANNATT, Andrew: Rugby League footballer; b. 20 November 1965, Hull; player Hull 1982–93, St Helens 93– ; with Hull: winners Premiership 1991; GB debut v. France 1985. *Address*: St Helens RLFC, Dunriding Lane, St Helens, Merseyside WA10 4AD.

DARBY, Julian: footballer; b. 3 October 1967, Bolton; player Bolton Wanderers 1986–93, Coventry City 93– . *Address*: Coventry City FC, Highfield Rd Stadium, King Richard St, Coventry CV2 4FW.

DARBYSHIRE, Paul: Rugby League footballer; b. 3 December 1969, Wigan; player Wigan St Pats ARLFC, Warrington 1989– ; GB U-21 debut v. France 1991. *Address*: Warrington RLFC, Wilderspool Stadium, Wilderspool Causeway, Warrington WA4 6PY.

DARE, Alison: point-to-point rider; b. 23 November 1957, Bristol; GB ladies' champ. 1986, 87, 90–92; holds record for ladies' career wins (over 180), rode record 26 wins in season 1991; NH ladies' champ.

1982/83. *Leisure interests*: fly fishing, cinema, DIY/home decorating. *Address*: c/o Upper Hill Farm, Hill, nr Berkeley, Glos. GL13 9EE.

DAUNT, Brett: Rugby League footballer; b. 8 October 1965; player Featherstone Rovers 1992– . *Address*: Featherstone Rovers RLFC, The Croft, Batley Rd, W. Ardsley, Wakefield WF3 1DX.

DAVENPORT, Angela Jayne: synchronized swimmer; b. 11 October 1969, Bloxwich; GB solo jnr champ. 1984, Scottish duet champ. 1991; England and GB jnr debuts 1984, snr debuts 1987 (capt. 1989); European Jnr Champs. team gold medal 1984; Europa Cup team silver medal 1992. *Leisure interests*: dancing, reading, cookery, jigsaws. *Address*: c/o ASA, Harold Fern House, Derby Square, Loughborough, Leics. LE11 0AL.

DAVENPORT, Peter: footballer; b. 24 March 1961, Birkenhead; m. Lesley Jayne Reid; 1 s.; player Nottingham Forest 1982–86, Manchester Utd 86–88, Middlesbrough 88–90, Sunderland 90– ; 1 England B cap, 1 full England cap. *Leisure interests*: cricket, tennis, golf, home computing, marine art and antiques. *Address*: Sunderland FC, Roker Park Ground, Sunderland, Tyne and Wear SR6 9SW.

DAVIDSON, Paul: Rugby League footballer; b. 1 August 1969, Whitehaven; player Hensingham ARLFC, Widnes 1990– ; rep. Cumbria. *Address*: Widnes RLFC, Naughton Park, Lowerhouse Lane, Widnes WA8 7DZ.

DAVIES, Adrian: Rugby Union footballer; b. 9 February 1969, Bridgend; player Neath, Cardiff; Wales debut v. Barbarians 1990, tour Zimbabwe/Namibia 1993. *Address*: Cardiff RFC, Cardiff Arms Park, Westgate St, Cardiff CF1 1JA.

DAVIES, Adrian Leigh: squash player; b. 6 January 1966, Carmarthen; 1 s., 1 d.; player Llanelli 1977–82, Manchester N. 83–88, Leekes Wizards 88– (capt.); with Leekes Wizards: League champs. 1988/89, 1990/91; Welsh open champ. 1988; Wales debut 1981 (youngest-ever snr Welsh int.); winner Dutch Open 1988, 90. *Leisure interests*: golf, tennis, rugby. *Address*: 7 Llys Westfa, Swiss Valley, Llanelli, Dyfed SA14 8BG.

DAVIES, Andrew: weightlifter (+108kg); b. 17 July 1967, Newport; m. Alison Davies 1992; Welsh U-16 champ. 1983, U-18 champ. 1983–85, jnr champ. 1983–87, snr champ. 1984–92; GB U-16 champ. 1983, U-18 champ. 1983–85, jnr champ. 1984–87, snr champ. 1985–92; Commonwealth champ. 1987, 88; European Jnr Champs. silver medal 1987; World Jnr Champs. silver medal 1987; Commonwealth Games bronze medal 1986, gold 1990; European Champs. silver medal 1989, bronze 1991; World Champs. silver, bronze medals 1989; Olympic squad 1988, 92; 1st Briton to total +400kg. *Address*: Caldicot School of Weightlifting, Caldicot Leisure Centre, Calicot, Gwent.

DAVIES, Brian Rhys: Rugby Union footballer; b. 22 January 1966, Nairobi, Kenya; player Barry 1982–84, Swansea Univ. 85–88, Southend 89–90 (capt.), Saracens 90– (capt. 92–); rep. Welsh Exiles 1992/93, E. Counties 1991/92, London and S.E. Div. B 1992/93; London Div. tour Aus. 1991. *Leisure interests*: golf, squash, pubs. *Address*: Saracens FC, Bramley Rd Sports Ground, Chaseside, Southgate, London N14 4AB.

DAVIES, Claire Elizabeth: oarswoman; b. 17 June 1972, Bebington; rep. Royal Chester RC 1980–90, Univ. of London Women's BC 90– ; GB debut 1989, World Champs. lightweight women's coxless fours silver medals 1991, 92; youngest snr Brit. World Champs. medallist. *Leisure interests*: discovering new flavours of ice-cream. *Address*: 1 St John's Rd, Queen's Park, Chester CH4 7AL.

DAVIES, Geraint: Rugby Union footballer; b. 20 May 1971; player Bridgend; Wales U-21 debut v. Ireland U-21 1991. *Address*: Bridgend RFC, Brewery Field, Tondu Rd, Bridgend, Mid Glamorgan.

DAVIES, John David: Rugby Union footballer; b. 1 February 1969, Carmarthen; player Cwmgwrach, Neath (capt.); Wales and Five Nations debut v. Ireland 1991, tour Zimbabwe/Namibia 1993. *Address*: Neath RFC, The Gnoll, Gnoll Park Rd, Neath, W. Glamorgan.

DAVIES, Jonathan: Rugby League footballer; b. 24 October 1962, Llanelli; player Neath (RU), Llanelli (RU), Canterbury Bankstown, Widnes 1989–93, Warrington 93– ; with Widnes: winners Regal Trophy 1992; 27 Wales RU caps; Wales RL debut v. Papua New Guinea 1991; GB debut v. Papua New Guinea 1990, Brit. Lions tour NZ/Papua New Guinea 1990. *Address*: Warrington RLFC, Wilderspool Stadium, Wilderspool Causeway, Warrington WA4 6PY.

DAVIES, Laura: golfer; b. 5 October 1963; English ladies' intermediate champ. 1983, Welsh ladies' open amateur strokeplay champ. 1984; England debut 1983; Curtis Cup team 1984; prof. debut 1985; Solheim Cup team 1990, 92, winners 1992; winner Belgian Ladies' Open 1985, Ladies' Brit. Open 1986, US Ladies' Open 1987, Italian Open 1987, 88, Ford Classic, Biarritz Ladies' Open 1988, European Open 1992, Thailand Ladies' Open 1993, 94, English Open, Australian Ladies' Masters 1993. *Address*: c/o Women's Prof. Golf European Tour, The Tytherington Club, Dorchester Way, Tytherington, Macclesfield, Cheshire SK10 2JP.

DAVIES, Mandy Joanna: hockey player; b. 29 September 1966, Birmingham; m. Mark Graham Davies 1992; player Sutton Coldfield 1980– , winners European Cup Winners' Cup 1992; rep. Warks. 1988– ; England U-21 debut 1986, snr debut 1988, European Champs. gold medallist 1991; GB debut 1990, 1st reserve Olympic squad 1992, Champions Trophy squad 1993. *Leisure interests*: skiing, sailing, golf, music. *Address*: First Personnel Sutton Coldfield HC, Rectory Park, Sutton Coldfield, W. Midlands.

DAVIES, Mark: cricketer; b. 18 April 1969, Neath; player Glamorgan 1990–91, Glos. 92– . *Address*: Glos. CCC, Phoenix County Ground, Nevil Rd, Bristol BS6 9EJ.

DAVIES, Mary Eileen: flat green bowler; b. 21 July 1935, Carmarthen; m. Ormond Davies 1960; Welsh women's pairs champ. (outdoor) 1977, women's triples champ. (outdoor) 1990, 91, women's fours champ. (outdoor and indoor) 1993; GB women's triples champ. 1991; Wales debut (outdoor) 1978, (indoor) 1993, World Champs. women's triples bronze medal 1992. *Leisure interests*: foreign holidays, crossword puzzles. *Address*: `Ormary', Hillcrest Rise, Llandrindod Wells, Powys LD1 6BN.

DAVIES, Nigel Gareth: Rugby Union footballer; b. 29 March 1965; player Llanelli, winners Welsh Cup 1993, Welsh League champs. 1992/93; Wales debut v. NZ 1988, Five Nations debut v. Scotland 1989. *Address*: Llanelli RFC, Stradey Park, Llanelli, Dyfed.

DAVIES, Philip Thomas: Rugby Union footballer; b. 19 October 1963, Seven Sisters; m. Caroline Davies; 2 d.; player S. Wales Police, Llanelli (vice-capt.); with Llanelli: winners Welsh Cup 1988, 91–93, Welsh League champs. 1992/93; Wales and Five Nations debut v. England 1985, tours Aus. 1992, Zimbabwe/Namibia 1993. *Address*: Llanelli RFC, Stradey Park, Llanelli, Dyfed.

DAVIES, Sharron Elizabeth, MBE: swimmer; b. 1 November 1962, Plymouth; m. Derek Redmond (qv) 1994; 1 s.; GB women's 200m individ. medley and 50m butterfly champ. 1991, 92; GB jnr debut 1973, snr debut 1976, Olympic squad 1976 (youngest mem.), women's 400m individ. medley silver medal 1980, squad 1992; GB women's 200m and 400m individ. medley record-holder; Sports Writers' Sportswoman of the Year 1978, 80. *Publications: Against the Tide*, 1982, *Learn to Swim in a Weekend*, 1991. *Leisure interests*: most sports, thrillers, music. *Address*: c/o ASA, Harold Fern House, Derby Square, Loughborough, Leics. LE11 0AL.

DAVIES, Stuart: Rugby Union footballer; b. 2 September 1965, Swansea; m. Lorna Davies 1989; player Swansea 1984– (capt. 92–), Welsh League champs. 1991/92; Barbarians tour USSR 1992; Wales and Five Nations debut v. Ireland 1992, tour Zimbabwe/Namibia 1993. *Leisure interests*: golf, cinema, DIY, socializing. *Address*: Swansea RFC, St Helens, Swansea SA2 0AR.

DAVIES, William John Charles: tennis player; b. 24 May 1972, Bristol; rep. S. Wales 1990– ; Welsh jnr hard court singles and doubles champ. 1990, snr hard court doubles champ. 1992; Wales debut 1992. *Leisure interests*: sampling beverages, golf, the philosophy of gamesmanship. *Address*: 14 Baneswell Court Yard, N. Street, Baneswell, Newport, Gwent.

DAVIES, William Simon: Rugby Union footballer; b. 19 January 1967; player Llanelli, winners Welsh Cup 1993, Welsh League champs. 1992/93; Wales B int. *Address*: Llanelli RFC, Stradey Park, Llanelli, Dyfed.

DAVIS, Andrew John: glider pilot; b. 13 June 1956, Bath; m. Lyn Davis; 1 s.; GB 15m-class champ. 1978 (youngest ever); GB debut 1981, World Champs. standard-class silver medal 1989, gold 1993. *Leisure interests*: cycling, rugby, physical fitness. *Address*: Clarebourne House, Shortwood, Nailsworth, Glos. GL6 0SJ.

DAVIS, Mark Edwin: Rugby Union footballer; b. 18 September 1970, Newport; player Pontypool, Newport; with Newport: Welsh League champs. 1990/91; Wales U-21 debut v. NZ Youth XV 1991, snr debut and tour Aus. 1991. *Address*: Newport RFC, Rodney Parade, Newport, Gwent.

DAVIS, Paul: footballer; b. 9 December 1961, Dulwich; player Arsenal 1979– , winners League Cup 1987, 93, FA Cup 1993, League champs. 1988/89, 90/91; 11 England U-21 caps. *Address*: Arsenal FC, Arsenal Stadium, Highbury, London N5 1BU.

DAVIS, Richard Peter: cricketer; b. 18 March 1966, Margate; m. Samantha Jane Davis 1990; player Kent 1986–93, Warks. 94– . *Address*: Warks. CCC, County Ground, Edgbaston, Birmingham B5 7QU.

DAVIS, Steve, MBE: snooker player; b. 22 August 1957, Plumstead; m. Judith Lyn Davis 1990; 1 s.; prof. debut 1978, UK champ. 1980, 81, 84–87, world champ. 1981, 83, 84, 87–89, winner Mercantile Credit Classic 1980, 84, 87, 88, 92, Brit. Open 1981, 82, 84, 86, 93, Pot Black 1982, 83, Masters 1982, 88, Scottish Masters 1982, 83, 84, Irish Masters 1983, 84, 87, 88, 90, 91, 93, Rothmans GP 1985, 88, 89, World Matchplay Champs. 1988, Asian Open 1992, European Open 1993, Welsh Open 1994; made 1st televised 147 break, Lada Classic 1982; 1st player to score 200 100s in major prof. tournaments; BBC Sports Personality of the Year 1988. *Publications*: *Steve Davis – Snooker Champion, Frame and Fortune, Successful Snooker, How to Be Really Interesting. Leisure interests*: collecting soul records, helping to run a soul collectors' magazine, *Voices from the Shadows*. *Address*: Matchroom, 10 Western Rd, Romford, Essex RM1 3JT.

DAVISON, Aidan: footballer; b. 11 May 1968, Sedgefield; player Notts County 1988–89, Bury 89–91, Millwall 91–93, Bolton Wanderers 93– . *Address*: Bolton Wanderers FC, Burnden Park, Manchester Rd, Bolton, Lancs. BL3 2QR.

DAVISON, John: boxer; b. 30 September 1958; England debut 1985; prof. debut 1988; titles won: WBC int. featherweight 1990, WBC int. super-bantamweight 1991, GB featherweight 1992; over 14 prof. wins. *Address*: c/o Tommy Conroy, 144 High St E., Sunderland, Tyne and Wear SR1 2BL.

DAVISON, Richard John: equestrianist (dressage); b. 20 September 1955, Nottingham; m. Gillian Mary Davison 1985; 2 s.; GB debut 1989; European Champs. team silver medal (Master JCB) 1993; Fellow, Brit. Horse Soc. 1984– . *Address*: c/o Brit. Horse Soc., Brit. Equestrian Centre, Stoneleigh Park, Kenilworth, Warks. CV8 2LR.

DAWE, Richard Graham Reed: Rugby Union footballer; b. 4 September 1959, Plymouth; player Bath; rep. S.W. Div., Div. champs. 1993/94; England debut v. Ireland 1987. *Address*: Bath FC, Recreation Ground, Bath, Avon.

DAWES, Ian: footballer; b. 22 February 1963, Croydon; player Queens Park Rangers 1980–88, Millwall 88– ; with Queens Park Rangers: 2nd Div. champs. 1982/83. *Address*: Millwall FC, The Den, Zampa Rd, Bermondsey, London SE16 3LH.

DAWSON, Robert Ian: cricketer; b. 29 March 1970, Exmouth; player Glos. 1991– . *Address*: Glos. CCC, Phoenix County Ground, Nevil Rd, Bristol BS6 9EJ.

DAY, Mervyn: footballer; b. 26 June 1955, Chelmsford; player W. Ham Utd 1973–79, Leyton Orient 79–83, Aston Villa 83–85, Leeds Utd 85–93, Carlisle Utd 93– ; with W. Ham Utd: winners FA Cup 1975; with Leeds Utd: 2nd Div. champs. 1989/90; 5 England U-23 caps. *Address*: Carlisle Utd FC, Brunton Park, Warwick Rd, Carlisle, Cumbria CA1 1LL.

DE FREITAS, Phillip Anthony Jason: cricketer; b. 18 February 1966, Scotts Head, Dominica; m. Nicola de Freitas 1990; 1 d.; player Leics. 1985–88, Lancs. 89–93, Derbys. 94– ; Test debut 1986, tours Aus. 1986/87, Pakistan/Aus./NZ 1987/88, India/WI 1989/90, Aus. 1990/91, NZ 1991/92, India/Sri Lanka 1992/93. *Address*: Derbys. CCC, County Cricket Ground, Nottingham Rd, Derby DE2 6DA.

DE GLANVILLE, Philip Ranulph: Rugby Union footballer; b. 1 October 1968, Loughborough; player Durham Univ., Oxford Univ., Bath; with Bath: winners Pilkington Cup 1992, League champs. 1992/93; rep. S.W. Div.; England U-21 debut v. Romania 1989, England B debut v. Italy 1989, tour NZ 1992, snr debut v. SA 1992, Five Nations debut v. Wales 1993, England A tour Canada 1993 (aborted). *Address*: Bath RFC, Recreation Ground, Bath BA2 6PW.

DE GRAAFF, Daniel George: powerboat racer; b. 21 June 1978, Chertsey; GB sports-boat J250 champ. 1993. *Leisure interests*: water skiing, swimming, para-kiting, go-karting, fishing, boating. *Address*: 'The Pantiles', Oakfield Glade, Weybridge, Surrey KT13 9DP.

DE HAVILLAND, John Anthony: full-bore rifle shooter; b. 14 April 1938, Horkesley, Essex; m. Hilary Anne de Havilland 1964; 1 s., 2 d.; rep. Cambridge Univ. 1957–59 (capt. 1959); GB match rifle champ. 1963, 68–70, 81, 82, 84, 86, 87; England debut 1961, Elcho Shield team 1961–92 (capt. 1993); held record for highest score in Elcho 1978–90; chairman Nat. Rifle Assoc. 1990– . *Address*: c/o Nat. Rifle Assoc., Bisley Camp, Brookwood, Woking, Surrey GU24 0PB.

DE POURTALES, Claire: Alpine skier; b. 20 April 1969, Paris, France; GB jnr women's champ. 1985, 86; Scottish women's champ. 1988; GB women's downhill, slalom, giant slalom, super giant slalom, combined champ. 1991; GB debut 1988, World Champs. squad 1989, 91, 93, Olympic squad 1992, 94. *Leisure interests*: piano, French horn, windsurfing, tennis, squash. *Address*: 103 Comeragh Rd, London W14 9HS.

DEACON, Andrew: Rugby Union footballer; b. 31 July 1965; player Longlevens, Gloucester. *Address*: Gloucester RUFC, Kingsholm, Worcester St, Gloucester GL3 3AX.

DEACON, John William: motorcyclist (off-road); b. 30 November 1962, Plymouth; m. Tracey Ann Deacon 1984; GB expert solo enduro champ. 1985, 4-stroke solo enduro champ. 1986, 88–93; ISDE team silver medal 1986 (Italy), gold 1987 (Poland), 1988 (France), 1989 (Germany), 1990 (Sweden), 1991 (Czechoslovakia). *Leisure interests*: golf, jet skiing, diving. *Address*: Plymouth Off-Road, 176 Union St, Plymouth, Devon PL3 1HL.

DEAKINS, Joanne: swimmer; b. 20 November 1972, Worcester; rep. Glos. 1982–92, Warks. 92– ; England debut 1988; Commonwealth Games women's 4 x 100m medley relay silver medal 1990; GB debut 1989, Olympic squad 1992 (200m backstroke); GB women's 200m backstroke record-holder. *Leisure interests*: music. *Address*: c/o ASA, Harold Fern House, Derby Square, Loughborough, Leics. LE11 0AL.

DEAN, Christopher Colin, MBE: ice dancer; b. 27 July 1958, Nottingham; with Sandra Elsen: GB primary champ. 1974; with Jayne Christensen (Torvill) (qv): GB champ. 1978–83, 94; GB debut 1976; European Champs. gold medals 1981, 82, 84, 94; World Champs. gold medals

1981–84; Olympic gold medal 1984, bronze 1994; world prof. champ. 1984, 85, 90; winner Vandervell Trophy 1981–84, European Trophy 1981, 82, 84, Jacques Favart Trophy 1986; BBC Sports Personality of the Year 1984. *Leisure interests*: motor racing, cars, cinema, dance, theatre. *Address*: c/o Debbie Turner, 59 Goodwin Ave, Swalecliffe, Kent CT5 2RA.

DEAN, Darren Francis: judo player (U-65kg); b. 4 April 1970; rep. N.W. England 1983–88, Clwyd, Welsh county champs. 1991, 92; Welsh champ. 1990–92; GB sombo wrestling champ. 1990, 91; Wales jnr debut 1981, snr debut 1992; GB sombo wrestling debut 1989. *Leisure interests*: mountain biking. *Address*: 10 Bryn Rd, Connahs Quay, Deeside, Clwyd CH5 4UU.

DEANE, Brian: footballer; b. 7 February 1968, Leeds; player Doncaster Rovers 1985–88, Sheffield Utd 88–93, Leeds Utd 93– ; 2 England caps. *Address*: Leeds Utd FC, Elland Rd, Leeds, W. Yorks. LS11 0ES.

DEAS, Paul: footballer; b. 22 February 1972, Perth; player St Johnstone 1990– ; Scotland U-21 int. *Address*: St Johnstone FC, McDiarmid Park, Crieff Rd, Perth PH1 2SJ.

DELANEY, Laurance: Rugby Union footballer; b. 8 May 1956, Llanelli; m. Lynne Delaney; 1 s., 1 d.; player Llanelli 1977– , winners Welsh Cup 1991, 92, Welsh League champs. 1992/93; Wales and Five Nations debut v. Ireland 1989. *Address*: Llanelli RFC, Stradey Park, Llanelli, Dyfed.

DELGADO-CORREDOR, Jamie: tennis player; b. 21 March 1977, Birmingham; rep. Warks.; GB U-14 hard court champ. 1990, U-16 doubles champ. 1991, U-18 doubles champ. 1991; Orange Bowl U-14 champ. 1991; GB U-14 and U-16 debuts 1989; semi-finalist Aus. Jnr Open U-18 singles 1993. *Address*: 11 Dorchester Close, Pinkneys Green, Maidenhead, Berks. SL6 6RX.

DENMARK, Robert Neil: athlete; b. 23 November 1968; m. Victoria Kennison 1993; AAA 10km champ. 1993; European Cup 5000m gold medal 1993; UK 3000m indoor record-holder. *Leisure interests*: Southend Utd and Liverpool FCs, cinema, fishing, ten-pin bowling, computer games. *Address*: c/o Brit. Athletic Fed., 225A Bristol Rd, Edgbaston, Birmingham B5 7UB.

DENNIS, Shaun: footballer; b. 20 December 1969, Kirkcaldy; player Raith Rovers 1988– ; Scotland U-21 int. *Address*: Raith Rovers FC, Stark's Park, Pratt St, Kirkcaldy, Fife KY1 1SA.

DENNISON, Robert: footballer; b. 30 April 1963, Banbridge, NI; player W. Bromwich Albion 1985–87, Wolverhampton Wanderers 87– ; with Wolverhampton Wanderers: 4th Div. champs. 1987/88, 3rd Div. champs. 1988/89; 15 NI caps. *Address*: Wolverhampton Wanderers FC, Molineux Stadium, Waterloo Rd, Wolverhampton WV1 4QR.

DERMOTT, Martin: Rugby League foot-baller; b. 25 September 1967, Wigan; player Wigan St Pats ARLFC, Wigan 1984– ; with Wigan: winners World Sevens, Sydney 1991, Challenge Cup 1990–93, John Player Special Trophy 1987, Regal Trophy 1989, 90, 93, Premiership 1992, League champs. 1986/87, 89/90, 90/91, 91/92, 92/93; GB debut v. NZ 1990, Brit. Lions tours NZ/Papua New Guinea 1990, Aus./NZ/Papua New Guinea 1992, over 13 caps. *Address*: Wigan RLFC, The Pavilion, Central Park, Wigan WN1 1XF.

DESSAUR, Wayne Anthony: cricketer; b. 4 February 1971, Nottingham; player Notts. 1992– . *Address*: Notts. CCC, Trent Bridge, Nottingham NG2 6AG.

DEVEREUX, John: Rugby League foot-baller; b. 30 March 1966, Pontycymmer; player Bridgend (RU), Widnes 1989– ; with Widnes: winners Regal Trophy 1992; Wales int. and Brit. Lion (RU); Wales RL debut v. Papua New Guinea 1991; GB debut v. France and Brit. Lions tour Aus./NZ/Papua New Guinea 1992. *Address*: Widnes RLFC, Naughton Park, Lowerhouse Lane, Widnes WA8 7DZ.

DEVINE, Scott Peter: basketball player; b. 19 July 1973, Ely; player Glasgow City 1985–89, Northeastern Univ. (Boston, USA) 92–93; Scotland U-19 int. *Address*: 15 Faskin Crescent, Crookston, Glasgow G53 7HD.

DEVLIN, Paul: footballer; b. 14 April 1972, Birmingham; player Notts County 1992– . *Address*: Notts County FC, Meadow Lane Ground, Nottingham NG2 3HJ.

DICKS, Julian: footballer; b. 8 August 1968, Bristol; player Birmingham City 1986–88, W. Ham Utd 88–93, Liverpool 93– ; 4 England U-21 caps. *Address*: Liverpool FC, Anfield Rd, Liverpool L4 0TH.

DICKSON, Roderick McEwan (Rory): Rugby Union footballer; b. 31 January 1970, Haddington, E. Lothian; player Kelso Harlequins 1987–88, Royal High School FPs 88–91, Currie 91– ; Scottish Schools tour NZ 1988. *Leisure interests*: skiing, water sports, travel, reading, music, eating out. *Address*: Currie RFC, Malleny Park, Balerno EH14 5HA.

DIGBY, Fraser: footballer; b. 23 April 1967, Sheffield; player Swindon Town 1986– ; 5 England U-21 caps. *Address*: Swindon Town FC, The County Ground, Swindon, Wilts. SN1 2ED.

DIGHTON, Gary John: cyclist; b. 18 May 1968, Whittlesey, Cambs.; RTTC 50-mile team time trial champ. 1990, 91, 100km team champ. 1991; GB debut and World Champs. squad (100km team time trial) 1991, Olympic squad (100km team time trial) 1992. *Leisure interests*: football, athlet-ics, travel, eating out. *Address*: 5 Snoots Rd, Whittlesey, Peterborough PE7 1LA.

DIGWEED, George Hickman: clay pigeon shooter; b. 21 April 1964, Hastings; English open sporting champ. 1989; GB open sporting champ. 1989, 91, open skeet champ. 1991; UK FITASC sporting champ. 1989; European FITASC Sporting Champs. bronze medals 1991, 93, gold 1992; World Sporting Champs. gold medals 1987, 89; World FITASC Sporting Champs. gold medals 1992, 93; World Cup double trap gold medal 1993. *Leisure interests*: cricket, golf, game-shooting. *Address*: Merlins, Ewhurst Lane, Northiam, E. Sussex.

DILL, James William: table tennis player; b. 1 June 1963, Belfast, NI; m. Melanie Dill 1989; 1 s.; Ulster champ. 1990, 92, 93; NI debut 1985; Ireland debut 1987; winner Belfast Open 1989, 90, 93. *Leisure interests*: water skiing, cycling. *Address*: 52 Lyndhurst Park, Belfast BT13 3PG.

DILLON, Terence Grant: oarsman; b. 8 May 1964, Skipton; rep. Univ. of London BC 1983–85, Oxford Univ. BC 1989, Leander Club 1987– ; with Oxford: winners Univ. Boat Race 1989; winning crew, Grand Challenge Cup, Henley Royal Regatta 1986, 88; Commonwealth Games eights silver medal 1986; World U-23 Champs. coxed fours bronze medal 1984; World Champs. coxed fours bronze medal 1989; Olympic squad 1988 (eights), 1992 (coxed fours). *Leisure interests*: basketball, Alfa Romeo cars, feature films and cinema. *Address*: 39 St Marks Rd, Henley-on-Thames, Oxon RG9 1LP.

DINNIE, Alan: footballer; b. 14 May 1963, Glasgow; player Partick Thistle 1987–89, Dundee 89– . *Address*: Dundee FC, Dens Park, Dundee DD3 7JY.

DIVET, Daniel: Rugby League footballer; b. 11 December 1966; player Hull 1993– . *Address*: Hull RLFC, The Boulevard Ground, Airlie St, Hull HU3 3JD.

DIVORTY, Gary: Rugby League footballer; b. 28 January 1966, York; player Hull, Leeds, Halifax 1992– ; GB debut v. France 1985. *Address*: Halifax RLFC, The Pavilion, Thrum Hall, Gibbet St, Halifax, W. Yorks. HX1 4TL.

DIXON, John: Rugby Union footballer; b. 5 October 1961, Middlesbrough; player Acklam, W. Hartlepool 1986– ; rep. Durham, N. Div. *Address*: W. Hartlepool RFC, Brierton Lane, Hartlepool, Cleveland TS25 5DR.

DIXON, Karen Elizabeth: equestrianist (three-day eventing); b. 17 September 1964, Newcastle-upon-Tyne; m. Andrew Dixon 1991; European Jnr Champs. individ. and team gold medals 1982; European Young Rider Champs. team gold and individ. silver medals 1983; European Champs. team gold and individ. bronze medals 1991; World Champs. team silver medal 1990; Olympic team silver medal 1988, squad 1992. *Leisure interests*: skiing, sailing, tennis, being an industrious housewife. *Address*: c/o Brit. Horse Soc., Brit. Equestrian Centre, Stoneleigh Park, Kenilworth, Warks. CV8 2LR.

DIXON, Kerry: footballer; b. 24 July 1961, Luton; player Reading 1980–83, Chelsea 83–92, Southampton 92–93, Luton Town 93– ; with Chelsea: 2nd Div. champs. 1983/84, 88/89; 1 England U-21 cap, 8 full England caps. *Address*: Luton Town FC, Kenilworth Stadium, 1 Maple Rd, Luton, Beds. LU4 8AW.

DIXON, Lee Michael: footballer; b. 17 March 1964, Manchester; m. Joanne Dixon 1987; 1 s., 1 d.; player Burnley 1983–84, Chester City 84–85, Bury 85–86, Stoke City 86–87, Arsenal 87– ; with Arsenal: winners League Cup, FA Cup 1993, League champs. 1988/89, 90/91; 5 England B caps, over 20 full England caps. *Leisure interests*: golf, cricket. *Address*: Arsenal FC, Arsenal Stadium, Highbury, London N5 1BU.

DIXON, Michael Francis: Nordic skier/biathlete; b. 21 November 1962, Achnacarry; m. Dulcie Dixon 1991; 1 d.; GB 30km cross-country champ. 1985, 86, 90, 15km cross-country champ. 1989, 90, 20km biathlon champ. 1987, 89, 91, 93, 10km biathlon champ. 1993, 10-mile rollerski champ. 1990–93; World Champs. squad (Nordic skiing) 1985, 89, (biathlon) 1987, 89, 90, 91, 93; Olympic squad (Nordic skiing) 1984, (biathlon) 1988, 92. *Leisure interests*: hill-walking, nature photography. *Address*: 10 Railway Terrace, Aviemore, Inverness-shire.

DIXON, Mike: Rugby League footballer; b. 6 April 1971; player E. Park ARLFC, Hull 1989– . *Address*: Hull RLFC, The Boulevard Ground, Airlie St, Hull HU3 3JD.

DIXON, Paul Andrew: Rugby League footballer; b. 28 October 1963, Huddersfield; player Huddersfield, Halifax 1985–89, Leeds 89–93, Bradford Northern 93– ; GB debut v. France 1987. *Address*: Bradford Northern RLFC, Odsal Stadium, Bradford BD6 1BS.

DOBBIN, James: footballer; b. 17 September 1963, Dunfermline; player Celtic 1980–84, Doncaster Rovers 84–86, Barnsley 86–91, Grimsby Town 91– . *Address*: Grimsby Town FC, Blundell Park, Cleethorpes, S. Humberside DN35 7PY.

DOBSON, Anthony: footballer; b. 5 February 1969, Coventry; player Coventry City 1986–90, Blackburn Rovers 90–93, Portsmouth 93– ; 4 England U-21 caps. *Address*: Portsmouth FC, Fratton Park, Frogmore Rd, Portsmouth PO4 8RA.

DOBSON, Helen: golfer; b. 25 February 1971, Skegness; rep. Lincs. 1985–90, Lincs. ladies' champ. 1985, 87, 88, 89; English ladies' amateur champ., GB ladies' open amateur champ., GB ladies' U-21 and snr open amateur strokeplay champ. 1989;

England debut 1987; Curtis Cup team 1990; prof. debut 1990; winner European Masters 1993. *Address*: The Ship, Castleton Boulevard, Skegness, Lincs.

DOCHERTY, Drew: boxer; b. 29 November 1965; Scotland debut 1986; prof. debut 1989; titles won: GB bantamweight 1992; over 7 prof. wins. *Address*: St Andrew's Sporting Club, Forte Crest Hotel, Bothwell St, Glasgow G2 7EN.

DODD, Jason: footballer; b. 2 November 1970, Bath; player Southampton 1989– ; 8 England U-21 caps. *Address*: Southampton FC, The Dell, Milton Rd, Southampton SO9 4XX.

DODDS, William: footballer; b. 5 February 1969, New Cumnock; player Chelsea 1986–89, Dundee 89– . *Address*: Dundee FC, Dens Park, Dundee DD3 7JY.

DODS, Michael: Rugby Union footballer; b. 30 December 1968, Galashiels; m. Louise Dods 1991; player Gala; rep. S. of Scotland; Scotland A debut v. NZ 1993. *Leisure interests*: shooting, golf, touring. *Address*: Gala RUFC, Netherdale, Nether Rd, Galashiels TD1 3HE.

DOGGART, Audrey: flat green bowler; b. 10 June 1945, Belfast; NI women's pairs champ. (outdoor) 1987, triples champ. (indoor) 1992, 93; GB women's fours champ. (indoor) 1992, 93; Ireland debut (outdoor and indoor) 1988. *Address*: 35 Orpen Park, Finaghy, Belfast 10, NI.

DOLAN, Jim: footballer; b. 22 February 1969, Salsburgh; player Motherwell 1987– . *Address*: Motherwell FC, Fir Park, Fir Park St, Motherwell ML1 2QN.

DOLING, Stuart: footballer; b. 28 October 1972, Newport, Isle of Wight; player Portsmouth 1990– . *Address*: Portsmouth FC, Fratton Park, Frogmore Rd, Portsmouth PO4 8RA.

D'OLIVEIRA, Damian Basil: cricketer; b. 19 October 1960, Cape Town, SA; m. Tracey Michele D'Oliveira 1983; 2 s.; player Worcs. 1982– , county champs. 1988, 89, Sunday League champs. 1987, 88; English Counties XI tour Zimbabwe 1985. *Address*: Worcs. CCC, County Ground, New Rd, Worcester WR2 4QQ.

DONAGHY, Malachy: footballer; b. 13 September 1957, Belfast; player Luton Town 1978–88, Manchester Utd 88–92, Chelsea 92– ; with Luton Town: winners League Cup 1988, 2nd Div. champs. 1981/82; with Manchester Utd: winners European Cup Winners' Cup 1991; 1 NI U-21 cap, over 84 full NI caps. *Address*: Chelsea FC, Stamford Bridge, Fulham Rd, London SW6 1HS.

DONALD, Allan Anthony: cricketer; b. 20 October 1966, Bloemfontein, SA; m. Tina Donald 1991; player Warks. 1989– ; Test debut 1992, SA tours India 1991/92, Aus./NZ/WI (World Cup) 1991/92. *Address*: Warks. CCC, County Ground, Edgbaston, Birmingham B5 7QU.

DONALD, Graeme: footballer; b. 14 April 1974, Stirling; player Hibernian 1991– ; Scotland U-21 int. *Address*: Hibernian FC, Easter Rd Stadium, 64 Albion Rd, Edinburgh EH7 5QG.

DONALD, Nicola Jean: hockey player; b. 21 July 1971, Newport; player Newport 1984–89, Swansea 89–93, Clifton 93– ; with Swansea: winners Welsh Cup 1993; rep. Univ. College, Swansea 1989–93 (capt. 90–92), Welsh Univ. 1989–93 (capt. 1993), Bristol Univ. 93–94, S. Univ. 93–94 (capt.); Wales U-18 debut 1987 (vice-capt. 1989), U-21 debut 1989, snr debut 1992. *Leisure interests*: tennis, swimming, golf. *Address*: 9 The Paddocks, Lodge Hill, Caerleon, Newport NP6 1BZ.

DONALDSON, Robert Lindsey (Dip): basketball player; b. 4 September 1959, Heacham, Norfolk; m. Beth Ann Donaldson 1983; 3 s.; player Birmingham Bullets 1982–84, Team Glasgow 84–85, Birmingham Bullets 85–86, Leicester Riders 88–89, Oldham Celtics 89–90, Leicester Riders 90–92, Coventry Flyers 92– ; over 25 England caps; GB squad, World Student Games 1983. *Leisure interests*: gospel music, American football. *Address*: Coventry Flyers Basketball Club, Coventry Sports Centre, Fairfax St, Coventry CV1 5RY.

DONOHUE, Jason: Rugby League footballer; b. 18 April 1972, Leigh; player Golborne ARLFC, Leigh 1988– . *Address*: Leigh RLFC, Hilton Park, Kirkhall Lane, Leigh WN7 1RN.

DONOHUE, Nigel John Patrick: judo player (U-60kg); b. 20 December 1969, Leigh; GB U-18 champ. 1981–87, Austrian U-21 open champ. 1988, 89, German U-21 open champ. 1989; Belgian open champ. 1989, US open champ. 1990, Scottish open champ., GB open champ. 1991, GB champ. 1992; European U-21 Champs. bronze medal 1988, silver 1989; European Champs. silver medal 1990, bronze 1993; Multi-Nations bronze medal 1990, gold 1993 (1st Brit. gold); GB U-18, U-21 and snr Olympic freestyle wrestling champ. and Commonwealth Games bronze medal 1986. *Leisure interests*: Rugby League, football, computer games, eating out, cinema. *Address*: 3 Schofield Gardens, Leigh, Lancs. WN7 4JD.

DORIGO, Anthony: footballer; b. 31 December 1965, Melbourne, Aus.; player Aston Villa 1983–87, Chelsea 87–91, Leeds Utd 91– ; with Chelsea: 2nd Div. champs. 1988/89; with Leeds Utd: League champs. 1991/92; 11 England U-21 caps, over 14 full England caps. *Address*: Leeds Utd FC, Elland Rd, Leeds, W. Yorks. LS11 0ES.

DOUCE, Steve: cyclist; b. 15 November 1963, Caterham; m. Sharon Julie Douce 1993; 1 d.; rep. Dauphin Sport 1985–87, Raleigh 87–91, Dawes 91–92, Saracen 93– ; GB jnr cyclo-cross champ. 1981, snr open champ. 1983, 85–89, 93; winner Nat. Trophy (cyclo-cross) 1985–87, 92–94. *Leisure interests*: classic cars. *Address*: 14 Somerset Rd, Meadvale, Redhill, Surrey RH1 6LS.

DOUGLAS, Kitrina Joanne: golfer; b. 6 September 1960, Bristol; m. Richard Guy Thomas 1992; Glos. ladies' champ. 1980–84; GB ladies' open amateur champ. 1982, Portuguese ladies' open amateur champ. 1983; England debut and European U-23 team champs. 1982; Curtis Cup team 1982; prof. debut 1984; Solheim Cup team (winners) 1992; winner Ford Classic, Swedish Ladies' Open 1984, Jersey Open 1986, Hennessy Cup 1987, St Moritz Classic 1989, European Masters 1989, 92, English Open 1991; 1st woman to win her 1st prof. event. *Publications*: *100 Tips for Lady Golfers*, 1993. *Leisure interests*: interior design, painting, scuba diving, sailing, watching rugby and football, learning to play the drums. *Address*: 68 Hillside Rd, Redcliffe Bay, Portishead, Avon.

DOW, Andrew: footballer; b. 7 February 1973, Dundee; player Dundee 1990–93, Chelsea 93– ; Scotland U-21 int. *Address*: Chelsea FC, Stamford Bridge, Fulham Rd, London SW6 1HS.

DOWIE, Iain: footballer; b. 9 January 1965, Hatfield; player Luton Town 1988–91, W. Ham Utd 1991, Southampton 1991– ; 1 NI U-21 cap, over 18 full NI caps. *Address*: Southampton FC, The Dell, Milton Rd, Southampton SO9 4XX.

DOWLING, Deborah: golfer; b. 26 July 1962, Wimbledon; Surrey ladies' champ. 1980; England debut 1981; prof. debut 1981; winner Jersey Open 1983, Portuguese Ladies' Open 1985. *Address*: c/o Women's

Prof. Golf European Tour, The Tytherington Club, Dorchester Way, Tytherington, Macclesfield, Cheshire SK10 2JP.

DOWMAN, Matthew Peter: cricketer; b. 10 May 1974, Grantham; player Notts. 1992– . *Address*: Notts. CCC, Trent Bridge, Nottingham NG2 6AG.

DOWNING, Keith: footballer; b. 23 July 1965, Oldbury; player Notts County 1984–87, Wolverhampton Wanderers 87–93, Birmingham City 93– ; with Wolverhampton Wanderers: 4th Div. champs. 1987/88, 3rd Div. champs. 1988/89. *Address*: Birmingham City FC, St Andrews Ground, Birmingham B9 4NH.

DOYLE, Anthony Paul, MBE: cyclist; b. 19 May 1958, Hampton Court; m. Anne Margaret Doyle 1980; 1 s.; rep. Viscount 1980–82, RMC 83–85, Ammaco 86–90, European 91–92, Neilson-Tivoli 93– ; GB 4000m pursuit and madison champ. 1977–79, points champ. 1979, prof. pursuit champ. 1980, 81, 87, 88; Commonwealth Games squad 1978; GB jnr debut 1976, snr debut 1977; European Champs. prof. madison gold medals 1985, 89, 90, omnium gold 1989; Olympic squad 1980; Milk Race stage-winner 1989; holds Brit. record for number of 6-day race wins. *Leisure interests*: family, concerts. *Address*: c/o Brit. Cycling Fed., 36 Rockingham Rd, Kettering, Northants. NN16 8HG.

DOYLE, Maurice: footballer; b. 17 October 1969, Ellesmere Port; player Crewe Alexandra 1988–89, Queens Park Rangers 89– . *Address*: Queens Park Rangers FC, Rangers Stadium, S. Africa Rd, London W12 7PA.

DOZZELL, Jason: footballer; b. 9 December 1967, Ipswich; player Ipswich Town 1983–93, Tottenham Hotspur 93– ; 9 England U-21 caps. *Address*: Tottenham Hotspur FC, 748 High Rd, Tottenham, London N17 0AP.

DRAPER, Mark: footballer; b. 11 November 1970, Long Eaton; player Notts County 1988– ; 3 England U-21 caps. *Address*: Notts County FC, Meadow Lane Ground, Nottingham NG2 3HJ.

DREYER, John: footballer; b. 11 June 1963, Alnwick; player Oxford Utd 1985–88, Luton Town 88– . *Address*: Luton Town FC, Kenilworth Stadium, 1 Maple Rd, Luton, Beds. LU4 8AW.

DRINKELL, Kevin: footballer; b. 18 June 1960, Grimsby; player Grimsby Town 1976–85, Norwich City 85–88, Rangers 88–89, Coventry City 89–92, Falkirk 92– ; with Rangers: winners Scottish League Cup 1989. *Address*: Falkirk FC, Brockville Park, Hope St, Falkirk FK1 5AX.

DRYDEN, Anna Marie: oarswoman; b. 24 May 1966, Kingsbury; rep. Cambridge Univ. Women's BC 1987–89, Thames Tradesmen's RC 89–91, Queen's Tower BC 92– ; GB lightweight women's coxless fours champ. 1990, women's lightweight indoor champ. 1991–93; GB debut 1991, World Champs. lightweight women's coxless fours silver medals 1991, 92, gold 1993, World Indoor Champs. women's lightweight gold medals 1992, 93. *Leisure interests*: good food and wine, art, reading. *Address*: Queen's Tower BC, Imperial College Boat House, The Embankment, Putney, London SW15.

DRYDEN, Richard: footballer; b. 14 June 1969, Stroud; player Bristol Rovers 1987–89, Exeter City 89–91, Notts County 91–92, Birmingham City 92– ; with Exeter City: 4th Div. champs. 1989/90. *Address*: Birmingham City FC, St Andrews Ground, Birmingham B9 4NH.

DRYSDALE, Jason: footballer; b. 17 November 1970, Bristol; player Watford 1988– . *Address*: Watford FC, Vicarage Rd Stadium, Watford, Herts. WD1 8ER.

DUBLIN, Dion: footballer; b. 22 April 1969, Leicester; player Cambridge Utd 1988–92, Manchester Utd 92– ; with Cambridge Utd: 3rd Div. champs. 1990/91; with Manchester Utd: League champs. 1992/93. *Address*: Manchester Utd FC, Old Trafford, Manchester M16 0RA.

DUBLIN, Keith: footballer; b. 29 January 1966, High Wycombe; player Chelsea 1984–87, Brighton and Hove Albion 87–90, Watford 90– . *Address*: Watford FC, Vicarage Rd Stadium, Watford, Herts. WD1 8ER.

DUCKETT, Jayne Margaret: lacrosse player; b. 11 September 1959, Birmingham; m. Graham Reid Duckett 1987; 1 d.; player Worcester Ladies 1980–82, Luton Sprites 83–86, Beckenham Beetles 86– ; rep. Worcs. 1980–82, Beds. 83–86 (capt.), Kent 86– (capt. 87–89), Midlands 77–90 (capt. 84–87), East 92– ; Scotland debut 1983; World Cup bronze medal 1986, squad 89, 93 (capt. 1986, 89, vice-capt. 1993); tour USA 1993; GB debut and tour Aus. 1985. *Leisure interests*: netball, photography, athletics, tennis. *Address*: The Willows, 2 Kilnwood, Knockholt Rd, Halstead, Kent TN14 7ET.

DUFFIELD, Peter: footballer; b. 4 February 1969, Middlesbrough; player Sheffield Utd 1987– . *Address*: Sheffield Utd FC, Bramall Lane, Sheffield, S. Yorks S2 4SU.

DUFFY, Jim: football player/manager; b. 27 April 1959, Glasgow; player Morton 1981–85, Dundee 85–88, 89–90, Partick Thistle 90–92, Dundee 92– ; manager Falkirk 1988–89, player/manager Dundee 1993– . *Address*: Dundee FC, Dens Park, Dundee DD3 7JY.

DUGDALE, William Paul: athlete (cross-country); b. 13 May 1965, Bolton; rep. Lancs. 1988–90, Greater Manchester 1992– ; Scottish univ. 5000m champ. 1987; Lancs. cross-country champ. 1990, N. counties champ. 1991, Greater Manchester champ. 1992; England debut 1989; GB debut 1992; World Champs. team bronze medal 1992. *Address*: 506 Darwen Rd, Bromley Cross, Bolton BL7 9DX.

DUGGIN, Patricia: karate player (+60kg); b. 21 July 1972, Hackney; English champ. 1992; European Champs. team gold medal 1993; World Champs. team gold medal 1992. *Leisure interests*: fitness training, photography, playing the drums. *Address*: 13 Wycombe Rd, Gants Hill, Ilford, Essex IG2 6UT.

DUNCAN, Brian: crown green bowler; b. 24 October 1943, Orrell; m. Gail Duncan 1968; 1 s., 1 d.; rep. Lancs.; winner Waterloo Handicap 1979, 86, 87, 89, 92, Bass Masters 1984, 90, 92, 93, Spring Waterloo 1988, 92, Champion of Champions 1991; 1st player to win the Waterloo 3 times, only player to hold both Waterloo trophies at same time. *Leisure interests*: Rugby League. *Address*: 30 Badger Way, Lostock Hall, Preston PR5 5QU.

DUNCAN, John: basketball player; b. 19 August 1963, Kilmarnock; m. Jane Duncan 1990; 1 s., 1 d.; player Cumnock, Glasgow, Falkirk, Glasgow Rangers; with Glasgow Rangers: nat. play-off champs. 1989, League champs. 1988/89; Scotland debut 1984, European Champs. squad 1985, 89, 91, 93. *Leisure interests*: bird-watching. *Address*: 2 Teviot St, Ayr KA8 9JE.

DUNDAS, Stephen: golfer; b. 20 December 1973, Glasgow; Glasgow boys' strokeplay and matchplay champ. 1988, 89, W. of Scotland boys' champ. 1988; GB amateur champ. 1992. *Address*: c/o Scottish Golf Union, The Cottage, 181A Whitehouse Rd, Edinburgh EH4 6BY.

DUNLOP, John Leeper: racehorse trainer (Flat); b. 10 July 1939, Tetbury; m. Susan Jennifer Dunlop 1965; 2 s.; 1st licence 1966; winner Derby, Irish Derby 1978 (Shirley

Heights), 1000 Guineas 1980 (Quick as Lightning), 1990 (Salsabil), 1991 (Shadayid), Irish 2000 Guineas 1983 (Wassl), Irish St Leger 1983 (Mountain Lodge), Oaks 1984 (Circus Plume), 1990 (Salsabil), St Leger 1986 (Moon Madness), Irish Derby 1990 (Salsabil). *Address*: Castle Stables, Arundel, W. Sussex BN18 9AB.

DUNWOODY, Thomas Richard, MBE: jockey (NH); b. 18 January 1964, Belfast; m. Carol Ann Abraham 1988; winner Mackeson Gold Cup 1986 (Very Promising), 1991 (Another Coral), Grand National 1986 (West Tip), Cheltenham Gold Cup 1988 (Charter Party), Champion Hurdle 1990 (Kribensis), Whitbread Gold Cup 1993 (Topsham Bay); champ. jockey 1992/93; rode 173 winners in season 1992/93, 1000th winner at Cheltenham 1994; NH Jockey of the Year 1989/90, 91/92. *Publications*: contributor to *Horse and Hound*, 1989– . *Leisure interests*: playing and watching most sports. *Address*: Hyperion House, Church Way, Sparsholt, Wantage, Oxon OX12 9PU.

DURIE, Gordon: footballer; b. 6 December 1965, Paisley; player E. Fife 1981–85, Hibernian 85–86, Chelsea 86–91, Tottenham Hotspur 91–93, Rangers 93– ; with Chelsea: 2nd Div. champs. 1988/89; 4 Scotland U-21 caps, over 23 full Scotland caps. *Address*: Rangers FC, Ibrox Stadium, 150 Edmiston Drive, Glasgow G51 2XD.

DURIE, Joanna Mary: tennis player; b. 27 July 1960, Bristol; rep. Glos., Avon; GB girls' U-12 grass court champ. 1972, U-14 grass court champ. 1973, U-18 covered court, grass court and hard court champ. 1976, ladies' champ. 1983, 84, 86, 87, 90, 91, 92; GB debut 1981, Federation Cup team 1981–87, 89– , European Cup team 1989– (winners 1992), Wightman Cup team 1979, 81–89; winner Wimbledon mixed doubles 1987, Aus. Champs. mixed doubles 1991; semi-finalist French Champs., US Champs. 1983; Sports

Writers' Sportswoman of the Year 1983. *Leisure interests*: skiing, golf. *Address*: c/o LTA, The Queen's Club, W. Kensington, London W14 9EG.

DURNIN, John: footballer; b. 18 August 1965, Bootle; player Oxford Utd 1989–93, Portsmouth 93– . *Address*: Portsmouth FC, Fratton Park, Frogmore Rd, Portsmouth PO4 8RA.

DURRANT, Iain: footballer; b. 29 October 1966, Glasgow; player Rangers 1984– , winners Scottish League Cup 1987, 88, Scottish Cup 1992, 93; over 10 Scotland caps. *Address*: Glasgow Rangers FC, Ibrox Stadium, 150 Edmiston Drive, Glasgow G51 2XD.

DWYER, Bernard: Rugby League footballer; b. 20 April 1967, St Helens; player St Helens 1984– , winners Premiership 1993. *Address*: St Helens RLFC, Dunriding Lane, St Helens, Merseyside WA10 4AD.

DWYER, Mark Peter: jockey; b. 9 August 1963; m. Jane Dwyer 1990; winner Hennessy Gold Cup 1985 (Galway Blaze), Cheltenham Gold Cup 1985 (Forgive 'n' Forget), 1993 (Jodami). *Address*: c/o BHB, 42 Portman Square, London W1H 0EN.

DYER, Alexander: footballer; b. 14 November 1965, W. Ham; player Blackpool 1983–87, Hull City 87–88, Crystal Palace 88–90, Charlton Athletic 90–93, Oxford Utd 93– . *Address*: Oxford Utd FC, Manor Ground, London Rd, Headington, Oxford OX3 7RS.

DYER, Darren: boxer; b. 31 July 1966; ABA welterweight champ. 1986; Commonwealth Games welterweight gold medal 1986; prof. debut 1986; over 17 prof. wins. *Address*: c/o Brit. Boxing Board of Control, Jack Petersen House, 52A Borough High St, London SE1 1XW.

EALHAM, Mark Alan: cricketer; b. 27 August 1969, Ashford; player Kent 1989– . *Address*: Kent CCC, St Lawrence Ground, Canterbury CT1 3NZ.

EARLE, Robert: footballer; b. 27 January 1965, Newcastle-under-Lyme; player Port Vale 1982–91, Wimbledon 91– . *Address*: Wimbledon FC, Selhurst Park, London SE25 6PY.

EARNSHAW, Robert: racehorse trainer; b. 13 July 1960; m. Denise Earnshaw 1979; prof. jockey 1977–88; 1st trainer's licence 1987. *Address*: c/o BHB, 42 Portman Square, London W1H 0EN.

EASTWOOD, Damon Charles: water skier (racing); b. 24 April 1971, Peterborough; GB F2, overall offshore and inland champ. 1992, F1 and overall offshore champ. 1993; GB debut 1992; European Champs. gold medal 1992; European Cup gold medal 1992. *Leisure interests*: jet skiing, gym training, motocross. *Address*: 34 Postland Rd, Crowland, Peterborough PE6 0JB.

EASTWOOD, Paul: Rugby League footballer; b. 3 December 1965, Hull; player Hull 1985– , winners Premiership 1991; GB debut v. Papua New Guinea 1990, Brit. Lions tours NZ/Papua New Guinea 1990, Aus./NZ/Papua New Guinea 1992. *Address*: Hull RLFC, The Boulevard Ground, Airlie St, Hull HU3 3JD.

EBBRELL, John: footballer; b. 1 October 1969, Bromborough; player Everton 1986– ; 14 England U-21 caps. *Address*: Everton FC, Goodison Park, Liverpool L4 4EL.

EBDON, Marc: footballer; b. 17 October 1970, Pontypool; player Peterborough Utd 1991– ; 2 Wales U-21 caps. *Address*: Peterborough Utd FC, London Rd Ground, Peterborough, Cambs. PE2 8AL.

EDDERY, Patrick James John: jockey (Flat); b. 18 March 1952, Newbridge, Ireland; m. Carolyn Mercer 1978; winner Oaks 1974 (Polygamy), 1979 (Scintillate), Derby 1975 (Grundy), 1982 (Golden Fleece), 1990 (Quest for Fame), Irish Derby 1975 (Grundy), 1984 (El Gran Senor), 1985 (Law Society), 1993 (Commander In Chief), King George VI and Queen Elizabeth Diamond Stakes 1975 (Grundy), 1986 (Dancing Brave), Prix de l'Arc de Triomphe 1980 (Detroit), 1985 (Rainbow Quest), 1986 (Dancing Brave), 1987 (Trempolino), Irish 2000 Guineas 1981 (Kings Lake), 1990 (Tirol), 2000 Guineas 1983 (Lomond), 1984 (El Gran Senor), 1993 (Zafonic), Irish Oaks 1986 (Colorspin), 1993 (Wemyss Bight); champ. jockey 1974–77, 86, 88–91, 93; rode 209 winners in season 1990, 3000th winner at Bath 1991. *Address*: c/o BHB, 42 Portman Square, London W1H 0EN.

EDGAR, Marie: equestrianist (show jumping); b. 20 January 1970; GB jnr debut 1987; European Jnr Champs. individ. gold medals 1988, 89; European Young Rider Champs. individ. and team gold medals 1990, 91. *Address*: c/o Brit. Horse Soc., Brit. Equestrian Centre, Stoneleigh Park, Kenilworth, Warks. CV8 2LR.

EDINBURGH, Justin: footballer; b. 18 December 1969, Brentwood; player Southend Utd 1988–90, Tottenham Hotspur 90– ; with Tottenham Hotspur: winners FA Cup 1991. *Address*: Tottenham Hotspur FC, 748 High Rd, Tottenham, London N17 0AP.

EDMONDSON, Paul: motorcyclist (off-road); b. 17 July 1969, Otley; GB 80cc solo enduro champ. 1986, 125cc champ. 1987–89, 125cc and overall champ. 1990, 250cc and overall champ. 1991, 92; European 125cc enduro champ. 1989; world 125cc enduro champ. 1990, 93; ISDE team silver medal 1986 (Italy), gold 1987 (Poland), 1988 (France), 1989 (Germany), 1990 (Sweden), 1991 (Czechoslovakia), 1992 (Aus.); only Brit. rider to win European or world enduro title. *Leisure interests*: squash, mountain biking, running. *Address*: c/o ACU, ACU House, Wood St, Rugby CV21 2YX.

EDWARDS, Andrew: footballer; b. 17 September 1971, Epping; player Southend Utd 1989– . *Address*: Southend Utd FC, Roots Hall, Victoria Ave, Southend-on-Sea, Essex SS2 6NQ.

EDWARDS, Jonathan David: athlete (triple jump); b. 10 May 1966, Westminster; m. Alison Joy Edwards 1990; 1 s.; English schools champ. 1984, AAA champ. 1989, UK champ. 1989, 92; Commonwealth Games silver medal 1990; GB debut 1988; European Cup silver medal 1993; World Cup bronze medal 1989, gold 1992; World Champs. bronze medal 1993; Olympic squad 1988, 92; AAA and UK all-comers indoor record-holder. *Leisure interests*: tennis, golf, music, playing the guitar, eating out. *Address*: c/o Brit. Athletic Fed., 225A Bristol Rd, Edgbaston, Birmingham B5 7UB.

EDWARDS, Mark Sydney (Cedric): motorcyclist; b. 28 September 1961, St Athan; Midlands 2-stroke champ. 1987; Welsh 250cc champ. 1985, 86, solo champ. 1987. *Address*: Cambrian Council of Welsh Motorcycle Clubs, 13 Parret Walk, Bettws, Newport, Gwent.

EDWARDS, Neil George Barry: Rugby Union footballer; b. 20 August 1964, Carshalton; player Rosslyn Park, Harlequins, Northampton; with Harlequins: winners John Player Special Cup 1988; Scotland and Five Nations debut v. England 1992, tour Aus. 1992. *Address*: Northampton RUFC, Franklins Gardens, Weedon Rd, Northampton NN5 5BG.

EDWARDS, Nicholas Quentin: powerboat racer (navigator); b. 30 December 1959, Bristol; m. Lynda Edwards 1991; GB off-shore circuit racing production class PII champ., overall champ. navigator 1993. *Leisure interests*: classic cars. *Address*: c/o Powerboat Secretary, RYA, RYA House, Romsey Rd, Eastleigh, Hants. SO5 4YA.

EDWARDS, Shaun: Rugby League foot-baller; b. 17 October 1966, Wigan; player Wigan St Pats ARLFC, Wigan 1983– ; with Wigan: winners Challenge Cup 1985, 88 (capt.), 89–93, John Player Special Trophy 1986, 87, Regal Trophy 1989, 90, 93, Premiership 1987, 92, League champs. 1986/87, 89/90, 90/91, 91/92, 92/93; GB debut v. France 1985, youngest-ever Test player, Brit. Lions tours Aus./NZ/Papua New Guinea 1988 (aborted), 92, over 30 caps; Young Player of the Year an unprece-dented 3 years running; Int. Player of the Year 1989; winner Man of Steel 1990; top try-scorer in Rugby League 1991/92; achieved 1000 career points v. Leeds 1994. *Leisure interests*: golf, martial arts, going to dance clubs. *Address*: Wigan RLFC, The Pavilion, Central Park, Wigan WN1 1XF.

EDYVEAN, Jeremy (Jed): glider pilot; b. 15 December 1954, Woodbridge; GB standard-class champ. 1990, 91 (joint); UK multi-seat 100km triangular speed record-holder 1985–88. *Leisure interests*: angling, flying. *Address*: RAFGSA Centre, RAF Bicester, Oxon OX9 6AA.

EHIOGU, Ugochuku: footballer; b. 3 November 1972, Hackney; player W. Bromwich Albion 1990–91, Aston Villa 91– ; England U-21 debut v. Hungary 1992, over 3 caps. *Leisure interests*: snooker, golf, resting. *Address*: Aston Villa FC, Villa Park, Trinity Rd, Birmingham B6 6HE.

EKOKU, Efan: footballer; b. 7 June 1967, Manchester; player Bournemouth 1990–92, Norwich City 92– . *Address*: Norwich City FC, Carrow Rd, Norwich NR1 1JE.

ELKINS, Gary: footballer; b. 4 May 1966, Wallingford; player Fulham 1983–90, Wimbledon 90– . *Address*: Wimbledon FC, Selhurst Park, London SE25 6PY.

ELLIOT, Virginia Helen Antoinette, MBE: equestrianist (three-day eventing); b. 1 February 1955, Malta; m. Michael Tomas Elliot 1993; European Jnr Champs. team gold medal 1973; GB open champ. 1987, 93 (Welton Houdini); European Champs. team gold medal 1981, team silver 1983, individ. and team gold 1985 (Priceless), 1987 (Nightcap), 1989 (Master Craftsman); World Champs. team gold medal 1982, individ. and team gold 1986 (Priceless); Olympic individ. bronze and team silver medals 1984 (Priceless), 1988 (Master Craftsman); winner Badminton Horse Trials 1985 (Priceless), 1989 (Master Craftsman), 1993 (Welton Houdini), Burghley Horse Trials 1983 (Priceless), 1984 (Nightcap), 1986 (Murphy Himself); Sports Writers' Sportswoman of the Year 1985. *Publications*: Ginny, Ginny and Her Horses, Training the Event Horse, Priceless, A Free Rein. *Leisure interests*: cooking, skiing, antiques, fox-hunting, racing. *Address*: New Barn, Steeple Aston, Oxon OX5 3QH.

ELLIOTT, Alice Mary: flat green bowler; b. 7 November 1942, Ballymoney, NI; 2 d.; Irish women's pairs champ. (outdoor) 1989, (indoor) 1991, women's triples champ. (outdoor) 1983, 90, (indoor) 1987, 90, women's fours champ. (outdoor) 1990; GB women's pairs champ. (indoor) 1991, triples champ. (indoor) 1987; Ireland debut (outdoor) 1984, (indoor) 1988. *Leisure inter-ests*: reading, knitting, walking, country music. *Address*: 46 Huey Crescent, Bushmills, Co. Antrim BT57 8QZ.

ELLIOTT, Malcolm: cyclist; b. 1 July 1961, Sheffield; rep. Raleigh 1984–86, ANC 86–88, Fagor 88–89, Teka 89–91, Seur 91–93, LA Sheriff 93– ; RTTC hill-climb champ. 1980; GB prof. criterium champ. 1984, pursuit champ. 1985, road race champ. 1993; Commonwealth Games road race and team time trial gold medals 1982; GB jnr debut 1979, snr debut and Olympic squad (4000m team pursuit) 1980; Tour de France debut 1987; winner Milk Race 1987, Kelloggs Tour of Britain 1988, Tour of the Americas 1990. *Address:* c/o Brit. Cycling Fed., 36 Rockingham Rd, Kettering, Northants. NN16 8HG.

ELLIOTT, Paul: footballer; b. 18 March 1964, Lewisham; player Charlton Athletic 1981–83, Luton Town 83–85, Aston Villa 85–87, Pisa (Italy), Celtic 1989–91, Chelsea 91– ; 3 England U-21 caps. *Address:* Chelsea FC, Stamford Bridge, Fulham Rd, London SW6 1HS.

ELLIOTT, Peter: athlete; b. 4 October 1962, Rotherham; Commonwealth Games 1500m gold medal 1990; World Champs. 800m silver medal 1987; Olympic 1500m silver medal 1988. *Address:* c/o Brit. Athletic Fed., 225A Bristol Rd, Edgbaston, Birmingham B5 7UB.

ELLIS, Kevin: Rugby League footballer; b. 29 May 1965, Bridgend; player Bridgend (RU), Warrington 1990– ; with Warrington: winners Regal Trophy 1991; 3 Wales B RU caps; Wales RL debut v. Papua New Guinea 1991; GB debut v. France 1991, Brit. Lions tour Aus./NZ/Papua New Guinea 1992. *Address:* Warrington RLFC, Wilderspool Stadium, Wilderspool Causeway, Warrington WA4 6PY.

ELLIS, Louise: hockey player; b. 12 June 1974, Chester; player Buckley 1989–93, Clifton 93– ; Wales U-16 debut 1990, U-18 and U-21 debuts 1991, snr debut 1992; youngest goalkeeper to gain snr Wales cap. *Leisure interests:* tennis, football, reading, travel. *Address:* 9 Highcroft, Higher Shotton, Deeside, Clwyd CH5 1QZ.

ELLIS, St John: Rugby League footballer; b. 3 October 1964, Fulford; player Southlands ARLFC, York, Castleford 1989– ; with Castleford: winners Regal

Trophy 1994; GB debut v. France 1991. *Address:* Castleford RLFC, Wheldon Rd, Castleford WF10 2SD.

ELLISON, Adrian Charles: coxswain; b. 11 September 1958, Solihull; m. Clare Louise Ellison 1988; rep. Reading Univ. 1977–79, Thames Tradesmen RC 79–80, Leander Club 80–81, Tideway Scullers School 81–91, Leander Club 91– ; Commonwealth Games coxed fours gold medal 1986; GB debut and World Champs. coxed pairs bronze medal 1981, eights bronze medal 1989, Olympic coxed fours gold medal 1984, squad (eights) 1992; only Brit. cox to have won Commonwealth, World and Olympic medals. *Leisure interests:* driving, tropical fish, food and drink. *Address:* Leander Club, Henley-on-Thames, Oxon.

ELSWORTH, David Raymond Cecil: race-horse trainer; b. 12 December 1939; m. Jane Elsworth 1969; 2 s., 1 d.; prof. NH jockey 1957–72; 1st trainer's licence 1978/79; winner Grand National 1988 (Rhyme 'n' Reason), Whitbread Gold Cup 1988 (Desert Orchid), Cheltenham Gold Cup 1989 (Desert Orchid), Hennessy Gold Cup 1989 (Ghofar), Irish 1000 Guineas 1990 (In the Groove); leading NH trainer 1987/88. *Address:* c/o BHB, 42 Portman Square, London W1H 0EN.

EMBUREY, John Ernest: cricketer; b. 20 August 1952, Peckham; m. Susie Elizabeth Anne Booth 1980; 2 d.; player Middx 1973– (vice-capt. 83–), winners Gillette Cup 1977, 80, NatWest Trophy 1984, 88, Benson and Hedges Cup 1983, 86, county champs. 1976, 77, 80, 82, 85, 90, 93, Sunday League champs. 1992; Test debut 1978, tours Aus. 1978/79, Aus./India 1979/80, WI 1980/81, India/Sri Lanka 1981/82, WI 1985/86, Aus. 1986/87, Pakistan/Aus./NZ (World Cup) 1987/88, India/Sri Lanka 1992/93. *Publications: Emburey*, 1986, *Spinning in a Fast World*, 1989. *Leisure interests:* golf, reading, gardening. *Address:* Middx CCC, Lord's Cricket Ground, London NW8 8QN.

ENGLAND, Brian Stuart: water skier; b. 29 December 1949, Belfast, NI; m. Patricia Anne England 1993; Ireland capt., World Champs. 1987, 93; chairman NI section, Irish Water Ski Fed. *Address*: c/o Irish Water Ski Fed., House of Sport, Upper Malone Rd, Belfast, NI.

ENGLAND, Keith: Rugby League footballer; b. 27 February 1964, Castleford; player Castleford 1981– ; GB debut v. France 1987. *Address*: Castleford RLFC, Wheldon Rd, Castleford WF10 2SD.

ENGLISH, Isaac: footballer; b. 12 November 1971, Paisley; player Partick Thistle 1989– . *Address*: Partick Thistle FC, Firhill Stadium, 80 Firhill Rd, Glasgow G20 7BA.

ERRAUGHT, Maria: synchronized swimmer; b. 1 March 1970, Bristol; England and GB jnr debuts 1986, snr debuts 1990; Europa Cup team silver medal 1992. *Leisure interests*: weight training, DIY. *Address*: c/o ASA, Harold Fern House, Derby Square, Loughborough, Leics. LE11 0AL.

ETHERIDGE, Christopher John: motorcyclist (moto-cross); b. 26 October 1965, Maidstone; GB sidecar moto-cross champ. 1991–93. *Leisure interests*: swimming, watching motor sports. *Address*: c/o ACU, ACU House, Wood St, Rugby CV21 2YX.

EUBANK, Christopher Livingston: boxer; b. 8 August 1966; prof. debut 1985; titles won: WBC int. middleweight 1990, WBO middleweight 1990, WBO super-middleweight 1991; over 36 prof. wins. *Address*: Matchroom Ltd, 10 Western Rd, Romford, Essex RM1 3JT.

EVANS, Ceri: footballer; b. 2 October 1963, Christchurch, NZ; player Oxford Utd 1989– . *Address*: Oxford Utd FC, Manor Ground, London Rd, Headington, Oxford OX3 7RS.

EVANS, Gareth: footballer; b. 14 January 1967, Coventry; player Coventry City 1985–86, Rotherham Utd 86–88, Hibernian 88– ; with Hibernian: winners Scottish League Cup 1992. *Address*: Hibernian FC, Easter Rd Stadium, 64 Albion Rd, Edinburgh EH7 5QG.

EVANS, Ieuan Cenydd: Rugby Union footballer; b. 21 March 1964, Pontardulais; player Carmarthen Quins, Llanelli; with Llanelli: winners Welsh Cup 1991, 92, 93, Welsh League champs. 1992/93; Wales and Five Nations debut v. France 1987, capt. 1991– ; Brit. Lions tours Aus. 1989, NZ 1993; Whitbread/*Rugby World* Player of the Year 1993. *Address*: Llanelli RFC, Stradey Park, Llanelli, Dyfed.

EVANS, Kevin Paul: cricketer; b. 10 September 1963, Nottingham; m. Sandra Evans 1988; player Notts. 1984– , county champs. 1987, Sunday League champs. 1991. *Address*: Notts. CCC, Trent Bridge, Nottingham NG2 6AG.

EVANS, Linda: flat green bowler; b. 14 March 1942, Briton Ferry; m. Keith Evans 1971; rep. Glamorgan (outdoor) 1979– ; Welsh women's pairs champ. (outdoor) 1986, 92, (indoor) 1992, women's triples champ. (outdoor) 1980, 81, (indoor) 1983, 87, women's fours champ. (outdoor) 1979, (indoor) 1979, 88; GB women's fours champ. 1979; Wales debut (outdoor) 1982, (indoor) 1980, Commonwealth Games women's fours gold medal 1986. *Leisure interests*: TV, theatre, knitting. *Address*: 278 Old Rd, Briton Ferry, Neath, W. Glamorgan SA11 2ET.

EVANS, Owen: Rugby Union footballer; b. 22 October 1965, Hartlepool; player W. Hartlepool 1984– ; rep. Durham U-19 and snr squad, N. Div. U-19. *Address*: W. Hartlepool RFC, Brierton Lane, Hartlepool, Cleveland TS25 5DR.

EVANS, Paul: Rugby Union footballer; b. 3 January 1967, Bridlington; player W. Hartlepool 1989– ; rep. Durham. *Address*: W. Hartlepool RFC, Brierton Lane, Hartlepool, Cleveland TS25 5DR.

EVANS, Richard Lloyd: Rugby Union footballer; b. 23 June 1961, Cardigan; player Cardigan, Llanelli; with Llanelli: winners Welsh Cup 1993, Welsh League champs. 1992/93; Wales B tour Canada 1989, snr and Five Nations debut v. England 1993. *Address*: Llanelli RFC, Stradey Park, Llanelli, Dyfed.

EVANS, Terence: footballer; b. 12 April 1965, Shepherd's Bush; player Brentford 1985–93, Wycombe Wanderers 93– ; with Brentford: 3rd Div. champs. 1991/92. *Leisure interests*: boxing. *Address*: Wycombe Wanderers FC, Adams Park, Hillbottom Rd, Sands, High Wycombe HP12 4HJ.

EYRE, Sally Louise: hockey player; b. 14 November 1971; player Portsmouth 1986–91, Ealing 91– ; rep. Hants. U-18 1987–90, U-21 86–92, U-21 indoor county champs. 1989 (capt.), snr squad 1988– ; England U-18 debut 1988, U-21 debut 1989, European Indoor Cup U-21 silver medallist 1991, snr training squad 1992/93; England indoor debut 1989; GB development squad 1990. *Leisure interests*: water sports, tennis, mountain-climbing, travel, fashion, comedy clubs. *Address*: Ealing HC, Ealing CC, Crofton Rd, London W5.

EYRES, Richard: Rugby League footballer; b. 7 December 1966, St Helens; player Widnes Tigers ARLFC, Widnes 1984–93, Leeds 93– ; rep. Lancs.; GB debut v. France 1989. *Address*: Leeds RLFC, Bass Headingley, St Michael's Lane, Leeds LS6 3BR.

FAIMALO, Esene: Rugby League footballer; b. 11 October 1966, Christchurch, NZ; player Widnes 1990– ; NZ debut v. Papua New Guinea 1988, tour GB 1989. *Address*: Widnes RLFC, Naughton Park, Lowerhouse Lane, Widnes WA8 7DZ.

FAIRBANK, Karl: Rugby League footballer; b. 1 June 1964, Greetland; player Elland ARLFC, Bradford Northern 1986– ; rep. Yorks.; GB debut v Papua New Guinea 1987, Brit. Lions tour Aus./NZ/Papua New Guinea 1992. *Address*: Bradford Northern RLFC, Odsal Stadium, Bradford BD6 1BS.

FAIRBROTHER, Neil Harvey: cricketer; b. 9 September 1963, Warrington; m. Audrey Fairbrother 1988; 1 d.; player Lancs. 1982– (capt. 92–93); Test debut 1987, tours India/Pakistan (World Cup), Aus./NZ 1987/88, Pakistan (England A) 1990/91, NZ 1991/92, India 1992/93. *Address*: Lancs. CCC, Old Trafford, Manchester M16 0PX.

FAIRBROTHER, Nicola Kim: judo player (U-56kg); b. 14 May 1970, Henley-on-Thames; GB women's open champ. 1990, 93; European Jnr Champs. silver medal 1986, gold 1987; European Champs. gold medals 1992, 93; World Champs. gold medal 1993; Olympic silver medal 1992. *Leisure interests*: squash, reading, writing. *Address*: c/o Brit. Judo Assoc., 7A Rutland St, Leicester LE1 1RB.

FAIRBROTHER, Paul: motorcyclist (off-road); b. 6 November 1962, Kirby Muxloe, Leics.; m. Denise Margot Fairbrother 1983; 1 s., 1 d.; ACU 500cc expert solo enduro champ. 1991; ISDE team bronze medal 1985 (Spain), silver 1986 (Italy), gold 1988 (France), 1989 (Germany), 1990 (Sweden), 1991 (Czechoslovakia), 1992 (Aus.). *Leisure interests*: cycling, road racing, DIY. *Address*: c/o ACU, ACU House, Wood St, Rugby CV21 2YX.

FAIRCLOUGH, Courtney (Chris): footballer; b. 12 April 1964, Nottingham; player Nottingham Forest 1981–87, Tottenham Hotspur 87–89, Leeds Utd 89– ; with Leeds Utd: 2nd Div. champs. 1989/90, League champs. 1991/92; 7 England U-21 caps. *Address*: Leeds Utd FC, Elland Rd, Leeds, W. Yorks. LS11 0ES.

FAIRIE, Michele Frances: netball player; b. 15 January 1973, Glasgow; player Scotstoun; rep. Glasgow District; Scotland U-18 debut 1989, U-21 debut 1992, snr debut 1993. *Leisure interests*: football, canoeing, meeting people. *Address*: c/o Scottish Netball Assoc., Kelvin Hall, Argyle St, Glasgow G3 8AW.

FAIRWEATHER, Carlton: footballer; b. 22 September 1961, Camberwell; player Wimbledon 1984– . *Address*: Wimbledon FC, Selhurst Park, London SE25 6PY.

FALCONER, William: footballer; b. 5 April 1966, Aberdeen; player Aberdeen 1982–88, Watford 88–91, Middlesbrough 91–93, Sheffield Utd 93– . *Address*: Sheffield Utd FC, Bramall Lane, Sheffield, S. Yorks S2 4SU.

FALDO, Nicholas Alexander, MBE: golfer; b. 18 July 1957, Welwyn Garden City; m. Gillian Faldo 1986; 1 s., 2 d.; English amateur champ. 1975; prof. debut 1976; world matchplay champ. 1989, 92, world champ. 1992; Dunhill Cup team 1985–88, 91, 93 (winners 1987); Ryder Cup team 1977–93, winners 1985, 87, youngest-ever competitor 1977; winner French Open 1983, 88, 89, Swiss Masters 1983, Spanish Open 1987, Open 1987, 90, 92, US Masters 1989, 90, Brit. Masters 1989, Asian Classic 1990, 93, Irish Open 1991, 92, 93, Scandinavian Masters, European Open 1992; Sports Writers Sportsman of the Year 1987, 89, 90, BBC Sports Personality of the Year 1989. *Leisure interests*: fly fishing, rallying, motor sport. *Address*: Int. Management Group, Pier House, Strand on the Green, London W4 3NN.

FALLON, James Anthony: Rugby League footballer; b. 27 March 1965, Windsor; player Bath (RU) 1990–92, Leeds 92– ; RU: with Bath: League champs. 1991/92; England B debut v. France 1990, 5 caps. *Address*: Leeds RLFC, Bass Headingley, St Michael's Lane, Leeds LS6 3BR.

FANSHAWE, James Robert: racehorse trainer; b. 6 August 1961, Moreton in Marsh; m. Jacqueline Fanshawe 1990; 1st licence 1990; winner Coral-Eclipse Stakes 1991 (Environment Friend), Champion Hurdle 1992 (Royal Gait). *Address*: Pegasus Stables, Snailwell Rd, Newmarket, Suffolk CB8 7DJ.

FARISH, Stephen Edward: flat green bowler; b. 12 August 1970, Wigton; rep. Cumbria (outdoor) 1988– , (indoor) 1991– ; English singles champ. (outdoor) 1992, fours champ. (indoor) 1992; GB fours champ. (indoor) 1993; England debut (outdoor) 1993. *Leisure interests*: snooker, football, golf, films and TV. *Address*: 18 Waver Lane, Wigton, Cumbria CA7 9RU.

FARNINGHAM, Ray: footballer; b. 10 April 1961, Dundee; player Forfar Athletic 1978–87, Motherwell 87–89, Dunfermline 89–92, Partick Thistle 92–93, Dundee 93– . *Address*: Dundee FC, Dens Park, Dundee DD3 7JY.

FARRELL, Andrew: Rugby League footballer; b. 30 May 1975; player Wigan 1992– , winners Challenge Cup 1993; GB debut v. NZ 1993. *Address*: Wigan RLFC, The Pavilion, Central Park, Wigan WN1 1XF.

FARRELL, Anthony: Rugby League footballer; b. 17 January 1969, Huddersfield; player Huddersfield, Sheffield Eagles 1989– . *Address*: Sheffield Eagles RLFC, Stadium Corner, 824 Attercliffe Rd, Sheffield S9 3RS.

FARRELL, David: footballer; b. 29 October 1969, Glasgow; player Hibernian 1988– . *Address*: Hibernian FC, Easter Rd Stadium, 64 Albion Rd, Edinburgh EH7 5QG.

FASHANU, John: footballer; b. 18 September 1962, Kensington; player Norwich City 1979–83, Lincoln City 83–84, Millwall 84–86, Wimbledon 86– (capt.); with Wimbledon: winners FA Cup 1988; 2 England caps. *Address*: Wimbledon FC, Selhurst Park, London SE25 6PY.

FASHANU, Justin: footballer; b. 19 February 1961, Hackney; player Norwich City 1978–81, Nottingham Forest 81–82, Notts County 82–85, Brighton and Hove Albion 85–86, Manchester City 1989, W. Ham Utd 1989, Leyton Orient 1990, Torquay Utd 1991–92, Airdrieonians 92–93, Heart of Midlothian 93– ; 11 England U-21 caps. *Address*: Heart of Midlothian FC, Tynecastle Park, Gorgie Rd, Edinburgh EH11 2NL.

FAULDS, Richard Bruce: clay pigeon shooter; b. 16 March 1977, Guildford; English jnr all-round champ., FITASC sporting champ. 1992, open sporting champ., open skeet champ. 1993; GB jnr FITASC sporting champ., open skeet champ., all-round champ. 1992; European Jnr FITASC Sporting Champs. team silver medals 1991–93, individ. gold 1992; World Jnr FITASC Sporting Champs. team gold medals 1991, 92, silver 1993, individ. bronze 1992, gold 1993; World Jnr Beretta Sporting Champs. gold medal 1993; World FITASC Sporting Champs. individ. silver medal 1993 (1st jnr medal-winner). *Leisure interests*: game-shooting, trout-fishing. *Address*: Rivers End, Mill Lane, Longparish, Andover, Hants. SP11 6PH.

FAWCETT, Vince: Rugby League footballer; b. 13 November 1970; player Middleton ARLFC, Leeds 1987– ; GB U-21 debut v. France 1990. *Address*: Leeds RLFC, Bass Headingley, St Michael's Lane, Leeds LS6 3BR.

FEHERTY, David: golfer; b. 13 August 1958, Bangor, NI; prof. debut 1976; Dunhill Cup team (Ireland) 1986, 90, 91, 93; winners 1990; Ryder Cup team 1991; winner Italian Open, Scottish Open 1986, BMW Int. Open 1989, Cannes Open 1991, Madrid Open 1992. *Address*: c/o PGA European Tour, Wentworth Club, Wentworth Drive, Virginia Water, Surrey GU25 4LS.

FELGATE, David: footballer; b. 4 March 1960, Blaenau Ffestionog; player Lincoln City 1980–85, Grimsby Town 85–87, Bolton Wanderers 87– ; 1 Wales cap. *Address*: Bolton Wanderers FC, Burnden Park, Manchester Rd, Bolton, Lancs. BL3 2QR.

FELLENGER, David: footballer; b. 6 June 1969, Edinburgh; player Hibernian 1987– . *Address*: Hibernian FC, Easter Rd Stadium, 64 Albion Rd, Edinburgh EH7 5QG.

FELTHAM, Mark Andrew: cricketer; b. 26 June 1963, London; m. Debra Elizabeth Feltham 1990; 1 d.; player Surrey 1983–92, Middx 93– ; with Middx: county champs. 1993. *Address*: Middx CCC, Lord's Cricket Ground, London NW8 8QN.

FELTON, Nigel Alfred: cricketer; b. 24 October 1960, Guildford; m. Jill-Marie Felton 1989; player Somerset 1982–88, Northants. 89– ; with Somerset: tours Barbados 1986, Sierra Leone 1988; England YC tour Aus. 1979. *Address*: Northants. CCC, County Cricket Ground, Wantage Rd, Northampton NN1 4TJ.

FELTON, Sally Louise: squash player; b. 22 November 1973, Northampton; player Overstone 1986– ; rep. Northants. 1985– , E. Midlands 1986–89; Northants. girls' U-16 champ. 1989, U-19 champ. 1989–91, ladies' champ. 1989, 91; GB girls' U-16 open champ. 1988; England U-16 debut 1989, U-19 debut 1991; European Jnr Champs. team gold medal 1992; World Jnr

Champs. team gold medal 1991. *Leisure interests*: tennis, aerobics, swimming, athletics, films, design. *Address*: 1 Pear Tree Close, Orchard Hill, Little Billing, Northampton NN3 9TH.

FENWICK, Sarah Jane: paraglider pilot; b. Newport, Isle of Wight; GB women's champ. 1992; World Champs. team bronze medal 1993; world women's distance record-holder. *Leisure interests*: hang gliding, sailing, riding, cycling, swimming, photography, travel, reading. *Address*: Lower Rill Farm, Chillerton, Isle of Wight PO30 3HQ.

FENWICK, Terence: footballer; b. 17 November 1959, Camden, Durham; player Crystal Palace 1976–80, Queens Park Rangers 80–87, Tottenham Hotspur 87–93, Swindon Town 93– ; with Crystal Palace: 2nd Div. champs. 1978/79; with Queens Park Rangers: 2nd Div. champs. 1982/83; 11 England U-21 caps, 20 full England caps. *Address*: Swindon Town FC, The County Ground, Swindon, Wilts. SN1 2ED.

FERA, Rick: ice hockey player; b. 13 August 1964; player Murrayfield Racers 1985–87, Solihull Barons 87–88, Tayside Tigers 88–89, Fife Flyers 89–91, Trafford Metros 91–92, Basingstoke Beavers 92– ; with Murrayfield Racers: winners Autumn Cup 1986, Scottish Cup 1987, GB champs. 1985/86, League champs. 1986/87. *Address*: The Playground, W. Ham Park, W. Ham, Basingstoke, Hants.

FERDINAND, Leslie: footballer; b. 18 December 1966, Acton; player Queens Park Rangers 1987– ; England debut v. San Marino 1993. *Address*: Queens Park Rangers FC, Rangers Stadium, S. Africa Rd, London W12 7PA.

FEREDAY, Wayne: footballer; b. 16 June 1963, Warley; player Queens Park Rangers 1980–89, Newcastle Utd 89–90, Bournemouth 90–91, W. Bromwich Albion

91– ; 5 England U-21 caps. *Address*: W. Bromwich Albion FC, The Hawthorns, W. Bromwich B71 4LF.

FERGUS, Jason Robert: athlete; b. 11 October 1973, Paddington; S. of England 100m, 200m and 60m indoor champ. 1992; English schools 100m champ. 1992; UK U-20 Champs. 100m silver and 200m bronze medals 1992; World Jnr Champs. 4 x 100m relay gold medal 1992. *Leisure interests*: cricket, altar serving, reading, music. *Address*: c/o Brit. Athletic Fed., 225A Bristol Rd, Edgbaston, Birmingham B5 7UB.

FERGUSON, Alexander Chapman: football manager; b. 31 December 1941, Govan, Glasgow; m. Catherine Russell Ferguson 1966; 3 s.; player Queen's Park 1958–60, St Johnstone 60–64, Dunfermline Athletic 64–67, Rangers 67–69, Falkirk 69–73, Ayr Utd 73–74; manager East Stirling August–October 1974, St Mirren 74–78, Aberdeen 78–86, Manchester Utd 86– ; as manager: Scottish 1st Div. champs. 1976/77 (St Mirren), Scottish League champs. 1979/80, 83/84, 84/85 (Aberdeen), winners Scottish Cup 1982, 83, 84, 86 (Aberdeen), European Cup Winners' Cup and European Super Cup 1983 (Aberdeen) and 1991 (Manchester Utd), Scottish League Cup 1986 (Aberdeen), FA Cup and Charity Shield 1990 (Manchester Utd), League Cup 1992 (Manchester Utd), League champs. 1992/93 (Manchester Utd). *Publications*: *Alight in the North, 1985, Six Years at United, 1992, Just Champion, 1993. Leisure interests*: golf, snooker, films. *Address*: Manchester Utd FC, Old Trafford, Manchester M16 0RA.

FERGUSON, Darren: footballer; b. 9 February 1972, Glasgow; player Manchester Utd 1990–94, Wolverhampton Wanderers 94– ; Scotland U-21 int. *Address*: Wolverhampton Wanderers FC, Molineux Stadium, Waterloo Rd, Wolverhampton WV1 4QR.

FERGUSON, Derek: footballer; b. 31 July 1967, Glasgow; player Rangers 1983–90, Heart of Midlothian 90–93, Sunderland 93– ; with Rangers: winners Scottish League Cup 1987, 88. *Address*: Sunderland FC, Roker Park Ground, Sunderland, Tyne and Wear SR6 9SW.

FERGUSON, Duncan: footballer; b. 27 December 1971, Stirling; player Dundee Utd 1990–93, Rangers 93– ; 3 Scotland caps. *Address*: Glasgow Rangers FC, Ibrox Stadium, 150 Edmiston Drive, Glasgow G51 2XD.

FERGUSON, Iain: footballer; b. 4 August 1962, Newarthill; player Dundee 1979–84, Rangers 84–86, Dundee Utd 86–88, Heart of Midlothian 88–90, Motherwell 90– ; with Rangers: winners Scottish League Cup 1985; with Motherwell: winners Scottish Cup 1991. Scotland U-21 int. *Address*: Motherwell FC, Fir Park, Fir Park St, Motherwell ML1 2QN.

FERGUSON, Ian: footballer; b. 15 March 1967, Glasgow; player Clyde 1984–87, St Mirren 87–88, Rangers 88– ; with Rangers: winners Scottish League Cup 1989, 91, 93, Scottish Cup 1993; over 6 Scotland caps. *Address*: Glasgow Rangers FC, Ibrox Stadium, 150 Edmiston Drive, Glasgow G51 2XD.

FERREYRA, Victor: footballer; b. 24 February 1965, Buenos Aires, Argentina; player San Lorenzo (Argentina), Dundee Utd 1991– ; Argentina int. *Address*: Dundee Utd FC, Tannadice Park, Dundee DD3 7JW.

FETTIS, Alan: footballer; b. 1 February 1971, Belfast, NI; player Hull City 1991– ; over 3 NI caps. *Address*: Hull City FC, Boothferry Park, Boothferry Rd, Hull, N. Humberside HU4 6EU.

FIBBENS, Michael Wenham: swimmer; b. 31 May 1968, Harlow; GB 50m and 100m freestyle, 100m butterfly champ. 1993; European Champs. 50m freestyle bronze medal 1991, 4 x 100m medley relay bronze 1993; World Short-Course Champs. 4 x 100m medley relay bronze medal 1993; Olympic squad 1988, 92; GB 100m freestyle record-holder. *Leisure interests*: dance, music, cooking, cars. *Address*: c/o ASA, Harold Fern House, Derby Square, Loughborough, Leics. LE11 0AL.

FIELD-BUSS, Michael Gwyn: cricketer; b. 23 September 1964, Mtarfa, Malta; player Essex 1987–88, Notts. 89– ; with Notts.: Sunday League champs. 1991. *Leisure interests*: family, Leyton Orient FC, Arsenal FC, music. *Address*: Notts. CCC, Trent Bridge, Nottingham NG2 6AG.

FIELDHOUSE, John: Rugby League footballer; b. 28 June 1962, Wigan; player Wigan St Pats ARLFC, Warrington, Widnes, St Helens, Oldham, Halifax 1991– ; GB debut v. NZ 1985. *Address*: Halifax RLFC, The Pavilion, Thrum Hall, Gibbet St, Halifax, W. Yorks HX1 4TL.

FIFIELD, Darren: boxer; b. 9 October 1969; ABA jnr champ. 1986; ABA light-flyweight champ. 1992; England debut 1991; prof. debut 1992; titles won: Commonwealth flyweight 1993. *Address*: c/o Brit. Boxing Board of Control, Jack Petersen House, 52A Borough High St, London SE1 1XW.

FILSELL, Vikki Caroline: oarswoman; b. 30 April 1967, Bedford; rep. Univ. of London Women's BC 1986–88, Thames Tradesmen's RC 91– ; GB lightweight women's double sculls champ. 1986, lightweight and open coxless fours champ. 1991–93; GB jnr debut 1984, U-23 debut 1986, snr debut 1988; rep. Beds. hockey and cross-country 1984–85. *Address*: c/o ARA, The Priory, 6 Lower Mall, London W6 9DJ.

FINDLAY, William: footballer; b. 29 August 1970, Kilmarnock; player Hibernian 1987– ; Scotland U-21 int. *Address*: Hibernian FC, Easter Rd Stadium, 64 Albion Rd, Edinburgh EH7 5QG.

FISHER, Allison: snooker player; b. 24 February 1968, Cheshunt; UK women's champ. 1986–90, world women's champ. 1985, 86, 88, 89, 91, 93; prof. debut 1991, winner World Mixed Doubles and World Masters mixed doubles (with Steve Davis) 1991, European Masters 1991, Brit. Open 1992; 1st prof. woman player to compete against men. *Leisure interests*: walking. *Address*: Matchroom, 10 Western Rd, Romford, Essex RM1 3JT.

FISHER, Andy: Rugby League footballer; b. 17 November 1967, Wakefield; player Eastmoor ARLFC, Featherstone Rovers, Castleford 1993– . *Address*: Castleford RLFC, Wheldon Rd, Castleford WF10 2SD.

FISHER, Jodi Victor: water skier; b. 4 July 1970, Mansfield; GB U-21 slalom, jump champ. 1990; European U-21 slalom champ. 1991; English overall champ. 1991; GB debut 1984; European Champs. team bronze medal 1992; World Champs. squad 1993. *Address*: Princes Club, Clockhouse Lane, Bedfont, Middx TW14 8QA.

FISHER, Neil: footballer; b. 7 November 1970, St Helens; player Bolton Wanderers 1989– . *Address*: Bolton Wanderers FC, Burnden Park, Manchester Rd, Bolton, Lancs. BL3 2QR.

FITZGERALD, James Gerard: racehorse trainer; b. 22 May 1935; m. Jane Fitzgerald 1978; 1 s., 2 d.; 1st licence 1969; winner Hennessy Gold Cup 1985 (Galway Blaze), Cheltenham Gold Cup 1985 (Forgive 'n' Forget). *Address*: c/o BHB, 42 Portman Square, London W1H 0EN.

FITZGERALD, Scott: footballer; b. 13 August 1969, Westminster; player Wimbledon 1987– ; 1 Ireland U-21 cap. *Address*: Wimbledon FC, Selhurst Park, London SE25 6PY.

FLECK, Robert: footballer; b. 11 August 1965, Glasgow; player Partick Thistle 1983–84, Rangers 84–87, Norwich City 87–92, Chelsea 92– ; with Rangers: winners Scottish League Cup 1987, 88; 7 Scotland U-21 caps, 4 full Scotland caps. *Address*: Chelsea FC, Stamford Bridge, Fulham Rd, London SW6 1HS.

FLEMING, Craig: footballer; b. 6 October 1971, Halifax; player Halifax Town 1990–91, Oldham Athletic 1991– . *Address*: Oldham Athletic FC, Boundary Park, Oldham, Lancs. OL1 2PA.

FLEMING, Curtis: footballer; b. 8 October 1968, Manchester; player St Patrick's (Ireland) 1987–91, Middlesbrough 91– ; 1 Ireland U-21 cap. *Address*: Middlesbrough FC, Ayresome Park, Middlesbrough, Cleveland TS1 4PB.

FLEMING, Gary: footballer; b. 17 February 1967, Derry, NI; player Nottingham Forest 1984–88, Manchester City 1989, Barnsley 1989– ; over 14 NI caps. *Address*: Barnsley FC, Oakwell Ground, Barnsley, S. Yorks. S71 1ET.

FLEMING, Gerard: karate player (U-80kg); b. 14 July 1959, Glasgow; m. Marion Fleming; 1 s.; Scottish champ. 1981, 83, 86, 88, 91, English open champ. 1988, 89; Scotland debut 1980; Commonwealth Champs. silver medal 1984; GB debut 1981; European Champs. team gold medals 1983, 84, 87, individ. bronze 1985; World Champs. team gold medals 1984, 86, 88. *Leisure interests*: tennis, cycling, football, running, swimming. *Address*: 2 Linacre Drive, Meadowlea Estate, Sandyhills, Glasgow G32 0EH.

FLEMING, Matthew Valentine: cricketer; b. 12 December 1964, Macclesfield; m. Caroline Fleming 1989; player Kent 1988– . *Address*: Kent CCC, St Lawrence Ground, Canterbury CT1 3NZ.

FLETCHER, Graham: equestrianist (show jumping); b. 9 January 1951; m. Karen Fletcher; 3 d.; GB debut 1971, Olympic squad 1976, team silver medal 1980. *Address*: c/o Brit. Horse Soc., Brit. Equestrian Centre, Stoneleigh Park, Kenilworth, Warks. CV8 2LR.

FLETCHER, Ian: cricketer; b. 31 August 1971, Sawbridgeworth; player Somerset 1991– ; rep. Herts. NatWest Trophy 1990, Combined Univ. Benson and Hedges Cup 1991. *Address*: Somerset CCC, The County Ground, Taunton, Somerset TA1 1JT.

FLETCHER, Michael: Rugby League footballer; b. 14 April 1967, Hull; player Hull Kingston Rovers 1985– ; GB U-21 debut v. France 1988. *Address*: Hull Kingston Rovers RLFC, Craven Park, Preston Rd, Hull HU9 5HE.

FLETCHER, Paul: Rugby League footballer; b. 26 January 1962, Salford; player Hull, Castleford 1990–93, Oldham 93– . *Address*: Oldham RLFC, The Pavilion, Watersheddings, Oldham OL4 2PB.

FLETCHER, Paul: Rugby League footballer; b. 17 March 1970, Hull; player Eureka ARLFC, Hull Kingston Rovers 1987– . *Address*: Hull Kingston Rovers RLFC, Craven Park, Preston Rd, Hull HU9 5HE.

FLINT, Darren Peter John: cricketer; b. 14 June 1970; player Hants. 1993– . *Address*: Hants. CCC, County Cricket Ground, Northlands Rd, Southampton SO9 2TY.

FLITCROFT, Gary: footballer; b. 6 November 1972, Bolton; player Manchester City 1991– . *Address*: Manchester City FC, Maine Rd, Moss Side, Manchester M14 7WN.

FLOWERS, Timothy: footballer; b. 3 February 1967, Kenilworth; player Wolverhampton Wanderers 1984–86, Southampton 86–93, Blackburn Rovers 93– ; 3 England U-21 caps, snr debut v. Brazil, US Cup 1993. *Address*: Blackburn Rovers FC, Ewood Park, Blackburn, Lancs. BB2 4JF.

FLYNN, Adrian: Rugby League footballer; b. 9 September 1974; player Wakefield Trinity 1992– . *Address*: Wakefield Trinity RLFC, 171 Doncaster Rd, Belle Vue, Wakefield WF1 5EZ.

FLYNN, Sean: footballer; b. 13 March 1968, Birmingham; player Coventry City 1991– . *Address*: Coventry City FC, Highfield Rd Stadium, King Richard St, Coventry CV2 4FW.

FOGARTY, Carl George: motorcyclist; b. 1 July 1966, Blackburn; m. Michaela Fogarty 1991; 1 d.; F1 world champ. 1988–90, world endurance champ. 1992; winner Isle of Man snr TT, FI TT 1990, Le Mans 24-hour race 1992. *Leisure interests*: running, squash, moto-cross, jet skiing. *Address*: Bolton Rd, Blackburn, Lancs. BB1 3PX.

FOGERTY, Adam: Rugby League footballer; b. 6 March 1969; player Halifax 1991–93, St Helens 93– . *Address*: St Helens RLFC, Dunriding Lane, St Helens, Merseyside WA10 4AD.

FOGERTY, Jason: Rugby League footballer; b. 4 October 1967; player Huddersfield 1992–93, Oldham 93– . *Address*: Oldham RLFC, The Pavilion, Watersheddings, Oldham OL4 2PB.

FOGGO, Samantha Jane: swimmer; b. 14 January 1974, Newcastle-upon-Tyne; GB girls' 800m freestyle jnr champ. 1989, snr women's champ. 1991; England debut 1989; GB debut 1991, Olympic squad 1992 (women's 400m and 800m freestyle). *Leisure interests*: cycling, weight training, music, reading, drawing. *Address*: c/o ASA, Harold Fern House, Derby Square, Loughborough, Leics. LE11 0AL.

FOLLAND, Nicholas Arthur: cricketer; b. 17 September 1963, Bristol; m. Diane Folland 1992; player Devon 1980–92 (capt. 1992), Somerset 92– ; rep. Minor Counties 1987–92 (capt. v. Pakistan 1992); maiden 1st-class 100 v. Sussex 1993. *Leisure interests*: all sport, film, the coastline of Devon, coaching rugby/cricket. *Address*: Somerset CCC, The County Ground, Taunton, Somerset TA1 1JT.

FORBER, Paul: Rugby League footballer; b. 29 April 1964, St Helens; player St Helens, Salford 1993– ; with St Helens: winners Premiership 1985, John Player Special Trophy 1988. *Address*: Salford RLFC, The Willows, Willows Rd, Weaste, Salford M5 2ST.

FORD, Michael: footballer; b. 9 February 1966, Bristol; player Cardiff City 1984–88, Oxford Utd 88– . *Address*: Oxford Utd FC, Manor Ground, London Rd, Headington, Oxford OX3 7RS.

FORD, Mike: Rugby League footballer; b. 18 November 1965, Oldham; player Wigan, Leigh, Oldham, Castleford 1991– ; with Castleford: winners Regal Trophy 1994; GB debut v. France 1993. *Address*: Castleford RLFC, Wheldon Rd, Castleford WF10 2SD.

FORD, Philip: Rugby League footballer; b. 16 March 1961, Cardiff; player Warrington, Wigan, Bradford Northern, Leeds, Salford 1992– ; Wales debut v. England 1984; GB debut v. France 1985. *Address*: Salford RLFC, The Willows, Willows Rd, Weaste, Salford M5 2ST.

FORD, Stephen Paul: Rugby Union footballer; b. 15 August 1965, Cardiff; player Cardiff; Wales and Five Nations debut v.

Ireland 1990, tours Canada (Wales B) 1989, Namibia 1990, Aus. 1991; holds Welsh try-scoring record (7 for Wales B v. Saskatchewan 1989); 1st RU player to be banned for having RL trial. *Address*: Cardiff RFC, Cardiff Arms Park, Westgate St, Cardiff CF1 1JA.

FORD, Tony: footballer; b. 14 May 1959, Grimsby; player Grimsby Town 1977–86, Stoke City 86–89, W. Bromwich Albion 89–91, Grimsby Town 91– ; with Grimsby Town: 3rd Div. champs. 1979/80. *Address*: Grimsby Town FC, Blundell Park, Cleethorpes, S. Humberside DN35 7PY.

FORDHAM, Alan: cricketer; b. 9 November 1964, Bedford; player Northants. 1986– , tour Natal 1992; Christians in Sport tour India 1990, MCC tour Leeward Islands 1992. *Address*: Northants. CCC, County Cricket Ground, Wantage Rd, Northampton NN1 4TJ.

FORSHAW, Mike: Rugby League footballer; b. 5 January 1970, Wigan; player Wigan 1987–93, Wakefield Trinity 93– ; GB U-21 debut v. France 1991. *Address*: Wakefield Trinity RLFC, 171 Doncaster Rd, Belle Vue, Wakefield WF1 5EZ.

FORSTER, Mark: Rugby League footballer; b. 25 November 1964, Warrington; player Woolston ARLFC, Warrington 1981– ; with Warrington: winners Regal Trophy 1991; GB debut v. France 1987. *Address*: Warrington RLFC, Wilderspool Stadium, Wilderspool Causeway, Warrington WA4 6PY.

FOSTER, Andrew Lee: tennis player; b. 16 March 1972, Stoke-on-Trent; rep. Staffs.; winner Stella Artois Jnr Champs. 1990; youngest Brit. player to reach last 16 at Wimbledon 1993. *Leisure interests*: golf. *Address*: c/o LTA, The Queen's Club, W. Kensington, London W14 9EG.

FOSTER, Colin: footballer; b. 16 July 1964, Chislehurst; player Leyton Orient 1982–87, Nottingham Forest 87–89, W. Ham Utd 89– . *Address*: W. Ham Utd FC, Boleyn Ground, Green St, Upton Park, London E13 9AZ.

FOSTER, Frankie: boxer; b. 25 May 1968; prof. debut 1988; titles won: Northern super-featherweight champ. 1990, 92; over 10 prof. wins. *Address*: c/o Tommy Conroy, 144 High St E., Sunderland, Tyne and Wear SR1 2BL.

FOSTER, Mark Andrew: swimmer; b. 12 May 1970, Billericay; GB 50m butterfly champ. 1993; Commonwealth Games 4 x 100m freestyle relay bronze medal 1986, 50m freestyle bronze 1990; European Champs. 4 x 100m medley relay bronze medal 1993; World Cup 50m butterfly gold and 50m freestyle silver medals 1992; World Short-Course Champs. 50m freestyle gold, 4 x 100m medley relay bronze medals 1993; Olympic squad 1988, 92; UK and Commonwealth 50m freestyle and 50m butterly record-holder. *Leisure interests*: all sport, cars, music. *Address*: c/o ASA, Harold Fern House, Derby Square, Loughborough, Leics. LE11 0AL.

FOSTER, Michael: cricketer; b. 17 September 1972, Leeds; player Yorks. 1993– ; England U-19 tour Pakistan 1991/92. *Address*: Yorks. CCC, Headingley Cricket Ground, Leeds LS6 3BU.

FOTHERGILL, Andrew Robert: cricketer; b. 10 February 1962, Newcastle-upon-Tyne; player Durham 1992– . *Address*: Durham CCC, County Ground, Riverside, Chester-le-Street, Co. Durham DH3 3QR.

FOULDS, Neal Robert: snooker player; b. 13 July 1963, Perivale; prof. debut 1983, winner Scottish Masters 1992. *Address*: c/o World Prof. Billiards and Snooker Assoc., 27 Oakfield Rd, Clifton, Bristol BS8 2AT.

FOWKE, Robert: Rugby Union footballer; b. 15 June 1963; player Spartans, Gloucester. *Address*: Gloucester RUFC, Kingsholm, Worcester St, Gloucester GL3 3AX.

FOWLER, David George William: hockey player; b. 14 January 1970, Glasgow; player Kelburne 1987– , winners Scottish Cup 1992, Scottish League champs. 1990, 91, 92; Scotland U-21 debut 1989, U-21 indoor debut 1990, snr outdoor and indoor debuts 1992. *Leisure interests*: football, squash, badminton, TV, music. *Address*: Kelburne HC, Kelburne CC, Whitehaugh, Greenlaw Drive, Paisley.

FOWLER, Graeme: cricketer; b. 20 April 1957, Accrington; player Lancs. 1979–92, Durham 93– ; 21 Tests, debut 1982, 26 1-day ints, tours Aus./NZ 1982/83, NZ/Pakistan 1983/84, India/Aus. 1984/85. *Address*: Durham CCC, County Ground, Riverside, Chester-le-Street, Co. Durham DH3 3QR.

FOX, David Clifford: Rugby Union footballer; b. 4 December 1959, Swansea; m. Sian Fox; 1 s., 1 d.; player Bonymaen, Llanelli 1983– ; with Llanelli: winners Welsh Cup 1985, 88, 91, 92, 93, Welsh League champs. 1992/93. *Address*: Llanelli RFC, Stradey Park, Llanelli, Dyfed.

FOX, Deryck: Rugby League footballer; b. 17 September 1964, Dewsbury; player St John Fisher ARLFC, Featherstone Rovers, Bradford Northern 1992– ; rep. Yorks.; GB debut v. France 1985. *Address*: Bradford Northern RLFC, Odsal Stadium, Bradford BD6 1BS.

FOX, Richard Munro, MBE: canoeist; b. 5 June 1960, Winsford, Cheshire; m. Myriam Jérusalmi; World Champs. KI slalom individ. gold medals 1981, 83, 85, 89, 93; team gold 1979, 81, 83, 87, 93; World Cup K1 slalom gold medals 1988, 89, 91. *Address*: c/o Brit. Canoe Union, John Dudderidge House, Adbolton Lane, W. Bridgford, Nottingham NG2 5AS.

FOX, Ruel: footballer; b. 14 January 1968, Ipswich; player Norwich City 1986–94, Newcastle Utd 94– . *Address:* Newcastle Utd FC, St James' Park, Newcastle-upon-Tyne, Tyne & Wear NE1 4ST.

FRAIL, Stephen: footballer; b. 10 August 1969, Glasgow; player Dundee 1985– . *Address:* Dundee FC, Dens Park, Dundee DD3 7JY.

FRAME, Derek George: basketball player; b. 28 December 1962, Musselburgh; m. Deborah Lee Frame 1992; 2 s.; player Cavalry Park 1977–80, Murray Int. Metals 80–82, Merrimack College 82–86, Murray Int. Metals/Livingston 86–89, City of Edinburgh 89– ; Scotland debut 1980, European Champs. squad 1985, 89, 91, 93; GB squad, World Student Games 1987, Olympic squad 1984, 88. *Leisure interests:* golf, watching other sports, walking the dog. *Address:* c/o Scottish Basketball Assoc., Caledonia House, S. Gyle, Edinburgh EH12 9DQ.

FRANCIS, Gerald: football manager; b. 6 December 1951, Chiswick; player Queens Park Rangers 1969–79, Crystal Palace 79–81, Queens Park Rangers 81–82, Coventry City 82–83, Exeter City 83–84, Cardiff City 1984, Swansea City 1984, Portsmouth 1984–85, Bristol Rovers 85–87; 6 England U-23 caps, 12 full England caps; manager Bristol Rovers 1987–91, Queens Park Rangers 91– ; with Bristol Rovers: 3rd Div. champs. 1989/90. *Address:* Queens Park Rangers FC, Rangers Stadium, S. Africa Rd, London W12 7PA.

FRANCIS, Janice Pauline: karate player (U-60kg/+60kg); b. 24 September 1964, London; English women's team champ. 1991, 92; GB women's team champ. 1987–90, 92; GB debut 1990; European Champs. team silver and individ. bronze medals 1991, team open ippon shobu gold 1992, team silver 1993; World Champs. squad 1990, team gold medal 1992; World Cup team gold medal 1992, silver 1993; winner Dutch Open, English Open 1991. *Publications:* contributor to *Martial Arts Today. Leisure interests:* black music, circuit training, learning French. *Address:* 21 Emerald Gardens, Dagenham, Essex RM8 1LH.

FRANCIS, Trevor: football manager; b. 19 April 1954, Plymouth; player Birmingham City 1971–79, Nottingham Forest 79–81, Manchester City 81–82, Sampdoria (Italy), Atlanta, Rangers 1987–88, Queens Park Rangers 88–90, Sheffield Wednesday 90–92; with Nottingham Forest: winners European Cup 1979, 80; with Rangers: winners Scottish League Cup 1988; with Sheffield Wednesday: winners League Cup 1991; 5 England U-23 caps, snr debut v. Holland 1977, 52 caps; manager Sheffield Wednesday 1991– . *Address:* Sheffield Wednesday FC, Hillsborough, Sheffield, S. Yorks. S6 1SW.

FRASER, Alastair Gregory James: cricketer; b. 17 October 1967, Edgware; player Middx 1986–90, Essex 91–93; with Essex: county champs. 1991, 92; England YC tour Sri Lanka 1987. *Address:* Essex CCC, County Cricket Ground, New Writtle St, Chelmsford DM2 0PG.

FRASER, Angus Robert Charles: cricketer; b. 8 August 1965, Billinge; player Middx 1984– , county champs. 1985, 90, 93, Sunday League champs. 1992; Test debut 1989, tours India/WI 1989/90, Aus. 1990/91, WI 1994. *Address:* Middx CCC, Lord's Cricket Ground, London NW8 8QN.

FRASER, Louise: athlete; b. 10 October 1970, Manchester; European U-23 Champs. women's 400m hurdles gold medal 1992. *Address:* c/o Brit. Athletic Fed., 225A Bristol Rd, Edgbaston, Birmingham B5 7UB.

FRASER, Susan Barbara: hockey player; b. 15 July 1966, Aberdeen; player Bon Accord, Glasgow Western; Scotland U-16,

U-18, U-21 and snr int., top Scotland goal-scorer European Cup 1991; GB squad, Olympic bronze medallist 1992. *Leisure interests*: film, cooking, racket sports, golf, music, eating out. *Address*: Willowburn, Pitroddie, Perth.

FRASER, Wendy Katrina: hockey player; b. 23 April 1963, Bukoba, Tanzania; player Glasgow Western 1980– , Scottish League champs. 1982–93; Scotland U-23 debut 1981, Scotland B debut 1983, snr debut 1984, over 85 caps; GB debut 1985, Olympic squad 1988, bronze medallist 1992. *Leisure interests*: hockey coaching, skiing, dining out. *Address:* 1443 Paisley Rd W., Bellahouston, Glasgow G52 1SX.

FREELAND, Richard John: hockey player; b. 16 January 1971, Aberdeen; player Gordonians; Scotland U-21 and snr debuts 1988; rep. GB Students 1991, 92; Scottish Young Player of the Year 1990. *Leisure interests*: running, cycling, golf, music, guitar-playing. *Address*: Gordonians HC, Seafield Club, 12 Seafield Rd, Aberdeen.

FRENCH, Terence James: boxer; b. 15 January 1967, Newcastle; m. Dawn French 1985; 1 s., 1 d.; prof. debut 1988; titles won: Northern light-heavyweight 1990; over 14 prof. wins. *Leisure interests*: squash, running. *Address*: c/o Tommy Conroy, 144 High St E., Sunderland, Tyne and Wear SR1 2BL.

FRITH, Stanley: crown green bowler; b. 7 April 1938, Northwich; m. Wendy Frith 1961; 2 d.; rep. Cheshire 1961– ; All England champ. 1983, 92; winner Waterloo Handicap 1983, Champion of Champions 1983, Crown King 1986, 87, 93, Spring Waterloo 1993; only bowler to have won the Grand Slam of All England, Waterloo and Champion of Champions in same year. *Publications*: `How to Practise a Green' in *Crown Green Manual*, 1984. *Leisure interests*: swimming, gardening, grandchildren. *Address*: 41 Green Park, Weaverham, Northwich, Cheshire CW8 3EH.

FROGGATT, Stephen: footballer; b. 9 March 1973, Lincoln; player Aston Villa 1991– . *Address*: Aston Villa FC, Villa Park, Trinity Rd, Birmingham B6 6HE.

FROST, James Douglas: jockey (NH); b. 31 July 1958, Torbay; m. Nicola Frost 1986; 2 s.; winner Grand National 1989 (Little Polveir), Champion Hurdle 1991 (Morley Street). *Leisure interests*: water skiing, breeding and showing cattle. *Address*: c/o BHB, 42 Portman Square, London W1H 0EN.

FROST, Mark: cricketer; b. 21 October 1962, Barking; m. Janet Frost 1991; player Staffs. 1986–87, Surrey 88–89, Glamorgan 90–93; with Glamorgan: tours Trinidad 1990, Zimbabwe 1991, SA 1993. *Leisure interests*: Christians in Sport, hill-walking, all music. *Address*: Glamorgan CCC, Sophia Gardens, Cardiff CF1 9XR.

FRY, Barry: football manager; b. 7 April 1945, Bedford; player Bolton Wanderers 1964–65, Luton Town 1965, Leyton Orient 1966, 67; manager Maidstone Utd 1985, Barnet 1986–93, Southend Utd 1993, Birmingham City 1993– . *Address*: Birmingham City FC, St Andrews Ground, Birmingham B9 4NH.

FRY, Laura Barbara Mansel: equestrianist (dressage); b. 13 January 1967, Totnes; m. Simon Fry 1991; GP champ. 1992 (youngest ever); GB debut 1991; European Champs. team silver medal 1993 (Quarryman); Olympic squad 1992. *Publications*: *Discovering Dressage*, 1993. *Leisure interests*: riding and training horses, teaching dressage, spectating at equestrian events. *Address*: 89 Pilgrims Way W., Otford, Sevenoaks, Kent TN14 5JL.

FULFORD, Robert Ian: croquet player; b. 26 August 1969, Colchester; GB open champ. 1991, 92, doubles champ. 1990–93; world champ. 1990, 92, invitational champ. 1992, 93; GB debut and winners

MacRobertson Int. Shield 1990; winner
Brit. Masters 1989, NZ Open, Canadian
Open, French Open 1993; achieved record
43 consecutive wins 1993. *Leisure interests*:
bridge, chess, cinema, travel. *Address*:
Ramparts Farm, Bakers Lane, Colchester
CO4 5BB.

FULTON, David Paul: cricketer; b. 15
November 1971, Lewisham; player Kent
1992– . *Address*: Kent CCC, St Lawrence
Ground, Canterbury CT1 3NZ.

FULTON, Stephen: footballer; b. 10
August 1970, Greenock; player Celtic
1986–93, Bolton Wanderers 93– ; Scotland
U-21 int. *Address*: Bolton Wanderers FC,
Burnden Park, Manchester Rd, Bolton,
Lancs. BL3 2QR.

FURLONG, Paul: footballer; b. 1 October
1968, Wood Green; player Coventry City
1991–92, Watford 92– . *Address*: Watford
FC, Vicarage Rd Stadium, Watford, Herts.
WD1 8ER.

FURY, Sarah Jayne: squash player; b. 24
August 1970, Swansea; player Swansea;
Welsh ladies' champ. 1989–92; Wales U-16
and U-19 debuts 1983, snr debut 1985;
European Champs. squad 1987, 88, 90, 91,
World Champs. squad 1985, 87, 89
(youngest-ever player 1985). *Leisure inter-
ests*: tennis, surfing, holidays, keeping fit,
cooking. *Address*: Swansea Lawn Tennis
and Squash Rackets Club, King George V
Playing Fields, Mumbles Rd, Swansea, W.
Glamorgan.

FUTCHER, Paul: footballer; b. 25
September 1956, Chester; player Chester
City 1972–74, Luton Town 74–78,
Manchester City 78–80, Oldham Athletic
80–83, Derby County 83–84, Barnsley
84–90, Halifax Town 90–91, Grimsby Town
91– ; 11 England U-21 caps. *Address*:
Grimsby Town FC, Blundell Park,
Cleethorpes, S. Humberside DN35 7PY.

GABBIADINI, Marco: footballer; b. 20
January 1968, Nottingham; player York
City 1985–87, Sunderland 87–91, Crystal
Palace 91–92, Derby County 92– ; with
Sunderland: 3rd Div. champs. 1987/88; 2
England U-21 caps. *Address*: Derby County
FC, The Baseball Ground, Shaftesbury
Crescent, Derby DE3 8NB.

GAGE, Kevin: footballer; b. 21 April 1964,
Chiswick; player Wimbledon 1982–87,
Aston Villa 87–91, Sheffield Utd 91– ;
with Wimbledon: 4th Div. champs.
1982/83. *Address*: Sheffield Utd FC,
Bramall Lane, Sheffield, S. Yorks S2 4SU.

GALE, Anthony: footballer; b. 19
November 1959, Westminster; player
Fulham 1977–84, W. Ham Utd 84– ; 1
England U-21 cap. *Address*: W. Ham Utd
FC, Boleyn Ground, Green St, Upton Park,
London E13 9AZ.

GALE, Shaun: footballer; b. 8 October
1969, Reading; player Portsmouth 1988– .
Address: Portsmouth FC, Fratton Park,
Frogmore Rd, Portsmouth PO4 8RA.

GALLACHER, Bernard: golfer; b. 9
February 1949, Bathgate; m. Lesley
Gallacher; 1 s., 2 d.; Scottish open amateur
strokeplay champ. 1967; Scotland debut
1967; prof. debut 1967; Scottish prof.
champ. 1971, 73, 74, 77; Ryder Cup team
1969–83, non-playing capt. 1991, 93;
winner Spanish Open 1977, French Open
1979, Jersey Open 1982, 84. *Address*: c/o
PGA European Tour, Wentworth Club,
Wentworth Drive, Virginia Water, Surrey
GU25 4LS.

GALLACHER, Kevin: footballer; b. 23
November 1966, Clydebank; player
Dundee Utd 1983–89, Coventry City 89–93,
Blackburn Rovers 93– ; 7 Scotland U-21
caps, over 17 full Scotland caps. *Address*:
Blackburn Rovers FC, Ewood Park,
Blackburn, Lancs. BB2 4JF.

GALLOWAY, Michael: footballer; b. 30 May 1965, Oswestry; player Mansfield Town 1983–86, Halifax Town 86–87, Heart of Midlothian 87–89, Celtic 89– ; 1 Scotland cap. *Address*: Celtic FC, Celtic Park, 95 Kerrydale St, Glasgow G40 3RE.

GAMSON, Mark Edward: Rugby League footballer; b. 17 August 1965, Leeds; player Crigglestone ARLFC, Sheffield Eagles 1984– . *Address*: Sheffield Eagles RLFC, Stadium Corner, 824 Attercliffe Rd, Sheffield S9 3RS.

GANNON, John: footballer; b. 18 December 1966, Wimbledon; player Wimbledon 1984–89, Sheffield Utd 89– ; with Wimbledon: winners FA Cup 1988. *Address*: Sheffield Utd FC, Bramall Lane, Sheffield, S. Yorks S2 4SU.

GARDNER, James: footballer; b. 27 September 1967, Dunfermline; player Queen's Park 1986–88, Motherwell 88– . *Address*: Motherwell FC, Fir Park, Fir Park St, Motherwell ML1 2QN.

GARFORTH, Darren James: Rugby Union footballer; b. 9 April 1966, Coventry; player Coventry Saracens 1984–87, Nuneaton 87–90, Leicester 90– ; with Leicester: winners Pilkington Cup 1993; rep. Midland Div. 1992– ; England A tour Canada 1993. *Leisure interests*: training, squash, swimming. *Address*: Leicester FC, Welford Rd, Leicester LE2 7LF.

GARNER, Simon: footballer; b. 23 November 1959, Boston; player Blackburn Rovers 1977–92, W. Bromwich Albion 92– . *Address*: W. Bromwich Albion FC, The Hawthorns, W. Bromwich B71 4LF.

GARNER, Tim John: squash player; b. 24 April 1970, Crawley; player Lingfield 1984– ; rep. Sussex 1988– ; GB student champ. 1990; winner Ipoh Open 1991, Bern Open 1993. *Leisure interests*: golf, soccer, hockey, cricket, music, films, travel. *Address*: Shawlands Farm, Newchapel Rd, Lingfield, Surrey RH76 6BL.

GARNETT, Shaun: footballer; b. 22 November 1969, Wallasey; player Tranmere Rovers 1988– . *Address*: Tranmere Rovers FC, Prenton Park, Prenton Rd West, Birkenhead, Merseyside L42 9PN.

GARNHAM, Michael Anthony: cricketer; b. 20 August 1960, Johannesburg, SA; m. Lorraine Garnham 1984; 2 d.; player Glos. 1979, Leics. 1980–85, Essex 89– ; with Essex: county champs. 1991, 92; England Schools tour India 1977/78, England YC tour Aus. 1979. *Address*: Essex CCC, County Cricket Ground, New Writtle St, Chelmsford DM2 0PG.

GARSIDE, Alexandra Jane: real tennis player; b. 7 October 1959, Aldershot; m. Ian Norman Garside 1990; 1 s.; Scottish ladies' open doubles champ. 1989; GB ladies' open doubles champ. 1987–93; US ladies' open doubles champ. 1989; French ladies' open doubles champ. 1989, 90; Aus. ladies' open doubles champ. 1991; world ladies' doubles champ. 1989, 91. *Leisure interests*: squash, aerobics, swimming, cooking, gardening. *Address*: White Lee Cottage, 31 Victoria Ave, Hayling Island, Hants. PO11 9AJ.

GASCOIGNE, Paul John: footballer; b. 27 May 1967, Gateshead; player Newcastle Utd 1985–88, Tottenham Hotspur 88–92, Lazio (Italy) 92– ; with Tottenham Hotspur: winners FA Cup 1991; 13 England U-21 caps, over 26 full England caps; BBC Sports Personality of the Year 1990. *Address*: c/o PFA, 2 Oxford Court, Bishopsgate, Manchester M2 3WQ.

GASELEE, Nicholas Auriol: racehorse trainer; b. 30 January 1939, London; m. Judith Mary Gaselee 1966; 1 s., 1 d.; 1st licence 1977; winner Grand National (Party Politics) 1992. *Leisure interests*: fishing, coursing. *Address*: Saxon Cottage, Upper Lambourn, Newbury, Berks. RG16 7QN.

GATTING, Michael William, OBE: cricketer; b. 6 June 1957, Kingsbury, Middx; m. Elaine Elizabeth Gatting 1980; 2 s.; player Middx 1975– (capt. 83–), county champs. 1976, 77, 80, 82, 85, 90, 93, Sunday League champs. 1992; Test debut 1977, tours NZ/Pakistan 1977/78, WI 1980/81, India/Sri Lanka 1981/82, NZ/Pakistan 1983/84, India/Aus. 1984/85, WI 1985/86, Aus. 1986/87, India/Pakistan/Aus./NZ (World Cup) 1987/88, India/Sri Lanka 1992/93; England vice-capt. 1984–86, capt. 86–88; has scored 1000 runs in season 12 times, 2000 runs in season 3 times. *Publications: Limited Overs*, 1986, *Triumph in Australia*, 1987, *Leading from the Front*, 1988. *Leisure interests*: golf, football, squash, swimming, tennis. *Address*: Middx CCC, Lord's Cricket Ground, London NW8 8QN.

GATTING, Stephen: footballer; b. 29 May 1959, Willesden; player Arsenal 1978–81, Brighton and Hove Albion 81–91, Charlton Athletic 91– . *Address*: Charlton Athletic FC, The Valley, Floyd Rd, London SE7 8BL.

GATTY SAUNT, Sarah: water skier; b. 12 June 1976, Wimbledon; GB girls' dauphin slalom, tricks, jump and overall champ. 1990, jnr slalom and overall champ. 1991, 92; GB jnr debut 1989; European Jnr Champs. girls' dauphin slalom and overall silver, team gold medals 1990, jnr slalom and team gold 1992; European U-21 Champs. ladies' slalom and team gold medals 1992; European Youth Cup team gold medal 1992. *Leisure interests*: skiing, riding, tennis. *Address*: Fern Cottage, Tandridge Lane, Tandridge, Surrey RH8 9NY.

GAULT, Michael: pistol shooter; b. 2 May 1954, Sheffield; m. Janet Gault 1974; 1 s., 2 d.; GB air pistol champ. 1992, 94, .22 long-range and short-range champ. 1991, 93, free pistol champ. 1991, 93, standard pistol champ. 1993; England debut 1993; GB debut 1990, World Champs. squad 1990,

Mayleigh Cup team 1991–93; World Cup free pistol bronze medal 1991. *Leisure interests*: home and family. *Address*: c/o Nat. Small-Bore Rifle Assoc., Lord Roberts House, Bisley Camp, Brookwood, Woking, Surrey GU24 0NP.

GAVIN, Patrick: footballer; b. 5 June 1967, Hammersmith; player Gillingham 1989, Leicester City 1989–91, Peterborough Utd 91–93, Wigan Athletic 93– . *Address*: Wigan Athletic FC, Springfield Park, Wigan WN6 7BA.

GAY, Richard: Rugby League footballer; b. 9 March 1969, Hull; player Hull 1989– , winners Premiership 1991. *Address*: Hull RLFC, The Boulevard Ground, Airlie St, Hull HU3 3JD.

GAYLE, Brian: footballer; b. 6 March 1965, Kingston; player Wimbledon 1984–88, Manchester City 88–90, Ipswich Town 90–91, Sheffield Utd 91– . *Address*: Sheffield Utd FC, Bramall Lane, Sheffield, S. Yorks S2 4SU.

GAYLE, John: footballer; b. 30 July 1964, Bromsgrove; player Wimbledon 1989–90, Birmingham City 90–93, Coventry City 93– . *Address*: Coventry City FC, Highfield Rd Stadium, King Richard St, Coventry CV2 4FW.

GAYLE, Marcus Anthony: footballer; b. 27 September 1970, Hammersmith; player Brentford 1988– ; 1 England Youth cap. *Leisure interests*: socializing, tennis. *Address*: Brentford FC, Griffin Park, Braemar Rd, Brentford, Middx TW8 0NT.

GAYNOR, Thomas: footballer; b. 29 January 1963, Limerick, Ireland; player Limerick City, Doncaster Rovers 1986–87, Nottingham Forest 87– ; with Nottingham Forest: winners League Cup 1989. *Address*: Nottingham Forest FC, City Ground, Nottingham NG2 5FJ.

GAYWOOD, Linzi: water polo player; b. 4 December 1961, Sheffield; m. Nicholas Richard Gaywood 1990; 1 d.; player City of Sheffield; rep. N.E. Counties 1986– ; GB debut 1985, European Champs. squad 1987, 91, 93, World Champs. squad 1986; rep. Wales swimming 1975–83, Commonwealth Games squad 1978, GB swimming 1978–93. *Leisure interests:* playing with my daughter, squash, mixed hockey. *Address:* 4 Stenton Rd, Greenhill, Sheffield S8 7RN.

GEAVES, Fiona Jane: squash player; b. 6 December 1967, Gloucester; player Courtlands; Glos. girls' U-19 champ. 1983, 84, ladies' champ. 1991; GB ladies' U-23 open champ. 1988; England U-19 debut 1984, snr debut 1988; European Champs. team gold medals 1991, 92, 94; winner Zambian Open 1986, Berlin Open 1987, Dutch Open 1989. *Leisure interests:* Liverpool FC, golf, bungee jumping, photography, cinema, reading, music, eating out. *Address:* 49 Spencer Close, Hucclecote, Gloucester GL3 3EA.

GEE, Mark: biathlete; b. 21 February 1972, Southend; GB jnr champ. 1991; GB jnr debut 1990, World Jnr Champs. squad 1991, 92, snr debut 1993, World Cup squad 1992/93. *Leisure interests:* mountain biking, snowboarding, travel. *Address:* 205 Ambleside Drive, Southend-on-Sea SS1 2UE.

GEMMILL, Scot: footballer; b. 2 January 1971, Paisley; player Nottingham Forest 1988– ; 4 Scotland U-21 caps. *Address:* Nottingham Forest FC, City Ground, Nottingham NG2 5FJ.

GEOGHEGAN, Simon Patrick: Rugby Union footballer; b. 1 September 1968, Barnet; player London Irish; Ireland U-25 debut v. Spain 1990, Ireland B debut v. Argentina 1990, snr and Five Nations debut v. France 1991, tour Namibia 1991. *Address:* London Irish RUFC, The Avenue, Sunbury-on-Thames, Middx TW16 5EQ.

GIBBS, Ian Scott: Rugby Union footballer; b. 23 January 1971, Bridgend; player Pencoed (capt. 1989/90), Bridgend, Neath, Swansea 1992– ; with Swansea: Welsh League champs. 1991/92; Wales B debut v. The Netherlands 1990, snr and Five Nations debut v. England 1991, tour Aus. 1991; Brit. Lions tour NZ 1993. *Address:* Swansea RFC, St Helens, Swansea SA2 0AR.

GIBBS, Nigel: footballer; b. 20 November 1965, St Albans; player Watford 1983– ; 5 England U-21 caps. *Address:* Watford FC, Vicarage Rd Stadium, Watford, Herts. WD1 8ER.

GIBSON, Carl: Rugby League footballer; b. 23 April 1963, Batley; player Batley, Leeds 1986–93, Featherstone Rovers 93– ; GB debut v. France 1985, Brit. Lions tour Aus./NZ/Papua New Guinea 1988. *Address:* Featherstone Rovers RLFC, The Croft, Batley Rd, W. Ardsley, Wakefield WF3 1DX.

GIBSON, Sally: hockey player; b. 7 December 1969; player Trojans; England debut 1993; GB debut and Champions Trophy squad 1993. *Address:* c/o All England Women's Hockey Assoc., 51 High St, Shrewsbury SY1 1ST.

GIBSON, Terence: footballer; b. 23 December 1962, Walthamstow; player Tottenham Hotspur 1980–83, Coventry City 83–86, Manchester Utd 86–87, Wimbledon 87– ; with Wimbledon: winners FA Cup 1988; 11 England U-21 caps. *Address:* Wimbledon FC, Selhurst Park, London SE25 6PY.

GIBSON, Walter: Rugby League footballer; b. 5 April 1967, Aus.; player Newcastle Knights, Huddersfield, Oldham 1992– . *Address:* Oldham RLFC, The Pavilion, Watersheddings, Oldham OL4 2PB.

GIDDINS, Edward Simon Hunter: cricketer; b. 20 July 1971, Eastbourne; player Sussex 1991– . *Leisure interests*: golf, fashion, reading, clubbing, travel. *Address*: Sussex CCC, County Ground, Eaton Rd, Hove, E. Sussex BN3 3AN.

GIFFORD, Joshua Thomas, MBE: racehorse trainer; b. 3 August 1941, Huntingdon; m. Althea Roger-Smith 1969; 1 s., 1 d.; as jockey: winner Mackeson Gold Cup 1967 (Charlie Worcester), Whitbread Gold Cup 1969 (Larbawn), champ. NH jockey 1962/63, 63/64, 66/67, 67/68; rode 122 winners in season 1966/67; as trainer: 1st licence 1970; winner Grand National 1981 (Aldaniti), Whitbread Gold Cup 1982 (Shady Deal), Mackeson Gold Cup 1993 (Bradbury Star). *Address*: c/o BHB, 42 Portman Square, London W1H 0EN.

GIGGS, Ryan: footballer; b. 29 November 1973, Cardiff; player Manchester Utd 1990– , League champs. 1992/93; 1 Wales U-21 cap, over 8 full Wales caps; PFA Young Player of the Year 1992, 93. *Address*: Manchester Utd FC, Old Trafford, Manchester M16 0RA.

GILBERT, David: footballer; b. 22 June 1963, Lincoln; player Lincoln City 1981–82, Scunthorpe Utd 1982, Northampton Town 1986–89, Grimsby Town 89– ; with Northampton Town: 4th Div. champs. 1986/87. *Address*: Grimsby Town FC, Blundell Park, Cleethorpes, S. Humberside DN35 7PY.

GILDART, Ian: Rugby League footballer; b. 14 October 1969, Billinge; player Wigan 1986– , winners Challenge Cup, Regal Trophy 1990. *Address*: Wigan RLFC, The Pavilion, Central Park, Wigan WN1 1XF.

GILFORD, David: golfer; b. 14 September 1965; English amateur champ. 1984; England debut 1983; Walker Cup team 1985; prof. debut 1986; Dunhill Cup team (winners) 1992; Ryder Cup team 1991; winner Johnnie Walker Int. 1990, English Open 1991, Moroccan Open, Tobago Int. 1992, Portuguese Open 1993, Tenerife Open 1994. *Address*: c/o PGA European Tour, Wentworth Club, Wentworth Drive, Virginia Water, Surrey GU25 4LS.

GILLESPIE, Gary: footballer; b. 5 July 1960, Bonnybridge; player Falkirk 1977–78, Coventry City 78–83, Liverpool 83–91, Celtic 91– ; 8 Scotland U-21 caps, 13 full Scotland caps. *Address*: Celtic FC, Celtic Park, 95 Kerrydale St, Glasgow G40 3RE.

GILLINGHAM, Nicholas, MBE: swimmer; b. 22 January 1967, Walsall; GB 100m and 200m breaststroke champ. 1993; Commonwealth Games 200m breaststroke bronze medals 1986, 90; European Champs. 200m breaststroke gold medals 1989, 91, 92, 93, 100m breaststroke silver and 4 x 100m medley relay bronze medals 1993; World Champs. 200m breaststroke bronze medal 1991; World Short-Course Champs. 200m breaststroke gold, 4 x 100m medley relay bronze medals 1993; Olympic 200m breaststroke silver medal 1988. *Leisure interests*: photography, clay pigeon shooting, running, tennis, golf. *Address*: c/o ASA, Harold Fern House, Derby Square, Loughborough, Leics. LE11 0AL.

GILZEAN, Ian: footballer; b. 10 December 1969, London; player Dundee 1992– . *Address*: Dundee FC, Dens Park, Dundee DD3 7JY.

GITTENS, Jonathan: footballer; b. 22 January 1964, Birmingham; player Southampton 1985–87, Swindon Town 87–91, Southampton 91–92, Middlesbrough 92–93, Portsmouth 93– . *Address*: Portsmouth FC, Fratton Park, Frogmore Rd, Portsmouth PO4 8RA.

GLOVER, Andrea Elizabeth: table tennis player; b. 14 March 1979, Belfast, NI; N. Wales girls' U-14 open champ., Irish girls' U-17 open champ., W. of Scotland girls'

U-14 open champ. 1993; Ireland U-14 debut 1992, U-16 debut 1993. *Leisure interests*: cricket, hockey, tennis. *Address*: 75 Drumaghlis Rd, Crossgar, Downpatrick, Co. Down BT30 9JS.

GLOVER, Lee: footballer; b. 24 April 1970, Kettering; player Nottingham Forest 1986– ; 2 Scotland U-21 caps. *Address*: Nottingham Forest FC, City Ground, Nottingham NG2 5FJ.

GODDARD, Richard: Rugby League footballer; b. 28 April 1974, Wakefield; player Wakefield Trinity 1990– ; rep. Yorks. *Address*: Wakefield Trinity RLFC, 171 Doncaster Rd, Belle Vue, Wakefield WF1 5EZ.

GOLDING, Michael Redvers: yachtsman (ocean racing); b. 27 August 1960, Gt Yarmouth; skipper *Group 4 Securitas*, overall runners-up and winners legs 3 and 4, Brit. Steel Challenge 1992/93. *Address*: 24 John Taylor Court, Tuns Lane, Slough, Berks. SL1 3UN.

GOLDSMITH, Bruce: hang glider/ paraglider pilot; b. 27 March 1960, Hemel Hempstead; GB hang gliding champ. 1991, 92; GB debut (hang gliding) 1986, (paragliding) 1991, winners Bleriot Cup 1987; European Champs. hang gliding silver medal 1988; world hang gliding triangular speed record-holder 1988–91. *Publications*: contributor to *Cross Country* magazine. *Leisure interests*: squash, windsurfing. *Address*: 34 Birmingham Rd, Cowes, Isle of Wight PO31 7BM.

GOMER, Sara Louise: tennis player; b. 13 May 1964, Torquay; rep. Devon; GB ladies' doubles champ. 1988; GB debut 1985, European Cup team 1986–88, 90, Wightman Cup team 1985–89, Federation Cup team 1987, 88, 92, Olympic squad 1988, 92; winner San Antonio Open 1985, Wimbledon ladies' plate 1987, N.

Californian Open 1988. *Leisure interests*: music, film, all sport. *Address*: Field End, Woodside Green, Gt Hallingbury, Bishop's Stortford, Herts. CM22 7UG.

GOMM, Sarah Jane: lacrosse player; b. 7 March 1966, Bolton; m. Philip Gomm 1989; player Liverpool Ladies 1984–87, Trent Bridge Ladies 87– ; rep. Notts. 1987– , North 84– ; England U-21 debut 1984 (capt. 1987), U-24 debut (capt.) 1987; Wales debut 1990, World Cup squad 1993, tours USA 1991, 92, 93. *Leisure interests*: skiing, fives, cooking. *Address*: 25 Bayley Close, Uppingham, Leics.

GOOCH, Graham Alan, OBE: cricketer; b. 23 July 1953, Leytonstone; m. Brenda Gooch 1976; 3 d.; player Essex 1973– (capt. 86–87, 89–), county champs. 1979, 83, 84, 86, 91, 92, Sunday League champs. 1984, 85; Test debut 1975, tours Aus. 1978/79, Aus./India 1979/80, WI 1980/81, India/Sri Lanka 1981/82, India/Pakistan (World Cup) 1987/88, India/WI 1989/90, Aus. 1990/91, Aus./NZ (World Cup) 1991/92, India 1992/93; England capt. 1988, 90–93; 100th 1st-class century v. Cambridge Univ. 1993; 100th Test appearance v. India 1993; became England's leading run-scorer Test v. Aus. 1993; passed 2000 runs in a season for 5th time 1993. *Publications*: *Out of the Wilderness*, 1988, *Test of Fire*, 1990, *Captaincy*, 1992. *Address*: Essex CCC, County Cricket Ground, New Writtle St, Chelmsford DM2 0PG.

GOOCH, Nicholas: short-track speed skater; b. 30 January 1973, Roehampton; GB overall champ. 1993, 1500m, 3000m and overall champ. 1994; Europa Cup 1000m gold medal 1990, overall gold 1994; European Champs. team gold medals 1992, 93; World Champs. team bronze medal 1991, silver 1992; Olympic squad 1992, 500m bronze medal 1994. *Leisure interests*: jet skiing, cycling, all sport. *Address*: 107 Brookwood Ave, London SW13 0LU.

GOODALL, Katherine Tamara: table tennis player; b. 19 March 1975, Leeds; rep. Yorks.; English girls' U-14 champ. 1989, U-17 champ. 1992, U-18 champ. 1992, 93, U-21 singles and doubles champ. 1993, snr ladies' doubles champ. 1993; England debut 1991. *Leisure interests*: tennis, TV, pop music. *Address*: 21 Parkside Place, Meanwood, Leeds LS6 4NX.

GOODCHILD, Mark Jonathan: canoe sailor; b. 29 December 1957, Rochester; GB canoe sailing champ. 1991, 92, European champ. 1991. *Leisure interests*: cycling, gardening, boat-building, fixing anything. *Address*: 58 Tradescant Drive, Meopham, Gravesend, Kent DA13 0EF.

GOODMAN, Donald: footballer; b. 9 May 1966, Leeds; player Bradford City 1983–87, W. Bromwich Albion 87–91, Sunderland 91– ; with Bradford City: 3rd Div. champs. 1984/85. *Address*: Sunderland FC, Roker Park Ground, Sunderland, Tyne and Wear SR6 9SW.

GOODMAN, Jonathan: footballer; b. 2 June 1971, Walthamstow; player Millwall 1990– . *Address*: Millwall FC, The Den, Zampa Rd, Bermondsey, London SE16 3LH.

GOODWAY, Andrew: Rugby League footballer; b. 6 June 1961, Castleford; player Oldham, Wigan 1992, Leeds 1992–93, Oldham 93– ; England debut v. Wales 1984; GB debut v. France 1983, Brit. Lions tour Aus./NZ/Papua New Guinea 1984. *Address*: Oldham RLFC, The Pavilion, Watersheddings, Oldham OL4 2PB.

GOODWIN, Nicola Yvette: swimmer; b. 20 August 1969, Shipston-on-Stour; m. Robert William Goodwin 1992; GB women's 50m freestyle champ. 1987, 50m butterfly champ. 1991; England youth debut 1983, intermediate debut and World School Games women's 100m butterfly silver medal 1986, snr debut 1991; GB B

and snr debuts 1986. *Address*: c/o ASA, Harold Fern House, Derby Square, Loughborough, Leics. LE11 0AL.

GORAM, Andrew: footballer; b. 13 April 1964, Bury; player Oldham Athletic 1981–88, Hibernian 88–91, Rangers 91– ; with Rangers: winners Scottish Cup 1992, 93; 1 Scotland U-21 cap, over 25 full Scotland caps. *Address*: Glasgow Rangers FC, Ibrox Stadium, 150 Edmiston Drive, Glasgow G51 2XD.

GORDON, Dale: footballer; b. 9 January 1967, Gt Yarmouth; player Norwich City 1984–91, Rangers 91–93, W. Ham Utd 93– ; with Rangers: winners Scottish Cup 1992; 4 England U-21 caps. *Address*: W. Ham Utd FC, Boleyn Ground, Green St, Upton Park, London E13 9AZ.

GORE, Robert Carlos James: fencer (épée); b. 9 September 1961, Bromley; UAU champ. 1986, 88, Brit. Univ. Sports Fed. champ. 1988; England debut 1991; GB debut 1991, World Champs. squad 1991, 93. *Leisure interests*: music, reading, cinema, driving in the countryside. *Address*: c/o AFA, 1 Barons Gate, 33–35 Rothschild Rd, London W4 5HT.

GORMAN, John: football manager; b. 16 August 1949, Winchburgh; player Celtic, Carlisle Utd 1970–76, Tottenham Hotspur 76–78; manager Swindon Town 1993– . *Address*: Swindon Town FC, The County Ground, Swindon, Wilts. SN1 2ED.

GORMAN, Paul: footballer; b. 18 September 1968, Macclesfield; player Doncaster Rovers 1987–88, Charlton Athletic 91– . *Address*: Charlton Athletic FC, The Valley, Floyd Rd, London SE7 8BL.

GORRINGE, John Pennington: glider pilot; b. 28 September 1953, Eastbourne; 1 d.; GB handicapped-class open champ. 1992; GB debut and European Champs. squad 1992. *Address*: 11 Evelyn Terrace, Richmond, Surrey TW9 2TQ.

GOSS, Jeremy: footballer; b. 11 May 1965, Cyprus; player Norwich City 1983– ; over 3 Wales caps. *Address*: Norwich City FC, Carrow Rd, Norwich NR1 1JE.

GOUGH, Darren: cricketer; b. 18 September 1970, Barnsley; player Yorks. 1989– , tours Barbados 1990, SA 1992; England YC tour Aus. 1989/90, England A tour SA 1993/94. *Address*: Yorks. CCC, Headingley Cricket Ground, Leeds LS6 3BU.

GOUGH, Richard: footballer; b. 5 April 1962, Stockholm, Sweden; player Dundee Utd 1980–86, Tottenham Hotspur 86–88, Rangers 88– (capt.); with Rangers: winners Scottish League Cup 1988, 89, 91, 94, Scottish Cup 1992; 5 Scotland U-21 caps, over 60 full Scotland caps; Scottish Football Writers' Assoc. Player of the Year 1989. *Address*: Glasgow Rangers FC, Ibrox Stadium, 150 Edmiston Drive, Glasgow G51 2XD.

GOULD, Jonathan: footballer; b. 18 July 1968, Paddington; player Halifax Town 1990–92, Coventry City 92– . *Address*: Coventry City FC, Highfield Rd Stadium, King Richard St, Coventry CV2 4FW.

GOULDING, Robert: Rugby League footballer; b. 4 February 1972, Widnes; player Wigan, Leeds, Widnes 1992– ; GB debut v. Papua New Guinea and Brit. Lions tour NZ/Papua New Guinea 1990. *Address*: Widnes RLFC, Naughton Park, Lowerhouse Lane, Widnes WA8 7DZ.

GOURLAY, Archibald: footballer; b. 29 June 1969, Greenock; player Morton 1987–88, Newcastle Utd 88–91, Motherwell 91– . *Address*: Motherwell FC, Fir Park, Fir Park St, Motherwell ML1 2QN.

GOWERS, Gillian Carol: badminton player; b. 9 April 1964; rep. Herts.; English U-15 mixed doubles champ. 1979, jnr mixed doubles champ. 1982, U-21 ladies'

doubles champ. 1983, snr ladies' doubles champ. 1985–88, 90, 91, 93, 94, mixed doubles champ. 1986, 89, 91; England U-23 debut 1981, snr debut 1983; Commonwealth Games ladies' doubles gold medal 1986, silver 1990; European Champs. ladies' doubles gold medal, mixed doubles silver 1986; World Champs. mixed doubles bronze medal 1985; Olympic squad 1992; winner Scottish Open ladies' doubles 1989, 90, mixed doubles 1990, Japan Open ladies' doubles 1989, 91, German Open mixed doubles 1990, Singapore Open ladies' doubles 1991, World Cup mixed doubles 1993. *Address*: c/o Badminton Assoc. of England, 5 Picketts, Picketts Lane, Salfords, Surrey RH1 5RG.

GOWSHALL, Amy: flat green bowler; b. 20 March 1979, Grimsby; Humberside U-25 champ. 1991; English Women's Bowling Fed. pairs champ. 1993; youngest-ever nat. bowls champ. *Leisure interests*: hockey, netball, javelin. *Address*: 97 Brigsley Rd, Waltham, Grimsby DN37 0LB.

GRAHAM, Alastair: footballer; b. 11 August 1966, Glasgow; player Clydebank 1984–87, Albion Rovers 87–90, Ayr Utd 90–92, Motherwell 92– . *Address*: Motherwell FC, Fir Park, Fir Park St, Motherwell ML1 2QN.

GRAHAM, George: football manager; b. 30 November 1944, Coatbridge; player Aston Villa 1961–64, Chelsea 64–66, Arsenal 66–72, Manchester Utd 72–74, Portsmouth 74–76, Crystal Palace 76–77; manager Millwall 1982–86, Arsenal 86– ; as player: winner League Cup 1965 (Chelsea), FA Cup 1971, League champs. 1970/71 (Arsenal), 2 Scotland U-23 caps, 12 full Scotland caps; as manager: winner League Cup 1987, 93, FA Cup 1993, League champs. 1988/89, 90/91 (Arsenal). *Address*: Arsenal FC, Arsenal Stadium, Highbury, London N5 1BU.

GRAHAM, Helena Jane: lacrosse player; b. 9 November 1968, Edinburgh; rep. Cambs. 1988–89, Middx 1991– , East 88–89, South 91– ; England U-18 debut 1986 (vice-capt. 1986–87); Scotland B debut 1988, U-21 debut 1989, snr debut 1990, World Cup squad 1993, tours USA 1992, 93. *Leisure interests*: skiing, fun runs, squash, tennis, travel. *Address*: 35 Blackford Rd, Edinburgh EH9 2DT.

GRANT, Brian: footballer; b. 19 June 1964, Bannockburn; player Stirling Albion 1981–84, Aberdeen 84– ; with Aberdeen: winners Scottish League Cup, Scottish Cup 1990. *Address*: Aberdeen FC, Pittodrie Stadium, Pittodrie St, Aberdeen AB2 1QH.

GRANT, Dalton: athlete (high jump); b. 8 April 1966, London; AAA champ. 1989, 90; UK champ. 1990, 91, 93; Commonwealth Games silver medal 1990; European Cup gold medals 1989, 91; European Indoor Champs. silver medal 1989; World Cup silver medal 1989. *Address*: c/o Brit. Athletic Fed., 225A Bristol Rd, Edgbaston, Birmingham B5 7UB.

GRANT, Frank: boxer; b. 22 May 1965; prof. debut 1986; titles won: GB middle-weight 1992; over 19 prof. wins. *Address*: c/o Phil Martin, 79 Buckingham Rd, Chorlton, Manchester M21 1QT.

GRANT, James: Rugby League footballer; b. 22 May 1964; player Hull 1992– . *Address*: Hull RLFC, The Boulevard Ground, Airlie St, Hull HU3 3JD.

GRANT, Peter: footballer; b. 30 August 1965, Bellshill; player Celtic 1982– , winners Scottish Cup 1989; 2 Scotland caps. *Address*: Celtic FC, Celtic Park, 95 Kerrydale St, Glasgow G40 3RE.

GRAVENEY, David Anthony: cricketer; b. 2 January 1953, Bristol; player Glos. 1972–91 (capt. 81–88), Somerset 1991, Durham 1992– . *Publications: Durham CCC: Past, Present and Future* (co-author), 1993. *Address*: Durham CCC, County Ground, Riverside, Chester-le-Street, Co. Durham DH3 3QR.

GRAY, Andrew: footballer; b. 22 February 1964, Lambeth; player Crystal Palace 1984–87, Aston Villa 87–89, Queens Park Rangers 1989, Crystal Palace 1989–92, Tottenham Hotspur 92– ; 2 England U-21 caps, 1 full England cap. *Address*: Tottenham Hotspur FC, 748 High Rd, Tottenham, London N17 0AP.

GRAY, Christopher Anthony: Rugby Union footballer; b. 11 July 1960, Haddington; m. Judith Gray; 1 s.; player Edinburgh Academicals, Nottingham (capt. 1989–91); Scotland and Five Nations debut v. Wales 1989, Grand Slam champs. 1990, tours NZ 1990, Aus. 1992, Fiji/Tonga/W. Samoa 1993. *Address*: Nottingham RFC, Ireland Ave, Beeston, Nottingham NG9 1JD.

GRAY, Philip: footballer; b. 2 October 1968, Belfast; player Tottenham Hotspur 1986–91, Luton Town 91–93, Sunderland 93– ; over 4 NI caps. *Address*: Sunderland FC, Roker Park Ground, Sunderland, Tyne and Wear SR6 9SW.

GRAY, Stuart: footballer; b. 19 April 1960, Withernsea; player Nottingham Forest 1978–83, Barnsley 83–87, Aston Villa 87–91, Southampton 91– . *Address*: Southampton FC, The Dell, Milton Rd, Southampton SO9 4XX.

GRAYSON, Adrian Paul: cricketer; b. 31 March 1971, Ripon; player Yorks. 1990– , tours Barbados 1990, Cape Town (SA) 1992; England YC tour Aus. 1989/90. *Address*: Yorks. CCC, Headingley Cricket Ground, Leeds LS6 3BU.

GREEN, Alan Richard: powerboat racer (navigator); b. 3 June 1964, Isle of Wight; European offshore circuit racing class III 2-litre champ. 1993. *Leisure interests*: squash, mountain biking, reading, travel. *Address*: 19 Place Rd, Cowes, Isle of Wight PO31 7UA.

GREEN, Elizabeth: water polo player; b. 21 October 1969, Leicester; player City of Coventry; GB debut 1992. *Leisure interests*: aerobics, watching videos. *Address*: c/o ASA, Harold Fern House, Derby Square, Loughborough, Leics. LE11 0AL.

GREEN, Joanne: hockey player; b. 4 August 1973; player Chelmsford; England U-21 debut (outdoor and indoor) 1991, snr debut (outdoor) 1992, (indoor) 1990, European Indoor Cup silver medallist 1993. *Address*: Chelmsford HC, Chelmer Park, Beehive Lane, Chelmsford, Essex.

GREEN, Lucinda Jane, MBE: equestrianist (three-day eventing); b. 7 November 1953, London; m. David Green 1981; European Jnr Champs. team gold medal 1971; European Champs. individ. gold medal 1975 (Be Fair), 1977 (George); World Champs. individ. and team gold medals 1982 (Regal Realm); Olympic squad 1976, team silver medal 1984; winner Badminton Horse Trials 1973 (Be Fair), 1976 (Wideawake), 1977 (George), 1979 (Killaire), 1983 (Regal Realm), 1984 (Beagle Bay), Burghley Horse Trials 1977 (George), 1981 (Beagle Bay); Sports Writers' Sportswoman of the Year 1975. *Address*: c/o Brit. Horse Soc., Brit. Equestrian Centre, Stoneleigh Park, Kenilworth, Warks. CV8 2LR.

GREEN, Scott: footballer; b. 15 January 1970, Walsall; player Bolton Wanderers 1990– . *Address*: Bolton Wanderers FC, Burnden Park, Manchester Rd, Bolton, Lancs. BL3 2QR.

GREENFIELD, Keith: cricketer; b. 6 December 1968, Brighton; m. Caroline Susannah Greenfield 1992; player Sussex 1987– . *Address*: Sussex CCC, County Ground, Eaton Rd, Hove, E. Sussex BN3 3AN.

GREENFIELD, Myles Thomas: flat green bowler; b. 14 January 1972, Lurgan, NI; Irish fours champ. 1992; Ireland U-21 debut 1989, U-25 debut 1992, snr debut 1993; Ireland Young Player of the Year 1990. *Leisure interests*: tennis, swimming. *Address*: Dunbarton Bowling Club, Dunbarton St, Gilford, Co. Armagh, NI.

GREENMAN, Christopher: footballer; b. 22 December 1968, Bristol; player Coventry City 1988–92, Peterborough Utd 92– . *Address*: Peterborough Utd FC, London Rd Ground, Peterborough, Cambs. PE2 8AL.

GREENWAY, Carol Margaret: fencer (épée); b. 26 September 1966, Ross-on-Wye; England debut 1991; GB debut and winning team Oslo Cup 1993. *Leisure interests*: horseracing, travel and expeditions, cinema, massage. *Address*: 8C Hereford Mews, London W2 5AN.

GREENWOOD, Matthew: Rugby Union footballer; b. 25 September 1964; player Wasps; rep. N. Div., London Div. 1993– ; England A debut v. Spain 1992, tours NZ 1992, Canada 1993. *Address*: Wasps FC, Wasps Football Ground, Repton Ave, Sudbury, Wembley, Middx HA0 3DW.

GREGORY, Andrew: Rugby League footballer; b. 10 August 1961, Wigan; player Widnes, Warrington, Wigan, Leeds 1992–93, Salford 93– ; with Widnes: winners Challenge Cup 1981, 84, Premiership 1982, 83; with Warrington: winners Premiership 1986; with Wigan: winners Premiership 1987, Challenge Cup 1988–92, Regal Trophy 1989, 90; GB debut v. France 1981, Brit. Lions tours Aus./NZ/Papua New Guinea 1984, 88, NZ/Papua New Guinea 1990, Aus./Papua New Guinea 1992. *Address*: Salford RLFC, The Willows, Willows Rd, Weaste, Salford M5 2ST.

GREGORY, Martin: Rugby Union footballer; b. 3 August 1962, Dagenham; player Southend, Saracens 1989– ; rep. E. Counties. *Address*: Saracens FC, Bramley Rd Sports Ground, Chaseside, Southgate, London N14 4AB.

GREGORY, Michael: Rugby League footballer; b. 20 May 1964, Wigan; player Wigan St Pats ARLFC, Warrington; rep. Lancs.; GB debut v. France 1987, Brit. Lions tour Aus./NZ/Papua New Guinea 1988. *Address*: Warringon RLFC, Wilderspool Stadium, Wilderspool Causeway, Warrington WA4 6PY.

GRESSWELL, Charles John: motorcyclist (off-road); b. 22 February 1959, Cirencester; m. Angela Lock 1993; ACU expert U-350cc 4-stroke enduro champ. 1991, 92. *Leisure interests*: keep-fit, road motorcycling. *Address*: 1 Stockwell Farm Cottages, Birdlip, Glos. GL4 8JZ.

GRICE, John: clay pigeon shooter; b. 18 May 1954, Stretton-en-le-Field; m. Hilary Grice 1973; 2 s.; rep. Leics. 1977– ; English open universal trap champ. 1981, 89, 92, double-rise champ. 1987, 91, Olympic trap champ. 1993; GB open universal trap champ. 1981, 89, 90, open double-rise champ. 1992; England debut 1977; GB debut 1981; European Champs. universal trap bronze medal 1990; World Champs. universal trap gold medal 1990. *Publications*: contributor to *Successful Clay Pigeon Shooting*, 1991. *Leisure interests*: deer-stalking, snooker, trout-fishing, game-shooting. *Address*: 53 Top St, Appleby Magna, Swadlincote, Derbys. DE12 7AH.

GRIFFIN, James: footballer; b. 1 January 1967, Hamilton; player Motherwell 1985– , winners Scottish Cup 1991. *Address*: Motherwell FC, Fir Park, Fir Park St, Motherwell ML1 2QN.

GRIFFITH, Frank Alexander: cricketer; b. 15 August 1968, Leyton; player Derbys. 1988– , winners Benson and Hedges Cup 1993, Sunday League champs. 1990. *Address*: Derbys. CCC, County Cricket Ground, Nottingham Rd, Derby DE2 6DA.

GRIFFITH, Michelle Amanda: athlete (long and triple jump); b. 6 October 1971, Wembley; UK women's triple jump champ. 1990, 93; GB debut 1990; UK and Commonwealth women's triple jump record-holder. *Leisure interests*: socializing, travel. *Address*: 11 Kirton Walk, Burnt Oak, Edgware, Middx HA8 0TY.

GRIFFITHS, Jonathan: Rugby League footballer; b. 23 August 1964, Carmarthen; player Llanelli (RU), St Helens 1989– ; with St Helens: winners Premiership 1993; Wales RU int.; Wales RL debut v. Papua New Guinea 1991; GB debut v. France 1992. *Address*: St Helens RLFC, Dunriding Lane, St Helens, Merseyside WA10 4AD.

GRIFFITHS, Michael: Rugby Union footballer; b. 18 March 1962, Tonypandy; m. Anne Griffiths; 2 s.; player Bridgend, Cardiff; Wales debut v. W. Samoa 1988, Five Nations debut v. Scotland 1989, tour Zimbabwe/Namibia 1993; Brit. Lions tour Aus. 1989. *Address*: Cardiff RFC, Cardiff Arms Park, Westgate St, Cardiff CF1 1JA.

GRIFFITHS, Terence Martin: snooker player; b. 16 October 1947, Llanelli; Welsh amateur champ. 1975, English amateur champ. 1977, 78; prof. debut 1978, Welsh champ. 1985, UK champ. 1982, world champ. 1979; rep. Wales, winners World Cup 1979, 80; winner Masters 1980, Irish Masters 1980–82, Mercantile Credit Classic 1982, Pot Black 1984. *Address*: c/o World Prof. Billiards and Snooker Assoc., 27 Oakfield Rd, Clifton, Bristol BS8 2AT.

GRIMOLDY, Nic: Rugby League footballer; b. 31 January 1962, Doncaster; player Fulham, Sheffield Eagles. *Address*: Sheffield Eagles RLFC, Stadium Corner, 824 Attercliffe Rd, Sheffield S9 3RS.

GRINDLEY, David: athlete; b. 29 October 1972; 400m GP champ. 1993; European Jnr Champs. 400m and 4 x 400m relay gold medals 1991; World Jnr Champs. 4 x 400m relay silver medal 1990; European Cup 400m and 4 x 400m relay gold medals 1993;

European Indoor Champs. 400m bronze medal 1992; Olympic 4 x 400m relay bronze medal 1992; UK 400m record-holder. *Address*: c/o Brit. Athletic Fed., 225A Bristol Rd, Edgbaston, Birmingham B5 7UB.

GRITT, Stephen: football manager; b. 31 October 1957, Bournemouth; player Bournemouth 1975–77, Charlton Athletic 1977–89, Walsall 89–90, Charlton Athletic 90–91; joint player/manager Charlton Athletic 1991– . *Address*: Charlton Athletic FC, The Valley, Floyd Rd, London SE7 8BL.

GROBBELAAR, Bruce: footballer; b. 6 October 1957, Durban, SA; player Crewe Alexandra 1979–80, Vancouver W. (Canada) 80–81, Liverpool 81– ; with Liverpool: winners European Cup 1981, 84, League Cup 1982, 83, 84, FA Cup 1986, 89, 92, League champs. 1981/82, 82/83, 83/84, 85/86, 87/88, 89/90; Zimbabwe int. *Address*: Liverpool FC, Anfield Rd, Liverpool L4 0TH.

GROVES, Paul: Rugby League footballer; b. 25 May 1965, Salford; player Salford, St Helens 1987–93, Oldham 93– ; GB debut v. Papua New Guinea 1987, Brit. Lions tour Aus./NZ/Papua New Guinea 1988. *Address*: Oldham RLFC, The Pavilion, Watersheddings, Oldham OL4 2PB.

GRUNFELD, Amanda Louise: tennis player; b. 1 March 1967, Manchester; rep. Lancs., indoor county champs. 1992; GB girls' U-18 covered court champ. 1984; England debut 1984; GB debut 1985, Wightman Cup team 1989; winner Texaco Ladies Challenger 1991. *Leisure interests*: cross-country running, reading, collecting tennis paraphernalia, eating pizzas. *Address*: c/o LTA, The Queen's Club, W. Kensington, London W14 9EG.

GULBRANDSEN, Laura Jane: hockey player; b. 10 March 1972, Toronto, Canada; player Edinburgh Ladies 1988– ; Scotland U-21 debut 1991, snr debut 1992, tour Germany 1993. *Leisure interests*: water sports, socializing, travel. *Address*: 28 Ladebraes, St Andrews, Fife KY16 9DA.

GUNN, Bryan James: footballer; b. 22 December 1963, Thurso; m. Susan Gunn 1989; 1 d.; player Aberdeen 1980–86, Norwich City 86– ; with Aberdeen: winners European Cup Winners' Cup 1983; 8 Scotland U-21 caps, snr debut v. Egypt 1990, over 3 full caps. *Leisure interests*: golf, tennis. *Address*: Norwich City FC, Carrow Rd, Norwich NR1 1JE.

GUNN, Richard: Rugby League footballer; b. 25 February 1967; player Leeds, Featherstone Rovers 1992– . *Address*: Featherstone Rovers RLFC, The Croft, Batley Rd, W. Ardsley, Wakefield WF3 1DX.

GUNNELL, Sally Janet Jane, MBE: athlete; b. 29 July 1966, Chigwell; m. Jon Bigg 1992; Commonwealth Games women's 100m hurdles gold medal 1986, 400m hurdles and 4 x 400m relay gold 1990; European Cup women's 400m hurdles silver medal 1989, gold 1993; European Indoor Champs. women's 400m gold medal 1989; World Cup women's 400m hurdles bronze medal 1989; World Champs. women's 400m hurdles silver medal 1991, 400m hurdles gold and 4 x 400m relay bronze 1993; Olympic women's 400m hurdles gold and 4 x 400m bronze medals 1992; world women's 400m hurdles and UK women's 100m hurdles record-holder; Sports Writers' Sportswoman of the Year 1992, 93, Brit. Athletics Writers' Assoc. Woman Athlete of the Year 1993. *Leisure interests*: home, cats, husband, cooking, gardening, eating out, shopping. *Address*: c/o Brit. Athletic Fed., 225A Bristol Rd, Edgbaston, Birmingham B5 7UB.

GUNNING, John: Rugby League footballer; b. 30 March 1969; player Leigh 1993– . *Address*: Leigh RLFC, Hilton Park, Kirkhall Lane, Leigh WN7 1RN.

GUSCOTT, Jeremy Clayton: Rugby Union footballer; b. 7 July 1965, Bath; m. Jayne Guscott; player Bath, winners Pilkingon Cup 1987, 89, 90, 92, League champs. 1990/91, 91/92, 92/93; England B debut 1988, snr debut v. Romania 1989, Five Nations debut v. Ireland 1990, Grand Slam champs. 1991, 92, tour Aus. 1991; Brit. Lions tours Aus. 1989, NZ 1993. *Address:* Bath RFC, Recreation Ground, Bath BA2 6PW.

GYNN, Michael: footballer; b. 19 August 1961, Peterborough; player Peterborough Utd 1978–83, Coventry City 83–93, Stoke City 93– ; with Coventry City: winners FA Cup 1987. *Address:* Stoke City FC, Victoria Ground, Stoke on Trent, Staffs. ST4 4EG.

HACKETT, Gary: footballer; b. 11 October 1962, Stourbridge; player Shrewsbury Town 1983–87, Aberdeen 87–88, Stoke City 88–90, W. Bromwich Albion 90–93, Peterborough Utd 93– . *Address:* Peterborough Utd FC, London Rd Ground, Peterborough, Cambs. PE2 8AL.

HACKNEY, Stephen Thomas: Rugby Union footballer; b. 13 June 1968; player Leicester; rep. Midland Div.; England B debut v. Aus. 1988, England A tour Canada 1993. *Address:* Leicester FC, Welford Rd, Leicester LE2 7LF.

HADDOCK, Neil: boxer; b. 22 June 1964; Welsh ABA lightweight champ. 1986; Commonwealth Games super-feather-weight silver medal 1986; prof. debut 1987; titles won: Welsh super-featherweight, GB super-featherweight 1992; over 11 prof. wins. *Address:* c/o Brit. Boxing Board of Control, Jack Petersen House, 52A Borough High St, London SE1 1XW.

HADLEY, Adrian: Rugby League footballer; b. 1 March 1963, Cardiff; player Cardiff (RU), Salford, Widnes 1992– ; 27 Wales RU caps; Wales RL debut v. Papua New Guinea 1991. *Address:* Widnes RLFC, Naughton Park, Lowerhouse Lane, Widnes WA8 7DZ.

HALL, Alison Jane: oarswoman; b. 23 August 1966, Bristol; m. Mark Patrick Hall 1992; rep. Upper Thames RC and Tideway Scullers School; GB women's single sculls champ. 1989, open indoor champ. 1993; GB debut 1988, World Student Games women's single sculls bronze medal 1989, Olympic squad (women's double sculls) 1988, 92. *Publications: The Yanks at Oxford,* 1990, `The Psychology of Racing' in *Steven Redgrave's Complete Book of Rowing,* 1992. *Leisure interests:* scuba diving, horseracing, skiing. *Address:* `Badgers', 7 Badgemore Lane, Henley-on-Thames, Oxon RG9 2JH.

HALL, Darren James: badminton player; b. 25 October 1965; rep. Essex; English U-15 singles, doubles and mixed doubles champ. 1981, jnr champ. 1983, 84, jnr mixed doubles champ. 1984, snr champ. 1986, 88–91, 93, 94; Welsh champ. 1993; England U-23 debut 1983, snr debut 1984; European Jnr Champs. team gold medal 1983; Commonwealth Games team gold medal, individ. bronze 1990; European Champs. gold medal 1988 (1st English winner), silver 1990; Olympic squad 1988; winner German Open 1988, Welsh Open 1989, Danish Open 1993, Hants. Open 1994. *Address:* c/o Badminton Assoc. of England, 5 Picketts, Picketts Lane, Salfords, Surrey RH1 5RG.

HALL, Gareth: footballer; b. 20 March 1969, Croydon; player Chelsea 1986– , 2nd Div. champs. 1988/89; 1 Wales U-21 cap, 9 full Wales caps. *Address:* Chelsea FC, Stamford Bridge, Fulham Rd, London SW6 1HS.

HALL, Jane Lucy: oarswoman; b. 20 October 1973, Kingston-upon-Thames; GB jnr debut 1990, U-23 debut and World U-23 Champs. lightweight women's double sculls bronze medal 1991, snr debut and World Champs. lightweight women's coxless fours gold medal 1993; youngest Briton to win World Champs. gold medal. *Leisure interests*: cycling, reading, music, TV, having a good time. *Address*: 31 Herne Rd, Surbiton, Surrey KT6 5BX.

HALL, Jonathan Peter: Rugby Union footballer; b. 15 March 1962; player Bath (capt.); rep. S.W. Div.; England and Five Nations debut v. Scotland 1984, tour Canada (England A) 1993. *Address*: Bath FC, Recreation Ground, Bath, Avon.

HALL, Julie Pauline: golfer; b. 10 March 1967, Ipswich; m. Michael Hall 1989; Suffolk ladies' champ. 1986, 89–93, ladies' strokeplay champ. 1985–87, 89–93; English ladies' strokeplay champ. 1987, 93, ladies' amateur champ. 1988, Welsh ladies' open amateur strokeplay champ. 1993; GB ladies' open amateur champ. 1990, ladies' open amateur strokeplay champ. 1993; Spanish ladies' open amateur champ. 1992; world fourball champ. 1987; England debut 1987; Curtis Cup team 1988, 90, 92, winners 1988, 92; *Daily Telegraph* Woman Golfer of the Year (joint) 1993. *Address*: c/o Ladies' Golf Union, The Scores, St Andrews, Fife KY16 9AT.

HALL, Martin: Rugby League footballer; b. 5 December 1968, Oldham; player Oldham, Rochdale Hornets, Wigan; rep. Lancs. U-17, England Schools. *Address*: Wigan RLFC, The Pavilion, Central Park, Wigan WN1 1XF.

HALL, Michael Robert: Rugby Union footballer; b. 13 October 1965, Bridgend; player Bridgend, Maesteg, Cardiff (capt.); Wales debut v. NZ 1988, Five Nations debut v. Scotland 1989, tours NZ 1988, Aus. 1991; Brit. Lions tour Aus. 1989. *Address*: Cardiff RFC, Cardiff Arms Park, Westgate St, Cardiff CF1 1JA.

HALL, Richard: footballer; b. 14 March 1972, Ipswich; player Scunthorpe Utd 1990–91, Southampton 91– ; 2 England U-21 caps. *Address*: Southampton FC, The Dell, Milton Rd, Southampton SO9 4XX.

HALL-CRAGGS, Wade: oarsman; b. 9 January 1966, N. Heath, Berks.; rep. Leander Club 1984–85, Durham Univ. BC 85–88, Tideway Scullers School 89– ; GB quadruple sculls champ. 1991, amateur sculling champ. 1993; World U-23 Champs. coxless fours bronze medal 1985; Olympic squad (single sculls) 1992; winner World Sculling Challenge 1993. *Leisure interests*: tennis, skiffing, railways. *Address*: Tideway Scullers School, Dukes Meadow, Chiswick, London W4 2SH.

HALLAS, Graham: Rugby League footballer; b. 27 February 1971, Leeds; player Hull Kingston Rovers, Halifax 1992– . *Address*: Halifax RLFC, The Pavilion, Thrum Hall, Gibbet St, Halifax, W. Yorks. HX1 4TL.

HALLE, Gunnar: footballer; b. 11 August 1965, Oslo, Norway; player Lillestrom (Norway), Oldham Athletic 1991– ; Norway int. *Address*: Oldham Athletic FC, Boundary Park, Oldham, Lancs. OL1 2PA.

HALLETT, Michael William: snooker player; b. 6 July 1959, Grimsby; GB jnr champ. 1978; prof. debut 1979, English champ. 1989, winner World Doubles 1987, Hong Kong Open 1989, Scottish Masters 1991. *Address*: c/o Cuemasters Ltd, Kerse Rd, Stirling, Scotland FK7 7SG.

HALLWORTH, Jonathan: footballer; b. 26 October 1965, Stockport; player Ipswich Town 1983–89, Oldham Athletic 89– . *Address*: Oldham Athletic FC, Boundary Park, Oldham, Lancs. OL1 2PA.

HALPIN, Garrett Francis: Rugby Union footballer; b. 14 February 1966; player London Irish; Ireland and Five Nations debut v. England 1990. *Address*: London Irish RUFC, The Avenue, Sunbury-on-Thames, Middx.

HALSALL, Michael: footballer; b. 21 July 1961, Bootle; player Birmingham City 1983–84, Carlisle Utd 84–87, Grimsby Town 1987, Peterborough Utd 1987– . *Address*: Peterborough Utd FC, London Rd Ground, Peterborough, Cambs. PE2 8AL.

HAMER, Jonathan: Rugby League footballer; b. 23 February 1966, Halifax; player Siddall ARLFC, Elland ARLFC, Bradford Northern 1984– . *Address*: Bradford Northern RLFC, Odsal Stadium, Bradford BD6 1BS.

HAMILTON, Brian: footballer; b. 5 August 1967, Paisley; player St Mirren 1985–89, Hibernian 89– ; with St Mirren: winners Scottish Cup 1987; with Hibernian: winners Scottish League Cup 1992; Scotland U-21 int. *Address*: Hibernian FC, Easter Rd Stadium, 64 Albion Rd, Edinburgh EH7 5QG.

HAMILTON, Bryan: football manager; b. 21 December 1946, Belfast, NI; player Ipswich Town 1971–75, Everton 75–77, Millwall 77–78, Swindon Town 78–80, Tranmere Rovers 80–84; 2 NI U-23 caps, 50 full NI caps; manager Wigan Athletic, NI 1994– . *Address*: c/o Irish FA, 20 Windsor Ave, Belfast BT9 6EE.

HAMILTON, Hilda: flat green bowler; b. Belfast; m. Andrew Hamilton 1955; 2 s.; Irish women's singles champ. (outdoor) 1983, women's triples champ. (outdoor) 1985, 87, 89, women's fours champ. (outdoor) 1984, 85; GB women's triples champ. (outdoor) 1988, women's fours champ. (outdoor) 1985, 86; Ireland debut (outdoor and indoor) 1978, NI Commonwealth Games squad 1986. *Leisure interests*: reading, knitting, charity work. *Address*: 23 Richill Park, Belfast BT5 6HG.

HAMILTON, Ian: footballer; b. 14 December 1967, Stevenage; player Cambridge Utd 1988, Scunthorpe Utd 1988–92, W. Bromwich Albion 92– . *Address*: W. Bromwich Albion FC, The Hawthorns, W. Bromwich B71 4LF.

HAMMOND, Karl: Rugby League footballer; b. 25 April 1974; player Widnes 1990– . *Address*: Widnes RLFC, Naughton Park, Lowerhouse Lane, Widnes WA8 7DZ.

HAMMOND, Nicholas: footballer; b. 7 September 1967, Hornchurch; player Swindon Town 1987– . *Address*: Swindon Town FC, The County Ground, Swindon, Wilts. SN1 2ED.

HAMMOND, Roger Edward: cyclist; b. 30 January 1974, Oxford; rep. Invicta; GB univ. cyclo-cross champ. 1993; GB juvenile cyclo-cross champ. 1989, 90, jnr champ. 1990–92, snr open champ. 1994; world jnr cyclo-cross champ. 1992; London criterium champ. 1992; mem. GB cyclo-cross, road and time trial squads; winner Tour of Assen 1990, 91. *Leisure interests*: cross-country running, judo, football, table tennis. *Address*: Arlington, Amersham Rd, Chalfont St Peter, Bucks. SL9 0NZ.

HAMPSON, Steve: Rugby League footballer; b. 14 August 1961, Cyprus; player Wigan 1983–93, Halifax 93– ; GB debut v. Papua New Guinea 1987, Brit. Lions tour Aus./NZ/Papua New Guinea 1992. *Address*: Halifax RLFC, The Pavilion, Thrum Hall, Gibbet St, Halifax, W. Yorks HX1 4TL.

HANBURY, Benjamin: racehorse trainer; b. 25 March 1946; m. Moira Elizabeth Hanbury 1969; 2 d.; 1st licence 1974; winner Oaks, 1000 Guineas 1986 (Midway Lady). *Address*: c/o BHB, 42 Portman Square, London W1H 0EN.

HANCOCK, Timothy Harold Coulter: cricketer; b. 20 April 1972; player Glos. 1991– , tour Kenya 1991. *Address*: Glos. CCC, Phoenix County Ground, Nevil Rd, Bristol BS6 9EJ.

HAND, Paul Terence Jack: tennis player; b. 3 July 1965, Wokingham; rep. Berks.; GB doubles champ. 1992; GB debut and World Student Games squad 1986, European Cup team 1990; leading player, Reebok Tour 1992; winner Bristol Trophy doubles 1993. *Leisure interests*: fishing, windsurfing, softball, reading. *Address*: 24 Coombe Pine, Crown Wood, Bracknell, Berks. RG12 3TJ.

HAND, Tony: ice hockey player; b. 15 August 1967; player Murrayfield Racers 1983– , winners Autumn Cup 1986, 90, 94, Scottish Cup 1987–91, GB champs. 1985/86, League champs. 1986/87, 87/88; World Champs. debut 1989. *Address*: The Ice Rink, Riversdale Crescent, Edinburgh EH12 5XN.

HANGER, Dean: Rugby League footballer; b. 24 February 1970; player Leigh 1993– . *Address*: Leigh RLFC, Hilton Park, Kirkhall Lane, Leigh WN7 1RN.

HANLAN, Lee: Rugby League footballer; b. 6 October 1971, Leeds; player Hull, Batley 1992–93, Wakefield Trinity 93– . *Address*: Wakefield Trinity RLFC, 171 Doncaster Rd, Belle Vue, Wakefield WF1 5EZ.

HANLEY, Ellery, MBE: Rugby League footballer; b. 27 March 1961, Leeds; player Bradford Northern 1978–85, Wigan 85–91, Leeds 91– (capt.); England debut v. Wales 1984; GB debut v. France 1984, Brit. Lions tours Aus./NZ/Papua New Guinea 1984, 88 (capt.), 1992 (capt.), 36 caps; 1st-ever black GB capt. *Address*: Leeds RLFC, Bass Headingley, St Michael's Lane, Leeds LS6 3BR.

HANNAFORD, Marcus: Rugby Union footballer; b. 27 April 1963; player Gloucester; England B int. *Address*: Gloucester RUFC, Kingsholm, Worcester St, Gloucester GL3 3AX.

HANNON, Richard Michael: racehorse trainer; b. 30 May 1945; m. Josephine Hannon 1966; 2 s., 4 d.; 1st licence 1970; winner 2000 Guineas 1973 (Mon Fils), 1987 (Don't Forget Me), 1990 (Tirol), Irish 2000 Guineas 1987 (Don't Forget Me), 1990 (Tirol); leading trainer 1992; trained record number of winners (182) in season 1993. *Address*: c/o BHB, 42 Portman Square, London W1H 0EN.

HANSON, Moray: ice hockey player; b. 21 June 1964; player Murrayfield Racers 1983– , winners Autumn Cup 1986, 90, 94, Scottish Cup 1987–91, GB champs. 1985/86, League champs. 1986/87, 87/88; World Champs. debut 1989. *Address*: The Ice Rink, Riversdale Crescent, Edinburgh EH12 5XN.

HARDCASTLE, Sarah Lucy: swimmer; b. 9 April 1969, Chelmsford; GB women's 400m and 800m freestyle champ. 1993; European Jnr Champs. girls' 800m freestyle silver medal 1981, 400m and 800m freestyle gold and 400m individ. medley bronze 1982; Commonwealth Games women's 400m and 800m freestyle gold, 4 x 200m freestyle relay silver and 400m individ. medley bronze medals 1986; European Champs. women's 800m freestyle bronze medal 1983, 800m freestyle silver 1985, 4 x 200m freestyle relay bronze 1993; World Champs. women's 400m freestyle bronze medal 1986; Olympic women's 400m freestyle silver and 800m freestyle bronze medals 1984 (youngest-ever Brit. medal-winner); UK and Commonwealth and European women's 800m freestyle record-holder 1986–87. *Leisure interests*: watching rugby, interior design, cycling, running. *Address*: c/o ASA, Harold Fern House, Derby Square, Loughborough, Leics. LE11 0AL.

HARDEN, Richard John: cricketer; b. 16 August 1965, Bridgwater; m. Nicola Rae Harden 1992; player Somerset 1985– (vice-capt. 92–). *Leisure interests*: golf, watching most sports. *Address*: Somerset CCC, The County Ground, Taunton, Somerset TA1 1JT.

HARDIMAN, Marie: swimmer; b. 21 July 1975, Walsall; GB women's 200m breaststroke and 400m individ. medley champ. 1993; England youth debut 1990, snr debut 1991, World Cup GP squad 1991, 93; GB debut and European Champs. women's 200m breaststroke bronze medal 1993. *Leisure interests*: watching all sport, music. *Address*: c/o ASA, Harold Fern House, Derby Square, Loughborough, Leics. LE11 0AL.

HARDING, Kim Anne: water skier (barefoot); b. 18 March 1962, Romford; m. Peter Harding 1991; GB ladies' jump champ. 1991, 92; European Champs. ladies' jump silver medal 1991, gold 1992. *Leisure interests*: swimming, callanetics, aerobics, socializing, gardening, reading. *Address*: 32 East Rd, Chadwell Heath, Romford, Essex RM6 6XP.

HARDING, Paul: footballer; b. 6 March 1964, Mitcham; player Barnet, Notts County 1990–94, Birmingham City 94– . *Address*: Birmingham City FC, St Andrews Ground, Birmingham B9 4NH.

HARDY, Billy: boxer; b. 15 September 1964; ABA jnr champ. 1981; England debut 1982; prof. debut 1983; titles won: GB bantamweight 1987, Commonwealth featherweight 1992; over 26 prof. wins. *Address*: Nat. Promotions, Nat. House, 60–66 Wardour St, London W1V 3HP.

HARFORD, Michael: footballer; b. 12 February 1959, Sunderland; player Lincoln City 1977–80, Newcastle Utd 80–81, Bristol City 81–82, Birmingham City 82–84, Luton Town 84–90, Derby County 90–91, Luton Town 91–92, Chelsea 92–93, Sunderland 1993, Coventry 1993– ; with Luton Town: winners League Cup 1988; 2 England caps. *Address*: Coventry City FC, Highfield Rd Stadium, King Richard St, Coventry CV2 4FW.

HARGRAVES, Spencer: surfer; b. 22 January 1973, Truro; English jnr champ. 1987; GB jnr champ. 1987–89, open champ. 1988, 89, Cup champ. 1989; European pro-jnr champ. 1991, pro-am champ. 1990–92; world pro-jnr champ. 1992; GB debut 1988. *Leisure interests*: swimming, tennis, snowboarding. *Address*: 23 St Thomas Rd, Newquay, Cornwall TR7 1RS.

HARGREAVES, Christian: footballer; b. 12 May 1972, Cleethorpes; player Grimsby Town 1989– . *Address*: Grimsby Town FC, Blundell Park, Cleethorpes, S. Humberside DN35 7PY.

HARKES, John: footballer; b. 8 March 1967, New Jersey, USA; player N. Carolina (USA), Sheffield Wednesday 1990–93, Derby County 93– ; USA int. *Address*: Derby County FC, The Baseball Ground, Shaftesbury Crescent, Derby DE3 8NB.

HARLAND, Lee: Rugby League footballer; b. 4 September 1973; player Leeds 1992–93, Halifax 93– . *Address*: Halifax RLFC, The Pavilion, Thrum Hall, Gibbet St, Halifax, W. Yorks. HX1 4TL.

HARMON, Neil: Rugby League footballer; b. 9 January 1969, St Helens; player Blackbrook ARLFC, Warrington 1986–93, Leeds 93– ; GB U-21 debut v. France 1988. *Address*: Leeds RLFC, Bass Headingley, St Michael's Lane, Leeds LS6 3BR.

HAROLD, David William: snooker player; b. 9 December 1966, Stoke on Trent; prof. debut 1991, winner Asian Open 1993; lowest-ranked player to win a major ranking tournament. *Leisure interests*: all sport, keeping fit, Stoke City FC. *Address*: World Prof. Billiards and Snooker Assoc., 27 Oakfield Rd, Clifton, Bristol BS8 2AT.

HARPER, Alan: footballer; b. 1 November 1960, Liverpool; player Everton 1983–88, Sheffield Wednesday 88–89, Manchester City 89–91, Everton 91–92, Luton Town 92– ; with Everton: League champs. 1984/85, 86/87. *Address*: Luton Town FC, Kenilworth Stadium, 1 Maple Rd, Luton, Beds. LU4 8AW.

HARPER, Laurent Olivier: fencer (foil); b. 24 March 1968, Edmonton; GB U-14 champ. 1982, U-16 champ. 1984, U-18 champ. 1986, snr champ. 1992, 93, 94, team champ. 1985 (Salle Goodall), 1991 (Salle Boston); GB U-20 debut 1982, snr debut and World Champs. squad 1993; winner Birmingham Int. 1993. *Leisure interests*: music, food, Thai boxing, football, weight and circuit training. *Address*: c/o AFA, 1 Barons Gate, 33–35 Rothschild Rd, London W4 5HT.

HARRIMAN, Andrew Tuoyo: Rugby Union footballer; b. 13 July 1964; player Harlequins; England debut v. Aus. 1988, winning squad World Cup Sevens 1993 (capt.); GB U-16 tennis doubles champ. *Address*: Harlequins FC, Stoop Memorial Ground, Craneford Way, Twickenham, Middx.

HARRIS, Martin Clifford: swimmer; b. 21 May 1969, Bow; GB 50m and 100m backstroke champ. 1990–93; GB debut 1989; European Champs. 4 x 100m medley relay and 100m backstroke bronze medals 1993; World Short-Course Champs. 100m backstroke silver, 4 x 100m medley relay bronze medals 1993; Olympic squad 1992; GB 100m backstroke record-holder. *Leisure interests*: snooker, boxing. *Address*: c/o ASA, Harold Fern House, Derby Square, Loughborough, Leics. LE11 0AL.

HARRIS, Sylvia: target archer; b. 17 March 1965, Chorley; rep. Cheshire 1980–88, ladies' county champ. 1979–81, Warks. 88– , county champ. 1992; GB U-13 outdoor and indoor champ. 1977, U-16 champ. 1979, 80, girls' champ. 1981, 82, ladies' champ. 1985; attained Grand Master Bowman status 1982; Brit. Indoor Champs. silver medal 1981, Brit. Target Champs. bronze medal 1983; England debut 1981; GB jnr debut 1982, snr debut 1983; Olympic reserve 1984, squad 1992. *Leisure interests*: design, architectural design. *Address*: 2 Heath End Rd, Alsager, Stoke on Trent ST7 2SQ.

HARRISON, Chris: Rugby League footballer; b. 28 September 1967; player Eureka ARLFC, Hull Kingston Rovers 1991– . *Address*: Hull Kingston Rovers RLFC, Craven Park, Preston Rd, Hull HU9 5HE.

HARRISON, John: Rugby League footballer; b. 10 March 1965, Ashton-in-Makerfield; player Parkside ARLFC, St Helens 1987– . *Address*: St Helens RLFC, Dunriding Lane, St Helens, Merseyside WA10 4AD.

HARRISON, Karl: Rugby League footballer; b. 20 February 1964, Morley; player Bramley, Featherstone Rovers, Hull, Halifax 1991– ; GB debut v. Aus. 1990. *Address*: Halifax RLFC, The Pavilion, Thrum Hall, Gibbet St, Halifax, W. Yorks HX1 4TL.

HART, Karen: netball player; b. 17 March 1973, Glasgow; player Castlemilk 1987– ; rep. Glasgow District U-21 1991– , snr inter-district champs. 1992/93; Scotland U-18 debut 1989, U-21 debut 1990, snr debut 1992. *Leisure interests*: badminton, racketball, reading, socializing, watching sport on TV. *Address*: c/o Scottish Netball Assoc., Kelvin Hall, Argyle St, Glasgow G3 8AW.

HARTLEY, Peter John: cricketer; b. 18 April 1960, Keighley; m. Sharon Hartley 1988; 1 d.; player Warks. 1982–84, Yorks. 85– . *Address*: Yorks. CCC, Headingley Cricket Ground, Leeds LS6 3BU.

HARVEY, Peter James: hang glider pilot; b. 14 October 1958, Worthing; GB champ. 1993; GB debut 1980; European Champs. team gold medal 1990; World Champs. team gold medal 1991. *Leisure interests*: building my own house, gliding, paragliding, keep-fit, reading. *Address*: 3 Ashpole Furlong, Loughton, Milton Keynes MK5 8EA.

HARWOOD, Guy: racehorse trainer; b. 10 June 1939, Pulborough; m. Gillian Rosalind Lawson 1965; 3 d.; 1st licence 1966; winner 2000 Guineas 1981 (To Agori Mou), 1986 (Dancing Brave), King George VI and Queen Elizabeth Diamond Stakes 1982 (Kalaglow), 1986 (Dancing Brave), Prix de l'Arc de Triomphe 1986 (Dancing Brave). *Leisure interests*: tennis, golf, 4-wheel driving. *Address*: Coombelands Racing Stables, Pulborough, W. Sussex RH20 1BP.

HASTINGS, Andrew Gavin, OBE: Rugby Union footballer; b. 3 January 1962, Edinburgh; player Cambridge Univ. (Blue 1984, 85), Watsonians; Scotland and Five Nations debut v. France 1986, Grand Slam champs., capt. 1993– , tours N. America 1985, NZ (World Cup) 1987, 90, Aus. 1992, over 44 caps; Brit. Lions tours Aus. 1989, NZ 1993 (capt.); holds Scottish records for most points scored in Five Nations season (52 in 1986) and for points scored in one game (27 v. Romania, World Cup 1987). *Leisure interests*: golf, squash, tennis, travel. *Address*: Carnegie Partnership Ltd, 46 Charlotte Square, Edinburgh EH2 4HQ.

HASTINGS, Scott: Rugby Union footballer; b. 4 December 1964, Edinburgh; m. Jenny Hastings 1990; 1 s.; player Northern 1982–85, Watsonians 1986– (capt. 1987/88, 89/90); Scotland B debut v. Italy B 1985, snr and Five Nations debut v. France 1986, Grand Slam champs. 1990, tour NZ 1990, Aus. 1992, over 45 caps; Brit. Lions tours Aus. 1989, NZ 1993; shares with Sean Lineen world's most-capped centre partnership (27). *Leisure interests*: golf, mixed mud wrestling. *Address*:

Watsonians RFC, Myreside, Myreside Rd, Edinburgh EH10 5DB.

HATELEY, Mark: footballer; b. 7 November 1961, Liverpool; player Coventry City 1978–83, Portsmouth 83–84, AC Milan (Italy), AS Monaco, Rangers 1990– ; with Rangers: winners Scottish League Cup 1991, 93, Scottish Cup 1992, 93; 10 England U-21 caps, 32 full England caps. *Address*: Glasgow Rangers FC, Ibrox Stadium, 150 Edmiston Drive, Glasgow G51 2XD.

HAUSER, Thomas: footballer; b. 10 April 1965, W. Germany; player FC Basel (Switzerland), Sunderland 1989– . *Address*: Sunderland FC, Roker Park Ground, Sunderland, Tyne and Wear SR6 9SW.

HAVELOCK, Robert Gary: motorcyclist (speedway); b. 4 November 1966, Eaglescliffe; rep. Middlesbrough, Bradford (capt.); with Middlesbrough: Nat. League fours champs. 1985; with Bradford: winners Div. 1 Cup 1991–93; Nat. League grand slam champ. 1986; GB U-21 champ. 1986, snr champ. 1991, 92; overseas champ. 1992; world champ. 1992. *Leisure interests*: night clubs, rave music, helping charities, promoting speedway. *Address*: c/o Philip Lanning, 17 Whitcroft, Langdon Hills, Laindon SS16 6LR.

HAVERY, Steve: Rugby Union footballer; b. 13 February 1962, Newcastle; player W. Hartlepool 1992– ; rep. Durham U-16 and snr squad, N. Div. colts, England colts. *Address*: W. Hartlepool RFC, Brierton Lane, Hartlepool, Cleveland TS25 5DR.

HAWES, Katherine Elizabeth Alice: flat green bowler; b. 9 December 1969, Oxford; English women's triples champ. 1992; UK mixed triples champ. 1991; England jnr debut 1988. *Leisure interests*: swimming, music, drawing and painting, dress-making. *Address*: `Mainlands', Water Lane, Drayton St Leonard, Wallingford, Oxon OX10 7BE.

HAWKE, Warren: footballer; b. 20 September 1970, Durham; player Sunderland 1988– . *Address*: Sunderland FC, Roker Park Ground, Sunderland, Tyne and Wear SR6 9SW.

HAWKINS, Jamie Fenton: windsurfer; b. 8 February 1973, Rustington; World Youth Champs. funboard gold medal 1991; World Champs. funboard gold medal 1992. *Leisure interests*: surfing, tennis, squash, weight training, music. *Address*: 3 Angmering Lane, E. Preston, Littlehampton, W. Sussex BN16 2SN.

HAY, Andy: Rugby League footballer; b. 5 November 1973, Castleford; player Castleford 1990– , winners Regal Trophy 1994. *Address*: Castleford RLFC, Wheldon Rd, Castleford WF10 2SD.

HAYHURST, Andrew Neil: cricketer; b. 23 November 1962, Manchester; m. April Hayhurst 1990; 1 s.; player Lancs. 1985–89, Somerset 1990– (capt. 94–); with Lancs.: tours Jamaica 1987, 88, Zimbabwe 1989; with Somerset: tour Bahamas 1990. *Address*: Somerset CCC, The County Ground, Taunton, Somerset TA1 1JT.

HAYNES, Desmond Leo: cricketer; b. 15 February 1956, St James, Barbados; m. Dawn Haynes 1991; player Middx 1989– , county champs. 1990, 93, Sunday League champs. 1992; Test debut 1977, WI tours Aus./NZ 1979/80, England 1980, Pakistan 1980/81, Aus. 1981/82, India 1983/84, England 1984, Aus. 1984/85, NZ/Pakistan 1986/87, India 1987/88, England 1988, Aus. 1988/89, India 1989/90, Pakistan 1990/91, England 1991, Pakistan/Aus. (World Cup) 1991/92, Aus./SA 1992/93; Britannic Assurance Player of the Year 1990. *Address*: Middx CCC, Lord's Cricket Ground, London NW8 8QN.

HAYNES, Gavin Richard: cricketer; b. 29 September 1969; player Worcs. 1991– ; rep. England Schools U-15. *Address*: Worcs.

CCC, County Ground, New Rd, Worcester WR2 4QQ.

HAZARD, Michael: footballer; b. 5 February 1960, Sunderland; player Tottenham Hotspur 1978–85, Chelsea 85–90, Portsmouth 1990, Swindon Town 1990–93, Tottenham Hotspur 93– ; with Tottenham Hotspur: winners FA Cup 1982, UEFA Cup 1984. *Address*: Tottenham Hotspur FC, 748 High Rd, Tottenham, London N17 0AP.

HAZEL, Shannon Mark: rackets player; b. 6 July 1961, Bristol; GB prof. champ. 1982, 84, 90, 91, U-24 champ. 1983, 84, open champ. 1992, open doubles champ. 1991, 92; US prof. singles champ. 1984–86, open singles champ. 1986, open doubles champ. 1986–90; world doubles champ. 1992, 93; winner Canadian Jnr Open (squash) 1977. *Leisure interests*: reading, music, beach holidays, conversation, films. *Address*: The Rackets Court, Clifton College, 32 College Rd, Clifton, Bristol BS8 3JH.

HAZLITT, Simon Charles: hockey player; b. 16 October 1966, Woking; player Hounslow 1988– (capt.), club champs. 1988/89, 90/91, 91/92, 92/93, League champs. 1989/90, 92/93; England and GB debuts 1987. *Leisure interests*: literature, golf. *Address*: Hounslow HC, Chiswick Boat House, Dukes Meadows, London W4 2SH.

HEAD, Hilary: Alpine skier; b. 16 October 1974, Paris, France; GB jnr women's super giant slalom champ. 1992, snr women's slalom champ. 1990; GB debut 1991, World Jnr Champs. squad 1991, 92. *Leisure interests*: cross-country running, athletics, horseriding, swimming. *Address*: Bernwood House, Holton, Oxford OX33 1PY.

HEAD, Robbie: rally driver; b. 28 May 1968; rep. Ford; Scottish class A 1300cc champ. 1988; GB N2 champ. 1990; group N winner, Ulster Rally, RAC Rally 1991,

Scottish Rally 1991, 93. *Leisure interests*: water skiing, mountain biking. *Address*: c/o Stuart McCrudden Associates Ltd, 10 The Street, Wickham Bishops, Witham, Essex CM8 3NN.

HEADLEY, Dean Warren: cricketer; b. 27 January 1970, Stourbridge; player Middx 1991–92, Kent 93– . *Address*: Kent CCC, St Lawrence Ground, Canterbury CT1 3NZ.

HEATH, Martin Robert: squash player; b. 31 January 1973, Stirling; player Oban, Glasgow Univ. 1990–92, Glasgow Academicals 1991– ; rep. W. of Scotland 1989– ; Scottish U-14 champ. 1985, U-19 champ. 1991, univ. champ. 1993; Scotland jnr debut 1985, snr debut 1992; European Champs. team gold medal 1992; Scottish Player of the Year 1992/93. *Leisure interests*: parachuting, skydiving, anthropology, travel, writing poetry and children's stories, music, reptile-breeding. *Address*: Corry Lynn, Laurel Rd, Oban, Argyll PA34 5EB.

HEATHCOTE, Michael: footballer; b. 10 September 1965, Kelloe, Durham; player Sunderland 1987–90, Shrewsbury Town 90–91, Cambridge Utd 91– . *Address*: Cambridge Utd FC, Abbey Stadium, Newmarket Rd, Cambridge CB5 8LL.

HEBBARD, Steven David: powerboat racer (navigator); b. 14 November 1963, London; GB offshore circuit racing C class champ. 1993; winner Duckhams Trophy 1993. *Leisure interests*: driving and rebuilding cars, jet skiing. *Address*: The Firs, Roding Way, Rainham, Essex.

HEBDEN, David John: Rugby fives player; b. 30 June 1948, Shoreham-by-Sea; m. Katherine Bridget Hebden 1974; 2 d.; rep. Alleyn's School 1960–67, Cambridge Univ. 67–70 (Blue 68–70), Alleyn Old Boys 70– ; with Alleyn Old Boys: club champs. 1989; GB univ. doubles champ. 1967, 69; GB

amateur singles champ. 1979, doubles champ. 1980–85, 87–90 (record number of wins). *Leisure interests*: family, soccer, golf, running, skiing, walking, watching all sports, guitar, gardening, reading. *Address*: The Coolins, 118 Holly Lane E., Banstead, Surrey SM7 2BE.

HEGG, Warren Kevin: cricketer; b. 23 February 1968, Radcliffe; player Lancs. 1986– ; England U-19 tours Sri Lanka 1986/87, Aus. (Youth World Cup) 1988, England A tour Pakistan/Sri Lanka 1990/91. *Address*: Lancs. CCC, Old Trafford, Manchester M16 0PX.

HEMMINGS, Andrew: yachtsman; b. 9 August 1964, Reading; m. Gina Hemmings 1992; UK J-24 champ. 1985, 470-class champ. 1986–88, 91; US J-24 champ. 1991, 92; European Champs. Fireball gold medal 1985, J-24 gold 1990, CHS gold 1993; World Champs. 420-class gold medal 1983, bronze 1991, J-24 gold 1990; Olympic squad (470 class) 1988, 92. *Publications*: contributor to *Yachts and Yachting, Portsmouth Evening News*. *Leisure interests*: walking, fishing, the house. *Address*: 'The Gateway', Woodgreen Common, Woodgreen, Hants.

HEMMINGS, Edward Ernest: cricketer; b. 20 February 1949, Leamington Spa; m. Christine Mary Hemmings 1971; 2 s.; player Warks. 1966–78, Notts. 79–92, Sussex 93– ; 16 Tests, debut 1982, 33 1-day ints, tours Aus./NZ 1982/83, Pakistan/Aus./NZ (World Cup) 1987/88, India/WI 1989/90, Aus. 1990/91; maiden 1st-class 100 v. Yorks. 1982. *Address*: Sussex CCC, County Ground, Eaton Rd, Hove, E. Sussex BN3 3AN.

HEMP, David Lloyd: cricketer; b. 15 November 1970, Bermuda; player Glamorgan 1991– ; Welsh Schools U-19 tour Aus. 1986/87. *Address*: Glamorgan CCC, Sophia Gardens, Cardiff CF1 9XR.

HEMSLEY, David Michael: cyclist (cycle speedway); b. 16 December 1969, Leicester; GB U-18 outdoor and indoor champ. 1987, U-21 indoor champ. 1988, 89, snr outdoor champ. 1992, indoor champ. 1988, 89, 91; S. hemisphere champ. 1990, 93; world masters champ. 1991; England debut 1988, winners World Cup 1991, 93. *Leisure interests*: motorcycle speedway. *Address*: 68 Oakfield Ave, Markfield, Leicester LE67 9WG.

HENDER, Jason Brian: swimmer; b. 26 April 1971, Manchester; England debut 1991; GB debut and Olympic squad 1992 (200m breaststroke). *Leisure interests*: music, bowling, Liverpool FC, cricket, art, film. *Address*: c/o ASA, Harold Fern House, Derby Square, Loughborough, Leics. LE11 0AL.

HENDERSON, Fergus Michael: Rugby Union footballer; b. 5 July 1969, Edinburgh; player Trinity Academicals 1987–90, Watsonians 90– ; rep. Edinburgh U-21 1988–90; Scotland U-19 squad 1987/88. *Leisure interests*: climbing, skiing, golf, drinking Guinness. *Address*: Watsonians RFC, Myreside, Myreside Rd, Edinburgh EH10 5DB.

HENDERSON, Nicholas John: racehorse trainer (NH); b. 10 December 1950, London; m. Diana Thorne 1978; 3 d.; amateur NH jockey 1970–78, rode 75 winners; 1st trainer's licence 1978; winner Champion Hurdle 1985, 86, 87 (See You Then), Whitbread Gold Cup 1989 (Brown Windsor); leading trainer 1985/86, 86/87. *Leisure interests*: golf. *Address*: Seven Barrows, Lambourn, Newbury, Berks. RG16 7UJ.

HENDON, Ian: footballer; b. 5 December 1971, Ilford; player Tottenham Hotspur 1989–93, Leyton Orient 93– ; 4 England U-21 caps. *Address*: Leyton Orient FC, Leyton Stadium, Brisbane Rd, Leyton, London E10 5NE.

HENDRIE, John: footballer; b. 24 October 1963, Lennoxtown; player Coventry City 1981–84, Bradford City 84–88, Newcastle Utd 88–89, Leeds Utd 89–90, Middlesbrough 90– ; with Bradford City: 3rd Div. champs. 1984/85; with Leeds Utd: 2nd Div. champs. 1989/90. *Address*: Middlesbrough FC, Ayresome Park, Middlesbrough, Cleveland TS1 4PB.

HENDRY, Colin: footballer; b. 7 December 1965, Keith; player Dundee, Blackburn Rovers 1986–89, Manchester City 89–91, Blackburn Rovers 91– ; over 2 Scotland caps. *Address*: Blackburn Rovers FC, Ewood Park, Blackburn, Lancs. BB2 4JF.

HENDRY, John: footballer; b. 6 January 1970, Glasgow; player Dundee 1988–90, Tottenham Hotspur 90– ; 1 Scotland U-21 cap. *Address*: Tottenham Hotspur FC, 748 High Rd, Tottenham, London N17 0AP.

HENDRY, Stephen Gordon, MBE: snooker player; b. 13 January 1969, Edinburgh; Scottish amateur champ. 1984, 85; prof. debut 1985, Scottish champ. 1986–88, UK champ. 1989, 90, world champ. 1990 (youngest-ever winner), 92, 93, 94, winner Rothmans GP 1987, 90, 91, World Doubles 1987, Brit. Open 1988, 91, Asian Open 1989, 90, 91, Dubai Classic 1989, 90, 93, Scottish Masters 1989, 90, Masters 1989–93, Irish Masters 1992, Int. Open 1993; holds record for 100 breaks (over 205); 1st player to win all 9 world-ranking tournaments. *Leisure interests*: golf, music, film. *Address*: Cuemasters Ltd, Kerse Rd, Stirling FK7 7SG.

HENRY, Nicholas: footballer; b. 21 February 1969, Liverpool; player Oldham Athletic 1987– . *Address*: Oldham Athletic FC, Boundary Park, Oldham, Lancs. OL1 2PA.

HEPWORTH, Peter Nash: cricketer; b. 4 May 1967, Ackworth, W. Yorks.; player Leics. 1988– . *Address*: Leics. CCC, County Ground, Grace Rd, Leicester LE2 8AD.

HERBERT, Garry Gerard Paul, MBE:
coxswain; b. 3 October 1969, London; rep.
Thames RC 1985–87, Leander Club 88– ;
with Leander: winners Grand Challenge
Cup, Henley Royal Regatta 1991; GB jnr
debut 1987, U-23 debut 1988; World U-23
Champs. eights bronze medals 1988, 90;
snr debut 1991; World Champs. eights
bronze medal 1991, coxed pairs gold 1993;
Olympic coxed pairs gold medal 1992.
Leisure interests: travel, law, broadcasting,
eating in good restaurants. *Address*: 75
Netheravon Rd, Chiswick, London
W4 2NB.

HERBERT, John Paul (Johnny): F1 driver;
b. 25 June 1964; m. Rebecca Cross 1990; 2
d.; GB jnr go-kart champ. 1979, snr champ.
1982; F3 debut 1986, GB F3 champ. 1987;
F1 debut 1989, rep. Benetton 1989, Lotus
1991– ; winner Le Mans 24-hour race
1991. *Address*: c/o Team Lotus Int.,
Ketteringham Hall, Wymondham, Norfolk
NR18 9RS.

HERBERT, Niki Jane: water polo player;
b. 22 January 1967, Farnborough; m. Mark
Alan Herbert 1991; player Beckenham
1982– ; GB debut 1984 (ladies' capt.
1991–92), European Champs. squad 1985,
87, 91, World Champs. squad 1986. *Leisure
interests*: skiing, water skiing, travel, good
food, music. *Address*: 134 Aylesford Ave,
Beckenham, Kent BR3 3RY.

HERN, William Richard, CVO: racehorse
trainer (Flat); b. 20 January 1921, Holford;
m. Sheilah Hern 1956; amateur jockey
1938–56; 1st trainer's licence 1957; winner
2000 Guineas 1971 (Brigadier Gerard), 1989
(Nashwan), King George VI and Queen
Elizabeth Diamond Stakes 1972 (Brigadier
Gerard), 1979 (Troy), 1980 (Ela Mana
Mou), 1985 (Petoski), 1989 (Nashwan),
1000 Guineas 1974 (Highclere), St Leger
1962 (Hethersett), 1974 (Bustino), 1977
(Dunfermline), 1981 (Cut Above), 1983
(Sun Princess), Oaks 1977 (Dunfermline),

1980 (Bireme), 1983 (Sun Princess),
Derby 1979 (Troy), 1980 (Henbit), 1989
(Nashwan); leading trainer 1962, 72, 80, 83.
Address: c/o BHB, 42 Portman Square,
London W1H 0EN.

HERON, David Colin: Rugby League
footballer; b. 1 March 1958, Leeds; player
Hunslet Parkside, Leeds, Bradford
Northern 1992– ; rep. Yorks.; GB debut
v. Aus. 1982. *Address*: Bradford Northern
RLFC, Odsal Stadium, Bradford BD6 1BS.

HERRERA, Roberto: footballer; b. 12 June
1970, Torquay; player Queens Park
Rangers 1988– . *Address*: Queens Park
Rangers FC, Rangers Stadium, S. Africa
Rd, London W12 7PA.

HESLOP, Nigel John: Rugby League foot-
baller; b. 4 December 1963, Hartlepool; m.
Denise Heslop; RU: player Waterloo,
Liverpool, Orrell; rep. Lancs., county
champs. 1989/90; England debut v.
Argentina 1990, Grand Slam champs. 1991,
92, tours Argentina 1990, Aus./Fiji 1991;
RL: player Oldham 1993– . *Address*:
Oldham RLFC, The Pavilion,
Watersheddings, Oldham OL4 2PB.

HESSENTHALER, Andrew: footballer;
b. 17 August 1965, Dartford; player
Watford 1991– . *Address*: Watford FC,
Vicarage Rd Stadium, Watford, Herts.
WD1 8ER.

HESTER, Carl Rupert: equestrianist (dressage); b. 29 June 1967, Barnet; nat. U-21
champ. 1985, GP champ. 1992; GB U-21
debut 1988, snr debut 1990, European
Champs. squad 1991, World Champs.
squad 1990 (youngest-ever rider selected),
Olympic squad 1992; youngest-ever rider
to win a GP 1990; Dressage Rider of the
Year 1992. *Leisure interests*: eating out,
travel, squash. *Address*: Stable Cottage,
Eastington House, Ampney St Peter,
Cirencester, Glos.

HETHERSTON, Peter: footballer; b. 6 November 1964, Bellshill; player Falkirk 1984–87, Watford 87–88, Sheffield Utd 88–89, Falkirk 89–91, Raith Rovers 91–   . *Address*: Raith Rovers FC, Stark's Park, Pratt St, Kirkcaldy, Fife KY1 1SA.

HICK, Graeme Ashley: cricketer; b. 23 May 1966, Trelawney, Zimbabwe; m. Jackie Hick 1991; 1 d.; player Worcs. 1984–   , county champs. 1988, 89, Sunday League champs. 1987, 88; Zimbabwe tours England (World Cup) 1983, Sri Lanka 1983/84; Test debut 1991, England tours NZ/Aus. (World Cup) 1991/92, India/Sri Lanka 1992/93, WI 1994; youngest player to score 2000 1st-class runs in season 1986; made highest individ. score in England since 1985 (405 n.o.) v. Somerset 1988; completed 10,000 runs in 1st-class cricket and became youngest batsman to obtain 50 1st-class 100s 1990; maiden Test and 1-day int. 100s v. India 1993; became youngest batsman to score 20,000 1st-class runs 1993. *Address*: Worcs. CCC, County Ground, New Rd, Worcester WR2 4QQ.

HICKEY, Daryl John: Rugby Union footballer; b. 3 November 1959, Bristol; m. Susan Elizabeth Hickey 1992; player Bristol 1982–   . *Leisure interests*: squash, badminton, tennis, walking, DIY, travel, sunworshipping. *Address*: Bristol FC, Memorial Ground, Filton Ave, Horfield, Bristol BS7 0AQ.

HICKMAN, James Paul: swimmer; b. 2 February 1976, Stockport; GB 200m butterfly jnr champ. 1993; England youth debut 1992, snr debut 1993; GB jnr debut 1992; European Jnr Champs. 4 x 100m medley relay silver medal 1992, 4 x 100m medley relay and 200m butterfly gold 1993. *Leisure interests*: writing, music, travel. *Address*: Flat 5, Thorne House, 279 Wilmslow Rd, Fallowfield, Manchester M14 6HW.

HIDE, Herbie: boxer; b. 27 August 1971; prof. debut 1989; titles won: WBC int. heavyweight 1992, WBO penta-continental heavyweight, GB heavyweight 1993; over 25 prof. wins. *Address*: Matchroom Ltd, 10 Western Rd, Romford, Essex RM1 3JT.

HIGGINS, David: footballer; b. 19 August 1961, Liverpool; player Tranmere Rovers 1983–84, 87–   . *Address*: Tranmere Rovers FC, Prenton Park, Prenton Rd W., Birkenhead, Merseyside L42 9PN.

HIGNETT, Craig: footballer; b. 21 January 1970, Whiston; player Crewe Alexandra 1988–92, Middlesbrough 92–   . *Address*: Middlesbrough FC, Ayresome Park, Middlesbrough, Cleveland TS1 4PB.

HILEY, Scott: footballer; b. 27 September 1968, Plymouth; player Exeter City 1987–93, Birmingham City 93–   ; with Exeter City: 4th Div. champs. 1989/90. *Leisure interests*: most sports. *Address*: Birmingham City FC, St Andrews Ground, Birmingham B9 4NH.

HILL, Colin: footballer; b. 12 November 1963, Uxbridge; player Arsenal 1981–84, Maritima (Portugal), Colchester Utd 1987–89, Sheffield Utd 89–92, Leicester City 92–   ; 6 NI caps. *Address*: Leicester City FC, City Stadium, Filbert St, Leicester LE2 7FL.

HILL, Damon Graham Devereux: F1 driver; b. 17 September 1960, Hampstead; m. Georgie Hill; 2 s.; F3 debut 1986; F3000 debut 1988, rep. GA Motosport 1988, Footwork 1989, Middlebridge 1990–91; F1 debut 1992, rep. Brabham 1992, Williams 93–   , winner Hungarian, Belgian, Italian GP, 2nd place Brazilian, European, Monaco and French GP 1993. *Leisure interests*: motorcycles, golf, guitar-playing, Arsenal FC. *Address*: c/o Williams GP Engineering Ltd, Basil Hill Rd, Didcot, Berks. OX11 7HW.

HILL, Graeme Everitt: basketball player; b. 28 January 1964, Ayr; player Murray Int. Metals/Livingston 1984– , winners Scottish Cup 1987–93, League Cup 1988, Scottish League champs. 1984/85–92/93, nat. play-off champs. 1988; Scotland and GB debut 1984. *Leisure interests*: rugby, swimming, squash. *Address*: 32C Cadogan Park, Belfast BT9 6HH.

HILL, Michael: athlete (javelin); b. 22 October 1964, Leeds; AAA champ. 1987, 90, 91; UK champ. 1985–87, 93; Commonwealth Games silver medals 1986, 90; European Cup silver medal 1993; World Champs. bronze medal 1993. *Address*: c/o Brit. Athletic Fed., 225A Bristol Rd, Edgbaston, Birmingham B5 7UB.

HILL, Richard John: Rugby Union footballer; b. 4 May 1961, Birmingham; m. Karen Hill; 1 s., 1 d.; player Exeter Univ., Salisbury, Bath 1983– ; with Bath: winners Pilkington Cup 1984, 85, 86, 87, 89, 90, 92, League champs. 1990/91, 91/92, 92/93; rep. S.W. Div., Div. champs. 1993/94; England B debut 1986, snr debut v. SA 1984, Five Nations debut v. Ireland 1985, Grand Slam champs. 1991, tours SA 1984, NZ 1985, Aus./NZ (World Cup) 1987, Argentina 1990, Aus. 1991. *Address*: Bath RFC, Recreation Ground, Bath BA2 6PW.

HILL, Robert William: hockey player; b. 11 June 1967, Maidstone; m. Nicky Hill 1991; player Taunton Vale 1986–89, Havant 89–92, Firebrands 92–93, Havant 93– ; with Havant: European Cup Winners' Cup silver medallist 1991, club champs. 1990, League champs. 1991, 92; rep. Somerset; England indoor debut 1987, European Champs. U-21 silver medallist and capt. 1988, World Cup squad 1990; GB debut 1988, World Student Games gold medallist 1991, Olympic squad 1992. *Leisure interests*: shooting. *Address*: Havant HC, Havant Park, Havant, Hants.

HILLS, Barrington William: racehorse trainer (Flat); b. 2 April 1937; m. Penelope Hills; 5 s.; 1st licence 1969; winner Prix de l'Arc de Triomphe 1973 (Rheingold), 1000 Guineas 1978 (Enstone Spark), 2000 Guineas 1979 (Tap on Wood), Irish Derby 1987 (Sir Harry Lewis), Irish 1000 Guineas 1993 (Nicer). *Address*: c/o BHB, 42 Portman Square, London W1H 0EN.

HILLS, Michael Patrick: jockey (Flat); b. 22 January 1963; m. Christine Hills 1989; 1 d.; winner Irish 1000 Guineas 1993 (Nicer). *Address*: c/o BHB, 42 Portman Square, London W1H 0EN.

HILLIER, David: footballer; b. 19 December 1969, Woolwich; player Arsenal 1988– , winners FA Youth Cup 1988, League Cup 1993, League champs. 1990/91; England U-21 debut 1991. *Leisure interests*: all sport except bowls. *Address*: Arsenal FC, Arsenal Stadium, Highbury, London N5 1BU.

HILLYER, Anthea: clay pigeon shooter; b. 9 April 1951, Templecombe, Somerset; 1 s.; English ladies' sporting champ. 1977, 78, 80–83, 92; GB ladies' sporting champ. 1981–83, 85; GB debut 1980; European FITASC Sporting Champs. gold medals 1980, 83, 93; World FITASC Sporting Champs. gold medals 1980, 82, 83, 86, 88, 90, 93; World Beretta Sporting Champs. gold medals 1987–89. *Address*: The Studio, Church Rd, Thornford, Sherborne, Dorset DT9 6QE.

HILTON, Paul: footballer; b. 8 October 1959, Oldham; player Bury 1978–84, W. Ham Utd 84– . *Address*: W. Ham Utd FC, Boleyn Ground, Green St, Upton Park, London E13 9AZ.

HINCHCLIFFE, Andrew: footballer; b. 5 February 1969, Manchester; player Manchester City 1987–90, Everton 90– ; 1 England U-21 cap. *Address*: Everton FC, Goodison Park, Liverpool L4 4EL.

HINDMARCH, Robert: footballer; b. 27 April 1961, Morpeth; player Sunderland 1978–84, Derby County 84–90, Wolverhampton Wanderers 90– ; with Derby County: 2nd Div. champs. 1986/87. *Address*: Wolverhampton Wanderers FC, Molineux Stadium, Waterloo Rd, Wolverhampton WV1 4QR.

HINDSON, James Edward: cricketer; b. 13 September 1973, Huddersfield; player Notts. 1992– ; England U-19 tour India 1992/93; took 5 wickets on 1st-class debut. *Address*: Notts. CCC, Trent Bridge, Nottingham NG2 6AG.

HINKS, Simon Graham: cricketer; b. 12 October 1960, Northfleet; m. Vicki Hinks 1990; 1 d.; player Kent 1982–91, Glos. 92– . *Address*: Glos. CCC, Phoenix County Ground, Nevil Rd, Bristol BS6 9EJ.

HIRST, David: footballer; b. 7 December 1967, Cudworth; player Barnsley 1985–86, Sheffield Wednesday 86– ; with Sheffield Wednesday: winners League Cup 1991; 7 England U-21 caps, 3 full England caps. *Address*: Sheffield Wednesday FC, Hillsborough, Sheffield, S. Yorks. S6 1SW.

HIRST, Lee: footballer; b. 26 January 1969, Sheffield; player Scarborough 1990–93, Coventry City 93– . *Address*: Coventry City FC, Highfield Rd Stadium, King Richard St, Coventry CV2 4FW.

HITCHCOCK, Kevin: footballer; b. 5 October 1962, Canning Town; player Nottingham Forest 1983–84, Mansfield Town 84–88, Chelsea 88– . *Address*: Chelsea FC, Stamford Bridge, Fulham Rd, London SW6 1HS.

HITCHEN, Robert: crown green bowler; b. 11 December 1958, Halifax; m. Ruth Hitchen 1986; 2 d.; rep. Yorks. 1976– ; winner Top Crown pairs 1982, 85, Champion of Champions 1985, Crown King 1990. *Address*: 'Royd House', 10 Savile Park Rd, Halifax HX1 2EY.

HOBBS, Peter David: jockey (NH); b. 9 February 1962, Minehead; m. Angela Hobbs 1989; 1 s.; only jockey to ride 4 winners in 1 day at Cheltenham. *Leisure interests*: golf, most sports. *Address*: c/o BHB, 42 Portman Square, London W1H 0EN.

HOBSON, Richard Paul Joseph: triathlete; b. 9 May 1965, Torquay; GB middle-distance champ. 1990; GB debut 1989; European Champs. middle-distance team gold medal 1992; World Champs. squad 1992; Triathlete of the Year 1990; GB speed sailing champ. 1982, 83. *Leisure interests*: surfing, windsurfing. *Address*: 72 Ferry Rd, Langston Marina, Southsea PO4 9UD.

HOCKLEY, Joanne: golfer; b. 9 February 1973, Ipswich; rep. Suffolk 1986– ; Suffolk girls' champ. 1987–91; Midland ladies' champ. 1990; GB ladies' open amateur strokeplay champ. 1992; England jnr debut 1989, snr debut 1991; GB debut 1992. *Leisure interests*: swimming, cycling, watching football. *Address*: 69 Western Ave, Felixstowe, Suffolk IP11 9NX.

HODDER, Paul: Rugby Union footballer; b. 13 April 1965, Hamilton, NZ; player W. Hartlepool 1988– (capt. 93–); NZ U-17 and U-19 int; NZ U-19 cricket int. *Address*: W. Hartlepool RFC, Brierton Lane, Hartlepool, Cleveland TS25 5DR.

HODDLE, Glenn: football player/ manager; b. 27 October 1957, Hayes, Middx; player Tottenham Hotspur 1975–87, AS Monaco, Swindon Town 1991–92; with Tottenham Hotspur: winners FA Cup 1981, 82, UEFA Cup 1984; 12 England U-21 caps, snr debut v. Bulgaria 1979, 53 caps; player/manager Swindon Town 1992–93, Chelsea 93– . *Address*: Chelsea FC, Stamford Bridge, Fulham Rd, London SW6 1HS.

HODGE, Stephen: footballer; b. 25 October 1962, Nottingham; player Nottingham Forest 1980–85, Aston Villa 85–86, Tottenham Hotspur 86–88, Nottingham Forest 88–91, Leeds Utd 91–   ; with Nottingham Forest: winners League Cup 1989, 90; with Leeds Utd: League champs. 1991/92; 8 England U-21 caps, 24 full England caps. *Address*: Leeds Utd FC, Elland Rd, Leeds, W. Yorks. LS11 0ES.

HODGES, Carole Anne: cricketer; b. 1 September 1959, Blackpool; player Leyland Motors WCC 1974–88, Fylde CC 84–88, Wakefield WCC 90–   ; with Wakefield: winners Nat. Cup 1990, 93, League champs. 1990, 92, 93; rep. Lancs. and Cheshire U-19 1974–78 (capt. 77–78), snr 74–   (capt. 87–88, 92–   ); England U-25 tours India 1981, Ireland 1984; Test debut 1984, tours NZ (World Cup) 1982, Aus. 1984/85, 88 (World Cup), Ireland 1990, The Netherlands 1991, Aus./NZ 1992, winners European Cup 1990, 91, World Cup 1993; most-capped English woman cricketer; leading wicket-taker for England in women's World Cup cricket; Sports Writers' Team of the Year award-winner 1993. *Leisure interests*: squash, badminton, golf, watching rugby and cricket, Christians in Sport, travel, TV. *Address*: c/o Women's Cricket Assoc., 41 St Michael's Lane, Headingley, Leeds LS6 3BR.

HODGES, Glyn: footballer; b. 30 April 1963, Streatham; player Wimbledon 1981–87, Newcastle Utd 1987, Watford 1987–90, Crystal Palace 90–91, Sheffield Utd 91–   ; with Wimbledon: 4th Div. champs. 1982/83; 5 Wales U-21 caps, 16 full Wales caps. *Address*: Sheffield Utd FC, Bramall Lane, Sheffield, S. Yorks S2 4SU.

HODGSON, Geoffrey Dean: cricketer; b. 22 October 1966, Carlisle; player Warks. 1987–88, Glos. 89–   ; with Glos.: tours Namibia 1990, Kenya 1991. *Address*: Glos. CCC, Phoenix County Ground, Nevil Rd, Bristol BS6 9EJ.

HODGSON, Neil Stuart: motorcyclist; b. 20 November 1973, Burnley; GB 125cc Supercup champ., U-21 and snr 125cc champ. 1992. *Leisure interests*: mountain biking, moto-cross. *Address*: Adamson's Farm House, Royle Burnley, Lancs. BB12 0RU.

HODKINSON, Paul: boxer; b. 14 September 1965; ABA jnr champ. 1982; ABA featherweight champ. 1986; England debut 1985; prof. debut 1986; titles won: GB featherweight 1988, European feather-weight 1989, WBC featherweight 1991; over 20 prof. wins. *Address*: c/o Brit. Boxing Board of Control, Jack Petersen House, 52A Borough High St, London SE1 1XW.

HODSON, Simeon: footballer; b. 5 March 1966, Lincoln; player Notts County 1984–85, Charlton Athletic 85–86, Lincoln City 86–87, Newport County 87–88, W. Bromwich Albion 88–   . *Address*: W. Bromwich Albion FC, The Hawthorns, W. Bromwich B71 4LF.

HOENIGMANN, Paul Francis: fencer (sabre); b. 3 November 1969, Los Angeles, USA; Scottish champ. 1991–93; Scotland debut 1990; GB debut 1992, World Champs. squad 1993 (1st Scottish sabre representative in GB team); winner Meadowbank Open 1991–93, Inverclyde Open 1992, 93, Highland Open 1992, Essex Open 1993. *Leisure interests*: all sport. *Address*: 19 Hillington Gardens, Cardonald, Glasgow G52 2TP.

HOGG, Carl David: Rugby Union foot-baller; b. 5 July 1969; player Melrose, Scottish League champs. 1991/92; rep. S. of Scotland; Scotland U-21 debut v. Wales 1990 (capt.), Scotland B debut v. France B 1991, snr tours Aus. 1992, Fiji/Tonga/W. Samoa 1993. *Address*: Melrose RFC, The Greenyards, Melrose TD6 9SA.

HOLDEN, Andrew: footballer; b. 14 September 1962, Flint; player Chester City 1983–86, Wigan Athletic 86–89, Oldham Athletic 89– ; 1 Wales U-21 cap, 1 full Wales cap. *Address*: Oldham Athletic FC, Boundary Park, Oldham, Lancs. OL1 2PA.

HOLDEN, Richard: footballer; b. 9 September 1964, Skipton; player Halifax Town 1986–88, Watford 88–89, Oldham Athletic 89–92, Manchester City 92–93, Oldham Athletic 93– . *Address*: Oldham Athletic FC, Boundary Park, Oldham, Lancs. OL1 2PA.

HOLDING, Neil: Rugby League footballer; b. 15 December 1961, St Helens; player St Helens, Rochdale Hornets, St Helens, Bradford Northern 1993– ; rep. Lancs.; GB debut v. Aus. 1984. *Address*: Bradford Northern RLFC, Odsal Stadium, Bradford BD6 1BS.

HOLDSWORTH, David: footballer; b. 8 November 1968, Walthamstow; player Watford 1986– ; 1 England U-21 cap. *Address*: Watford FC, Vicarage Rd Stadium, Watford, Herts. WD1 8ER.

HOLDSWORTH, Dean: footballer; b. 8 November 1968, Walthamstow; player Watford 1986–89, Brentford 89–92, Wimbledon 92– ; with Brentford: 3rd Div. champs. 1991/92. *Address*: Wimbledon FC, Selhurst Park, London SE25 6PY.

HOLFORD, Paul: Rugby Union footballer; b. 2 December 1969; player Gloucester; rep. S.W. Div., Div. champs. 1993/94. *Address*: Gloucester RUFC, Kingsholm, Worcester St, Gloucester GL3 3AX.

HOLLIGAN, Andy: boxer; b. 6 June 1967; ABA light-welterweight champ. 1987; prof. debut 1987; titles won: GB and Commonwealth light-welterweight 1991; over 21 prof. wins. *Address*: Brit. Boxing Board of Control, Jack Petersen House, 52A Borough High St, London SE1 1XW.

HOLLIOAKE, Adam John: cricketer; b. 5 September 1971, Melbourne, Aus.; player Surrey 1992– . *Address*: Surrey CCC, The Oval, Kennington, London SE11 5SS.

HOLLOWAY, Ian: footballer; b. 12 March 1963, Kingswood; player Bristol Rovers 1981–85, Wimbledon 85–86, Brentford 86–87, Bristol Rovers 87–91, Queens Park Rangers 91– ; with Bristol Rovers: 3rd Div. champs. 1989/90. *Address*: Queens Park Rangers FC, Rangers Stadium, S. Africa Rd, London W12 7PA.

HOLLOWAY, Piran Christopher Laity: cricketer; b. 1 October 1970, Helston; player Warks. 1988–93, Somerset 94– ; England U-19 tour Aus. 1990; maiden 1st-class 100 v. Worcs. 1992. *Address*: Somerset CCC, The County Ground, Taunton, Somerset TA1 1JT.

HOLROYD, Graham: Rugby League footballer; b. 25 October 1975; player Siddal ARLFC, Leeds 1992– . *Address*: Leeds RLFC, Bass Headingley, St Michael's Lane, Leeds LS6 3BR.

HOLT, Andrea Mary: table tennis player; b. 11 November 1970, Radcliffe, Manchester; English girls' jnr singles, doubles and mixed doubles champ. 1985, 86, ladies' champ. 1991, 93, doubles champ. 1993; England debut (as cadet) 1984; Olympic squad 1992; semi-finalist Italian Open 1990, women's doubles and team finalist English Open 1992. *Leisure interests*: golf, tennis, listening to music, driving fast cars, eating out, going to discos. *Address*: 72 Victoria St, Ramsbottom, Bury, Lancs. BL0 9EB.

HONEYGHAN, Lloyd: boxer; b. 22 April 1960; England debut 1980; prof. debut 1980; titles won: GB welterweight 1983, Commonwealth and European welter-weight 1985, WBC welterweight 1986, 88, IBF welterweight 1987, Commonwealth light-middleweight 1993; over 41 prof.

wins; Sports Writers' Sportsman of the Year 1986. *Address*: Nat. Promotions, Nat. House, 60–66 Wardour St, London W1V 3HP.

HOOD, Garry: flat green bowler; b. 30 June 1961, Kilmarnock; rep. Ayrshire 1985– ; Scottish triples champ. (indoor) 1989; winner Scottish Cup (outdoor) 1985, 86, 89, (indoor) 1989; Scotland debut 1986. *Leisure interests*: fishing, modelling, reading, youth work. *Address*: 51 Mary Morison Drive, Mauchline, Ayrshire KA5 6BA.

HOOPER, Carl Llewellyn: cricketer; b. 15 December 1966, Guyana; player Kent 1992– ; Test debut 1987, WI tours India/Pakistan 1987/88, Aus. 1988/89, Pakistan 1990/91, England 1991, Pakistan/Aus. (World Cup) 1991/92, Aus./SA 1992/93. *Address*: Kent CCC, St Lawrence Ground, Canterbury CT1 3NZ.

HOPE, Shannon: ice hockey player; b. 25 November 1962; player Peterborough Pirates 1984–85, Cardiff Devils 85– ; with Peterborough Pirates: Div. 1 champs. 1984/85; with Cardiff Devils: winners Autumn Cup 1993, Div. 1 champs. 1988/89, League champs., GB champs. 1989/90, 92/93; World Champs. debut 1992. *Address*: Wales Nat. Ice Rink, Hayes Bridge Rd, Cardiff CF1 2GH.

HOPKINS, Kevin: Rugby Union footballer; b. 29 September 1961, Cwmllynfell; player Ystradgynlais, Neath, Cardiff, Swansea 1981– ; Wales and Five Nations debut v. England 1985. *Address*: Swansea RFC, St Helen's, Bryn Rd, Swansea SA2 0AR.

HOPLEY, Damian Paul: Rugby Union footballer; b. 12 April 1970; player Wasps; England B debut v. Emerging Aus. 1990, tour NZ 1992, snr tours Aus./Fiji 1991, Canada (England A) 1993, winning squad World Cup Sevens 1993. *Address*: Wasps FC, Wasps Football Ground, Repton Ave, Sudbury, nr Wembley, Middx HA0 3DW.

HORE, Stephen Michael: powerboat racer; b. 6 January 1960, Looe; 1 s.; GB offshore circuit racing 1.8-litre champ. 1990, class III 2-litre champ. 1993. *Leisure interests*: golf, badminton, water skiing. *Address*: Hayloft Restaurant, Menheniot Station, nr Liskeard, Cornwall PL14 3PU.

HORNE, Barry: footballer; b. 18 May 1962, St Asaph; player Wrexham 1984–87, Portsmouth 87–89, Southampton 89–92, Everton 92– ; over 38 Wales caps. *Address*: Everton FC, Goodison Park, Liverpool L4 4EL.

HORNE, Brian: footballer; b. 5 October 1967, Billericay; player Millwall 1985–92, Portsmouth 92– ; with Millwall: 2nd Div. champs. 1987/88; 5 England U-21 caps. *Address*: Portsmouth FC, Fratton Park, Frogmore Rd, Portsmouth PO4 8RA.

HORNER, Victoria Elizabeth: swimmer; b. 11 May 1976, Newcastle; England youth debut 1990, snr debut 1992; GB jnr debut 1990, European Jnr Champs. squad 1990, 91, Olympic triallist 1992. *Leisure interests*: drawing, painting, reading, social events. *Address*: c/o ASA, Harold Fern House, Derby Square, Loughborough, Leics. LE11 0AL.

HORRELL, Janet Elizabeth: netball player; b. 2 September 1972, Neath; rep. W. Glamorgan, Brit. Univ.; with Brit. Univ.: tour Barbados 1993 (capt.); Wales U-18 debut 1988, U-21 debut 1990, World Youth Champs. squad 1992 (capt.), snr debut and World Games squad 1993; rep. W. Glamorgan tennis. *Leisure interests*: tennis, badminton. *Address*: 10 Station Rd, Cymer, Port Talbot, W. Glamorgan SA13 3HR.

HORTON, Brian: football manager; b. 4 February 1949, Hednesford; player Port Vale 1970–76, Brighton and Hove Albion 76–81, Luton Town 81–84, player/manager Hull City 84–88; manager Oxford Utd 1988–93, Manchester City 93– . *Address*: Manchester City FC, Maine Rd, Moss Side, Manchester M14 7WN.

HORTON, Josephine Louise: judo player (U-72kg); b. 17 November 1968, Croydon; Scottish women's open champ. 1992, 93; GB debut 1986, World Champs. squad 1993, Olympic squad 1992. *Leisure interests*: music, film, squash. *Address*: 83 Westcombe Ave, W. Croydon, Surrey CR0 3DF.

HOUGHTON, Raymond James: footballer; b. 9 January 1962, Glasgow; m. Brenda Houghton 1983; 3 s.; player W. Ham Utd 1981–82, Fulham 82–85, Oxford Utd 85–87, Liverpool 87–92, Aston Villa 92– ; with Oxford Utd: winners League Cup 1986; with Liverpool: winners FA Cup 1989, 92, League champs. 1987/88; over 53 Ireland caps. *Leisure interests*: golf, snooker, darts. *Address*: Aston Villa FC, Villa Park, Trinity Rd, Birmingham B6 6HE.

HOUSTON, Valerie Helen: lacrosse player; b. 15 April 1964, Dumfries; rep. W. of Scotland; Scotland debut 1982, World Cup bronze medal 1986, squad 1989, 93 (capt.), tours Aus. 1983, USA 1993. *Leisure interests*: hill-walking, golf, gardening, DIY, travel, music, horseriding. *Address*: 1 Smithy Cottages, Fintry Rd, Ballikinrain, Balfron, Glasgow G63 0LL.

HOWARD, Harvey: Rugby League footballer; b. 29 August 1968, Whiston; player Waterloo (RU), Widnes 1990–94, Leeds 94– ; with Widnes: winners Regal Trophy 1992. *Address*: Leeds RLFC, Bass Headingley, St Michael's Lane, Leeds LS6 3BR.

HOWELL, David: footballer; b. 10 October 1958, Hammersmith; player Barnet 1991–93, player/coach Southend Utd 1993– . *Address*: Southend Utd FC, Roots Hall, Victoria Ave, Southend-on-Sea, Essex SS2 6NQ.

HOWELL, Val: flat green bowler; b. 26 April 1943, Merthyr Tydfil; m. Martin Howell 1966; rep. S. Wales and Monmouthshire 1980– ; Welsh women's triples champ. (outdoor) 1986, (indoor)

1985, 93; Wales debut (outdoor) 1985, (indoor) 1983, World Champs. women's triples bronze medal 1992. *Leisure interests*: art, theatre, film. *Address*: `The Croft', 12 Penydarren Park, Merthyr Tydfil, Mid Glamorgan CF47 8YW.

HOWELLS, David: footballer; b. 15 December 1967, Guildford; player Tottenham Hotspur 1985– , FA Cup winners 1991. *Address*: Tottenham Hotspur FC, 748 High Rd, Tottenham, London N17 0AP.

HOWEY, Kate Louise: judo player (U-66–U-72kg); b. 31 May 1973, Andover; European women's U-19 champ. 1989–91, world women's U-19 champ. 1990; GB women's champ. 1993, open champ. 1990, 91, 93, 94, Belgian women's open champ. 1992, Hiroshima women's open champ., World Masters women's open champ. 1993; European Jnr Champs. gold medals 1989, 90, 91; World Jnr Champs. gold medal 1990; European Champs. silver medals 1990, 91, bronze 1993, 94; World Champs. bronze medal 1991, silver 1993; Olympic bronze medal 1992 (1st Brit. women's judo medal-winner). *Leisure interests*: sport, reading, music, computers. *Address*: 6 Linton Drive, Andover, Hants. SP10 3TT.

HOWEY, Stephen: footballer; b. 26 October 1971, Sunderland; player Newcastle Utd 1989– . *Address*: Newcastle Utd FC, St James' Park, Newcastle-upon-Tyne, Tyne & Wear NE1 4ST.

HOWLEY, Robert: Rugby Union footballer; b. 13 October 1970, Bridgend; player Bridgend, Cardiff 1993– ; Welsh Schools U-18 capt. 1989; Wales U-21 debut 1991, snr tour Zimbabwe/Namibia 1993. *Address*: Cardiff RFC, Cardiff Arms Park, Westgate St, Cardiff CF1 1JA.

HOYLAND, Jamie: footballer; b. 23 January 1966, Sheffield; player Manchester City 1983–86, Bury 86–90, Sheffield Utd 90– . *Address*: Sheffield Utd FC, Bramall Lane, Sheffield, S. Yorks S2 4SU.

HUGHES, Ceri: footballer; b. 26 February 1971, Pontypridd; player Luton Town 1989– ; 2 Wales U-21 caps, 1 full Wales cap. *Address*: Luton Town FC, Kenilworth Stadium, 1 Maple Rd, Luton, Beds. LU4 8AW.

HUGHES, Dale Robert: target archer (recurve); b. 14 January 1967, Newport; GB jnr champ. 1984, snr outdoor champ. 1992, indoor champ. 1993; GB jnr debut 1983, snr debut 1987; European GP team silver medal 1993; World Champs. squad 1993; Welsh mixed pairs aerobics champ. 1990. *Address*: 17 Coverack Rd, Newport, Gwent NP9 0DS.

HUGHES, Gareth: Rugby Union foot-baller; b. 25 July 1964, Llandysul; player Fylde, Blackheath, London Welsh, Askeans, Saracens 1992– . *Address*: Saracens FC, Bramley Rd Sports Ground, Chaseside, Southgate, London N14 4AB.

HUGHES, Ian: Rugby League footballer; b. 13 March 1972; player E. Leeds ARLFC, Sheffield Eagles 1991– . *Address*: Sheffield Eagles RLFC, Stadium Corner, 824 Attercliffe Rd, Sheffield S9 3RS.

HUGHES, Mark: footballer; b. 3 February 1962, Port Talbot; player Bristol Rovers 1980–84, Swansea City 84–85, Bristol City 1985, Tranmere Rovers 1985– . *Address*: Tranmere Rovers FC, Prenton Park, Prenton Rd W., Birkenhead, Merseyside L42 9PN.

HUGHES, Mark: footballer; b. 1 November 1963, Wrexham; player Manchester Utd 1980–86, Barcelona (Spain) 86–88, Manchester Utd 88– ; with Manchester Utd: winners FA Cup 1985, 90, European Cup Winners' Cup 1991, League champs. 1992/93; 5 Wales U-21 caps, over 50 full Wales caps. *Address*: Manchester Utd FC, Old Trafford, Manchester M16 0RA.

HUGHES, Michael: footballer; b. 2 August 1971, Larne, NI; player Manchester City 1988–92, Strasbourg (France) 92– ; over 11 NI caps. *Address*: c/o Prof. Footballers Assoc., 2 Oxford Court, Bishopsgate, Manchester M2 3WQ.

HUGHES, Mickey: boxer; b. 13 June 1962; ABA jnr champ. 1978, 79; ABA welter-weight champ. 1984; Olympic squad 1984; prof. debut 1985; titles won: Commonwealth light-middleweight 1992; over 23 prof. wins. *Address*: c/o Brit. Boxing Board of Control, Jack Petersen House, 52A Borough High St, London SE1 1XW.

HUGHES, Paul: Rugby Union footballer; b. 25 July 1967, Hitchin; player Letchworth, Royston, Wasps, Saracens 1988– ; rep. Herts. *Address*: Saracens FC, Bramley Rd Sports Ground, Chaseside, Southgate, London N14 4AB.

HUGHES, Roger Edward: Alpine skier; b. 29 July 1969, Bangor; Welsh jnr champ. 1987, snr champ. 1989, 90, 92; Scottish slalom champ. 1990; Belgian combined champ. 1992; Wales debut 1986 (capt. 1992–); GB debut 1991. *Leisure interests*: hill-climbing, hill-running, canoeing, water skiing, rollerblading, surfing, golf. *Address*: Summer Hill, Betws-y-Coed, Gwynedd LL24 0BL.

HUGHES, Simon Peter: cricketer; b. 20 December 1959, Kingston; player Middx 1980–91, Durham 92–93; with Middx: tour Zimbabwe 1980. *Publications*: *From Minor to Major*, 1992. *Address*: Durham CCC, County Ground, Riverside, Chester-le-Street, Co. Durham DH3 3QR.

HUGHTON, Christopher William Gerard: footballer; b. 11 December 1958, Forest Gate; m. Cheryl Hughton 1980; 1 s., 3 d.; player Tottenham Hotspur 1979–90, W. Ham Utd 90–92, Brentford 92–93; with Tottenham Hotspur: winners FA Cup 1981,

82, UEFA Cup 1984; with Brentford: 3rd Div. champs. 1991/92; 1 Ireland U-21 cap, 53 full Ireland caps; 1st black player to play for Ireland; coach Tottenham Hotspur 1993– . *Leisure interests*: anything to do with my children. *Address*: Tottenham Hotspur FC, 748 High Rd, Tottenham, London N17 0AP.

HUISTRA, Pieter Egge: footballer; b. 16 January 1967, Goënga, The Netherlands; m. Mirjam Broerse 1993; player FC Groningen (The Netherlands) 1983–86, BV Veendam (The Netherlands) 86–87, FC Twente Enschede (The Netherlands) 87–90, Rangers 90– ; with Rangers: winners Scottish League Cup 1991, 93, 94, Scottish Cup 1993, Scottish League champs. 1990/91, 91/92, 92/93; over 7 Holland caps. *Leisure interests*: tennis, golf. *Address*: Glasgow Rangers FC, Ibrox Stadium, 150 Edmiston Drive, Glasgow G51 2XD.

HULL, Paul Anthony: Rugby Union footballer; b. 17 May 1968, Lambeth; m. Lesley Ann Hull 1991; player Bristol 1988– (vice-capt. 1991–); rep. S.W. Div., Div. champs. 1993/94; England B debut 1990. *Leisure interests*: all sport, night life. *Address*: Bristol FC, Memorial Ground, Filton Ave, Horfield, Bristol BS7 0AQ.

HULME, David: Rugby League footballer; b. 6 February 1964, Widnes; player Widnes 1980– , winners Premiership 1983, 88–90; rep. Lancs.; GB debut v. Papua New Guinea and tour Aus./NZ/Papua New Guinea 1988. *Address*: Widnes RLFC, Naughton Park, Lowerhouse Lane, Widnes WA8 7DZ.

HULME, Paul: Rugby League footballer; b. 19 April 1966, Widnes; player Widnes 1983– , winners Premiership 1988–90, Regal Trophy 1992; rep. Lancs.; GB debut v. Aus. 1988, Brit. Lions tour (replacement) Aus./NZ 1992. *Address*: Widnes RLFC, Naughton Park, Lowerhouse Lane, Widnes WA8 7DZ.

HUMBY, Alison: badminton player; b. 7 December 1972, Southampton; rep. Hants. 1985– ; European ladies' circuit champ. 1993; England debut 1992; winner Hungarian Open ladies' singles 1993. *Leisure interests*: all sports, cinema, animals. *Address*: 2 Harewood Close, Boyatt Wood, Eastleigh, Southampton SO5 4NZ.

HUMPHREY, John: footballer; b. 31 January 1961, Paddington; player Wolverhampton Wanderers 1979–85, Charlton Athletic 85–90, Crystal Palace 90– . *Address*: Crystal Palace FC, Selhurst Park Stadium, London SE25 6PU.

HUMPHREYS, Marika: ice dancer; b. 3 January 1977, Chester; with Justin Lanning (qv): GB jnr champ. 1989; Welsh open champ. 1991, 92; GB champ. 1992; European and World Champs. squads 1993. *Leisure interests*: ballet, music. *Address*: Sports Unlimited, 12–13 Lyon Way, Greenford, Middx UB6 6BN.

HUNT, Caroline Mary: tennis player; b. 29 August 1973, Poole; rep. Dorset 1986– , ladies' champ. 1989; GB girls' U-18 champ. 1991; England debut 1990. *Leisure interests*: drawing, horseriding, dancing, reading, music, cinema. *Address*: 2 Poplar Close, Wimborne, Dorset BH21 1TZ.

HUNT, Christopher John: badminton player; b. 1 December 1968, Bolton; rep. Lancs.; English doubles champ. 1992, 94, Welsh mixed doubles champ. 1993; England debut 1989; winner Hants. Open doubles, mixed doubles 1994. *Leisure interests*: tennis, squash, running, physical training, golf. *Address*: Wimbledon Squash and Badminton Club, Cranbrook Rd, Wimbledon, London SW19 4HD.

HUNT, Paul: footballer; b. 8 October 1970, Swindon; player Swindon Town 1989– . *Address*: Swindon Town FC, The County Ground, Swindon, Wilts. SN1 2ED.

HUNT, Simon: ice hockey player; b. 16 April 1973; player Nottingham Panthers 1988– , winners Autumn Cup 1992, GB champs. 1988/89. *Address*: The Ice Stadium, Lower Parliament St, Nottingham, Notts.

HUNT-DAVIS, Francis Benedict: oarsman; b. 15 March 1972, Tidworth; rep. Shiplake College 1989–90, Leander Club 1991– ; GB jnr debut 1990, U-23 debut 1991, snr debut and Olympic squad (eights) 1992; rep. Oxon U-18 rugby 1988/89. *Leisure interests*: walking, windsurfing, water skiing. *Address*: Leander Club, Henley-on-Thames, Oxon.

HUNTE, Alan: Rugby League footballer; b. 11 July 1970, Wakefield; player Eastmoor ARLFC, Wakefield Trinity, St Helens 1989– ; with St Helens: winners Premiership 1993; GB debut v. France 1992, Brit. Lions tour Aus./NZ/Papua New Guinea 1992. *Address*: St Helens RLFC, Dunriding Lane, St Helens, Merseyside WA10 4AD.

HUNTER, Gordon: footballer; b. 3 May 1967, Wallyford; player Hibernian 1983– , winners Scottish League Cup 1992; Scotland U-21 int. *Address*: Hibernian FC, Easter Rd Stadium, 64 Albion Rd, Edinburgh EH7 5QG.

HUNTER, Ian: Rugby Union footballer; b. 15 February 1969, Harrow; player Windermere, Carlisle, Nottingham, Northampton; rep. N. Div.; England B tour NZ 1992, snr tour Aus./Fiji 1991; Brit. Lions tour NZ 1993 (aborted). *Address*: Northampton FC, Franklins Gardens, Weedon Rd, Northampton NN5 5BG.

HUNTER-ROWE, Carolyn: athlete (long distance); b. 25 January 1964, Leicester; UK women's 100km champ. 1992, 93; World Champs. women's 100km bronze medal 1992, gold 1993; winner London to Brighton race 1991, 93; UK,

Commonwealth and European women's 50 mile, world women's 30 mile, 40 mile and 50km record-holder. *Leisure interests*: cycling, reading, music, good food, red wine. *Address*: c/o Brit. Athletic Fed., 225A Bristol Rd, Edgbaston, Birmingham B5 7UB.

HUNTRIDGE, Nicola Jane: water skier; b. 19 February 1975, Doncaster; English dauphin and jnr girls' jump, slalom champ. 1989; GB ladies' U-21 jump champ. 1993, open slalom champ. 1992, overall champ. 1993; GB dauphin debut 1989, jnr debut 1991, snr debut 1993; European Jnr Champs. girls' jump silver medal 1989; World Jnr Champs. girls' jump, slalom and overall team silver medals 1992; World Champs. squad 1993. *Leisure interests*: skiing, aerobics, gym, swimming. *Address*: 142 Bawtry Rd, Bessacarr, Doncaster, Yorks. DN4 7BP.

HURLOCK, Terence: footballer; b. 22 September 1958, Hackney; player Brentford 1980–86, Reading 86–87, Millwall 87–90, Rangers 90–91, Southampton 91– ; with Millwall: 2nd Div. champs. 1987/88; with Rangers: winners Scottish League Cup 1991. *Address*: Southampton FC, The Dell, Milton Rd, Southampton SO9 4XX.

HURST, Lee: footballer; b. 21 September 1970, Nuneaton; player Coventry City 1989– . *Address*: Coventry City FC, Highfield Rd Stadium, King Richard St, Coventry CV2 4FW.

HUSSAIN, Nasser: cricketer; b. 28 March 1968, Madras, India; player Essex 1987– , county champs. 1991, 92; Test debut 1989, England A tours Pakistan/Sri Lanka 1990/91, WI 1991/92, snr tours India/WI 1989/90, WI 1994. *Address*: Essex CCC, County Cricket Ground, New Writtle St, Chelmsford DM2 0PG.

HUTCHCROFT, Jonathan Mark: windsurfer; b. 19 August 1968, Bridlington; UK Olympic-class champ. 1993; European Champs. Mistral silver medal (lightweight) 1986, gold 1987, 89, 90; World Champs. Mistral bronze medal 1986, gold 1990. *Leisure interests*: mountain biking, skiing, triathlon, rock climbing. *Address*: 2 Palatine Rd, Worthing, Sussex BN12 6JP.

HUTCHINSON, Rob: Rugby League footballer; b. 20 September 1968, Hull; player Norland ARLFC, Halifax, Hull Kingston Rovers 1992– . *Address*: Hull Kingston Rovers RLFC, Craven Park, Preston Rd, Hull HU9 5HE.

HUTCHISON, Donald: footballer; b. 9 May 1971, Gateshead; player Hartlepool Utd 1990, Liverpool 1990– . *Address*: Liverpool FC, Anfield Rd, Liverpool L4 0TH.

HUTCHISON, Hugh: freestyle skier; b. 17 November 1964, Dunfermline; Army, Combined Services, Commonwealth Services Alpine champ. 1989–91; GB moguls champ. 1989, 92, 93; GB debut 1989, World Champs. squad 1989, 91, 93, Olympic squad 1992. *Leisure interests*: tennis, diving, mountain biking, cinema, theatre. *Address*: Officers' Mess, Minley Manor, Blackwater, Surrey GU17 9LP.

HUTTON, Stewart: cricketer; b. 30 November 1969, Stockton-on-Tees; player Durham 1992– , tour Zimbabwe 1991/92. *Address*: Durham CCC, County Ground, Riverside, Chester-le-Street, Co. Durham DH3 3QR.

HYNES, Martin Peter: Rugby Union footballer; b. 23 August 1968, Wigan; player Durban Crusaders (SA), Orrell; rep. N. Div.; England U-21 debut v. Romania 1989, England B tour NZ 1992, England A tour Canada 1993. *Address*: Orrell RUFC, Edgehall Rd, Orrell, Wigan WN5 8TL.

HYSLOP, Christian: footballer; b. 14 June 1972, Watford; player Southend Utd 1990– . *Address*: Southend Utd FC, Roots Hall, Victoria Ave, Southend-on-Sea, Essex SS2 6NQ.

IGGLESDEN, Alan Paul: cricketer; b. 8 October 1964, Farnborough; m. Hilary Moira Igglesden 1990; player Kent 1986– ; England A tour Zimbabwe/Kenya 1989/90, Test debut 1989, snr tour WI 1994. *Address*: Kent CCC, St Lawrence Ground, Canterbury CT1 3NZ.

ILLINGWORTH, Matthew: cyclist; b. 25 July 1968, Rochford; RTTC 25- and 50-mile team time trial champ. 1992; GB debut and World Champs. squad (individ. and team pursuit) 1991, Olympic squad (team time trial) 1992. *Leisure interests*: music, watching sport on TV. *Address*: 289 Carlton Ave, Westcliff-on-Sea, Essex SS0 0PX.

ILLINGWORTH, Richard Keith: cricketer; b. 23 August 1963, Bradford; m. Anne Illingworth 1985; 2 s.; player Worcs. 1982– , county champs. 1988, 89, Sunday League champs. 1987, 88; England A tours Zimbabwe/Kenya 1989/90, Pakistan/Sri Lanka 1990/91, Test debut 1991, tour NZ/Aus. (World Cup) 1991/92; MCC tour Kenya 1992/93. *Address*: Worcs. CCC, County Ground, New Rd, Worcester WR2 4QQ.

ILOTT, Mark Christopher: cricketer; b. 27 August 1970, Watford; player Essex 1988– , county champs. 1991, 92; England A tours Sri Lanka 1990/91, Aus. 1992/93, SA 1993/94, Test debut v. Aus. 1993. *Leisure interests*: badminton, squash, reading, drinking real ale, keeping fit. *Address*: Essex CCC, County Cricket Ground, New Writtle St, Chelmsford DM2 0PG.

IMPEY, Andrew: footballer; b. 30 September 1971, Hammersmith; player Queens Park Rangers 1990– . *Address*: Queens Park Rangers FC, Rangers Stadium, S. Africa Rd, London W12 7PA.

INCE, Paul: footballer; b. 21 October 1967, Ilford; m. Clare Ince; player W. Ham Utd 1985–89, Manchester Utd 89– ; with Manchester Utd: winners FA Cup 1990, European Cup Winners' Cup 1991, League champs. 1992/93; 2 England U-21 caps, over 9 full England caps; first black player to captain England, US Cup 1993. *Address*: Manchester Utd FC, Old Trafford, Manchester M16 0RA.

INGLIS, John: footballer; b. 16 October 1966, Edinburgh; player E. Fife 1983–87, Brechin City 87–89, Meadowbank Thistle 89–90, St Johnstone 90– . *Address*: St Johnstone FC, McDiarmid Park, Crieff Rd, Perth PH1 2SJ.

INGS, David John: figure skater; b. 28 December 1973, Ely; Scottish champ. 1993; GB jnr debut 1991, snr debut 1992. *Leisure interests*: weight training, circuit training, music, dancing. *Address*: 6 Nyland Rd, Nythe, Swindon SN3 3RD.

INNES, Craig: Rugby League footballer; b. 10 September 1969; player Leeds 1992– ; NZ int. (RU). *Address*: Leeds RLFC, Bass Headingley, St Michael's Lane, Leeds LS6 3BR.

IREDALE, John: ice hockey player; b. 8 October 1966; player Whitley Warriors 1983–86, Solihull Barons 1986, Whitley Warriors 1987– ; with Whitley Warriors: winners Scottish Cup 1992; World Champs. debut 1989. *Address*: The Ice Rink, Hillheads Rd, Whitley Bay, Tyne & Wear.

IRELAND, Andy: Rugby League footballer; b. 6 December 1971; player Golborne ARLFC, Widnes 1991– . *Address*: Widnes RLFC, Naughton Park, Lowerhouse Lane, Widnes WA8 7DZ.

IRO, Kevin: Rugby League footballer; player Leeds 1992– ; NZ debut v. Papua New Guinea 1987. *Address*: Leeds RLFC, Bass Headingley, St Michael's Lane, Leeds LS6 3BR.

IRONS, David: footballer; b. 18 July 1961, Glasgow; player Ayr Utd 1984–87, Clydebank 87–88, Dunfermline 88–92, Partick Thistle 92– . *Address*: Partick Thistle FC, Firhill Stadium, 80 Firhill Rd, Glasgow G20 7BA.

IRONS, Kenneth: footballer; b. 4 November 1970, Liverpool; player Tranmere Rovers 1989– . *Address*: Tranmere Rovers FC, Prenton Park, Prenton Rd W., Birkenhead, Merseyside L42 9PN.

IRONSIDE, Ian: footballer; b. 8 March 1964, Sheffield; player Scarborough 1988–91, Middlesbrough 91– . *Address*: Middlesbrough FC, Ayresome Park, Middlesbrough, Cleveland TS1 4PB.

IRVINE, Brian Alexander: footballer; b. 24 May 1965, Bellshill, Lanarkshire; m. Donna Frances Irvine 1988; 1 d.; player Falkirk 1983–85, Aberdeen 85– ; with Aberdeen: winners Scottish League Cup, Scottish Cup 1990; Scotland debut v. Romania 1990, over 4 full caps. *Publications*: `Winning Is Not Enough' in *Christians in Sport*, Stuart Weir and Andrew Wingfield Digby (eds), 1991, *Aberdeen: The Final Years*, 1991. *Address*: Aberdeen FC, Pittodrie Stadium, Pittodrie St, Aberdeen AB2 1QH.

IRVING, Simon: Rugby League footballer; b. 22 March 1967, Cleckheaton; player Headingley RUFC, Leeds 1990– ; England B RU int. *Address*: Leeds RLFC, Bass Headingley, St Michael's Lane, Leeds LS6 3BR.

IRWIN, Dennis: footballer; b. 31 October 1965, Cork, Ireland; player Leeds Utd 1983–86, Oldham Athletic 86–90, Manchester Utd 90–   ; with Manchester Utd: winners European Cup Winners' Cup 1991, League champs. 1992/93; 3 Ireland U-21 caps, over 21 full Ireland caps. *Address:* Manchester Utd FC, Old Trafford, Manchester M16 0RA.

IRWIN, Shaun: Rugby League footballer; b. 8 December 1968, Castleford; player Redhill ARLFC, Castleford 1986–93, Oldham 93–   ; GB debut v. France 1990, Brit. Lions tour NZ/Papua New Guinea 1990. *Address:* Oldham RLFC, The Pavilion, Watersheddings, Oldham OL4 2PB.

ISAAC, Gary Ronald: Rugby Union footballer; b. 15 February 1966; m. Antonya Isaac; player Gala; Scotland U-21 debut v. Italy 1986, Scotland A debut v. Spain 1990, snr tour Fiji/Tonga/W. Samoa 1993. *Address:* Gala RFC, Netherdale, Nether Rd, Galashiels TD1 3HE.

IVES, Michael Frederick Jeffrey: cyclist; b. 10 August 1939, Longdon, Staffs.; m. Sheila Joan Bateman; 1 d.; rep. Saracen (and team manager); GB prof. cyclo-cross champ. 1968, mountain bike masters cross-country, downhill and hill climb champ. 1991, point series champ. 1992; world veteran time trial champ. 1991; World Mountain Bike Champs. squad 1991 (oldest GB rider ever selected); only rider to represent GB at road, track, cyclo-cross and mountain bike events; world's oldest registered prof. racing cyclist. *Leisure interests:* fishing, cycle touring, gardening. *Address:* 78 Mill Hill, Baginton, Coventry CV8 3AG.

JACKETT, Yvonne: netball player; b. 20 March 1972, Glasgow; player Castlemilk 1987–   ; rep. Glasgow District U-21 1990–93, snr inter-district champs. 1992/93; Scotland U-21 debut 1990, snr debut 1991. *Leisure interests:* badminton, racketball, golf, swimming, football, volleyball. *Address:* c/o Scottish Netball Assoc., Kelvin Hall, Argyle St, Glasgow G3 8AW.

JACKMAN, Cassandra: squash player; b. 22 December 1972, N. Walsham; player N. Walsham 1982–86, Barnham Broom 86–89, Colets 89–91, Courtlands 91–   , Bamberg (Germany) 91–   ; rep. Norfolk 1984–   ; Surrey women's open champ. 1990; English ladies' champ. 1993; GB girls' U-16 open champ. 1988, U-19 open champ. 1990, 91, ladies' U-23 champ. 1989, 92, 93, doubles champ. 1987 (youngest ever); European girls' U-19 champ. 1989, 91; world girls' U-19 champ. 1991; England U-19 debut 1987, snr debut 1990; European Jnr Champs. team gold medals 1989–91; World Jnr Champs. team gold medals 1987, 89, 91; European Champs. team gold medals 1990–94; winner Swiss Open 1991, US Open 1993; SRA Young Player of the Year 1991/92. *Leisure interests:* water skiing, wildlife, whales and dolphins, cinema, TV, true-life murder books, going out. *Address:* c/o SRA, Westpoint, 33–34 Warple Way, London W3 0RQ.

JACKSON, Anthony: Rugby League footballer; b. 20 November 1969; player Greatfield ARLFC, Hull 1988–   . *Address:* Hull RLFC, The Boulevard Ground, Airlie St, Hull HU3 3JD.

JACKSON, Colin, MBE: athlete; b. 18 February 1967, Cardiff; Commonwealth Games 110m hurdles gold medal 1990; European Indoor Champs. 60m hurdles gold medal 1989; European Champs. 110m hurdles gold medal 1990; European Cup 110m hurdles gold medal 1993; World Cup 110m hurdles silver medal 1989, gold 1992; World Indoor Champs. 60m hurdles silver medal 1989, 93; World Champs. 110m hurdles gold and 4 x 100m relay silver medals 1993; Olympic 110m hurdles silver medal 1988; world 110m hurdles, UK, Commonwealth and European 60m hurdles indoor record-holder; Brit. Athletics Writers' Assoc. Male Athlete of the Year 1993. *Address:* `Nuff' Respect, Rosedale House, Rosedale Rd, Richmond, Surrey TW9 2SZ.

JACKSON, Darren: footballer; b. 25 July 1966, Edinburgh; player Meadowbank Thistle 1985–86, Newcastle Utd 86–88, Dundee Utd 88–92, Hibernian 92– . *Address*: Hibernian FC, Easter Rd Stadium, 64 Albion Rd, Edinburgh EH7 5QG.

JACKSON, Darren: footballer; b. 24 September 1971, Keynsham; player Oxford Utd 1990– . *Address*: Oxford Utd FC, Manor Ground, London Rd, Headington, Oxford OX3 7RS.

JACKSON, Joanna: equestrianist (dressage); b. 26 February 1970, Chatburn, Lancs.; nat. young riders champ. 1989–91; GB debut 1992. *Leisure interests*: dancing, aerobics, theatre, cinema. *Address*: c/o Brit. Horse Soc., Brit. Equestrian Centre, Stoneleigh Park, Kenilworth, Warks. CV8 2LR.

JACKSON, Lee: Rugby League footballer; b. 12 March 1969, Hull; player Villa ARLFC, Hull 1986–93, Sheffield Eagles 93– ; with Hull: winners Premiership 1991; GB debut v. Papua New Guinea 1990, Brit. Lions tours NZ/Papua New Guinea 1990, Aus./NZ/Papua New Guinea 1992. *Address*: Sheffield Eagles RLFC, Stadium Corner, 824 Attercliffe Rd, Sheffield S9 3RS.

JACKSON, Matthew: footballer; b. 19 October 1971, Leeds; player Luton Town 1990–91, Everton 91– ; 4 England U-21 caps. *Address*: Everton FC, Goodison Park, Liverpool L4 4EL.

JACKSON, Michael: Rugby League footballer; b. 11 October 1969, Heckmondwyke; player Dewsbury Moor ARLFC, Hunslet, Wakefield Trinity 1991–93, Halifax 93– ; GB debut v. Papua New Guinea 1991, Brit. Lions tour Aus./NZ/Papua New Guinea 1992. *Address*: Halifax RLFC, The Pavilion, Thrum Hall, Gibbet St, Halifax, W. Yorks HX1 4TL.

JACKSON, Robert: Rugby League footballer; b. 13 August 1960, Sydney, Aus.; player Fulham (Aus.), Warrington 1989– . *Address*: Warrington RLFC, Wilderspool Stadium, Wilderspool Causeway, Warrington WA4 6PY.

JACKSON, Wayne: Rugby League footballer; b. 19 September 1967, Hull; player W. Hull ARLFC, Hull Kingston Rovers 1990– . *Address*: Hull Kingston Rovers RLFC, Craven Park, Preston Rd, Hull HU9 5HE.

JACOBS, Gary: boxer; b. 10 December 1965; prof. debut 1985; titles won: Scottish welterweight 1987, Commonwealth welterweight, WBC int. welterweight 1988, GB welterweight 1992, European welterweight 1993; over 34 prof. wins. *Address*: Nat. Promotions, Nat. House, 60–66 Wardour St, London W1V 3HP.

JAMES, David: footballer; b. 1 August 1970, Welwyn Garden City; player Watford 1990–92, Liverpool 92– ; 10 England U-21 caps. *Address*: Liverpool FC, Anfield Rd, Liverpool L4 0TH.

JAMES, Julian: footballer; b. 22 March 1970, Tring; player Luton Town 1988– ; 2 England U-21 caps. *Address*: Luton Town FC, Kenilworth Stadium, 1 Maple Rd, Luton, Beds. LU4 8AW.

JAMES, Kevan David: cricketer; b. 18 March 1961, Lambeth; m. Debbie James 1987; player Middx 1980–84, Hants. 85– ; with Hants.: Sunday League champs. 1986; England YC tours Aus. 1978/79, WI 1979/80. *Address*: Hants. CCC, County Cricket Ground, Northlands Rd, Southampton SO9 2TY.

JAMES, Marie Elizabeth: ice dancer; b. 29 November 1971, Nottingham; with Philip Askew: GB northern champ. 1992. *Leisure interests*: dancing, swimming, gym, cycling, skiing, art, fashion design, music. *Address*: Nottingham Ice Dance and Figure Skating Club, Nottingham Ice Stadium, Nottingham.

JAMES, Mark: golfer; b. 28 October 1953, Manchester; English amateur champ. 1974; England debut 1974; Walker Cup team 1975; prof. debut 1975; Dunhill Cup team 1988–90, 93; Ryder Cup team 1977–81, 89–93; winner Lusaka Open 1977, Irish Open 1979, 80, Italian Open 1980, Sao Paulo Open 1981, Tunisian Open 1983, Benson and Hedges Int. Open 1986, Spanish Open 1988, English Open 1989, 90, Brit. Masters 1990. *Address*: c/o PGA European Tour, Wentworth Club, Wentworth Drive, Virginia Water, Surrey GU25 4LS.

JAMES, Stephen Peter: cricketer; b. 7 September 1967, Lydney; player Cambridge Univ. (Blue 1989, 90), Glamorgan 1985– ; with Glamorgan: Sunday League champs. 1993, tours Trinidad 1990, Zimbabwe 1991; rep. Combined Univ. 1989–90, tour Barbados 1989; player Gloucester RUFC 1989–90. *Leisure interests*: sports journalism, reading, videos, socializing. *Address*: Glamorgan CCC, Sophia Gardens, Cardiff CF1 9XR.

JAMES, Steve: snooker player; b. 2 May 1961; prof. debut 1986, winner Mercantile Credit Classic 1990. *Address*: c/o World Prof. Billiards and Snooker Assoc., 27 Oakfield Rd, Clifton, Bristol BS8 2AT.

JARDINE, Ian Carrick: Rugby Union footballer; b. 20 October 1964, Dunfermline; m. Ann Jardine; player Stirling County; Scotland B debut v. Ireland 1989, snr debut v. NZ 1993, tours N. America 1991, Fiji/Tonga/W. Samoa 1993. *Address*: Stirling County RFC, Bridgehaugh, Causewayhead Rd, Stirling.

JARRETT, Anthony: athlete; b. 13 August 1968, Enfield; UK 110m hurdles champ. 1987, 88; European Jnr Champs. 110m hurdles and 4 x 100m relay gold medals 1987; Commonwealth Games 110m hurdles

silver medal 1990; European Champs. 110m hurdles silver medal 1990; European Cup 4 x 100m relay gold medals 1989, 93; European Indoor Champs. 110m hurdles silver medal 1990; World Champs. 110m hurdles and 4 x 100m relay bronze medals 1991, silver 1993. *Address*: c/o Brit. Athletic Fed., 225A Bristol Rd, Edgbaston, Birmingham B5 7UB.

JARVIS, Paul William: cricketer; b. 29 June 1965, Redcar; m. Wendy Jayne Jarvis 1988; 1 s.; player Yorks. 1981–93, Sussex 94– ; with Yorks.: tour St Lucia/Barbados 1987; Test debut 1987, tours India/Pakistan (World Cup) 1986/87, Aus./NZ 1987/88, India/Sri Lanka 1992/93. *Address*: Sussex CCC, County Ground, Eaton Rd, Hove, E. Sussex BN3 3AN.

JAVER, Monique Alicia: tennis player; b. 22 July 1967, Burlingame, California, USA; GB debut 1988, Wightman and European Cup teams 1988, Federation Cup team 1990– , Olympic squad 1992; winner Singapore Open ladies' singles 1988. *Leisure interests*: water sports, ballet, music, animals, fashion, hiking, gourmet cooking. *Address*: c/o LTA, The Queen's Club, W. Kensington, London W14 9EG.

JEMSON, Nigel: footballer; b. 10 August 1969, Preston; player Preston N. End 1987–88, Nottingham Forest 88–91, Sheffield Wednesday 91– ; with Nottingham Forest: winners League Cup 1990; 1 England U-21 cap. *Address*: Sheffield Wednesday FC, Hillsborough, Sheffield, S. Yorks. S6 1SW.

JENKINS, Garin Richard: Rugby Union footballer; b. 18 August 1967, Ynysybwl; player Ynysybwl, Pontypridd, King Country (NZ), Pontypool, Swansea; with Swansea: Welsh League champs. 1991/92; over 9 Wales caps. *Address*: Swansea RFC, St Helens, Swansea SA2 0AR.

JENKINS, Neil Roger: Rugby Union footballer; b. 8 July 1971, Pontypridd; player Pontypridd; Wales U-21 debut v. NZ U-21 1991, snr and Five Nations debut v. England 1991, tour Zimbabwe/Namibia 1993. *Address*: Pontypridd RFC, Sardis Rd, Pwllgwaun, Pontypridd, Mid Glamorgan.

JENKINSON, Julian: triathlete; b. 10 January 1967; European Champs. middle-distance team gold medal 1992. *Address*: c/o Brit. Triathlon Assoc., 4 Tynemouth Terrace, Tynemouth NE30 4BH.

JENKINSON, Leigh: footballer; b. 9 July 1969, Thorne; player Hull City 1987–92, Coventry City 92– . *Address*: Coventry City FC, Highfield Rd Stadium, King Richard St, Coventry CV2 4FW.

JENNINGS, Joanne: athlete (high jump); b. 20 September 1969, Pakenham; English schools champ. 1984–87; England and GB debuts 1985, Commonwealth Games squad 1990, European Indoor Champs. squad 1992, World and World Indoor Champs. squad 1993, Olympic squad 1988, 92; UK jnr high jump record-holder. *Leisure interests*: eating out, cinema, driving, shopping, music, watching most sports. *Address*: c/o Mr A. Stokes, Essex Ladies Athletic Club, 57 Roundmead Ave, Loughton, Essex IG10 1PZ.

JENSEN, John: footballer; b. 3 May 1965, Denmark; player Brondby (Denmark), Arsenal 1992– ; Denmark int. *Address*: Arsenal FC, Arsenal Stadium, Highbury, London N5 1BU.

JESS, Eoin: footballer; b. 13 December 1970, Aberdeen; player Aberdeen 1987– , winners Scottish League Cup 1990; Scotland int. *Address*: Aberdeen FC, Pittodrie Stadium, Pittodrie St, Aberdeen AB2 1QH.

JOBLING, Kevin: footballer; b. 1 January 1968, Sunderland; player Leicester City

1986–88, Grimsby Town 88– . *Address*: Grimsby Town FC, Blundell Park, Cleethorpes, S. Humberside DN35 7PY.

JOBSON, Richard: footballer; b. 9 May 1963, Holderness; player Watford 1982–85, Hull City 85–90, Oldham Athletic 90– ; with Oldham Athletic: 2nd Div. champs. 1990/91. *Address*: Oldham Athletic FC, Boundary Park, Oldham, Lancs. OL1 2PA.

JOHNSEN, Erland: footballer; b. 5 April 1967, Frederikstad, Norway; player Moss FK, Bayern Munich (Germany), Chelsea 1989– ; 19 Norway U-21 caps, 18 full Norway caps. *Address*: Chelsea FC, Stamford Bridge, Fulham Rd, London SW6 1HS.

JOHNSON, Andrew: footballer; b. 2 May 1974, Bath; player Norwich City 1992– . *Address*: Norwich City FC, Carrow Rd, Norwich NR1 1JE.

JOHNSON, Anthony: ice hockey player; b. 4 January 1969; player Durham Wasps 1983–90, Humberside Seahawks 90– ; with Durham Wasps: winners Autumn Cup 1985, 88, 89, League champs. 1984/85, 85/86, 88/89, GB champs. 1986/87, 87/88; World Champs. debut 1990. *Address*: Humberside Ice Arena, Kingston St, Hull HU1 2DZ.

JOHNSON, David: footballer; b. 29 October 1970, Dinnington; player Sheffield Wednesday 1989–93, Lincoln City 93– . *Address*: Lincoln City FC, Sincil Bank, Lincoln LN5 8LD.

JOHNSON, Gavin: footballer; b. 10 October 1970, Eye; player Ipswich Town 1989– . *Address*: Ipswich Town FC, Portman Rd, Ipswich, Suffolk IP1 2DA.

JOHNSON, Grant: footballer; b. 24 March 1972, Dundee; player Dundee Utd 1990– ; Scotland U-21 int. *Address*: Dundee Utd FC, Tannadice Park, Dundee DD3 7JW.

JOHNSON, Kathryn: hockey player; b. 21 January 1967; player Balsam Leicester; England U-21 debut 1986, snr debut (outdoor) 1988, (indoor) 1990, World Cup squad 1990, European Champs. gold medallist 1991; GB debut 1991, Olympic bronze medallist 1992, Champions Trophy squad 1993. *Address*: c/o All England Women's Hockey Assoc., 51 High St, Shrewsbury SY1 1ST.

JOHNSON, Martin Osborne: Rugby Union footballer; b. 9 March 1970, Solihull; player Leicester, winners Pilkington Cup 1993; rep. Midland Div.; England U-21 debut v. Belgium 1991, England B debut v. France 1992, tour NZ 1992, England A tour Canada 1993, snr and Five Nations debut v. France 1993; Brit. Lions tour NZ 1993 (late call). *Address*: Leicester FC, Welford Rd, Leicester LE2 7LF.

JOHNSON, Marvin: footballer; b. 29 October 1968, Wembley; player Luton Town 1986– . *Address*: Luton Town FC, Kenilworth Stadium, 1 Maple Rd, Luton, Beds. LU4 8AW.

JOHNSON, Patricia (Trish): golfer; b. 17 January 1966, Bristol; Devon girls' champ. 1982; S.W. ladies' champ. 1984; English ladies' amateur champ. and ladies' stroke-play champ. 1985; England debut 1984; Curtis Cup team (winners) 1986; prof. debut 1987; Solheim Cup team 1990, 92, winners 1992; winner Hennessy Cup, European Open 1990, Spanish Classic 1992. *Address*: c/o Women's Professional Golf European Tour, The Tytherington Club, Dorchester Way, Tytherington, Macclesfield, Cheshire SK10 2JP.

JOHNSON, Paul: cricketer; b. 24 April 1965, Newark; player Notts. 1981– , winners NatWest Trophy 1987, Benson and Hedges Cup 1989, county champs. 1981, 87, Sunday League champs. 1991; England A tour WI 1991/92. *Leisure interests*: Nottingham Forest FC, Nottingham

Panthers (ice hockey). *Address*: Notts. CCC, Trent Bridge, Nottingham NG2 6AG.

JOHNSON, Richard Leonard: cricketer; b. 29 December 1974, Chertsey; player Middx 1992– , county champs. 1993; England U-18 tour SA 1992/93. *Address*: Middx CCC, Lord's Cricket Ground, London NW8 8QN.

JOHNSON, Shaun: ice hockey player; b. 22 March 1973; player Durham Wasps 1988–90, Humberside Seahawks 90– ; with Durham Wasps: winners Autumn Cup 1989, League champs. 1988/89; World Champs. debut 1992. *Address*: Humberside Ice Arena, Kingston St, Hull HU1 2DZ.

JOHNSON, Sian Margaret: squash player; b. 8 October 1957, Llanelli; m. Arthur Johnson; 1 d.; player Llanelli, Swansea, Sophia Gardens, Cardiff; rep. S. Glamorgan, S. Wales; Dyfed ladies' champ. 1976–84, S. Glamorgan ladies' champ. 1987–92; Welsh ladies' champ. 1981, 84, 86, 87, open champ. 1982, doubles champ. 1993; Wales debut 1978 (ladies' capt. 1984–); European Champs. team bronze medal 1981; most-capped Welsh player. *Leisure interests*: fitness training, reading, family. *Address*: c/o Welsh Squash Rackets Fed., 7 Kymin Terrace, Penarth, S. Glamorgan CF6 1AP.

JOHNSON, Stephen: ice hockey player; b. 19 June 1967; player Durham Wasps 1983–90, Humberside Seahawks 90– ; with Durham Wasps: winners Autumn Cup 1985, 88, 89, League champs. 1984/85, 85/86, 88/89, GB champs. 1986/87, 87/88; World Champs. debut 1990. *Address*: Humberside Ice Arena, Kingston St, Hull HU1 2DZ.

JOHNSON, Thomas: footballer; b. 15 January 1971, Newcastle; player Notts County 1989–92, Derby County 92– ; 7 England U-21 caps. *Address*: Derby County FC, The Baseball Ground, Shaftesbury Crescent, Derby DE3 8NB.

JOHNSTON, Margaret, MBE: flat green bowler; b. 2 May 1943, Londonderry, NI; 2 s., 1 d.; Irish women's singles champ. (outdoor) 1984, (indoor) 1987, 88, 90, 92, women's pairs champ. (outdoor) 1984, (indoor) 1988, 89, 93, women's triples champ. (outdoor) 1991, women's fours champ. (outdoor) 1983, (indoor) 1989; GB women's singles champ. (outdoor) 1985, (indoor) 1987, 90, women's pairs champ. (outdoor) 1985, (indoor) 1989, women's triples champ. (outdoor) 1992; Ireland debut (outdoor) 1981, (indoor) 1987; Commonwealth Games women's pairs gold medal 1986, bronze 1990; World Champs. women's singles silver medal 1988, gold 1992, women's pairs gold 1988, 92; World Indoor Champs. women's singles gold medals 1988, 89. *Leisure interests*: reading, knitting, gardening. *Address*: 26 Beatrice Villas, Bellaghy, Co. Londonderry BT45 8JA.

JOHNSTON, Maurice (Mo): footballer; b. 30 April 1963, Glasgow; player Partick Thistle 1981–83, Watford 83–85, Celtic 85–87, Nantes (France) 87–89, Rangers 89–91, Everton 91–93, Heart of Midlothian 93– ; with Celtic: winners Scottish Cup 1985; 3 Scotland U-21 caps, 38 full Scotland caps. *Address*: Heart of Midlothian FC, Tynecastle Park, Gorgie Rd, Edinburgh EH11 2NL.

JOHNSTON, Sammy: footballer; b. 13 April 1967, Glasgow; player St Johnstone 1984–91, Partick Thistle 91– . *Address*: Partick Thistle FC, Firhill Stadium, 80 Firhill Rd, Glasgow G20 7BA.

JONES, David: Rugby League footballer; b. 7 December 1967, Chorley; player Wakefield Trinity 1990–93, Oldham 93– ; rep. Lancs. *Address*: Oldham RLFC, The Pavilion, Watersheddings, Oldham OL4 2PB.

JONES, Gary: Rugby Union footballer; b. 17 July 1960; player Llanelli, winners Welsh Cup 1993, Welsh League champs. 1992/93; 5 Wales caps. *Address*: Llanelli RFC, Stradey Park, Llanelli, Dyfed.

JONES, Ian Wynn: Rugby Union footballer; b. 12 May 1971, Carmarthen; player Llanelli, winners Welsh Cup 1991, 92, 93, Welsh League champs. 1992/93; Wales tours Aus. 1991, Zimbabwe/Namibia 1993; Wales jnr javelin champ. 1987. *Address*: Llanelli RFC, Stradey Park, Llanelli, Dyfed.

JONES, Isobel Diana Whitfield: jockey; b. 27 September 1958, Oswestry; ladies' amateur champ. 1994; winner Ladies' Derby 1983 (Prince Reviewer). *Leisure interests*: reading. *Address*: Pentre David, Oswestry, Shropshire SY10 7EA.

JONES, Keith: footballer; b. 14 October 1965, Dulwich; player Chelsea 1983–87, Brentford 87–91, Southend Utd 91– . *Address*: Southend Utd FC, Roots Hall, Victoria Ave, Southend-on-Sea, Essex SS2 6NQ.

JONES, Mark: Rugby League footballer; b. 22 June 1965; player Neath RUFC, Hull 1990– ; Wales debut v. Papua New Guinea 1991. *Address*: Hull RLFC, The Boulevard Ground, Airlie St, Hull HU3 3JD.

JONES, Melvyn: canoeist; b. 26 January 1964, Stourbridge; m. Lisa Micheler-Jones 1993; GB K1 slalom champ. 1992; GB jnr debut 1981, snr debut 1984; European Jnr Champs. K1 slalom silver medal 1982; Europa Cup K1 slalom silver medal 1988; World Cup K1 slalom bronze medals 1988, 92; World Champs. K1 slalom team gold medal 1987, team gold and individ. bronze 1993; Olympic squad 1992. *Leisure interests*: skiing, cycling. *Address*: Metzstrasse 50, 86316 Friedberg, Germany.

JONES, Paul Courtney: Rugby Union footballer; b. 24 March 1967; player Llanelli, winners Welsh Cup 1993, Welsh League champs. 1992/93. *Address*: Llanelli RFC, Stradey Park, Llanelli, Dyfed.

JONES, Peter Martin: Rugby Union footballer; b. 28 December 1964, Arbroath; m. Sarah Jones; player Longlevens, Gloucester; Scotland B debut v. Ireland 1990, snr and Five Nations debut v. Wales 1992, tour Aus. 1992. *Address*: Gloucester RUFC, Kingsholm, Worcester St, Gloucester GL3 3AX.

JONES, Rhodri Jason: Rugby Union footballer; b. 22 August 1971; player Neath. *Address*: Neath RFC, The Gnoll, Gnoll Park Rd, Neath, W. Glamorgan.

JONES, Richard Lyn: Rugby Union footballer; b. 5 June 1964; player Llanelli, winners Welsh Cup 1993, Welsh League champs. 1992/93; Wales tour Zimbabwe/Namibia 1993. *Address*: Llanelli RFC, Stradey Park, Llanelli, Dyfed.

JONES, Rita: flat green bowler; b. 28 September 1937, Bargoed; m. Kenneth James Jones 1962; 1 s.; rep. Mid Glamorgan 1973– ; Welsh women's singles champ. (outdoor) 1989, (indoor) 1977, 84, 91, 92, women's triples champ. (indoor) 1989, women's fours champ. (outdoor) 1991, 92, (indoor) 1990; GB women's pairs champ. (indoor) 1993, women's triples champ. (indoor) 1989, women's fours champ. (outdoor) 1992; Wales debut (outdoor) 1980, (indoor) 1976; Commonwealth Games women's fours gold medal 1986, squad 1990; Atlantic Rim Champs. singles silver medal 1993; World Champs. women's triples bronze medal 1985. *Leisure interests*: walking. *Address*: 23 Maesygraig St, Gilfach, Bargoed, Mid Glamorgan.

JONES, Robert: footballer; b. 5 November 1971, Wrexham; player Crewe Alexandra 1988–91, Liverpool 91– ; with Liverpool: winners FA Cup 1992; England U-21 and snr int. *Address*: Liverpool FC, Anfield Rd, Liverpool L4 0TH.

JONES, Robert Nicholas: Rugby Union footballer; b. 10 November 1965, Trebanos; m. Megan Jones; player Swansea

1983– (capt. 1989–91), Welsh League champs. 1991/92; Wales and Five Nations debut v. England 1986, tours Fiji/Tonga/W. Samoa 1986, NZ 1988, Aus. 1991; Brit. Lions tours Aus. 1989, NZ 1993. *Address*: Swansea RFC, St Helens, Swansea SA2 0AR.

JONES, Sally: real tennis player; b. Coventry; m. John Wallace Grant 1989; 1 s., 1 d.; GB ladies' open champ. 1987, 89, open doubles champ. 1993; US ladies' open singles and doubles champ. 1986; world ladies' doubles champ. 1991, singles champ. 1993; won 5 Oxford Blues (tennis, squash, netball, cricket, modern pentathlon) 1974–76; rep. Warks. lawn tennis 1971– (capt. 91–), Wimbledon jnr ladies' doubles semi-finalist 1973, S. Wales squash 1985–86; real tennis and rackets correspondent, *The Times*, 1988– . *Publications*: *Legends of Cornwall*, 1983, *Legends of Devon*, 1984, *Legends of Somerset*, 1986, *Mysteries in the Somerset Landscape*, 1987, *First Team at Tennis*, 1988, *The Ladybird Book of Riding and Pony Care*, 1988. *Leisure interests*: lawn tennis, netball, reading and researching legends. *Address*: Crane Hill, Newbold Pacey, nr Leamington Spa, Warks.

JONES, Vincent: footballer; b. 5 January 1965, Watford; player Wimbledon 1986–89, Leeds Utd 89–90, Sheffield Utd 90–91, Chelsea 91–92, Wimbledon 92– ; with Wimbledon: winners FA Cup 1988; with Leeds Utd: 2nd Div. champs. 1989/90. *Address*: Wimbledon FC, Selhurst Park, London SE25 6PY.

JONES, Vivien Aileen: lacrosse player; b. 21 June 1951, Glasgow; m. Anthony Graham Jones 1970; 2 d.; player Putney Ladies 1969– ; rep. Middx 1977– , South 1978– ; Wales debut 1977, World Cup squad 1982, 86, 89, 93, tours USA 1991, 92, 93, Japan/Aus. 1992; GB debut and tour Aus. 1985; most-capped int. player. *Leisure interests*: family, rounders, marathon-running, driving, reading. *Address*: 6 Oaks Rd, Stanwell, Staines, Middx TW19 7LG.

JONES, Zachary Damon: hockey player; b. 2 December 1973, Kisumu, Kenya; player Llanishen and Llandaff, Bournville 1992– ; rep. Mid Glamorgan U-16, U-18, Combined Univ. 1992/93, UAU Champs. gold medallist 1993; Wales U-21 and snr debuts 1992; GB U-21 debut 1991. *Leisure interests*: squash, reading, tennis, rugby, trout-fishing, swimming. *Address*: 9 Bedwas Rd, Caerphilly, Mid Glamorgan CF8 3AP.

JORDAN, Joseph: football manager; b. 15 December 1951, Carluke; player Morton, Leeds Utd 1970–78, Manchester Utd 78–80, Verona (Italy), Southampton 1984–87, Bristol City 87–89; 1 Scotland U-23 cap, 52 full Scotland caps; manager Bristol City 1988–90, Heart of Midlothian 90–93, assistant manager Celtic 1993, manager Stoke City 1993– . *Address*: Stoke City FC, Victoria Ground, Stoke on Trent, Staffs. ST4 4EG.

JOSEPH, David John: Rugby Union footballer; b. 20 September 1963; player Llanelli, Aberavon, Neath, Swansea, Llanelli; with Llanelli: winners Welsh Cup 1993, Welsh League champs. 1992/93; Wales B debut v. Italy 1986; unbeaten as amateur boxer. *Address*: Llanelli RFC, Stradey Park, Llanelli, Dyfed.

JOSEPH, Roger: footballer; b. 21 December 1965, Paddington; player Brentford 1984–88, Wimbledon 88– . *Address*: Wimbledon FC, Selhurst Park, London SE25 6PY.

JOYNT, Christopher: Rugby League footballer; b. 7 December 1971, Wigan; player Oldham, St Helens 1992– ; with St Helens: winners Premiership 1993; rep. Lancs.; GB debut v. France 1993. *Address*: St Helens RLFC, Dunriding Lane, St Helens, Merseyside WA10 4AD.

KAMARA, Christopher: footballer; b. 25 December 1957, Middlesbrough; player Portsmouth 1975–77, Swindon Town 77–81, Portsmouth 1981, Brentford 1981–85, Swindon Town 85–88, Stoke City 88–90, Leeds Utd 90–91, Luton Town 91–93, Sheffield Utd 93– ; with Swindon Town: 4th Div. champs. 1985/86. *Address*: Sheffield Utd FC, Bramall Lane, Sheffield, S. Yorks. S2 4SU.

KANCHELSKIS, Andrei: footballer; b. 23 January 1969, Kirowograd, USSR; player Shakhtyor (USSR), Manchester Utd 1991– ; with Manchester Utd: League champs. 1992/93. *Address*: Manchester Utd FC, Old Trafford, Manchester M16 0RA.

KANE, Paul: footballer; b. 20 June 1965, Edinburgh; player Hibernian 1982–91, Oldham Athletic 91–92, Aberdeen 92– . *Address*: Aberdeen FC, Pittodrie Stadium, Pittodrie St, Aberdeen AB2 1QH.

KARDOONI, Aadel: Rugby Union footballer; b. 17 May 1968, Tehran, Iran; player Leicester, winners Pilkington Cup 1993; rep. Midland Div.; England B tour NZ 1992. *Address*: Leicester FC, Welford Rd, Leicester LE2 7LF.

KAY, John: footballer; b. 29 January 1964, Gt Lumley, Durham; player Arsenal 1981–84, Wimbledon 84–87, Sunderland 87– ; with Sunderland: 3rd Div. champs. 1987/88. *Address*: Sunderland FC, Roker Park Ground, Sunderland, Tyne and Wear SR6 9SW.

KEANE, Roy: footballer; b. 10 August 1971, Cork, Ireland; player Cobh Ramblers (Ireland), Nottingham Forest 1990–93, Manchester Utd 93– ; over 16 Ireland caps. *Address*: Manchester Utd FC, Old Trafford, Manchester M16 0RA.

KEARSEY, David: Rugby Union footballer; b. 18 April 1967; player Cheltenham, Gloucester. *Address*: Gloucester RUFC, Kingsholm, Worcester St, Gloucester GL3 3AX.

KEARTON, Jason: footballer; b. 9 July 1969, Ipswich, Aus.; player Brisbane Lions (Aus.), Everton 1988– . *Address*: Everton FC, Goodison Park, Liverpool L4 4EL.

KEBBIE, Brimah: Rugby League footballer; b. 21 September 1965, London; player Widnes, St Helens, Huddersfield, Bradford Northern 1992– . *Address*: Bradford Northern RLFC, Odsal Stadium, Bradford BD6 1BS.

KEE, Paul: footballer; b. 8 November 1969, Belfast; player Oxford Utd 1988– ; 7 NI caps. *Address*: Oxford Utd FC, Manor Ground, London Rd, Headington, Oxford OX3 7RS.

KEECH, Matthew: cricketer; b. 21 October 1970, Hampstead; player Middx 1991–93, Hants. 94– ; England U-19 tour Aus. 1989/90. *Address*: Hants. CCC, County Cricket Ground, Northlands Rd, Southampton SO9 2TY.

KEEGAN, Joseph Kevin, OBE: football manager; b. 14 February 1951, Armthorpe, Yorks.; player Scunthorpe Utd 1968–71, Liverpool 71–77, SV Hamburg (Germany) 77–80, Southampton 80–82, Newcastle Utd 82–84; with Liverpool: winners FA Cup 1974, European Cup 1977, UEFA Cup 1973, 76, League champs. 1972/73, 75/76, 76/77; 5 England U-23 caps, snr debut v. Wales 1972, 63 full England caps; Footballer of the Year 1975/76, European Footballer of the Year 1977/78, 78/79, PFA Player of the Year 1975/76, 81/82; manager Newcastle Utd 1992– , 1st Div. champs. 1992/93. *Address*: Newcastle Utd FC, St James' Park, Newcastle-upon-Tyne, Tyne & Wear NE1 4ST.

KEELEY, John: footballer; b. 27 July 1961, Plaistow; player Southend Utd 1979–85, Brighton and Hove Albion 86–90, Oldham Athletic 90–93, Colchester Utd 93– . *Address*: Colchester Utd FC, Layer Rd, Colchester, Essex CO2 7JJ.

KEEN, Kevin: footballer; b. 25 February 1967, Amersham; player W. Ham Utd 1984–93, Wolverhampton Wanderers 93– . *Address*: Wolverhampton Wanderers FC, Molineux Stadium, Waterloo Rd, Wolverhampton WV1 4QR.

KELLAND, Chris: ice hockey player; b. 22 December 1957; player Murrayfield Racers 1983–91, Nottingham Panthers 91– (capt.); with Murrayfield Racers: winners Autumn Cup 1986, 90, Scottish Cup 1987–91, GB champs. 1985/86, League champs. 1986/87, 87/88; with Nottingham Panthers: winners Autumn Cup 1992; World Champs. debut 1990. *Address*: The Ice Stadium, Lower Parliament St, Nottingham, Notts.

KELLETT, Simon Andrew: cricketer; b. 16 October 1967, Mirfield; player Yorks. 1989– . *Address*: Yorks. CCC, Headingley Cricket Ground, Leeds LS6 3BU.

KELLY, Alan: footballer; b. 11 August 1968, Preston; player Preston N. End 1985–92, Sheffield Utd 92– ; Ireland int. *Address*: Sheffield Utd FC, Bramall Lane, Sheffield, S. Yorks S2 4SU.

KELLY, Anthony: footballer; b. 1 January 1964, Prescot; player Wigan Athletic 1984–86, Stoke City 86–87, W. Bromwich Albion 87–89, Shrewsbury Town 89–91, Bolton Wanderers 91– . *Address*: Bolton Wanderers FC, Burnden Park, Manchester Rd, Bolton, Lancs. BL3 2QR.

KELLY, David: footballer; b. 25 November 1965, Birmingham; player Walsall 1983–88, W. Ham Utd 88–90, Leicester City 90–91, Newcastle Utd 91–93, Wolverhampton Wanderers 93– ; 1 Ireland U-21 cap, 13 full Ireland caps. *Address*: Wolverhampton Wanderers FC, Molineux Stadium, Waterloo Rd, Wolverhampton WV1 4QR.

KELLY, Garry: footballer; b. 9 July 1974, Drogheda, Ireland; player Leeds Utd 1991– ; Ireland U-21 int. *Address*: Leeds Utd FC, Elland Rd, Leeds, W. Yorks LS11 0ES.

KELLY, Mark: footballer; b. 27 November 1969, Sutton; player Portsmouth 1986– ; 2 Ireland U-21 caps, 4 full Ireland caps. *Address*: Portsmouth FC, Fratton Park, Frogmore Rd, Portsmouth PO4 8RA.

KENDRICK, Neil Michael: cricketer; b. 11 November 1967, Bromley; player Surrey 1988– , U-19 tour Aus. 1985/86. *Leisure interests*: most ball sports, football for Old Wilsonians FC. *Address*: Surrey CCC, The Oval, Kennington, London SE11 5SS.

KENNA, Jeffrey: footballer; b. 27 August 1970, Dublin, Ireland; player Southampton 1989– ; 3 Ireland U-21 caps. *Address*: Southampton FC, The Dell, Milton Rd, Southampton SO9 4XX.

KENNEDY, Andrew: footballer; b. 8 October 1964, Stirling; player Rangers 1983–85, Birmingham City 85–88, Blackburn Rovers 88–90, Watford 90– . *Address*: Watford FC, Vicarage Rd Stadium, Watford, Herts. WD1 8ER.

KENNEDY, Peter Terence: yachtsman; b. 3 May 1964, Belfast, NI; m. Carolyn Anne Louise Kennedy 1993; rep. Cambridge Univ. 1983–86 (Blue 1985, 86), Oxford Univ. 87–88 (Blue 1987); Irish Laser champ. 1985; UK Flying Dutchman open champ. 1989, 90; Ireland debut 1986; World Team Racing Champs. bronze medal 1989; Olympic squad 1988, 92. *Address*: Blackwater Rocks, Saintfield Rd, Killinchy, Co. Down BT23 6RL.

KENT, Steven Paul: powerboat racer (navigator); b. 16 April 1958, Redruth; m. Karen Kent; 2 d.; GB offshore circuit racing A class champ. 1990–93. *Leisure interests*: boats, water sports. *Address*: Outboard

Services, The Boat Market, Mill Hill, Lostwithiel, Cornwall.

KENYON, Neil: Rugby League footballer; b. 26 October 1967, St Helens; player Bold ARLFC, Warrington 1988– . *Address*: Warrington RLFC, Wilderspool Stadium, Wilderspool Causeway, Warrington WA4 6PY.

KEOUGH, Linda: athlete; b. 26 December 1963, London; AAA women's 800m indoor champ. 1993; Commonwealth Games women's 4 x 400m relay silver medal 1986, 400m silver 1990; European Cup women's 400m silver medal 1989, bronze 1993; European Champs. women's 4 x 400m relay bronze medal 1990; World Champs. women's 4 x 400m relay bronze medal 1993. *Address*: c/o Brit. Athletic Fed., 225A Bristol Rd, Edgbaston, Birmingham B5 7UB.

KEOWN, Martin: footballer; b. 24 July 1966, Oxford; player Arsenal 1985–86, Aston Villa 86–89, Everton 89–92, Arsenal 92– ; with Arsenal: winners Coca-Cola Cup 1993; 8 England U-21 caps, over 9 full England caps. *Address*: Arsenal FC, Arsenal Stadium, Highbury, London N5 1BU.

KERNAGHAN, Alan: footballer; b. 25 April 1967, Otley; player Middlesbrough 1985–93, Manchester City 93– ; over 6 Ireland caps. *Address*: Manchester City FC, Maine Rd, Moss Side, Manchester M 14 7WN.

KERR, Dylan: footballer; b. 14 January 1967, Malta; player Leeds Utd 1989–93, Reading 93– . *Address*: Reading FC, Elm Park, Norfolk Rd, Reading, Berks. RG3 2EF.

KERR, Jason Ian Douglas: cricketer; b. 7 April 1974, Bolton; player Somerset 1993– ; England U-19 tour India 1992/93. *Address*: Somerset CCC, The County Ground, Taunton, Somerset TA1 1JT.

KERSEY, Graham James: cricketer; b. 19 May 1971, Greenwich; player Kent 1991–92, Surrey 93– ; Kent Schools U-17 tour Singapore/NZ 1987/88. *Address:* Surrey CCC, The Oval, Kennington, London SE11 5SS.

KERSLAKE, David: footballer; b. 19 June 1966, Stepney; player Queens Park Rangers 1983–89, Swindon Town 89–92, Leeds Utd 92–93, Tottenham Hotspur 93– ; 1 England U-21 cap. *Address:* Tottenham Hotspur FC, 748 High Rd, Tottenham, London N17 0AP.

KETTERIDGE, Martin: Rugby League footballer; b. 2 October 1964, Dundee; player Moorends ARLFC, Castleford 1983– ; with Castleford: winners Regal Trophy 1994. *Address:* Castleford RLFC, Wheldon Rd, Castleford WF10 2SD.

KHARINE, Dmitri: footballer; b. 18 August 1968, USSR; m. Lilla Kharine; 1 s.; player Torpedo Moscow, Dynamo Moscow, CSKA Moscow (all USSR), Chelsea 1992– ; 8 USSR U-21 caps, 6 full USSR caps, 9 CIS caps. *Address:* Chelsea FC, Stamford Bridge, Fulham Rd, London SW6 1HS.

KIDDIE, Alan: basketball player; b. 5 June 1969, Falkirk; player Falkirk 1985–86, Murray Int. Metals/Livingston 86–87, Glasgow Rangers 87–88, Glasgow City 88– ; Scotland U-19 and snr int. *Leisure interests:* volleyball. *Address:* c/o Scottish Basketball Assoc., Caledonia House, S. Gyle, Edinburgh EH12 9DQ.

KILCLINE, Brian: footballer; b. 7 May 1962, Nottingham; player Notts County 1980–84, Coventry City 84–91, Oldham Athletic 91–92, Newcastle Utd 92–94, Swindon Town 94– ; with Coventry City: winners FA Cup 1987; 2 England U-21 caps. *Address:* Swindon Town FC, The County Ground, Swindon, Wilts. SN1 2ED.

KIMBERLEY, Scott: Rugby Union footballer; b. 24 March 1965, Bristol; player Chingford, Saracens 1991– . *Address:* Saracens FC, Bramley Rd Sports Ground, Chaseside, Southgate, London N14 4AB.

KIMBLE, Alan Frank: footballer; b. 6 August 1966, Dagenham; m. Perry Anne Kimble 1992; player Charlton Athletic 1984–86, Cambridge Utd 86–93, Wimbledon 93– . *Leisure interests:* horseracing, snooker, golf, greyhound racing. *Address:* Wimbledon FC, Selhurst Park, London SE25 6PY.

KINANE, Michael Joseph: jockey (Flat); b. 22 June 1959; m. Catherine Kinane 1982; 2 d.; winner Irish Oaks 1989 (Alydaress), Prix de l'Arc de Triomphe 1989 (Carroll House), 2000 Guineas 1990 (Tirol), Derby 1993 (Commander In Chief), Irish St Leger, Melbourne Cup 1993 (Vintage Crop); rode 113 winners in season 1988. *Address:* c/o BHB, 42 Portman Square, London W1H 0EN.

KING, Jaime Anne: swimmer; b. 18 December 1976, Swindon; GB women's 100m breaststroke champ. 1993; GB debut and Olympic squad (100m breaststroke) 1992; GB women's 50m breaststroke jnr record-holder. *Leisure interests:* cycling, tennis. *Address:* c/o ASA, Harold Fern House, Derby Square, Loughborough, Leics. LE11 0AL.

KING, John: football manager; b. 15 April 1938, St John's Wood; player Everton 1956–60, Bournemouth 60–61, Tranmere Rovers 61–68, Port Vale 68–70; manager Tranmere Rovers 1975–80, 87– . *Address:* Tranmere Rovers FC, Prenton Park, Prenton Rd W., Birkenhead, Merseyside L42 9PN.

KING, Philip: footballer; b. 28 December 1967, Bristol; player Exeter City 1985–86, Torquay Utd 86–87, Swindon Town 87–89, Sheffield Wednesday 89– ; with Sheffield Wednesday: winners League Cup 1991. *Address:* Sheffield Wednesday FC, Hillsborough, Sheffield, S. Yorks. S6 1SW.

KINNAIRD, Paul: footballer; b. 11 November 1966, Glasgow; player Dundee Utd 1985–88, Motherwell 88–89, St Mirren 89–92, Partick Thistle 92–93, Shrewsbury Town 1993, St Johnstone 1993– . *Address*: St Johnstone FC, McDiarmid Park, Crieff Rd, Perth PH1 2SJ.

KINNEAR, Joseph: football manager; b. 27 December 1946, Dublin, Ireland; player Tottenham Hotspur 1965–75, Brighton and Hove Albion 75–76; 25 Ireland caps; manager Wimbledon 1991– . *Address*: Wimbledon FC, Selhurst Park, London SE25 6PY.

KIRK, Stephen: footballer; b. 3 January 1963, Kirkcaldy; player E. Fife 1979–80, Stoke City 80–82, Partick Thistle 1982, E. Fife 1982–86, Motherwell 86– ; with Motherwell: winners Scottish Cup 1991. *Address*: Motherwell FC, Fir Park, Fir Park St, Motherwell ML1 2QN.

KIRKLAND, Darren Keith: water skier (racing); b. 4 August 1967, London; GB U-14 champ. 1978, 79, F4 champ. 1981, 82, F2 champ. 1984–86, F1 champ. 1990–92; European Jnr Champs. gold medals 1981, 82; European Champs. F2 bronze medal 1983, gold 1984–86, F1 bronze 1987, silver 1988, 89, 91, 92, gold 1990; GB 1km record-holder. *Leisure interests*: circuit training, aerobics, windsurfing, jet skiing. *Address*: 27 Stambourne Way, Upper Norwood, London SE19 2PY.

KITE, Philip: footballer; b. 26 October 1962, Bristol; player Bristol Rovers 1980–84, Southampton 84–87, Gillingham 87–89, Bournemouth 89–90, Sheffield Utd 90–93, Cardiff City 93– . *Address*: Cardiff City FC, Ninian Park, Sloper Rd, Cardiff CF1 8SX.

KITSON, Paul: footballer; b. 9 January 1971, Peterlee; player Leicester City 1988–92, Derby County 92– ; 7 England U-21 caps. *Address*: Derby County FC, The Baseball Ground, Shaftesbury Crescent, Derby DE3 8NB.

KITSON, Suzie Jane: cricketer; b. 1 May 1969, Kingston, Cambs.; player Cambridge LCC 1984– ; rep. E. Anglia Ladies 1985– ; England jnr debut 1986; Test debut 1992, tours Ireland 1990, Aus./NZ 1992, winners European Cup 1989, 91, World Cup 1993; Sports Writers' Team of the Year award-winner 1993. *Leisure interests*: badminton, music, TV, films. *Address*: 89 Bramley Way, Hardwick, Cambs.

KIWOMYA, Andrew: footballer; b. 1 October 1967, Huddersfield; player Dundee 1992– . *Address*: Dundee FC, Dens Park, Dundee DD3 7JY.

KIWOMYA, Christopher: footballer; b. 2 December 1969, Huddersfield; player Ipswich Town 1987– . *Address*: Ipswich Town FC, Portman Rd, Ipswich, Suffolk IP1 2DA.

KNIGHT, Alan: footballer; b. 3 July 1961, Balham; player Portsmouth 1979– , 3rd Div. champs. 1982/83; 2 England U-21 caps. *Address*: Portsmouth FC, Fratton Park, Frogmore Rd, Portsmouth PO4 8RA.

KNIGHT, Gary Stephen: motorcyclist; b. 22 September 1957, Swanley; m. Susan Knight 1987; 1 s., 3 d.; European sidecar road racing champ. 1992. *Leisure interests*: cycling, trumpet-playing, flying, collecting (signed copies, brass instruments, Brit. coins, stamps), attending steam rallies and antique fairs. *Address*: Redline Superbikes, 151 London Rd, Macclesfield, Cheshire SK11 7SP.

KNIGHT, Henrietta Catherine: racehorse trainer; b. 15 December 1946, London; 1st licence 1989. *Leisure interests*: farming, hunting, cooking, gardening. *Address*: W. Lockinge Farm, Wantage, Oxon OX12 8QF.

KNIGHT, Nicholas Verity: cricketer; b. 28 November 1969, Watford; player Essex 1991– , county champs. 1991, 92; capt. England Schools 1987–88, Combined Univ. 1991; rep. Essex (hockey), E. Counties (rugby). *Address*: Essex CCC, County Cricket Ground, New Writtle St, Chelmsford DM2 0PG.

KNOX, Grant: flat green bowler; b. 8 June 1960, Armadale, W. Lothian; rep. W. Lothian (outdoor) 1980– , (indoor) 1981– ; Scotland debut (outdoor) 1983, (indoor) 1991, Commonwealth Games pairs gold medal 1986. *Address*: 58 Honeyman Court, Armadale, W. Lothian EH48 3RG.

KOHN, Patricia Anne: yachtswoman; b. 28 September 1975, Glasgow; Scottish schools champ. 1990, 91, 93, jnr champ. 1987, 89, Optimist champ. 1990, Europe champ. 1991; UK youth champ. 1992; Scotland debut 1987; GB debut 1992. *Leisure interests*: skiing, Italian food. *Address*: 97 Boghead Rd, Lenzie, Glasgow G66 4UB.

KOLOTO, Emosi: Rugby League footballer; b. 23 January 1965, Tonga; player Wellington (NZ) (RU), Widnes 1988– ; with Widnes: winners Premiership 1989, 90; NZ debut v. France 1991. *Address*: Widnes RLFC, Naughton Park, Lowerhouse Lane, Widnes WA8 7DZ.

KRIKKEN, Karl Matthew Giles: cricketer; b. 9 April 1969, Bolton; player Derbys. 1987– , winners Benson and Hedges Cup 1993, Sunday League champs. 1990. *Address*: Derbys. CCC, County Cricket Ground, Nottingham Rd, Derby DE2 6DA.

KRIVOKAPIC, Miodrag: footballer; b. 6 September 1959, Niksic, Yugoslavia; player Red Star Belgrade (Yugoslavia), Dundee Utd 1988– ; Yugoslavia int. *Address*: Dundee Utd FC, Tannadice Park, Dundee DD3 7JW.

KROMHEER, Elroy: footballer; b. 15 January 1970, Amsterdam, The Netherlands; player FC Volendam (The Netherlands), Motherwell 1992– . *Address*: Motherwell FC, Fir Park, Fir Park St, Motherwell ML1 2QN.

KUBICKI, Dariusz: footballer; b. 6 June 1963, Warsaw, Poland; player Legia Warsaw (Poland), Aston Villa 1991– ; over 40 Poland caps. *Address*: Aston Villa FC, Villa Park, Trinity Rd, Birmingham B6 6HE.

KUHL, Martin: footballer; b. 10 January 1965, Frimley; player Birmingham City 1983–87, Sheffield Utd 87–88, Watford 1988, Portsmouth 1988–92, Derby County 92– . *Address*: Derby County FC, The Baseball Ground, Shaftesbury Crescent, Derby DE3 8NB.

KUITI, Michael James: Rugby League footballer; b. 18 March 1963, Foxton, NZ; player Leeds, Rochdale Hornets 1991–93, Oldham 93– ; NZ debut v. France 1989. *Address*: Oldham RLFC, The Pavilion, Watersheddings, Oldham OL4 2PB.

KUZNETSOV, Oleg: footballer; b. 2 March 1963, Kiev, USSR; player Dynamo Kiev (USSR), Rangers 1990– ; CIS int. *Address*: Rangers FC, Ibrox Stadium, 150 Edmiston Drive, Glasgow G51 2XD.

LAKE, Michael: footballer; b. 15 November 1966, Denton; player Sheffield Utd 1989– . *Address*: Sheffield Utd FC, Bramall Lane, Sheffield, S. Yorks S2 4SU.

LAMB, Allan Joseph: cricketer; b. 20 June 1954, Langebaanweg, Cape Province, SA; m. Lindsay Lamb 1979; 1 s., 1 d.; player Northants. 1978– (capt. 89–); Test debut 1982, tours Aus./NZ 1982/83, NZ/Pakistan 1983/84, India/Aus. 1984/85, WI 1985/86, Aus. 1986/87, India/Pakistan (World Cup) 1987/88, India/WI 1989/90, Aus. 1990/91, NZ 1991/92; scored 3 100s in consecutive Tests v. WI 1984. *Address*: Northants. CCC, County Cricket Ground, Wantage Rd, Northampton NN1 4TJ.

LAMBERT, Catriona Isobel: golfer; b. 25 August 1969, Edinburgh; rep. E. Lothian 1987– ; Scottish girls' champ. 1986, schools champ. 1986, 87, ladies' U-21 open strokeplay champ. 1988, 89, univ. champ. 1989–91, amateur champ. 1991, 93; Welsh ladies' open amateur strokeplay champ. 1992; GB univ. champ. 1990, ladies' open amateur champ. 1993; Spanish ladies' open amateur champ. 1993; Scotland jnr debut 1988, snr debut 1989; GB debut 1989, Curtis Cup team 1990, 92, winners 1992; *Daily Telegraph* Woman Golfer of the Year (joint) 1993. *Leisure interests*: squash, badminton, swimming, keep-fit, reading, cinema. *Address*: c/o Scottish Ladies' Golfing Assoc., Room 1010, Terminal Building, Prestwick Airport, Prestwick KA9 2PL.

LAMERTON, Andrew Edwin: Rugby Union footballer; b. 28 May 1970; player Llanelli, winners Welsh Cup 1993, Welsh League champs. 1992/93; Wales debut v. France 1993, tour Zimbabwe/Namibia 1993. *Address*: Llanelli RFC, Stradey Park, Llanelli, Dyfed.

LAMPITT, Stuart Richard: cricketer; b. 29 July 1966, Wolverhampton; player Worcs. 1985– , county champs. 1988, 89, Sunday League champs. 1987, 88, tours Bahamas 1990, Zimbabwe 1991, SA 1992. *Address*: Worcs. CCC, County Ground, New Rd, Worcester WR2 4QQ.

LANCASTER, Philip: Rugby Union footballer; b. 15 January 1964, Hartlepool; player W. Hartlepool 1984– ; rep. Durham colts and snr squad, N. Div., tour Zimbabwe/Namibia 1992. *Address*: W. Hartlepool RFC, Brierton Lane, Hartlepool, Cleveland TS25 5DR.

LANE, Barry: golfer; b. 21 June 1960, Hayes, Middx; prof. debut 1976; Dunhill Cup team 1988; Ryder Cup team 1993; winner Jamaica Open 1983, Equity and Law Challenge 1987, Scottish Open 1988,

German Masters 1992, European Masters 1993. *Address*: c/o PGA European Tour, Wentworth Club, Wentworth Drive, Virginia Water, Surrey GU25 4LS.

LANGLEY, Mark: Rugby Union footballer; b. 9 June 1967, Cardiff; player Penarth, Bridgend, Swansea, Swansea Univ., Saracens 1989– ; Wales U-21 int. *Address*: Saracens FC, Bramley Rd Sports Ground, Chaseside, Southgate, London N14 4AB.

LANNING, Justin: ice dancer; b. 21 February 1973, Pinner; with Marika Humphreys (qv): GB jnr champ. 1989; Welsh open champ. 1991, 92; GB champ. 1992; European and World Champs. squads 1993. *Leisure interests*: Watford FC, motor racing, music. *Address*: Sports Unlimited, 12–13 Lyon Way, Greenford, Middx UB6 6BN.

LAPWORTH, Christine: windsurfer; b. 26 August 1959, Pembroke; UK women's Mistral champ. 1986, 88, 91, nat. series champ. 1987–89; European Champs. Mistral gold medals 1989–91; World Champs. Mistral gold medal 1990. *Leisure interests*: skiing, snowboarding, horseriding, aerobics. *Address*: 2 Rowley Court, Rowley Drive, Botley, Southampton SO3 2SN.

LARBY, Verity: race walker; b. 13 November 1970, Salisbury; m. David Snook 1993; Hants. women's 3km champ. 1990, 92; GB women's 3km indoor champ. 1991, 10km champ. 1993; Scotland jnr debut 1989, snr debut 1990; GB U-23 debut 1990, World Champs. squad 1993. *Leisure interests*: life-saving. *Address*: c/o Race Walking Assoc., 9 Whitehouse Close, Rectory Rd, Sutton Coldfield B75 7SD.

LARKINS, Wayne: cricketer; b. 22 November 1953; m. Jane Elaine Larkins 1975; 1 d.; player Northants. 1972–91, Durham 92– ; 13 Tests, debut 1979, 25 1-day ints, tours Aus./India 1979/80,

India/Sri Lanka 1981/82, India/WI 1989/90, Aus. 1990/91. *Address*: Durham CCC, County Ground, Riverside, Chester-le-Street, Co. Durham DH3 3QR.

LASLETT, Jason George: hockey player; b. 1 July 1969, Canterbury; player Teddington (capt.); rep. Kent; European Cup bronze and European Indoor Cup silver medallist 1991, Champions Trophy squad 1990, 91, 92; Olympic squad 1992; Poundstretcher Nat. League Player of the Year and Norwich Union Player of the Year 1990/91; youngest nat. league capt. *Leisure interests*: football, cricket, squash, tennis, surfing, reading, TV, sleeping, eating. *Address*: Teddington HC, Bushy Park, Teddington, Middx.

LATHWELL, Mark Nicholas: cricketer; b. 26 December 1971, Bletchley; player Somerset 1991– ; England A tours Aus. 1992/93, SA 1993/94, Test debut v. Aus. 1993. *Address*: Somerset CCC, The County Ground, Taunton, Somerset TA1 1JT.

LAUGHTON, Dale: Rugby League footballer; b. 10 October 1970; player Dodworth ARLFC, Sheffield Eagles 1989– . *Address*: Sheffield Eagles RLFC, Stadium Corner, 824 Attercliffe Rd, Sheffield S9 3RS.

LAW, Bobby: footballer; b. 24 December 1965, Bellshill; player Partick Thistle 1984– . *Address*: Partick Thistle FC, Firhill Stadium, 80 Firhill Rd, Glasgow G20 7BA.

LAW, Brian: footballer; b. 1 January 1970, Merthyr Tydfil; player Queens Park Rangers 1987– ; 1 Wales U-21 cap, 1 full Wales cap. *Address*: Queens Park Rangers FC, Rangers Stadium, S. Africa Rd, London W12 7PA.

LAW, Danny Richard Charles: cricketer; b. 15 July 1975, London; player Sussex 1993– ; England U-18 tour SA 1992. *Address*: Sussex CCC, County Ground, Eaton Rd, Hove, E. Sussex BN3 3AN.

LAWLER, Ivan: canoeist; b. 19 November 1966, Addlestone; GB jnr debut 1981, snr debut 1985; World Cup K2 marathon silver medal 1987, gold 1989, 91, K1 marathon gold 1993; World Champs. K2 marathon silver medals 1988, 90, K2 10,000m silver 1989, gold 1990, K1 marathon gold 1992; Olympic squad 1988, 92. *Address*: 93 Chertsey Lane, Staines, Middx TW18 3LQ.

LAWRENCE, Lennie: football manager; b. 14 December 1947, Brighton; player/manager Plymouth Argyle 1978, Charlton Athletic 1982–91; manager Middlesbrough 1991–94. *Address*: Middlesbrough FC, Ayresome Park, Middlesbrough, Cleveland TS1 4PB.

LAWRENCE, Sarah Penelope: lacrosse player; b. 18 August 1967, Croydon; player Purley 1981– (capt. 91–); rep. Surrey 1987– , South 88–89; Wales debut 1986, World Cup squad 1989, 93, tours USA 1991, 92. *Leisure interests*: skiing, tennis, athletics, mountain biking, fitness training, travel, DIY, childcare. *Address*: 78 Foxley Lane, Purley, Surrey CR8 3EE.

LAWS, Brian: footballer; b. 14 October 1961, Wallsend; player Burnley 1979–83, Huddersfield Town 83–85, Middlesbrough 85–88, Nottingham Forest 88– ; with Burnley: 3rd Div. champs. 1981/82; with Nottingham Forest: winners League Cup 1989, 90. *Address*: Nottingham Forest FC, City Ground, Nottingham NG2 5FJ.

LAY, Stephen: Rugby League footballer; b. 28 March 1968, Dewsbury; player Hunslet 1987–93, Halifax 93– . *Address*: Halifax RLFC, The Pavilion, Thrum Hall, Gibbet St, Halifax, W. Yorks HX1 4TL.

LE MOIGNAN, Martine, MBE: squash player; b. 28 October 1962; player Windsor; rep. Essex; English ladies' champ. 1984, 88, 91; European ladies' champ. 1991, champ. of champs. 1989; world ladies' open champ. 1989; England debut 1980; World Champs. team gold medals 1985, 87, 89, 90. *Address*: c/o SRA, Westpoint, 33–34 Warple Way, London W3 0RQ.

LE SAUX, Graeme: footballer; b. 17 October 1968, Jersey; player St Pauls (Jersey), Chelsea 1988–93, Blackburn Rovers 93– ; 4 England U-21 caps. *Address*: Blackburn Rovers FC, Ewood Park, Blackburn, Lancs. BB2 4JF.

LE TISSIER, Matthew: footballer; b. 14 October 1968, Guernsey; player Southampton 1986– . *Address*: Southampton FC, The Dell, Milton Rd, Southampton SO9 4XX.

LEADBITTER, Christopher Jon: footballer; b. 17 October 1967, Middlesbrough; m. Cordelia Leadbitter 1992; player Hereford Utd 1986–88, Cambridge Utd 88–93, Bournemouth 93– ; with Cambridge Utd: 3rd Div. champs. 1990/91. *Leisure interests*: golf, snooker. *Address*: Bournemouth FC, Dean Court, Bournemouth, Dorset BH7 7AF.

LEADER, Gruffudd James Llewelyn: Alpine skier; b. 18 November 1971, Caerphilly; Welsh U-15 champ., schools champ. 1987, open champ. 1991; Celtic Nations champ. 1992, 93; GB jnr champ. 1987; Wales debut 1987. *Leisure interests*: mountain biking, tennis, golf, circuit training, music, playing the guitar. *Address*: 55 Penylan Rd, Roath, Cardiff CF2 5HZ.

LEASK, Perry: motorcyclist (moto-cross); b. 29 May 1961, Cuckfield; m. Deborah Lynne Leask 1991; 1 s., 1 d.; GB 100cc schoolboy champ. 1973, 125cc schoolboy champ. 1975; ACU 125cc youth champ. 1976; GB 4-stroke champ. 1992; NZ 250cc champ. 1983, 84. *Leisure interests*: squash, swimming. *Address*: Crawley and District Motorcycle Club, 'Rowan', Bonehurst Rd, Horley, Surrey RH6 8QG.

LEATHERDALE, David Anthony: cricketer; b. 26 November 1967, Bradford; m. Vanessa Leatherdale; 1 s.; player Worcs. 1988– . *Address*: Worcs. CCC, County Ground, New Rd, Worcester WR2 4QQ.

LEDEN, Judy, MBE: hang glider pilot; b. 23 December 1959, London; GB women's champ. 1983, 88–91; GB debut 1984 (1st woman selected), capt. 1990; European Champs. gold medal 1986; World Champs. individ. and team gold medals 1987, individ. gold 1991; prof. debut 1988; winner Venezuelan Open 1988, Bulgarian Open 1989; 1st woman to cross English Channel by hang glider; world women's triangular distance record-holder. *Leisure interests*: microlight flying, fitness training, reading, photography. *Address*: 8 Burnham Manor, Gibbet Lane, Camberley, Surrey GU15 3UP.

LEE, Andrew: Rugby Union footballer; b. 10 November 1968, Wanstead; player Woodford, Saracens 1989– ; rep. London Div. U-21 and B, E. Counties U-21 (capt.), Middx; England U-21 int. *Address*: Saracens FC, Bramley Rd Sports Ground, Chaseside, Southgate, London N14 4AB.

LEE, Craig: Rugby Union footballer; b. 7 May 1971, Stockton; player W. Hartlepool 1991– ; rep. Durham U-19 and snr squad, N. Div. colts; England U-21 int. *Address*: W. Hartlepool RFC, Brierton Lane, Hartlepool, Cleveland TS25 5DR.

LEE, David: footballer; b. 5 November 1967, Blackburn; player Bury 1986–91, Southampton 91–92, Bolton Wanderers 92– . *Address*: Bolton Wanderers FC, Burnden Park, Manchester Rd, Bolton, Lancs. BL3 2QR.

LEE, David: footballer; b. 26 November 1969, Kingswood; player Chelsea 1988– ; with Chelsea: 2nd Div. champs. 1988/89; 10 England U-21 caps. *Address*: Chelsea FC, Stamford Bridge, Fulham Rd, London SW6 1HS.

LEE, Fiona: hockey player; b. 6 January 1971; player Hightown Ladies; England U-21 debut (outdoor) 1989, (indoor) 1991, snr debut (outdoor) 1990, (indoor) 1993, European Champs. gold medallist 1991, European Indoor Cup silver medallist 1993. *Address*: Hightown Ladies HC, Thirlmere Rd, Hightown, Merseyside.

LEE, Jason: footballer; b. 9 May 1971, Forest Gate; player Charlton Athletic 1989–91, Lincoln City 91–93, Southend Utd 93– . *Address*: Southend Utd FC, Roots Hall, Victoria Ave, Southend-on-Sea, Essex SS2 6NQ.

LEE, Mark: Rugby League footballer; b. 27 March 1968, St Helens; player St Helens, Salford 1990– . *Address*: Salford RLFC, The Willows, Willows Rd, Weaste, Salford M5 2ST.

LEE, Robert: footballer; b. 1 February 1966, W. Ham; player Charlton Athletic 1983–92, Newcastle Utd 92– ; 2 England U-21 caps. *Address*: Newcastle Utd FC, St James' Park, Newcastle-upon-Tyne, Tyne & Wear NE1 4ST.

LEE, Stephen: snooker player; b. 12 October 1974, Bromsgrove; GB U-16 champ. 1990, GB U-18 and English amateur champ. 1992; prof. debut 1992. *Leisure interests*: badminton, golf, pop music. *Address*: Elite Squad Ltd, Valtony, The Ridges, Finchampstead, Berks. RG11 3SS.

LEEVES, Donia Erminia: squash player; b. 11 March 1976, Tehran, Iran; player Dunnings Mill 1985– ; rep. Sussex 1988– ; Sussex girls' U-14 champ. 1987, U-16 champ. 1989–90, U-19 champ. 1991, 92; S.E. girls' U-19 open champ. 1990, 92; GB girls' U-19 champ. 1993; England U-16 debut 1990, U-19 debut 1992; European Jnr Champs. squad 1992; World Jnr Champs. squad 1991, 93. *Leisure interests*: rounders, hockey, tennis, badminton, reading, nightclubbing, cinema, theatre. *Address*: Ranlea,

Furzefield Chase, Dormans Park, E. Grinstead, W. Sussex RH19 2LY.

LEFEBVRE, Roland Philippe: cricketer; b. 7 February 1963, Rotterdam, The Netherlands; player Somerset 1990–92, Glamorgan 93– ; with Glamorgan: Sunday League champs. 1993; MCC tour Leeward Islands 1992; Holland int., 1st Dutch player to score 1st-class 100. *Address*: Glamorgan CCC, Sophia Gardens, Cardiff CF1 9XR.

LEGG, Andrew: footballer; b. 28 July 1966, Neath; player Swansea City 1988–93, Notts County 93– . *Address*: Notts County FC, Meadow Lane Ground, Nottingham NG2 3HJ.

LEIGHTON, James: footballer; b. 24 July 1958, Johnstone; player Aberdeen 1978–88, Manchester Utd 88–91, Dundee 91–93, Hibernian 93– ; with Aberdeen: winners Scottish Cup 1982, 83, 84, 86, Scottish League Cup 1986; over 58 Scotland caps. *Address*: Hibernian FC, Easter Rd Stadium, 64 Albion Rd, Edinburgh EH7 5QG.

LENG, Virginia: see ELLIOT, Virginia

LENHAM, Neil John: cricketer; b. 17 December 1965, Worthing; player Sussex 1984– ; England U-19 tour WI 1985 (capt.). *Address*: Sussex CCC, County Ground, Eaton Rd, Hove, E. Sussex BN3 3AN.

LENNON, Daniel: footballer; b. 6 April 1969, Whitburn; player Hibernian 1987– . *Address*: Hibernian FC, Easter Rd Stadium, 64 Albion Rd, Edinburgh EH7 5QG.

LEONARD, Jason: Rugby Union footballer; b. 14 August 1968, Barking; player Barking 1985–89, Saracens 89–91, Harlequins 91– ; with Saracens: 2nd Div. champs. 1989/90; England U-19 debut v. Italy 1987, England B debut v. Fiji 1989, snr debut v. Argentina 1990, Five Nations debut v. Wales 1991, Grand Slam champs. 1991, 92, tours Argentina 1990, Aus./Fiji 1991; Brit. Lions tour NZ 1993. *Address*: Harlequins FC, Stoop Memorial Ground, Craneford Way, Twickenham, Middx.

LESSING, Simon Christopher: triathlete; b. 12 February 1971, Cape Town, SA; SA champ. 1988; GB champ. 1992; European Jnr Champs. gold medal 1991; European Champs. individ. gold medals 1991, 93, silver 1992, team gold 1991, 92; World Champs. gold medal 1992 (1st European winner); European Triathlete of the Year 1992. *Leisure interests*: sailing, hiking, reading. *Address*: 19 rue de Bourgogne, 13300 Salon de Provence, France.

LEVEIN, Craig: footballer; b. 22 October 1964, Dunfermline; player Cowdenbeath 1981–83, Heart of Midlothian 83– (capt.); over 10 Scotland caps. *Address*: Heart of Midlothian FC, Tynecastle Park, Gorgie Rd, Edinburgh EH11 2NL.

LEVER, Mark: footballer; b. 29 March 1970, Beverley; player Grimsby Town 1988– . *Address*: Grimsby Town FC, Blundell Park, Cleethorpes, S. Humberside DN35 7PY.

LEWIS, Christopher Clairmonte: cricketer; b. 14 February 1968, Georgetown, Guyana; player Leics. 1987–91, Notts. 92– ; Test debut 1990, tours WI 1989/90, Aus./NZ 1990/91, NZ 1991/92, India/Sri Lanka 1992/93, WI 1994; maiden Test century v. India 1993. *Address*: Notts. CCC, Trent Bridge, Nottingham NG2 6AG.

LEWIS, David Colin: athlete; b. 15 October 1961, Haslingden; m. Susan Lewis 1987; inter-counties jnr cross-country champ. 1980, 81, AAA youth steeplechase champ. 1987, 88, English youth cross-country champ. 1979; English cross-country champ. 1985, 89, 94; AAA 5000m champ. 1985, 3000m indoor champ. 1985, 86, 10-mile road-race champ. 1987, half-marathon

champ. 1992; UK 3000m steeplechase champ. 1983, 10,000m champ. 1988; World Half-Marathon Champs. team bronze medal 1993. *Publications*: *Enjoy Athletics the Dave Lewis Way*, 1990. *Leisure interests*: Blackburn Rovers FC, cricket, travel, cooking, relaxing. *Address*: Age Concern Metro Bury, 132 The Rock, Bury BL9 0PP.

LEWIS, Emyr Wyn: Rugby Union footballer; b. 29 August 1968, Carmarthen; player Carmarthen Athletic, Llanelli; with Llanelli: winners Welsh Cup 1991–93, Welsh League champs. 1992/93; Wales and Five Nations debut v. Ireland 1991, tours Aus. 1991, Zimbabwe/Namibia 1993. *Address*: Llanelli RFC, Stradey Park, Llanelli, Dyfed.

LEWIS, Geoffrey: racehorse trainer; b. 21 December 1935, Talgarth; m. Noelene Munro 1959; 1 s. (deceased), 1 d.; Flat jockey 1953–79, winner 2000 Guineas, Irish 2000 Guineas 1969 (Right Tack), Derby 1971 (Mill Reef), Oaks 1971 (Altesse Royale), 1973 (Mysterious), Irish Oaks 1971 (Altesse Royale), King George VI and Queen Elizabeth Diamond Stakes, Prix de l'Arc de Triomphe 1971 (Mill Reef), 1000 Guineas 1973 (Mysterious); rode 146 winners in season 1969; 1st trainer's licence 1980. *Leisure interests*: golf, squash, fishing. *Address*: c/o BHB, 42 Portman Square, London W1H 0EN.

LEWIS, Jonathan James Benjamin: cricketer; b. 21 May 1970; player Essex 1990– , county champs. 1991, 92. *Address*: Essex CCC, County Cricket Ground, New Writtle St, Chelmsford DM2 0PG.

LEWIS, Lennox Claudius: boxer; b. 2 September 1965; world jnr super-heavyweight champ. 1983; Canada debut 1984; Commonwealth Games super-heavyweight gold medal 1986; Pan-American Games super-heavyweight silver medal 1987; World Cup super-heavyweight silver medal 1985; Olympic squad 1984, super-heavyweight gold medal 1988; prof. debut 1989; titles won: European heavyweight 1990, GB heavyweight 1991, Commonwealth heavyweight, WBC heavyweight 1992; over 24 prof. wins. *Address*: Champion Enterprises, 84 Green Lanes, London N16 9EJ.

LEWIS, Michael: footballer; b. 15 February 1965, Birmingham; player W. Bromwich Albion 1982–84, Derby County 84–88, Oxford Utd 88–   . *Address*: Oxford Utd FC, Manor Ground, London Rd, Headington, Oxford OX3 7RS.

LIEBREICH, Michael David: freestyle skier; b. 11 August 1963, Northolt; GB moguls champ. 1988; England debut 1986; GB debut 1987; Europa Cup moguls silver medals 1988; Olympic squad 1992. *Publications*: *The Complete Skier*, 1993. *Leisure interests*: ski mountaineering, reading, visiting art galleries, writing, business. *Address*: 5 Monks Drive, London W3 0EG.

LIGHTBODY, Alexander: flat green bowler; b. 25 June 1966, Newtownards, NI; m. Maeve Bernadette O'Hara 1993; NI singles champ. (outdoor) 1992, fours champ. (outdoor) 1983; Irish singles champ. (outdoor) 1992; GB singles champ. (outdoor) 1993; NI (outdoor) and Ireland U-25 (indoor) int. *Leisure interests*: film, music, painting and drawing, snooker. *Address*: c/o Irish Bowling Assoc., 55 Beechgrove Park, Belfast BT6 0NQ.

LILEY, John Garin: Rugby Union footballer; b. 21 August 1967, Wakefield; m. Melanie Jane Liley 1991; player Sandal 1982–87, Wakefield 87–88, Leicester 88–   ; with Leicester: winners Pilkington Cup 1993; rep. Yorks. U-21, county U-21 champs. 1987/88, N. Div. U-21 1987/88, Midlands Div. 1991–   ; England tour Argentina 1990; holds Leicester record for points scored in one season. *Leisure interests*: cricket, football, golf, tennis, badminton, volleyball, photography, ten-pin

bowling, classical music. *Address*: Leicester FC, Welford Rd, Leicester LE2 7LF.

LILLYWHITE, Christopher John: cyclist; b. 15 June 1966, Wimbledon; m. Jane Lillywhite 1992; rep. ANC 1987, Raleigh 1988–89, Falcon 90–91, MET 1992, Banana 1993–   ; GB jnr 1km sprint champ. 1983, jnr road race champ. 1984, prof. criterium champ. 1993; Commonwealth Games squad 1986; prof. debut 1987; GB debut 1989, World Champs. squad 1989, 93; Nissan Classic King of the Mountains 1987, 91, Milk Race King of the Mountains 1988; winner Tour of Lancs. 1989, Milk Race 1993. *Leisure interests*: Chelsea FC, real ale, travel. *Address*: c/o Brit. Cycling Fed., 36 Rockingham Rd, Kettering, Northants. NN16 8HG.

LIMPAR, Anders: footballer; b. 24 August 1965, Sweden; player Cremonese (Italy), Arsenal 1990–   ; with Arsenal: League Champions 1990/91, winners League Cup 1993; Swedish int. *Address*: Arsenal FC, Arsenal Stadium, Highbury, London N5 1BU.

LINDORES, Joyce: flat green bowler; b. 2 May 1944, Galashiels; 3 d.; Scottish women's singles champ. (outdoor) 1988, (indoor) 1987, women's pairs champ. (outdoor) 1993; UK women's singles champ. (indoor) 1988; GB mixed pairs champ. (indoor) 1989; Scotland debut (outdoor and indoor) 1987; Commonwealth Games squad 1990; World Champs. women's team gold medal 1992. *Leisure interests*: walking, keep-fit, knitting. *Address*: 'Dinsburn', 1 Shawpark Rd, Selkirk TD7 4DS.

LINDSAY, Todd James: fencer (épée); b. 27 April 1970, Edinburgh; rep. St Andrews Univ. 1988–92 (Blue 1988); Scottish univ. champ. 1992, 93; Scottish U-20 champ. 1988; GB U-16 champ. 1985; Scotland jnr debut 1989, snr debut 1991; GB U-20 debut 1990, snr debut and World

Student Games squad 1991. *Leisure interests*: golf. *Address*: Middleton Lodge, Middleton Hall Lane, Brentwood, Essex CM15 8AJ.

LINEEN, Sean Raymond Patrick: Rugby Union footballer; b. 25 December 1961, Auckland, NZ; m. Lynne Lineen 1992; player Pakuranga, Papakura, Counties (all NZ), Bombay, Pontypool, Boroughmuir; with Boroughmuir: Scottish League champs. 1990/91; Scotland and Five Nations debut v. Wales 1989, Grand Slam champs. 1990, tours NZ 1990, Aus. 1992; shares with Scott Hastings world's most-capped centre partnership (27). *Leisure interests*: tennis, golf, squash. *Address*: Boroughmuir RFC, Meggetland, Colinton Rd, Edinburgh EH14 1AS.

LING, Martin: footballer; b. 15 July 1966, W. Ham; player Exeter City 1984–86, Swindon Town 1986, Southend Utd 1986–91, Swindon Town 91– . *Address*: Swindon Town FC, The County Ground, Swindon, Wilts. SN1 2ED.

LINIGHAN, Andrew: footballer; b. 18 June 1962, Hartlepool; player Hartlepool Utd 1980–84, Leeds Utd 84–85, Oldham Athletic 85–87, Norwich City 87–90, Arsenal 90– ; with Arsenal: League Champions 1990/91, winners League Cup, FA Cup 1993. *Address*: Arsenal FC, Arsenal Stadium, Highbury, London N5 1BU.

LINIGHAN, David: footballer; b. 9 January 1965, Hartlepool; player Hartlepool Utd 1981–86, Shrewsbury Town 86–88, Ipswich Town 88– (capt.). *Address*: Ipswich Town FC, Portman Rd, Ipswich, Suffolk IP1 2DA.

LISTER, Sandra Denise: hockey player; b. 16 August 1961, Halifax; player Bradford Ladies 1976–83, Chelsea CPE 79–83, Ipswich Ladies 83– ; with Ipswich: club champs. 1985, League champs. 1993, indoor club champs. 1990, European Indoor Cup silver medallist 1991; rep. Yorks. Jnrs 1976–79,

Sussex 79–84, Essex 84–89, Essex indoor 85–89; England U-18 debut 1978, U-21 debut 1981, snr debut 1982 (snr capt. 1989–   ), tour Aus. 1985, European Champs. silver medallist 1987, gold 1991, World Cup squad 1983, 86, 90; England indoor debut 1987 (capt. 1989/90), European Indoor Cup bronze medallist 1987, silver 1993; GB debut 1989, Olympic bronze medal 1992; 3rd-highest capped England player (over 106); most-capped England capt. (over 60). *Leisure interests*: all sport, music, travel. *Address*: Ipswich Ladies HC, Tuddenham Rd, Ipswich, Suffolk IP4 3QJ.

LITTLE, Brian: football manager; b. 25 November 1953, Horden; player Aston Villa 1971–80, winners League Cup 1975, 77; 1 England cap; manager Darlington, Wolverhampton Wanderers 1986, Leicester City 1991– . *Address*: Leicester City FC, City Stadium, Filbert St, Leicester LE2 7FL.

LITTLEJOHN, Adrian: footballer; b. 26 September 1970, Wolverhampton; player Walsall 1989–91, Sheffield Utd 91– . *Address*: Sheffield Utd FC, Bramall Lane, Sheffield, S. Yorks S2 4SU.

LIVINGSTONE, Stephen: footballer; b. 8 September 1968, Middlesbrough; player Coventry City 1986–91, Blackburn Rovers 91–93, Chelsea 93–94, Grimsby Town 94– . *Address*: Grimsby Town FC, Blundell Park, Cleethorpes, S. Humberside DN35 7PY.

LLEWELLYN, Carl: jockey (NH); b. 29 July 1965; winner Grand National 1992 (Party Politics), Mackeson Gold Cup 1992 (Tipping Tim). *Address*: c/o BHB, 42 Portman Square, London W1H 0EN.

LLEWELLYN, Gareth Owen: Rugby Union footballer; b. 27 February 1969, Cardiff; player Llanharan, Neath; Wales debut v. NZ 1989, Five Nations debut v. England 1990, tours Aus. 1991, Zimbabwe/Namibia 1993 (capt.). *Address*: Neath RFC, The Gnoll, Gnoll Park Rd, Neath, W. Glamorgan.

LLEWELLYN, Glyn David: Rugby Union footballer; b. 9 August 1965, Bradford on Avon; player London Welsh, Llanelli, Neath; Wales debut v. Namibia 1990, Five Nations debut v. England 1991, tour Aus. 1991. *Address:* Neath RFC, The Gnoll, Gnoll Park Rd, Neath, W. Glamorgan.

LLONG, Nigel James: cricketer; b. 11 February 1969, Ashford; player Kent 1991– . *Address:* Kent CCC, St Lawrence Ground, Canterbury CT1 3NZ.

LLOYD, Graham David: cricketer; b. 1 July 1969, Accrington; player Lancs. 1988– ; England A tour Aus. 1992/93. *Address:* Lancs. CCC, Old Trafford, Manchester M16 0PX.

LLOYD, Owain Stradling: Rugby Union footballer; b. 26 September 1970; player Bridgend; Wales U-21 debut v. Scotland U-21 1991. *Address:* Bridgend RFC, Brewery Field, Tondu Rd, Bridgend, Mid Glamorgan.

LLOYD, Timothy Andrew: cricketer; b. 5 November 1956, Oswestry; m. Gilly Lloyd; 2 d.; player Warks. 1977–93 (capt. 88–92); English Counties XI tour Zimbabwe 1984/85; 1 Test (1984), 3 1-day ints. *Address:* Warks. CCC, County Ground, Edgbaston, Birmingham B5 7QU.

LOCKE, Adam: footballer; b. 20 August 1970, Croydon; player Southend 1990– . *Address:* Southend Utd FC, Roots Hall, Victoria Ave, Southend-on-Sea, Essex SS2 6NQ.

LOCOCK, Jeffery Mark: powerboat racer (navigator); b. 15 December 1953, Plymouth; GB offshore circuit racing class III 2-litre champ. 1993. *Leisure interests:* golf, water skiing, football. *Address:* 80 Knighton Rd, St Judes, Plymouth, Devon.

LOGAN, Kenneth: Rugby Union footballer; b. 3 April 1972, Stirling; player Stirling County; Scotland debut v. Aus. 1992, Five Nations debut v. England 1993, tours Aus. 1992, Fiji/Tonga/W. Samoa 1993; 1st Stirling County player to gain int. cap. *Leisure interests:* golf, snooker, football, socializing. *Address:* Stirling County RFC, Bridgehaugh, Causewayhead Rd, Stirling.

LOMAS, Lisa: table tennis player; b. 9 March 1967; m. Andrew Lomas; English women's singles and doubles champ. 1994; European Champs. women's singles bronze medal 1986, silver 1992, team bronze 1994; World Champs. squad 1991; Olympic squad 1992. *Address:* c/o English Table Tennis Assoc., 3rd Floor, Queensbury House, Havelock Rd, Hastings, E. Sussex TN34 1HF.

LONGBOTTOM, Peter: cyclist; b. 13 May 1959, Huddersfield; m. Lyn Longbottom 1989; RTTC 100-mile time trial individ. champ. 1990, team champ. 1991, 100km team champ. 1991, team hill-climb champ. 1985–91; Commonwealth Games team time trial bronze medal 1990; GB jnr debut 1977, snr debut 1979, World Champs. squad (road race) 1982, 83, (team time trial) 1985, 91, Olympic squad (team time trial) 1992. *Leisure interests:* mountain biking, badminton. *Address:* 7 Pasture Lane, Malton, N. Yorks. YO17 0BS.

LONGLEY, Jonathan Ian: cricketer; b. 12 April 1969, New Brunswick, USA; player Kent 1989–93, Durham 94– . *Address:* Durham CCC, County Ground, Riverside, Chester-le-Street, Co. Durham DH3 3QR.

LONGSTAFFE, David: ice hockey player; b. 26 August 1974; player Whitley Warriors 1989– , winners Scottish Cup 1992. *Address:* The Ice Rink, Hillheads Rd, Whitley Bay, Tyne & Wear.

LOOSEMORE, Sarah Jane: tennis player; b. 15 June 1971, Cardiff; rep. S. Wales; Welsh ladies' champ. 1985; GB girls' U-16 champ. 1986, U-18 champ. 1987, ladies' champ. 1988 (youngest ever); GB debut and Federation Cup team 1990; finalist Singapore Open 1990. *Leisure interests*: hockey, rowing, golf, skiing. *Address*: High Trees, Druidstone Rd, St Mellons, Cardiff.

LORD, Gary Robert: Rugby League footballer; b. 6 July 1966, Wakefield; player Leeds, Halifax 1991– ; GB U-19 and U-21 int. *Address*: Halifax RLFC, The Pavilion, Thrum Hall, Gibbet St, Halifax, W. Yorks. HX1 4TL.

LOTHIAN, Jackie: hockey player; b. 6 January 1969, Blairgowrie; player Blairgowrie FP 1983–86, Moray House College SCPE 86–90, Royal High Gymnasts 90–93 (capt.); Scotland U-21 debut 1986 (capt. 89–90), snr debut 1992. *Leisure interests*: cycling, hill-walking, swimming. *Address*: 40/15 Caledonian Crescent, Edinburgh.

LOUGHLAN, Anthony: footballer; b. 19 January 1970, Croydon; player Nottingham Forest 1989– . *Address*: Nottingham Forest FC, City Ground, Nottingham NG2 5FJ.

LOUGHLIN, Paul: Rugby League footballer; b. 28 July 1966, St Helens; player St Helens 1983– , winners John Player Special Trophy 1988, Premiership 1993; GB debut v. France 1988, Brit. Lions tours Aus./NZ/Papua New Guinea 1988, Aus./Papua New Guinea 1992. *Address*: St Helens RLFC, Dunriding Lane, St Helens, Merseyside WA10 4AD.

LOUGHRAN, Eamonn: boxer; b. 5 June 1970; Ireland debut 1987; World Jnr Champs. welterweight silver medal 1987; prof. debut 1987; titles won: Commonwealth welterweight 1992, WBO welterweight 1993; over 22 prof. wins. *Address*: Matchroom Ltd, 10 Western Rd, Romford, Essex RM1 3JT.

LOUGHRIDGE, Christopher Bryce: surfer; b. 22 March 1959, Belfast, NI; Ireland debut 1990. *Leisure interests*: windsurfing, skiing, water skiing, snowboarding. *Address*: 116 Upper Lisburn Rd, Belfast BT10 0BD.

LOUIS LANE, Suzanne: badminton player; b. 7 October 1965, Hitchin; m. Richard Lane 1992; rep. Devon; English ladies' champ. 1993, 94; England debut 1990, Uber Cup team 1992; European Champs. team bronze medal 1992; winner Spanish Open ladies' singles 1992, Welsh Open, Irish Open ladies' singles 1993, Hants. Open ladies' singles 1994. *Leisure interests*: squash, tennis, cookery, shopping for clothes, interior decorating. *Address*: 9 Sopwith Ave, Chessington, Surrey KT9 1QE.

LOVELL, Lindsay: ice hockey player; b. 4 January 1966; player Murrayfield Racers 1983–87, Fife Flyers 87–91, Murrayfield Racers 91– ; with Murrayfield Racers: winners Autumn Cup 1986, 94, Scottish Cup 1987, GB champs. 1985/86, League champs. 1986/87. *Address*: The Ice Rink, Riversdale Crescent, Edinburgh EH12 5XN.

LOVELL, Patricia Anne: field archer; b. 16 March 1952, Purley; m. Derrick John Lovell 1971; 3 s.; rep. Kent (target archery) 1980–82; attained Grand Master Bowman status (ladies' bare bow) 1991; GB debut 1990; World Champs. team silver medal 1992; World Games ladies' bare bow gold medal 1993. *Leisure interests*: swimming. *Address*: c/o Grand Nat. Archery Soc., Nat. Agricultural Centre, Seventh St, Stoneleigh Park, Kenilworth, Warks. CV8 2LG.

LOWE, John: darts player; b. 21 July 1945, Chesterfield; m. Diana Lowe 1966; 1 s., 1 d.; world prof. champ. 1979, 87, 93, pairs champ. 1986; England debut 1979, winners World Cup 1979–91, Nations Cup 1979, 80, 82–84, 86–88; winner World Masters 1976, 80, Brit. Open 1977, 88, Brit. Matchplay

1978, 85, World Cup singles 1981, 91, *News of the World* Champs. 1981, World Matchplay 1984; 1st play to throw perfect televised 9-dart 501 1984; chairman World Prof. Darts Players Assoc. *Publications: The John Lowe Story, Darts the John Lowe Way, The Lowe Profile. Leisure interests*: golf, motor sport, Sparks and Variety Club. *Address*: John Lowe Sports Enterprises Ltd, 5 Hayfield Close, Wingerworth, Chesterfield, Derbys. S42 6QF.

LOWE, Kendra: netball player; b. 11 November 1962, Sedgefield; player Pioneers/Stockton Ladies 1974–81, Vauxhall Golds 82– , Linden 88– ; rep. S. Durham and Cleveland 1973–81, Herts. 85–86, Beds. 87– (capt.), North U-21 76–80, East U-21 81–84, snr 84– ; with Herts.: inter-county champs. 1985/86; with Beds.: League champs. 1989/90; with East: regional champs. 1989/90, 1991/92; England U-18 debut 1980 (capt. 1981), U-21 and snr debuts 1982 (U-21 capt. 1982–84, snr capt. 1990–); World Champs. squad 1983, 87, 91; World Games bronze medal 1989, squad 1985, 93; tours Fiji/NZ 1987, NZ 1991, Spain 1992, Jamaica 1993; holds record number of England caps (over 101). *Leisure interests*: skiing, swimming, athletics, wine-making, reading, pen pals. *Address*: 32 Braemar Court, 40 Ashburnham Rd, Bedford MK40 1DZ.

LOWE, Kenneth: footballer; b. 6 November 1961, Sedgefield; player Hartlepool Utd 1978–84, Scarborough 1988, Barnet 1991–93, Stoke City 93– . *Address*: Stoke City FC, Victoria Ground, Stoke on Trent, Staffs. ST4 4EG.

LOWES, James: Rugby League footballer; b. 11 October 1969, Leeds; player Hunslet, Leeds 1992– . *Address*: Leeds RLFC, Bass Headingley, St Michael's Lane, Leeds LS6 3BR.

LOYE, Malachy Bernard: cricketer; b. 27 September 1972, Northampton; player Northants. 1991– ; England U-19 tour Pakistan 1992, England A tour SA 1993/94. *Address*: Northants. CCC, County Cricket Ground, Wantage Rd, Northampton NN1 4TJ.

LUBIN, Jonathan Mark: weightlifter (64kg); b. 15 February 1974, Chertsey; GB jnr champ. 1991, 93; GB debut 1991, European Jnr Champs., World Jnr Champs. squads 1993. *Address*: 21 Albany Rd, Hersham, Walton on Thames, Surrey KT12 5QG.

LUCKES, David James: hockey player; b. 24 April 1969, Newport; player E. Grinstead 1987–93, indoor club champs. 1993; rep. Somerset 1987, Sussex 1988–90; England U-21 debut and European Cup U-21 silver medallist 1988, snr debut 1989, European Cup bronze medallist 1991; GB debut 1990, Champions Trophy squad 1989, 90, 91, 92, World Student Games gold medallist 1991, Olympic squad 1992; rep. Somerset U-18 cricket. *Leisure interests*: cricket, squash, badminton, 20th-century history, modern theatre, parapsychology. *Address*: c/o The Hockey Assoc., Norfolk House, 102 Saxon Gate W., Milton Keynes MK9 2EP.

LUKE, Noel: footballer; b. 28 December 1964, Birmingham; player W. Bromwich Albion 1982–84, Mansfield Town 84–86, Peterborough Utd 86– . *Address*: Peterborough Utd FC, London Rd Ground, Peterborough, Cambs. PE2 8AL.

LUKIC, John: footballer; b. 11 December 1960, Chesterfield; player Leeds Utd 1978–83, Arsenal 83–90, Leeds Utd 90– ; with Arsenal: winners League Cup 1987, League champs. 1988/89; with Leeds Utd: League champs. 1991/92; 7 England U-21 caps. *Address*: Leeds Utd FC, Elland Rd, Leeds, W. Yorks. LS11 0ES.

LUMLEY, Penelope Christine: real tennis player; b. 13 May 1963, Frinton; m. Colin

John Lumley 1991; 1 s.; Scottish ladies' open singles champ. 1989; GB ladies' open singles champ. 1988, 91, 93, doubles champ. 1991; French ladies' open singles champ. 1988–90, doubles champ. 1990; Aus. ladies' open singles champ. 1991; world ladies' champ. 1989, 91, 93, doubles champ. 1993. *Leisure interests*: golf, cinema. *Address*: Royal County of Berks. Real Tennis Club, Holyport St, Holyport, Maidenhead, Berks. SL6 2JR.

LUND, Gary: footballer; b. 13 September 1964, Grimsby; player Grimsby Town 1983–86, Lincoln City 86–87, Notts County 87– ; 3 England U-21 caps. *Address*: Notts County FC, Meadow Lane Ground, Nottingham NG2 3HJ.

LUPTON, Victoria Ann: race walker; b. 17 April 1972, Sheffield; AAA women's 5km champ. 1993; World Cup squad 1991, 93, World Champs. squad 1993, Olympic squad 1992; GB women's jnr 3km, 5km and 10km track record-holder. *Leisure interests*: most sport, reading. *Address*: 15 Newlands Grove, Intake, Sheffield S12 2FU.

LUSCOMBE, Lee: footballer; b. 16 July 1971, Guernsey; player Brentford 1991–93, Millwall 93– ; with Brentford: 3rd Div. champs. 1991/92. *Address*: Millwall FC, The Den, Zampa Rd, Bermondsey, London SE16 3LH.

LUSCOMBE, Robin: motorcyclist (sidecar trials); b. 4 August 1961, Shipley; m. Karen Tracey Luscombe 1987; 1 s.; GB champ. 1986–88, 91, 92, expert champ. 1986, 87, 91, 92; FIM coupe-winner 1989, 91, 92; winner Isle of Man 2 days trial 1985–90, 92, 93. *Address*: c/o ACU, ACU House, Wood St, Rugby CV21 2YX.

LYDON, Joseph: Rugby League footballer; b. 26 November 1963, Wigan; player Widnes, Wigan 1986– ; with Widnes: winners Premiership 1983, Challenge Cup 1984; with Wigan: winners Premiership

1987, 92, 94, Challenge Cup 1988–90, 92, 93, John Player Special Trophy 1987, Regal Trophy 1989, 90, 93, League champs. 1986/87, 89/90, 90/91, 91/92, 92/93; rep. Lancs., England Schools (RU), tour Zimbabwe 1982; GB debut v. France 1983, Brit. Lions tours Aus./NZ/Papua New Guinea 1984, 92, NZ/Papua New Guinea 1990. *Address*: Wigan RLFC, The Pavilion, Central Park, Wigan WN1 1XF.

LYLE, Alexander Walter Barr (Sandy), MBE: golfer; b. 9 February 1958, Shrewsbury; Shropshire and Herefordshire champ. 1974, 76, Midland open champ. 1975; English open amateur strokeplay champ. 1975, 77; England debut 1975; Walker Cup team 1977; prof. debut 1977; Scottish prof. champ. 1979; world match-play champ. 1988; Dunhill Cup team (Scotland) 1985–90, 92, 93; Ryder Cup team 1979–87, winners 1985, 87; winner Nigerian Open 1978, Jersey Open, Scandinavian Open, European Open 1979, French Open 1981, Madrid Open 1983, Italian Open 1984, 92, Open, Benson and Hedges Int. Open 1985, German Masters 1987, US Masters, Brit. Masters 1988, BMW Int. Open 1991, Volvo Masters 1992; Sports Writers' Sportsman of the Year 1988. *Address*: c/o PGA European Tour, Wentworth Club, Wentworth Drive, Virginia Water, Surrey GU25 4LS.

LYNCH, Monte Allan: cricketer; b. 21 May 1958, Georgetown, Guyana; player Surrey 1977– ; England 1-day int. debut v. WI 1988. *Address*: Surrey CCC, The Oval, Kennington, London SE11 5SS.

LYON, David: Rugby League footballer; b. 3 September 1965, Billinge; player Widnes, Warrington, St Helens 1992– ; with Warrington: winners Regal Trophy 1991; with St Helens: winners Premiership 1993; GB U-21 debut v. NZ 1985. *Address*: St Helens RLFC, Dunriding Lane, St Helens, Merseyside WA10 4AD.

LYON, Sharyn Ann: netball player; b. 18 August 1969, Paisley; m. Andrew Rae Lyon 1993; player Moneycounts; rep. Renfrewshire U-16 and U-18 1982–85, Glasgow District U-21 86–88, snr 89–91; Scotland U-18 and U-21 debuts 1986, snr debut and World Champs. squad 1987, World Games squad 1989, tour Aus. 1987. *Leisure interests*: watching athletics and football, reading, eating out. *Address*: c/o Scottish Netball Assoc., Kelvin Hall, Argyle St, Glasgow G3 8AW.

McALLISTER, Brian: footballer; b. 30 November 1970, Glasgow; player Wimbledon 1989– . *Address*: Wimbledon FC, Selhurst Park, London SE25 6PY.

McALLISTER, Gary: footballer; b. 25 December 1964, Motherwell; player Motherwell 1981–85, Leicester City 85–90, Leeds Utd 90–   (capt.); with Leeds Utd: League champs. 1991/92; 1 Scotland U-21 cap, over 22 full Scotland caps. *Address*: Leeds Utd FC, Elland Rd, Leeds, W. Yorks. LS11 0ES.

McALLISTER, Kevin: footballer; b. 8 November 1962, Falkirk; player Falkirk 1983–85, Chelsea 85–91, Falkirk 91–93, Hibernian 93–   . *Address*: Hibernian FC, Easter Rd Stadium, 64 Albion Rd, Edinburgh EH7 5QG.

McATEER, Jason: footballer; b. 18 June 1971, Liverpool; player Bolton Wanderers 1991– . *Address*: Bolton Wanderers FC, Burnden Park, Manchester Rd, Bolton, Lancs. BL3 2QR.

McAVENNIE, Frank: footballer; b. 22 November 1959, Glasgow; player St Mirren 1981–85, W. Ham Utd 85–87, Celtic 87–89, W. Ham Utd 89–92, Aston Villa 1992, Celtic 1992–   ; with Celtic: winners Scottish Cup 1988; 5 Scotland U-21 caps, 5 full Scotland caps. *Address*: Celtic FC, Celtic Park, 95 Kerrydale St, Glasgow G40 3RE.

McBRYDE, Robin Currie: Rugby Union footballer; b. 3 July 1970, Bangor; player Bangor 1985–86, Menai Bridge 86–88, Mold 88–90, Swansea 90–   ; with Swansea: Welsh League champs. 1991/92; Wales tour Zimbabwe/Namibia 1993. *Leisure interests*: squash, target shooting, weight training, cycling, night-clubbing. *Address*: Swansea RFC, St Helens, Swansea SA2 0AR.

McCAGUE, Martin John: cricketer; b. 24 May 1969, Larne, NI; player Kent 1991–   ; England A tour SA 1993/94, Test debut v. Aus. 1993. *Address*: Kent CCC, St Lawrence Ground, Canterbury CT1 3NZ.

McCALL, Stuart: footballer; b. 10 June 1964, Leeds; player Bradford City 1982–88, Everton 88–91, Rangers 91–   ; with Rangers: winners Scottish Cup 1992, 93, Scottish League Cup 1993; 2 Scotland U-21 caps, over 23 full Scotland caps. *Address*: Glasgow Rangers FC, Ibrox Stadium, 150 Edmiston Drive, Glasgow G51 2XD.

McCANDLISH, Lynne Helen: netball player; b. 27 May 1968, Glasgow; player Moneycounts 1986–   ; rep. Glasgow District, inter-district champs. 1991/92; Scotland U-18 and U-21 debuts 1986 (U-21 capt. 1988/89), snr debut 1992 (vice-capt. 1991/92). *Leisure interests*: 5-a-side football, tennis, table tennis, badminton. *Address*: c/o Scottish Netball Assoc., Kelvin Hall, Argyle St, Glasgow G3 8AW.

McCARRISON, Dugald: footballer; b. 22 December 1969, Lanark; player Celtic 1987–92, Kilmarnock 92–   . *Address*: Kilmarnock FC, Rugby Park, Kilmarnock KA1 2DP.

McCART, Chris: footballer; b. 17 April 1967, Motherwell; player Motherwell 1984–   , winners Scottish Cup 1991. *Address*: Motherwell FC, Fir Park, Fir Park St, Motherwell ML1 2QN.

McCARTHY, Alan: footballer; b. 11 January 1972, Wandsworth; player Queens Park Rangers 1989– . *Address*: Queens Park Rangers FC, Rangers Stadium, S. Africa Rd, London W12 7PA.

McCARTHY, Matthew: Rugby Union footballer; b. 16 April 1971; player Neath; Wales U-21 debut v. Scotland U-21 1992. *Address*: Neath RFC, The Gnoll, Gnoll Park Rd, Neath, W. Glamorgan.

McCARTHY, Michael: football player/manager; b. 7 February 1959, Barnsley; player Barnsley 1977–83, Manchester City 83–87, Celtic 87–89, Olympique Lyon (France) 89–90, Millwall 1990– , player/manager 1992– ; with Celtic: winners Scottish Cup 1988, 89; 55 Ireland caps. *Address*: Millwall FC, The Den, Zampa Rd, Bermondsey, London SE16 3LH.

McCLAIR, Brian: footballer; b. 8 December 1963, Bellshill; player Motherwell 1981–83, Celtic 83–87, Manchester Utd 87– ; with Celtic: winners Scottish Cup 1985; with Manchester Utd: winners FA Cup 1990, European Cup Winners' Cup 1991, League champs. 1992/93; 8 Scotland U-21 caps, over 25 full Scotland caps; Scottish Football Writers' Assoc. Player of the Year 1987. *Address*: Manchester Utd FC, Old Trafford, Manchester M16 0RA.

McCLOY, Gary Samuel: flat green bowler; b. 28 May 1969, Ballymoney, NI; m. Jayne Margaret McCloy 1992; Irish triples champ. (outdoor and indoor) 1991; Ireland debut (outdoor and indoor) 1991. *Publications*: *Skilful Bowls*, 1991. *Leisure interests*: golf, snooker, football, tennis, fishing. *Address*: 84 Shellbridge Park, Coleraine, Co. Londonderry BT52 2HP.

McCLUSKEY, George: footballer; b. 19 September 1957, Hamilton; player Celtic 1975–83, Leeds Utd 83–86, Hibernian 86–89, Hamilton Academical 89–92, Kilmarnock 92– ; with Celtic: winners Scottish Cup 1980; 6 Scotland U-21 caps. *Address*: Kilmarnock FC, Rugby Park, Kilmarnock KA1 2DP.

McCOIST, Alistair Murdoch: footballer; b. 24 September 1962, E. Kilbride; m. Allison McCoist; player St Johnstone 1978–81, Sunderland 81–83, Rangers 83– ; with Rangers: winners Scottish League Cup 1984, 85, 87, 88, 89, 91, 94, Scottish Cup 1992; 1 Scotland U-21 cap, over 45 full Scotland caps; BBC Scotland's Sports Personality of the Year and Scottish Football Writers' Assoc. Player of the Year 1992. *Address*: Glasgow Rangers FC, Ibrox Stadium, 150 Edmiston Drive, Glasgow G51 2XD.

McCOLGAN, Elizabeth, MBE: athlete; b. 24 May 1964, Dundee; m. Peter McColgan 1987; 1 d.; Scottish women's 3000m champ. 1985, 86, UK women's 10,000m champ. 1986, 5000m champ. 1988, 3000m champ. 1989, 91; Commonwealth Games women's 10,000m gold medal 1986, 10,000m gold, 3000m bronze 1990; World Cross-Country Champs. silver medal 1987, bronze 1991; World Indoor Champs. women's 3000m silver medal 1989; World Champs. women's 10,000m gold medal 1991; Olympic women's 10,000m silver medal 1988; winner New York Marathon 1991, Tokyo Marathon 1992, World Half-Marathon 1992; UK and Commonwealth women's 10,000m, world women's 5000m indoor record-holder; Sports Writers' Sportswoman of the Year 1988, 91, BBC Sports Personality of the Year 1991, AIMS Female Athlete of the Year 1992. *Address*: c/o Brit. Athletic Fed., 225A Bristol Rd, Edgbaston, Birmingham B5 7UB.

McCRACKEN, Robert: boxer; b. 31 May 1968; England debut 1988, Commonwealth Games squad 1990, World Cup silver medal 1990; prof. debut 1991; titles won: GB light-middleweight 1994; over 14 prof. wins. *Address*: Nat. Promotions, Nat. House, 60–66 Wardour St, London W1V 3HP.

McCRONE, John: ice hockey player; b. 26 February 1963; player Ayr Raiders 1983–92, Fife Flyers 92– ; World Champs. debut 1989. *Address*: The Ice Rink, Rosslyn St, Kirkcaldy, Fife.

McCRONE, Senga: flat green bowler; b. 11 June 1934, Kilmarnock; m. James McCrone 1955; 2 s.; Scottish women's pairs champ. (indoor) 1992, women's triples champ. (indoor) 1993; GB women's fours champ. (outdoor) 1972; Ireland debut (outdoor) 1972, Scotland debut (outdoor) 1981; Commonwealth Games women's singles silver medal 1986, squad 1990; World Champs. women's fours gold medal 1992. *Leisure interests*: cycling, gardening, crosswords, reading. *Address*: 5 Weensgate Drive, Hawick TD9 9PF.

McCULLOUGH, Heather: hockey player; b. 5 January 1971, Belfast, NI; player Randalstown Ladies 1982– , European Div. B Champs. silver medallist 1991, European Indoor Div. B gold medallist 1992; Ulster U-21 and Ireland U-21 debuts 1989, snr debuts 1992. *Leisure interests*: football, swimming, badminton, tennis, horseriding, sunbathing, trampolining. *Address*: 2 Bracken Ave, Glenburn, Co. Antrim BT41 1PU.

McCULLOUGH, Robert: karate player (U-60–U-65kg); b. 8 September 1966, Kilmarnock; m. Janet McCullough 1991; Scottish champ. 1988, team champ. 1993; Scotland debut 1991; European Champs. bronze medal 1993; winner Cumbrian Open 1990, 91, Sakai Open 1991–93. *Leisure interests*: marathon running, circuit and weight training, football. *Address*: 42 Whatriggs Rd, Bellfield, Kilmarnock KA1 3RA.

McCUNE, Velda: fencer (foil); b. 30 November 1971, Glasgow; rep. Edinburgh Univ. 1991–93 (women's capt. 92–93), Univ. of Pennsylvania 93–94; Scottish jnr champ. 1990; Scotland debut 1992. *Leisure*

interests: horseriding, reading, flute. *Address*: c/o AFA, 1 Barons Gate, 33–35 Rothschild Rd, London W4 5HT.

McCURRIE, Steve: Rugby League footballer; b. 1 June 1973, Whitehaven; player Hensingham ARLFC, Widnes 1990– ; GB debut v. France 1993. *Address*: Widnes RLFC, Naughton Park, Lowerhouse Lane, Widnes WA8 7DZ.

McDAID, Anthony: basketball player; b. 31 January 1969, Glasgow; m. Carolyne McDaid 1990; player Glasgow City 1984–87, Glasgow Rangers 87–88, Glasgow City 88– ; Scotland U-17, U-19 and snr int., Commonwealth Champs. silver medallist 1991. *Leisure interests*: football, swimming, reading. *Address*: c/o Scottish Basketball Assoc., Caledonia House, S. Gyle, Edinburgh EH12 9DQ.

McDERMOTT, John: footballer; b. 3 February 1969, Middlesbrough; player Grimsby Town 1987– . *Address*: Grimsby Town FC, Blundell Park, Cleethorpes, S. Humberside DN35 7PY.

McDONALD, Alan: footballer; b. 12 October 1963, Belfast, NI; player Queens Park Rangers 1981– (capt.); over 41 NI caps (capt.). *Address*: Queens Park Rangers FC, Rangers Stadium, S. Africa Rd, London W12 7PA.

MacDONALD, Andrew Edward Douglas: Rugby Union footballer; b. 17 January 1966, Nairn; player London Scottish, Cambridge Univ., Heriot's FP; Scotland B debut v. Ireland 1989, Scotland A debut v. Spain 1991, snr debut v. NZ 1993, tour Fiji/Tonga/W. Samoa 1993. *Address*: Heriot's FP, Goldenacre, Bangholm Terrace, Edinburgh EH3 5QN.

MacDONALD, Kyle: fencer (épée); b. 23 March 1964, Inverness; rep. Glasgow Univ. 1981–87, Scottish univ. 84–87; Scottish univ. champ. 1986, 88; W. of Scotland champ. 1985–87; Scotland debut 1992; winner NI Open 1992. *Leisure interests*: mountaineering, paragliding, travel, photography. *Address*: c/o Scottish Amateur Fencing Union, 11 Eyre Crescent, Edinburgh EH3 5ET.

McDONALD, Neil: footballer; b. 2 November 1965, Wallsend; player Newcastle Utd 1983–88, Everton 88–91, Oldham Athletic 91– ; 5 England U-21 caps. *Address*: Oldham Athletic FC, Boundary Park, Oldham, Lancs. OL1 2PA.

MacDONALD, Susan Christina: hockey player; b. 12 August 1968, Glasgow; player Edinburgh Univ. 1987–90, Glasgow Western 1985– ; with Glasgow Western: European Cup silver medallist 1991, 92, Scottish League champs. 1985–93; Scotland debut 1991; GB squad, World Student Games 1991 (top GB goal-scorer), Olympic training squad 1992. *Leisure interests*: most sports, travel, cinema, eating out, current affairs. *Address*: 2 The Cottages, Lower Craigton, Milngavie, Glasgow G62 7HQ.

McDONOUGH, Darron: footballer; b. 7 November 1962, Antwerp, Belgium; player Oldham Athletic 1980–86, Luton Town 86–92, Newcastle Utd 92– . *Address*: Newcastle Utd FC, St James' Park, Newcastle-upon-Tyne, Tyne & Wear NE1 4ST.

McELVEEN, Karen: netball player; b. 28 November 1972, Glasgow; player Castlemilk 1987– ; rep. Glasgow District U-21 1991– , snr inter-district champs. 1992/93; Scotland U-18 debut 1989, U-21 debut 1990 (capt. 1991–93), snr debut 1991. *Leisure interests*: badminton, racketball, tennis, football, swimming, volleyball. *Address*: c/o Scottish Netball Assoc., Kelvin Hall, Argyle St, Glasgow G3 8AW.

McEVOY, Peter Aloysius: golfer; b. 22 March 1953, London; m. Dorothy Lanier McEvoy 1978; 2 s.; Brit. univ. strokeplay champ. 1973, W. of England open amateur strokeplay champ. 1977, 80, 83, Midland open amateur strokeplay champ. 1978; joint English open amateur strokeplay champ. 1980; GB amateur champ. 1977, 78; England debut 1976, most-capped player (over 140); GB debut 1977, Walker Cup team 1977, 79, 81, 85, 89, leading individ., World Amateur Team Champs. 1988; leading amateur in Open 1978, 79; 1st Brit. amateur to complete 72 holes in US Masters 1978. *Address*: c/o English Golf Union, 1–3 Upper King St, Leicester LE1 6XF.

McEWEN, Doug: ice hockey player; b. 2 October 1963; player Peterborough Pirates 1986–87, Lee Valley Lions 87–89, Cardiff Devils 89– ; with Peterborough Pirates: Div. 1 champs. 1986/87; with Cardiff Devils: winners Autumn Cup 1993, League champs., GB champs. 1992/93. *Address*: Wales Nat. Ice Rink, Hayes Bridge Rd, Cardiff CF1 2GH.

McFARLAND, Roy: football manager; b. 5 April 1948, Liverpool; player Tranmere Rovers 1966–67, Derby County 67–81, Bradford City 81–83, Derby County 1983; with Derby County: 2nd Div. champs. 1968/69, League champs. 1971/72, 74/75; 5 England U-23 caps, 28 full England caps; assistant manager Derby County 1983–93, manager 93– , 2nd Div. champs. 1986/87. *Address*: Derby County FC, The Baseball Ground, Shaftesbury Crescent, Derby DE3 8NB.

McGEACHIE, George: footballer; b. 5 February 1959, Bothkennar; player Dundee 1977–90, Raith Rovers 90– . *Address*: Raith Rovers FC, Stark's Park, Pratt St, Kirkcaldy, Fife KY1 1SA.

McGEE, Paul: footballer; b. 17 May 1968, Dublin, Ireland; player Colchester Utd 1989, Wimbledon 1989– ; 3 Ireland U-21 caps. *Address*: Wimbledon FC, Selhurst Park, London SE25 6PY.

McGIBBON, Kirsteen: Alpine skier; b. 18 December 1975, Paisley; N.W. Scotland women's jnr slalom, giant slalom champ. 1993; GB women's jnr super giant slalom champ. 1993; Scotland squad 1993/94. *Leisure interests*: badminton, cycling, reading, writing. *Address*: 10 Vardar Ave, Clarkston, Glasgow G76 7QP.

McGIMPSEY, Garth: golfer; b. 17 July 1955; N. of Ireland champ. 1978, 84, 91, W. of Ireland champ. 1984, 88, E. of Ireland champ. 1988; Irish amateur champ. 1985, 88; GB amateur champ. 1985; Ireland debut 1978; GBI debut 1984, Walker Cup team 1985, 89, 91, winners 1989. *Address*: c/o Irish Golf Union, 58A High St, Holywood, Co. Down BT18 9AE.

McGINLAY, Patrick: footballer; b. 30 May 1967, Glasgow; player Blackpool 1985–87, Hibernian 87–93, Celtic 93– ; with Hibernian: winners Scottish League Cup 1992. *Address*: Celtic FC, Celtic Park, 95 Kerrydale St, Glasgow G40 3RE.

McGINNIS, Gary: footballer; b. 21 October 1963, Dundee; player Dundee Utd 1981–90, St Johnstone 90– ; Scotland U-21 int. *Address*: St Johnstone FC, McDiarmid Park, Crieff Rd, Perth PH1 2SJ.

McGINTY, William: Rugby League footballer; b. 6 December 1964, Widnes; player Widnes Tigers ARLFC, Warrington, Wigan 1991– ; with Warrington: winners Premiership 1986, Regal Trophy 1991; with Wigan: winners Challenge Cup, Premiership 1992, Regal Trophy 1993; rep. Lancs.; GB debut v. Aus. and Brit. Lions tour Aus./NZ/Papua New Guinea 1992. *Address*: Wigan RLFC, The Pavilion, Central Park, Wigan WN1 1XF.

McGIVEN, Michael: football manager; b. 7 February 1951, Newcastle; player Sunderland 1968–73, W. Ham Utd 73–77; manager Ipswich Town 1993–94. *Address*: Ipswich Town FC, Portman Rd, Ipswich, Suffolk IP1 2DA.

McGLASHAN, Colin: footballer; b. 17 March 1964, Perth; player Dundee 1980–84, Dunfermline Athletic 84–85, Cowdenbeath 85–87, Clyde 87–90, Partick Thistle 90– . *Address*: Partick Thistle FC, Firhill Stadium, 80 Firhill Rd, Glasgow G20 7BA.

McGLASHAN, John: footballer; b. 3 June 1967, Dundee; player Montrose 1988–90, Millwall 90–92, Peterborough Utd 92– . *Address*: Peterborough Utd FC, London Rd Ground, Peterborough, Cambs. PE2 8AL.

McGOLDRICK, Edward: footballer; b. 30 April 1965, Corby; player Northampton Town 1986–89, Crystal Palace 89–93, Arsenal 93– ; over 8 Ireland caps. *Address*: Arsenal FC, Arsenal Stadium, Highbury, London N5 1BU.

McGOWAN, Jamie: footballer; b. 5 December 1970, Morecambe; player Dundee 1992– . *Address*: Dundee FC, Dens Park, Dundee DD3 7JY.

McGOWAN, Stephen: Rugby League footballer; b. 25 February 1964, Leeds; player W. Leeds RUFC, N. Sydney (Aus.), Bradford Northern 1983– . *Address*: Bradford Northern RLFC, Odsal Stadium, Bradford BD6 1BS.

McGOWNE, Kevin: footballer; b. 16 December 1969, Kilmarnock; player St Mirren 1989–92, St Johnstone 92– . *Address*: St Johnstone FC, McDiarmid Park, Crieff Rd, Perth PH1 2SJ.

McGRATH, Lloyd: footballer; b. 24 February 1965, Birmingham; player Coventry City 1982– , winners FA Cup 1987; 1 England U-21 cap. *Address*: Coventry City FC, Highfield Rd Stadium, King Richard St, Coventry CV2 4FW.

McGRATH, Paul: footballer; b. 4 December 1959, Ealing; player Manchester Utd 1982–89, Aston Villa 89– ; with Manchester Utd: winners FA Cup 1985;

over 60 Ireland caps. *Address*: Aston Villa FC, Villa Park, Trinity Rd, Birmingham B6 6HE.

McGRAW, Mark: footballer; b. 5 January 1971, Rutherglen; player Morton 1988–90, Hibernian 90– . *Address*: Hibernian FC, Easter Rd Stadium, 64 Albion Rd, Edinburgh EH7 5QG.

MacGREGOR, George: golfer; b. 19 August 1944, Edinburgh; S.E. Scotland amateur champ. 1972, 75, 79–81, E. of Scotland open amateur champ. 1979, 82; Scottish open amateur strokeplay champ. 1982; Scotland debut 1969; GB debut 1970, Walker Cup team 1971, 75, 83–87, non-playing capt. 1991, 93, winners 1971. *Address*: c/o Scottish Golf Union, The Cottage, 181A Whitehouse Rd, Edinburgh EH4 6BY.

McGRILLEN, Paul: footballer; b. 19 August 1971, Glasgow; player Motherwell 1990– . *Address*: Motherwell FC, Fir Park, Fir Park St, Motherwell ML1 2QN.

McGUIRE, Bruce: Rugby League footballer; b. 31 January 1962; player Sheffield Eagles 1992– . *Address*: Sheffield Eagles RLFC, Stadium Corner, 824 Attercliffe Rd, Sheffield S9 3RS.

McINALLY, James: footballer; b. 19 February 1964, Glasgow; player Celtic 1982–84, Nottingham Forest 84–85, Coventry City 85–86, Dundee Utd 86– ; over 9 Scotland caps. *Address*: Dundee Utd FC, Tannadice Park, Dundee DD3 7JW.

MacINNES, Fiona Elizabeth: hockey player; b. 17 March 1971, Inverness; player Heriot-Watt SCPE, European Cup Winners' Cup bronze medallists 1993, Scottish Univ. League champs. 1992, GB Univ. champs. 1992, 93; Scotland U-16 debut and European Champs. U-16 silver medallist 1986, U-21 debut 1990. *Leisure interests*:

running, swimming, windsurfing, canoeing, basketball, badminton, aerobics. *Address*: 18 Ross-Hill Drive, Maryburgh, Dingwall, Ross-shire IV7 8EH.

McINTOSH, Dale Lynsay: Rugby Union footballer; b. 23 November 1969, Turangi, NZ; player Pontypridd 1990– ; Scotland B debut v. Ireland 1991. *Address*: Pontypridd RFC, Sardis Rd, Pwllgwaun, Pontypridd, Mid Glamorgan.

McINTOSH, Fiona Jane: fencer (foil); b. 24 June 1960, Edinburgh; m. Matthew David Holt 1992; rep. Cambridge Univ. 1980–84 (Blue); GB ladies' champ. 1993, 94; Scotland debut 1975; Commonwealth Champs. ladies' individ. gold medal 1990; GB debut 1979, Olympic squad 1984, 88, 92 (finalist); rep. Surrey hockey. *Leisure interests*: walking, climbing, skiing, cinema, travel, eating out. *Address*: Queens College, 43–49 Harley St, London W1N 2BT.

McINTYRE, Tom: footballer; b. 26 December 1963, Bellshill; player Aberdeen 1983–86, Hibernian 86– ; with Hibernian: winners Scottish League Cup 1992. *Address*: Hibernian FC, Easter Rd Stadium, 64 Albion Rd, Edinburgh EH7 5QG.

McIVOR, David John: Rugby Union footballer; b. 29 June 1964, Kirkcaldy; m. Pauline McIvor; 2 s.; player Dunfermline, Glenrothes, Edinburgh Academicals; Scotland B debut v. France 1991, snr and Five Nations debut v. England 1992, tours Aus. 1992, Fiji/Tonga/W. Samoa 1993. *Address*: Edinburgh Academicals RFC, Raeburn Place, Stockbridge, Edinburgh EH4 1HQ.

McKAY, Martin: ice hockey player; b. 27 April 1968; player Dundee 1984–87, Solihull Barons 87–88, Fife Flyers 88–89, Murrayfield Racers 89– ; World Champs. debut 1990. *Address*: The Ice Rink, Riversdale Crescent, Edinburgh EH12 5XN.

McKAY, Mhairi Louise: golfer; b. 18 April 1975, Glasgow; Scottish girls' champ. 1990, 92; GB girls' champ. 1992, 93; Scotland debut 1991; GB debut 1993. *Leisure interests*: art, chess, squash. *Address*: 7 Gardenside Ave, Uddingston, Glasgow G71 7BU.

McKAY, Michael Joseph: fencer (foil); b. 23 September 1967; m. Siân McKay 1991; rep. W. of Scotland, winners Winton Cup 1991; Scotland debut 1988. *Leisure interests*: hill-walking, reading. *Address*: c/o Scottish Amateur Fencing Union, 11 Eyre Crescent, Edinburgh EH3 5ET.

McKEAN, Tom: athlete; b. 27 October 1963; AAA 800m champ. 1991, indoor champ. 1994; UK 800m champ. 1985; GP champ. 1988; Commonwealth Games 800m silver medal 1986, 4 x 400m relay silver medal 1990; European Champs. 800m silver medal 1986, gold 1990; European Cup 800m gold medals 1985, 87, 89, 91, bronze 1993; European Indoor Champs. 800m gold medal 1990; World Cup 800m gold medal 1989; World Indoor Champs. 800m gold medal 1993. *Address*: c/o Brit. Athletic Fed., 225A Bristol Rd, Edgbaston, Birmingham B5 7UB.

MacKENZIE, Alan: footballer; b. 8 August 1966, Edinburgh; player Cowdenbeath 1984–86, Berwick Rovers 86–87, Cowdenbeath 88–91, Raith Rovers 91– . *Address*: Raith Rovers FC, Stark's Park, Pratt St, Kirkcaldy, Fife KY1 1SA.

McKENZIE, Donald Allan: fencer (foil); b. 3 June 1960, Edinburgh; m. Louise Christine Kean 1993; 1 d.; GB U-18 champ. 1976, univ. champ. 1981, snr champ. 1989; Commonwealth Champs. individ. silver medal 1986; GB U-20 debut 1977, snr debut 1981, Olympic squad 1988, 92; winner Brit. Open 1986, Birmingham Int. 1990, 91, 94, Welsh Open 1993. *Leisure interests*: science, tennis, badminton, table tennis, chess,

family, food, travel, music, films, reading. *Address*: c/o Scottish Amateur Fencing Union, 11 Eyre Crescent, Edinburgh EH3 5ET.

McKENZIE, Duke: boxer; b. 5 May 1963, Croydon; prof. debut 1982; titles won: GB flyweight 1985, European flyweight 1986, IBF flyweight 1988, WBO bantamweight 1991, WBO super-bantamweight 1992, GB featherweight 1993; over 34 prof. wins; only Brit. boxer to win world titles at 3 different weights. *Address*: Nat. Promotions, Nat. House, 60–66 Wardour St, London W1V 3HP.

MacKENZIE, Louise Mhairi Catriona: Nordic skier/biathlete; b. 31 March 1964, Grantown-on-Spey; UK women's jnr Nordic skiing champ. 1985; GB women's 10km cross-country, 15km biathlon champ. 1993; Lowlander women's 5km, 10km cross-country champ. 1988; World Cup squad (biathlon) (1st Brit. woman competitor) 1991– , World Champs. squad (biathlon) 1993; Olympic squad (Nordic skiing) 1988; Scottish women's triathlon champ. 1985, 86. *Leisure interests*: languages, training men's football and shinty teams, letter-writing, socializing, music. *Address*: 10 Dalfaber Rd, Aviemore, Inverness-shire PH22 1PU.

MacKENZIE, Niall MacFarlane: motorcyclist; b. 19 July 1961, Stirling; m. Jan MacKenzie 1991; 1 s.; rep. Honda 1987–88, Yamaha 1989, Suzuki 1990, Honda 1991, Yamaha 1991–92, Team Valvoline 1993– ; Scottish 500cc production-class champ. 1982; GB 350cc champ. 1984, 250cc and 350cc champ. 1985; winner Yamaha Pro-Am World Cup 1983; achieved highest Brit. position in World Champs. (4th) since Barry Sheene's 1977 victory 1990. *Leisure interests*: all motor sports, mountain biking, moto-cross, running. *Address*: 14 Deanston Gardens, Deanston, nr Doune, Perthshire FK16 6AZ.

McKEOWN, Gary: footballer; b. 19 October 1970, Oxford; player Dundee 1992– . *Address*: Dundee FC, Dens Park, Dundee DD3 7JY.

McKEOWN, Mary Ellen: water skier; b. 3 March 1959, Belfast, NI; m. Nigel McKeown 1984; 2 s.; Irish ladies' overall champ. 1984, slalom, tricks champ. 1993; Ireland debut 1984. *Leisure interests*: horseriding, badminton, squash. *Address*: 39 Beechgrove Gardens, Belfast BT6 0NN.

McKIMMIE, Stuart: footballer; b. 27 October 1962, Aberdeen; player Dundee 1980–83, Aberdeen 83– ; with Aberdeen: winners Scottish Cup 1984, 86, 90, Scottish League Cup 1986, 90; over 21 Scotland caps. *Address*: Aberdeen FC, Pittodrie Stadium, Pittodrie St, Aberdeen AB2 1QH.

McKINLAY, Tosh: footballer; b. 3 December 1964, Glasgow; player Dundee 1981–88, Heart of Midlothian 88– ; Scotland U-21 int. *Address*: Heart of Midlothian FC, Tynecastle Park, Gorgie Rd, Edinburgh EH11 2NL.

McKINLAY, William: footballer; b. 22 April 1969, Glasgow; player Dundee Utd 1986– ; Scotland U-21 and B int., snr debut v. Malta 1993. *Address*: Dundee Utd FC, Tannadice Park, Dundee DD3 7JW.

McKINNON, Darren: Rugby Union footballer; b. 29 January 1972, Durham; player W. Hartlepool 1991– ; rep. N. Div. U-21, England colts. *Address*: W. Hartlepool RFC, Brierton Lane, Hartlepool, Cleveland TS25 5DR.

McKINNON, Ray: footballer; b. 5 August 1970, Dundee; player Dundee Utd 1989–92, Nottingham Forest 92–94, Aberdeen 94– ; 6 Scotland U-21 caps. *Address*: Aberdeen FC, Pittodrie Stadium, Pittodrie St, Aberdeen AB2 1QH.

McKINNON, Rob: footballer; b. 31 July 1966, Glasgow; player Newcastle Utd 1984–86, Hartlepool Utd 86–91, Motherwell 91– ; Scotland debut v. Malta 1993. *Address*: Motherwell FC, Fir Park, Fir Park St, Motherwell ML1 2QN.

McKNIGHT, Margaret Mary: lacrosse player; b. 15 August 1963, Newport; player Penarth 1982–85, Hatch End 89–91, W. London 91– ; rep. Middx 1989– , West 88– ; with Middx: county champs. 1992; Wales debut 1985, World Cup squad 1986, 89, 93, tours USA 1991, 92, Japan/Aus. 1992. *Leisure interests*: running, cycling, sports photography, watching Rugby Union. *Address*: c/o Welsh Lacrosse Assoc., 3 Tyla Teg, Pantmawr, Cardiff.

McLAREN, Alan: footballer; b. 4 January 1971, Edinburgh; player Heart of Midlothian 1987– ; over 9 Scotland caps. *Address*: Heart of Midlothian FC, Tynecastle Park, Gorgie Rd, Edinburgh EH11 2NL.

McLAREN, Andrew: footballer; b. 5 June 1973, Glasgow; player Dundee Utd 1989– . *Address*: Dundee Utd FC, Tannadice Park, Dundee DD3 7JW.

McLAREN, Ross: footballer; b. 14 April 1962, Edinburgh; player Shrewsbury Town 1980–85, Derby County 85–88, Swindon Town 88– ; with Derby County: 2nd Div. champs. 1986/87. *Address*: Swindon Town FC, The County Ground, Swindon, Wilts. SN1 2ED.

McLAREN, Stephen: footballer; b. 3 May 1961, York; player Hull City 1979–85, Derby County 85–88, Bristol City 88–89, Oxford Utd 89– . *Address*: Oxford Utd FC, Manor Ground, London Rd, Headington, Oxford OX3 7RS.

McLAUGHLIN, Joseph: footballer; b. 2 June 1960, Greenock; player Morton 1977–83, Chelsea 83–89, Charlton Athletic 89–90, Watford 90–92, Falkirk 92– ; with Chelsea: 2nd Div. champs. 1983/84, 88/89; 10 Scotland U-21 caps. *Address*: Falkirk FC, Brockville Park, Hope St, Falkirk FK1 5AX.

McLAUGHLIN, Paul: footballer; b. 9 December 1965, Johnstone; player Queen's Park 1983–90, Celtic 90–91, Partick Thistle 91– . *Address*: Partick Thistle FC, Firhill Stadium, 80 Firhill Rd, Glasgow G20 7BA.

McLEAN, Fiona Helen: netball player; b. 2 December 1965, Glasgow; player Bellahouston; rep. Glasgow City 1980– ; Scotland U-21 debut 1984, snr debut 1989 (capt. 1992/93), World Games squad 1989, World Champs. squad 1991. *Leisure interests*: watching all other sports, reading, socializing. *Address*: c/o Scottish Netball Assoc., Kelvin Hall, Argyle St, Glasgow G3 8AW.

MacLEAN, Iain: basketball player; b. 5 February 1965, Greenock; player Paisley, N. Arizona Univ. (USA), Murray Int. Metals/Livingston; with Livingston: winners League Cup 1988, Scottish Cup 1989–93, Scottish League champs. 1988/89–92/93, nat. play-off champs. 1988; Scotland int.; GB debut and World Student Games squad 1987, Olympic squad 1988, 92. *Leisure interests*: football, golf, coaching basketball. *Address*: Livingston Basketball Club, c/o Livingston Forum, Almondvale, Livingston.

McLEARY, Alan: footballer; b. 6 October 1964, Lambeth; player Millwall 1981–93, Charlton Athletic 93– ; with Millwall: 2nd Div. champs. 1987/88; 1 England U-21 cap. *Address*: Charlton Athletic FC, The Valley, Floyd Rd, London SE7 8BL.

McLEISH, Alex: footballer; b. 21 January 1959, Glasgow; player Aberdeen 1977– , winners Scottish Cup 1982, 83, 84, 86, 90, Scottish League Cup 1986, 90; 77 Scotland caps; Scottish Football Writers' Assoc. Player of the Year 1990. *Address*: Aberdeen FC, Pittodrie Stadium, Pittodrie St, Aberdeen AB2 1QH.

MacLENNAN, Calman Alexander: oarsman; b. 25 May 1968, Taplow; rep. Oxford Univ. BC 1988–92, Leander Club 90– ; with Oxford: winners Univ. Boat Race 1989, 91, 92; GB single sculls champ. 1992; GB U-23 debut 1990, snr debut 1993. *Leisure interests*: mountaineering, skiing, Christians in Sport. *Address*: Leander Club, Henley-on-Thames, Oxon.

MacLEOD, Ian: footballer; b. 19 November 1959, Glasgow; player Motherwell 1977–86, Falkirk 86–89, Raith Rovers 89– . *Address*: Raith Rovers FC, Stark's Park, Pratt St, Kirkcaldy, Fife KY1 1SA.

McLEOD, Joe: footballer; b. 30 December 1967, Edinburgh; player Dundee Utd 1984–91, Motherwell 91– . *Address*: Motherwell FC, Fir Park, Fir Park St, Motherwell ML1 2QN.

MacLEOD, Murdo: footballer; b. 24 September 1958, Glasgow; player Dumbarton 1974–78, Celtic 78–87, Borussia Dortmund, Hibernian 1990– ; with Celtic: winners Scottish Cup 1980, 85, Scottish League Cup 1983; with Hibernian: winners Scottish League Cup 1992; 20 Scotland caps. *Address*: Hibernian FC, Easter Rd Stadium, 64 Albion Rd, Edinburgh EH7 5QG.

McLOUGHLIN, Alan: footballer; b. 20 April 1967, Manchester; player Swindon Town 1986–90, Southampton 90–92, Portsmouth 92– ; over 13 Ireland caps. *Address*: Portsmouth FC, Fratton Park, Frogmore Rd, Portsmouth PO4 8RA.

McLOUGHLIN, Theresa: netball player; b. 28 October 1966, Glasgow; Scotland debut 1993; Irish dancing World Champs. medallist. *Leisure interests*: football, reading, eating out. *Address*: c/o Scottish Netball Assoc., Kelvin Hall, Argyle St, Glasgow G3 8AW.

McMAHON, Stephen: footballer; b. 20 August 1961, Liverpool; player Everton 1979–83, Aston Villa 83–85, Liverpool 85–91, Manchester City 91– ; with Liverpool: winners FA Cup 1986, 89, League champs. 1985/86, 87/88, 89/90; 6 England U-21 caps, 17 full England caps. *Address*: Manchester City FC, Maine Rd, Moss Side, Manchester M14 7WN.

McMANAMAN, Steven: footballer; b. 11 February 1972, Bootle; player Liverpool 1990– , winners FA Cup 1992; England U-21 int. *Address*: Liverpool FC, Anfield Rd, Liverpool L4 0TH.

McMANUS, Alan: snooker player; b. 21 January 1971; prof. debut 1991, winner Masters 1994. *Address*: c/o Masters Snooker Club, 164 Craig Park, Dennistown, Glasgow G31 2HE.

McMARTIN, Grant: footballer; b. 31 December 1970, Linlithgow; player Dundee 1989– . *Address*: Dundee FC, Dens Park, Dundee DD3 7JY.

McMILLAN, Colin Bernard: boxer; b. 12 February 1966, London; m. Susan McMillan 1992; 2 ch.; England debut 1986; prof. debut 1988; titles won: GB feather-weight 1991, Commonwealth feather-weight 1992, WBO featherweight 1992; over 22 prof. wins. *Leisure interests*: reading, music. *Address*: Frank Warren Productions, Centurion House, Bircherley Green, Hertford, Herts. SG14 1HP.

McMINN, Kevin (Ted): footballer; b. 28 September 1962, Castle Douglas; player Queen of the S. 1982–84, Rangers 84–87, Seville (Spain), Derby County 1988–93, Birmingham City 93– ; with Rangers: winners Scottish League Cup 1987. *Address*: Birmingham City FC, St Andrews Ground, Birmingham B9 4NH.

McMURRUGH, Michael Ernest: real tennis player; b. 24 May 1942, Burton upon Trent; m. Margaret Rose McMurrugh 1964;

1 s.; GB over-40 open doubles champ. 1989, amateur doubles champ. 1991–93, Masters amateur champ. 1993; world over-40 champ. 1989, over-40 doubles champ. 1990; GB debut 1982, winners Bathurst Cup 1987, 89, 91; Derbys. jnr table tennis champ. 1957–58, rep. Derbys. jnr lawn tennis, colt cricket 1959, golf 1967–71. *Leisure interests*: all sport. *Address*: The Paddock, Glenfield Stud, Furzeley Rd, Denmead, Hants. PO7 6TS.

McNAB, Neil: footballer; b. 4 June 1957, Greenock; player Tottenham Hotspur 1974–78, Bolton Wanderers 78–80, Brighton and Hove Albion 80–83, Manchester City 83–90, Tranmere Rovers 90–93, Ayr Utd 93– ; 1 Scotland U-21 cap. *Address*: Ayr Utd FC, Somerset Park, Tryrield Place, Ayr KA8 9NB.

McNALLY, Bernard: footballer; b. 17 February 1963, Shrewsbury; player Shrewsbury Town 1981–89, W. Bromwich Albion 89– ; 5 NI caps. *Address*: W. Bromwich Albion FC, The Hawthorns, W. Bromwich B71 4LF.

McNALLY, Mark: footballer; b. 10 March 1971, Bellshill; player Celtic 1987– ; Scotland U-21 int. *Address*: Celtic FC, Celtic Park, 95 Kerrydale St, Glasgow G40 3RE.

McNAMARA, Steve: Rugby League foot-baller; b. 18 September 1971, Hull; player Skirlaugh ARLFC, Hull 1989– ; England schoolboy int.; GB debut v. France 1992. *Address*: Hull RLFC, The Boulevard Ground, Airlie St, Hull HU3 3JD.

MacNAUGHTON, Robert Carlo: Rugby Union footballer; b. 21 September 1965, Guildford; m. Sally Anne MacNaughton 1989; player Liverpool St Helens 1988–91, Northampton 91– ; Scotland tour Fiji/Tonga/W. Samoa 1993. *Leisure interests*: all sport, walking, house restoration, travel. *Address*: Northampton FC, Franklins Gardens, Weedon Rd, Northampton NN5 5BG.

McNIVEN, James: oarsman; b. 3 June 1965, Dumbarton; m. Louise McNiven 1990; rep. Nottinghamshire County Rowing Assoc. 1989–90; GB coxed pairs champ. 1989, lightweight coxed fours and coxless fours champ. 1990, eights champ. 1992; Scotland debut 1981, England debut 1989; GB debut 1990, World Champs. lightweight eights silver medal 1992. *Leisure interests*: cross-country skiing, golf, mountaineering. *Address*: Flat 4, 13 Newcastle Drive, The Park, Nottingham NG7 1AA.

McPHERSON, Andrew: Rugby Union footballer; b. 2 November 1967; player Ebbw Vale, Saracens 1991– ; rep. Monmouthshire U-21. *Address*: Saracens FC, Bramley Rd Sports Ground, Chaseside, Southgate, London N14 4AB.

MacPHERSON, Angus: footballer; b. 11 October 1968, Glasgow; player Rangers 1988–90, Kilmarnock 90– . *Address*: Kilmarnock FC, Rugby Park, Kilmarnock KA1 2DP.

McPHERSON, David: footballer; b. 28 January 1964, Paisley; player Rangers 1980–88, Heart of Midlothian 88–92, Rangers 92– ; with Rangers: winners Scottish League Cup 1984, 85, 93; over 25 Scotland caps. *Address*: Glasgow Rangers FC, Ibrox Stadium, 150 Edmiston Drive, Glasgow G51 2XD.

McPHERSON, Vikki: athlete; b. 1 June 1971, Dunbartonshire; Scottish women's cross-country champ. 1992, 93; Brit. univ. women's cross-country champ. 1992; AAA women's 10,000m champ. 1993; Scotland jnr debut 1989, snr debut 1990; GB debut 1992; World Student Cross-Country Champs. team gold and individ. silver medals 1992. *Address*: 4 The Glen, Torphican Rd, Bathgate, E. Lothian EH48 4LJ.

McQUEEN, Robert Dale: field archer; b. 7 April 1953, Uphall, Lothian; Scottish

recurve freestyle indoor champ. 1989, 91–93, outdoor champ. 1989–93; GB recurve freestyle champ. 1993; Scotland debut 1991; World Champs. individ. bronze medal 1990. *Leisure interests*: tai chi chuan, golf, bonsai. *Address*: 10 Murray Place, Linlithgow EH49 6DP.

McQUILLAN, John: footballer; b. 20 July 1970, Stranraer; player Dundee 1987– . *Address*: Dundee FC, Dens Park, Dundee DD3 7JY.

McSKIMMING, Shaun: footballer; b. 29 May 1970, Stranraer; player Stranraer 1986–87, Dundee 87–91, Kilmarnock 91– . *Address*: Kilmarnock FC, Rugby Park, Kilmarnock KA1 2DP.

McSTAY, John: footballer; b. 24 December 1965, Larkhall; player Motherwell 1982–87, Raith Rovers 87– . *Address*: Raith Rovers FC, Stark's Park, Pratt St, Kirkcaldy, Fife KY1 1SA.

McSTAY, Paul: footballer; b. 22 October 1964, Hamilton; player Celtic 1981– (capt.), winners Scottish League Cup 1983, Scottish Cup 1985, 88, 89; over 65 Scotland caps; Scottish Football Writers' Assoc. Player of the Year 1988. *Address*: Celtic FC, Celtic Park, 95 Kerrydale St, Glasgow G40 3RE.

McSTAY, William: footballer; b. 26 November 1961, Hamilton; player Celtic 1979–87, Huddersfield Town 87–88, Notts County 88–90, Kilmarnock 90– ; with Celtic: winners Scottish Cup 1985. *Address*: Kilmarnock FC, Rugby Park, Kilmarnock KA1 2DP.

McVICAR, Donald: footballer; b. 6 November 1962, Perth; player St Johnstone 1981–85, Tranmere Rovers 85–86, Montrose 86–87, St Johnstone 87–91, Partick Thistle 91– . *Address*: Partick Thistle FC, Firhill Stadium, 80 Firhill Rd, Glasgow G20 7BA.

McVIE, Malcolm: Rugby Union footballer; b. 24 June 1971; player Edinburgh Academicals; Scotland U-21 debut v. Wales 1992. *Address*: Edinburgh Academicals RFC, Raeburn Place, Stockbridge, Edinburgh EH4 1HQ.

McWALTER, Mark: footballer; b. 20 June 1968, Arbroath; player Arbroath 1984–87, St Mirren 87–91, Partick Thistle 91– . *Address*: Partick Thistle FC, Firhill Stadium, 80 Firhill Rd, Glasgow G20 7BA.

MABBUTT, Gary, MBE: footballer; b. 23 August 1961, Bristol; player Bristol Rovers 1979–82, Tottenham Hotspur 82– (capt.); with Tottenham Hotspur: winners UEFA Cup 1984, FA Cup 1991; 7 England U-21 caps, 16 full England caps. *Address*: Tottenham Hotspur FC, 748 High Rd, Tottenham, London N17 0AP.

MACARI, Luigi (Lou): football manager; b. 4 June 1949, Aberdeen; player Celtic, Manchester Utd 1973–84, Swindon Town 84–85; 2 Scotland U-23 caps, 24 full Scotland caps; manager Swindon Town 1984–89, W. Ham Utd 89–90, Birmingham City 1991, Stoke City 1991–93, Celtic 93– ; with Swindon Town: 4th Div. champs. 1985/86. *Address*: Celtic FC, Celtic Park, 95 Kerrydale St, Glasgow G40 3RE.

MACKAY, Gary: footballer; b. 23 January 1964, Edinburgh; player Heart of Midlothian 1980– ; 4 Scotland caps. *Address*: Heart of Midlothian FC, Tynecastle Park, Gorgie Rd, Edinburgh EH11 2NL.

MACKEY, Greg: Rugby League footballer; b. 20 October 1961, Sydney, Aus.; player Warrington, Hull, Warrington 1992– ; with Hull: winners Premiership 1990/91. *Address*: Warrington RLFC, Wilderspool Stadium, Wilderspool Causeway, Warrington WA4 6PY.

MACREE, Rebecca Claire: squash player; b. 19 June 1971, Barking; player Bremfield, Nottingham, Courtlands; with Bremfield: club champs. 1988/89, League champs. 1987/88, 88/89; with Courtlands: Superleague champs. 1991/92, 92/93; rep. Essex 1986– ; Essex girls' U-19 champ. 1988, 89, ladies' champ. 1989, 90; England U-19 debut 1990. *Leisure interests*: dancing, films, eating out. *Address*: Connaught Squash Club, Barn Hoppett, Rangers Rd, N. Chingford, London E4 7QH.

MADDEN, Lawrence: footballer; b. 28 September 1955, Hackney; player Mansfield Town 1975, Charlton Athletic 1978–82, Millwall 82–83, Sheffield Wednesday 83–91, Wolverhampton Wanderers 91– ; with Sheffield Wednesday: winners League Cup 1991. *Address*: Wolverhampton Wanderers FC, Molineux Stadium, Waterloo Rd, Wolverhampton WV1 4QR.

MADDISON, Neil: footballer; b. 2 October 1969, Darlington; player Southampton 1988– . *Address*: Southampton FC, The Dell, Milton Rd, Southampton SO9 4XX.

MADDIX, Daniel: footballer; b. 11 October 1967, Ashford; player Queens Park Rangers 1987– . *Address*: Queens Park Rangers FC, Rangers Stadium, S. Africa Rd, London W12 7PA.

MADDOCKS, Christopher Lloyd: race walker; b. 28 March 1957, Tiverton; rep. Devon 1972– ; Commonwealth Games squad 1986, 90; GB debut 1978, World Cup squad 1979, 83, 87, 89, 91, 93, World Champs. squad 1987, 91, 93, Olympic squad 1984, 88, 92; GB 35km and 50km record-holder. *Leisure interests*: athletics, football, boxing, Rugby Union, F1 motor racing, tennis, weightlifting, cycling, music. *Address*: 94/96 Hyde Park Rd, Peverell, Plymouth PL3 4RE.

MADEN, Jonathon Richard: swimmer; b. 21 September 1972, Littleborough; GB 100m and 200m breaststroke champ. 1990, 91; England youth debut 1988, snr debut 1990; GB jnr debut 1988, European Jnr Champs. 200m breaststroke silver medal 1989, snr debut 1990. *Leisure interests:* music, films. *Address:* 15 Longacres Drive, Whitworth, Rochdale, Lancs. OL12 8JT.

MAGILTON, James: footballer; b. 6 May 1969, Belfast; player Oxford Utd 1990–94, Southampton 94– ; 1 NI U-23 cap, over 17 full NI caps. *Address:* Southampton FC, The Dell, Milton Rd, Southampton SO9 4XX.

MAGUIRE, Adrian Edward: jockey (NH); b. 29 April 1971; champ. point-to-point rider 1990/91; winner Irish Grand National 1991 (Omerta) (youngest-ever winner), Hennessy Gold Cup 1992 (Sibton Abbey), Cheltenham Gold Cup 1992 (Cool Ground); rode 124 winners in season 1992/93. *Address:* c/o BNB, 42 Portman Square, London W1H 0EN.

MAGUIRE, Gavin: footballer; b. 24 November 1967, Hammersmith; player Queens Park Rangers 1985–89, Portsmouth 89– ; 7 Wales caps. *Address:* Portsmouth FC, Fratton Park, Frogmore Rd, Portsmouth PO4 8RA.

MAIN, Alan: footballer; b. 5 December 1967, Elgin; player Dundee Utd 1986– ; Scotland U-21 and snr int. *Address:* Dundee Utd FC, Tannadice Park, Dundee DD3 7JW.

MAIN, Stephanie: figure skater; b. 20 September 1976, Edinburgh; Scottish novice ladies' champ. 1988, primary ladies' champ. 1989, jnr ladies' champ. 1990, snr ladies' champ. 1991–93; GB primary ladies' champ. 1990, snr champ. 1993; Scotland debut 1986; GB debut 1990, World Jnr Champs. squad 1993, Olympic training squad 1992. *Leisure interests:* trampolining, ballet, aerobics, ice hockey. *Address:* Stable House, 4 Gogarbank, Edinburgh EH12 9BU.

MAINWARING, Richard Charles: water skier (barefoot); b. 4 June 1953, London; m. Josephine Ann Mainwaring 1980; 1 d.; GB overall champ. 1984–90, 92, 93; European overall champ. 1983–87, 89; GB debut 1979; World Champs. team bronze medals 1986, 88, 90; GB tricks, veterans' jump, tricks and slalom, world 250m speed record-holder. *Publications:* contributor to *Sportsboat and Waterski International. Leisure interests:* sports boating. *Address:* 11 Arlington Row, Bibury, Glos. GL7 5NJ.

MALCOLM, Devon Eugene: cricketer; b. 22 February 1963, Kingston, Jamaica; m. Jennifer Malcolm 1989; player Derbys. 1984– , winners Benson and Hedges Cup 1993, Sunday League champs. 1990; Test debut 1989, tours WI 1989/90, Aus. 1990/91, WI (England A) 1991/92, India/Sri Lanka 1992/93, WI 1994. *Address:* Derbys. CCC, County Cricket Ground, Nottingham Rd, Derby DE2 6DA.

MALCOLM, Lindsay Anne: netball player; b. 30 October 1971, Cheadle; player Birmingham Athletic Institute 1986–92, Bishopbriggs 92– ; with Bishopbriggs: winners Scottish Cup 1993, Glasgow League champs. 1992/93; rep. Birmingham District 1987–92, Glasgow District 92– ; Scotland U-21 debut 1991, snr debut 1992, World Games squad 1993. *Leisure interests:* skiing, climbing, badminton, reading, cinema, playing the piano. *Address:* c/o Scottish Netball Assoc., Kelvin Hall, Argyle St, Glasgow G3 8AW.

MALIK, Farhana Tegwen: squash player; b. 21 January 1975, London; Welsh ladies' champ. 1992 (youngest ever); Wales U-16 debut 1987, U-19 debut 1988, snr debut 1989. *Leisure interests:* music, hockey, completing Duke of Edinburgh's Award. *Address:* 216 Swansea Rd, Waunarlwydd, Swansea SA5 4SN.

MALKIN, Christopher: footballer; b. 4 June 1967, Bebington; player Tranmere Rovers 1987– . *Address*: Tranmere Rovers FC, Prenton Park, Prenton Rd West, Birkenhead, Merseyside L42 9PN.

MALLENDER, Neil Alan: cricketer; b. 13 August 1961, Kirk Sandall, Doncaster; m. Caroline Mallender 1983; 1 s., 1 d.; player Northants. 1980–86, Somerset 87– ; rep. England Schools 1979/80; England U-19 tour WI 1980/81, Test debut v. Pakistan 1992 (Headingley record for Test debutant of 8 wickets). *Leisure interests*: golf. *Address*: Somerset CCC, The County Ground, Taunton, Somerset TA1 1JT.

MALLON, Maureen: flat green bowler; b. 21 May 1935, Lisburn, NI; m. Thomas Mallon 1958; 2 s., 3 d.; NI women's triples champ. (outdoor) 1984, 85, 86, 91, 92, Irish women's triples champ. (outdoor) 1984, 92; GB women's triples champ. (outdoor) 1985; Ireland debut (outdoor and indoor) 1981, Commonwealth Games squad 1986, World Champs. squad 1992. *Leisure interests*: reading, knitting, family. *Address*: 20 Causeway End Rd, Lisburn, Co. Antrim BT28 1UB.

MALO, André: ice hockey player; b. 10 May 1965; player Ayr Raiders 1986–87, Cleveland/Billingham Bombers 87–93, Nottingham Panthers 93– . *Address*: The Ice Stadium, Lower Parliament St, Nottingham, Notts.

MALONE, Niall Gareth: Rugby Union footballer; b. 30 April 1971, Leeds; player Collegians (NI), Loughborough Students, London Irish, Leicester 1993– ; Ireland U-21 debut v. The Netherlands 1990. *Address*: Leicester FC, Welford Rd, Leicester LE2 7LF.

MALONEY, Francis John: Rugby League footballer; b. 26 May 1973, Dewsbury; player Leeds, Featherstone Rovers 1992– . *Address*: Featherstone Rovers RLFC, The Croft, Batley Rd, W. Ardsley, Wakefield WF3 1DX.

MALPAS, Maurice: footballer; b. 3 August 1962, Dunfermline; player Dundee Utd 1979– , Scottish League champs. 1982/83; 55 Scotland caps; Scottish Football Writers' Assoc. Player of the Year 1991. *Address*: Dundee Utd FC, Tannadice Park, Dundee DD3 7JW.

MANN, George: Rugby League footballer; b. 31 July 1965, Auckland, NZ; player Mangere E. (NZ), St Helens 1989– ; with St Helens: winners Premiership 1993; NZ debut v. GB 1990. *Address*: St Helens RLFC, Dunriding Lane, St Helens, Merseyside WA10 4AD.

MANNING, Terry: Rugby League footballer; b. 4 December 1965, Elland; player Keighley, Featherstone Rovers 1989– . *Address*: Featherstone Rovers RLFC, The Croft, Batley Rd, W. Ardsley, Wakefield WF3 1DX.

MANUEL, William Albert James: footballer; b. 28 June 1969, Hackney; 1 d.; player Gillingham 1989–91, Brentford 91– ; with Brentford: 3rd Div. champs. 1991/92. *Leisure interests*: golf, fishing, snooker, ice hockey, bungee jumping. *Address*: Brentford FC, Griffin Park, Braemar Rd, Brentford, Middx TW8 0NT.

MARCHANT, Tony: Rugby League footballer; b. 22 December 1962, Castleford; player Castleford RUFC, Castleford RLFC, Bradford Northern 1989– ; rep. Yorks.; GB debut v. France 1986. *Address*: Bradford Northern RLFC, Odsal Stadium, Bradford BD6 1BS.

MARKER, Nicholas: footballer; b. 3 May 1965, Budleigh Salterton; player Exeter City 1981–87, Plymouth Argyle 87–92, Blackburn Rovers 92– . *Address*: Blackburn Rovers FC, Ewood Park, Blackburn, Lancs. BB2 4JF.

MARLOW, Ian: Rugby League footballer; b. 18 January 1963, Aylesbury; player Lincoln (RU), Beverley (RU), Hull 1990–93, Wakefield Trinity 93– ; Wales debut v. France 1992. *Address*: Wakefield Trinity RLFC, 171 Doncaster Rd, Belle Vue, Wakefield WF1 5EZ.

MARRIOTT, Andrew: footballer; b. 11 October 1970, Sutton-in-Ashfield; player Nottingham Forest 1989–93, Wrexham 93– ; 1 England U-21 cap. *Address*: Wrexham FC, Racecourse Ground, Mold Rd, Wrexham, Clwyd LL11 2AN.

MARRIOTT, Gareth John: canoeist; b. 14 July 1970, Mansfield; GB jnr debut 1985, snr debut 1987; World Jnr Champs. C1 slalom gold medal 1988; World Cup C1 slalom gold medal 1991, silver 1992; World Champs. C1 slalom team bronze medal 1991, silver 1993; Olympic C1 slalom silver medal 1992; 1st Brit. canoeist to win Olympic medal. *Leisure interests*: snowboarding, mountain biking, music, reading. *Address*: c/o Brit. Canoe Union, John Dudderidge House, Adbolton Lane, W. Bridgford, Nottingham NG2 5AS.

MARSH, Michael: footballer; b. 21 July 1969, Liverpool; player Liverpool 1988–93, W. Ham Utd 93– . *Address*: W. Ham Utd FC, Boleyn Ground, Green St, Upton Park, London E13 9AZ.

MARSH, Steven Andrew: cricketer; b. 27 January 1961, Westminster; m. Julie Marsh 1986; 1 s., 1 d.; player Kent 1982– (vice-capt. 91–); equalled world record of 8 catches in innings v. Middx 1991. *Address*: Kent CCC, St Lawrence Ground, Canterbury CT1 3NZ.

MARSHALL, Georgina: lacrosse player; b. 12 April 1959, Glasgow; player Edinburgh Ladies 1978–86, Kingston Kingfishers 87–89, W. London 92–93, Beckenham Beetles 93– ; rep. South 1986–89, 92– ; Scotland debut 1980,

World Cup bronze medal 1986, squad 1982, 89, 93. *Leisure interests*: most sports. *Address*: 3 Doverfield Rd, London SW2.

MARSHALL, Gordon: footballer; b. 19 April 1964, Edinburgh; player E. Stirling 1982–83, E. Fife 83–86, Falkirk 86–91, Celtic 91– ; 1 Scotland cap. *Address*: Celtic FC, Celtic Park, 95 Kerrydale St, Glasgow G40 3RE.

MARSHALL, Ian: footballer; b. 20 March 1966, Liverpool; player Everton 1984–88, Oldham Athletic 88–93, Ipswich Town 93– . *Address*: Ipswich Town FC, Portman Rd, Ipswich, Suffolk IP1 2DA.

MARSHALL, Kathryn Christine: golfer; b. 8 June 1967, Rochford; m. Scott Marshall 1990; Scottish schools champ. 1981, 84, Scottish girls' matchplay champ. 1983, girls' open strokeplay champ. 1985, 86, 87; Scotland debut 1984; Curtis Cup team 1990; prof. debut 1990; leading amateur in Ladies' Brit. Open 1988. *Leisure interests*: all sport, hill-walking, working out. *Address*: 490/9 The Stables, Gilmerton Rd, Edinburgh EH17 7SA.

MARTI, Debora Jane: athlete (high jump); b. 14 May 1968, Zofingen, Switzerland; AAA and UK women's champ. 1993; GB debut v. E. Germany 1984, European Jnr Champs. bronze medal 1985, Olympic squad 1992. *Leisure interests*: music, dancing, shopping, stoolball. *Address*: 120 Earlsbrook Rd, Redhill, Surrey RH1 6HZ.

MARTIN, Brian: footballer; b. 24 February 1963, Bellshill; player Falkirk 1985–86, Hamilton Academical 86–87, St Mirren 87–91, Motherwell 91– . *Address*: Motherwell FC, Fir Park, Fir Park St, Motherwell ML1 2QN.

MARTIN, David: footballer; b. 25 April 1963, E. Ham; player Millwall 1980–84, Wimbledon 84–86, Southend Utd 86–93, Bristol City 93– . *Address*: Bristol City FC, Ashton Gate, Bristol BS3 2EJ.

MARTIN, Eamonn Thomas: athlete; b. 9 October 1958, Basildon; m. Julie Teresa Martin 1985; 1 s., 2 d.; English schools cross-country champ. 1973, 1500m champ. 1975; English cross-country champ. 1984, 92; AAA 5000m champ. 1988, 90, 91, 10km road-race champ. 1988, 10,000m champ. 1989, 92; UK 5000m champ. 1984, 85, cross-country trial champ. 1988; 5000m GP champ. 1988; Commonwealth Games 10,000m gold medal 1990; European Cup 10,000m gold medal 1991; winner London Marathon 1993 (1st attempt); UK 10,000m record-holder. *Address*: c/o Brit. Athletic Fed., 225A Bristol Rd, Edgbaston, Birmingham B5 7UB.

MARTIN, John: figure skater; b. 13 December 1967, Ayr; Scottish primary champ. 1984, intermediate champ. 1985, 86, snr champ. 1987, 90–92; GB intermediate champ. 1986; European Champs. squad 1989, 92, 93, World Champs. squad 1992, reserve 1993, Olympic reserve 1992; winner Jennings Trophy 1988 (only Scottish winner). *Leisure interests*: the arts, reading, travel, music. *Address*: 105 Glendale Crescent, Ayr KA7 3RX.

MARTIN, Lee: footballer; b. 5 February 1968, Hyde; player Manchester Utd 1986–94, Celtic 94– ; with Manchester Utd: winners FA Cup 1990, League champs. 1992/93; 2 England U-21 caps. *Address*: Celtic FC, Celtic Park, 95 Kerrydale St, Glasgow G40 3RE.

MARTIN, Peter James: cricketer; b. 15 November 1968, Accrington; player Lancs. 1989– ; England YC tour Aus. (Youth World Cup) 1988; rep. England A v. Sri Lanka 1991. *Address*: Lancs. CCC, Old Trafford, Manchester M16 0PX.

MARTIN, Scott: Rugby League footballer; b. 29 December 1974; player Leigh 1991– . *Address*: Leigh RLFC, Hilton Park, Kirkhall Lane, Leigh WN7 1RN.

MARTINDALE, David: footballer; b. 9 April 1964, Liverpool; player Tranmere Rovers 1987– . *Address*: Tranmere Rovers FC, Prenton Park, Prenton Rd W., Birkenhead, Merseyside L42 9PN.

MARTYN, Nigel: footballer; b. 11 August 1966, St Austell; player Bristol Rovers 1987–89, Crystal Palace 89– ; 11 England U-21 caps, 2 full England caps. *Address*: Crystal Palace FC, Selhurst Park Stadium, London SE25 6PU.

MARTYN, Tommy: Rugby League footballer; b. 4 June 1971; player Oldham 1989–93, St Helens 1993– . *Address*: St Helens RLFC, Dunriding Lane, St Helens, Merseyside WA10 4AD.

MARU, Rajesh Jamnadass: cricketer; b. 28 October 1962, Nairobi, Kenya; m. Amanda Jane Maru 1991; player Middx 1980–83, Hants. 84– ; with Hants.: Sunday League champs. 1986, tours Barbados 1987, 88, Dubai 1989, Barbados 1990; MCC tour Leeward Islands 1992. *Address*: Hants. CCC, County Cricket Ground, Northlands Rd, Southampton SO9 2TY.

MARWOOD, Brian: footballer; b. 5 February 1960, Seaham; player Hull City 1978–84, Sheffield Wednesday 84–88, Arsenal 88–90, Sheffield Utd 90– ; with Arsenal: League champs. 1988/89; 1 England cap. *Address*: Sheffield Utd FC, Bramall Lane, Sheffield, S. Yorks S2 4SU.

MASKELL, Craig: footballer; b. 10 April 1968, Aldershot; player Southampton 1986–88, Huddersfield Town 88–90, Reading 90–92, Swindon Town 92–94, Southampton 94– . *Address*: Southampton FC, The Dell, Milton Rd, Southampton SO9 4XX.

MASON, Andrew: Rugby League footballer; b. 10 November 1962, Hunslet; player Leeds, Wakefield Trinity 1987– ; rep. Yorks. *Address*: Wakefield Trinity RLFC, 171 Doncaster Rd, Belle Vue, Wakefield WF1 5EZ.

MASON, Brian: ice hockey player; b. 1 April 1965; player Whitley Warriors 1985–87, Solihull Barons 87–88, Slough Jets 88–92, Milton Keynes Kings 92– ; World Champs. debut 1990. *Address*: Milton Keynes Leisure Plaza, Childs Way H8, Milton Keynes, Beds.

MASON, Paul: footballer; b. 3 September 1963, Liverpool; player FC Groningen (The Netherlands), Aberdeen 1988–93, Ipswich Town 93– ; with Aberdeen: winners Scottish Cup, Scottish League Cup 1990. *Address*: Ipswich Town FC, Portman Rd, Ipswich, Suffolk IP1 2DA.

MATHER, Barrie-Jon: Rugby League footballer; b. 15 January 1973; player Wigan. *Address*: Wigan RLFC, The Pavilion, Central Park, Wigan WN1 1XF.

MATHERS, Paul: footballer; b. 17 January 1970, Aberdeen; player Dundee 1989– . *Address*: Dundee FC, Dens Park, Dundee DD3 7JY.

MATHIE, Alex: footballer; b. 20 December 1968, Bathgate; player Celtic 1987–91, Morton 91–93, Newcastle Utd 93– . *Address*: Newcastle Utd FC, St James' Park, Newcastle-upon-Tyne, Tyne & Wear NE1 4ST.

MATTHEW, Damian: footballer; b. 23 September 1970, Islington; player Chelsea 1989–94, Crystal Palace 94– ; 9 England U-21 caps. *Address*: Crystal Palace FC, Selhurst Park Stadium, London SE25 6PU.

MATTHEWS, Brian Curtis: Eton fives player; b. 15 August 1957, Highgate; player Cambridge Univ. 1975–78, 80 (capt. 77–78), Citizens 76–86, Village 87– ; with Citizens: League champs. 1980; with Village: League champs. 1987–90; rep. Middx 1981– , county champs. 1984–86, 88–91, 93 (capt. 1981, 82, 89); winner Kinnaird Cup 1981–90, London Tournament 1981, 83–86, 89, Midland Tournament 1980–82, 84, Northern Tournament 1982, 86, Individ. Challenge 1993. *Leisure interests*: squash, cricket, chess. *Address*: 24A Broadlands Rd, London N6 4AG.

MATTHEWS, Neil John: Rugby Union footballer; b. 11 April 1970, Gloucester; player Gloucester, Bristol 1993– ; England U-21 debut v. Ireland 1990, England B tour NZ 1992. *Address*: Bristol FC, Memorial Ground, Filton Ave, Horfield, Bristol BS7 0AQ.

MAXWELL, Alistair: footballer; b. 16 February 1965, Hamilton; player Motherwell 1981–92, Rangers 92– ; with Rangers: winners Scottish League Cup 1993; Scotland int. *Address*: Glasgow Rangers FC, Ibrox Stadium, 150 Edmiston Drive, Glasgow G51 2XD.

MAY, Andrew: footballer; b. 26 February 1964, Bury; player Manchester City 1982–87, Huddersfield Town 87–90, Bristol City 90–92, Millwall 92– ; 1 England U-21 cap. *Address*: Millwall FC, The Den, Zampa Rd, Bermondsey, London SE16 3LH.

MAY, David: footballer; b. 24 June 1970, Oldham; player Blackburn Rovers 1988– . *Address*: Blackburn Rovers FC, Ewood Park, Blackburn, Lancs. BB2 4JF.

MAY, Philip Stephen: Rugby Union footballer; b. 1 July 1956, Llanelli; m. Ann May; 2 s.; player Llanelli; Wales B debut v. France 1986, snr and Five Nations debut v. England 1988. *Address*: Llanelli RFC, Stradey Park, Llanelli, Dyfed.

MAY, Robin: glider pilot; b. 28 July 1951, E. Grinstead; m. Siobhan May 1990; 1 s., 1 d.; GB open-class champ. 1988–90; GB debut 1988, European Champs. squad . 1988, World Champs. squad 1989, 91; UK multi-seat 100km, 200km and 600km triangular speed record-holder. *Leisure interests*: flying, computers. *Address*: 42 Welland Rd, Totternhoe, Dunstable, Beds LU6 1QS.

MAYBURY, Debra: cricketer; b. 8 August 1971, Huddersfield; player Wakefield WCC 1987–90, City of Leeds LCC 91– ; with Wakefield: winners Nat. Cup, League champs. 1990; rep. Yorks. Ladies 1988– , county champs. 1988, 92, 93; Test debut 1992, tours Aus. (World Cup) 1988, Ireland 1990, Aus./NZ 1992, winners European Cup 1989 (vice-capt.), 90, 91, World Cup 1993; youngest woman to win cap for England 1988; Sports Writers' Team of the Year award-winner 1993. *Leisure interests*: driving, hockey, watching sport. *Address*: c/o Women's Cricket Assoc., 41 St Michael's Lane, Headingley, Leeds LS6 3BR.

MAYNARD, Matthew Peter: cricketer; b. 21 March 1966, Oldham; m. Susan Maynard 1986; 1 s.; player Glamorgan 1985– , Sunday League champs. 1993, tour Barbados 1989; Test debut v. WI 1988, tour WI 1994; scored 1000 runs in 1st full season with Glamorgan. *Address*: Glamorgan CCC, Sophia Gardens, Cardiff CF1 9XR.

MAYO, Paul Michael: golfer; b. 6 January 1963, Newport; m. Hazel Mayo 1992; 1 s.; Welsh boys' champ. 1979; GB youths' open amateur champ. 1983; Gwent amateur champ. 1982; Welsh amateur champ. 1987; GB amateur champ. 1987; Wales debut 1982; Walker Cup team 1985, 87; prof. debut 1988; Welsh prof. champ. 1990, 91; Dunhill Cup team (Wales) 1993; leading amateur in Open 1987. *Leisure interests*: cooking, music, travel, gardening, family. *Address*: 30 Goodrich Crescent, Newport, Gwent NP9 5PF.

MAYOCK, John: athlete; b. 26 October 1970; European Jnr Champs. 5000m silver medal 1989; World Student Games 5000m gold medal 1991; European Indoor Champs. 3000m silver medal 1992; World Road Relay Champs. team bronze medal 1992. *Address*: c/o Brit. Athletic Fed., 225A Bristol Rd, Edgbaston, Birmingham B5 7UB.

MEAKER, Michael: footballer; b. 18 August 1971, Greenford; player Queens Park Rangers 1989– . *Address*: Queens Park Rangers FC, Rangers Stadium, S. Africa Rd, London W12 7PA.

MEDLEY, Paul: Rugby League footballer; b. 21 September 1966, Leeds; player Leeds, Halifax, Bradford Northern 1989– ; rep. Yorks.; GB debut v. Papua New Guinea 1987. *Address*: Bradford Northern RLFC, Odsal Stadium, Bradford BD6 1BS.

MEDNICK, Dana Joy: figure skater; b. 14 August 1973, Freehold, New Jersey, USA; with Jason Briggs: GB pairs champ. 1993. *Leisure interests*: roller-blading, swimming, shopping, family, travel. *Address*: c/o 3 Gordondale Rd, Mansfield, Nottingham NG19 7DF.

MEGSON, Gary: footballer; b. 2 May 1959, Manchester; player Plymouth Argyle 1977–79, Everton 79–81, Sheffield Wednesday 81–84, Newcastle Utd 84–85, Sheffield Wednesday 85–89, Manchester City 89–92, Norwich City 92– . *Address*: Norwich City FC, Carrow Rd, Norwich NR1 1JE.

MELLOR, Stanley Thomas Edward, MBE; racehorse trainer (NH); b. 10 April 1937, Manchester; m. Mary Elain Williams 1963; 2 ch.; as jockey: winner Whitbread Gold Cup 1962 (Frenchman's Cove), Mackeson Gold Cup 1964 (Super Flash), Hennessy Gold Cup 1966 (Stalbridge Colonist); champ. NH jockey 1959/60, 60/61, 61/62; 1st amateur jockey to ride over 1000 winners; as trainer: 1st licence 1972; winner Whitbread Gold Cup 1987 (Lean Ar Aghaidh). *Leisure interests*: training jockeys, snooker, cricket, swimming, reading. *Address*: Pollardstown, Foxhill, Swindon, Wilts. SN4 0DR.

MELVILLE, Andrew: footballer; b. 29 November 1968, Swansea; player Swansea City 1986–90, Oxford Utd 90–93,

Sunderland 93– ; 1 Wales U-21 cap, over 15 full Wales caps. *Address*: Sunderland FC, Roker Park Ground, Sunderland, Tyne and Wear SR6 9SW.

MENDONCA, Clive: footballer; b. 9 September 1968, Islington; player Sheffield Utd 1986–88, Rotherham Utd 88–91, Sheffield Utd 91–92, Grimsby Town 92– . *Address*: Grimsby Town FC, Blundell Park, Cleethorpes, S. Humberside DN35 7PY.

MEO, Anthony Christian: snooker player; b. 2 October 1959, Hampstead; m. Denise Meo 1981; 5 ch.; prof. debut 1979, Aus. champ. 1981, 85, English champ. 1985, 86, winner World Doubles 1982, 83, 85, 86, Brit. Open 1989. *Leisure interests*: cricket, table tennis, horseracing, music, dining out, cooking. *Address*: Elite Squad Ltd, Valtony, The Ridges, Finchampstead, Berks. RG11 3SS.

MERCER, Gary Ivan: Rugby League footballer; b. 22 June 1966, Tauranga, NZ; player Bradford Northern, Warrington, Leeds 1992– ; NZ debut v. Papua New Guinea 1987. *Address*: Leeds RLFC, Bass Headingley, St Michael's Lane, Leeds LS6 3BR.

MERSON, Paul: footballer; b. 20 March 1968, Harlesden; player Arsenal 1986– , League champs. 1988/89, winners League Cup, FA Cup 1993; 4 England U-21 caps, over 12 full England caps. *Address*: Arsenal FC, Arsenal Stadium, Highbury, London N5 1BU.

METSON, Colin Peter: cricketer; b. 2 July 1963, Cuffley, Herts.; m. Stephanie Leslie Metson 1991; player Durham Univ. (capt. 1984), Middx 1981–86, Glamorgan 87– ; with Middx: county champs. 1985; with Glamorgan: Sunday League champs. 1993; rep. England YC v. India 1981; Young Wicketkeeper of the Year 1981, Glamorgan Cricketer of the Year 1991. *Leisure interests*: most sports, reading, drinking good wine, travel. *Address*: Glamorgan CCC, Sophia Gardens, Cardiff CF1 9XR.

MICKLEWHITE, Gary: footballer; b. 21 March 1961, Southwark; m. Kate Micklewhite 1982; 2 d.; player Queens Park Rangers 1979–85, Derby County 85–93, Gillingham 93– ; with Queens Park Rangers: 2nd Div. champs. 1982/83; with Derby County: 2nd Div. champs. 1986/87. *Leisure interests*: golf, cars, snooker, family. *Address*: Gillingham FC, Priestfield Stadium, Redfern Ave, Gillingham, Kent ME7 4DD.

MIDDLETON, Graham: Rugby League footballer; b. 2 November 1970, Leeds; player E. Leeds ARLFC, Leeds 1989– . *Address*: Leeds RLFC, Bass Headingley, St Michael's Lane, Leeds LS6 3BR.

MIDDLETON, Simon: Rugby League footballer; b. 2 February 1966; player Knottingley RUFC, Castleford 1991– ; with Castleford: winners Regal Trophy 1994. *Address*: Castleford RLFC, Wheldon Rd, Castleford WF10 2SD.

MIDDLETON, Tony Charles: cricketer; b. 1 February 1964, Winchester; m. Sherralyn Middleton 1989; player Hants. 1984– , Sunday League champs. 1986, tour Barbados 1989; England A tour Aus. 1992/93; scored 6 consecutive 100s, May 1990; 1st batsman to score 1000 1st-class runs 1992. *Address*: Hants. CCC, County Cricket Ground, Northlands Rd, Southampton SO9 2TY.

MIKHAILICHENKO, Alexei: footballer; b. 30 March 1963, Kiev, USSR; player Sampdoria (Italy), Rangers 1991– ; with Rangers: winners Scottish Cup 1992; USSR and CIS int. *Address*: Rangers FC, Ibrox Stadium, 150 Edmiston Drive, Glasgow G51 2XD.

MIKLOSKO, Ludek: footballer; b. 9 December 1961, Czechoslovakia; player Banik Ostrava (Czechoslovakia), W. Ham Utd 1990– ; Czechoslovakia int. *Address*: W. Ham Utd FC, Boleyn Ground, Green St, Upton Park, London E13 9AZ.

MILES, Peter: Rugby Union footballer; b. 4 June 1965; player Bath, Gloucester. *Address*: Gloucester RUFC, Kingsholm, Worcester St, Gloucester GL3 3AX.

MILLAR, Michael Rendall: canoeist; b. 25 August 1963, Edinburgh; Scottish C2 slalom champ. 1991, 92; Scotland debut 1987; GB intermediate debut 1989, snr debut 1990. *Address*: c/o Scottish Canoe Assoc., Caledonia House, S. Gyle, Edinburgh EH12 9DQ.

MILLARD, David Bruce: Rugby Union footballer; b. 19 September 1964, Guildford; player London Scottish, 2nd Div. champs. 1991/92; Scotland tour Aus. 1992. *Address*: London Scottish FC, Richmond Athletic Ground, Kew Foot Rd, Richmond, Surrey TW9 2SS.

MILLEN, Keith: footballer; b. 26 September 1966, Croydon; player Brentford 1984– , 3rd Div. champs. 1991/92. *Leisure interests*: golf, snooker. *Address*: Brentford FC, Griffin Park, Braemar Rd, Brentford, Middx TW8 0NT.

MILLER, Joe: footballer; b. 8 December 1967, Glasgow; player Aberdeen 1984–87, Celtic 87– ; Scotland U-21 int. *Address*: Celtic FC, Celtic Park, 95 Kerrydale St, Glasgow G40 3RE.

MILLER, Kevin: footballer; b. 15 March 1969, Falmouth; player Exeter City 1989–93, Birmingham City 93– ; with Exeter City: 4th Div. champs. 1989/90. *Address*: Birmingham City FC, St Andrews Ground, Birmingham B9 4NH.

MILLER, Paul: footballer; b. 31 January 1968, Woking; player Wimbledon 1987– . *Address*: Wimbledon FC, Selhurst Park, London SE25 6PY.

MILLER, Tammy: hockey player; b. 21 June 1967; player Clifton; England U-21 debut 1986, snr debut 1988, European Champs. gold medallist 1991, World Cup squad 1990; GB debut 1991, Olympic bronze medallist 1992. *Address*: Clifton HC, Bristol University Astroturf, Coombe Dingle, Stoke Bishop, Bristol.

MILLER, William: footballer; b. 1 November 1969, Edinburgh; player Hibernian 1989– , winners Scottish League Cup 1992; Scotland U-21 int. *Address*: Hibernian FC, Easter Rd Stadium, 64 Albion Rd, Edinburgh EH7 5QG.

MILLIGAN, Kenneth: Rugby Union footballer; b. 19 July 1972; player Stewart's Melville FP; Scotland A debut v. France A 1993, snr tour Fiji/Tonga/W. Samoa 1993. *Address*: Stewart's Melville FP, Inverleith, Ferry Rd, Edinburgh.

MILLIGAN, Michael: footballer; b. 20 February 1967, Manchester; player Oldham Athletic 1985–90, Everton 90–91, Oldham Athletic 91– ; 1 Ireland U-21 cap, 1 full Ireland cap. *Address*: Oldham Athletic FC, Boundary Park, Oldham, Lancs. OL1 2PA.

MILLNS, David James: cricketer; b. 27 February 1965, Mansfield; player Notts. 1988–89, Leics. 90– ; England A tour Aus. 1992/93. *Address*: Leics. CCC, County Ground, Grace Rd, Leicester LE2 8AD.

MILLS, Gary: footballer; b. 11 November 1961, Northampton; player Nottingham Forest 1978–81, Derby County 1982, Nottingham Forest 1983–87, Notts County 87–89, Leicester City 89– ; with Nottingham Forest: winners European Cup 1980; 2 England U-21 caps. *Address*: Leicester City FC, City Stadium, Filbert St, Leicester LE2 7FL.

MILNE, Callum: footballer; b. 27 August 1965, Edinburgh; player Hibernian 1983– . *Address*: Hibernian FC, Easter Rd Stadium, 64 Albion Rd, Edinburgh EH7 5QG.

MILNE, Kenneth Stuart: Rugby Union footballer; b. 1 December 1961, Edinburgh; m. Eleanor Milne; 1 s., 1 d.; player Heriot's FP; Scotland and Five Nations debut v. Wales 1989, Grand Slam champs. 1990, tours N. America 1985, 91, NZ 1990; Brit. Lions tour NZ 1993. *Address*: Heriot's FP, Goldenacre, Bangholm Terrace, Edinburgh EH3 5QN.

MIMMS, Robert: footballer; b. 12 October 1963, York; player Rotherham Utd 81–85, Everton 85–88, Tottenham Hotspur 88–90, Blackburn Rovers 90–   ; 3 England U-21 caps. *Address*: Blackburn Rovers FC, Ewood Park, Blackburn, Lancs. BB2 4JF.

MINTO, Scott: footballer; b. 6 August 1971, Heswell; player Charlton Athletic 1989–   ; over 3 England U-21 caps. *Address*: Charlton Athletic FC, The Valley, Floyd Rd, London SE7 8BL.

MITCHELL, Alistair: footballer; b. 3 December 1968, Kirkcaldy; player E. Fife 1988–91, Kilmarnock 91–   . *Address*: Kilmarnock FC, Rugby Park, Kilmarnock KA1 2DP.

MITCHELL, David: Rugby Union footballer; b. 19 October 1971, Peterborough; player W. Hartlepool 1992–   ; rep. N. of England colts, N. Div. U-21; England U-19 int. *Address*: W. Hartlepool RFC, Brierton Lane, Hartlepool, Cleveland TS25 5DR.

MITCHELL, Graham: footballer; b. 2 November 1962, Glasgow; player Hamilton Academical 1980–86, Hibernian 86–   ; with Hibernian: winners Scottish League Cup 1992. *Address*: Hibernian FC, Easter Rd Stadium, 64 Albion Rd, Edinburgh EH7 5QG.

MITCHELL, James Johnstone: basketball player; b. 28 May 1961, Irvine; m. Jacqueline Bell 1991; 2 d.; player Cumnock 1977–86, Paisley 86–90, Glasgow Rangers 90–91, Paisley 91–   ; Scotland debut 1985,

Commonwealth Champs. silver medallist 1991; Ayrshire schools U-18 javelin record-holder. *Leisure interests*: golf. *Address*: c/o Scottish Basketball Assoc., Caledonia House, S. Gyle, Edinburgh EH12 9DQ.

MITCHELL, Paul: footballer; b. 20 October 1971, Bournemouth; player Bournemouth 1989–93, W. Ham Utd 93–   . *Address*: W. Ham Utd FC, Boleyn Ground, Green St, Upton Park, London E13 9AZ.

MITCHELL, Simon: Rugby Union footballer; b. 23 November 1965, Saltburn; player W. Hartlepool 1987–   ; rep. Durham, N. Div.; England B squad. *Address*: W. Hartlepool RFC, Brierton Lane, Hartlepool, Cleveland TS25 5DR.

MOHAN, Nicholas: footballer; b. 6 October 1970, Middlesbrough; player Middlesbrough 1987–   . *Address*: Middlesbrough FC, Ayresome Park, Middlesbrough, Cleveland TS1 4PB.

MOLES, Andrew James: cricketer; b. 12 February 1961, Solihull; m. Jacquie Moles 1988; 1 s.; player Warks. 1986–   , winners NatWest Trophy 1993. *Address*: Warks. CCC, County Ground, Edgbaston, Birmingham B5 7QU.

MOLLOY, Stephen John: Rugby League footballer; b. 11 March 1969, Manchester; player Warrington, Leeds 1990–93, Featherstone Rovers 93–   ; England debut v. Wales 1992; GB debut v. France 1993. *Address*: Featherstone Rovers RLFC, The Croft, Batley Rd, W. Ardsley, Wakefield WF3 1DX.

MONCRIEFF, Mark: Rugby Union footballer; b. 19 December 1968, Edinburgh; player Gala; Scotland A debut v. Spain 1990, Scotland B debut v. France 1991, snr tour Fiji/Tonga/W. Samoa 1993. *Address*: Gala RFC, Netherdale, Nether Rd, Galashiels TD1 3HE.

MONCUR, John: footballer; b. 22 September 1966, Stepney; player Tottenham Hotspur 1984–92, Swindon Town 92– . *Address*: Swindon Town FC, The County Ground, Swindon, Wilts. SN1 2ED.

MONTGOMERIE, Colin Stuart: golfer; b. 23 June 1963, Glasgow; m. Eimear Montgomerie 1990; 1 d.; Scottish open amateur strokeplay champ. 1985, amateur champ. 1987; Scotland debut 1985; Walker Cup team 1985, 87; prof. debut 1988; Scotland debut 1988, Dunhill Cup team 1988, 91–93; Ryder Cup team 1991, 93; winner Portuguese Open 1989, Scandinavian Masters 1991, Dutch Open, Volvo Masters 1993. *Leisure interests*: DIY, cars, music. *Address*: Int. Management Group, Pier House, Strand on the Green, London W4 3NN.

MONTGOMERIE, Ray: footballer; b. 17 April 1961, Irvine; player Dumbarton 1981–88, Kilmarnock 88– . *Address*: Kilmarnock FC, Rugby Park, Kilmarnock KA1 2DP.

MOODIE, Janice Christine: golfer; b. 31 May 1973, Glasgow; Scottish girls' champ. 1989, 91, ladies' champ. 1992; GB debut 1993. *Leisure interests*: keep-fit. *Address*: 7 Heather Ave, Hardgate, Clydebank, Glasgow.

MOODY, Paul: footballer; b. 13 June 1967, Portsmouth; player Southampton 1991– . *Address*: Southampton FC, The Dell, Milton Rd, Southampton SO9 4XX.

MOODY, Thomas Masson: cricketer; b. 2 October 1965, Adelaide, Aus.; player Warks. 1990, Worcs. 1991–92, 94– ; Test debut 1989, Aus. tours India/Pakistan (World Cup) 1987, England 1989, India 1989/90, Sri Lanka 1992. *Address*: Worcs. CCC, County Ground, New Rd, Worcester WR2 4QQ.

MOON, Benedick Joseph: rock climber; b. 13 June 1966, Kingston-upon-Thames; prof. debut 1988; GB debut 1989, World Cup squad 1989, 90, 91, 93; 1st ascents: 'Statement of Youth' (grade 8A) 1984, 'Zeke the Freak' (8B) 1986, 'Agincourt' (8C) and 'Maginot Line' (8C) 1989, 'Hubble' (8C+) 1990. *Publications*: *Extreme Rock*, 1987. *Leisure interests*: motor sports, walking, film, literature. *Address*: 29 Buttermere Rd, Sheffield S7 2AX.

MOON, Rupert Henry St John Barker: Rugby Union footballer; b. 1 February 1968, Birmingham; player Neath, Llanelli 1990– (capt.); with Llanelli: winners Welsh Cup 1991–93, Welsh League champs. 1992/93; England U-21 debut v. Romania 1989, England B debut v. Emerging Aus. 1990, Wales and Five Nations debut v. France 1993, tour Zimbabwe/Namibia 1993. *Address*: Llanelli RFC, Stradey Park, Llanelli, Dyfed.

MOONEY, Brian: footballer; b. 2 February 1966, Dublin, Ireland; player Preston N. End 1987–91, Sunderland 91– . *Address*: Sunderland FC, Roker Park Ground, Sunderland, Tyne and Wear SR6 9SW.

MOONEY, Thomas: footballer; b. 11 August 1971, Middlesbrough; player Scarborough 1990–93, Southend Utd 93– . *Address*: Southend Utd FC, Roots Hall, Victoria Ave, Southend-on-Sea, Essex SS2 6NQ.

MOORCROFT, David Robert: athlete; b. 10 April 1953, Coventry; m. Linda Ann Moorcroft 1975; 1 s., 1 d.; AAA 1500m jnr champ. 1971, snr champ. 1978; UK 1500m and 5000m champ. 1980, 3000m champ. 1989; GB debut v. E. Germany 1973; Commonwealth Games 1500m gold medal 1978, 5000m gold 1982; European Champs. 1500m bronze medal 1978, 5000m bronze 1982; European Cup 5000m gold medal 1981; UK 5000m record-holder. *Publications*: *Running Commentary*, 1984.

Leisure interests: reading, music. *Address*: c/o Brit. Athletic Fed., 225A Bristol Rd, Edgbaston, Birmingham B5 7UB.

MOORE, Alexander: Rugby Union footballer; b. 19 August 1963, Queensland, Aus.; 2 s.; player Livingston, Gala, Edinburgh Academicals; Scotland debut v. NZ 1990, Five Nations debut v. France 1991, tours Zimbabwe 1988, NZ 1990. *Address*: Edinburgh Academicals RFC, Raeburn Place, Stockbridge, Edinburgh EH4 1HQ.

MOORE, Brian Christopher: Rugby Union footballer; b. 11 January 1962, Birmingham; m. Dr Penny Sowden; player Nottingham 1981–90, Harlequins 90– ; England and Five Nations debut v. Scotland 1987, Grand Slam champs. 1991, 92, tours Aus. 1988, Argentina 1990, Aus./Fiji 1991; Brit. Lions tours Aus. 1989, NZ 1993; Whitbread/*Rugby World* Player of the Year 1991. *Address*: Harlequins FC, Stoop Memorial Ground, Craneford Way, Twickenham, Middx.

MOORE, Joanne: tennis player; b. 9 March 1976, Birmingham; rep. Warks.; GB girls' U-12 grass court doubles champ. 1988; student at Nick Bollettieri Tennis Academy 1988– . *Leisure interests*: reading, country and western music, shopping, surfing. *Address*: 474 Palm Tree Drive, Bradenton, Florida 34210, USA.

MOORE, Paul Martin: flat green and short mat bowler; b. 10 July 1965, Portadown, NI; NI and All Ireland U-25 singles champ. (outdoor flat green) 1989; GB U-25 singles champ. (outdoor flat green) 1990; world short mat singles champ. 1990, team champ. 1992; Ireland debut (outdoor flat green) 1990, (short mat) 1991. *Leisure interests*: rock music, golf. *Address*: 141 Pinebank, Tullygally, Craigavon BT65 5BY.

MOORES, Peter: cricketer; b. 18 December 1962, Macclesfield; m. Karen Moores 1989;

1 d.; player Worcs. 1983–84, Sussex 85– ; Christians in Sport tour India 1990, MCC tours Namibia 1991, Leeward Islands 1992. *Address*: Sussex CCC, County Ground, Eaton Rd, Hove, E. Sussex BN3 3AN.

MORAN, Kevin: footballer; b. 29 April 1956, Dublin; player Pegasus (Ireland), Manchester Utd 1978–88, Sporting Gijon (Spain) 88–89, Blackburn Rovers 90– ; over 68 Ireland caps. *Address*: Blackburn Rovers FC, Ewood Park, Blackburn, Lancs. BB2 4JF.

MORAN, Paul: footballer; b. 22 May 1968, Enfield; player Tottenham Hotspur 1985– . *Address*: Tottenham Hotspur FC, 748 High Rd, Tottenham, London N17 0AP.

MOREAU, Jemma Elizabeth: synchronized swimmer; b. 13 November 1975, Chertsey; Middx jnr solo champ. and S. Counties jnr figures champ. 1991; England and GB jnr debuts 1991, snr debuts 1993. *Leisure interests*: gym, weight training. *Address*: Hounslow Synchro Squad, 18 Chaplin Crescent, Sunbury, Middx.

MORGAN, Antony: weightlifter (70–76kg); b. 13 June 1969, Cambridge; m. Patricia Jane Connors 1993; GB U-16 champ. 1984, U-18 champ., jnr champ. 1985, 86, snr champ. 1985–93 (youngest ever 1985); Olympic squad 1992. *Address*: c/o Brit. Amateur Weightlifters Assoc., 3 Iffley Turn, Oxford OX4 4DU3.

MORGAN, Darren Thomas: snooker player; b. 3 May 1966, Cwmfelinfach, Gwent; Welsh and world amateur champ. 1987, winner Welsh Masters 1987; prof. debut 1988, Welsh champ. 1990, 91. *Leisure interests*: fishing, golf, tennis, music, tropical fish, old films. *Address*: Cuemasters Ltd, Kerse Rd, Stirling FK7 7SG.

MORGAN, David: weightlifter (67.5–83kg); b. 30 September 1964, Cambridge; GB 67.5kg champ. 1982, 75kg champ. 1984, 82.5kg champ. 1986–88, 90; EEC 67.5kg champ. 1982, 82.5kg champ. 1985–88; World Jnr Champs. 67.5kg bronze medals 1982, 75kg gold, silver and bronze 1984; Commonwealth Games 67.5kg gold medal 1982 (youngest weightlifting gold medallist), 82.5kg gold 1986, 90; Olympic squad 1984, 88, 92; youngest lifter to snatch double body weight. *Leisure interests*: athletics, judo, health and fitness, sports psychology, meeting new people, cinema, reading, travel. *Address*: 17 Perowne St, Cambridge CB1 2AY.

MORGAN, Kevin: Rugby Union footballer; b. 28 August 1964, Haverfordwest; player Llanelli 1983–87, Bristol 1988, Cardiff 1990–91, Bristol 91– ; with Llanelli: winners Aberavon Sevens 1983; former Welsh Schools and Welsh Students int.; Welsh Rugby'lympics 200m champ. 1985. *Leisure interests*: travel, car maintenance, DIY, sketching. *Address*: Bristol FC, Memorial Ground, Filton Ave, Horfield, Bristol BS7 0AQ.

MORGAN, Robert: diver; b. 27 March 1967, Cardiff; GB highboard champ. 1984– ; Commonwealth Games highboard bronze medal 1986, gold 1990; European Champs. highboard bronze medal 1991, silver 93; Olympic squad 1984, 88, 92. *Leisure interests*: golf, rugby. *Address*: 13 Windmill Close, Llantwit Major, S. Glamorgan CF6 9SW.

MORGAN, Stephen: footballer; b. 19 September 1968, Oldham; player Blackpool 1986–90, Plymouth Argyle 90–93, Coventry City 93– . *Address*: Coventry City FC, Highfield Rd Stadium, King Richard St, Coventry CV2 4FW.

MORIARTY, Paul: Rugby League footballer; b. 16 July 1964, Morriston; player Swansea (RU), Widnes 1989– ; Wales RU int.; Wales RL debut v. Papua New Guinea 1991; GB debut v. Papua New Guinea 1991. *Address*: Widnes RLFC, Naughton Park, Lowerhouse Lane, Widnes WA8 7DZ.

MORIARTY, Richard Daniel: Rugby Union footballer; b. 1 May 1957, Gorseinon; player Swansea (capt. 1986–89); Wales debut v. Aus. 1981, Five Nations debut v. Ireland 1982, tour N. America 1980. *Address*: Swansea RFC, St Helen's, Bryn Rd, Swansea SA2 0AR.

MORLEY, Joanne Lois: golfer; b. 30 December 1966, Sale; Cheshire ladies' champ. 1988–90, 92, 93; English ladies' strokeplay champ. 1991, 92; GB ladies' open amateur strokeplay champ. 1991; European women's amateur champ. 1992; England jnr debut 1984, snr debut 1990; Curtis Cup team (winners) 1992; prof. debut 1994; leading amateur in Ladies' Brit. Open 1989; *Daily Telegraph* Woman Golfer of the Year 1991. *Leisure interests*: keep-fit, music. *Address*: 197 Northenden Rd, Sale, Cheshire M33 2JB.

MORLEY, Trevor: footballer; b. 20 March 1961, Nottingham; player Northampton Town 1985–88, Manchester City 88–89, W. Ham Utd 89– ; with Northampton Town: 4th Div. champs. 1986/87. *Address*: W. Ham Utd FC, Boleyn Ground, Green St, Upton Park, London E13 9AZ.

MORRIS, Christopher: footballer; b. 24 December 1963, Newquay; player Sheffield Wednesday 1982–87, Celtic 87–92, Middlesbrough 92– ; with Celtic: winners Scottish Cup 1988, 89; 34 Ireland caps. *Address*: Middlesbrough FC, Ayresome Park, Middlesbrough, Cleveland TS1 4PB.

MORRIS, Colin Dewi: Rugby Union footballer; b. 9 February 1964, Crickhowell; player Liverpool St Helens, Orrell; rep. Lancs., county champs. 1989/90; England debut v. Aus. 1988, Five Nations debut v. Scotland 1989, Grand Slam champs. 1992, tours Argentina 1990, Aus./Fiji 1991. *Address*: Orrell RUFC, Edgehall Rd, Orrell, Wigan WN5 8TL.

MORRIS, Frank: ice hockey player; b. 22 March 1963; player Ayr Raiders 1987–91, Fife Flyers 91–92, Murrayfield Racers 92– ; with Fife Flyers: Div. 1 champs. 1991/92; with Murrayfield Racers: winners Autumn Cup 1994. *Address*: The Ice Rink, Riversdale Crescent, Edinburgh EH12 5XN.

MORRIS, Graham Robert: diver; b. 28 March 1964, Prestatyn; m. Alison Morris 1988; rep. N.E. Counties 1984– ; Welsh springboard champ. 1985, 87–90, 93, Scottish champ. 1988, 90; GB springboard champ. 1987, 90, 92; Wales debut 1983, England debut 1989; GB debut 1987, Olympic squad 1988. *Leisure interests*: DIY. *Address*: c/o 27 Buttermere Drive, Dalton, Huddersfield HD5 9EN.

MORRIS, Hugh: cricketer; b. 5 October 1963, Cardiff; player Glamorgan 1981– (capt. 86–89, 93–), Sunday League champs. 1993; England A tours Pakistan 1990/91 (capt.), WI 1991/92, SA 1993/94 (capt.), Test debut 1991. *Address*: Glamorgan CCC, Sophia Gardens, Cardiff CF1 9XR.

MORRIS, John Edward: cricketer; b. 1 April 1964, Crewe; m. Sally Morris 1990; 1 s.; player Derbys. 1982–93, Durham 94– ; with Derbys.: winners Benson and Hedges Cup 1993, Sunday League champs. 1990; Test debut 1990, tour Aus. 1990/91. *Address*: Durham CCC, County Ground, Riverside, Chester-le-Street, Co. Durham DH3 3QR

MORRIS, Martyn Stuart: Rugby Union footballer; b. 23 August 1962, Neath; m. Rhian Morris; 1 d.; player S. Wales Police, Neath; Wales and Five Nations debut v. Scotland 1985, tours Namibia 1990, Aus. 1991. *Address*: Neath RFC, The Gnoll, Gnoll Park Rd, Neath, W. Glamorgan.

MORRIS, Simon: Rugby Union footballer; b. 3 May 1969; player Lydney, Gloucester. *Address*: Gloucester RUFC, Kingsholm, Worcester St, Gloucester GL3 3AX.

MORRISON, Andrew: footballer; b. 30 July 1970, Inverness; player Plymouth Argyle 1988–93, Blackburn Rovers 93– . *Address*: Blackburn Rovers FC, Ewood Park, Blackburn, Lancs. BB2 4JF.

MORRISON, Anthony: Rugby League footballer; b. 17 December 1965, St Helens; player Swinton, Castleford 1992– ; with Castleford: winners Regal Trophy 1994; GB U-19 int. *Address*: Castleford RLFC, Wheldon Rd, Castleford WF10 2SD.

MORRISON, Iain Robert: Rugby Union footballer; b. 14 December 1962, Linlithgow; player Linlithgow, Cambridge Univ. (Blue 1983, 84), London Scottish 1985– ; with London Scottish: winners Middx Sevens 1991; Scotland A debut v. Ireland A 1992, snr and Five Nations debut v. Ireland 1993. *Address*: London Scottish FC, Richmond Athletic Ground, Kew Foot Rd, Richmond, Surrey TW9 2SS.

MORRISON, James: basketball player; b. 7 December 1962, Kilmarnock; m. Julie Morrison 1986; 1 s.; player Cumnock, Falkirk, Glasgow Rangers, Troon; with Glasgow Rangers: nat. play-off champs. 1989, League champs. 1988/89; Scotland debut 1980, European Champs. squad 1983, 85, 89, 91, 93. *Leisure interests*: golf, bird-watching. *Address*: c/o Scottish Basketball Assoc., Caledonia House, S. Gyle, Edinburgh EH12 9DQ.

MORRISON, Scott Kenneth: ice hockey player; b. 12 August 1964, Hamilton, Ontario, Canada; m. Jacqui Morrison 1991; player London Knights, Ottawa 67s (both Canada), Whitley Warriors 1987–89, Humberside Seahawks 89–92, Billingham Bombers 92–93, Whitley Warriors 93– ; with London Knights: winners Molson Cup 1985; with Humberside Seahawks: Div. 1 champs. 1990/91; World Champs. gold medal (Pool B) 1993; London Knights Most Valuable Player 1983/84, 84/85; Premier Div. Player of the Year 1987/88,

90/91. *Leisure interests*: golf, weight training, field hockey, reading, music. *Address*: The Ice Rink, Hillheads Rd, Whitley Bay, Tyne & Wear.

MORRISSEY, John: footballer; b. 8 March 1965, Liverpool; player Everton 1983–85, Wolverhampton Wanderers 1985, Tranmere Rovers 85– . *Address*: Tranmere Rovers FC, Prenton Park, Prenton Rd W., Birkenhead, Merseyside L42 9PN.

MORROW, Stephen: footballer; b. 2 July 1970, Carrickfergus, NI; m. Fiona Morrow 1991; player Cliftonville (NI) 1984–85, Bangor (NI) 85–87, Arsenal 87– ; with Arsenal: winners League Cup 1993; 1 NI U-21 cap, 10 full NI caps. *Leisure interests*: golf, snooker, cinema, theatre, travel, reading. *Address*: Arsenal FC, Arsenal Stadium, Highbury, London N5 1BU.

MORTENSEN, Ole Henrik: cricketer; b. 29 January 1958, Vejle, Denmark; m. Jette Jepmond Mortensen; 2 d.; player Derbys. 1983– , winners Benson and Hedges Cup 1993, Sunday League champs. 1990; rep. Rest of the World v. Aus. 1990; Denmark int. *Address*: Derbys. CCC, County Cricket Ground, Nottingham Rd, Derby DE2 6DA.

MORTON, Les: race walker; b. 1 July 1958, Sheffield; m. Jean Morton 1979; 1 d.; GB 20km champ. 1987, 35km champ. 1990, 92, 50km champ. 1985, 87–89, 91, 93, 10-mile champ. 1993; World Cup squad 1985, 87, 89, 91, 93, World Champs. squad 1991, 93, Olympic squad 1992. *Leisure interests*: classic cars. *Address*: c/o Race Walking Assoc., 9 Whitehouse Close, Rectory Rd, Sutton Coldfield, W. Midlands B75 7SD.

MOULAND, Mark: golfer; b. 23 April 1961; GB boys' champ. 1976; prof. debut 1981; Midland prof. strokeplay champ. 1984, 87; Dunhill Cup team (Wales) 1986–90, 93; winner Dutch Open 1988. *Address*: c/o PGA European Tour, Wentworth Club, Wentworth Drive, Virginia Water, Surrey GU25 4LS.

MOULDEN, Paul: footballer; b. 6 September 1967, Farnworth; player Manchester City 1984–89, Bournemouth 89–90, Oldham Athletic 90– . *Address*: Oldham Athletic FC, Boundary Park, Oldham, Lancs. OL1 2PA.

MOUNTFIELD, Derek: footballer; b. 2 November 1962, Liverpool; m. Julie Elizabeth Mountfield 1984; 1 s., 1 d.; player Tranmere Rovers 1980–82, Everton 82–88, Aston Villa 88–91, Wolverhampton Wanderers 91– ; with Everton: winners FA Cup 1984, European Cup Winners' Cup 1985, League champs. 1984/85, 86/87; 1 England U-21 cap. *Leisure interests*: golf, most sports. *Address*: Wolverhampton Wanderers FC, Molineux Stadium, Waterloo Rd, Wolverhampton WV1 4QR.

MOUNTJOY, Douglas James: snooker player; b. 8 June 1941, Tir-y-Berth, Rhymney; world amateur champ. 1976; prof. debut 1976; UK champ. 1978, 88; rep. Wales, winners World Cup 1979; winner Masters 1977, Pot Black 1978, 85, Irish Masters 1979, Mercantile Credit Classic 1989. *Address*: c/o World Prof. Billiards and Snooker Assoc., 27 Oakfield Rd, Clifton, Bristol BS8 2AT.

MOWBRAY, Anthony: footballer; b. 22 November 1963, Saltburn; player Middlesbrough 1981–92, Celtic 92– . *Address*: Celtic FC, Celtic Park, 95 Kerrydale St, Glasgow G40 3RE.

MOXON, Martyn Douglas: cricketer; b. 4 May 1960, Barnsley; m. Sue Moxon 1985; 1 d.; player Yorks. 1981– (capt. 90–); England B tour Sri Lanka 1985/86; 10 Tests, debut 1986, 8 1-day ints, tours India/Aus. 1984/85, Aus./NZ 1987/88, WI (England A) 1991/92 (capt.), Aus. (England A) 1992/93. *Address*: Yorks. CCC, Headingley Cricket Ground, Leeds LS6 3BU.

MUGLISTON, Luke William Thomas: fencer; b. 1 May 1972, Farnham; GB debut 1991, European Champs. squad 1991, 92, World Champs. squad 1993. *Leisure interests*: tennis, rally driving, fly fishing, cricket, volleyball. *Address*: Sussex House, 68 Cadogan Gardens, London SW1X 0EA.

MUIR, Ian: footballer; b. 5 May 1963, Coventry; player Queens Park Rangers 1980–83, Birmingham City 83–84, Brighton and Hove Albion 84–85, Tranmere Rovers 85– . *Address*: Tranmere Rovers FC, Prenton Park, Prenton Rd West, Birkenhead, Merseyside L42 9PN.

MULALLY, Alan David: cricketer; b. 12 July 1969, Southend; player Hants. 1988, Leics. 1990– ; W. Aus. tour India 1990. *Address*: Leics. CCC, County Ground, Grace Rd, Leicester LE2 8AD.

MULHOLLAND, Joyce: flat green bowler; b. 19 February, 1938, Bushmills, NI; m. Patrick Mulholland 1959; 2 s.; Irish women's pairs champ. (outdoor) 1989, (indoor) 1991, women's triples champ. (outdoor) 1983, 90, (indoor) 1987, women's fours champ. (outdoor) 1990; Ireland debut (outdoor) 1984, (indoor) 1988, World Champs. squad 1992. *Leisure interests*: walking, knitting, crossword puzzles. *Address*: 39 Huey Crescent, Bushmills, Co. Antrim BT57 8QZ.

MULLINS, Andrew Richard: Rugby Union footballer; b. 12 December 1964, Eltham; player Durham Univ., Harlequins 1987– (capt. 93–); England B debut v. Aus. 1988, snr debut v. Fiji 1989. *Address*: Harlequins FC, Stoop Memorial Ground, Craneford Way, Twickenham, Middx.

MUMBY, Keith: Rugby League footballer; b. 21 February 1957, Huddersfield; player Bradford Northern, Sheffield Eagles, Bradford Northern 1992– ; GB debut v. Aus. 1982. *Address*: Bradford Northern RLFC, Odsal Stadium, Bradford BD6 1BS.

MUNGALL, Steven: footballer; b. 22 May 1958, Bellshill; player Motherwell 1976–79, Tranmere Rovers 79– . *Address*: Tranmere Rovers FC, Prenton Park, Prenton Rd West, Birkenhead, Merseyside L42 9PN.

MUNRO, Alan Keith: jockey (Flat); b. 14 January 1967, Stevenage; winner Derby, Irish Derby, King George VI and Queen Elizabeth Diamond Stakes 1991 (Generous). *Leisure interests*: sport, music. *Address*: Rookdene, Dassels, Braughing, Herts. SG11 2RN.

MUNRO, Donald Shade: Rugby Union footballer; b. 19 November 1966; player Glasgow High/Kelvinside; Scotland A debut v. France A 1988, snr and Five Nations debut v. Wales 1994, tour Fiji/Tonga/W. Samoa 1993. *Address*: Glasgow High/Kelvinside RFC, Old Anniesland, Crow Rd, Glasgow.

MUNRO, Robert Neil: freestyle skier; b. 23 September 1967, Gasworth; Scottish moguls champ. 1987; GB moguls champ. 1990; Lowlanders moguls champ. 1988; GB debut 1987, World Champs. squad 1991, World Cup squad 1990– , Olympic squad 1992. *Leisure interests*: surfing, mountain biking, tennis, travel, speaking French. *Address*: c/o Brit. Ski Fed., 258 Main St, E. Calder, Livingston, W. Lothian EH53 0EE.

MUNTON, Timothy Alan: cricketer; b. 30 July 1965, Melton Mowbray; m. Helen Lesley Munton 1986; 1 s., 1 d.; player Warks. 1985– (vice-capt. 93–), winners NatWest Trophy 1989, 93; England A tours Pakistan 1990/91, WI 1991/92, Test debut v. Pakistan 1992. *Leisure interests*: family, most sports, home improvement. *Address*: Warks. CCC, County Ground, Edgbaston, Birmingham B5 7QU.

MURDOCH, Andrew: footballer; b. 20 July 1968, Greenock; player Celtic 1987–90, Partick Thistle 90– . *Address*: Partick Thistle FC, Firhill Stadium, 80 Firhill Rd, Glasgow G20 7BA.

MURPHY, Anthony John: cricketer; b. 6 August 1962, Manchester; player Lancs. 1985–88, Surrey 89– ; with Lancs.: tours Jamaica 1986, 87; with Surrey: tours Sharjah (UAE) 1989, 90, 93, Barbados 1989, 90, Lanzarote 1991, Rhodes 1992. *Address*: Surrey CCC, The Oval, Kennington, London SE11 5SS.

MURRAY, Neil: footballer; b. 21 February 1973, Bellshill; player Rangers 1989– , winners Scottish Cup 1993. *Address*: Glasgow Rangers FC, Ibrox Stadium, 150 Edmiston Drive, Glasgow G51 2XD.

MURRAY, Shaun: footballer; b. 7 December 1970, Newcastle; player Portsmouth 1989– . *Address*: Portsmouth FC, Fratton Park, Frogmore Rd, Portsmouth PO4 8RA.

MURRAY, Thomas: athlete; b. 18 May 1961, Greenock; m. Lesley Anne Murray 1986; 2 d.; W. of Scotland 5000m champ. 1987, 10,000m champ. 1986, 90, 3000m indoor champ. 1990, 91, cross-country champ. 1988–93; Scottish 10,000m champ. 1987, 92, 3000m indoor champ. 1992, cross-country champ. 1989, 92, 93; World Cross-Country Champs. team bronze medal 1992. *Leisure interests*: music, cycling, horse- and dog-racing, sketching, writing. *Address*: 97 Kilmacolm Rd, Greenock PA15 3LF.

MURRAY, Yvonne Carole Grace: athlete; b. 4 October 1964, Musselburgh; AAA women's 1500m champ. 1992, 3000m champ. 1988, 90, 91; UK women's 3000m champ. 1985, 87, 93, 5000m champ. 1983; Commonwealth Games women's 3000m bronze medal 1986, silver 1990; European Champs. women's 3000m bronze medal 1986, gold 1990; European Cup women's 3000m silver medals 1987, 89, 1500m bronze 1993; European Indoor Champs. women's 3000m bronze medal 1985, silver 1986, gold 1987; World Cup women's 3000m gold medal 1989; World Indoor Champs. women's 3000m gold medal 1993; Olympic women's 3000m bronze medal 1988; Sports Writers' Sportswoman of the Year 1989. *Address*: c/o Brit. Athletic Fed., 225A Bristol Rd, Edgbaston, Birmingham B5 7UB.

MUSHTAQ AHMED: cricketer; b. 28 June 1970, Sahival, Pakistan; player Somerset 1993– ; Test debut 1991, Pakistan tours NZ/Aus. (World Cup) 1992, England 1992, NZ/Aus./SA 1992/93. *Address*: Somerset CCC, The County Ground, Taunton, Somerset TA1 1JT.

MUSIKANT, Philippa Eve: gymnast (sports acrobatics); b. 2 December 1967, London; GB women's tumbling champ. 1987, 89, 91–93; GB jnr debut (artistic) 1981, snr debut (sports acrobatics) 1983; European Champs. combined silver medal 1988, bronze 1991; World Cup combined bronze medal 1991; World Champs. combined bronze medal 1988. *Leisure interests*: music, reading, jigsaw puzzles, all sport. *Address*: Hendon Youth Sports Centre, Algernon Rd, London NW4 3TA.

MUSTOE, Lyndon: Rugby Union footballer; b. 30 January 1969, Newport; player Pontypool, Cardiff; Wales A debut v. The Netherlands 1993. *Address*: Cardiff RFC, Cardiff Arms Park, Westgate St, Cardiff CF1 1JA.

MUSTOE, Robert: footballer; b. 28 August 1968, Witney; player Oxford Utd 1986–90, Middlesbrough 90– . *Address*: Middlesbrough FC, Ayresome Park, Middlesbrough, Cleveland TS1 4PB.

MUTCH, Andrew: footballer; b. 28 December 1963, Liverpool; player Wolverhampton Wanderers 1986–93, Swindon Town 93– ; with Wolverhampton Wanderers: 4th Div. champs. 1987/88, 3rd Div. champs. 1988/89; 1 England U-21 cap. *Address*: Swindon Town FC, The County Ground, Swindon, Wilts. SN1 2ED.

MYERS, Andrew: footballer; b. 3 November 1973, Hounslow; player Chelsea 1991– . *Address*: Chelsea FC, Stamford Bridge, Fulham Rd, London SW6 1HS.

MYERS, David: Rugby League footballer; b. 31 July 1971, Widnes; player Blackbrook (RU), Widnes (RU), Widnes, Warrington, Wigan, Widnes 1992– ; with Wigan: winners Premiership 1992; GB U-21 debut v. France 1991. *Address*: Widnes RLFC, Naughton Park, Lowerhouse Lane, Widnes WA8 7DZ.

MYLER, Robert: Rugby League footballer; b. 4 March 1970, Widnes; player Warrington 1989– . *Address*: Warrington RLFC, Wilderspool Stadium, Wilderspool Causeway, Warrington WA4 6PY.

NARBETT, Jonathan: footballer; b. 21 November 1968, Birmingham; player Shrewsbury Town 1986–88, Hereford Utd 88–92, Oxford Utd 92– . *Address*: Oxford Utd FC, Manor Ground, London Rd, Headington, Oxford OX3 7RS.

NAREY, David: footballer; b. 21 June 1956, Dundee; player Dundee Utd 1973– , winners Scottish League Cup 1980, 81; 35 Scotland caps. *Address*: Dundee Utd FC, Tannadice Park, Dundee DD3 7JW.

NAYLOR, Scott: Rugby League footballer; b. 2 February 1972; player Wigan 1988–93, Salford 93– . *Address*: Salford RLFC, The Willows, Willows Rd, Weaste, Salford M5 2ST.

NAYLOR, Stuart: footballer; b. 6 December 1962, Wetherby; player Lincoln City 1980–86, W. Bromwich Albion 86– . *Address*: W. Bromwich Albion FC, The Hawthorns, W. Bromwich B71 4LF.

NDLOVU, Peter: footballer; b. 25 February 1973, Bulawayo, Zimbabwe; player Highlanders (Zimbabwe), Coventry City 1991– ; Zimbabwe int. *Address*: Coventry City FC, Highfield Rd Stadium, King Richard St, Coventry CV2 4FW.

NEAL, Philip: football manager; b. 29 February 1951, Irchester; player Northampton Town 1968–74, Liverpool 74–85, Bolton Wanderers 85–88; 50 England caps; manager Coventry City 1993– . *Address*: Coventry City FC, Highfield Rd Stadium, King Richard St, Coventry CV2 4FW.

NEIL, Scott: ice hockey player; b. 1 August 1962; player Murrayfield Racers 1985–92, Sheffield Steelers 92– ; with Murrayfield Racers: winners Autumn Cup 1986, 90, Scottish Cup 1987–91, GB champs. 1985/86, League champs. 1986/87, 87/88; World Champs. debut 1981. *Address*: Sheffield Arena, Broughton Lane, Sheffield S9 2DF.

NEILL, Jonathan: Rugby League footballer; b. 19 December 1968, Whitehaven; player Kells ARLFC, St Helens 1987– ; with St Helens: winners Premiership 1993. *Address*: St Helens RLFC, Dunriding Lane, St Helens, Merseyside WA10 4AD.

NEILL, Warren: footballer; b. 21 November 1962, Acton; player Queens Park Rangers 1980–88, Portsmouth 88– ; with Portsmouth: 3rd Div. champs. 1982/83. *Address*: Portsmouth FC, Fratton Park, Frogmore Rd, Portsmouth PO4 8RA.

NEILSON, Alan: footballer; b. 26 September 1972, Wegberg, Germany; player Newcastle Utd 1991– ; 1 Wales cap. *Address*: Newcastle Utd FC, St James' Park, Newcastle-upon-Tyne, Tyne & Wear NE1 4ST.

NELSON, Craig: footballer; b. 28 May 1971, Coatbridge; player Partick Thistle 1990– . *Address*: Partick Thistle FC, Firhill Stadium, 80 Firhill Rd, Glasgow G20 7BA.

NELSON, David: Rugby League footballer; b. 8 September 1962, Leeds; player Queens Park ARLFC, Sheffield Eagles, Castleford 1991– . *Address*: Castleford RLFC, Wheldon Rd, Castleford WF10 2SD.

NELSON, Johnny: boxer; b. 4 January 1967; prof. debut 1986; titles won: Central cruiserweight 1988, GB cruiserweight 1989, European cruiserweight 1990; over 21 prof. wins. *Address*: c/o Brit. Boxing Board of Control, Jack Petersen House, 52A Borough High St, London SE1 1XW.

NELSON, Richard Shaun: motorcyclist; b. 31 January 1961, Holbrook; m. Teresa Nelson 1989; GB F2 sidecar champ. 1992. *Leisure interests*: motor sports, shooting, horseriding. *Address*: Two the Limit Racing, c/o Nelson Auto Electrical, Darley Abbey Mill, Derby DE3 1DZ.

NERURKAR, Richard David: athlete; b. 6 January 1964, Wolverhampton; English cross-country champ. 1990, 91, 93; AAA 10,000m champ. 1990; World Cross-Country Champs. squad 1989–92; Olympic squad (10,000m) 1992; winner Hamburg Marathon (debut), World Cup Marathon 1993. *Leisure interests*: travel, languages. *Address*: 33 MacNeice Drive, Marlborough, Wilts. SN8 1TR.

NEVIN, Patrick: footballer; b. 6 September 1963, Glasgow; player Clyde 1981–83, Chelsea 83–88, Everton 88–92, Tranmere Rovers 92– (capt.); with Chelsea: 2nd Div. champs. 1983/84; 5 Scotland U-21 caps, over 17 full Scotland caps. *Address*: Tranmere Rovers FC, Prenton Park, Prenton Rd W., Birkenhead, Merseyside L42 9PN.

NEW, Beverley Jayne: golfer; b. 30 July 1960, Bristol; Somerset ladies' champ. 1979–83, Bristol and District open champ. 1983; English ladies' amateur champ. 1980; England debut 1980; Curtis Cup team 1984; prof. debut 1984; winner Thailand Ladies' Open 1987, Malaysian Ladies' Open 1988.

Address: c/o Women's Prof. Golf European Tour, The Tytherington Club, Dorchester Way, Tytherington, Macclesfield, Cheshire SK10 2JP.

NEWELL, Michael: footballer; b. 27 January 1965, Liverpool; player Crewe Alexandra 1983, Wigan Athletic 1983–86, Luton Town 86–87, Leicester City 87–89, Everton 89–91, Blackburn Rovers 91– ; 4 England U-21 caps. *Address*: Blackburn Rovers FC, Ewood Park, Blackburn, Lancs. BB2 4JF.

NEWHOUSE, Aidan: footballer; b. 23 May 1972, Wallasey; player Chester City 1989–90, Wimbledon 90– . *Address*: Wimbledon FC, Selhurst Park, London SE25 6PY.

NEWLOVE, Paul: Rugby League footballer; b. 10 August 1971, Pontefract; player Travellers ARLFC, Featherstone Rovers 1988–93, Bradford Northern 93– ; rep. Yorks.; GB debut v. NZ 1989 (youngest ever snr cap), Brit. Lions tour Aus./NZ/Papua New Guinea 1992. *Address*: Bradford Northern RLFC, Odsal Stadium, Bradford BD6 1BS.

NEWMAN, Peter James: Rugby fives player; b. 25 August 1969; rep. Rugby Fives Assoc., Jesters, Manchester YMCA, Old Dunstonians, Manchester Univ.; with Manchester YMCA: club knockout champs. 1992; N. of England U-16 singles and doubles champ. 1986, U-19 singles champ. 1987, snr singles champ. 1991; GB U-19 singles and doubles champ. 1988, U-25 doubles champ. 1992. *Leisure interests*: cricket, tennis, squash, snooker, cinema, theatre, travel. *Address*: 12 Treewall Gardens, Bromley, Kent BR1 5BT.

NEWMAN, Robert: footballer; b. 13 December 1963, Bradford-on-Avon; player Bristol City 1981–91, Norwich City 91– . *Address*: Norwich City FC, Carrow Rd, Norwich NR1 1JE.

NEWPORT, Philip John: cricketer; b. 11 October 1962, High Wycombe; m. Christine Anne Newport 1985; 1 s.; player Worcs. 1982– , county champs. 1988, 89, Sunday League champs. 1987, 88; 3 Tests, debut 1988, tour Aus. 1990/91; Worcs. Player of the Year 1992. *Address*: Worcs. CCC, County Ground, New Rd, Worcester WR2 4QQ.

NEWSOME, Jonathan: footballer; b. 6 September 1970, Sheffield; player Sheffield Wednesday 1989–91, Leeds Utd 91– ; *Address*: Leeds Utd FC, Elland Rd, Leeds, W. Yorks. LS11 0ES.

NICHOLAS, Alison Margaret: golfer; b. 6 March 1962, Gibraltar; rep. Yorks. 1981–84; N. of England girls' champ. 1982, 83; Yorks. ladies' champ. 1984; GB ladies' open amateur strokeplay champ. 1983; prof. debut 1984; Solheim Cup team 1990, 92, winners 1992; winner Ladies' Brit. Open 1987, Guernsey Open 1988, German Open, Gislaved Ladies' Open 1989, Malaysian Open, W. Aus. Open, Paris Open 1992. *Leisure interests*: scuba diving, ornithology, photography, skiing. *Address*: c/o Women's Prof. Golf European Tour, The Tytherington Club, Dorchester Way, Tytherington, Macclesfield, Cheshire SK10 2JP.

NICHOLAS, Charles: footballer; b. 30 December 1961, Glasgow; player Celtic 1980–83, Arsenal 83–87, Aberdeen 87–90, Celtic 90– ; with Celtic: winners Scottish League Cup 1983; with Aberdeen: winners Scottish League Cup, Scottish Cup 1990; 6 Scotland U-21 caps, 20 full Scotland caps; Scottish Football Writers' Assoc. Player of the Year 1983. *Address*: Celtic FC, Celtic Park, 95 Kerrydale St, Glasgow G40 3RE.

NICHOLAS, Lilian: flat green bowler; b. 24 November 1907, Ebbw Vale; m. Horace Nicholas 1934; 1 s.; Welsh women's singles champ. (outdoor) 1963, 64, 67, 70, 71, 78, 82, (indoor) 1968, 70, women's pairs champ. (outdoor) 1965, 83, women's triples champ. (outdoor) 1962, 63, 68, 77, (indoor) 1991, women's fours champ. (outdoor) 1959, 60; 1st GB women's singles champ. (outdoor) 1972; Wales debut (outdoor) 1963, (indoor) 1974, World Champs. women's pairs bronze medal 1977. *Leisure interests*: dress-making, knitting, decorating, gardening, amateur dramatics, TV. *Address*: c/o Welsh Women's Bowling Assoc., Ffrydd Cottage, 2 Ffrydd Rd, Knighton, Powys.

NICHOLAS, Mark Charles Jefford: cricketer; b. 29 September 1957, London; player Hants. 1978– (capt. 85–), Sunday League champs. 1986; England B tour Sri Lanka 1985/86 (capt.), England A tour Zimbabwe/Kenya 1989/90. *Address*: Hants. CCC, County Cricket Ground, Northlands Rd, Southampton SO9 2TY.

NICHOLL, James: football player/manager; b. 28 February 1956, Hamilton, Canada; player Manchester Utd 1974–81, Toronto (Canada) 81–82, Sunderland 82–83, Toronto (Canada) 83–84, Rangers 1984, W. Bromwich Albion 1984–86, Rangers 86–89, Dunfermline Athletic 89–91, player/manager Raith Rovers 91– ; with Rangers: winners Scottish League Cup 1987, 88; 1 NI U-21 cap, 73 full NI caps. *Address*: Raith Rovers FC, Stark's Park, Pratt St, Kirkcaldy, Fife KY1 1SA.

NICHOLL, Pauline: squash player; b. 21 November 1966, Kendal; rep. Cumbria 1982–87, Durham and Cleveland 88– ; Cumbria ladies' champ. 1984–87, Durham and Cleveland ladies' champ. 1988–92; Scottish ladies' U-23 open champ. 1986; GB ladies' doubles champ. 1987; England B debut 1986. *Leisure interests*: most sports, driving. *Address*: 8 Howard St, Kendal, Cumbria LA9 5QZ.

NICHOLLS, Mandy: hockey player; b. 28 February 1968, Kingston; m. James Nicholls 1990; player Ealing 1987– , club champs. 1987, 89, indoor club champs. 1986, top goal-scorer 1991/92; England U-21 debut 1988, vice-capt. 1989, snr debut v. The Netherlands 1989, World Cup squad 1990; England indoor debut and European Indoor Cup silver medallist 1993; GB debut and Olympic bronze medal 1992, Champions Trophy squad 1993. *Leisure interests*: squash, keep-fit, cinema, cats, general fiction. *Address*: Ealing Ladies HC, Ealing CC, Crofton Rd, London W5.

NICHOLSON, David: racehorse trainer; b. 19 March 1939; m. Dinah Nicholson 1962; 2 s.; prof. jockey 1951–74, winner Whitbread Gold Cup 1967 (Mill House); 1st trainer's licence 1968; winner Mackeson Gold Cup 1986 (Very Promising), 1991 (Another Coral), Cheltenham Gold Cup 1988 (Charter Party). *Address*: c/o BHB, 42 Portman Square, London W1H 0EN.

NICKLE, Sonny: Rugby League footballer; b. 4 May 1969, Leeds; player Hunslet, Sheffield Eagles, St Helens 1991– ; with St Helens: winners Premiership 1993; GB debut and tour Papua New Guinea 1992. *Address*: St Helens RLFC, Dunriding Lane, St Helens, Merseyside WA10 4AD.

NICOL, Andrew Douglas: Rugby Union footballer; b. 12 March 1971, Dundee; player Heriot's FP, Dundee High School FP (vice-capt 1991–93, capt. 93–94); Scotland B debut v. France B 1991, snr and Five Nations debut v. England 1992, tours N. America 1991, Aus. 1992, Fiji/Tonga/W. Samoa (capt.) 1993; Brit. Lions tour NZ (replacement) 1993. *Leisure interests*: golf, cinema. *Address*: Dundee High School FP, Mayfield, Arbroath Rd, Dundee.

NICOL, Peter Franz: squash player; b. 5 April 1973, Inverurie; player Cannons 1992–93; rep. Yorks. 1991–92; Scottish champ. 1993 (youngest ever); GB U-19

champ. 1992; European champ. of champs. 1993; Scotland jnr debut 1985, snr debut 1991; European Champs. team gold medal 1992; winner Singapore Open 1993. *Leisure interests*: golf, music. *Address*: 12 St Egberts Way, Chingford, London E4 6QH.

NICOL, Stephen: footballer; b. 11 December 1961, Irvine; player Ayr Utd 1979–81, Liverpool 81– ; with Liverpool: winners European Cup 1984, FA Cup 1986, 89, 92, League champs. 1983/84, 85/86, 87/88, 89/90; 14 Scotland U-21 caps, 27 full Scotland caps. *Address*: Liverpool FC, Anfield Rd, Liverpool L4 0TH.

NICOLL, Ed: Nordic skier; b. 1 October 1964, Preston; GB 15km cross-country champ. 1992, 30km cross-country champ. 1992, 93; GB debut 1988, World Champs. squad 1991, 93. *Leisure interests*: coaching, cycling. *Address*: c/o Brit. Ski Fed., 258 Main St, E. Calder, Livingston, W. Lothian EH53 0EE.

NICOLL, Kurt: motorcyclist (moto-cross); b. 15 November 1964, Bishop's Stortford; m. Lisa Nicoll 1991; 1 d.; rep. Kawasaki 1983, KTM 84–85, Kawasaki 86–89, KTM 90–92, Honda 93– ; GB schoolboy moto-cross champ. 1980, snr champ. 1988–90, 92, 93; 3rd-placed team, Moto-Cross des Nations 1992; World Champs. 500cc runner-up 1987, 88, 90, 92. *Leisure interests*: carp fishing. *Address*: c/o ACU, ACU House, Wood St, Rugby CV21 2YX.

NIELSEN, Anders Ward: badminton player; b. 24 February 1967, Cape Town, SA; rep. Surrey, inter-county champs. 1983–85, 88–91, 93; English champ. 1992; England debut 1988, Thomas Cup team 1990, 92; European Champs. individ. bronze medals 1992, 94; Olympic squad 1992; winner European Masters 1992. *Leisure interests*: golf, horseracing, music. *Address*: 5 Savona Court, The Downs, Wimbledon, London SW20 8HY.

NIJHOLT, Luc: footballer; b. 29 July 1961, Zaandam, Switzerland; player Motherwell 1990–93, Swindon Town 93– . *Address*: Swindon Town FC, The County Ground, Swindon, Wilts. SN1 2ED.

NIKAU, Tawera: Rugby League footballer; b. 1 January 1967, Huntly, NZ; player Otahuhu (NZ), Sheffield Eagles, Ryedale-York, Castleford 1991– ; with Castleford: winners Regal Trophy 1994; NZ debut v. GB 1990. *Address*: Castleford RLFC, Wheldon Rd, Castleford WF10 2SD.

NIXON, Eric: footballer; b. 4 October 1962, Manchester; player Manchester City 1983–88, Tranmere Rovers 88– . *Address*: Tranmere Rovers FC, Prenton Park, Prenton Rd W., Birkenhead, Merseyside L42 9PN.

NIXON, Paul Andrew: cricketer; b. 21 October 1970, Carlisle; player Leics. 1989– , tour The Netherlands 1991. *Address*: Leics. CCC, County Ground, Grace Rd, Leicester LE2 8AD.

NOGAN, Lee: footballer; b. 21 May 1969, Cardiff; player Oxford Utd 1987–91, Watford 91– ; 1 Wales U-21 cap, 1 full Wales cap. *Address*: Watford FC, Vicarage Rd Stadium, Watford, Herts. WD1 8ER.

NOLAN, Gary: Rugby League footballer; b. 31 May 1966, Hull; player Nat. Docks Labour Board ARLFC, Hull 1991– ; with Hull: winners Premiership 1991. *Address*: Hull RLFC, The Boulevard Ground, Airlie St, Hull HU3 3JD.

NOLAN, Ian: footballer; b. 9 July 1970, Liverpool; player Tranmere Rovers 1991– . *Address*: Tranmere Rovers FC, Prenton Park, Prenton Rd W., Birkenhead, Merseyside L42 9PN.

NOLAN, Philippa Rachel (Pippa): equestrianist (three-day eventing); b. 7 October 1968, Crowborough; m. William Funnell

1993; GB open champ. 1992 (Sir Barnaby); European Jnr Champs. team bronze medal 1986 (Aibourne); European Young Rider Champs. individ. gold medal 1987, team gold 1988, individ. and team silver 1989 (Sir Barnaby); winner Blenheim Horse Trials 1993 (Metronome). *Leisure interests*: tennis, water sports. *Address*: Cobbetts Farm, Lyefield Lane, Forest Green, Dorking RH5 5SN.

NOLAN, Phillis: flat green bowler; b. 10 February 1946, Bray, Ireland; m. Philip Nolan 1967; 2 s., 1 d.; Irish women's singles champ. (outdoor) 1989, 91, 92, women's pairs champ. (outdoor) 1983, 92, women's triples champ. (outdoor) 1986, women's fours champ. (outdoor) 1979, 81, 82; GB women's singles champ. (outdoor) 1992, 93; Ireland debut (outdoor) 1976, World Champs. women's pairs gold medals 1988, 92. *Leisure interests*: tennis, reading. *Address*: 5 New Grange Park, Meath Rd, Bray, Co. Wicklow, Ireland.

NOLAN, Robert: Rugby League footballer; b. 2 October 1968, Hull; player Hull 1988– . *Address*: Hull RLFC, The Boulevard Ground, Airlie St, Hull HU3 3JD.

NOONE, James Martin: powerboat racer; b. 7 September 1958, Stevenage; GB inboard hydroplane champ. 1987, 90, 91, sprint champ. 1992; European HR 1000 hydroplane champ. 1993; world HR 1000 champ. 1992, 93; winner Bluebird Trophy 1993; world HR 1000 speed record-holder. *Leisure interests*: Rugby League, quizzes. *Address*: 10 Sutherland Crescent, Roundhay, Leeds LS8 1OA.

NORFOLK, James Howard: cyclist; b. 4 October 1973, Newport; Wessex cyclo-cross champ. 1991; RTTC 25-mile team time trial jnr champ. 1991; GB cyclo-cross debut 1992, World Champs. squad 1993. *Leisure interests*: TV, videos. *Address*: Hawthorns, 10 Main Rd, Tadley, Hants. RG26 6NL.

NORMAN, Anthony: footballer; b. 24 February 1958, Deeside; player Hull City 1980–88, Sunderland 88– ; 5 Wales caps. *Address*: Sunderland FC, Roker Park Ground, Sunderland, Tyne and Wear SR6 9SW.

O'BRIEN, Craig: Rugby League footballer; b. 4 April 1969, Hull; player W. Hull ARLFC, Hull Kingston Rovers 1988– . *Address*: Hull Kingston Rovers RLFC, Craven Park, Preston Rd, Hull HU9 5HE.

O'BRIEN, William (Liam): footballer; b. 5 September 1964, Dublin, Ireland; player Shamrock Rovers (Ireland), Manchester Utd 1986–88, Newcastle Utd 88–94, Tranmere Rovers 94– ; 9 Ireland caps. *Address*: Tranmere Rovers FC, Prenton Park, Prenton Rd W., Birkenhead, Merseyside L42 9PN.

O'BRYAN, Rachel Elizabeth: hockey player; b. 25 June 1971, Pontypridd; player Gloucester City 1986–89, Ealing 90– ; rep. Glos. U-21 (snr indoor), Middx U-21; Wales U-21 debut 1989, snr debut 1990. *Leisure interests*: tennis, squash, cricket, karate, socializing. *Address*: 275B Bristol Rd, Quedgeley, Glos. GL2 6QP.

O'CALLAGHAN, Kevin: footballer; b. 19 October 1961, Dagenham; player Millwall 1978–80, Ipswich Town 80–85, Portsmouth 85–87, Millwall 87–91, Southend Utd 91– ; with Millwall: 2nd Div. champs. 1987/88; 1 Ireland U-21 cap, 20 full Ireland caps. *Address*: Southend Utd FC, Roots Hall, Victoria Ave, Southend-on-Sea, Essex SS2 6NQ.

O'CONNOR, Mike: ice hockey player; b. 12 December 1961; player Durham Wasps 1984– , winners Autumn Cup 1985, 88, 89, 91, League champs. 1984/85, 85/86, 88/89, 90/91, 91/92, GB champs. 1986/87, 87/88, 90/91, 91/92; World Champs. debut 1992. *Address*: The Ice Rink, Walkersgate, Durham DH1 1SQ.

O'CONNOR, Scott: ice hockey player; b. 3 May 1969; player Kirkcaldy Kestrels 1986–88, Ayr Raiders 88–90, Peterborough Pirates 90– ; World Champs. debut 1992. *Address*: E. of England Ice Rink, Mallard Rd, Bretton, Peterborough PE3 8YN.

O'DONNELL, Augustine: Rugby League footballer; b. 11 December 1970, Billinge; player Wigan, St Helens 1992– ; with St Helens: winners Premiership 1993. *Address*: St Helens RLFC, Dunriding Lane, St Helens, Merseyside WA10 4AD.

O'DONNELL, Phillip: footballer; b. 25 March 1972, Bellshill; player Motherwell 1990– , winners Scottish Cup 1991; Scotland U-21 int. *Address*: Motherwell FC, Fir Park, Fir Park St, Motherwell ML1 2QN.

O'GORMAN, Timothy Joseph Gerard: cricketer; b. 15 May 1967, Woking; player Durham Univ. 1985–89, Derbys. 88– ; with Derbys.: winners Benson and Hedges Cup 1993, Sunday League champs. 1990; rep. England Schools 1981, 84; Surrey Young Cricketer of the Year 1984, Derbys. Young Cricketer of the Year 1989; rep. England Schools (hockey) 1981, 82. *Leisure interests*: most sports, music, theatre, reading. *Address*: Derbys. CCC, County Cricket Ground, Nottingham Rd, Derby DE2 6DA.

O'GORMAN, William Andrew: racehorse trainer; b. 22 March 1948, Newmarket; m. Elaine O'Gorman 1973; 3 ch.; 1st licence 1969; equalled world record of 16 wins with a 2-year-old with Provideo, 1984, and Timeless Times (USA), 1990. *Leisure interests*: sleeping. *Address*: Seven Springs, Newmarket, Suffolk CB8 7JQ.

O'LEARY, David: footballer; b. 2 May 1958, Stoke Newington; player Arsenal 1975–93, Leeds Utd 93–   ; with Arsenal: winners League Cup 1987, 93, FA Cup 1979, 93, League champs. 1988/89. 90/91; over 67 Ireland caps; first player to make 700 appearances for Arsenal; appeared in 3 consecutive Cup Finals 1978, 79, 80. *Address:* Leeds Utd FC, Elland Rd, Leeds, W. Yorks. LS11 0ES.

O'NEIL, Brian: footballer; b. 6 September 1972, Paisley; player Celtic 1991–   ; Scotland U-21 int. *Address:* Celtic FC, Celtic Park, 95 Kerrydale St, Glasgow G40 3RE.

O'NEIL, John: footballer; b. 6 July 1971, Bellshill; player Dundee Utd 1988–   ; Scotland U-21 int. *Address:* Dundee Utd FC, Tannadice Park, Dundee DD3 7JW.

O'NEILL, Janet Margaret: lacrosse player; b. 7 March 1963, Farnborough; m. Martin O'Neill 1984; player Beckenham Beetles 1977–   ; rep. Kent 1981–   , East 85–   ; Scotland debut 1990, tours USA 1992, 93. *Publications: Rules of Pop-Lacrosse,* 1987. *Leisure interests:* singing, tennis, squash, skiing, keeping fit, flower-arranging, watching rugby, eating and socializing. *Address:* Hewitts Farmhouse, Hewitts Rd, Chelsfield, Kent BR6 7QL.

O'NEILL, Michael: Rugby League footballer; b. 29 November 1960, Widnes; player Widnes, Rochdale Hornets, Leeds 1991–   ; GB debut v. Aus. 1982. *Address:* Leeds RLFC, Bass Headingley, St Michael's Lane, Leeds LS6 3BR.

O'NEILL, Michael: footballer; b. 5 July 1969, Portadown, NI; player Newcastle Utd 1987–89, Dundee Utd 89–93, Hibernian 93–   ; over 20 NI caps. *Address:* Hibernian FC, Easter Rd Stadium, 64 Albion Rd, Edinburgh EH7 5QG.

O'REGAN, Kieran: footballer; b. 9 November 1963, Cork, Ireland; player Brighton and Hove Albion 1983–87, Swindon Town 87–88, Huddersfield Town 88–93, W. Bromwich Albion 93–   ; 4 Ireland caps. *Address:* W. Bromwich Albion FC, The Hawthorns, Halfords Lane, W. Bromwich B71 4LF.

O'RIORDAN, Donal: footballer; b. 14 May 1957, Dublin, Ireland; player Derby County 1975–78, Tulsa Roughnecks (USA), Preston N. End 1978–83, Carlisle Utd 83–85, Middlesbrough 85–86, Grimsby Town 86–88, Notts County 88–   ; 1 Ireland U-21 cap. *Address:* Notts County FC, Meadow Lane Ground, Nottingham NG2 3HJ.

O'SHEA, Daniel: footballer; b. 26 March 1963, Kensington; player Arsenal 1982–84, Charlton Athletic 1984, Exeter City 1984–85, Southend Utd 85–89, Cambridge Utd 89–   ; with Cambridge Utd: 3rd Div. champs. 1990/91. *Address:* Cambridge Utd FC, Abbey Stadium, Newmarket Rd, Cambridge CB5 8LL.

O'SULLIVAN, Ronnie: snooker player; b. 5 December 1975; world jnr champ. 1991; prof. debut 1992; UK champ. 1993; winner Benson and Hedges Champs. 1993; holds record of 38 successive prof. wins; youngest-ever player to win major title. *Address:* Matchroom, 10 Western Rd, Romford, Essex RM1 3JT.

OAKES, David John: archer (crossbow); b. 19 January 1955, Harvington, Worcs.; m. Jill Oakes 1979; 2 ch.; Scottish open champ. 1991–93, Welsh open champ. 1992, 93; GB open champ. 1991. *Leisure interests:* computing, reading, walking, DIY. *Address:* 14 Kelvin Close, Kidderminster, Worcs. DY11 5NQ.

OAKES, Scott: footballer; b. 5 August 1972, Leicester; player Leicester City 1990–91, Luton Town 91–   . *Address:* Luton Town FC, Kenilworth Stadium, 1 Maple Rd, Luton, Beds. LU4 8AW.

OBREE, Douglas Graeme: cyclist; b. 11 September 1965; m. Anne Mary Obree 1989; Scottish 4000m individ. pursuit champ. 1989; GB 4000m individ. pursuit champ. 1993; RTTC 50-mile time trial champ. 1993; World Champs. 4000m individ. pursuit gold medal 1993; prof. debut 1993; world 4000m individ. pursuit record-holder. *Address*: c/o Brit. Cycling Fed., 36 Rockingham Rd, Kettering, Northants. NN16 8HG.

OFFIAH, Martin Nwokocha: Rugby League footballer; b. 29 December 1966, Hackney; player Ipswich (RU), Rosslyn Park (RU), Widnes, Wigan 1992– ; with Widnes: winners Premiership 1988–90; with Wigan: winners Premiership 1992, 94, Challenge Cup 1992–94, Regal Trophy 1993; GB debut v. France 1988, Brit. Lions tours Aus./NZ/Papua New Guinea 1988, 92, NZ/Papua New Guinea 1990; scored 300th try v. Hull Kingston Rovers 1993. *Address*: Wigan RLFC, The Pavilion, Central Park, Wigan WN1 1XF.

OGRIZOVIC, Steven: footballer; b. 12 September 1957, Mansfield; player Chesterfield 1977, Liverpool 1977–82, Shrewsbury Town 82–84, Coventry City 84– ; with Coventry City: winners FA Cup 1987. *Address*: Coventry City FC, Highfield Rd Stadium, King Richard St, Coventry CV2 4FW.

OJOMOH, Stephen Oziegbe: Rugby Union footballer; b. 25 May 1970, Benin City, Nigeria; player Bath, League champs. 1992/93; rep. S.W. Div., Div. champs. 1993/94; England A debut v. NZ 1992, tour Canada 1993, snr and Five Nations debut v. Ireland 1994. *Address*: Bath FC, Recreation Ground, Bath, Avon.

OLDFIELD, David: footballer; b. 30 May 1968, Aus.; player Luton Town 1986–89, Manchester City 89–90, Leicester City 90– ; 1 England U-21 cap. *Address*: Leicester City FC, City Stadium, Filbert St, Leicester LE2 7FL.

OLIPHANT, Kevan: Rugby Union footballer; b. 11 January 1967, Hartlepool; player W. Hartlepool 1986– ; rep. Durham. *Address*: W. Hartlepool RFC, Brierton Lane, Hartlepool, Cleveland TS25 5DR.

OLIVER, Greig Hunter: Rugby Union footballer; b. 12 September 1964, Hawick; player Hawick 1982– ; rep. S. of Scotland; Scotland debut v. Zimbabwe (World Cup) 1987, tours Aus./NZ (World Cup) 1987, Zimbabwe 1988, Japan 1989, NZ 1990, N. America 1991. *Leisure interests*: personal fitness, golf. *Address*: Hawick RFC, Mansfield Park, Mansfield Rd, Hawick.

OLNEY, Ian: footballer; b. 17 December 1969, Luton; player Aston Villa 1988–92, Oldham Athletic 92– ; 10 England U-21 caps. *Address*: Oldham Athletic FC, Boundary Park, Oldham, Lancs. OL1 2PA.

OLSSON, Sean Nicholas: bobsleigher; b. 2 March 1967, Beverley; GB 2-man champ. 1992; GB debut 1990; World Cup 2-man bronze medal 1993; Olympic squad 1992 (youngest driver). *Leisure interests*: fast cars, antique toy cars, DIY. *Address*: c/o Brit. Bobsleigh Assoc., Springfield House, Woodstock Rd, Coulsdon, Surrey CR5 3HS.

OPENSHAW, David Kay: croquet player; b. 31 October 1946, Nelson; m. Jacqueline Openshaw 1978; 1 s., 1 d.; GB men's champ. 1981, 91, open champ. 1979, 81, 85, open doubles champ. 1985, 87; winner US Open, Canadian Open 1991; England debut 1980; GB debut 1979 (capt. 1982–), winners MacRobertson Int. Shield 1982, 90, 93. *Address*: 45 Baring Rd, Beaconsfield, Bucks. HP9 2NF.

OPIE, Lisa Jane: squash player; b. 15 August 1963, Guernsey; player King's Club (Guernsey), Nottingham; GB ladies' open champ. 1991 (1st Brit. winner for 30 years); England U-19 debut 1976, snr debut 1980; World Jnr Champs. gold medal 1981;

World Champs. team gold medals 1985, 87, 89, 91; winner US Open 1986. *Leisure interests*: all sport, cooking, art, pop concerts. *Address*: Flat 1B, 1 Newcastle Drive, The Park, Nottingham NG7 1AA.

ORD, Richard: footballer; b. 3 March 1970, Murton; player Sunderland 1987– ; 3 England U-21 caps. *Address*: Sunderland FC, Roker Park Ground, Sunderland, Tyne and Wear SR6 9SW.

ORLYGSSON, Thorvaldur (Toddy): footballer; b. 2 August 1966, Odense, Denmark; player KA Akureyri (Iceland), Nottingham Forest 1989–93, Stoke City 93– ; Iceland int. *Address*: Stoke City FC, Victoria Ground, Stoke on Trent, Staffs. ST4 4EG.

ORMONDROYD, Ian: footballer; b. 22 September 1964, Bradford; player Bradford City 1985–89, Aston Villa 89–91, Derby County 91–92, Leicester City 92– . *Address*: Leicester City FC, City Stadium, Filbert St, Leicester LE2 7FL.

ORR, Neil: footballer; b. 13 May 1959, Greenock; player Morton 1975–82, W. Ham Utd 82–87, Hibernian 87– ; 7 Scotland U-21 caps. *Address*: Hibernian FC, Easter Rd Stadium, 64 Albion Rd, Edinburgh EH7 5QG.

OSBORN, Simon: footballer; b. 19 January 1972, Croydon; player Crystal Palace 1990– . *Address*: Crystal Palace FC, Selhurst Park Stadium, London SE25 6PU.

OSBORNE, Jamie: jockey (NH); b. 28 August 1967; winner Hennessy Gold Cup 1990 (Arctic Call). *Address*: c/o BHB, 42 Portman Square, London W1H 0EN.

OSHER, Katharine: swimmer; b. 30 June 1969, Gt Yarmouth; m. Michael Osher; GB women's 200m backstroke champ. 1984–87, 89, 91–93, 100m backstroke champ. 1984–87, 89, 91–93, 50m backstroke champ. 1991–93, 400m individ. medley champ.

1985, 86; England youth debut 1982, snr debut 1984; Commonwealth Games women's 200m backstroke silver medal 1986; GB debut 1983, Olympic squad 1984, 88, 92; GB women's 50m and 100m backstroke record-holder. *Leisure interests*: cooking, fitness training, promotions. *Address*: c/o ASA, Harold Fern House, Derby Square, Loughborough, Leics. LE11 0AL.

OSMAN, Russell: football player/manager; b. 14 February 1959, Repton; player Ipswich Town 1977–85, Leicester City 85–88, Southampton 88–91, Bristol City 91–92; player/manager Bristol City 93– . *Address*: Bristol City FC, Ashton Gate, Bristol BS3 2EJ.

OSTLER, Dominic Piers: cricketer; b. 15 July 1970, Solihull; player Warks. 1990– , winners NatWest Trophy 1993. *Address*: Warks. CCC, County Ground, Edgbaston, Birmingham B5 7QU.

OTI, Christopher: Rugby Union footballer; b. 16 June 1965, London; player Nottingham, Cambridge Univ. (Blue 1986, 87), Wasps; England and Five Nations debut v. Scotland 1988, tours Argentina 1990, Aus./Fiji 1991, Canada (England A) 1993; Brit. Lions tour Aus. 1989 (aborted). *Address*: Wasps FC, Wasps Football Ground, Repton Ave, Sudbury, nr Wembley, Middx HA0 3DW.

OTLEY, Suzanne: hockey player; b. 4 November 1970, Doncaster; player Doncaster Ladies 1990– ; rep. Yorks.; England U-21 debut (outdoor) 1987, (indoor) 1991, European U-21 Champs. silver medallist 1991. *Leisure interests*: training, cycling. *Address*: 75 Fernbank Drive, Armthorpe, Doncaster DN3 2HB.

OTTAWAY, John Martin: flat green bowler; b. 2 June 1955, Colton, Norfolk; rep. Norfolk 1983– ; English singles champ. (outdoor) 1989, pairs champ.

(outdoor) 1990; GB singles champ. (outdoor) 1990; England debut (outdoor and indoor) 1985; Commonwealth Games squad 1990; World Champs. triples and fours bronze medals, team gold 1988. *Address*: `Shotwood', The Street, Colton, Norwich NR9 5AB.

OTTO, Ricky: footballer; b. 9 November 1967, London; player Leyton Orient 1990–93, Southend 93– . *Address*: Southend Utd FC, Roots Hall, Victoria Ave, Southend-on-Sea, Essex SS2 6NQ.

OTTO, Wayne Colin Trevor: karate player (U-65–U-75kg); b. 18 May 1966, Hackney; English open champ. 1989, 90, U-75kg champ. 1991, 92, 93, open champ. 1992, 93, team champ. 1993; GB U-75kg jnr champ. 1986, snr champ. 1989; England debut 1984; European Jnr Champs. gold medal 1987; European Champs. gold medals 1988, 91, team gold 1992; World Champs. gold medals 1990, 92, team gold 1988, 90; World Games gold medal 1993. *Leisure interests*: music, dance, basketball, reading. *Address*: 14 Waterloo Close, Jack Dunning Estate, London E9 6EF.

OWERS, Gary: footballer; b. 3 October 1968, Newcastle; player Sunderland 1986– , 3rd Div. champs. 1987/88. *Address*: Sunderland FC, Roker Park Ground, Sunderland, Tyne and Wear SR6 9SW.

PAATELAINEN, Mixu: footballer; b. 3 February 1967, Helsinki, Finland; player Valkeakosken Haka (Finland), Dundee Utd 1987–91, Aberdeen 91– ; Finland int. *Address*: Aberdeen FC, Pittodrie Stadium, Pittodrie St, Aberdeen AB2 1QH.

PAGE, Carol Anne: pistol shooter; b. 19 October 1948, Gosport; m. Harry Page 1985; Army open air pistol champ. 1984, 90, 93, sport pistol champ. 1984, 90; Hants. open air pistol champ. 1984; Kent open air pistol champ. 1986; Dorset open air pistol champ. 1991, 93; English ladies' air pistol

champ. 1991, 92, sport pistol champ. 1993; GB ladies' air pistol champ. 1984, 85, 89, 91–94, open air pistol champ. 1991, ladies' sport pistol champ. 1988–91; GB debut 1976; Olympic squad (sport pistol) 1984. *Leisure interests*: walking along the clifftops at Sidmouth with my dog. *Address*: c/o Nat. Small-Bore Rifle Assoc., Lord Roberts House, Bisley Camp, Brookwood, Woking, Surrey GU24 0NP.

PAGE, Neil Sutherland Anderson: Rugby Union footballer; b. 12 June 1972, Edinburgh; player Watsonians 1992– ; rep. Edinburgh U-21 1992/93. *Leisure interests*: squash, keeping fit, speedway. *Address*: Watsonians RFC, Myreside, Myreside Rd, Edinburgh EH10 5DB.

PAGET, Leonard: motorcyclist; b. 12 July 1960, Hampshire; European pro-stock dragbike champ. 1990, 91. *Leisure interests*: moto-cross, tuning motorcycle engines. *Address*: 3 Swallow Close, Totton, Hants. SO4 2JA.

PALLISTER, Gary: footballer; b. 30 June 1965, Ramsgate; player Middlesbrough 1984–89, Manchester Utd 89– ; with Manchester Utd: winners FA Cup 1990, European Cup Winners' Cup 1991, League champs. 1992/93; over 9 England caps. *Address*: Manchester Utd FC, Old Trafford, Manchester M16 0RA.

PALMER, Carlton: footballer; b. 5 December 1965, Rowley Regis; player W. Bromwich Albion 1984–89, Sheffield Wednesday 89– ; with Sheffield Wednesday: winners League Cup 1991; 4 England U-21 caps, over 17 full England caps. *Address*: Sheffield Wednesday FC, Hillsborough, Sheffield, S. Yorks. S6 1SW.

PALMER, Charles: footballer; b. 10 July 1963, Aylesbury; player Watford 1981–84, Derby County 84–87, Hull City 87–89, Notts County 89– . *Address*: Notts County FC, Meadow Lane Ground, Nottingham NG2 3HJ.

PALMER, Paul: swimmer; b. 18 October 1974, Lincoln; GB 200m and 400m freestyle champ. 1993; World Schools Champs. 400m freestyle gold medal 1990; European Jnr Champs. 200m, 400m and 1500m freestyle gold medals 1991; European Champs. 400m freestyle silver medal 1993; World Cup 400m freestyle silver medal 1993; World Short-Course Champs. 400m freestyle bronze medal 1993; Olympic squad 1992 (200m and 400m freestyle, 4 x 200m freestyle relay; youngest Brit. male swimmer); GB 200m freestyle record-holder. *Address:* c/o ASA, Harold Fern House, Derby Square, Loughborough, Leics. LE11 0AL.

PALMER, Roger: footballer; b. 30 January 1959, Manchester; player Manchester City 1977–80, Oldham Athletic 80– . *Address:* Oldham Athletic FC, Boundary Park, Oldham, Lancs. OL1 2PA.

PANAPA, Sam: Rugby League footballer; b. 14 May 1962, Auckland, NZ; player Sheffield Eagles, Wigan 1991– ; with Wigan: winners Premiership 1992, Challenge Cup, Regal Trophy 1993; NZ debut v. GB 1990, tour Aus./Papua New Guinea 1987. *Address:* Wigan RLFC, The Pavilion, Central Park, Wigan WN1 1XF.

PANTON-LEWIS, Catherine: golfer; b. 14 June 1955, Bridge of Allan, Scotland; m. Philip Lewis 1991; rep. Stirling and Clackmannanshire 1970–77, Edinburgh Univ. Ladies 74–77; Stirlingshire girls' champ. 1968–73, Scottish girls champ. 1969; E. of Scotland ladies' champ., Scottish Univ. champ. 1976; GB ladies' open amateur champ. 1976; Scotland debut 1972; prof. debut 1978; winner Irish Classic 1983, Delsjî Open 1985, Portuguese Ladies' Open 1986, 87, Scottish Ladies' Open 1988; Scottish Sportswoman of the Year and Edinburgh Univ. Sportswoman of the Year 1976; winner Women's Prof. Golf European Tour Order of Merit 1979. *Leisure interests:* Scrabble, circuit training, cinema, horseracing, reading.

Address: 11 Georgina Court, Arlington Rd, E. Twickenham, Middx TW1 2AT.

PARDEW, Alan: footballer; b. 18 July 1961, Wimbledon; player Crystal Palace 1987–91, Charlton Athletic 91– . *Address:* Charlton Athletic FC, The Valley, Floyd Rd, London SE7 8BL.

PARIS, Alan: footballer; b. 15 August 1964, Slough; player Peterborough Utd 1985–88, Leicester City 88–91, Notts County 91– . *Address:* Notts County FC, Meadow Lane Ground, Nottingham NG2 3HJ.

PARIS, Carol: basketball player; b. 14 June 1962, Farnham Common; 1 s.; player Slough 1978–83, Crystal Palace 83–87, Northampton 87–89, Crystal Palace/Thames Valley Ladies 90– ; with Crystal Palace: winners women's Nat. Cup 1986, 87, women's League champs. 1985/86; with Northampton: winners women's Nat. Cup 1988, 89, women's League champs. 1988/89; England debut 1982, over 60 caps, Commonwealth Champs. gold medallist 1991; Olympic squad 1988; English Basketball Woman Player of the Year 1986, 91, Carlsberg Most Valuable Player 1992/93. *Leisure interests:* tennis, squash, horseriding, cycling, reading, cooking, gardening, walking. *Address:* 24 Rhyl Rd, Perivale, Middx UB6 8LD.

PARISH, Matthew Herbert Woodbine: oarsman; b. 30 November 1971, London; rep. Eton College 1988–90, Univ. of London BC 91–93; with Univ. of London: winners Grand Challenge Cup, Henley Royal Regatta 1992; GB jnr debut and World Jnr Champs. coxless fours gold medal 1989, U-23 debut 1991, snr debut and World Student Games eights silver medal 1993. *Leisure interests:* cricket, tennis, golf, sailing, windsurfing, science, travel. *Address:* Flat 3, 20 Marloes Rd, London W8 5LH.

PARKER, Garry: footballer; b. 7 September 1965, Oxford; player Luton Town 1982–85, Hull City 85–87, Nottingham Forest 87–91, Aston Villa 91– ; with Nottingham Forest: winners League Cup 1989, 90; 6 England U-21 caps. *Address*: Aston Villa FC, Villa Park, Trinity Rd, Birmingham B6 6HE.

PARKER, Malinda Florence Muriel (Linda): flat green bowler; b. 11 December 1925, Beckjay, Clungunford; rep. S. Wales and Monmouthshire 1969– ; Welsh women's singles champ. (outdoor) 1971, women's triples champ. (outdoor) 1982; Wales debut (outdoor) 1971; Commonwealth Games women's fours gold medal 1986; World Champs. women's triples bronze medal 1985, women's fours bronze 1988; Secretary, Welsh Women's Bowling Assoc. 1981– . *Leisure interests*: card games, bowls administration. *Address*: Ffrydd Cottage, 2 Ffrydd Rd, Knighton, Powys LD7 1DB.

PARKER, Paul William Giles: cricketer; b. 15 January 1956, Bulawayo, Rhodesia; m. Teresa Parker 1980; 1 s., 1 d.; player Sussex 1976–91 (capt. 88–91), Durham 92–93; 1 Test (1981). *Address*: Durham CCC, County Ground, Riverside, Chester-le-Street, Co. Durham DH3 3QR.

PARKER, Paul: footballer; b. 4 April 1964, W. Ham; player Fulham 1982–87, Queens Park Rangers 87–91, Manchester Utd 91– ; with Manchester Utd: League champs. 1992/93; 8 England U-21 caps, over 17 full England caps. *Address*: Manchester Utd FC, Old Trafford, Manchester M16 0RA.

PARKER, Wayne: Rugby League footballer; b. 2 April 1967, Hull; player Hull Kingston Rovers 1986– . *Address*: Hull Kingston Rovers RLFC, Craven Park, Preston Rd, Hull HU9 5HE.

PARKINSON, Gary: footballer; b. 10 January 1968, Thornaby; player

Middlesbrough 1986– . *Address*: Middlesbrough FC, Ayresome Park, Middlesbrough, Cleveland TS1 4PB.

PARKS, Robert James: cricketer; b. 15 June 1959, Cuckfield; m. Amanda Parks 1982; player Hants. 1980–92, Kent 93– ; with Hants.: Sunday League champs. 1986; English Counties tour Zimbabwe 1985. *Address*: Kent CCC, St Lawrence Ground, Canterbury CT1 3NZ.

PARLOUR, Ray: footballer; b. 7 March 1973, Romford, Essex; player Arsenal 1991– , winners League Cup 1993; over 5 England U-21 caps. *Leisure interests*: snooker, golf. *Address*: Arsenal FC, Arsenal Stadium, Highbury, London N5 1BU.

PARRACK, James Guy: swimmer; b. 10 March 1967, Cheltenham; GB 100m breaststroke champ. 1988; Commonwealth Games 100m breaststroke silver medal 1990; GB debut and Olympic squad 1988 (100m breaststroke); UK and Commonwealth 50m breaststroke record-holder. *Leisure interests*: backgammon, bridge, cooking, James Bond, hot chili and cold beer, travel. *Address*: c/o ASA, Harold Fern House, Derby Square, Loughborough, Leics. LE11 0AL.

PARRIS, George: footballer; b. 11 September 1964, Ilford; player W. Ham Utd 1982–92, Birmingham City 92– . *Address*: Birmingham City FC, St Andrews Ground, Birmingham B9 4NH.

PARROTT, John Stephen: snooker player; b. 11 May 1964, Liverpool; m. Karen Parrott; 1 s.; prof. debut 1983, UK and world champ. 1991, winner European Open 1989, 90, Dubai Classic 1991, 92, Int. Open 1994. *Address*: c/o Phil Miller, 186 Booker Ave, Allerton, Liverpool L18 9TB.

PARSONS, Carol Anne: equestrianist (dressage); b. 6 February 1956, St Helier, Jersey; m. Robin Parsons 1988; GB debut

1990, Olympic squad 1992. *Leisure interests*: water sports, gardening, decorating. *Address*: Little Wishford Farm, Stoford, Salisbury, Wilts.

PARSONS, Gordon James: cricketer; b. 17 October 1959, Slough; m. Hester Sophia Parsons 1991; 1 d.; player Leics. 1978–85, Warks. 86–88, Leics. 89– ; with Leics.: tour Zimbabwe 1981. *Address*: Leics. CCC, County Ground, Grace Rd, Leicester LE2 8AD.

PARTINGTON, Steve: race walker; b. 17 September 1965, Douglas, IoM; m. Cal Partington 1988; 1 s.; English schools 10km champ. 1985; UK 10km champ. 1991; Commonwealth Games squad (IoM) 1986, 90; GB jnr debut 1984, snr debut 1988, World Cup squad 1989, 93. *Leisure interests*: fell-running, cycling. *Address*: Smiler's Barn, Ballamilghyn Farm, Laxey, IoM.

PARTRIDGE, Mark Bernard: oarsman; b. 12 January 1967, Pontypool; m. Catherine Margaret Rooney 1991; rep. Leander Club 1989– ; Wales jnr debut 1984, snr debut 1988; GB lightweight and open eights champ. 1992; GB debut 1989, World Champs. lightweight eights silver medal 1992. *Leisure interests*: cinema, good food, spending time with my wife. *Address*: Leander Club, Henley-on-Thames, Oxon.

PASCOE, Colin: footballer; b. 9 April 1965, Port Talbot; player Swansea City 1983–88, Sunderland 88–93, Swansea City 93– ; 3 Wales U-21 caps, 10 full Wales caps. *Address*: Swansea City FC, Vetch Field, Swansea SA1 3SU.

PATERSON, Craig: footballer; b. 2 October 1959, S. Queensferry; player Hibernian 1978–82, Rangers 82–86, Motherwell 86–91, Kilmarnock 91– ; with Rangers: winners Scottish League Cup 1984, 85; with Motherwell: winners Scottish Cup 1991; Scotland U-21 int. *Address*: Kilmarnock FC, Rugby Park, Kilmarnock KA1 2DP.

PATERSON, Garry: footballer; b. 10 November 1969, Dunfermline; player Dundee 1992– . *Address*: Dundee FC, Dens Park, Dundee DD3 7JY.

PATES, Colin: footballer; b. 10 August 1961, Carshalton; player Chelsea 1979–88, Charlton Athletic 88–89, Arsenal 89–93, Brighton and Hove Albion 93– ; with Chelsea: 2nd Div. champs. 1983/84; with Arsenal: winners League Cup 1993. *Address*: Brighton and Hove Albion FC, Goldstone Ground, Newtown Rd, Hove, E. Sussex BN3 7DE.

PATTERSON, Mark: footballer; b. 24 May 1965, Darwen; player Blackburn Rovers 1983–88, Preston N. End 88–90, Bury 90–91, Bolton Wanderers 91– . *Address*: Bolton Wanderers FC, Burnden Park, Manchester Rd, Bolton, Lancs. BL3 2QR.

PATTON, Michael Brian: Rugby Union footballer; b. 15 July 1969; player Oxford Univ., London Irish; Ireland A debut v. Scotland A 1992. *Address*: London Irish RUFC, The Avenue, Sunbury-on-Thames, Middx.

PAUL, Lenny: bobsleigher; b. 25 May 1958, Ipswich; m. Stephanie Anne Paul 1988; GB 2-man champ. 1989–94, 4-man champ. 1989–93; GB debut 1986; European Champs. 4-man silver medal 1994; World Cup 4-man bronze medal 1992, 4-man gold and 2-man bronze 1993, 4-man overall bronze 1994; Olympic squad 1988, 92, 94. *Leisure interests*: reading, music, boxing. *Address*: c/o Brit. Bobsleigh Assoc., Springfield House, Woodstock Rd, Coulsdon, Surrey CR5 3HS.

PAYNE, Andrew: cricketer; b. 20 October 1973, Rawtenstall; player Somerset 1992– ; England U-19 tour Pakistan 1991/92. *Address*: Somerset CCC, The County Ground, Taunton, Somerset TA1 1JT.

PAYNE, Derek: footballer; b. 26 April 1967, Edgware; player Barnet 1988–93, Southend Utd 93– . *Address*: Southend Utd FC, Roots Hall, Victoria Ave, Southend-on-Sea, Essex SS2 6NQ.

PAYNE, James Robert: golfer; b. 17 April 1970, Louth; W. of England strokeplay champ. 1990, European amateur champ. 1991; England debut 1989; Walker Cup team 1991; prof. debut 1992; winner Balearic Open 1993; leading amateur in Open 1991. *Leisure interests*: Grimsby Town FC, snooker, tennis. *Address*: Advantage Int., 10 Blades Court, Deodar Rd, London SW15.

PAYNE, Nicholas Martin William: fencer (foil); b. 19 July 1971, Epsom; S. England U-14 champ. 1984, 85, U-16 champ. 1986, U-18 champ. 1988, snr champ. 1990; GB U-20 champ. 1989, team champ. 1993 (Salle Paul); GB U-17 debut 1987, U-20 debut 1989, Olympic reserve 1992, snr debut 1993; winner Bristol Open 1989. *Leisure interests*: travel, skiing, mountaineering, amateur radio. *Address*: 19 Ropery St, London E3 4QE.

PAYNE, Roger: mountaineer; b. 16 July 1956, Hammersmith; m. Julie-Ann Clyma 1987; 1st ascents: W. face of Milpoqraju, Peru 1985, S. face of Rusac, Peru 1986; 1st Brit. ascents: Khan Tengri and Pobeda, Tien Shan 1991; leader Brit./NZ Gasherbrum 2 expedition 1987, Brit. Broad Peak Traverse expedition 1992, Brit. K2 expedition 1993. *Publications*: contributor to *Alpine Journal, Expedition Planners' Handbook. Leisure interests*: photography, mountain environment and culture, history. *Address*: c/o Brit. Mountaineering Council, Crawford House, Precinct Centre, Booth St E., Manchester M13 9RZ.

PAYTON, Andrew: footballer; b. 3 October 1967, Whalley; player Hull City 1986–91, Middlesbrough 91–92, Celtic 92–93, Barnsley 93– . *Address*: Barnsley FC, Oakwell Ground, Barnsley, S. Yorks. S71 1ET.

PEACOCK, Darren: footballer; b. 3 February 1968, Bristol; player Newport County 1986–89, Hereford Utd 89–90, Queens Park Rangers 90– . *Address*: Queens Park Rangers FC, Rangers Stadium, S. Africa Rd, London W12 7PA.

PEACOCK, Gavin: footballer; b. 18 November 1967, Eltham; player Queens Park Rangers 1984–87, Gillingham 87–89, Bournemouth 89–90, Newcastle Utd 90–93, Chelsea 93– . *Address*: Chelsea FC, Stamford Bridge, Fulham Rd, London SW6 1HS

PEAKE, Andrew: footballer; b. 1 November 1961, Market Harborough; player Leicester City 1979–85, Grimsby Town 85–86, Charlton Athletic 86–91, Middlesbrough 91– ; with Leicester City: 2nd Div. champs. 1979/80; 1 England U-21 cap. *Address*: Middlesbrough FC, Ayresome Park, Middlesbrough, Cleveland TS1 4PB.

PEAKE, Trevor: footballer; b. 10 February 1957, Nuneaton; player Lincoln City 1979–83; Coventry City 83–91, Luton Town 91– (capt.); with Coventry City: winners FA Cup 1987. *Address*: Luton Town FC, Kenilworth Stadium, 1 Maple Rd, Luton, Beds. LU4 8AW.

PEARCE, Andrew: footballer; b. 20 April 1966, Bradford-on-Avon; player Coventry City 1990–93, Sheffield Wednesday 93– . *Address*: Sheffield Wednesday FC, Hillsborough, Sheffield, S. Yorks. S6 1SW.

PEARCE, Gary Stephen: Rugby Union footballer; b. 2 March 1956, Dinton, Bucks.; m. Susan Jean Pearce 1978; 2 s.; player Aylesbury 1973–77, Northampton 78– (capt. 1988–91); with Northampton: 2nd Div. champs. 1989/90; rep. Bucks. 1974–80, Midland Div.; England and Five Nations debut v. Scotland 1979, 36 caps, tours Japan/Fiji/Tonga 1979, Argentina 1981, N. America 1982, SA 1984, NZ 1985, Aus./NZ (World Cup) 1987, Aus. 1988,

Aus./Fiji 1991; most-toured int., only player to have played in 3 decades. *Address*: Northampton FC, Franklins Gardens, Weedon Rd, Northampton NN5 5BG.

PEARCE, Shaun David: canoeist; b. 13 December 1969, Reading; m. Christine Ann Chambers 1991; GB U-16 K1 slalom champ. 1985, U-18 champ. 1987; GB jnr debut 1985, snr debut 1991; World Champs. K1 slalom individ. gold medal 1991, team gold 1993. *Leisure interests*: golf, running, Manchester Utd FC. *Address*: 38 Lindum Rd, Basford, Nottingham.

PEARCE, Stuart: footballer; b. 24 April 1962, Shepherds Bush; player Coventry City 1983–85, Nottingham Forest 85– (capt.); with Nottingham Forest: winners League Cup 1989, 90; 1 England U-21 cap, over 53 full England caps, capt. 1993–94. *Address*: Nottingham Forest FC, City Ground, Nottingham NG2 5FJ.

PEARS, David: Rugby Union footballer; b. 6 December 1967, Workington; player Aspatria, Sale, Harlequins 1989– ; with Harlequins: winners Pilkington Cup 1991; England debut v. Argentina 1990, Five Nations debut v. France 1992, tours Argentina 1990, Aus./Fiji 1991, Canada (England A) 1993. *Address*: Harlequins FC, Stoop Memorial Ground, Craneford Way, Twickenham, Middx.

PEARS, Stephen: footballer; b. 22 January 1962, Brandon, Co. Durham; player Manchester Utd 1979–85, Middlesbrough 85– . *Address*: Middlesbrough FC, Ayresome Park, Middlesbrough, Cleveland TS1 4PB.

PEARSON, Joel Timothy Vernon: Rugby Union footballer; b. 8 March 1970; player Bristol; England U-21 debut v. The Netherlands 1991. *Address*: Bristol FC, Memorial Ground, Filton Ave, Horfield, Bristol BS7 0AQ.

PEARSON, Martin: Rugby League footballer; b. 24 October 1971, Sharlston; player Travellers ARLFC, Featherstone Rovers 1988– . *Address*: Featherstone Rovers RLFC, The Croft, Batley Rd, W. Ardsley, Wakefield WF3 1DX.

PEARSON, Nigel: footballer; b. 21 August 1963, Nottingham; player Shrewsbury Town 1981–87, Sheffield Wednesday 87– ; with Sheffield Wednesday: winners League Cup 1991. *Address*: Sheffield Wednesday FC, Hillsborough, Sheffield, S. Yorks. S6 1SW.

PEEBLES, Gary: footballer; b. 6 February 1967, Johnstone; player St Mirren 1984–88, Partick Thistle 88– . *Address*: Partick Thistle FC, Firhill Stadium, 80 Firhill Rd, Glasgow G20 7BA.

PEMBERTON, John: footballer; b. 18 November 1964, Oldham; player Crewe Alexandra 1985–88, Crystal Palace 88–90, Sheffield Utd 90–93, Leeds Utd 93– . *Address*: Leeds Utd FC, Elland Rd, Leeds, W. Yorks. LS11 0ES.

PEMBRIDGE, Mark: footballer; b. 29 November 1970, Merthyr Tydfil; player Luton Town 1989–92, Derby County 92– ; 1 Wales U-21 cap, over 6 full Wales caps. *Address*: Derby County FC, The Baseball Ground, Shaftesbury Crescent, Derby DE3 8NB.

PENBERTHY, Anthony Leonard: cricketer; b. 1 September 1969, Troon; player Northants. 1989– ; rep. England YC v. NZ 1989; scored 1st 1st-class 100 of 1990 season. *Address*: Northants. CCC, County Cricket Ground, Wantage Rd, Northampton NN1 4TJ.

PENDLEBURY, John: Rugby League footballer; b. 18 April 1961, Leigh; player Leigh Miners ARLFC, Wigan, Salford, Halifax, Bradford Northern, Leigh 1992– ; with Wigan: winners Regal Trophy 1983; with

Halifax: winners Challenge Cup 1987. *Address*: Leigh RLFC, Hilton Park, Kirkhall Lane, Leigh WN7 1RN.

PENDRY, John: hang glider pilot; b. 10 May 1957, Guildford; m. Dominique Gustin-Gex; 1 d.; prof. debut 1982; GB champ. 1986, 90; European Champs. gold medals 1986, 88, 90, 92; World Champs. gold medal 1985; World Paragliding Champs. bronze medal 1993. *Leisure interests*: windsurfing, catamaran sailing, trials motorcycling, mountain biking. *Address*: 7 Stanhope Lodge, Stanhope Drive, Cowes, Isle of Wight PO31 8BH.

PENN, Andrew Shaun: race walker; b. 31 March 1967, Nuneaton; GB 20km champ. 1993; GB jnr debut 1984, snr debut 1987, World Cup squad 1991, 93, Olympic squad 1992. *Leisure interests*: snooker, golf, tennis, eating out. *Address*: Federal Express, Sutherland House, 1 Matlock Rd, Foleshill, Coventry, W. Midlands.

PENNETT, David Barrington: cricketer; b. 26 October 1969, Leeds; player Notts. 1992– . *Address*: Notts. CCC, Trent Bridge, Nottingham NG2 6AG.

PENNEY, David: footballer; b. 17 August 1964, Wakefield; player Derby County 1985–89, Oxford Utd 89– . *Address*: Oxford Utd FC, Manor Ground, London Rd, Headington, Oxford OX3 7RS.

PENNEY, Trevor Lionel: cricketer; b. 12 June 1968, Harare, Zimbabwe; player Warks. 1992– ; Zimbabwe tour Sri Lanka 1987; rep. Zimbabwe hockey 1984–87. *Address*: Warks. CCC, County Ground, Edgbaston, Birmingham B5 7QU.

PENNY, Lee: Rugby League footballer; b. 24 September 1974; player Warrington 1991– . *Address*: Warrington RLFC, Wilderspool Stadium, Wilderspool Causeway, Warrington WA4 6PY.

PENRICE, Gary: footballer; b. 23 March 1964, Bristol; player Bristol Rovers 1984–89, Watford 89–91, Aston Villa 1991, Queens Park Rangers 1991– . *Address*: Queens Park Rangers FC, Rangers Stadium, S. Africa Rd, London W12 7PA.

PENTLAND, Paul: ice hockey player; b. 11 November 1964; player Murrayfield Racers 1983– , winners Autumn Cup 1986, 90, 94, Scottish Cup 1987–91, GB champs. 1985/86, League champs. 1986/87, 87/88; World Champs. debut 1989. *Address*: The Ice Rink, Riversdale Crescent, Edinburgh EH12 5XN.

PEREGO, Mark Angelo: Rugby Union footballer; b. 8 February 1964; player Llanelli, winners Welsh Cup 1993, Welsh League champs. 1992/93; Wales and Five Nations debut v. Scotland 1990, tour Zimbabwe/Namibia 1993. *Address*: Llanelli RFC, Stradey Park, Llanelli, Dyfed.

PERRATT, Linda: racehorse trainer; b. 10 October 1963, Glasgow; 1st licence 1991. *Leisure interests*: keep-fit, watching all sport. *Address*: Cree Lodge, 47 Craigie Rd, Ayr KA8 0HD.

PERRETT, Mark: Rugby League footballer; b. 18 July 1973; player Ovenden ARLFC, Halifax 1991– ; GB U-21 debut v. France 1993. *Address*: Halifax RLFC, The Pavilion, Thrum Hall, Gibbet St, Halifax, W. Yorks. HX1 4TL.

PERRY, Jason: footballer; b. 2 April 1970, Newport; player Cardiff City 1987– ; 3 Wales U-21 caps. *Address*: Cardiff City FC, Ninian Park, Sloper Rd, Cardiff CF1 8SX.

PERRY, Mark: footballer; b. 7 February 1971, Aberdeen; player Dundee Utd 1988– . *Address*: Dundee Utd FC, Tannadice Park, Dundee DD3 7JW.

PERRYMAN, Stephen, MBE: football manager; b. 21 December 1951, Ealing; player Tottenham Hotspur 1969–86, Oxford Utd 1986, Brentford 1986–90; with Tottenham Hotspur: winners League Cup 1971, 73, UEFA Cup 1972, FA Cup 1981, 82; 17 England U-23 caps, 1 full England cap; player/manager Brentford 1987–90, manager Watford 1990–93, assistant manager Tottenham Hotspur 1993–   . *Address*: Tottenham Hotspur FC, 748 High Rd, Tottenham, London N17 0AP.

PESCHISOLIDO, Paul: footballer; b. 25 May 1971, Canada; player Toronto Blizzards (Canada), Birmingham City 1992–   ; Canada int. *Address*: Birmingham City FC, St Andrews Ground, Birmingham B9 4NH.

PETCHEY, Mark: tennis player; b. 1 August 1970; rep. Essex; GB U-14 hard court and grass court champ. 1984, U-16 grass court champ. 1986, U-18 grass court champ. 1987, snr doubles champ. 1993; GB debut 1991, Davis and European Cup teams 1991–   ; winner Nagoya Challenger doubles, Kuala Lumpur Challenger doubles 1992. *Address*: c/o LTA, The Queen's Club, W. Kensington, London W14 9EG.

PEYTON, Gerald: footballer; b. 20 May 1956, Birmingham; player Burnley 1975–76, Fulham 76–86, Bournemouth 86–91, Everton 91–93, W. Ham Utd 93–   ; 33 Ireland caps. *Address*: W. Ham Utd FC, Boleyn Ground, Green St, Upton Park, London E13 9AZ.

PHELAN, Michael: footballer; b. 24 September 1962, Nelson; player Burnley 1980–85, Norwich City 85–89, Manchester Utd 89–   ; with Burnley: 3rd Div. champs. 1981/82; with Norwich City: 2nd Div. champs. 1985/86; with Manchester Utd: winners FA Cup 1990, European Cup Winners' Cup 1991, League champs. 1992/93; 1 England cap. *Address*: Manchester Utd FC, Old Trafford, Manchester M16 0RA.

PHELAN, Terence: footballer; b. 16 March 1967, Manchester; player Leeds Utd 1984–86, Swansea City 86–87, Wimbledon 87–92, Manchester City 92–   ; with Wimbledon: winners FA Cup 1988; 1 Ireland U-21 cap, over 15 full Ireland caps. *Address*: Manchester City FC, Maine Rd, Moss Side, Manchester M14 7WN.

PHELPS, Richard Charles: oarsman; b. 21 November 1965, London; rep. Cambridge Univ. BC, winners Univ. Boat Race 1993, 94; winning crew, Grand Challenge Cup, Henley Royal Regatta 1991; World U-23 Champs. coxed fours gold medal 1986; World Student Games eights silver medal 1993; World Champs. eights bronze medals 1989, 91; Olympic squad (eights) 1992; Oxford–Westminster rowing world record-holder. *Leisure interests*: golf, tennis, bears, CDs, a lousy sense of humour. *Address*: The Hawks Club, 18 Portugal Place, Cambridge CB5 8AF.

PHELPS, Richard Lawson: modern pentathlete; b. 19 April 1961, Gloucester; m. Teresa Purton; 1 s.; GB jnr champ. 1979, 81, 82, snr champ. 1979, 81–84, 86, 88, 90, 91, 93; GB jnr debut 1977, snr debut 1979; World Champs. gold medal 1993 (1st Brit. winner); Olympic team bronze medal 1988, squad 1984, 92. *Leisure interests*: surfing, skiing, triathlon, golf. *Address*: c/o Modern Pentathlon Assoc. of GB, Wessex House, Silchester Rd, Tadley, Basingstoke, Hants. RG26 6PX.

PHILLIBEN, John: footballer; b. 14 March 1964, Stirling; player Stirling Albion 1980–84, Doncaster Rovers 84–86, Motherwell 86–   . *Address*: Motherwell FC, Fir Park, Fir Park St, Motherwell ML1 2QN.

PHILLIPS, David Owen: footballer; b. 29 July 1963, Wegberg, Germany; m. Jeanette Phillips 1990; 1 s.; player Plymouth Argyle 1981–84, Manchester City 84–86, Coventry City 86–89, Norwich City 89–93,

Nottingham Forest 93– ; with Coventry City: winners FA Cup 1987; 4 Wales U-21 caps, over 46 full Wales caps. *Leisure interests*: golf, Aus. philately. *Address*: Nottingham Forest FC, City Ground, Nottingham NG2 5FJ.

PHILLIPS, James: footballer; b. 8 February 1966, Bolton; player Bolton Wanderers 1983–87, Rangers 87–88, Oxford Utd 88–90, Middlesbrough 90–93, Bolton Wanderers 93– . *Address*: Bolton Wanderers FC, Burnden Park, Manchester Rd, Bolton, Lancs. BL3 2QR.

PHILLIPS, Leslie: footballer; b. 7 January 1963, Lambeth; player Birmingham City 1980–84, Oxford Utd 1984–93, Northampton Town 93– ; with Oxford Utd: winners League Cup 1986. *Address*: Northampton Town FC, County Ground, Northampton NN1 4PS.

PHILLIPS, Robert: Rugby Union footballer; b. 22 January 1959; player Tredworth, Gloucester. *Address*: Gloucester RUFC, Kingsholm, Worcester St, Gloucester GL3 3AX.

PHILLIPS, Rowland David: Rugby League footballer; b. 28 July 1965, St David's; player Neath RUFC, Warrington 1990– ; with Warrington: winners Regal Trophy 1991; Wales RU int.; Wales RL debut v. Papua New Guinea 1991. *Address*: Warrington RLFC, Wilderspool Stadium, Wilderspool Causeway, Warrington WA4 6PY.

PHILLIPS, Sarah: cyclist; b. 3 July 1967, Stonehaven; Scottish women's 10- and 25-mile time trial champ. 1988, 90, 91; RTTC women's 50-mile time trial champ. 1992, 25-mile champ. 1993; Scotland debut 1988; GB debut and World Champs. squad (women's 50km team time trial) 1992. *Leisure interests*: horseriding, running, swimming, canoeing. *Address*: 10 Arbuthnott St, Stonehaven AB3 2JB.

PHILLISKIRK, Anthony: footballer; b. 10 February 1965, Sunderland; player Sheffield Utd 1983–88, Oldham Athletic 88–89, Preston N. End 1989, Bolton Wanderers 1989–92, Peterborough Utd 92– . *Address*: Peterborough Utd FC, London Rd Ground, Peterborough, Cambs. PE2 8AL.

PICKAVANCE, Ian: Rugby League footballer; b. 20 February 1968, St Helens; player St Helens, Swinton 1989–93, St Helens 93– ; rep. Lancs. U-19. *Address*: St Helens RLFC, Dunriding Lane, St Helens, Merseyside WA10 4AD.

PICKERING, Karen Denise: swimmer; b. 19 December 1971, Brighton; GB women's 50m, 100m and 200m freestyle champ. 1993; England youth debut 1986, snr debut 1987; Commonwealth Games women's 4 x 100m medley relay silver and 4 x 100m freestyle relay bronze medals 1990; GB youth and snr debuts 1986; US Nat. Champs. women's 100m freestyle silver and 200m freestyle bronze medals 1993; European Open Champs. women's 200m freestyle silver, 100m freestyle and 4 x 100m medley relay bronze medals 1990; European Champs. women's 200m freestyle and 4 x 200m freestyle relay bronze medals 1993; World Short-Course Champs. women's 200m freestyle gold medal, 100m freestyle bronze 1993; Olympic squad 1992; 1st Brit. woman to win world swimming title. *Leisure interests*: art and design, writing for local paper. *Address*: c/o ASA, Harold Fern House, Derby Square, Loughborough, Leics. LE11 0AL.

PIGGOTT, Lester Keith: jockey (Flat); b. 5 November 1935, Wantage; m. Susan Armstrong 1960; 2 d.; winner Derby 1954 (Never Say Die), 1957 (Crepello), 1960 (St Paddy), 1968 (Sir Ivor), 1970 (Nijinsky), 1972 (Roberto), 1976 (Empery), 1977 (The Minstrel), 1983 (Teenoso), 2000 Guineas 1957 (Crepello), 1968 (Sir Ivor), 1970

(Nijinsky), 1985 (Shadeed), 1992 (Rodrigo de Triano), Oaks 1957 (Carrozza), 1959 (Petit Etoile), 1966 (Valoris), 1975 (Juliette Marny), 1981 (Blue Wind), 1984 (Circus Plume), St Leger 1960 (St Paddy), 1961 (Aurelius), 1967 (Ribocco), 1968 (Ribero), 1970 (Nijinsky), 1971 (Athens Wood), 1972 (Boucher), 1984 (Commanche Run), King George VI and Queen Elizabeth Diamond Stakes 1965 (Meadow Court), 1966 (Aunt Edith), 1969 (Park Top), 1970 (Nijinsky), 1974 (Dahlia), 1977 (The Minstrel), 1984 (Teenoso), Irish Derby 1967 (Ribocco), 1968 (Ribero), 1977 (The Minstrel), 1981 (Shergar), 1000 Guineas 1970 (Humble Duty), 1981 (Fairy Footsteps), Prix de l'Arc de Triomphe 1973 (Rheingold), 1977, 78 (Alleged), Irish 2000 Guineas 1992 (Rodrigo de Triano); rode 191 winners in season 1966; champ. jockey 1960, 1964–71, 1981, 82. *Address*: c/o BHB, 42 Portman Square, London W1H 0EN.

PIGOTT, Anthony Charles Shackleton: cricketer; b. 4 June 1958, London; 1 s.; player Sussex 1978–93, Surrey 94– ; with Sussex: winners Gillette Cup 1978, NatWest Trophy 1986; 1 Test (1983), tour NZ 1983/84; MCC tours Leeward Islands 1992, Kenya 1993; 1st 3 1st-class wickets in 1978 a hat-trick. *Leisure interests*: squash (owns Sussex County Squash Club), watching all sport. *Address*: Surrey CCC, The Oval, Kennington, London SE11 5SS.

PILARSKI, Antoni: Alpine skier; b. 16 August 1975, Falkirk; Scottish children's slalom champ., dry-slope giant slalom champ. 1988, jnr dry-slope slalom, giant slalom champ. 1992; GB U-18 super giant slalom champ. 1993; Scotland debut 1990. *Leisure interests*: cycling, athletics, windsurfing, music. *Address*: 14 Elderslie Drive, Wallacestone, Falkirk FK2 0DN.

PILARSKI, Michal: Alpine skier; b. 31 May 1977, Falkirk; Scottish children's giant slalom champ. 1990, slalom champ. 1992, jnr slalom, giant slalom champ. 1993;

English children's slalom, giant slalom champ. 1992; GB children's slalom, giant slalom champ. 1992; Scotland debut 1993. *Leisure interests*: cycling, windsurfing, hockey, swimming, football. *Address*: 14 Elderslie Drive, Wallacestone, Falkirk FK2 0DN.

PINSENT, Matthew, MBE: oarsman; b. 10 October 1970, Norfolk; rep. Eton College 1987–88, Oxford Univ. BC, Leander Club; with Oxford: winners Univ. Boat Race 1990, 91; World Jnr Champs. coxless pairs gold medal 1988; World Champs. coxed fours bronze medal 1989, coxless pairs bronze medal 1990, gold 1991 (world record), 1993; Olympic coxless pairs gold medal 1992 (Olympic record). *Leisure interests*: golf. *Address*: Leander Club, Henley-on-Thames, Oxon.

PIPE, Martin Charles: racehorse trainer (NH); b. 29 May 1945, Taunton; m. Mary Caroline Pipe 1971; 1 s.; 1st licence 1977; winner Mackeson Gold Cup 1987 (Beau Ranger), Irish Grand National 1991 (Omerta), Hennessy Gold Cup 1988 (Strands of Gold), 1991 (Chatam), Champion Hurdle 1993 (Granville Again); achieved fastest-ever 200 wins in season 1990/91; leading trainer 1988/89, 89/90, 90/91, 91/92, 92/93. *Address*: c/o BHB, 42 Portman Square, London W1H 0EN.

PIPER, Keith John: cricketer; b. 18 December 1969; player Warks. 1989– , winners NatWest Trophy 1993, tours La Manga 1989, St Lucia 1990. *Address*: Warks. CCC, County Ground, Edgbaston, Birmingham B5 7QU.

PITMAN, Jennifer Susan: racehorse trainer (NH); b. 11 June 1946; 2 s.; 1st licence 1975; winner Grand National 1983 (Corbiere), Cheltenham Gold Cup 1984 (Burrough Hill Lad), 1991 (Garrison Savannah), Hennessy Gold Cup 1984 (Burrough Hill Lad); Piper-Heidsieck Trainer of the Year 1983/84, 89/90, Variety

Club of GB Sportswoman of the Year 1984. *Publications*: *Glorious Uncertainty* (autobiography), 1984. *Address*: Weathercock House, Upper Lambourn, nr Newbury, Berks. RG16 7QT.

PITT, Stewart Richard: canoeist; b. 19 March 1968, Ayr; Brit. univ. C2 slalom champ. 1988; Scottish C2 slalom champ. 1991, 92; Scotland debut 1987; GB intermediate debut 1989, snr debut 1990. *Leisure interests*: swimming, golf, cycling. *Address*: 13 Balfour St, Leith, Edinburgh EH6 5DG.

PITTMAN, Stephen: footballer; b. 18 July 1967, N. Carolina, USA; player E. Fife 1986–89, Shrewsbury Town 89–92, Dundee 92– . *Address*: Dundee FC, Dens Park, Dundee DD3 7JY.

PLANGE, David: Rugby League footballer; b. 24 July 1965, Hull; player Scunthorpe (RU), Doncaster, Castleford, Sheffield Eagles 1991– ; with Castleford: winners Challenge Cup 1986; GB debut v. France 1988. *Address*: Sheffield Eagles RLFC, Stadium Corner, 824 Attercliffe Rd, Sheffield S9 3RS.

PLATFOOT, Calvin John: motorcyclist (off-road); b. 19 April 1963, Braintree; m. Vivien Platfoot 1991; 1 d.; E. Anglian expert solo enduro champ. 1991; ACU 250cc expert solo enduro champ. 1992. *Leisure interests*: swimming. *Address*: Deveron Lodge, Sheepcotes Lane, Silver End, Witham, Essex CM8 3PJ.

PLATT, David: footballer; b. 10 June 1966, Oldham; player Crewe Alexandra 1985–88, Aston Villa 88–91, Bari (Italy) 91–92, Juventus (Italy) 92–93, Sampdoria (Italy) 93– ; 3 England U-21 caps, over 42 full England caps. *Address*: c/o PFA, 2 Oxford Court, Bishopsgate, Manchester M2 3WQ.

PLEAT, David: football manager; b. 15 January 1945, Nottingham; player Nottingham Forest 1962–64, Luton Town 64–67, Shrewsbury Town 67–68, Exeter City 68–70, Peterborough Utd 70–71; manager Nuneaton, Luton Town 1978–86, Tottenham Hotspur 86–87, Leicester City 87–91, Luton Town 91– ; with Luton Town: 2nd Div. champs. 1981/82. *Address*: Luton Town FC, Kenilworth Stadium, 1 Maple Rd, Luton, Beds. LU4 8AW.

PLIMMER, Helen Claire: cricketer; b. 3 June 1965, Brit. Solomon Islands; player City of Leeds LCC 1985– ; rep. Yorks. 1985– ; Test debut and tour NZ 1991 (capt.), winners European Cup 1991, World Cup 1993; Sports Writers' Team of the Year award-winner 1993. *Leisure interests*: skiing, walking, golf. *Address*: 17 Woodhall Rd, Carverley, Leeds LS28 5NL.

PLUMB, Howard Richard: windsurfer; b. 28 August 1971, Chichester; UK Mistral champ. 1989–91, nat. series Mistral champ. 1989, Olympic-class champ. 1990; French youth champ. 1989; European U-21 Champs. raceboard bronze medal 1990; European Champs. Mistral gold medals 1990, 91. *Leisure interests*: skiing, golf, 5-a-side football, surfing. *Address*: `Mayfield', 5 Breach Ave, Southborne, Emsworth, Hants. PO10 8NB.

POINTON, Neil: footballer; b. 28 November 1964, Warslip Vale; player Scunthorpe Utd 1982–85, Everton 85–90, Manchester City 90–92, Oldham Athletic 92– . *Address*: Oldham Athletic FC, Boundary Park, Oldham, Lancs. OL1 2PA.

POLLARD, Paul Raymond: cricketer; b. 24 September 1968, Carlton, Notts.; m. Kate Pollard 1992; player Notts. 1987– , Sunday League champs. 1991. *Address*: Notts. CCC, Trent Bridge, Nottingham NG2 6AG.

POLLOCK, Jamie: footballer; b. 16 February 1974, Stockton; player Middlesbrough 1991– . *Address*: Middlesbrough FC, Ayresome Park, Middlesbrough, Cleveland TS1 4PB.

POLSTON, Jonathan: footballer; b. 10 June 1968, Walthamstow; player Tottenham Hotspur 1985–90, Norwich City 90– . *Address*: Norwich City FC, Carrow Rd, Norwich NR1 1JE.

PONTING, Nicholas James: badminton player; b. 13 September 1966, London; rep. Glos.; English doubles champ. 1991, mixed doubles champ. 1992–94; England debut 1988; European Champs. team bronze medal 1992; World Champs. mixed doubles bronze medal 1993; winner Welsh Open doubles 1989, 90, 91, 93, mixed doubles 1991, 93, Austrian Open doubles 1990, 93, mixed doubles 1993, Irish Open doubles and mixed doubles 1992, Canadian Open mixed doubles 1992. *Leisure interests*: golf, Oriental and Indian food, cinema, music. *Address*: 33 Furlong Lane, Bishop's Cleeve, Cheltenham GL52 4AG.

POOLE, Kevin: footballer; b. 21 July 1963, Bromsgrove; player Aston Villa 1981–87, Middlesbrough 87–91, Leicester City 91– . *Address*: Leicester City FC, City Stadium, Filbert St, Leicester LE2 7FL.

POOLEY, Guy Richard: oarsman; b. 2 October 1965, Watford; rep. Imperial College BC 1984–87 (capt. 1986), Cambridge Univ. BC 87–91 (Vice-Pres. 1990), Leander Club 91– ; GB amateur sculling champ. 1991, 92; GB U-23 debut 1986, snr debut 1989, Olympic squad (quadruple sculls) 1992. *Leisure interests*: playing the piano, skiing, coaching, juggling. *Address*: Eton College, Windsor, Berks. SL8 4DB.

POOLEY, Jason Cavin: cricketer; b. 8 August 1969, Hammersmith; player Middx 1989– , county champs. 1990, 93, Sunday League champs. 1992. *Address*: Middx CCC, Lord's Cricket Ground, London NW8 8QN.

PORTEOUS, Ian: footballer; b. 21 November 1964, Glasgow; player Aberdeen 1981–89, Herfolge FC (Denmark) 89–90,

Kilmarnock 90– . *Address*: Kilmarnock FC, Rugby Park, Kilmarnock KA1 2DP.

PORTER, Gary: footballer; b. 6 March 1966, Sunderland; player Watford 1984– ; 12 England U-21 caps. *Address*: Watford FC, Vicarage Rd Stadium, Watford, Herts. WD1 8ER.

POTTER, Laurie: cricketer; b. 7 November 1962, Bexley Heath; m. Helen Louise Potter 1989; 1 s.; player Kent 1981–85, Leics. 86–93; Aus. U-19 tour Pakistan 1981 (capt.). *Address*: Leics. CCC, County Ground, Grace Rd, Leicester LE2 8AD.

POTTER, Stuart: Rugby Union footballer; b. 11 November 1967, Lichfield, Staffs.; player Lichfield 1980–90, Nottingham 90–92, Leicester 92– ; with Leicester: winners Pilkington Cup 1993; rep. Midland Div.; England A debut v. Italy A 1993, tour Canada 1993. *Address*: Leicester FC, Welford Rd, Leicester LE2 7LF.

POTTS, Steven: footballer; b. 7 May 1967, Hartford, USA; player W. Ham Utd 1984– . *Address*: W. Ham Utd FC, Boleyn Ground, Green St, Upton Park, London E13 9AZ.

POWELL, Christopher: footballer; b. 8 September 1969, Lambeth; player Crystal Palace 1987–90, Southend Utd 90– . *Address*: Southend Utd FC, Roots Hall, Victoria Ave, Southend-on-Sea, Essex SS2 6NQ.

POWELL, Daio: Rugby League footballer; b. 9 March 1973, Leeds; player Middleton Marauders ARLFC, Bradford Northern 1990– ; Wales debut v. France 1994. *Address*: Bradford Northern RLFC, Odsal Stadium, Bradford BD6 1BS.

POWELL, Darryl: footballer; b. 15 November 1971, Lambeth; player Portsmouth 1988– . *Address*: Portsmouth FC, Fratton Park, Frogmore Rd, Portsmouth PO4 8RA.

POWELL, Daryl: Rugby League footballer; b. 21 July 1965, Castleford; player Glenora (NZ), Sheffield Eagles 1984– ; rep. Yorks.; GB debut v. France 1990, Brit. Lion tours NZ/Papua New Guinea 1990, Aus./NZ/ Papua New Guinea 1992. *Address*: Sheffield Eagles RLFC, Stadium Corner, 824 Attercliffe Rd, Sheffield S9 3RS.

POWELL, Lee: footballer; b. 2 June 1973, Caerleon; player Southampton 1991– ; 2 Wales U-21 caps. *Address*: Southampton FC, The Dell, Milton Rd, Southampton SO9 4XX.

POWELL, Roy Colin: Rugby League footballer; b. 30 April 1965, Dewsbury; player Leeds, Bradford Northern 1992– ; rep. Yorks.; GB debut v. France 1985. *Address*: Bradford Northern RLFC, Odsal Stadium, Bradford BD6 1BS.

POWER, Lee: footballer; b. 30 June 1972, Lewisham; player Norwich City 1990– ; 5 Ireland U-21 caps. *Address*: Norwich City FC, Carrow Rd, Norwich NR1 1JE.

PRATT, Gareth: Rugby League footballer; b. 23 August 1969; player Mayfield ARLFC, Leigh 1992– . *Address*: Leigh RLFC, Hilton Park, Kirkhall Lane, Leigh WN7 1RN.

PREAN, Carl: table tennis player; b. 20 August 1967, Isle of Wight; rep. Hants.; English champ. 1991, 93; European U-14 champ. 1982, jnr champ. 1985; European Champs. team silver medals 1988, 92, bronze 1990; World Champs. team bronze medal 1983; Olympic squad 1988, 92; winner Belgian Open 1985. *Leisure interests*: music, TV. *Address*: The Barn, 12 Marlborough Rd, Ryde, Isle of Wight PO33 1AA.

PREECE, David: footballer; b. 28 May 1963, Bridgnorth; player Walsall 1980–84, Luton Town 84– ; with Luton Town: winners League Cup 1988. *Address*: Luton Town FC, Kenilworth Stadium, 1 Maple Rd, Luton, Beds. LU4 8AW.

PRENN, John Allen Nicholas: rackets player; b. 30 August 1953, London; m. Jane Thomlinson 1992; GB amateur champ. 1979, 80, 82, 83, 91, doubles champ. 1988–91, 93, open champ. 1977, 80–83, 85, open doubles champ. 1986–90, 93; Canadian amateur champ. 1979, 81–86, 92; US open champ. 1980, 82, 85; world champ. 1981–84, 86, 87, doubles champ. 1990. *Leisure interests*: golf, real tennis. *Address*: 21 Clifford St, London W1X 1RH.

PRESSLEY, Steven: footballer; b. 11 October 1973, Elgin; player Rangers 1991– , winners Scottish Cup 1993; Scotland U-21 int. *Address*: Glasgow Rangers FC, Ibrox Stadium, 150 Edmiston Drive, Glasgow G51 2XD.

PRESSMAN, Kevin: footballer; b. 6 November 1967, Fareham; player Sheffield Wednesday 1985– ; with Sheffield Wednesday: winners League Cup 1991; 1 England U-21 cap. *Address*: Sheffield Wednesday FC, Hillsborough, Sheffield, S. Yorks. S6 1SW.

PRESTON, Allan: footballer; b. 16 August 1968, Edinburgh; player Dundee Utd 1985–92, Heart of Midlothian 92– . *Address*: Heart of Midlothian FC, Tynecastle Park, Gorgie Rd, Edinburgh EH11 2NL.

PRESTON, Luke William: judo player (U-55kg); b. 26 May 1976, Kensington; Welsh jnr champ. 1987–91, youth champ. 1993; GB U-18 champ. 1990; Wales jnr debut 1988; GB U-19 debut 1991. *Leisure interests*: football, tennis, swimming, running, music, reading. *Address*: The Red House, Greenhill Bank, Dudleston Heath, nr Ellesmere, Shropshire SY12 9LU.

PRESTON, Mark: Rugby League footballer; b. 3 April 1967, Lytham St Annes; player Wigan, Halifax 1991– ; England B int (RU). *Address*: Halifax RLFC, The Pavilion, Thrum Hall, Gibbet St, Halifax, W. Yorks. HX1 4TL.

PRICE, Gary: Rugby League footballer; b. 28 October 1969, Wakefield; player Wakefield Trinity, Featherstone Rovers 1993– ; GB debut v. Papua New Guinea 1991. *Address*: Featherstone Rovers RLFC, The Croft, Batley Rd, W. Ardsley, Wakefield WF3 1DX.

PRICE, John Haydn: flat green bowler; b. 14 September 1960, Neath; m. Anne Rosser Mizen 1989; rep. W. Glamorgan, Welsh county champs. 1983, 90, 91; Welsh U-25 singles champ. (outdoor) 1983, U-35 singles champ. (outdoor) 1986, singles champ. (indoor) 1981 (youngest-ever winner), 87, 88, 91, 93, pairs champ. (outdoor) 1981, (indoor) 1984, 93, triples champ. (outdoor) 1982, (indoor) 1983, fours champ. (indoor) 1980, 84; GB singles champ. (indoor) 1993, pairs champ. (outdoor) 1982, (indoor) 1993, triples champ. (outdoor) 1983; Wales debut (outdoor) 1984, (indoor) 1979 (capt. 1987); Commonwealth Games squad 1990; World Indoor Champs. singles gold medal 1900; winner Scottish Masters singles and Scottish Indoor Masters singles 1991, Dundee Masters 1992. *Leisure interests*: football, watching all sports. *Address*: 129 Victoria Rd, Port Talbot, W. Glamorgan SA12 6QH.

PRICE, Katrina: motorcyclist (off-road); b. 2 April 1965, Llandovery; ISDE team silver medals 1989 (Germany), 1991 (Czechoslovakia), bronze 1992 (Aus.); Welsh Motorcycle Personality of the Year 1990. *Leisure interests*: keep-fit. *Address*: Why-not, Myddfai Rd, Llandovery, Dyfed SA20 0LQ.

PRICE, Mary Elizabeth: flat green bowler; b. 27 August 1943, Taplow; m. Peter Edwin 1969; rep. Bucks. (outdoor) 1971– , Berks. (indoor) 1991– ; English women's singles champ. (outdoor) 1988, (indoor) 1985, 91, women's triples champ. (outdoor) 1986, 88; UK women's singles champ. (indoor) 1991; GB women's singles champ. (outdoor) 1989, (indoor) 1992; England debut (outdoor) 1984, (indoor) 1982;

Commonwealth Games women's fours bronze medal 1986, pairs bronze 1990; World Champs. women's pairs bronze and fours silver medals 1988; World Indoor Champs. women's singles gold medal 1991; 1st woman to have won both English indoor and outdoor singles titles. *Leisure interests*: horseriding, cooking Chinese meals. *Address*: Heatherdene, Green Lane, Farnham Common, Slough SL2 3SP.

PRICE, Richard: Rugby League footballer; b. 26 June 1970; player Hull, Sheffield Eagles 1991– . *Address*: Sheffield Eagles RLFC, Stadium Corner, 824 Attercliffe Rd, Sheffield S9 3RS.

PRICE, Violet Helen Katie Marie: judo player (U-61kg); b. 27 June 1976, Carmarthen; Welsh women's open and closed champ. 1992; Wales jnr debut 1986, snr debut 1992. *Leisure interests*: reading, swimming, dancing. *Address*: 76 Bro-myrddin, Johnstown, Carmarthen SA31 3HF.

PRICHARD, Paul John: cricketer; b. 7 January 1965, Brentwood; m. Jo-Anne Prichard 1991; 1 d.; player Essex 1984– (vice-capt. 93–), winners NatWest Trophy 1985, county champs. 1984, 86, 91, 92, Sunday League champs. 1984, 85; England A tour Aus. 1992/93; Britannic Assurance Player of the Year 1992. *Leisure interests*: golf, music, W. Ham Utd FC. *Address*: Essex CCC, County Cricket Ground, New Writtle St, Chelmsford DM2 0PG.

PRIESTLEY, Dennis: darts player; b. 16 July 1950, Mexborough; m. Jenny Priestley 1972; 3 s., 1 d.; Welsh open champ. 1992; GB open champ. 1993; Aus. open champ. 1992; Canadian open champ. 1993; world prof. champ. 1991, WDC world champ. 1994; England debut 1990 (capt. 1993–); winner Brit. Matchplay 1991, World Masters 1992. *Leisure interests*: all sport, nature. *Address*: 87A Church St, Mexborough, S. Yorks. S64 0EX.

PRIOR, Spencer: footballer; b. 22 April 1971, Southend; player Southend Utd 1989–93, Norwich City 93– . *Address:* Norwich City FC, Carrow Rd, Norwich NR1 1JE.

PROBYN, Jeffrey Alan: Rugby Union footballer; b. 27 April 1956, London; m. Jennifer Probyn; 2 s., 1 d.; player Ilford Wanderers, Streatham/Croydon, Richmond, Askeans, Wasps; England and Five Nations debut v. France 1988, Grand Slam champs. 1991, 92, tours Aus. 1988, Argentina 1990, Aus./Fiji 1991. *Publications: Upfront – The Jeff Probyn Story* (with Barry Newcombe), 1993. *Address:* Wasps FC, Wasps Football Ground, Repton Ave, Sudbury, nr Wembley, Middx HA0 3DW.

PROCTOR, Mark: footballer; b. 30 January 1961, Middlesbrough; player Middlesbrough 1978–81, Nottingham Forest 81–83, Sunderland 83–87, Sheffield Wednesday 87–88, Middlesbrough 88–93, Tranmere Rovers 93– ; 4 England U-21 caps. *Address:* Tranmere Rovers FC, Prenton Park, Prenton Rd W., Birkenhead, Merseyside L42 9PN.

PROCTOR, Wayne Thomas: Rugby Union footballer; b. 12 June 1972, Bridgend; player Llanelli, winners Welsh Cup 1992, 93, Welsh League champs. 1992/93; Wales U-21 debut v. Scotland 1992, snr debut v. Aus. 1992, Five Nations debut v. England 1993, tour Zimbabwe/Namibia 1993. *Address:* Llanelli RFC, Stradey Park, Llanelli, Dyfed.

PRUDHOE, Mark: footballer; b. 11 November 1963, Washington; player Sunderland 1981–84, Birmingham City 84–86, Walsall 86–87, Carlisle Utd 87–89, Darlington 89–93, Stoke City 93– ; with Darlington: 4th Div. champs. 1990/91. *Address:* Stoke City FC, Victoria Ground, Stoke on Trent, Staffs. ST4 4EG.

PUGSLEY, Stuart: Rugby League footballer; b. 14 November 1967; player Whitehaven, Leigh 1992– . *Address:* Leigh RLFC, Hilton Park, Kirkhall Lane, Leigh WN7 1RN.

PUTNEY, Trevor: footballer; b. 9 April 1960, Harold Hill; player Ipswich Town 1980–86, Norwich City 86–89, Middlesbrough 89–91, Watford 91–93, Leyton Orient 93– . *Address:* Leyton Orient FC, Leyton Stadium, Brisbane Rd, Leyton, London E10 5NE.

PYATT, Christopher: boxer; b. 3 July 1963; ABA jnr champ. 1980; ABA welterweight champ. 1982; England debut 1982; Commonwealth Games welterweight gold medal 1982; prof. debut 1983; titles won: GB light-middleweight, European light-middleweight 1986, Commonwealth light-middleweight 1991, WBC int. middleweight 1992, WBO middleweight 1993; over 41 prof. wins. *Address:* c/o Brit. Boxing Board of Control, Jack Petersen House, 52A Borough High St, London SE1 1XW.

PYMAN, Iain David: golfer; b. 3 March 1973, Whitby; Yorks. boys' champ. 1991, amateur champ. 1992, youth champ. 1993; English boys' amateur open strokeplay champ. 1991; GB amateur champ. 1993; England debut 1991; GB youth debut and Walker Cup team 1993. *Leisure interests:* music, travel, TV. *Address:* 48 Barfield Crescent, Leeds LS17 8RU.

QUINN, James: footballer; b. 18 November 1959, Belfast, NI; player Swindon Town 1981–84, Blackburn Rovers 84–86, Swindon Town 86–88, Leicester City 88–89, Bradford City 1989, W. Ham Utd 1989–91, Bournemouth 91–92, Reading 92– ; over 34 NI caps. *Address:* Reading FC, Elm Park, Norfolk Rd, Reading, Berks. RG3 2EF.

QUINN, Michael: footballer; b. 2 May 1962, Liverpool; m. Sheila Quinn; 2 d.; player Wigan Athletic 1979–82, Stockport County 82–84, Oldham Athletic 84–86, Portsmouth 86–89, Newcastle Utd 89–92, Coventry City 92–   . *Address*: Coventry City FC, Highfield Rd Stadium, King Richard St, Coventry CV2 4FW.

QUINN, Niall: footballer; b. 6 October 1966, Dublin; player Arsenal 1983–90, Manchester City 90–   ; with Arsenal: winners League Cup 1987; 1 Ireland U-21 cap, over 39 full Ireland caps. *Address*: Manchester City FC, Maine Rd, Moss Side, Manchester M14 7WN.

QUINNELL, Leon (Scott): Rugby Union footballer; b. 20 August 1972, Llanelli; player Llanelli, winners Welsh Cup 1992, 93, Welsh League champs. 1992/93; Wales U-21 debut v. Scotland 1992, snr debut v. Canada 1993. *Address*: Llanelli RFC, Stradey Park, Llanelli, Dyfed.

QUIRK, Les: Rugby League footballer; b. 6 March 1965, Barrow; player Barrow, St Helens 1987–   ; with St Helens: winners John Player Special Trophy 1988; rep. Cumbria. *Address*: St Helens RLFC, Dunriding Lane, St Helens, Merseyside WA10 4AD.

RADCLIFFE, Paula Jane: athlete; b. 17 December 1973, Davenham; inter-counties and English women's intermediate cross-country champ., English schools women's 1500m champ. 1991, English, UK and world women's jnr cross-country champ., English schools women's 3000m champ. 1992, GB students women's cross-country champ. 1993; GB intermediate debut 1991; European Cup women's U-23 3000m gold medal 1992. *Leisure interests*: swimming, reading, socializing, music, travel. *Address*: 12 Lovell Rd, Oakley, Beds. MK43 7RZ.

RADFORD, Neal Victor: cricketer; b. 7 June 1957, Luanshya, Zambia; m. Lynne Mary Radford 1985; 2 s.; player Lancs. 1980–84, Worcs. 85–   ; with Lancs.: winners Benson and Hedges Cup 1984; with Worcs.: winners Benson and Hedges Cup 1991, county champs. 1988, 89, Sunday League champs. 1987, 88; 3 Tests, debut 1986, 6 1-day ints, tour NZ/Aus. 1987/88; Cricketers' Assoc. Cricketer of the Year and *Wisden* Cricketer of the Year 1985. *Leisure interests*: golf, family. *Address*: Worcs. CCC, County Ground, New Rd, Worcester WR2 4QQ.

RAE, Alexander: footballer; b. 30 September 1969, Glasgow; player Falkirk 1987–90, Millwall 90–   ; 5 Scotland U-21 caps. *Address*: Millwall FC, The Den, Zampa Rd, Bermondsey, London SE16 3LH.

RAESIDE, Robert: footballer; b. 7 July 1972, SA; player Raith Rovers 1990–   . *Address*: Raith Rovers FC, Stark's Park, Pratt St, Kirkcaldy, Fife KY1 1SA.

RAFFERTY, Ronan Patrick: golfer; b. 13 January 1964, Newry, NI; m. Clare Rafferty 1987; 1 s., 1 d.; Irish amateur champ., joint English open amateur strokeplay champ. 1980; Ireland debut 1980; GBI debut 1980, Walker Cup team 1981; prof. debut 1982; Aus. matchplay champ. 1988; Dunhill Cup team (Ireland) 1986–93, winners 1988, 90; Ryder Cup team 1989; winner Venezuelan Open 1982, S. Aus. Open, NZ Open 1987, Equity and Law Challenge 1988, Italian Open, Scandinavian Open, Volvo Masters 1989, Swiss Open 1990, Portuguese Open 1992, Austrian Open 1993. *Leisure interests*: wine-collecting, clay pigeon shooting. *Address*: Int. Management Group, Pier House, Strand on the Green, London W4 3NN.

RAMMELL, Andrew: footballer; b. 10 February 1967, Nuneaton; player Barnsley 1990–   . *Address*: Barnsley FC, Oakwell Ground, Barnsley, S. Yorks. S71 1ET.

RAMPRAKASH, Mark Ravindra: cricketer; b. 5 September 1969, Bushey; player Middx 1987– , winners NatWest Trophy 1988, county champs. 1990, 93, Sunday League champs. 1992; England A tour Pakistan 1990/91, WI 1991/92, Test debut 1991, tours NZ 1991/92, WI 1994. *Address*: Middx CCC, Lord's Cricket Ground, London NW8 8QN.

RAMSAY, Alison Gail: hockey player; b. 16 April 1959, London; player Glasgow Western, European Cup silver medallists 1990, 91, 92, Scottish League champs. 1980–93; Scotland debut 1982, European Cup squad 1987, 89, 91, World Cup squad 1983, 86; GB debut 1985, Olympic squad 1988, 92; highest-capped Scottish and GB player; holds world record for int. outdoor caps (214). *Leisure interests*: driving fast cars, gardening, sunbathing. *Address*: Willowburn, Pitroddie, Perthshire.

RANKINE, Mark: footballer; b. 30 September 1969, Doncaster; player Doncaster Rovers 1988–92, Wolverhampton Wanderers 92– . *Address*: Wolverhampton Wanderers FC, Molineux Stadium, Waterloo Rd, Wolverhampton WV1 4QR.

RATCLIFFE, Jason David: cricketer; b. 19 June 1969, Solihull; player Warks. 1988– , winners NatWest Trophy 1993, tour SA 1991/92. *Address*: Warks. CCC, County Ground, Edgbaston, Birmingham B5 7QU.

RATTRAY, Brian: flat green bowler; b. 8 July 1949, Tillicoultry, Clackmannanshire; m. Allyson Rattray 1974; 1 s.; Scottish singles champ. (outdoor) 1982; Scotland debut (outdoor) 1975; Commonwealth Games squad 1982; World Champs. team gold medal 1984. *Leisure interests*: watching movies at home. *Address*: 48 Gartmorn Rd, Sauchie, Clackmannanshire FK10 3NX.

RAVEN, Paul: footballer; b. 28 July 1970, Salisbury; player Doncaster Rovers 1988–89, W. Bromwich Albion 89– .

Address: W. Bromwich Albion FC, The Hawthorns, W. Bromwich B71 4LF.

RAVENSCROFT, Stephen: Rugby Union footballer; b. 2 November 1970, Bradford; player Northcote (NZ), Saracens 1990– ; England U-21 debut v. Ireland U-21 1991. *Address*: Saracens FC, Bramley Rd Sports Ground, Chaseside, Southgate, London N14 4AB.

RAW, Andrew: Rugby League footballer; b. 15 September 1967, Leeds; player Yew Tree ARLFC, Hunslet, Wakefield Trinity 1992– . *Address*: Wakefield Trinity RLFC, 171 Doncaster Rd, Belle Vue, Wakefield WF1 5EZ.

RAYER, Michael Anthony: Rugby Union footballer; b. 21 July 1965, Cardiff; player Llandudno, Cardiff 1984– ; Wales debut v. W. Samoa 1991, Five Nations debut v. England 1992, tour Zimbabwe/Namibia 1993. *Address*: Cardiff RFC, Cardiff Arms Park, Westgate St, Cardiff CF1 1JA.

RAYNOR, Paul: footballer; b. 29 April 1966, Nottingham; player Nottingham Forest 1984–85, Huddersfield Town 85–87, Swansea City 87–92, Cambridge Utd 92–93, Preston N. End 93– . *Address*: Preston N. End FC, Deepdale, Preston, Lancs. PR1 6RU.

REDFEARN, Neil: footballer; b. 20 June 1965, Dewsbury; player Bolton Wanderers 1982–83, Lincoln City 83–86, Doncaster Rovers 86–87, Crystal Palace 87–88, Watford 88–89, Oldham Athletic 89–91, Barnsley 91– ; with Oldham Athletic: 2nd Div. champs. 1990/91. *Address*: Barnsley FC, Oakwell Ground, Barnsley, S. Yorks. S71 1ET.

REDGRAVE, Steven Geoffrey: oarsman; b. 23 March 1962, Amersham; m. Elizabeth-Ann Redgrave; 1 d.; rep. Marlow RC 1976– , Leander Club 87– ; winner Diamond Sculls, Henley Royal Regatta

1983, 85; Commonwealth Games single sculls, coxless pairs and coxed fours gold medals 1986; World Champs. coxed pairs gold medal 1986, silver 1987, coxless pairs gold 1987, 91 (world record), 93, silver 1989, bronze 1990; World Indoor Champs. gold medal 1991; Olympic coxed fours gold medal 1984, coxless pairs gold 1988, 92 (Olympic record), coxed pairs bronze 1988; GB 4-man bobsleigh champ. 1989. *Publications: Steven Redgrave's Complete Book of Rowing*, 1992. *Leisure interests*: golf, skiing, bobsleigh. *Address*: c/o Brit. Olympic Assoc., 1 Wandsworth Plain, London SW18 1EH.

REDKNAPP, Jamie: footballer; b. 25 June 1973, Barton-on-Sea; player Bournemouth 1990–91, Liverpool 91–   . *Address*: Liverpool FC, Anfield Rd, Liverpool L4 0TH.

REDMAN, Nigel Charles: Rugby Union footballer; b. 16 August 1965, Cardiff; m. Lorinda Redman; player Weston-super-Mare, Bath 1983–   ; with Bath: winners Pilkington Cup 1984, 85, 86, 87, 90, 92, League champs. 1990/91, 91/92, 92/93; rep. S.W. Div.; England B debut 1986, snr debut v. Aus. 1984, Five Nations debut v. Scotland 1986, tours Aus./NZ (World Cup) 1987, Argentina 1990, Aus./Fiji 1991, Canada (England A) 1993. *Address*: Bath RFC, Recreation Ground, Bath BA2 6PW.

REDMOND, Derek: athlete; b. 3 September 1965, Bletchley; m. Sharron Davies (qv) 1994; 1 s.; European Cup 400m bronze medal 1985; European Champs. 4 x 400m relay gold medal 1986; World Champs. 4 x 400m relay silver medal 1987, gold 1991. *Address*: c/o Brit. Athletic Fed., 225A Bristol Rd, Edgbaston, Birmingham B5 7UB.

REDMOND, Stephen: footballer; b. 2 November 1967, Liverpool; player Manchester City 1984–92, Oldham Athletic 92–   ; 14 England U-21 caps. *Address*: Oldham Athletic FC, Boundary Park, Oldham, Lancs. OL1 2PA.

REDPATH, Bryan William: Rugby Union footballer; b. 2 July 1971, Galashiels; player Melrose, Scottish League champs. 1991/92; rep. S. of Scotland; Scotland U-21 debut v. Wales 1991, snr tour Fiji/Tonga/W. Samoa 1993. *Address*: Melrose RFC, The Greenyards, Melrose TD6 9SA.

REED, Andrew Ian: Rugby Union footballer; b. 4 May 1969, St Austell; m. Sarah Reed; player Bodmin, Camborne, Plymouth Albion, Bath 1990–   ; with Bath: tour Aus. 1990; rep. Cornwall, county champs. 1990/91; Scotland and Five Nations debut v. Ireland 1993; Brit. Lions tour NZ 1993. *Address*: Bath FC, Recreation Ground, Bath, Avon.

REES, Anthony: footballer; b. 1 August 1964, Merthyr Tydfil; player Birmingham City 1983–88, Barnsley 87–89, Grimsby Town 89–   ; 1 Wales U-21 cap, 1 full Wales cap. *Address*: Grimsby Town FC, Blundell Park, Cleethorpes, S. Humberside DN35 7PY.

REES, Jason: footballer; b. 22 December 1969, Aberdare; player Luton Town 1988–   ; 3 Wales U-21 caps, 1 full Wales cap. *Address*: Luton Town FC, Kenilworth Stadium, 1 Maple Rd, Luton, Beds. LU4 8AW.

REES, Melvyn: footballer; b. 25 January 1967, Cardiff; player Cardiff City 1984–87, Watford 87–90, W. Bromwich Albion 90–92, Sheffield Utd 92–   . *Address*: Sheffield Utd FC, Bramall Lane, Sheffield, S. Yorks S2 4SU.

REEVE, Dermot Alexander: cricketer; b. 2 April 1963, Hong Kong; m. Julie Reeve 1986; 1 d.; player Sussex 1983–87, Warks. 88–   (capt. 93–   ); with Sussex: winners NatWest Trophy 1986; with Warks.: winners NatWest Trophy 1989, 93; 3 Tests, 15 1-day ints, England tours NZ/Aus. (World Cup) 1991/92, India/Sri Lanka 1992/93. *Address*: Warks. CCC, County Ground, Edgbaston, Birmingham B5 7QU.

REEVES, David: footballer; b. 19 November 1967, Birkenhead; player Sheffield Wednesday 1986–89, Bolton Wanderers 89–92, Notts County 92–93, Carlisle Utd 93– . *Address:* Carlisle Utd FC, Brunton Park, Warwick Rd, Carlisle CA1 1LL.

REGAN, Robbie: boxer; b. 30 August 1968; Wales debut 1986; prof. debut 1989; titles won: Welsh flyweight, GB flyweight 1991, European flyweight 1992; over 10 prof. wins. *Address:* c/o Dai Gardiner, 13 Hengoed Hall Drive, Cefn Hengoed, Hengoed, Mid Glamorgan.

REGIS, Cyrille: footballer; b. 9 February 1958, Maripasoula, French Guyana; m. Beverley Marie Regis; 1 s., 1 d.; player W. Bromwich Albion 1977–84, Coventry City 84–91, Aston Villa 91–93, Wolverhampton Wanderers 93– ; with Coventry City: winners FA Cup 1987; 6 England U-21 caps, 5 England B caps, 5 full England caps; PFA Young Player of the Year 1978. *Address:* Wolverhampton Wanderers FC, Molineux Stadium, Waterloo Rd, Wolverhampton WV1 4QR.

REGIS, John: athlete; b. 13 October 1966, Lewisham; AAA 200m champ. 1986, 87, 90, 92; UK 200m champ. 1985 (joint), 86, 91, 93, 100m champ. 1988; European Jnr Champs. 100m bronze and 4 x 100m relay gold medals 1985; Commonwealth Games 200m silver and 4 x 100m relay gold medals 1990; European Champs. 200m gold, 4 x 100m relay silver, 4 x 400m relay gold, 100m bronze medals 1990; European Cup 200m and 4 x 100m relay gold medals 1989, 200m silver and 4 x 100m relay gold 1991, 200m, 4 x 100m relay and 4 x 400m relay gold 1993; European Indoor Champs. 200m bronze medal 1987, silver 1989; World Champs. 200m bronze medals 1987, 91, 4 x 100m relay bronze 1987, 4 x 400m relay gold 1987, 200m and 4 x 100m relay silver 1993; World Cup 4 x 100m relay silver medal 1989; World Indoor Champs. 200m gold medal 1989; Olympic 4 x 100m relay silver medal 1988, 4 x 400m relay bronze 1992; UK 200m record-holder. *Address:* c/o Brit. Athletic Fed., 225A Bristol Rd, Edgbaston, Birmingham B5 7UB.

REID, Carolyn Marie: hockey player; b. 28 March 1972, Liverpool; player Hightown Ladies 1986– , European Cup Winners' Cup silver medallist 1993, club champs. 1992, indoor club champs. 1991, 92, 93; rep. Merseyside U-18 1985–89, Lancs. indoor 1987– ; England U-18 debut 1989 (capt. 89/90), U-21 debut 1991 (capt. 92/93), snr debut and home countries champs. 1992; England U-21 indoor debut and European Indoor Cup U-21 silver medallist 1991, snr debut 1989, European Indoor Cup silver medallist 1993; youngest-ever snr England indoor player. *Leisure interests:* tennis, swimming, aerobics, reading, music, socializing. *Address:* Hightown Ladies HC, Thirlmere Rd, Hightown, Merseyside.

REID, Chris: footballer; b. 4 November 1971, Edinburgh; player Hibernian 1989– ; Scotland U-21 int. *Address:* Hibernian FC, Easter Rd Stadium, 64 Albion Rd, Edinburgh EH7 5QG.

REID, Dale: golfer; b. 20 March 1959, Ladybank, Fife; Fife girls' champ. 1973, 75; Scotland debut 1978; prof. debut 1979; Solheim Cup team 1990, 92, winners 1992; winner Guernsey Open 1982, European Open 1987, 88, Scottish Ladies' Open 1987, Ford Classic 1991. *Address:* c/o Women's Prof. Golf European Tour, The Tytherington Club, Dorchester Way, Tytherington, Macclesfield, Cheshire SK10 2JP.

REID, John Andrew: jockey (Flat); b. 6 August 1955, Banbridge, NI; m. Amanda Joy Reid 1983; 2 s., 1 d.; winner King George VI and Queen Elizabeth Diamond Stakes 1978 (Ile de Bourbon), 1000 Guineas 1982 (On the House), Irish Derby 1987 (Sir Harry Lewis), Prix de l'Arc de Triomphe

1988 (Tony Bin), Derby 1992 (Dr Devious). *Leisure interests*: working on my farm. *Address*: Middle Green Farm, Baulking Green, nr Faringdon, Oxon SN7 7QE.

REILLY, Mark: footballer; b. 30 March 1969, Bellshill; player Motherwell 1988–91, Kilmarnock 91– . *Address*: Kilmarnock FC, Rugby Park, Kilmarnock KA1 2DP.

RENDLE, Sharon Susan, MBE: judo player (U-52kg); b. 18 June 1966, Hull; Commonwealth Games gold medal 1990; European Champs. gold medal 1990; World Champs. gold medals 1987, 89, silver 1991; Olympic gold medal (demonstration) 1988, bronze 1992; only judo player to have held Brit., Commonwealth, European, world and Olympic titles simultaneously. *Leisure interests*: reading, bowling, music. *Address*: 10 Hawthorn Ave, New Waltham, Grimsby DN36 4PS.

RENNELL, Mark Ian: Rugby Union footballer; b. 17 January 1971, Stratford-upon-Avon; player Abbey, Bedford 1990–93, Rugby 93– ; rep. Midland Div. U-21 1991–93; England U-21 debut and tour France/The Netherlands 1991, England A tour Canada 1993; Berks. schools shot-put champ. 1987, Oxon cross-country champ. 1988. *Leisure interests*: cricket, volleyball, hang gliding, marine wildlife. *Address*: The Rugby FC, Webb Ellis Rd, off Bilton Rd, Rugby, Warks.

RENNIE, David: footballer; b. 29 August 1964, Edinburgh; player Leicester City 1983–86, Leeds Utd 86–89, Bristol City 89–92, Birmingham City 92–93, Coventry City 93– . *Address*: Coventry City FC, Highfield Rd Stadium, King Richard St, Coventry CV2 4FW.

REYNOLDS, John Patrick: Eton fives player; b. 9 August 1961, Whitechapel; m. Kathryn Clinkscales 1992; player Old Citizens 1976– , The Artists 84– ; rep. Essex 1980– ; GB schools champ. 1979;

England debut 1980; winner Kinnaird Cup 1981–91 (record). *Publications*: *Fives: How to Play Eton Fives*, 1993. *Leisure interests*: photography, cooking, drinking. *Address*: c/o The Eton Fives Assoc., P.O. Box 27, Farnham, Surrey.

RHODES, Andrew: footballer; b. 23 August 1964, Askern; player Barnsley 1982–85, Doncaster Rovers 85–88, Oldham Athletic 88–90, Dunfermline Athletic 90–92, St Johnstone 92– . *Address*: St Johnstone FC, McDiarmid Park, Crieff Rd, Perth PH1 2SJ.

RHODES, Jane Louise: Alpine skier; b. 7 November 1975, Perth; E. of Scotland women's jnr slalom champ. 1993; Scottish schoolgirls' champ. 1993; Scotland debut 1991. *Leisure interests*: athletics, badminton, singing. *Address*: `Ormiston', 16 Brompton Terrace, Perth PH2 7DH.

RHODES, Steven John: cricketer; b. 17 June 1964, Bradford; player Yorks. 1981–84, Worcs. 85– ; with Worcs.: county champs. 1988, 89, Sunday League champs. 1987, 88; England B tour Sri Lanka 1985/86, England A tours Zimbabwe/Kenya 1989/90, Pakistan 1990/91, WI 1991/92, SA 1993/94, 3 1-day ints. *Address*: Worcs. CCC, County Ground, New Rd, Worcester WR2 4QQ.

RICHARDS, Dean: Rugby Union footballer; b. 11 July 1963, Nuneaton; m. Nicky Richards; player Roanne (France), Leicester 1982– ; with Leicester: winners Pilkington Cup 1993; rep. Midland Div.; England and Five Nations debut v. Ireland 1986, Grand Slam champs. 1991, 92, tour Aus./Fiji 1991; Brit. Lions tour Aus. 1989; Whitbread/*Rugby World* Player of the Year 1991. *Address*: Leicester FC, Welford Rd, Leicester LE2 7LF.

RICHARDSON, Kevin: footballer; b. 4 December 1962, Newcastle; player Everton 1981–86, Watford 86–87, Arsenal 87–90, Real Sociedad (Spain) 90–91, Aston Villa

91– (capt.); with Everton: winners FA Cup 1984, European Cup Winners' Cup 1985, League champs. 1984/85; with Arsenal: League champs. 1988/89. *Address*: Aston Villa FC, Villa Park, Trinity Rd, Birmingham B6 6HE.

RICHARDSON, Lee: footballer; b. 12 March 1969, Halifax; player Halifax Town 1987–89, Watford 89–90, Blackburn Rovers 90–92, Aberdeen 92– . *Address*: Aberdeen FC, Pittodrie Stadium, Pittodrie St, Aberdeen AB2 1QH.

RICHARDSON, Richard Benjamin: cricketer; b. 12 January 1962, Antigua; player Yorks. 1993– ; Test debut 1983, WI tours India 1983/84, England 1984, Aus. 1984/85, Pakistan/NZ 1986/87, India 1987/88, England 1988, Aus. 1988/89, England 1991, Pakistan 1991/92, Aus./NZ (World Cup) 1991/92, Aus./SA 1992/93; WI capt. 1991– . *Address*: Yorks. CCC, Headingley Cricket Ground, Leeds LS6 3BU.

RICHARDSON, Steven: golfer; b. 24 July 1966, Windsor; English amateur champ. 1989; England debut 1986; prof. debut 1989; Dunhill Cup team 1991, 92, winners 1992; Ryder Cup team 1991; winner Girona Open, Portuguese Open 1991. *Address*: c/o PGA European Tour, Wentworth Club, Wentworth Drive, Virginia Water, Surrey GU25 4LS.

RICKETTS, Joan Vivien: flat green bowler; b. 14 September 1922, Hull; m. Ronald Edmund Ricketts; 2 s., 1 d.; Welsh women's triples champ. (outdoor) 1983; Wales debut (outdoor) 1977, (indoor) 1979, Commonwealth Games women's fours gold medal 1986. *Address*: 87 Park Crescent, Abergavenny, Gwent NP7 5TL.

RIDGEON, Jonathan Peter: athlete; b. 14 February 1967, Bury St Edmunds; European Jnr Champs. 110m hurdles gold medal 1985; World Jnr Champs. 4 x 100m relay gold and 110m hurdles silver medals 1986; World

Student Games 110m hurdles gold medal 1987; European Indoor Champs. 60m hurdles silver medal 1988; World Champs. 110m hurdles silver medal 1987; World Cup 400m hurdles silver and 4 x 400m relay bronze medals 1992. *Publications*: contributor to *Athletics Today*, 1989, *New Studies in Athletics*, 1990, *Coaching Focus*, 1991. *Leisure interests*: travel, hill-walking, seeing friends. *Address*: c/o Brit. Athletic Fed., 225A Bristol Rd, Edgbaston, Birmingham B5 7UB.

RIGG, Gordon Stirling: hang glider pilot; b. 2 December 1962, Warrington; m. Kathleen Rigg 1990; GB cross-country league champ. 1989, defined cross-country league champ. 1992; GB debut 1990; GB open distance record-holder. *Leisure interests*: training, mountain biking. *Address*: 57 New St, New Mills, Stockport, Cheshire SK12 4PD.

RIGG, Suzanne: athlete; b. Essex, Iowa, USA; m. John Rigg 1990; rep. Cheshire 1992– ; women's inter-counties cross-country champ. 1993; AAA women's 5000m champ. 1993; world women's cross-country trials champ. 1993; GB debut 1992, World Half-Marathon Champs. squad 1992, European Cup and World Cross-Country Champs. squads 1993. *Leisure interests*: DIY crafts, needlework, piano. *Address*: 9 Watton Close, Thelwall, Warrington, Cheshire.

RILEY, David: footballer; b. 8 December 1960, Northampton; player Nottingham Forest 1984–87, Port Vale 87–90, Peterborough Utd 90– . *Address*: Peterborough Utd FC, London Rd Ground, Peterborough, Cambs. PE2 8AL.

RILEY, Michael: Rugby League footballer; b. 20 November 1970, Widnes; player Widnes Tigers ARLFC, St Helens 1990– ; with St Helens: winners Premiership 1993. *Address*: St Helens RLFC, Dunriding Lane, St Helens, Merseyside WA10 4AD.

RING, Mark Gerarde: Rugby Union footballer; b. 15 October 1962, Cardiff; player Cardiff 1981–87, Pontypool 87–88, Cardiff 88–93, Pontypool 93– (capt.); Wales B tours Spain 1983, Canada 1989, snr and Five Nations debut v. England 1983, tours NZ 1988, Namibia 1990; Welsh Rugby Player of the Year 1985; Wales baseball int., 4 caps. *Leisure interests*: horseracing. *Address*: Pontypool RFC, Pontypool Park, HQ Elm House, Park Rd, Pontypool, Gwent.

RINGER, Thomas Antony: full-bore rifle shooter; b. 5 September 1966, Norwich; rep. Norfolk 1984– ; England debut 1992, Mackinnon Match team 1992, 93 (winners 1993); GB debut 1988, Palma Match team (winners) 1992, Kolapore Match team (winners) 1993; winner Queen's Prize, Bisley 1992; rep. Norfolk U-21 hockey. *Leisure interests*: hockey, golf, tennis, squash, cricket, studying, farming, vermin control. *Address*: The Grange, W. Rudham, King's Lynn, Norfolk PE31 8SY.

RIOCH, Bruce: football manager; b. 6 September 1947, Aldershot; player Luton Town 1964–69, Aston Villa 69–74, Derby County 74–76, Everton 76–77, Derby County 77–79, Seattle (USA) 79–80, Torquay Utd 80–83; 24 Scotland caps; player/manager Middlesbrough 1986–90, manager Millwall 90–92, Bolton Wanderers 92– . *Address*: Bolton Wanderers FC, Burnden Park, Manchester Rd, Bolton, Lancs. BL3 2QR.

RIPLEY, David: cricketer; b. 13 September 1966, Leeds; m. Jackie Ripley 1988; 1 s.; player Northants. 1984– , tour Durban (SA) 1992; England YC tour WI 1984/85. *Address*: Northants. CCC, County Cricket Ground, Wantage Rd, Northampton NN1 4TJ.

RIPLEY, Stuart: footballer; b. 20 November 1967, Middlesbrough; player Middlesbrough 1984–92, Blackburn Rovers 92– ; England debut v. San Marino 1993. *Address*: Blackburn Rovers FC, Ewood Park, Blackburn, Lancs. BB2 4JF.

RITCHIE, Andrew: footballer; b. 28 November 1960, Manchester; player Manchester Utd 1977–80, Brighton and Hove Albion 80–83, Leeds Utd 83–87, Oldham Athletic 87– ; with Oldham Athletic: 2nd Div. champs. 1990/91; 1 England U-21 cap. *Address*: Oldham Athletic FC, Boundary Park, Oldham, Lancs. OL1 2PA.

RITCHIE, Paul: footballer; b. 25 January 1969, St Andrews; player Dundee 1986– . *Address*: Dundee FC, Dens Park, Dundee DD3 7JY.

RIX, Graham: footballer; b. 23 October 1957, Askern; player Arsenal 1976–87, Dundee 92– ; 7 England U-21 caps, 17 full England caps. *Address*: Dundee FC, Dens Park, Dundee DD3 7JY.

ROBB, Curtis: athlete; b. 7 June 1972, Liverpool; AAA 1500m jnr champ. 1990, 91; AAA 800m champ. 1992; UK 800m champ. 1992, 1500m champ. 1993; European Jnr Champs. 800m gold medal 1991; World Student Games 800m silver medal 1991. *Address*: c/o Brit. Athletic Fed., 225A Bristol Rd, Edgbaston, Birmingham B5 7UB.

ROBERTS, Andrew: footballer; b. 20 March 1974, Dartford; player Millwall 1991– . *Address*: Millwall FC, The Den, Zampa Rd, Bermondsey, London SE16 3LH.

ROBERTS, Anthony: footballer; b. 4 August 1969, Holyhead; player Queens Park Rangers 1987– ; Wales int. *Address*: Queens Park Rangers FC, Rangers Stadium, S. Africa Rd, London W12 7PA.

ROBERTS, Martin John: Rugby Union footballer; b. 26 January 1968, Gloucester; 1 d.; player Cheltenham 1985–89, Gloucester 89– . *Leisure interests*: weight training, walking, DIY, local league football. *Address*: Gloucester RUFC, Kingsholm, Worcester St, Gloucester GL3 3AX.

ROBERTS, Michael Leonard: jockey (Flat); b. 17 May 1954, SA; m. Verna Roberts 1976; 2 d.; winner King George VI and Queen Elizabeth Diamond Stakes 1988 (Mtoto), 1993 (Opera House), 2000 Guineas 1991 (Mystiko), Oaks 1993 (Intrepidity), Irish 2000 Guineas 1993 (Barathea); champ. jockey 1992 (206 wins); 1st jockey to ride 200 winners in season in SA 1982. *Address*: c/o BHB, 42 Portman Square, London W1H 0EN.

ROBERTS, Neil Howarth: Rugby fives player; b. 14 July 1960, Settle; m. Gillian Eva Roberts 1992; rep. Rugby Fives Assoc., White Rose (capt.); with Rugby Fives Assoc.: tour USA 1987; with White Rose: club knockout champs. 1990, tour USA 1989; N. of England champ. 1990, W. of England champ. 1991, 92; Scottish open champ. 1989–92; GB doubles champ. 1991–93; GB Winchester fives doubles champ. 1992. *Leisure interests*: squash, fell-walking. *Address*: The Dalehead Veterinary Group, Station Rd, Settle, N. Yorks. BD24 9AA.

ROBERTS, Philippa Mary Elizabeth, MBE: water skier; b. 11 April 1960, Manchester; GB ladies' slalom champ. 1974, 93, jump champ. 1993, overall champ. 1977, 82, 85–92; GB debut 1974; European Jnr Champs. girls' overall gold medals 1974–78; European Champs. ladies' jump gold medal 1985, bronze 1992, slalom gold 1991, silver 1992, overall gold 1986, 90, silver 1993; European Masters ladies' jump gold medal 1990, slalom gold 1991, slalom and overall gold 1992; World Games ladies' slalom gold medals 1989, 93. *Leisure interests*: snow skiing. *Address*: 20 Gregory Drive, Old Windsor, Berks SL4 2RG.

ROBERTSON, David: footballer; b. 17 October 1968, Aberdeen; player Aberdeen 1986–91, Rangers 91– ; with Aberdeen: winners Scottish Cup, Scottish League Cup 1990; with Rangers: winners Scottish Cup 1992, 93, Scottish League Cup 1993; Scotland int. *Address*: Glasgow Rangers FC, Ibrox Stadium, 150 Edmiston Drive, Glasgow G51 2XD.

ROBERTSON, Graham: flat green bowler; b. 3 June 1957, Musselburgh, East Lothian; m. Helen Robertson 1982; 5 d.; Scottish singles champ. (outdoor) 1987, (indoor) 1989, 90, Scottish pairs champ. (indoor) 1989, 91, 94, triples champ. (indoor) 1992; Scottish int. debut (outdoor) 1985, (indoor) 1987; GB singles champ. (outdoor) 1988, (indoor) 1990, pairs champ. (indoor) 1991, triples champ. (indoor) 1992; World Champs. fours and team gold medals, triples bronze 1992; winner Irish Jack High and Scottish Masters (outdoor) 1989, Hong Kong Classic singles 1990, 93, pairs 1990, Dundee Masters 1991, Scottish Masters (indoor) 1992, 93; 1st Scotsman to win both GB indoor and outdoor singles titles. *Leisure interests*: watching all sports, swimming. *Address*: 7 Duncan Gardens, Tranent, E. Lothian EH33 1DD.

ROBERTSON, Iain Thompson: ice hockey player; b. 2 June 1969, Kirkcaldy; player Kirkcaldy Kestrels 1986–87, Fife Flyers 87–88, Ayr Raiders 88–90, Fife Flyers 90– ; with Fife Flyers: Div. 1 champs. 1991/92; Scotland debut 1991; GB U-19 and U-21 debuts 1986, World U-21 Champs. bronze medal (Pool C) 1987, snr debut 1990, World Champs. gold medals (Pool C) 1992, (Pool B) 1993; Young Brit. Player of the Year 1989/90. *Leisure interests*: golf, curling. *Address*: 186 St Clair St, Kirkcaldy, Fife KY1 2DG.

ROBERTSON, John: footballer; b. 2 October 1964, Edinburgh; player Heart of Midlothian 1980–88, Newcastle Utd 88–89, Heart of Midlothian 89– ; 1 Scotland U-21 cap, over 10 full Scotland caps. *Address*: Heart of Midlothian FC, Tynecastle Park, Gorgie Rd, Edinburgh EH11 2NL.

ROBERTSON, Julian Anthony:
badminton player; b. 9 October 1969,
Peterborough; English doubles champ.
1993; England debut 1991. *Leisure interests*:
golf, squash, gym, aerobics, swimming,
running, music. *Address*: 6 Kirkstone Walk,
Cakeview, Northampton NN8 1PY.

ROBERTSON, Michelle Alice: hockey
player; b. 24 May 1972, Liverpool; player
Cardiff Athletic Ladies, winners Welsh
Cup 1992; Wales U-18 debut 1988, U-21
debut 1990, snr debut 1993. *Leisure
interests*: all sport, sports psychology,
reading, travel. *Address*: Y'don, Beach Rd,
Morfa Bychan, Porthmadog, Gwynedd.

ROBERTSON, Pauline Judith: hockey
player; b. 28 December 1968, Dundee;
player Edinburgh Ladies 1989– ; Scotland
debut 1989, home countries champs. 1991,
93, Inter-Nations Cup silver medallists
1992; GB debut 1990. *Leisure interests*:
keeping fit, weight training, swimming.
Address: c/o Swinton Insurance, 280 High
St, Arbroath DD11 1JF.

ROBERTSON, Shirley Ann:
yachtswoman; b. 15 July 1968, Dundee;
Scotland debut 1983; UK debut 1986;
European Champs. Laser silver medal
1986, bronze 1988; World Champs. Europe
silver medal 1993; Olympic squad 1992;
winner Europe class, Spa, Anzio, Cork
Regattas 1993. *Leisure interests*: mountain
biking, flying kites. *Address*: c/o RYA, RYA
House, Romsey Rd, Eastleigh, Hants.
SO5 4YA.

ROBINS, Grant Alan: swimmer; b. 21 May
1969, Portsmouth; GB 400m individ.
medley champ. 1993; England youth debut
1984, snr debut 1985; GB youth debut 1984,
snr debut 1985; European Jnr Champs.
400m freestyle bronze medal 1985. *Leisure
interests*: triathlon. *Address*: Portsmouth
Northsea Swimming Club, Anglesea Rd,
Portsmouth, Hants.

ROBINS, Mark: footballer; b. 22 December
1969, Ashton-under-Lyne; player
Manchester Utd 1986–92, Norwich City
92– ; with Manchester Utd: winners FA
Cup 1990, European Cup Winners' Cup 1991;
6 England U-21 caps. *Address*: Norwich City
FC, Carrow Rd, Norwich NR1 1JE.

ROBINSON, Darren David John: crick-
eter; b. 2 March 1972, Braintree; player
Essex 1993– ; England U-18 tour Canada
1991, U-19 tour Pakistan 1991/92. *Address*:
Essex CCC, County Cricket Ground, New
Writtle St, Chelmsford DM2 0PG.

ROBINSON, David: footballer; b. 14
January 1965, Middlesbrough; player
Hartlepool Utd 1983–86, Halifax Town
86–89, Peterborough Utd 89– . *Address*:
Peterborough Utd FC, London Rd Ground,
Peterborough, Cambs. PE2 8AL.

ROBINSON, Grant: surfer; b. 14
November 1951, NI; Irish champ. 1981, 82,
84; European masters champ. 1987; Ireland
debut 1973. *Leisure interests*: music, playing
guitar, reading, martial arts. *Address*: 29
Underwood Park, Enniskillen, Co.
Fermanagh, NI.

ROBINSON, Jason: Rugby League foot-
baller; b. 30 July 1974; player Wigan
1991– , winners Challenge Cup, Regal
Trophy 1993; GB debut v. NZ 1993.
Address: Wigan RLFC, The Pavilion,
Central Park, Wigan WN1 1XF.

ROBINSON, Leslie: footballer; b. 1 March
1967, Shirebrook; player Mansfield Town
1984–86, Stockport County 86–88,
Doncaster Rovers 88–90, Oxford Utd 90– .
Address: Oxford Utd FC, Manor Ground,
London Rd, Headington, Oxford OX3 7RS.

ROBINSON, Liam: footballer; b. 29
December 1965, Bradford; player
Huddersfield Town 1984–86, Bury 86–93,
Bristol City 93– . *Address*: Bristol City FC,
Ashton Gate, Bristol BS3 2EJ.

ROBINSON, Mark: footballer; b. 21 November 1968, Rochdale; player W. Bromwich Albion 1985–87, Barnsley 87–93, Newcastle Utd 93– . *Address*: Newcastle Utd FC, St James' Park, Newcastle-upon-Tyne, Tyne & Wear NE1 4ST.

ROBINSON, Mark Andrew: cricketer; b. 23 November 1966, Hull; player Northants. 1987–90, Yorks. 91– ; with Yorks.: tour Cape Town (SA) 1992. *Address*: Yorks. CCC, Headingley Cricket Ground, Leeds LS6 3BU.

ROBINSON, Philip: footballer; b. 6 January 1967, Salford; player Aston Villa 1985–87, Wolverhampton Wanderers 87–89, Notts County 89– ; with Wolverhampton Wanderers: 4th Div. champs. 1987/88, 3rd Div. champs. 1988/89. *Address*: Notts County FC, Meadow Lane Ground, Nottingham NG2 3HJ.

ROBINSON, Phillip Edward: cricketer; b. 3 August 1963, Keighley; m. Jane Robinson 1986; player Yorks. 1984–91, Leics. 92– ; with Yorks.: tour St Lucia/ Barbados 1988. *Address*: Leics. CCC, County Ground, Grace Rd, Leicester LE2 8AD.

ROBINSON, Philip Peter: jockey (Flat); b. 10 January 1961, Newmarket; m. Gillian Robinson 1983; 1 s., 2 d.; winner 1000 Guineas 1984 (Pebbles), Irish 1000 Guineas 1984 (Katies), St Leger 1993 (Bob's Return); champ. jockey in Hong Kong 1989, 90. *Leisure interests*: golf, fishing, skiing, motorcycle trials. *Address*: Highfield House, 37 The Avenue, Newmarket, Suffolk.

ROBINSON, Robert Timothy: cricketer; b. 21 November 1958, Sutton-in-Ashfield; m. Patricia Robinson 1985; 2 s.; player Notts. 1978– (capt.), county champs. 1981, 87, Sunday League champs. 1991; 29 Tests, debut 1984, 26 1-day ints, tours India/Aus. 1984/85, WI 1985/86, India/NZ (World Cup) 1987/88. *Address*: Notts. CCC, Trent Bridge, Nottingham NG2 6AG.

ROBINSON, Ronald: footballer; b. 22 October 1966, Sunderland; player Leeds Utd 1985–87, Doncaster Rovers 87–89, W. Bromwich Albion 1989, Rotherham Utd 1989–91, Peterborough Utd 91–93, Exeter City 93– . *Address*: Exeter City FC, St James Park, Well St, Exeter EX4 6PX.

ROBINSON, Steve: boxer; b. 13 December 1968; prof. debut 1989; titles won: Welsh featherweight 1991, Welsh super-featherweight 1992, WBO featherweight 1993; over 13 prof. wins. *Address*: c/o Dai Gardiner, 13 Hengoed Hall Drive, Cefn Hengoed, Hengoed, Mid Glamorgan.

ROBSON, Bryan: footballer; b. 11 January 1957, Witton Gilbert, Durham; player W. Bromwich Albion 1974–81, Manchester Utd 81–94; with Manchester Utd: winners FA Cup 1983, 85, 90, European Cup Winners' Cup 1991, League champs. 1992/93; 7 England U-21 caps, 90 full England caps. *Address*: Manchester Utd FC, Old Trafford, Manchester M16 0RA.

ROCASTLE, David: footballer; b. 2 May 1967, Lewisham; player Arsenal 1984–92, Leeds Utd 92–93, Manchester City 93– ; with Arsenal: winners League Cup 1987, League champs. 1988/89, 90/91; 14 England U-21 caps, 14 full England caps. *Address*: Manchester City FC, Maine Rd, Moss Side, Manchester M14 7WN.

ROCHE, David: footballer; b. 13 December 1970, Wallsend; player Newcastle Utd 1988–93, Doncaster Rovers 93– . *Address*: Doncaster Rovers FC, Belle Vue, Doncaster, S. Yorks. DN4 5HT.

RODBER, Timothy Andrew: Rugby Union footballer; b. 2 July 1969, Richmond, Yorks.; player Petersfield, Northampton (capt. 1994–); rep. N. Div.; England U-21 debut v. Romania 1989, snr and Five Nations debut v. Scotland 1992, tour Argentina 1990, winning squad World Cup Sevens 1993. *Address*: Northampton FC, Franklins Gardens, Weedon Rd, Northampton NN5 5BG.

RODGER, Graham: footballer; b. 1 April 1967, Glasgow; player Wolverhampton Wanderers 1983–85, Coventry City 85–89, Luton Town 89–92, Grimsby Town 92– ; with Coventry City: winners FA Cup 1987; 4 England U-21 caps. *Address*: Grimsby Town FC, Blundell Park, Cleethorpes, S. Humberside DN35 7PY.

RODGER, Simon: footballer; b. 3 October 1971, Shoreham; player Crystal Palace 1990– . *Address*: Crystal Palace FC, Selhurst Park Stadium, London SE25 6PU.

RODGERSON, Ian: footballer; b. 9 April 1966, Hereford; player Hereford Utd 1985–88, Cardiff City 88–90, Birmingham City 90–93, Sunderland 93– . *Address*: Sunderland FC, Roker Park Ground, Sunderland, Tyne and Wear SR6 9SW.

ROEBUCK, Neil: Rugby League footballer; b. 4 October 1969, Hemsworth; player Travellers ARLFC, Bradford Northern, Castleford, Featherstone Rovers 1993– . *Address*: Featherstone Rovers RLFC, The Croft, Batley Rd, W. Ardsley, Wakefield WF3 1DX.

ROEDER, Glenn: football manager; b. 13 December 1955, Woodford; player Leyton Orient 1973–78, Queens Park Rangers 78–83, Newcastle Utd 83–89, Watford 89–91, Leyton Orient 1991; manager Gillingham, Watford 1993– . *Address*: Watford FC, Vicarage Rd Stadium, Watford, Herts. WD1 8ER.

ROGAN, Anton: footballer; b. 25 March 1966, Belfast; player Celtic 1986–91, Sunderland 91–93, Oxford Utd 93– ; with Celtic: winners Scottish Cup 1988, 89; 17 NI caps. *Address*: Oxford Utd FC, Manor Ground, London Rd, Headington, Oxford OX3 7RS.

ROGERS, Paul: footballer; b. 21 March 1965, Portsmouth; player Sheffield Utd 1992– . *Address*: Sheffield Utd FC, Bramall Lane, Sheffield, S. Yorks S2 4SU.

ROLLINGS, Christopher Charles: glider pilot; b. 19 March 1947, London; GB club-class champ. 1973, 15m-class champ. 1977, 21m-class open champ. 1984, 85, standard-class champ., overseas-class champ. 1992; GB debut and World Champs. squad 1993. *Address*: c/o Brit. Gliding Assoc., Kimberley House, 47 Vaughan Way, Leicester LE1 4SE.

ROLLINS, Robert John: cricketer; b. 30 January 1974, Plaistow; player Essex 1992– ; England U-18 tour Canada 1991, U-19 tours Pakistan 1991/92, India 1992/93. *Leisure interests*: swimming, golf, reading. *Address*: Essex CCC, County Cricket Ground, New Writtle St, Chelmsford DM2 0PG.

RONALDSON, Christopher James: real tennis player; b. 21 January 1950, Cambridge; m. Ann Lesley Pearson Ronaldson 1971; 3 s.; GB open champ. 1978, 80–85; French open champ. 1981–84, 86; Aus. open champ. 1977, 78, 82, 84, 85; US open champ. 1980, 84, 86; world champ. 1981–87; GB debut 1984 (capt. 1986); holds record number of Major wins (20); world's only Grand Slam winner 1984; rep. Oxon lawn tennis 1967–82, Surrey over-35 squash 1987. *Publications*: *Tennis – A Cut above the Rest*, 1985, 89. *Leisure interests*: family, education, real tennis administration, all sport except equestrian. *Address*: 53 Hampton Court Palace, E. Molesey, Surrey KT8 9AU.

ROOKS, Teawen Elizabeth: oarswoman; b. 25 April 1972, Newport; rep. Henley College 1988–89, Maidenhead RC 89–91, Univ. of London Women's BC 92– ; GB women's double sculls jnr champ. 1989, snr lightweight and open women's coxless fours champ. 1992; GB jnr debut 1990, snr debut 1993. *Leisure interests*: cycling, reading, juggling, cooking, painting and drawing. *Address*: 87 Hartington Rd, Chiswick, London W4 3TU.

ROSARIO, Robert: footballer; b. 4 March 1966, Hammersmith; player Norwich City 1983–91, Coventry City 91–92, Nottingham Forest 92– ; 4 England U-21 caps. *Address*: Nottingham Forest FC, City Ground, Nottingham NG2 5FJ.

ROSE, Graham David: cricketer; b. 12 April 1964, London; m. Teresa Julie Rose 1987; 1 d.; player Middx 1984–86, Somerset 87– ; rep. England YC v. Aus. 1983; completed double of 1000 runs and 50 wickets in 1st-class cricket and scored fastest 100s in 40- and 60-over cricket (v. Glamorgan and Devon respectively) 1990. *Leisure interests*: cooking, wine, golf, music. *Address*: Somerset CCC, The County Ground, Taunton, Somerset TA1 1JT.

ROSE, Hilary: hockey player; b. 9 July 1971; player Ipswich Ladies; England U-21 debut 1991, snr debut 1993; Champions Trophy squad 1993. *Address*: Ipswich Ladies HC, Tuddenham Rd, Ipswich, Suffolk IP4 3QJ.

ROSE, Jeanette Marie: weightlifter (67.5–70kg); b. 14 September 1959, Kingston, Jamaica; GB women's champ. 1987–91, 93; EEC women's champ. 1990–92; European Champs. silver medals 1990, 92, gold 1991; World Champs. bronze medal 1988. *Leisure interests*: parties, clubbing, music, watching videos, dancing, sleeping, reading. *Address*: c/o Brit. Amateur Weightlifters Assoc., 3 Iffley Turn, Oxford OX4 4DU3.

ROSEBERRY, Michael Anthony: cricketer; b. 28 November 1966, Houghton-le-Spring; m. Helen Louise Roseberry 1991; 1 d.; player Middx 1985– , county champs. 1990, 93, Sunday League champs. 1992; England YC tour WI 1985, England A tour Aus. 1992/93; Lord's Taverners/MCC Cricketer of the Year 1983; joint-highest run-scorer in 1st-class cricket 1992. *Address*: Middx CCC, Lord's Cricket Ground, London NW8 8QN.

ROSENTHAL, Ronny: footballer; b. 4 October 1963, Haifa, Israel; player Maccaba Haifa (Israel), Bruges (Belgium), Standard Liege (Belgium), Liverpool 1990–94, Tottenham Hotspur 94– ; Israel int. *Address*: Tottenham Hotspur FC, 748 High Rd, Tottenham, London N17 0AP.

ROSS, Michael: footballer; b. 2 September 1971, Southampton; player Portsmouth 1988–93, Exeter City 93– . *Address*: Exeter City FC, St James Park, Well St, Exeter EX4 6PX.

ROUND, Paul: Rugby League footballer; b. 24 September 1963, St Helens; player St Helens, Oldham, Wakefield Trinity 1991– ; rep. Lancs.; GB U-21 debut v. France 1984. *Address*: Wakefield Trinity RLFC, 171 Doncaster Rd, Belle Vue, Wakefield WF1 5EZ.

ROWE, Elizabeth Victoria (Vicky): modern pentathlete; b. 13 February 1965, Crosby; Aus. women's champ. 1992; GB women's champ. 1993; GB debut 1992, World Champs. squad 1993. *Leisure interests*: skiing, horseriding, parties, my family and other animals, music, TV. *Address*: The Grey House, Sandy Lane, Hightown, Merseyside L38 3RD.

ROWLAND, Keith: footballer; b. 1 September 1971, Portadown, NI; player Bournemouth 1989–93, W. Ham Utd 93– . *Address*: W. Ham Utd FC, Boleyn Ground, Green St, Upton Park, London E13 9AZ.

ROWLAND, Mark: athlete; b. 7 March 1963, Watersfield, W. Sussex; AAA 3000m steeplechase champ. 1988, 5000m champ. 1989; UK 1500m champ. 1985; European Champs. 3000m steeplechase silver medal 1990; Olympic 3000m steeplechase bronze medal 1988; UK 3000m steeplechase record-holder. *Address*: c/o Brit. Athletic Fed., 225A Bristol Rd, Edgbaston, Birmingham B5 7UB.

ROWLEY, Paul: Rugby League footballer; b. 12 March 1975; player Leigh Miners ARLFC, Leigh 1992– . *Address*: Leigh RLFC, Hilton Park, Kirkhall Lane, Leigh WN7 1RN.

ROWNTREE, Graham Christopher: Rugby Union footballer; b. 18 April 1971, Stockton-on-Tees; player Nuneaton, Leicester; with Leicester: winners Pilkington Cup 1993; rep. Midland Div.; England U-21 debut v. Ireland 1990, England A tour Canada 1993. *Address*: Leicester FC, Welford Rd, Leicester LE2 7LF.

ROY, Stuart: Rugby Union footballer; b. 25 December 1968, Ely; player Neath 1987–88, Cardiff 88– ; 2 Wales U-21 caps, 3 Wales B caps. *Leisure interests*: windsurfing, eating. *Address*: Cardiff RFC, Cardiff Arms Park, Westgate St, Cardiff CF1 1JA.

ROYLE, Joseph: football manager; b. 8 April 1949, Liverpool; player Everton 1966–74, Manchester City 74–77, Bristol City 77–80, Norwich City 80–81; with Everton: League champs. 1969/70; with Manchester City: winners League Cup 1976; 10 England U-23 caps, 6 full England caps; manager Oldham Athletic 1982– , 2nd Div. champs. 1990/91. *Address*: Oldham Athletic FC, Boundary Park, Oldham, Lancs. OL1 2PA.

RUCKWOOD, Adam: swimmer; b. 13 September 1974, Birmingham; 1 s.; GB 100m jnr backstroke champ. 1989, 90, 200m jnr backstroke champ. 1990, 200m snr backstroke champ. 1992, 93; World School Games 4 x 100m freestyle relay gold, 100m backstroke silver and 200m backstroke bronze medals 1990; European Jnr Champs. 100m backstroke silver and 200m backstroke bronze medals 1991; Olympic squad 1992 (100m and 200m backstroke); GB 200m backstroke record-holder. *Leisure interests*: social life, cinema, music, light reading, Aston Villa FC, Cradley Heathens speedway team. *Address*: c/o ASA, Harold Fern House, Derby Square, Loughborough, Leics. LE11 0AL.

RUDDOCK, Neil: footballer; b. 9 May 1968, Battersea; player Tottenham Hotspur 1986–88, Millwall 88–89, Southampton 89–92, Tottenham Hotspur 92–93, Liverpool 93– ; 4 England U-21 caps. *Address*: Liverpool FC, Anfield Rd, Liverpool L4 0TH.

RUSBY, David: Rugby Union footballer; b. 2 March 1971, N. Shields; player W. Hartlepool 1991– ; rep. Northumberland, N. Div. U-21, England Students. *Address*: W. Hartlepool RFC, Brierton Lane, Hartlepool, Cleveland TS25 5DR.

RUSH, David: footballer; b. 15 May 1971, Sunderland; player Sunderland 1989– . *Address*: Sunderland FC, Roker Park Ground, Sunderland, Tyne and Wear SR6 9SW.

RUSH, Ian James: footballer; b. 20 October 1961, St Asaph; player Chester City 1978–80, Liverpool 80–87, Juventus (Italy) 87–88, Liverpool 88– ; with Liverpool: winners European Cup 1984, League Cup 1981–84, FA Cup 1986, 89, 92, League champs. 1981/82, 82/83, 83/84, 85/86, 89/90; 2 Wales U-21 caps, snr debut v. Scotland (sub.) 1980, over 60 full caps. *Address*: Liverpool FC, Anfield Rd, Liverpool L4 0TH.

RUSH, Matthew: footballer; b. 6 August 1971, Hackney; player W. Ham Utd 1990– . *Address*: W. Ham Utd FC, Boleyn Ground, Green St, Upton Park, London E13 9AZ.

RUSSELL, Lee: footballer; b. 3 September 1969, Southampton; player Portsmouth 1988– . *Address*: Portsmouth FC, Fratton Park, Frogmore Rd, Portsmouth PO4 8RA.

RUSSELL, Mark: Rugby Union footballer; b. 16 December 1965, Nairobi, Kenya; player Harlequins; England B int. *Address*: Harlequins FC, Stoop Memorial Ground, Craneford Way, Twickenham, Middx.

RUSSELL, Richard: Rugby League footballer; b. 24 November 1967, Oldham; player Wigan, Oldham 1989–93, Castleford 93– ; with Castleford: winners Regal Trophy 1994; GB U-21 debut v. France 1987. *Address*: Castleford RLFC, Wheldon Rd, Castleford WF10 2SD.

RUSSELL, Robert Charles (Jack): cricketer; b. 15 August 1963, Stroud; m. Aileen Ann Russell 1985; 2 s., 2 d.; player Glos. 1981– ; Test debut 1988, tours Pakistan 1987/88, India/WI 1989/90, Aus. 1990/91, NZ 1991/92, Aus. (England A) 1992/93 (vice-capt.), WI 1994. *Publications*: *A Cricketer's Art*, 1988, *Sketches of a Season* (co-author), 1989. *Address*: Glos. CCC, Phoenix County Ground, Nevil Rd, Bristol BS6 9EJ.

RYAN, Dean: Rugby Union footballer; b. 22 June 1966, Tuxford; m. Wendy Ryan; player Saracens, Wasps (capt.); England debut and tour Argentina 1990. *Address*: Wasps FC, Wasps Football Ground, Repton Ave, Sudbury, Wembley, Middx HA0 3DW.

RYAN, Vaughan: footballer; b. 2 September 1968, Westminster; player Wimbledon 1986– . *Address*: Wimbledon FC, Selhurst Park, London SE25 6PY.

SALAKO, John: footballer; b. 11 February 1969, Nigeria; player Crystal Palace 1986– ; 5 England caps. *Address*: Crystal Palace FC, Selhurst Park Stadium, London SE25 6PU.

SALISBURY, Ian David Kenneth: cricketer; b. 2 January 1970, Northampton; player Sussex 1989– ; England A tours Pakistan/Sri Lanka 1990/91, WI 1991/92, Test debut 1992, tours India/Sri Lanka 1992/93, WI 1994; Sussex Player of the Year and Cricket Writers Young Cricketer of the Year 1992. *Leisure interests*: golf, squash, snooker, pool, eating out. *Address*: Sussex CCC, County Ground, Eaton Rd, Hove, E. Sussex BN3 3AN.

SALMON, Fred: cyclist; b. 1 June 1965, Stockport; rep. Peugeot 1988– ; Welsh mountain bike champ. 1988; GB debut 1987; World Uphill Champs. silver medal 1991; winner Three Peaks (cyclo-cross) 1990, 92. *Address*: 5 Crescent Row, Birch Vale, via Stockport, Cheshire SK12 5BW.

SALVESEN, Emily Vanessa Stuart: lacrosse player; b. 22 June 1970, Edinburgh; player Exeter Univ. 1988–91, Edinburgh Thistle 92– ; Scotland U-21 debut 1989, Scotland B debut 1990, snr debut and World Cup squad 1993, tour USA 1993. *Leisure interests*: various sports, cinema, port. *Address*: Edinburgh Thistle Lacrosse Club, The Grange Club, Raeburn Place, Stockbridge, Edinburgh.

SAMPSON, Dean: Rugby League footballer; b. 27 June 1967, Wakefield; player Castleford 1986– , winners Regal Trophy 1994; GB U-21 debut v. France 1988. *Address*: Castleford RLFC, Wheldon Rd, Castleford WF10 2SD.

SAMUEL, Mollie Irene: karate player (U-60kg); b. 12 September 1961, Paddington; 1 d.; English women's champ. 1985–89, 91, 92; GB women's champ. 1986–88, 90–92; European Champs. individ. gold medals 1986, 87, 89, 92, team gold 1989, 92; World Champs. individ. and team gold medals 1992; World Games gold medal 1993. *Leisure interests*: swimming, squash, badminton. *Address*: 45 Forest St, Forest Gate, London E7 0AP.

SAMWAYS, Claire: hockey player; b. 17 March 1971, Newtownards, NI; player Pegasus 1987– , winners European Cup Div. B 1993, All-Ireland Cup 1989, 91, 92, Ulster Shield 1989, All-Ireland League champs. 1989, 91; Ulster and Ireland U-21 and snr int., capt. Ireland U-21 European Cup squad 1992. *Leisure interests*: golf, tennis, cycling. *Address*: 21 Springhill Heights, Bangor, Co. Down BT20 3PB.

SAMWAYS, Vincent: footballer; b. 27 October 1968, Bethnal Green; player Tottenham Hotspur 1985– , winners FA Cup 1991; 5 England U-21 caps. *Address:* Tottenham Hotspur FC, 748 High Rd, Tottenham, London N17 0AP.

SANCHEZ, Lawrence: footballer; b. 22 October 1959, Lambeth; player Reading 1977–84, Wimbledon 84– ; with Reading: 4th Div. champs. 1978/79; with Wimbledon: FA Cup winners 1988; 3 NI caps. *Address:* Wimbledon FC, Selhurst Park, London SE25 6PY.

SANDERSON, Gary: Rugby League footballer; b. 21 February 1967, St Helens; player Thatto Heath ARLFC, Warrington 1985– ; GB U-21 debut v. France 1987. *Address:* Warrington RLFC, Wilderspool Stadium, Wilderspool Causeway, Warrington WA4 6PY.

SANDERSON, Jocky: paraglider pilot; b. 24 May 1967, London; Scottish champ. 1992, 93; GB debut 1989 (capt. 1990–); World Champs. team bronze medal 1993. *Leisure interests:* canoeing, sailing, climbing, surfing, swimming, skiing, riding, volleyball. *Address:* Eagle Quest, Rookin Farm House, Troutbeck, Penrith, Cumbria CA11 0SS.

SANSOM, Kenny: footballer; b. 26 September 1958, Camberwell; player Crystal Palace 1974–80, Arsenal 80–88, Newcastle Utd 88–89, Queens Park Rangers 89–90, Coventry City 90–93, Everton 93– ; with Crystal Palace: 2nd Div. champs. 1978/79; with Arsenal: winners League Cup 1987; 8 England U-21 caps, snr debut v. Wales 1979, 86 full caps. *Address:* Everton FC, Goodison Park, Liverpool L4 4EL.

SANSOME, Paul: footballer; b. 6 October 1961, New Addington; player Millwall 1980–88, Southend Utd 88– . *Address:* Southend Utd FC, Roots Hall, Victoria Ave, Southend-on-Sea, Essex SS2 6NQ.

SAPSFORD, Danny: tennis player; b. 3 April 1969; rep. Surrey; GB U-12 grass court champ. 1981, U-14 hard court champ. 1983, U-16 grass court champ. 1984, hard court champ. 1985, U-18 covered court champ. 1986, 87, hard court champ. 1987; GB debut 1990, Davis Cup team 1990, 91. *Address:* c/o LTA, The Queen's Club, W. Kensington, London W14 9EG.

SARGENT, Daniel Edward: judo player (U-95kg); b. 21 September 1970, Lambeth; London open champ. 1991–93; S. England champ. 1989–93; Welsh open champ. 1991, 92, Scottish open champ. 1992; Commonwealth champ. 1992; European Jnr Champs. bronze medal 1989, silver 1990; European Champs. team bronze medal 1992; rep. Kent U-18 rugby. *Leisure interests:* contact sports, canoeing. *Address:* 22 Albion Rd, Bexley Heath, Kent DA6 7LS.

SARTAIN, Hilary Kay: water polo player; b. 7 April 1970, Liverpool; player Everton 1986– , Stretford 1987–92; with Everton: ASA champs. 1993; with Stretford: League champs. 1988–92; rep. N. Counties 1987– ; GB debut 1987, European Champs. squad 1991, 93, World Cup squad 1993. *Leisure interests:* running, cycling, squash, badminton, travel, music, going out. *Address:* 1st Floor Flat, 219 Bebington Rd, Rock Ferry, Birkenhead L42 4QA.

SAUNDERS, Anthony Victor: mountaineer; b. 9 February 1950, Lossiemouth; m. Margaret Saunders 1987; 2 s.; 1st ascents: Conways Ogre 1980, W. face of Ushba 1986, 'Golden Pillar', Spantik 1987, Jitchu Drake 1988, Yaupa, W. Face of Makalu 1989, Panchuli V 1992; 1st traverse: Rajrambha 1992. *Publications: Elusive Summits,* 1989, *No Place to Fall,* 1993. *Leisure interests:* architecture, rock climbing, cooking. *Address:* Bamff, Alyth, Blairgowrie, Perthshire PH11 8LF.

SAUNDERS, Dean: footballer; b. 21 June 1964, Swansea; player Swansea City 1983–85, Brighton and Hove Albion 85–86, Oxford Utd 86–88, Derby County 88–91, Liverpool 91–92, Aston Villa 92– ; with Liverpool: winners FA Cup 1992; over 40 Wales caps. *Address*: Aston Villa FC, Villa Park, Trinity Rd, Birmingham B6 6HE.

SAUNDERS, Rob: Rugby Union footballer; b. 5 August 1968, Nottingham; player Queen's Univ. (NI), London Irish; Ireland U-21 debut v. Italy 1989, snr and Five Nations debut v. France 1991; rep. Ireland U-16 squash. *Address*: London Irish RUFC, The Avenue, Sunbury-on-Thames, Middx TW16 5EQ.

SAUNDERS, Steve: motorcyclist (off-road); b. 3 December 1964, Cheltenham; m. Sarah Jane Saunders; GB solo trials champ. 1982–92; World Champs. 3rd place 1985, 87, runner-up 1986; winner Scottish 6 Days Trial 1988–91. *Leisure interests*: snooker, jet skiing, radio-controlled cars. *Address*: c/o ACU, ACU House, Wood St, Rugby CV21 2YX.

SAWFORD, Steve James: motorcyclist; b. 1 July 1968, Bedford; GB 250cc Supercup champ. 1992. *Leisure interests*: jet and snow skiing, golf. *Address*: Sawfords Garage, Church St, Tempsford, Sandy, Beds. SG19 2AN.

SAXELBY, Mark: cricketer; b. 4 January 1969, Newark; player Notts. 1989–93, Sunday League champs. 1992. *Address*: Notts. CCC, Trent Bridge, Nottingham NG2 6AG.

SCALES, John: footballer; b. 4 July 1966, Harrogate; player Bristol Rovers 1985–87, Wimbledon 87– ; with Wimbledon: winners FA Cup 1988. *Address*: Wimbledon FC, Selhurst Park, London SE25 6PY.

SCHMEICHEL, Peter: footballer; b. 18 November 1968, Denmark; player Brøndby (Denmark), Manchester Utd 1991– ; with Manchester Utd: League champs. 1992/93; Denmark int. *Address*: Manchester Utd FC, Old Trafford, Manchester M16 0RA.

SCHOFIELD, Garry Edward: Rugby League footballer; b. 1 July 1965, Leeds; player Hunslet Parkside ARLFC, Hull 1983–87, Leeds 87– ; GB debut v. France 1984, Brit. Lions tours Aus./NZ/Papua New Guinea 1984, 88, 92, NZ/Papua New Guinea 1990. *Address*: Leeds RLFC, Bass Headingley, St Michael's Lane, Leeds LS6 3BR.

SCHWER, Billy: boxer; b. 12 April 1969; prof. debut 1990; titles won: GB and Commonwealth lightweight 1992, 93; over 23 prof. wins. *Address*: Nat. Promotions, Nat. House, 60–66 Wardour St, London W1V 3HP.

SCOPES, Lucy Karen: water skier (barefoot); b. 18 October 1980, Harold Wood; GB girls' dauphin tricks, slalom and overall champ. 1992, open ladies' tricks, slalom and overall champ. 1993; GB jnr debut 1991, snr debut 1992; European Jnr Champs. girls' slalom, tricks and overall gold medals 1991, 92, team gold 1992; European Champs., World Champs. squads 1992. *Leisure interests*: swimming, horseriding, trampolining. *Address*: 29 Redden Court Rd, Harold Wood, Romford, Essex RM3 0UR.

SCOTT, Archibald Bathgate: field archer; b. 24 February 1945, Dalkeith; m. Pamela Scott 1968; 3 d.; Scottish compound freestyle indoor champ. 1988, 89, 93, outdoor champ. 1988–92, indoor target champ. 1993; GB compound freestyle champ. 1988–91, 93; European Champs. gold medal 1991; World Champs. gold medal 1990. *Leisure interests*: art, photography. *Address*: 9 Clarinda Gardens, Dalkeith, Midlothian EH22 2LW.

SCOTT, Christopher Wilmot: cricketer; b. 23 January 1964, Lincoln; m. Jacqui Scott 1989; player Notts. 1981–91, Durham 92– ; with Durham: tour Zimbabwe 1991/92. *Address*: Durham CCC, County Ground, Riverside, Chester-le-Street, Co. Durham DH3 3QR.

SCOTT, Douglas Keith: mountaineer; b. 29 May 1941, Nottingham; 1 s., 2 d.; 1st ascents: Tarso Teiroko, Sahara 1965, Cilo Dag, S.E. Turkey 1966, S. face of Koh-i-Bandaka, Hindu Kush 1967, E. Pillar of Mt Asgard, Baffin Island 1972, Changabang, S.E. spur of Pic Lenin 1974, E. face of Mt Kenya direct 1976, Ogre, Karakoram 1977, N. ridge route, Kangchenjunga (without oxygen), N. summit of Kussum Kangguru, N. face of Nuptse 1979, Shivling E. pillar 1981, Pungpa Ri, S. face of Shishapangma, Lobsang Spire, Karakoram 1982, E. summit of Mt Chamlang 1984, Indian Aret Latok III 1990, Hanging Glacier Peak S., via S. ridge 1991; 1st Brit. ascent: Salathe Wall, El Capitan, Yosemite 1971; 1st Alpine ascents: S. face of Mt McKinley 1976, Kangchungste 1980, Diran 1985, S. face of Mt Jitchu Drake, Bhutan 1988; mem. European and Brit. S.W. face of Everest expeditions 1972; 1st Brit. to reach summit of Everest (with Dougal Haston), via S.W. face 1975. *Publications*: *Big Wall Climbing* (with Alex MacIntyre), 1974, *Shishapangma, Tibet*, 1984, *Himalayan Climber*, 1992. *Leisure interests*: rock climbing, photography, organic gardening. *Address*: Chapel House, Low Cotehill, Carlisle, Cumbria CA4 0EL.

SCOTT, Ian: Rugby League footballer; b. 20 April 1969, Workington; player Carlisle, Workington 1990–93, Leeds 93– . *Address*: Leeds RLFC, Bass Headingley, St Michael's Lane, Leeds LS6 3BR.

SCOTT, Kevin: footballer; 17 December 1966, Easington; player Newcastle Utd 1984–94, Tottenham Hotspur 94– . *Address*: Tottenham Hotspur FC, 748 High Rd, Tottenham, London N17 0AP.

SCOTT, Kevin Robert: badminton player; b. 3 July 1964, Dumfries; m. Gail Scott 1990; 1 s.; rep. Surrey; Scottish champ. 1992, 93, invitational champ. 1991; Scotland debut 1989, Commonwealth Games squad 1990, European Champs. squad 1990, 92, World Champs. squad 1989, 91, 93, Thomas Cup team 1990, 92; 1st Scottish player for 25 years to reach last 16 of All-England Champs. 1991. *Leisure interests*: golf, computing. *Address*: 7 Ockley Court, Burpham, Guildford GU4 7NE.

SCOTT, Martin William: Rugby Union footballer; b. 5 July 1966, Falkirk; m. Karen Scott; 2 d.; player Rosyth and District, Dunfermline, Edinburgh Academicals; Scotland B debut v. Ireland 1991, snr tours Aus. 1992, Fiji/Tonga/W. Samoa 1993. *Address*: Edinburgh Academicals RFC, Raeburn Place, Stockbridge, Edinburgh EH4 1HQ.

SCOTT, Richard James: cricketer; b. 2 November 1963, Bournemouth; m. Julie Scott 1991; player Hants. 1986–90, Glos. 1991–93. *Address*: Glos. CCC, Phoenix County Ground, Nevil Rd, Bristol BS6 9EJ.

SCOTT, Robb: Rugby Union footballer; b. 25 April 1966, Hong Kong; m. Anita Scott; player Heriot's FP, Dorking, Selkirk, London Scottish; with London Scottish: 2nd Div. champs. 1991/92; Scotland B debut v. Ireland B 1991, snr tour Fiji/Tonga/W. Samoa 1993. *Address*: London Scottish FC, Richmond Athletic Ground, Kew Foot Rd, Richmond, Surrey TW9 2SS.

SCULLY, David Andrew: Rugby Union footballer; b. 7 August 1965, Doncaster; m. Angela Scully 1989; 1 s.; player Wheatley Hills 1980–86, Wakefield 86– ; rep. Yorks. U-21 1985/86, snr squad 1988– , N. Div. 1990– ; with N. Div.: tour France 1993; England B debut v. Italy 1992, tour NZ

1992, winning squad World Cup Sevens 1993. *Leisure interests*: running, badminton, squash, golf, family. *Address*: Wakefield RUFC, College Grove, Eastmoor Rd, Wakefield, W. Yorks.

SCULLY, Patrick: footballer; b. 23 June 1970, Dublin, Ireland; player Southend Utd 1991– ; 3 Ireland U-21 caps, 1 full Ireland cap. *Address*: Southend Utd FC, Roots Hall, Victoria Ave, Southend-on-Sea, Essex SS2 6NQ.

SEAGRAVES, Mark: footballer; b. 22 October 1966, Bootle; player Manchester City 1987–90, Bolton Wanderers 90– . *Address*: Bolton Wanderers FC, Burnden Park, Manchester Rd, Bolton, Lancs. BL3 2QR.

SEAMAN, David: footballer; b. 19 September 1963, Rotherham; player Peterborough Utd 1982–84, Birmingham City 84–86, Queens Park Rangers 86–90, Arsenal 90– ; with Arsenal: League champions 1990/91; winners League Cup, FA Cup 1993; 10 England U-21 caps, over 10 full England caps. *Address*: Arsenal FC, Arsenal Stadium, Highbury, London N5 1BU.

SEARLE, Gregory Mark Pascoe, MBE: oarsman; b. 20 March 1972, Ashford, Middx; rep. Hampton School 1988–90, Molesey BC 91– ; GB jnr debut 1988, snr debut 1990, World Champs. eights bronze medal 1991, coxed pairs gold 1993, Olympic coxed pairs gold 1992. *Leisure interests*: off-road Land-Rover-driving, scuba diving, rock climbing, playing the guitar. *Address*: 85 Trinity Rd, Wimbledon, London SW19 8QZ.

SEARLE, Jonathan William Courtis, MBE: oarsman; b. 8 May 1969, Walton on Thames; rep. Hampton School 1982–87, Oxford Univ. BC 87–90, Molesey BC 90– ; with Oxford: winners Univ. Boat Race 1988–90; winning crew, Grand Challenge Cup, Henley Royal Regatta 1991; World Jnr

Champs. coxless fours silver medal 1986, gold 1987; World Champs. eights bronze medals 1989, 91, coxed pairs gold 1993; Olympic coxed pairs gold medal 1992. *Leisure interests*: going to work. *Address*: Molesey BC, Barge Walk, Molesey, Surrey.

SEDGLEY, Stephen: footballer; b. 26 May 1968, Enfield; player Coventry City 1986–89, Tottenham Hotspur 89– ; with Coventry City: winners FA Cup 1987; with Tottenham Hotspur: winners FA Cup 1991; 11 England U-21 caps. *Address*: Tottenham Hotspur FC, 748 High Rd, Tottenham, London N17 0AP.

SEELS, Jason James: water skier; b. 21 August 1976, Durban, SA; GB dauphin slalom champ. 1988, 89, jump champ. 1988–90, tricks champ. 1990, overall champ. 1988–90, jnr tricks, jump and overall champ. 1992, jump and overall champ. 1993; GB jnr debut 1989, snr debut 1992 (youngest-ever cap); European Dauphin Champs. jump bronze medal, team gold 1989, overall bronze, team gold 1990; European Jnr Champs. overall and team gold medals 1992; World Jnr Champs. team silver medal 1992. *Leisure interests*: badminton, football, basketball. *Address*: 86 Locks Heath Park Rd, Locks Heath, Southampton, Hants. SO3 6LZ.

SEGERS, Johannes (Hans): footballer; b. 30 October 1961, Eindhoven, The Netherlands; player PSV Eindhoven (The Netherlands), Nottingham Forest 1984–88, Wimbledon 88– . *Address*: Wimbledon FC, Selhurst Park, London SE25 6PY.

SELBY, Howard John: motorcyclist; b. 28 November 1960; m. Kate Selby 1987; Scottish 1300cc champ. 1984, 85, 1300cc production-class champ. 1985; European Supersport 600 champ. 1990. *Leisure interests*: squash, swimming, weight training, horses. *Address*: Howard Selby Auto Services, Heugh Rd, N. Berwick, E. Lothian EH39 5PS.

SELLARS, Scott: footballer; b. 27 November 1965, Sheffield; player Leeds Utd 1983–86, Blackburn Rovers 86–92, Leeds Utd 92–93, Newcastle Utd 93– ; 3 England U-21 caps. *Address*: Newcastle Utd FC, St James' Park, Newcastle-upon-Tyne, Tyne & Wear NE1 4ST.

SEYMOUR, Adam Charles Hilton: cricketer; b. 7 December 1967, Royston; player Essex 1988–91, Worcs. 92– ; with Worcs.: tour SA 1992. *Address*: Worcs. CCC, County Ground, New Rd, Worcester WR2 4QQ.

SHACKLOCK, Kerry: synchronized swimmer; b. 30 October 1971, Wokingham; GB debut 1988; European Champs. solo and duet bronze medals 1993. *Address*: c/o ASA, Harold Fern House, Derby Square, Loughborough, Leics. LE11 0AL.

SHAHID, Nadeem: cricketer; b. 23 April 1969, Karachi, Pakistan; player Essex 1989– , county champs. 1991, 92. *Address*: Essex CCC, County Cricket Ground, New Writtle St, Chelmsford DM2 0PG.

SHAKESPEARE, Craig: footballer; b. 26 October 1963, Birmingham; player Walsall 1981–89, Sheffield Wednesday 89–90, W. Bromwich Albion 90–93, Grimsby Town 93– . *Address*: Grimsby Town FC, Blundell Park, Cleethorpes, S. Humberside DN35 7PY.

SHARP, Alan Victor: Rugby Union footballer; b. 17 October 1968, Bristol; 1 d.; player Bristol; England B tour Spain 1989, Scotland and Five Nations debut v. England 1994. *Leisure interests*: swimming, running, watching rugby, family. *Address*: c/o Ian McLaughlan, 55 Chester St, Edinburgh EH3 7EN.

SHARP, Graeme: footballer; b. 16 October 1960, Glasgow; player Dumbarton, Everton 1980–91, Oldham Athletic 91– ; with Everton: winners FA Cup 1984, European Cup Winners' Cup 1985, League champs.

1984/85, 86/87; 1 Scotland U-21 cap, 12 full Scotland caps. *Address*: Oldham Athletic FC, Boundary Park, Oldham, Lancs. OL1 2PA.

SHARP, Jon: Rugby League footballer; b. 8 March 1967, Wakefield; player Travellers ARLFC, Hull 1984– ; with Hull: winners Premiership 1991. *Address*: Hull RLFC, The Boulevard Ground, Airlie St, Hull HU3 3JD.

SHARPE, David: athlete; b. 8 July 1967, Jarrow; UK 800m champ. 1990, 91; World Jnr Champs. 800m gold medal 1986; European Champs. 800m silver medal 1990; European Indoor Champs. 800m gold medal 1988; World Cup 800m gold medal 1992. *Address*: c/o Brit. Athletic Fed., 225A Bristol Rd, Edgbaston, Birmingham B5 7UB.

SHARPE, Lee: footballer; b. 27 May 1971, Halesowen; player Torquay Utd 1987–88, Manchester Utd 88– ; with Manchester Utd: winners European Cup Winners' Cup 1991, League champs. 1992/93; 8 England U-21 caps, over 6 full England caps. *Address*: Manchester Utd FC, Old Trafford, Manchester M16 0RA.

SHAW, George: footballer; b. 10 February 1969, Glasgow; player St Mirren 1987–91, Partick Thistle 91– . *Address*: Partick Thistle FC, Firhill Stadium, 80 Firhill Rd, Glasgow G20 7BA.

SHAW, Richard: footballer; b. 11 September 1968, Brentford; player Crystal Palace 1987– . *Address*: Crystal Palace FC, Selhurst Park Stadium, London SE25 6PU.

SHEALS, Mark: Rugby League footballer; b. 26 November 1966, Swinton; player Swinton, Leigh, Oldham 1992–93, Wakefield Trinity 93– . *Address*: Wakefield Trinity RLFC, 171 Doncaster Rd, Belle Vue, Wakefield WF1 5EZ.

SHEARER, Alan: footballer; b. 13 August 1970, Newcastle; player Southampton 1988–92, Blackburn Rovers 92– ; 11 England U-21 caps, over 6 full England caps. *Address*: Blackburn Rovers FC, Ewood Park, Blackburn, Lancs. BB2 4JF.

SHEARER, Duncan: footballer; b. 28 August 1962, Fort William; player Chelsea 1983–86, Huddersfield Town 86–88, Swindon Town 88–92, Blackburn Rovers 1992, Aberdeen 1992– . *Address*: Aberdeen FC, Pittodrie Stadium, Pittodrie St, Aberdeen AB2 1QH.

SHELFORD, Darrall: Rugby League footballer; b. 29 July 1962, Rotorua, NZ; player Bay of Plenty (NZ), Bradford Northern 1990– ; NZ B int. *Address*: Bradford Northern RLFC, Odsal Stadium, Bradford BD6 1BS.

SHELFORD, Kelly: Rugby League footballer; b. 4 May 1966; player Warrington 1991– ; NZ debut v. Aus. and tour GB 1989. *Address*: Warrington RLFC, Wilderspool Stadium, Wilderspool Causeway, Warrington WA4 6PY.

SHEPHERD, Ann: field archer; b. 27 April 1957, Wallasey; m. Michael Shepherd 1989; rep. Cheshire; English ladies' champ. 1986, 87, 89, 90, 92; GB ladies' champ. 1986–89, 91; attained Grand Master Bowman status 1986; GB debut 1989; World Champs. individ. gold medal 1990. *Leisure interests*: reading, crafts. *Address*: 56 Green Lane, Higher Poynton, nr Stockport, Cheshire SK12 1TJ.

SHEPHERD, Anthony: footballer; b. 16 November 1966, Glasgow; player Celtic 1983–89, Carlisle Utd 89–91, Motherwell 91– . *Address*: Motherwell FC, Fir Park, Fir Park St, Motherwell ML1 2QN.

SHEPHERD, Gordon John: hockey player; b. 11 October 1965, Dundee; m. Karen Elizabeth Shepherd 1991; 1 d.; player Linlathen 1970–83, Dundee Wanderers 84– ; with Dundee Wanderers: winners Scottish Cup 1990, Scottish League champs. 1993; Scotland U-21 debut 1982, snr outdoor and indoor debuts 1990, European Champs. indoor bronze medallist 1991; Scottish Player of the Year 1992. *Leisure interests*: golf, cards, snooker. *Address*: 60 Marlee Rd, Broughty Ferry, Dundee DD5 3EX.

SHEPHERD, Rowen James Stanley: Rugby Union footballer; b. 25 December 1970, Edinburgh; player Caithness, Edinburgh Academicals; Scotland U-21 debut v. Wales 1991, snr tour N. America 1991. *Address*: Edinburgh Academicals RFC, Raeburn Place, Stockbridge, Edinburgh EH4 1HQ.

SHEPPARD, Alison: swimmer; b. 5 November 1972, Glasgow; Scotland debut and Commonwealth Games squad 1990; GB jnr debut 1987, snr debut 1991, Olympic squad 1988, 92; Scottish women's 50m and 100m freestyle record-holder. *Leisure interests*: popular music, ten-pin bowling. *Address*: 1 Briarwell Rd, Milngavie, Glasgow G62 6AW.

SHEPSTONE, Paul: footballer; b. 8 November 1970, Coventry; player Blackburn Rovers 1990–92, Motherwell 92– . *Address*: Motherwell FC, Fir Park, Fir Park St, Motherwell ML1 2QN.

SHERIDAN, John: footballer; b. 1 October 1964, Manchester; player Leeds Utd 1982–89, Sheffield Wednesday 89– ; with Sheffield Wednesday: winners League Cup 1991; 1 Ireland U-21 cap, over 15 full Ireland caps. *Address*: Sheffield Wednesday FC, Hillsborough, Sheffield, S. Yorks. S6 1SW.

SHERIDAN, Ryan: Rugby League footballer; b. 24 May 1975; player Sheffield Eagles 1991– . *Address*: Sheffield Eagles RLFC, Stadium Corner, 824 Attercliffe Rd, Sheffield S9 3RS.

SHERINGHAM, Edward: footballer; b. 2 April 1966, Walthamstow; player Millwall 1984–91, Nottingham Forest 91–92, Tottenham Hotspur 92–   ; with Millwall: 2nd Div. champs. 1987/88; 1 England U-21 cap, snr debut v. Poland 1993. *Address*: Tottenham Hotspur FC, 748 High Rd, Tottenham, London N17 0AP.

SHERMAN, Jeremy Paul (Jez): water polo player; b. 26 July 1966, Bristol; player London Polytechnic 1985–   (capt. 1990–   ); rep. Glos., W. Counties jnr 1981–85, Univ. of London 1986–88 (capt.); England debut 1985; GB debut 1987, European Champs. squad 1989, 91. *Leisure interests*: rugby, squash, windsurfing. *Address*: Top Floor Flat, 19 Edgeley Rd, London SW4 6EH.

SHERON, Michael: footballer; b. 11 January 1972, Liverpool; player Manchester City 1990–   ; England U-21 int. *Address*: Manchester City FC, Maine Rd, Moss Side, Manchester M14 7WN.

SHERWOOD, Stephen: footballer; b. 10 December 1953, Selby; player Chelsea 1971–76, Watford 76–87, Grimsby Town 87–   ; with Watford: 4th Div. champs. 1977/78. *Address*: Grimsby Town FC, Blundell Park, Cleethorpes, S. Humberside DN35 7PY.

SHERWOOD, Timothy: footballer; b. 6 February 1969, St Albans; player Watford 1987–89, Norwich City 89–92, Blackburn Rovers 92–   ; 4 England U-21 caps. *Address*: Blackburn Rovers FC, Ewood Park, Blackburn, Lancs. BB2 4JF.

SHIEL, Andrew Graham: Rugby Union footballer; b. 13 August 1970, Galashiels; player Melrose, Scottish League champs. 1989/90, 91/92; rep. S. of Scotland; Scotland debut v. Ireland 1991, tours NZ 1990, N. America 1991, Aus. 1992. *Address*: Melrose RFC, The Greenyards, Melrose TD6 9SA.

SHILLABEER, Edmund Harold: race walker; b. 2 August 1939, Plymouth; m. Barbara Shillabeer 1963; 1 s., 2 d.; Devon 3km track champ. 1973; S.W. 10-mile champ. 1987, 20km champ. 1980, 82–84; GB 100km champ. 1985, 100-mile champ. 1989; European over-45 20km champ. 1984, over-50 champ. 1990; GB debut v. France (200km) 1991 (oldest-ever Brit. athletic debutant); UK and Commonwealth 100km track record-holder; achieved 3rd place in world's 1st quadrathon 1983. *Leisure interests*: conservation, Plymouth Argyle FC, family, St John Ambulance. *Address*: Plymouth City Walkers, 94/96 Hyde Park Rd, Peverell, Plymouth PL3 4RE.

SHINE, Kevin James: cricketer; b. 22 February 1969, Bracknell; player Hants. 1989–93, Middx 94–   . *Address*: Middx CCC, Lord's Cricket Ground, London NW8 8QN.

SHIRTLIFF, Peter: footballer; b. 6 April 1961, Hoyland; player Sheffield Wednesday 1978–86, Charlton Athletic 86–89, Sheffield Wednesday 89–93, Wolverhampton Wanderers 93–   ; with Sheffield Wednesday: winners League Cup 1991. *Address*: Wolverhampton Wanderers FC, Molineux Stadium, Waterloo Rd, Wolverhampton WV1 4QR.

SHORT, Christian: footballer; b. 9 May 1970, Munster, Germany; player Scarborough 1988–90, Notts County 90–   . *Address*: Notts County FC, Meadow Lane Ground, Nottingham NG2 3HJ.

SHORT, Craig: footballer; b. 25 June 1968, Bridlington; player Scarborough 1987–89, Notts County 89–92, Derby County 92–   . *Address*: Derby County FC, The Baseball Ground, Shaftesbury Crescent, Derby DE3 8NB.

SHORTMAN, Penny Jane: synchronized swimmer; b. 22 November 1970, Bristol; GB debut 1992; W. Counties biathlon champ. 1989. *Leisure interests*: water sports, jet skiing, aerobics, weight training. *Address*: c/o ASA, Harold Fern House, Derby Square, Loughborough, Leics. LE11 0AL.

SHUTT, Carl: footballer; b. 10 October 1961, Sheffield; player Sheffield Wednesday 1985–87, Bristol City 87–89, Leeds Utd 89–93, Birmingham City 93– ; with Leeds Utd: 2nd Div. champs. 1989/90, League champs. 1991/92. *Address*: Birmingham City FC, St Andrews Ground, Birmingham B9 4NH.

SIDDALL, Shirli-Ann: tennis player; b. 20 June 1974; rep. Dorset; GB girls' U-14 grass court champ. 1988, U-16 hard court and grass court champ. 1990, ladies' doubles champ. 1993; GB U-21 debut 1992, Maureen Connolly Trophy team 1992, 93, winners 1993, snr debut and European Cup team 1992. *Address*: c/o LTA, The Queen's Club, W. Kensington, London W14 9EG.

SIMMONS, Gavin Stuart: motorcyclist (sidecar passenger); b. 2 September 1960, York; m. Julie King 1982; 1 s., 1 d.; GB Supercup open champ. 1992; world champ. 1991, runner-up 1992, 93, 3rd place 1990. *Leisure interests*: weight training, swimming, jogging, moto-cross. *Address*: Mistral, Main St, Sutton on Derwent, York YO4 5BN.

SIMPSON, Fitzroy: footballer; b. 26 February 1970, Bradford-on-Avon; player Swindon Town 1988–92, Manchester City 92– . *Address*: Manchester City FC, Maine Rd, Moss Side, Manchester M14 7WN.

SIMPSON, Ian: motorcyclist; b. 21 August 1969, Edinburgh; GB Supercup Supersport 600 champ. 1991. *Leisure interests*: football, mountain bikes. *Address*: 47 William St, Dalbeattie DG5 4EN.

SIMPSON, Lynn Susan: canoeist; b. 16 February 1971, Scarborough; GB women's

jnr K1 slalom champ. 1988, 89, snr champ. 1990, 91, 93; GB jnr debut 1986, snr debut 1990; World Champs. women's K1 slalom team bronze medal 1993; World Cup women's K1 slalom bronze medal 1993; Olympic squad 1992. *Address*: 21 Wesley Close, S. Cave, Brough, N. Humberside HU15 2EJ.

SIMPSON, Neil: footballer; b. 15 November 1961, Hackney; player Aberdeen 1978–90, Newcastle Utd 90–91, Motherwell 91– ; with Aberdeen: winners Scottish Cup 1982, 83, 84, Scottish League Cup 1986; 11 Scotland U-21 caps, 4 full Scotland caps. *Address*: Motherwell FC, Fir Park, Fir Park St, Motherwell ML1 2QN.

SIMPSON, Owen: Rugby League footballer; b. 12 September 1965, Huddersfield; player Keighley, Featherstone Rovers 1990– . *Address*: Featherstone Rovers RLFC, The Croft, Batley Rd, W. Ardsley, Wakefield WF3 1DX.

SIMPSON, Paul David: footballer; b. 26 July 1966, Carlisle; m. Jacqueline Linda Osborne 1988; 2 s.; player Manchester City 1983–88, Oxford Utd 88–92, Derby County 92– ; 5 England U-21 caps. *Leisure interests*: golf, cricket. *Address*: Derby County FC, The Baseball Ground, Shaftesbury Crescent, Derby DE3 8NB.

SIMPSON, Rodney: racehorse trainer; b. 16 September 1945, Croydon; m. Eileen Jennings 1976; 1 s., 1 d.; 1st licence 1981; winner Cesarewitch 1983 (Bajan Sunshine). *Publications*: *Mainly Fun and Horses*, 1993. *Leisure interests*: all and every sport. *Address*: 17 Oxford St, Lambourn, Berks. RG16 7XS.

SIMPSON, Roger: Rugby League footballer; b. 27 August 1967, Huddersfield; player Moldgreen ARLFC, Bradford Northern 1985– ; GB tourist. *Address*: Bradford Northern RLFC, Odsal Stadium, Bradford BD6 1BS.

SIMS, David: Rugby Union footballer; b. 22 November 1969, Gloucester; player Longlevens, Sunnybank (Aus.), Gloucester; rep. S.W. Div., Div. champs. 1993/94; England U-21 debut v. The Netherlands 1990, England B debut v. Spain 1992, tour NZ 1992. *Address*: Gloucester RUFC, Kingsholm, Worcester St, Gloucester GL3 3AX.

SIMS, Robin Jason: cricketer; b. 22 November 1970, Hillingdon; player Middx 1992– , county champs. 1993. *Address*: Middx CCC, Lord's Cricket Ground, London NW8 8QN.

SINCLAIR, David: footballer; b. 6 October 1969, Dunfermline; player Raith Rovers 1990– . *Address*: Raith Rovers FC, Stark's Park, Pratt St, Kirkcaldy, Fife KY1 1SA.

SINCLAIR, Frank: footballer; b. 3 December 1971, Lambeth; player Chelsea 1990– . *Address*: Chelsea FC, Stamford Bridge, Fulham Rd, London SW6 1HS.

SINCLAIR, Trevor: footballer; b. 2 March 1973, Dulwich; player Blackpool 1990–93, Queens Park Rangers 93– . *Address*: Queens Park Rangers FC, Rangers Stadium, South Africa Rd, London W12 7PA.

SINNOTT, Lee: footballer; b. 12 July 1965, Pelsall; player Walsall 1982–83, Watford 83–87, Bradford City 87–91, Crystal Palace 91– ; 1 England U-21 cap. *Address*: Crystal Palace FC, Selhurst Park Stadium, London SE25 6PU.

SINTON, Andrew: footballer; b. 19 March 1966, Newcastle; player Cambridge Utd 1983–85, Brentford 85–89, Queens Park Rangers 89–93, Sheffield Wednesday 93– ; over 10 England caps. *Address*: Sheffield Wednesday FC, Hillsborough, Sheffield, S. Yorks S6 1SW.

SIXSMITH, Jane Teresa: hockey player; b. 5 September 1967, Sutton Coldfield; player Sutton Coldfield 1980– , European Cup Winners' Cup silver medallist 1991, gold 1992; rep. Warks. 1985– ; England U-18 debut 1983, U-21 debut 1985, snr debut and European Champs. silver medallist 1987, gold 1991, World Cup squad 1990; GB debut 1987, tour Aus./NZ 1990, Olympic squad 1988, bronze medallist 1992; top GB goal-scorer of all time; Hockey Writers Player of the Year 1992. *Leisure interests*: *Coronation Street*, Aston Villa FC, socializing, tennis. *Address*: First Personnel Sutton Coldfield HC, Rectory Park, Sutton Coldfield, W. Midlands.

SKELTON, Nick: equestrianist (show jumping); b. 30 December 1957; GB champ. 1981 (St James); GB debut 1978; European Champs. team gold medal 1985 (St James), 1987, team silver 1993; World Champs. team bronze medal 1982, team silver and individ. bronze 1986 (Apollo); Olympic squad 1988, 92; winner King George V Gold Cup 1984 (St James), 1993 (Limited Edition), Derby 1987 (J Nick), 1988, 89 (Apollo). *Address*: c/o Brit. Horse Soc., Brit. Equestrian Centre, Stoneleigh Park, Kenilworth, Warks. CV8 2LR.

SKERRETT, Kelvin: Rugby League footballer; b. 22 May 1966, Leeds; player Hunslet, Bradford Northern, Wigan 1990– ; with Wigan: winners Challenge Cup 1992, 93; rep. Yorks.; GB debut v. NZ 1989, Brit. Lions tours NZ/Papua New Guinea 1990, Aus./NZ/Papua New Guinea 1992. *Address*: Wigan RLFC, The Pavilion, Central Park, Wigan WN1 1XF.

SKIDMORE, Nicholas Alan: flat and crown green bowler; b. 15 April 1973, Coventry; rep. Warks. (flat green indoor) 1988– , N. Midlands (crown green) 1991– ; English U-25 singles champ. (flat green indoor) 1993; losing finalist, Champion of Champions (crown green) 1992. *Leisure interests*: football, golf, snooker, pool, darts, cricket. *Address*: Stoke Coventry Club, 7 Stoke Green, Coventry CV3 1FP.

SKILLING, Mark: footballer; b. 6 October 1972, Irvine; player Kilmarnock 1992– . *Address*: Kilmarnock FC, Rugby Park, Kilmarnock KA1 2DP.

SKLENAR, Jason Michael: biathlete; b. 27 March 1970, Cheltenham; GB debut 1991, World Champs. squad 1991, 93, Olympic squad 1992; GB 2-mile rollerblade champ. 1993. *Leisure interests*: cycling, canoeing, computing, learning German. *Address*: 40 Devon Ave, Rowanfield Rd, Cheltenham, Glos. GL51 8BJ.

SLATER, Richard: Rugby League footballer; b. 29 August 1970; player Normanton ARLFC, Wakefield Trinity 1988– . *Address*: Wakefield Trinity RLFC, 171 Doncaster Rd, Belle Vue, Wakefield WF1 5EZ.

SLATER, Stuart: footballer; b. 27 March 1969, Sudbury; player W. Ham Utd 1987–92, Celtic 92–93, Ipswich Town 93– ; 3 England U-21 caps. *Address*: Ipswich Town FC, Portman Rd, Ipswich, Suffolk IP1 2DA.

SLAVEN, Bernard: footballer; b. 13 November 1960, Paisley; player Morton 1981–83, Airdrieonians 83–84, Queen of the S. 1984, Albion Rovers 1984–85, Middlesbrough 1985– ; 7 Ireland caps. *Address*: Middlesbrough FC, Ayresome Park, Middlesbrough, Cleveland TS1 4PB.

SMAILES, Anthony Victor: motorcyclist (off-road); b. 2 April 1956, Saltburn; GB sand race trials and enduro champ. 1992. *Leisure interests*: football, road motorcycling. *Address*: 3 Bladon Drive, Marske, Cleveland TS11 6AT.

SMALES, Ian: Rugby League footballer; b. 26 September 1968, Featherstone; player

Featherstone Rovers 1987–93, Castleford 93– ; with Castleford: winners Regal Trophy 1994; Brit. Lions tour NZ/Papua New Guinea 1990. *Address*: Castleford RLFC, Wheldon Rd, Castleford WF10 2SD.

SMALL, Bryan: footballer; b. 15 November 1971, Birmingham; player Aston Villa 1991– . *Address*: Aston Villa FC, Villa Park, Trinity Rd, Birmingham B6 6HE.

SMALL, Gladstone Cleophas: cricketer; b. 18 October 1961, St George, Barbados; m. Lois Small; 1 s.; player Warks. 1980– , winners NatWest Trophy 1993; England YC tour NZ 1979/80, Test debut 1986, tours Aus./India/Pakistan (World Cup) 1986/87, India/WI 1989/90, Aus. 1990/91, Aus./NZ (World Cup) 1991/92. *Address*: Warks. CCC, County Ground, Edgbaston, Birmingham B5 7QU.

SMALL, Michael: footballer; b. 2 January 1962, Birmingham; player PAOK Salonika (Greece), Brighton and Hove Albion 1990–91, W. Ham Utd 91– . *Address*: W. Ham Utd FC, Boleyn Ground, Green St, Upton Park, London E13 9AZ.

SMART, Gary: footballer; b. 29 April 1964, Totnes; player Oxford Utd 1988– . *Address*: Oxford Utd FC, Manor Ground, London Rd, Headington, Oxford OX3 7RS.

SMILLIE, Neil: footballer; b. 19 July 1958, Barnsley; m. Penelope Lynn Smillie 1980; 3 s.; player Crystal Palace 1976–82, Brighton and Hove Albion 82–85, Watford 85–87, Reading 87–88, Brentford 88– ; with Brentford: 3rd Div. champs. 1991/92. *Leisure interests*: golf, holidays in Portugal, family life, eating out. *Address*: Brentford FC, Griffin Park, Braemar Rd, Brentford, Middx TW8 0NT.

SMIT, Jane: cricketer; b. 24 December 1972, Ilkeston; player Newark and Sherwood WCC 1989– ; rep. E. Midlands Ladies 1989– , county champs. 1989–91;

England jnr debut 1990; Test debut and tour Aus./NZ 1992, winners World Cup 1993; rep. Notts hockey, Derbys. U-21 golf; Sports Writers' Team of the Year award-winner 1993. *Leisure interests*: hockey, tennis, squash, Derby County FC. *Address*: 173 Longfield Lane, Ilkeston, Derbys. DE7 4DD.

SMITH, Alan: footballer; b. 21 November 1962, Bromsgrove; player Leicester City 1982–87, Arsenal 87– ; with Arsenal: League champs. 1988/89, 90/91, winners League Cup, FA Cup 1993; 13 England caps. *Address*: Arsenal FC, Arsenal Stadium, Highbury, London N5 1BU.

SMITH, Andrew: motorcyclist (speedway); b. 22 May 1966, York; 1 d.; rep. Belle Vue 1982–88, Bradford 89–90, Swindon 1991, Coventry 1992– ; with Belle Vue: GB League champs. 1982; GB jnr grass-track champ. 1981; GB speedway champ. 1993; England debut 1985, tours Aus. 1985, 87. *Leisure interests*: go-kart racing, cycling, swimming, travel. *Address*: 136 Firwood Ave, Urmston, Manchester M31 1PN.

SMITH, Andrew Michael: cricketer; b. 1 October 1967, Dewsbury; player Glos. 1991– , tour Kenya 1990. *Address*: Glos. CCC, Phoenix County Ground, Nevil Rd, Bristol BS6 9EJ.

SMITH, Andrew William: cricketer; b. 30 May 1969, Sutton, Surrey; player Surrey 1992– . *Address*: Surrey CCC, The Oval, Kennington, London SE11 5SS.

SMITH, Barry: footballer; b. 19 February 1974, Paisley; player Celtic 1991– ; Scotland U-21 int. *Address*: Celtic FC, Celtic Park, 95 Kerrydale St, Glasgow G40 3RE.

SMITH, Benjamin Francis: cricketer; b. 3 April 1972, Corby; player Leics. 1990– ; England U-19 tour NZ 1990/91. *Address*: Leics. CCC, County Ground, Grace Rd, Leicester LE2 8AD.

SMITH, Carl Bernard: oarsman; b. 1 December 1961, Lagos, Nigeria; m. Rosalind Ann Smith 1985; 1 s., 1 d.; GB lightweight coxless fours champ. 1992; Commonwealth Games lightweight single sculls and open double sculls bronze medals 1986; World Champs. lightweight coxless fours silver medal 1983, bronze 1984, double sculls gold 1986, bronze 1987, eights bronze 1990, coxless fours gold 1991, 92. *Publications*: contributor to *A Year to Remember: A Celebration of the 150th Henley Regatta*, ed. Richard Burnell, 1989. *Leisure interests*: marathon-running, stamp-collecting, my children. *Address*: Nottingham County Rowing Assoc., 60 Green Lane, Ockbrook, Derbys. DE7 3SE.

SMITH, Claire McDougall: oarswoman; b. 1 April 1966, Durham; rep. Univ. of London Women's BC 1984–87, 89–92, Thames Tradesmen's RC 87–89, 92– ; GB light-weight women's double sculls champ. 1988, women's coxed fours champ. 1990; GB debut 1987. *Leisure interests*: cycling, swimming, art, reading, cooking. *Address*: Thames Tradesmen's RC, Chiswick Boathouse, Dukes Meadows, London W4 2SH.

SMITH, Damian: ice hockey player; b. 8 October 1971; player Durham Wasps 1987– , winners Autumn Cup 1989, 91, GB champs. 1987/88, 90/91, 91/92, League champs. 1988/89, 90/91, 91/92; World Champs. debut 1992. *Address*: The Ice Rink, Walkersgate, Durham DH1 1SQ.

SMITH, David: Rugby League footballer; b. 15 March 1968; player Widnes 1987– , winners Regal Trophy 1992. *Address*: Widnes RLFC, Naughton Park, Lowerhouse Lane, Widnes WA8 7DZ.

SMITH, David: footballer; b. 29 March 1968, Stonehouse, Glos.; player Coventry City 1987–93, Birmingham City 93– ; 10 England U-21 caps. *Address*: Birmingham City FC, St Andrews Ground, Birmingham B9 4NH.

SMITH, David Mark: cricketer; b. 9 January 1956, Balham; m. Jacqui Smith 1977; 1 d.; player Surrey 1973–83, Worcs. 84–87, Surrey 87–88, Sussex 89– ; 2 Tests, debut 1985, 2 1-day ints, tours WI 1985/86, 89/90. *Address*: Sussex CCC, County Ground, Eaton Rd, Hove, E. Sussex BN3 3AN.

SMITH, Gary: footballer; b. 25 March 1971, Glasgow; player Falkirk 1988–91, Aberdeen 91– ; Scotland int. *Address*: Aberdeen FC, Pittodrie Stadium, Pittodrie St, Aberdeen AB2 1QH.

SMITH, Gary Andrew: flat green bowler; b. 13 October 1958, Lewisham; m. Jayne Leslie Smith 1990; 1 s., 2 step-d.; rep. Kent (outdoor and indoor) 1977– ; English singles champ. (indoor) 1988, pairs champ. (outdoor) 1992, (indoor) 1986, 91, mixed pairs champ. (outdoor) 1991, fours champ. (indoor) 1983, 84, 88, 89, 90; UK singles champ. (indoor) 1988; GB pairs champ. (outdoor) 1993, (indoor) 1987, 92, fours champ. (indoor) 1989, 90, 91; England debut (outdoor) 1982, (indoor) 1984; Commonwealth Games squad and Test debut 1990; World Indoor Champs. pairs gold medal 1993. *Leisure interests*: snooker, gardening, music, musical theatre. *Address*: 100 High St, Henlow, Beds. SG16 6AE.

SMITH, Ian: cricketer; b. 11 March 1967, Consett; player Glamorgan 1985–91, Durham 92– ; England YC tour WI 1985. *Address*: Durham CCC, County Ground, Riverside, Chester-le-Street, Co. Durham DH3 3QR.

SMITH, Ian Richard: Rugby Union footballer; b. 16 March 1965, Gloucester; m. Karen Smith; player Longlevens, Gloucester (capt.); England B debut v. Spanish Select 1989, tour Spain 1990, Scotland B debut v. Ireland 1990, snr and Five Nations debut v. England 1994 (replacement), tours Aus. 1992, Fiji/Tonga/W. Samoa 1993. *Address*: Gloucester RUFC, Kingsholm, Worcester St, Gloucester GL3 3AX.

SMITH, James: football manager; b. 17 October 1940, Sheffield; player Aldershot 1961–65, Halifax Town 65–68, Lincoln City 68–69, Colchester Utd 72–73; manager Colchester Utd, Blackburn Rovers 1975–78, Birmingham City 78–82, Oxford Utd 82–85, Queens Park Rangers 85–88, Portsmouth 91– ; with Oxford Utd: 3rd Div. champs. 1983/84, 2nd Div. champs. 1984/85. *Address*: Portsmouth FC, Fratton Park, Frogmore Rd, Portsmouth PO4 8RA.

SMITH, Jane: hockey player; b. 5 April 1969; player Chelmsford; England U-21 debut 1989, snr debut (outdoor and indoor) 1990, European Champs. gold medallist 1991; Champions Trophy squad 1993. *Address*: Chelmsford HC, Chelmer Park, Beehive Lane, Chelmsford, Essex.

SMITH, Lawrie Edward: yachtsman; b. 18 February 1956, Manchester; m. Penelope Jane Smith 1991; 1 s.; UK Fireball champ. 1977, Ultra 30 champ. 1991–93; French 470-class champ. 1976, 77; European Champs. Fireball gold medal 1976, J-24 gold 1984; World Cup 470-class gold medal 1976; World Champs. Enterprise, Fireball gold medals 1978, 6m gold 1981, 82, 86; Olympic squad 1988, Soling bronze medal 1992; America's Cup team 1980 (skipper *Lionheart*), 1983 (skipper *Victory*), 1987 (Aus.) (*Kookaburra III*); Admiral's Cup team 1985 (skipper *Panda*, winners Fastnet Race), 1987, 89 (winners 1989) (skipper *Jamarella*), 1991 (skipper *Port Pendennis*); Whitbread Round the World Race competitor 1985/86 (helmsman *Drum*, leg 1), 1989/90 (skipper *Rothmans*), 1993/94 (skipper *Fortuna* (withdrawn), *Intrum Justitia*, winners leg 2, record time); Whitbread 60-class world 24-hour record-holder; only Briton to have skippered yachts in the America's Cup, Admiral's Cup, Olympic Games and Whitbread. *Publications*: Dinghy Training, Dinghy Helming, Yacht Tuning. *Leisure interests*: golf, tennis. *Address*: c/o RYA, RYA House, Romsey Rd, Eastleigh, Hants. SO5 4YA.

SMITH, Mark: footballer; b. 19 December 1961, Sheffield; player Rochdale 1988–89, Huddersfield Town 89–91, Grimsby Town 91–93, Scunthorpe Utd 93– . *Address*: Scunthorpe Utd FC, Glanford Park, Doncaster Rd, Scunthorpe, S. Humberside DN15 8TD.

SMITH, Michael: footballer; b. 28 October 1958, Sunderland; player Lincoln City 1977–79, Wimbledon 79–86, Hartlepool Utd 89–92, Tranmere Rovers 92– . *Address*: Tranmere Rovers FC, Prenton Park, Prenton Rd W., Birkenhead, Merseyside L42 9PN.

SMITH, Neil Michael Knight: cricketer; b. 27 July 1967, Solihull; player Warks. 1987– , winners NatWest Trophy 1993. *Address*: Warks. CCC, County Ground, Edgbaston, Birmingham B5 7QU.

SMITH, Neil Philip Alwyne: rackets player; b. 22 March 1963, Godalming; m. Sarah Dunn Curran 1993; GB open champ. 1990, 93, 94, open doubles champ. 1991, 92, prof. champ. 1985–89, 92, 93; US prof. champ. 1991–94, open singles and doubles champ. 1991–94; world doubles champ. 1992, 93. *Leisure interests*: cooking, brewing beer. *Address*: 980 Second Ave, Apartment 2A, New York, NY10022, USA.

SMITH, Paul: footballer; b. 18 September 1971, Lenham, Kent; player Southend Utd 1990–93, Brentford 93– . *Address*: Brentford FC, Griffin Park, Braemar Rd, Brentford, Middx TW8 0NT.

SMITH, Paul Andrew: cricketer; b. 15 April 1964, Newcastle-upon-Tyne; m. Caroline Jayne Smith 1987; 2 s.; player Warks. 1982– , winners NatWest Trophy 1989, 93, tours La Manga 1989, Trinidad and Tobago 1991, Cape Town (SA) 1992, 93; holds world record (with Andrew Moles) for highest number of consecutive 50+ partnerships. *Leisure interests*: gym training, restoring cars, reading. *Address*: Warks. CCC, County Ground, Edgbaston, Birmingham B5 7QU.

SMITH, Pauline: tenpin bowler; b. 9 July 1956, Chessington; 1 s., 1 d.; Irish women's open champ. 1992; Welsh women's open champ. 1993; GB women's open champ. 1992, 93, masters champ. 1993; European Champs. women's all-events silver medal 1973, doubles and team gold, all-events silver 1993; World Games women's gold medal 1993; winner European Cup 1993, World Cup 1981, 1993; Brit. Bowler of the Year 1991–93. *Leisure interests*: spending time with my children, coaching juniors. *Address*: 46 Ravenswood Ave, Tolworth, Surrey KT6 7NP.

SMITH, Richard: footballer; b. 3 October 1970, Lutterworth; player Leicester City 1988– . *Address*: Leicester City FC, City Stadium, Filbert St, Leicester LE2 7FL.

SMITH, Robin Arnold: cricketer; b. 13 September 1963, Durban, SA; m. Katherine Smith 1988; 1 s.; player Hants. 1982– , Sunday League champs. 1986; Test debut 1988, tours India/WI 1989/90, Aus. 1990/91, Aus./NZ (World Cup) 1991/92, India/Sri Lanka 1992/93, WI 1994. *Address*: Hants. CCC, County Cricket Ground, Northlands Rd, Southampton SO9 2TY.

SMITH, Spencer William Thomas: triathlete; b. 11 May 1973, Hounslow; GB jnr champ. 1990–92, snr champ. 1991, 93, sprint champ., duathlon champ. 1992; European Jnr Champs. gold medals 1990, 91; World Jnr Champs. gold medal 1992; European Champs. Olympic-distance individ. and team gold, duathlon individ. gold and team silver medals 1992; World Champs. gold medal 1993; Triathlete of the Year 1991, European Jnr Triathlete of the Year 1992. *Leisure interests*: music, cinema, giant hamburgers, fruit cake. *Address*: c/o Brit. Triathlon Assoc., 4 Tynemouth Terrace, Tynemouth NE30 4BH.

SMITH, Steve: athlete (high jump); b. 29 March 1973, Liverpool; AAA champ. 1992; European Jnr Champs. gold medal 1991;

World Jnr Champs. gold medal 1992; World Champs. bronze medal 1993; World Indoor Champs. bronze medal 1993; UK and Commonwealth indoor and outdoor record-holder. *Address*: c/o Brit. Athletic Fed., 225A Bristol Rd, Edgbaston, Birmingham B5 7UB.

SMITH, Steven David: Rugby Union footballer; b. 20 June 1968, Solihull; player Solihull, Coventry 1988–91, Rugby 91– ; rep. Warks. 1989– . *Leisure interests*: weight training. *Address*: The Rugby FC, Webb Ellis Rd, off Bilton Rd, Rugby, Warks.

SMITH, Timothy: Rugby Union footballer; b. 10 May 1962, Gloucester; m. Imelda Frances Smith 1990; player Brockworth 1978–79, Gordon League 79–82, Gloucester 82– ; rep. England Students v. England U-23 1985; 300th appearance for Gloucester v. Wasps 1994. *Leisure interests*: basketball, barbecues, tropical fish, travel. *Address*: Gloucester RUFC, Kingsholm, Worcester St, Gloucester GL3 3AX.

SMITH, Tony: Rugby League footballer; b. 16 July 1970, Wakefield; player Castleford 1988– ; GB U-21 int. *Address*: Castleford RLFC, Wheldon Rd, Castleford WF10 2SD.

SMITHIES, Karen, OBE: cricketer; b. 20 March 1969, Ashby de la Zouch; m. Dean Smithies 1990; player Leicester WCC 1985–87, Newark and Sherwood WCC 88– ; rep. E. Midlands Ladies 1985– (capt. 89–); England jnr tour Denmark 1984; Test debut v. Aus. 1987, tours Aus. (World Cup) 1988, Ireland/The Netherlands 1990, NZ 1991, winners European Cup 1991, World Cup 1993 (capt.); holds women's world record for 7th-wicket partnership with Jo Chamberlain (110); Sports Writers' Team of the Year award-winner 1993. *Leisure interests*: running, reading, eating out. *Address*: c/o Women's Cricket Assoc., 41 St Michael's Lane, Headingley, Leeds LS6 3BR.

SMYTH, Michael: boxer; b. 22 February 1970, Barry; Welsh light-welterweight champ. 1988, 89, welterweight champ. 1990; Wales debut 1988, Commonwealth Games squad 1990; prof. debut 1991; over 8 prof. wins. *Leisure interests*: water sports. *Address*: Rhoose Boxing Club, Rhoose, S. Glamorgan.

SMYTH, William Jackson: flat green bowler; b. 18 December 1966, Magherafelt, NI; m. Joanne Smyth 1991; Irish U-25 singles champ. (outdoor) 1986, 87, 91, snr triples champ. (outdoor) 1992; GB U-25 singles champ. (outdoor) 1992, snr triples champ. (outdoor) 1993; Ireland debut (outdoor) 1992, (indoor) 1986. *Leisure interests*: Manchester Utd FC, eating out. *Address*: 4 Parkmore, Magherafelt, Co. Londonderry BT45 6EZ.

SNEDDON, Alan: footballer; b. 12 March 1958, Baillieston; player Celtic 1977–80, Hibernian 80–92, Motherwell 92– ; with Celtic: winners Scottish Cup 1980; Scotland U-21 int. *Address*: Motherwell FC, Fir Park, Fir Park St, Motherwell ML1 2QN.

SNELDERS, Theo: footballer; b. 7 December 1963, Westervoort, The Netherlands; player Twente (The Netherlands), Aberdeen 1988– ; with Aberdeen: winners Scottish League Cup, Scottish Cup 1990; Holland int. *Address*: Aberdeen FC, Pittodrie Stadium, Pittodrie St, Aberdeen AB2 1QH.

SNODIN, Glynn: footballer; b. 14 February 1960, Rotherham; player Doncaster Rovers 1977–85, Sheffield Wednesday 85–87, Leeds Utd 87–92, Heart of Midlothian 92–93, Barnsley 93– . *Address*: Barnsley FC, Oakwell Ground, Barnsley, S. Yorks. S71 1ET.

SNODIN, Ian: footballer; b. 15 August 1963, Rotherham; player Doncaster Rovers 1979–85, Leeds Utd 85–87, Everton 87– ; with Everton: League champs. 1986/87; 4 England U-21 caps. *Address*: Everton FC, Goodison Park, Liverpool L4 4EL.

SNOW, Julian Piercy: real tennis player; b. 16 June 1964, Hereford; GB U-21 open champ. 1985, U-24 open singles and doubles champ. 1985–88, amateur champ. 1987–89, 91–94, doubles champ. 1987, 91–93, open champ. 1992, 93; US amateur champ. 1992, doubles champ. 1992–94, open doubles champ. 1992, 93; Aus. open singles and doubles champ. 1992; French open champ. 1992, doubles champ. 1985, 91; GB team, winners Bathurst Cup 1986–92; winner Hayman Classic singles 1991, 92, doubles 1992, Laurent Perrier Masters 1992, 93, Ballarat Silver Racket 1989, 92, Leamington Silver Racket 1990–92, Coupe de Bordeaux 1993; ranked world no. 1. *Leisure interests*: futures trading, horseracing, betting. *Address*: 35 Canonbury Rd, London N1 2DG.

SODJE, Bright: Rugby League footballer; b. 21 April 1966, Aldershot; player Blackheath (RU), Hull Kingston Rovers 1990– ; rep. London Div. (RU). *Address*: Hull Kingston Rovers RLFC, Craven Park, Preston Rd, Hull HU9 5HE.

SOLOMAN, Jason: footballer; b. 6 October 1970, Welwyn Garden City; player Watford 1988– . *Address*: Watford FC, Vicarage Rd Stadium, Watford, Herts. WD1 8ER.

SOUTHALL, Neville: footballer; b. 16 September 1958, Llandudno; player Bury 1980–81, Everton 81– ; with Everton: winners FA Cup 1984, European Cup Winners' Cup 1985, League champs. 1984/85, 86/87; over 68 Wales caps. *Address*: Everton FC, Goodison Park, Liverpool L4 4EL.

SOUTHBY, David Edward: judo player (U-78–U-86kg); b. 21 April 1965, Exeter; Welsh open champ. 1985, 88, Scottish open champ. 1989, 92, 91, Austrian open champ. 1990, GB open champ. 1993; Common-wealth Games gold medal 1990; European Champs. team bronze medal 1991; World Champs. squad 1989. *Leisure interests*:

chess, golf, water polo, rugby. *Address*: 53 High St, Little Shelford, Cambs. CB2 5ES.

SOUTHERNWOOD, Graham: Rugby League footballer; b. 5 November 1971, Hemsworth; player Redhill ARLFC, Castleford 1988– ; GB U-21 debut v. France 1990. *Address*: Castleford RLFC, Wheldon Rd, Castleford WF10 2SD.

SOUTHERNWOOD, Roy: Rugby League footballer; b. 23 June 1968, Wakefield; player Castleford, Halifax 1990– ; GB U-21 debut v. France 1989. *Address*: Halifax RLFC, The Pavilion, Thrum Hall, Gibbet St, Halifax, W. Yorks. HX1 4TL.

SOUTHGATE, Gareth: footballer; b. 3 September 1970, Watford; player Crystal Palace 1989– . *Address*: Crystal Palace FC, Selhurst Park Stadium, London SE25 6PU.

SPACKMAN, Nigel: footballer; b. 2 December 1960, Romsey; player Bournemouth 1980–83, Chelsea 83–87, Liverpool 87–89, Queens Park Rangers 89–90, Rangers 90–92, Chelsea 92– ; with Liverpool: winners FA Cup 1989, League champs. 1987/88; with Rangers: winners Scottish League Cup 1991, Scottish Cup 1992, Scottish League champs. 1989/90, 90/91, 91/92. *Address*: Chelsea FC, Stamford Bridge, Fulham Rd, London SW6 1HS.

SPEAK, Nicholas Jason: cricketer; b. 21 October 1966, Manchester; m. Michelle Speak 1993; player Lancs. 1987– , tours Jamaica 1987/88, Zimbabwe 1989, Perth (Aus.) 1990/91, Johannesburg (SA) 1992. *Address*: Lancs. CCC, Old Trafford, Manchester M16 0PX.

SPEED, Gary: footballer; b. 8 September 1969, Hawarden; player Leeds Utd 1988– , 2nd Div. champs. 1989/90, League champs. 1991/92; 3 Wales U-21 caps, over 20 full Wales caps. *Address*: Leeds Utd FC, Elland Rd, Leeds, W. Yorks. LS11 0ES.

SPEEDIE, David: footballer; b. 20 February 1960, Glenrothes; player Barnsley 1978–80, Darlington 80–82, Chelsea 82–87, Coventry City 87–91, Liverpool 1991, Blackburn Rovers 1991–92, Southampton 92–93, Leicester City 93– ; with Chelsea: 2nd Div. champs. 1983/84; 1 Scotland U-21 cap, 10 full Scotland caps. *Address*: Leicester City FC, City Stadium, Filbert St, Leicester LE2 7FL.

SPEIGHT, Martin Peter: cricketer; b. 24 October 1967, Walsall; player Durham Univ. 1986–89, Sussex 86– ; rep. Combined Univ. 1987–89; NCA U-19 tour Bermuda 1985; England YC tour Sri Lanka 1987; scored fastest 1st-class 100 of 1992 v. Lancs. *Leisure interests*: painting, hockey, squash, Brit. TV comedy, music, photography, ancient history. *Address*: Sussex CCC, County Ground, Eaton Rd, Hove, E. Sussex BN3 3AN.

SPENCER, Gary: Rugby League footballer; b. 16 September 1966, Leeds; player Leeds, Wakefield Trinity 1991– ; rep. Yorks. *Address*: Wakefield Trinity RLFC, 171 Doncaster Rd, Belle Vue, Wakefield WF1 5EZ.

SPENCER, John: footballer; b. 11 September 1970, Glasgow; player Rangers 1986–92, Chelsea 92– ; Scotland U-21 int. *Address*: Chelsea FC, Stamford Bridge, Fulham Rd, London SW6 1HS.

SPENCER, Kirsten: hockey player; b. 17 June 1969; player Ipswich Ladies; England U-21 debut 1989, snr debut 1990. *Address*: Ipswich Ladies HC, Tuddenham Rd, Ipswich, Suffolk IP4 3QJ.

SPINK, Nigel: footballer; b. 8 August 1958, Chelmsford; player Aston Villa 1979– , winners European Cup 1982; 1 England cap. *Address*: Aston Villa FC, Villa Park, Trinity Rd, Birmingham B6 6HE.

SPOONER, Nicholas: footballer; b. 5 June 1971, Manchester; player Bolton Wanderers 1989– . *Address*: Bolton Wanderers FC, Burnden Park, Manchester Rd, Bolton, Lancs. BL3 2QR.

SPRECKLEY, Brian Tom: glider pilot; b. 10 June 1948, Nottingham; m. Gillian Spreckley 1986; 2 s., 1 d.; GB racing-class champ. 1981, 86, 91, standard-class champ. 1984; French club-class champ. 1990, multi-seat champ. 1988, 89; GB debut 1981, World Champs. 15m-class gold medal 1987, open-class bronze 1993; Brit. Gliding Assoc. nat. coach 1974–81. *Leisure interests*: bridge, sailing. *Address*: 106 High St, Tetsworth, Oxon OX9 4AS.

SPREITER, Christine: windsurfer; b. 28 January 1964; UK women's wave champ. 1992, 93; highest-ranked UK woman prof. sailor 1990–93. *Publications*: contributor to *Boards, Windsurf* magazines. *Leisure interests*: drawing, painting, printing, skiing, cycling, swimming, surfing, diving, sailing, reading, music. *Address*: Greycotes, Belle Vue Lane, Ambleside, Cumbria LA22 9EZ.

SPRINGMAN, Sarah Marcella: triathlete; b. 26 December 1956, London; GB women's champ. 1985–88, 92, middle-distance champ. 1984–88, 91, Ironman champ. 1990, 91; GB debut 1984 (capt. 1986); European Champs. Olympic-distance individ. gold medals 1985, 86, team gold 1986, 87, middle-distance team gold 1987, Ironman team gold 1987, 89; Vice-Pres. Int. Triathlon Union 1992– ; mem. Sports Council 1993– . *Leisure interests*: opera. *Address*: Magdalene College, Cambridge CB3 0AG.

SPRUCE, Stuart: Rugby League footballer; b. 3 January 1971, Widnes; player Widnes Tigers ARLFC, Widnes 1990– ; GB debut v. France 1993. *Address*: Widnes RLFC, Naughton Park, Lowerhouse Lane, Widnes WA8 7DZ.

SRNICEK, Pavel: footballer; b. 10 March 1968, Ostrava, Czechoslovakia; player Banik Ostrava (Czechoslovakia), Newcastle Utd 1991– ; Czechoslovakia U-21 int. *Address*: Newcastle Utd FC, St James' Park, Newcastle-upon-Tyne, Tyne & Wear NE1 4ST.

STABLER, John: Rugby Union footballer; b. 5 February 1963, Hartlepool; player W. Hartlepool 1981– (capt. 1989–93); rep. Durham colts and snr squad, N. Div. *Address*: W. Hartlepool RFC, Brierton Lane, Hartlepool, Cleveland TS25 5DR.

STANFORD, Matthew: golfer; b. 14 July 1969, Pontypool; rep. Glos. 1986– ; England debut 1991; GB debut 1992, Walker Cup team 1993; prof. debut 1993. *Leisure interests*: music, Bath RFC. *Address*: Saltford Golf Club, nr Bath, Avon.

STANGER, Anthony George: Rugby Union footballer; b. 14 May 1968, Hawick; m. Laura Stanger; player Hawick; rep. S. of Scotland; Scotland debut v. Fiji 1989, Five Nations debut v. Ireland 1990, Grand Slam champs. 1990, tours Japan 1989, NZ 1990, N. America 1991, Aus. 1992. *Address*: Hawick RFC, Mansfield Park, Mansfield Rd, Hawick.

STANHOPE, Richard Courtney: oarsman; b. 27 April 1957, Blackpool; m. Rachel Clare Hirst 1992; rep. Molesey BC, Tideway Scullers School, Leander Club, Royal Chester RC, Liverpool Univ. BC; winning crew, Grand Challenge Cup, Henley Royal Regatta 1982, 83, 86, 88; Commonwealth Games eights silver medal 1986; GB debut 1980, World Champs. eights silver medal 1981, bronze 1991, Olympic eights silver medal 1980, squad 1984, 88, 92. *Leisure interests*: Liverpool FC, cycling, swimming, running. *Address*: c/o ARA, The Priory, 6 Lower Mall, London W6 9DJ.

STANLEY, Andrew Anthony: Rugby Union footballer; b. 15 September 1965, Gloucester; player Gordon League 1974–83, Gloucester 83– ; rep. Glos. and S.W. colts 1981. *Leisure interests*: all sport, Indian food, kitty money. *Address*: Gloucester RUFC, Kingsholm, Worcester St, Gloucester GL3 3AX.

STAPLES, James Edward: Rugby Union footballer; b. 20 October 1965, London; player London Irish; Ireland B debut v. Scotland 1989, snr and Five Nations debut v. Wales 1991, tours Namibia 1991, NZ 1992. *Address*: London Irish RUFC, The Avenue, Sunbury-on-Thames, Middx TW16 5EQ.

STAPLES, Katharine Joanna: athlete (pole vault); b. 2 November 1965, London; AAA women's champ. 1993, indoor champ. 1994; UK women's champ. 1993; UK women's indoor and outdoor record-holder. *Leisure interests*: swimming, skiing, windsurfing, horseriding, walking. *Address*: c/o Brit. Athletic Fed., 225A Bristol Rd, Edgbaston, Birmingham B5 7UB.

STARK, Derek Alexander: Rugby Union footballer; b. 13 April 1966, Johnstone; player Kilmarnock, Ayr, Boroughmuir; Scotland U-21 debut 1987, Scotland B debut v. France 1988, snr tours Zimbabwe 1988, Aus. 1992. *Address*: Boroughmuir RFC, Meggetland, Colinton Rd, Edinburgh EH14 1AS.

STARK, Ian David, MBE: equestrianist (three-day eventing); b. 22 February 1954, Galashiels, Scotland; m. Janet Dixon McAulay 1979; 1 s., 1 d.; European Champs. team gold and individ. silver medals 1985, 87, team gold 1989, team and individ. gold 1991; World Champs. team gold medal 1986, team and individ. silver 1990; Olympic team silver medal 1984, team and individ. silver 1988, squad 1992; winner Badminton Horse Trials 1986, 88. *Publications*: *The Flying Scot* (with Jenny

Stark), 1988. *Leisure interests*: skiing, water skiing, flying, reading. *Address*: Haughhead, Ashkirk, Selkirk TD7 4NT.

STARK, William: footballer; b. 1 December 1956, Glasgow; player St Mirren 1975–83, Aberdeen 83–87, Celtic 87–90, Kilmarnock 90–91, Hamilton Academical 91–92, Kilmarnock 92– ; with Aberdeen: winners Scottish Cup 1984, 86, Scottish League Cup 1986; with Celtic: winners Scottish Cup 1990; Scotland U-21 int. *Address*: Kilmarnock FC, Rugby Park, Kilmarnock KA1 2DP.

STAUNTON, Stephen: footballer; b. 19 January 1969, Drogheda, Ireland; player Liverpool 1988–91, Aston Villa 91– ; with Liverpool: winners FA Cup 1989, League champs. 1990; 2 Ireland U-21 caps, over 40 full Ireland caps. *Address*: Aston Villa FC, Villa Park, Trinity Rd, Birmingham B6 6HE.

STEADMAN, Graham: Rugby League footballer; b. 8 December 1961, Castleford; player Knottingley RUFC, York, Featherstone Rovers, Castleford 1989– ; with Castleford: winners Regal Trophy 1994; GB debut v. France 1990, Brit. Lions tour Aus./NZ/Papua New Guinea 1992. *Address*: Castleford RLFC, Wheldon Rd, Castleford WF10 2SD.

STEELE, John David: Rugby Union footballer; b. 9 August 1964, Cambridge; m. Sophie Steele 1991; player Northampton 1986– , 2nd Div. champs. 1989/90; rep. Sandhurst 1982/83, Army 1984–88, Combined Services 1986–88, tour NZ 1988, Midland Div. 1986–88, 90–93; England B debut v. Namibia 1990; holds Northampton points record. *Leisure interests*: golf, cricket. *Address*: Northampton FC, Franklins Gardens, Weedon Rd, Northampton NN5 5BG.

STEELE, Martin Douglas: athlete; b. 30 September 1962, Huddersfield; 1 d.; AAA 800m champ. 1993, 800m indoor champ. 1991–93; UK 800m champ. 1993. *Leisure interests*: car maintenance, comedy videos, music. *Address*: c/o Brit. Athletic Fed., 225A Bristol Rd, Edgbaston, Birmingham B5 7UB.

STEELE, Mavis Mary, MBE: flat green bowler; b. 9 September 1928, Kenton, Middx; English women's singles champ. (outdoor) 1961, 62, 69, (indoor) 1989, women's pairs champ. (outdoor) 1964, 71, women's triples champ. (outdoor) 1968, women's fours champ. (outdoor) 1963, 69, (indoor) 1991; England debut (outdoor) 1959, (indoor) 1979; Commonwealth Games women's triples bronze medal 1982, squad 1990; World Champs. women's singles and pairs silver medals 1973, women's fours and team gold, triples silver 1981, women's fours bronze 1985; World Indoor Champs. women's singles silver medal 1989; Pres. English Women's Indoor Bowling Assoc. 1989–90. *Address*: 45C Woodthorpe Rd, Ashford, Middx TW15 2RP.

STEELE, Timothy: footballer; b. 1 December 1967, Coventry; player Shrewsbury Town 1985–89, Wolverhampton Wanderers 89–93, Bradford City 93– . *Address*: Bradford City FC, Valley Parade, Bradford, W. Yorks. BD8 7DY.

STEIN, Mark: footballer; b. 28 January 1966, Cape Town, SA; player Luton Town 1984–88, Queens Park Rangers 88–89, Oxford Utd 89–91, Stoke City 91–93, Chelsea 93– ; with Luton Town: winners League Cup 1988. *Address*: Chelsea FC, Stamford Bridge, Fulham Rd, London SW6 1HS.

STEJSKAL, Jan: footballer; b. 15 January 1962, Brunn, Czecholslovakia; player Sparta Prague (Czechoslovakia), Queens Park Rangers 1990– ; Czechoslovakia int. *Address*: Queens Park Rangers FC, Rangers Stadium, S. Africa Rd, London W12 7PA.

STEMP, Richard David: cricketer; b. 11 December 1967, Erdington; player Yorks. 1990–   ; 1st English non-Yorkshireman to be signed by county. *Address*: Yorks. CCC, Headingley Cricket Ground, Leeds LS6 3BU.

STEPHENS, Colin John: Rugby Union footballer; b. 29 November 1969, Morriston; player Llanelli, winners Welsh Cup 1993, Welsh League champs. 1992/93; Wales U-21 debut v. Scotland 1988, snr and Five Nations debut v. Ireland 1992. *Address*: Llanelli RFC, Stradey Park, Llanelli, Dyfed.

STEPHENS, Gareth: Rugby League footballer; b. 15 April 1974, Castleford; player Lock Lane ARLFC, Leeds 1990–   . *Address*: Leeds RLFC, Bass Headingley, St Michael's Lane, Leeds LS6 3BR.

STEPHENS, Rebecca Lucy, MBE: mountaineer; b. 3 October 1961, Sevenoaks; 1st ascent by Brit. woman: Everest via S. col and S.E. ridge 1993. *Leisure interests*: skiing, photography. *Address*: c/o Neville Shulman, 4 St Georges House, 15 Hanover Square, London W1R 9AJ.

STEPHENSON, Franklyn Dacosta: cricketer; b. 8 April 1959, St James, Barbados; m. Julia Stephenson 1981; 3 d.; player Glos. 1982–87, Notts. 88–91, Sussex 92–   ; WI U-19 tour England 1978; achieved 1st-class double of 1000 runs and 100 wickets in season 1988. *Address*: Sussex CCC, County Ground, Eaton Rd, Hove, E. Sussex BN3 3AN.

STEPHENSON, John Patrick: cricketer; b. 14 March 1965, Stebbing; player Essex 1985–   , county champs. 1986, 91, 92, Sunday League champs. 1985; England A tours Kenya/Zimbabwe 1989/90, WI 1991/92, Test debut 1989. *Address*: Essex CCC, County Cricket Ground, New Writtle St, Chelmsford DM2 0PG.

STEPHENSON, Paul: footballer; b. 2 January 1968, Wallsend; player Newcastle Utd 1985–88, Millwall 88–93, Brentford 93–   . *Address*: Brentford FC, Griffin Park, Braemar Rd, Brentford, Middx TW8 0NT.

STERLING, Worrell: footballer; b. 8 June 1965, Bethnal Green; player Watford 1983–89, Peterborough Utd 89–93, Bristol Rovers 93–   . *Address*: Bristol Rovers FC, Twerton Park, Bath.

STEVEN, Trevor: footballer; b. 21 September 1963, Berwick; player Burnley 1981–83, Everton 83–89, Rangers 89–91, Marseille (France) 91–92, Rangers 92–   ; with Rangers: winners Scottish League Cup 1991, 93; 2 England U-21 caps, 36 full England caps. *Address*: Glasgow Rangers FC, Ibrox Stadium, 150 Edmiston Drive, Glasgow G51 2XD.

STEVENS, Gary: footballer; b. 27 March 1963, Barrow; player Everton 1981–88, Rangers 88–   ; with Rangers: winners Scottish League Cup 1989, 91, 93, Scottish Cup 1992; 1 England U-21 cap, 46 full England caps. *Address*: Glasgow Rangers FC, Ibrox Stadium, 150 Edmiston Drive, Glasgow G51 2XD.

STEVENS, Keith: footballer; b. 21 June 1964, Merton; player Millwall 1981–   , 2nd Div. champs. 1987/88. *Address*: Millwall FC, The Den, Zampa Rd, Bermondsey, London SE16 3LH.

STEVENSON, Peter: cyclist (cyclocross/mountain bike); b. 8 March 1959, Northallerton; rep. Saracen 1993–   ; GB amateur cyclo-cross champ. 1992, 93; GB jnr cyclo-cross debut 1977; prof. road and cyclo-cross racer 1985–89, reinstated as amateur 1990. *Address*: Palmer Hargreaves PR Ltd, 18 The Parade, Leamington Spa CV32 4DW.

STEWART, Alec James: cricketer; b. 8 April 1963, Merton; m. Lynn Stewart 1991;

1 s.; player Surrey 1981–   ; Test debut 1989, tours India 1989, WI 1989/90, Aus. 1990/91, Aus./NZ (World Cup) 1991/92, India/Sri Lanka 1992/93, WI 1994. *Address*: Surrey CCC, The Oval, Kennington, London SE11 5SS.

STEWART, Gavin Blakely: oarsman; b. 25 February 1963, Belfast, NI; rep. Oxford Univ. BC 1986–88, winners Univ. Boat Race 1987, 88; winning crew, Grand Challenge Cup, Henley Royal Regatta 1988; GB debut 1988, World Champs. coxed fours bronze medal 1989, Olympic squad 1988, 92. *Leisure interests*: cinema, sport, N. American literature, drinking strong coffee and watching the world go by. *Address*: 6 Camden Terrace, London NW1 9DP.

STEWART, Gillian: golfer; b. 21 October 1958, Inverness; Scottish U-19 strokeplay champ. 1975; GB girls champ. 1976; N. Counties ladies' champ. 1976, 78, 82, N. of Scotland ladies' champ. 1975, 78, 80, 82, 83; Scottish ladies' champ. 1979, 83, 84; European ladies' open champ. 1984; Scotland debut 1979; Curtis Cup team 1980, 82; prof. debut 1985; winner Ford Classic 1985, 87. *Publications*: contributor to *Golf Weekly*. *Leisure interests*: cooking, keep-fit, hill-walking, cycling. *Address*: 14 Annfield Rd, Inverness IV2 3HX.

STEWART, Julie Cynthia: hockey player; b. 3 September 1973, Belfast, NI; player Holywood 1988–89, Newtownards 90–   ; Ulster and Ireland U-21 and snr int. *Leisure interests*: tennis, golf. *Address*: 31 Old Cultra Rd, Cultra, Holywood, Co. Down BT18 0AE.

STEWART, Ossie: yachtsman; b. 31 January 1954, Surbiton; m. Karen Stewart 1992; UK GP-14 champ. 1976, Fireball champ. 1980, 470-class champ. 1982, 83, 87; French Soling champ. 1992; Dutch Soling champ. 1992; European Champs. Fireball gold medal 1981; Olympic reserve (470-class) 1984, bronze medal 1992. *Leisure*

interests: squash, restoring vintage boats. *Address*: Harts Boatyard, Portsmouth Rd, Surbiton, Surrey KT6 4HJ.

STIMSON, Mark: footballer; b. 27 December 1967, Plaistow; player Tottenham Hotspur 1985–89, Newcastle Utd 89–93, Portsmouth 93–   . *Address*: Portsmouth FC, Fratton Park, Frogmore Rd, Portsmouth PO4 8RA.

STOCK, Debra Ann: cricketer; b. 17 July 1962, Oxford; player Blewbury & Upton WCC 1984–86, Gunnersbury WCC 1987–   ; rep. Thames Valley 1985–   ; Test debut and tour Aus./NZ 1992, winners World Cup 1993; Sports Writers' Team of the Year award-winner 1993. *Leisure interests*: football, squash, hockey, horseracing, crosswords, quizzes, competitions. *Address*: Maple Bank, Letcombe Bassett, Wantage, Oxon OX12 9LR.

STOCKWELL, Michael: footballer; b. 14 February 1965, Chelmsford; player Ipswich Town 1985–   . *Address*: Ipswich Town FC, Portman Rd, Ipswich, Suffolk IP1 2DA.

STONE, Darrell Richard: race walker; b. 2 February 1968, Kensington; GB jnr 10km champ. 1985, 86, snr 10km track champ. 1993; GB jnr debut 1985, World Jnr Champs. squad 1986, snr debut 1988, European Champs. squad 1990, World Cup squad 1989, 93, World Champs. squad 1993; GB 5km, 10km and mile track record-holder. *Leisure interests*: films, watching sport. *Address*: Steyning Athletic Club, Charlton St, Steyning, W. Sussex.

STONEHOUSE, Pauline Patricia: fencer; b. 16 February 1952, Woking; rep. Surrey 1976–   ; NI ladies' open foil champ. 1987–93; Irish ladies' foil champ. 1987–93; NI debut 1979 (capt. 1990–   ); Ireland debut 1981. *Leisure interests*: all sport, music, reading. *Address*: 30 Station Rd, Shalford, Guildford, Surrey GU4 8HB.

STORER, Stuart: footballer; b. 16 January 1967, Rugby; player Birmingham City 1985–87, Everton 1987, Bolton Wanderers 1987– . *Address*: Bolton Wanderers FC, Burnden Park, Manchester Rd, Bolton, Lancs. BL3 2QR.

STOTT, Lynton: Rugby League footballer; b. 9 May 1971; player Halifax, Sheffield Eagles 1992– . *Address*: Sheffield Eagles RLFC, Stadium Corner, 824 Attercliffe Rd, Sheffield S9 3RS.

STOUTE, Michael Ronald: racehorse trainer (Flat); b. 22 October 1945, Barbados; 1 s., 1 d.; 1st licence 1972; winner Oaks 1978 (Fair Salinia), 1987 (Unite), Derby 1981 (Shergar), 1986 (Shahrastani), Irish Derby 1981 (Shergar), 1983 (Shareef Dancer), 1986 (Shahrastani), 2000 Guineas 1985 (Shadeed), 1988 (Doyoun), Irish Oaks 1986 (Colorspin), 1987 (Unite), 1988 (Melodist), Irish 1000 Guineas 1986 (Sonic Lady), 1000 Guineas 1989 (Musical Bliss), Irish 2000 Guineas 1989 (Shaadi), King George VI and Queen Elizabeth Diamond Stakes 1993 (Opera House); leading trainer 1981, 86, 89; became 1st trainer this century to win English Classics in 5 successive seasons 1989. *Leisure interests*: cricket, hunting. *Address*: Freemason Lodge, Bury Rd, Newmarket, Suffolk CB8 7BT.

STOWELL, Michael: footballer; b. 19 April 1965, Portsmouth; m. Joanne Stowell 1992; 1 d.; player Everton 1985–90, Wolverhampton Wanderers 90– . *Leisure interests*: golf, tennis. *Address*: Wolverhampton Wanderers FC, Molineux Stadium, Waterloo Rd, Wolverhampton WV1 4QR.

STRACHAN, Gordon David, OBE: footballer; b. 9 February 1957, Edinburgh; m. Lesley Strachan; 3 ch.; player Dundee 1974–77, Aberdeen 77–84, Manchester Utd 84–89, Leeds Utd 89– ; with Aberdeen: winners Scottish Cup 1982, 83, 84, European Cup Winners' Cup 1983; with

Manchester Utd: winners FA Cup 1985; with Leeds Utd: 2nd Div. champs. 1989/90, League champs. 1991/92; 1 Scotland U-21 cap, 50 full Scotland caps; Scottish Football Writers' Assoc. Player of the Year 1980. *Address*: Leeds Utd FC, Elland Rd, Leeds, W. Yorks. LS11 0ES.

STRACHAN, Linda Caroline: fencer (fcil); b. 18 October 1961, Forest Gate; GB ladies' foil champ. 1990; England debut 1982; Commonwealth Games squad 1982, 86, 90; Commonwealth Champs. team gold medals 1982, 86; GB debut 1985, Olympic squad 1988, 92; winner Welsh Open 1989, 93, Leicester Open 1989, Birmingham Open 1990, Essex Open 1993. *Leisure interests*: keep-fit, soul music. *Address*: 15 Brock Rd, Plaistow, London E13 8NA.

STRANGE, Nicholas John: oarsman; b. 15 August 1966, Canterbury; rep. Reading Univ. 1984–87; GB eights champ. 1992; GB jnr debut 1984, U-23 debut and World U-23 Champs. lightweight coxless fours silver medal 1987, snr debut 1988, World Champs. lightweight coxless fours bronze medal 1989, eights silver 1992. *Leisure interests*: gym decathlons, cross-training competitions, squash, tennis, walking. *Address*: Hillmead, St Stephen, Canterbury CT2 7LB.

STREET, Tim: Rugby League footballer; b. 29 June 1968; player Oldham, Leigh 1992–93, Hull 93– . *Address*: Hull RLFC, The Boulevard Ground, Airlie St, Hull HU3 3JD.

STRODDER, Gary: footballer; b. 1 April 1965, Cleckheaton; player Lincoln City 1983–87, W. Ham Utd 87–90, W. Bromwich Albion 90– . *Address*: W. Bromwich Albion FC, The Hawthorns, W. Bromwich B71 4LF.

STRONGE, Tamara Elizabeth Louise: hockey player; b. 2 December 1971, Belfast, NI; player Loughborough Univ., Ards

Ladies; with Loughborough: UAU champs. (indoor and outdoor) 1992, 93; with Ards: Ulster indoor League champs. 1988–93, All-Ireland indoor champs. 1991; Ulster indoor debut 1989, outdoor 1991, Ireland U-21 debut 1990, snr debut 1991. *Leisure interests*: horseriding, water skiing. *Address*: Cadew Point, Killinchy, Co. Down BT23 6QB.

STUART, Graham: footballer; b. 24 October 1970, Tooting; player Chelsea 1989–93, Everton 93– ; 5 England U-21 caps. *Address*: Everton FC, Goodison Park, Liverpool L4 4EL.

STUBBS, Alan: footballer; b. 6 October 1971, Liverpool; player Bolton Wanderers 1990– . *Address*: Bolton Wanderers FC, Burnden Park, Manchester Rd, Bolton, Lancs. BL3 2QR.

SUCH, Peter Mark: cricketer; b. 12 June 1964, Helensburgh; player Notts. 1982–86, Leics. 87–89, Essex 90– ; with Essex: county champs. 1991, 92; England A tours Aus. 1992/93, SA 1993/94, Test debut v. Aus. 1993. *Leisure interests*: golf, music, reading. *Address*: Essex CCC, County Cricket Ground, New Writtle St, Chelmsford DM2 0PG.

SUCKLING, Perry: footballer; b. 12 October 1965, Leyton; player Coventry City 1983–86, Manchester City 86–88, Crystal Palace 88–92, Watford 92– ; 10 England U-21 caps. *Address*: Watford FC, Vicarage Rd Stadium, Watford, Herts. WD1 8ER.

SULLIVAN, Anthony Clive: Rugby League footballer; b. 23 November 1968, Hull; player Hull Kingston Rovers, St Helens 1991– ; Wales debut v. Papua New Guinea 1991; GB debut v. Papua New Guinea 1991. *Address*: St Helens RLFC, Dunriding Lane, St Helens, Merseyside WA10 4AD.

SUMMERBEE, Nicholas: footballer; b. 26 August 1971, Altrincham; player Swindon Town 1989– . *Address*: Swindon Town FC, The County Ground, Swindon, Wilts. SN1 2ED.

SUMMERS, Neil: Rugby League footballer; b. 10 October 1968, Leeds; player Headingley RUFC, Bradford Northern 1990– ; England U-21 and B int. (RU). *Address*: Bradford Northern RLFC, Odsal Stadium, Bradford BD6 1BS.

SUSSEX, Andrew: footballer; b. 23 November 1964, Enfield; player Leyton Orient 1982–88, Crewe Alexandra 88–91, Southend Utd 91– . *Address*: Southend Utd FC, Roots Hall, Victoria Ave, Southend-on-Sea, Essex SS2 6NQ.

SUTCH, Daryl: footballer; b. 11 September 1971, Beccles; player Norwich City 1990– ; 3 England U-21 caps. *Address*: Norwich City FC, Carrow Rd, Norwich NR1 1JE.

SUTTON, Christopher: footballer; b. 10 March 1973, Nottingham; player Norwich City 1991– . *Address*: Norwich City FC, Carrow Rd, Norwich NR1 1JE.

SWAN, Charles Francis Thomas: jockey (NH); b. 20 January 1968, Cloughjordan, Ireland; m. Tina Swan 1989; winner Irish Champion Hurdle 1991 (Nordic Surprise), Irish Grand National 1993 (Ebony Jane); Irish champ. jockey 1989/90, 90/91, 91/92, 92/93; 1st Irish NH jockey to ride 100 winners in season 1992/93 (104); Texaco Racing Sports Star of the Year 1992. *Leisure interests*: golf, tennis, squash, swimming, walking. *Address*: The Cobbs, Modreeny, Cloughjordan, Co. Tipperary, Ireland.

SWANN, Angela: netball player; b. 17 November 1962, Glasgow; m. Andrew Swann 1985; player Bishopbriggs 1981– , winners Scottish Cup 1993, Glasgow League champs. 1992/93; rep. Glasgow

District 1978– ; Scotland U-21 debut 1984, snr debut 1992, World Tournament squad 1983, 91. *Leisure interests*: swimming, learning sign language, watching football. *Address*: c/o Scottish Netball Assoc., Kelvin Hall, Argyle St, Glasgow G3 8AW.

SWINBURN, Walter Robert John: jockey (Flat); b. 7 August 1961, Oxford; winner Derby 1981 (Shergar), 1986 (Shahrastani), Irish Oaks 1981 (Blue Wind), 1987 (Unite), 1988 (Melodist), Irish 1000 Guineas 1982 (Prince's Polly), 1986 (Sonic Lady), 1992 (Marling), Irish Derby 1983 (Shareef Dancer), 1986 (Shahrastani), Prix de l'Arc de Triomphe 1983 (All Along), Oaks 1987 (Unite), 1000 Guineas 1989 (Musical Bliss), 1992 (Hatoof), 1993 (Sayyedati), Irish 2000 Guineas 1989 (Shaadi); rode 111 winners in season 1990. *Address*: c/o BHB, 42 Portman Square, London W1H 0EN.

SWINDLEHURST, Alison: hockey player; b. 10 August 1970; player Clifton; England U-21 debut 1989, snr debut 1990; GB debut 1990, Champions Trophy squad 1993. *Address*: Clifton HC, Bristol University Astroturf, Coombe Dingle, Stoke Bishop, Bristol.

SYED, Matthew Philip: table tennis player; b. 2 November 1970, Bromley; English U-14 champ. 1984, 85, U-17 champ. 1987; US U-22 open champ. 1990; Czechoslovak champ. 1991; Commonwealth team champ. 1994; European Youth Champs. silver and bronze medals 1985; European Champs. silver medal 1992; Olympic squad 1992. *Leisure interests*: boxing, Christianity. *Address*: 28 Shottery Rd, Stratford-upon-Avon CV37 9QA.

SYKES, Nathan: Rugby League footballer; b. 8 September 1974; player Moldgreen ARLFC, Castleford 1991– ; GB U-21 debut v. France U-21 1993. *Address*: Castleford RLFC, Wheldon Rd, Castleford WF10 2SD.

SYMONDS, Christopher Mark: bobsleigher; b. 15 November 1970, Oxford; GB debut 1992, World Cup 4-man gold medal 1993; GB Jnr Champs. weighlifting silver medals 1988, 90; UK U-17 discus record-holder. *Leisure interests*: golf, Nintendo games, videos. *Address*: c/o Brit. Bobsleigh Assoc., Springfield House, Woodstock Rd, Coulsdon, Surrey CR5 3HS.

SYMONS, Christopher (Kit): footballer; b. 8 March 1971, Basingstoke; player Portsmouth 1988– ; 2 Wales U-21 caps, over 10 full Wales caps. *Address*: Portsmouth FC, Fratton Park, Frogmore Rd, Portsmouth PO4 8RA.

TAGGART, Gerald: footballer; b. 18 October 1970, Belfast; player Manchester City 1988–89, Barnsley 89– ; 1 NI U-21 cap, over 21 full NI caps. *Address*: Barnsley FC, Oakwell Ground, Barnsley, S. Yorks. S71 1ET.

TAIT, Alan: Rugby League footballer; b. 2 July 1964, Kelso; player Kelso RUFC, Widnes, Leeds 1992– ; Scotland int. (RU); GB debut v. France 1989, Brit. Lions tour NZ/Papua New Guinea 1990. *Address*: Leeds RLFC, Bass Headingley, St Michael's Lane, Leeds LS6 3BR.

TANNER, Nicholas: footballer; b. 24 May 1965, Kingswood; player Bristol Rovers 1985–88, Liverpool 88–94. *Address*: Liverpool FC, Anfield Rd, Liverpool L4 0TH.

TARBUCK, Chris: Rugby Union footballer; b. 20 August 1968, Harlow; player Harlow, Southend, Saracens 1989–93, Leicester 93– . *Address*: Leicester FC, Welford Rd, Leicester LE2 7LF.

TAYLOR, Bleddyn: Rugby Union footballer; b. 17 January 1959, Bangor; m. Pamela Taylor 1987; 1 s., 1 d.; player Pontypool 1976–77, Neath 77–81, Llanelli 1981, Pontypool 81–87, Swansea 87–93, Pontypool 93– ; with Pontypool: winners Welsh Cup 1983; Wales B int. *Leisure interests*: golf, gardening. *Address*: Pontypool RFC, Pontypool Park, HQ Elm House, Park Rd, Pontypool, Gwent.

TAYLOR, Charles William: cricketer; b. 12 August 1966, Banbury; player Middx 1990– , county champs. 1990, 93, Sunday League champs. 1992. *Address*: Middx CCC, Lord's Cricket Ground, London NW8 8QN.

TAYLOR, Clare Elizabeth: footballer / cricketer; b. 22 May 1965, Huddersfield; as footballer: player Bronte Ladies 1976–91, Knowsley Utd 1992– ; with Bronte Ladies: winners N.W. League Cup 1982, 89, 91; England debut 1991; as cricketer: player Wakefield WCC 1987– , winners Nat. Cup, League champs. 1989, 90, 93; rep. Yorks. 1988– , county champs. 1988, 92, 93; England debut 1988, European Cup team (winners) 1989–91, World Cup team 1988, 1993, winners 1993; rep. W. Yorks. hockey 1979–81; only English woman double int. at football and cricket; Sports Writers' Team of the Year award-winner 1993. *Leisure interests*: any sport, music, socializing. *Address*: 1 Mount Pleasant, Lockwood, Huddersfield HD1 3QS.

TAYLOR, Colin: footballer; b. 25 December 1971, Liverpool; player Wolverhampton Wanderers 1990– . *Address*: Wolverhampton Wanderers FC, Molineux Stadium, Waterloo Rd, Wolverhampton WV1 4QR.

TAYLOR, Dennis James: snooker player; b. 19 January 1949, Coalisland, NI; 2 s., 1 d.; prof. debut 1971, Irish champ. 1982, 85–87, world champ. 1985; rep. Ireland,

winners World Cup 1985–87; winner Rothmans GP 1984, Canadian Masters 1985, 86, Tokyo Masters 1986, Aus. Masters 1987, Masters 1987. *Publications: Frame by Frame*, 1985, *Natural Break Funny Stories Book*, 1985, *Play Snooker*, 1990. *Leisure interests*: golf. *Address*: Cuemasters Ltd, Kerse Rd, Stirling FK7 7SG.

TAYLOR, Jonathan Paul: cricketer; b. 8 August 1964, Ashby-de-la-Zouch; player Derbys. 1988, Staffs. 1989–90, Northants. 91– ; England A tour SA 1993/94 (replacement), snr tour India/Sri Lanka 1992/93. *Address*: Northants. CCC, County Cricket Ground, Wantage Rd, Northampton NN1 4TJ.

TAYLOR, Neil Royston: cricketer; b. 21 July 1959, Farnborough; m. Jane Claire Taylor 1982; 2 d.; player Kent 1979– ; England Schools tour India 1977/78; rep. England B v. Pakistan 1982. *Address*: Kent CCC, St Lawrence Ground, Canterbury CT1 3NZ.

TAYLOR, Robert: footballer; b. 3 February 1967, Horden; player Leeds Utd 1986–89, Bristol City 89–92, W. Bromwich Albion 92– . *Address*: W. Bromwich Albion FC, The Hawthorns, W. Bromwich B71 4LF.

TAYLOR, Shaun: footballer; b. 26 March 1963, Plymouth; player Exeter City 1986–91, Swindon Town 91– ; with Exeter City: 4th Div. champs. 1989/90. *Address*: Swindon Town FC, The County Ground, Swindon, Wilts. SN1 2ED.

TEAGUE, Michael Clive: Rugby Union footballer; b. 8 October 1959, Gloucester; m. Lorraine Teague; player Cardiff, Gloucester, Moseley; England and Five Nations debut v. France 1984, Grand Slam champs. 1991, 92, tours SA 1984, NZ 1985, Aus./Fiji 1991; Brit. Lions tours Aus. 1989 (Player of the Series), NZ 1993. *Address*: Moseley FC, The Reddings, Reddings Rd, Moseley, Birmingham B13 8LW.

TEALE, Shaun: footballer; b. 10 March 1964, Southport; m. Carol Anne Teale 1990; 3 s.; player Bournemouth 1989–91, Aston Villa 91– . *Leisure interests*: golf, swimming, snooker. *Address*: Aston Villa FC, Villa Park, Trinity Rd, Birmingham B6 6HE.

TELFER, Paul: footballer; b. 21 October 1971, Edinburgh; player Luton Town 1988– . *Address*: Luton Town FC, Kenilworth Stadium, 1 Maple Rd, Luton, Beds. LU4 8AW.

TERRY, Simon Duncan: target archer; b. 27 March 1974, Stirling; Olympic individ. bronze medal 1992. *Leisure interests*: clay pigeon shooting. *Address*: c/o Grand Nat. Archery Soc., Nat. Agricultural Centre, Seventh St, Stoneleigh Park, Kenilworth, Warks. CV8 2LG.

TERRY, Vivian Paul: cricketer; b. 14 January 1959, Osnabruck, W. Germany; m. Bernadette Mary Terry 1986; 1 s., 1 d.; player Hants. 1978– , Sunday League champs. 1986; 2 Tests, debut 1984; English Counties tour Zimbabwe 1985. *Address*: Hants. CCC, County Cricket Ground, Northlands Rd, Southampton SO9 2TY.

THACKRAY, Richard: cyclist (cyclo-cross/mountain bike); b. 17 February 1973, Bradford; rep. Pace 1992– ; N. of England jnr cyclo-cross champ. 1991; GB jnr mountain bike cross-country and points series champ. 1991; GB cyclo-cross debut 1990; winner jnr Nat. Trophy (cyclo-cross) 1991. *Address*: 193 Windhill Old Rd, Thackley, Bradford BD10 0TR.

THACKRAY, Robert: cyclist (cyclo-cross/mountain bike); b. 25 September 1975, Bradford; rep. Saracen; GB juvenile cyclo-cross champ. 1991; GB debut (mountain bike) 1992, (cyclo-cross) 1993; winner jnr Nat. Trophy (cyclo-cross) 1993. *Address*: 193 Windhill Old Rd, Thackley, Bradford BD10 0TR.

THISTLE, John: archer (crossbow); b. 7 March 1956, Hillingdon; m. Deborah Joy Thistle 1989; 1 s., 1 d.; World Champs. team bronze medal 1982. *Leisure interests*: children, most sports. *Address*: 301 Longstone Rd, Iver Heath, Bucks SL0 0RN.

THOMAS, Ceri John: Rugby Union footballer; b. 8 March 1969, Tonyrefail, Mid Glamorgan; player Cardiff; Wales U-19 tour NZ 1987, U-21 debut v. Scotland 1990. *Leisure interests*: all sport, watching cartoons. *Address*: Cardiff RFC, Cardiff Arms Park, Westgate St, Cardiff CF1 1JA.

THOMAS, Dean: footballer; b. 19 December 1961, Bedworth; player Wimbledon 1981–83, Aachen (Germany), Fortuna Dusseldorf (Germany), Northampton Town 1988–90, Notts County 90– . *Address*: Notts County FC, Meadow Lane Ground, Nottingham NG2 3HJ.

THOMAS, Geoffrey: footballer; b. 5 August 1964, Manchester; player Rochdale 1982–84, Crewe Alexandra 84–87, Crystal Palace 87–93 (capt.), Wolverhampton Wanderers 93– (capt.); 9 England caps. *Address*: Wolverhampton Wanderers FC, Molineux Stadium, Waterloo Rd, Wolverhampton WV1 4QR.

THOMAS, Graham: motorcyclist (grass-track); b. 26 May 1968, Shrewsbury; Midland centre champ. 1992, 93, inter-centre team champ. 1991–93; GB 250cc champ. 1992, 93. *Leisure interests*: football, golf. *Address*: 18 The Grove, Minsterley, Shrewsbury SY5 0AG.

THOMAS, Karl Augustine: boxer; b. 11 March 1969, Cardiff; Welsh ABA welterweight champ. 1993; Wales debut 1992; GB debut 1993. *Leisure interests*: swimming, shooting, badminton, basketball, football, dancing. *Address*: Pentwyn Amateur Boxing Club, Power House, Pentwyn, Cardiff.

THOMAS, Michael: footballer; b. 24 August 1967, Lambeth; player Arsenal 1986–91, Liverpool 91– ; with Arsenal: winners League Cup 1987, League champs. 1988/89, 90/91; with Liverpool: winners FA Cup 1992; 12 England U-21 caps, 2 full England caps. *Address*: Liverpool FC, Anfield Rd, Liverpool L4 0TH.

THOMAS, Mitchell: footballer; b. 2 October 1964, Luton; player Luton Town 1982–86, Tottenham Hotspur 86–91, W. Ham Utd 91– ; 3 England U-21 caps. *Address*: W. Ham Utd FC, Boleyn Ground, Green St, Upton Park, London E13 9AZ.

THOMAS, Neil Roderick: gymnast; b. 6 April 1968, Chirk; Irish open champ. 1989; GB floor, horse vault, horizontal bar champ. 1986, combined champ. 1990, 92; England U-16 debut 1980, snr debut 1986; Commonwealth Games floor gold and team silver medals 1990; GB jnr debut 1984, snr debut 1986; European Champs. horse vault bronze medal 1990; World Champs. floor silver medal 1993 (1st Brit. medal-winner); Olympic squad 1992; 1st gymnast to win every individ. event in GB champs. 1992. *Leisure interests*: true crime stories, swimming, watching most Olympic sports. *Address*: c/o Brit. Amateur Gymnastics Assoc., Lilleshall Nat. Sports Centre, Newport, Shropshire TF10 9NB.

THOMAS, Roderick: footballer; b. 10 October 1970, Brent; player Watford 1988–93, Carlisle Utd 93– ; 1 England U-21 cap. *Address*: Carlisle Utd FC, Brunton Park, Warwick Rd, Carlisle, Cumbria CA1 1LL.

THOMAS, Stuart Darren: cricketer; b. 25 January 1975, Morriston; player Glamorgan 1992– ; youngest player to take 5 1st-class wickets on debut. *Address*: Glamorgan CCC, Sophia Gardens, Cardiff CF1 9XR.

THOMAS, Tony: footballer; b. 12 July 1971, Liverpool; player Tranmere Rovers

1989– . *Address*: Tranmere Rovers FC, Prenton Park, Prenton Rd W., Birkenhead, Merseyside L42 9PN.

THOMAS, William Alfred: flat green bowler; b. 21 October 1954, Neath; m. Catherine Thomas 1976; 2 s.; rep. W. Glamorgan 1977– ; Welsh singles champ. (outdoor) 1990, fours champ. (indoor) 1986; GB singles champ. (outdoor) 1991; Wales debut (outdoor and indoor) 1985 (capt. 1988–90); Commonwealth Games fours gold medal 1986, squad 1990; World Champs. pairs bronze medal 1988; winner Aus. Bicentennial Tournament pairs 1988, Jersey Int. Classic triples 1989. *Leisure interests*: gardening, DIY, rugby. *Address*: 40 Mayfield St, Port Talbot, W. Glamorgan SA13 1EY.

THOMPSON, Adrian (Carl): boxer; b. 26 May 1964; prof. debut 1988; titles won: GB cruiserweight 1992, European cruiserweight 1994; over 11 prof. wins. *Address*: c/o Phil Martin, 79 Buckingham Rd, Chorlton, Manchester M21 1QT.

THOMPSON, Alan: footballer; b. 22 December 1973, Newcastle; player Newcastle Utd 1991–93, Bolton Wanderers 93– . *Address*: Bolton Wanderers FC, Burnden Park, Manchester Rd, Bolton, Lancs. BL3 2QR.

THOMPSON, Andrew: footballer; b. 9 November 1967, Cannock; player W. Bromwich Albion 1985–86, Wolverhampton Wanderers 86– ; with Wolverhampton Wanderers: 4th Div. champs. 1987/88, 3rd Div. champs. 1988/89. *Address*: Wolverhampton Wanderers FC, Molineux Stadium, Waterloo Rd, Wolverhampton WV1 4QR.

THOMPSON, Andrew: Rugby League footballer; b. 29 June 1968, Hull; player Hull Kingston Rovers 1987– . *Address*: Hull Kingston Rovers RLFC, Craven Park, Preston Rd, Hull HU9 5HE.

THOMPSON, Garry: footballer; b. 7 October 1959, Birmingham; player Coventry City 1977–83, W. Bromwich Albion 83–85, Sheffield Wednesday 85–86, Aston Villa 86–88, Watford 88–90, Crystal Palace 90–91, Queens Park Rangers 91–93, Cardiff City 93– ; 6 England U-21 caps. *Address*: Cardiff City FC, Ninian Park, Sloper Rd, Cardiff CF1 8SX.

THOMPSON, Gavin John: Rugby Union footballer; b. 30 August 1969; player Harlequins; England A debut v. Emerging Aus. 1990, snr tour Argentina 1990. *Address*: Harlequins FC, Stoop Memorial Ground, Craneford Way, Twickenham, Middx.

THOMPSON, Joanne: hockey player; b. 13 May 1965; player Ipswich Ladies; England U-21 debut 1985, snr debut 1989, European Champs. gold medallist 1991, World Cup squad 1990; England indoor debut 1986, European Indoor Cup silver medallist 1993; GB debut and Olympic bronze medallist 1992. *Address*: Ipswich Ladies HC, Tuddenham Rd, Ipswich, Suffolk IP4 3QJ.

THOMPSON, Karen Jane: synchronized swimmer; b. 21 April 1973, Essex; W. Counties duet champ. 1989, 91; GB jnr debut 1989, snr debut 1991; Europa Cup team silver medal 1992. *Leisure interests*: speed swimming, sewing, coaching younger sister. *Address*: c/o ASA, Harold Fern House, Derby Square, Loughborough, Leics. LE11 0AL.

THOMPSON, Neil: footballer; b. 2 October 1963, Beverley; player Hull City 1981–83, Scarborough 83–89, Ipswich Town 89– . *Address*: Ipswich Town FC, Portman Rd, Ipswich, Suffolk IP1 2DA.

THOMPSON, Stephen: footballer; b. 2 November 1964, Oldham; player Bolton Wanderers 1982–91, Luton Town 1991, Leicester City 1991– . *Address*: Leicester City FC, City Stadium, Filbert St, Leicester LE2 7FL.

THOMSON, Andrew Edward: flat green bowler; b. 26 November 1955, St Andrews; m. Linda June Thomson 1982; 2 s.; rep. Fife 1975–79, Kent 81– ; English singles champ. (outdoor) 1981, (indoor) 1989–91, pairs champ. (outdoor) 1992, (indoor) 1986, 91, triples champ. (indoor) 1981, fours champ. (indoor) 1983, 84, 88, 89, 90; GB singles champ. (indoor) 1991, 92, pairs champ. (outdoor) 1993, (indoor) 1987, 92, fours champ. (indoor) 1989, 90, 91; Scotland debut (indoor) 1979, England debut (outdoor) 1982, (indoor) 1981; Commonwealth Games squad 1986, 90; World Indoor Champs. pairs gold medal 1993; Test debut 1983; has won more English indoor titles than any player. *Leisure interests*: cricket, football. *Address*: 71 Gerda Rd, New Eltham, London SE9 3SJ.

THOMSON, Ian: footballer; b. 24 September 1965, Coatbridge; player Stenhousemuir 1985–88, Partick Thistle 88–89, Queen of the S. 89–92, Raith Rovers 92– . *Address*: Raith Rovers FC, Stark's Park, Pratt St, Kirkcaldy, Fife KY1 1SA.

THOMSON, Mary Elizabeth: equestrianist (three-day eventing); b. 8 June 1961, Newark; GB open champ. 1990, 91; European Champs. team gold medal 1991; Olympic squad 1992; winner Windsor Horse Trials 1988, 89, 92, Badminton Horse Trials 1992; ranked world no. 1 1990, no. 2 1992; holds world record for consecutive 3-day event wins (5 in 1991/92). *Publications*: *Mary Thomson's Eventing Year*, 1993. *Leisure interests*: tennis, snow and water skiing, sailing, deep-sea diving. *Address*: School House, Salcombe Regis, Sidmouth, Devon EX10 0JQ.

THOMSON, William: footballer; b. 10 February 1958, Linwood; player Partick Thistle 1975–78, St Mirren 78–84, Dundee Utd 84–91, Motherwell 91– ; 7 Scotland caps. *Address*: Motherwell FC, Fir Park, Fir Park St, Motherwell ML1 2QN.

THORBURN, Paul Huw: Rugby Union footballer; b. 24 November 1962, Rheindalen, W. Germany; m. Ann Thorburn; 1 d.; player Swansea Univ., Ebbw Vale, Neath; Wales and Five Nations debut v. France 1985, tour Aus. 1991, 37 caps. *Address*: Neath RFC, The Gnoll, Gnoll Park Rd, Neath, W. Glamorgan.

THORN, Andrew: footballer; b. 12 November 1966, Carshalton; player Wimbledon 1984–88, Newcastle Utd 88–89, Crystal Palace 89–   ; with Wimbledon: winners FA Cup 1988; 5 England U-21 caps. *Address*: Crystal Palace FC, Selhurst Park Stadium, London SE25 6PU.

THORNE, William Joseph: snooker player; b. 4 March 1954, Leicester; GB jnr champ. 1973; prof. debut 1975, winner Mercantile Credit Classic 1985. *Address*: Warrior Management, Broadway House, 149–51 St Neots Rd, Hardwick, Cambridge CB3 7QJ.

THORNEYCROFT, Harvey Spencer: Rugby Union footballer; b. 22 February 1969; player Northampton 1987–89, Nottingham 89–90, Northampton 90–   ; rep. Midland Div.; England U-21 debut v. Romania 1989, England B tour NZ 1992. *Leisure interests*: water sports, bungee jumping, skiing, horse-riding. *Address*: Northampton FC, Franklins Gardens, Weedon Rd, Northampton NN5 5BG.

THORNILEY, Anthony: Rugby League footballer; b. 10 October 1966, Warrington; player Woolston ARLFC, Warrington 1986–   ; with Warrington: winners Regal Trophy 1991. *Address*: Warrington RLFC, Wilderspool Stadium, Wilderspool Causeway, Warrington WA4 6PY.

THORPE, Graham Paul: cricketer; b. 1 August 1969, Farnham; player Surrey 1988–   ; England A tours Zimbabwe/Kenya 1989/90, Pakistan 1990/91, WI 1991/92, Aus. 1992/93, Test debut and maiden Test 100 v. Aus. 1993, tour WI 1994. *Address*: Surrey CCC, The Oval, Kennington, London SE11 5SS.

THORSTVEDT, Erik: footballer; b. 28 October 1962, Stavanger, Norway; player Viking Stavanger (Norway), Borussia Moenchengladbach (Germany) 1985–87, IFK Gothenburg (Sweden) 87–88, Tottenham Hotspur 1988–   ; with Tottenham Hotspur: winners FA Cup 1991; Norway int. *Address*: Tottenham Hotspur FC, 748 High Rd, Tottenham, London N17 0AP.

THURSFIELD, John: Rugby League footballer; b. 22 October 1969, Warrington; player Warrington. *Address*: Warrington RLFC, Wilderspool Stadium, Wilderspool Causeway, Warrington WA4 6PY.

TIERNEY, Grant: footballer; b. 11 October 1961, Falkirk; player Cowdenbeath 1980–85, Meadowbank Thistle 85–89, Dunfermline Athletic 89–90, Partick Thistle 90–   . *Address*: Partick Thistle FC, Firhill Stadium, 80 Firhill Rd, Glasgow G20 7BA.

TILER, Carl: footballer; b. 11 January 1970, Sheffield; player Barnsley 1988–91, Nottingham Forest 91–   ; 13 England U-21 caps. *Address*: Nottingham Forest FC, City Ground, Nottingham NG2 5FJ.

TILL, Andy: boxer; b. 22 August 1963; N.W. London ABA middleweight champ. 1986; prof. debut 1986; titles won: Southern light-middleweight 1989, WBC int. light-middleweight 1991, GB light-middleweight 1992; over 17 prof. wins. *Address*: c/o Brit. Boxing Board of Control, Jack Petersen House, 52A Borough High St, London SE1 1XW.

TILSON, Stephen: footballer; b. 27 July 1966, Wickford; player Southend Utd 1989–   . *Address*: Southend Utd FC, Roots Hall, Victoria Ave, Southend-on-Sea, Essex SS2 6NQ.

TILLSON, Andrew: footballer; b. 30 June 1966, Huntingdon; player Grimsby Town 1988–90, Queens Park Rangers 90– . *Address*: Queens Park Rangers FC, Rangers Stadium, S. Africa Rd, London W12 7PA.

TITCHARD, Stephen Paul: cricketer; b. 17 December 1967, Warrington; player Lancs. 1990– . *Address*: Lancs. CCC, Old Trafford, Manchester M16 0PX.

TOLLEY, Christopher Mark: cricketer; b. 30 December 1967, Kidderminster; player Worcs. 1989– ; Brit. Univ. Sports Fed. tour Barbados 1989. *Address*: Worcs. CCC, County Ground, New Rd, Worcester WR2 4QQ.

TOLSON, Neil: footballer; b. 25 October 1973, Wordsley; player Walsall 1991–92, Oldham Athletic 1992–93, Bradford City 93– . *Address*: Bradford City FC, Valley Parade, Bradford, W. Yorks. BD8 7DY.

TOON, Joanna: hockey player; b. 14 August 1971; player Sutton Coldfield; England U-21 debut (outdoor) 1990, (indoor) 1991, snr debut (outdoor) 1992. *Address*: First Personnel Sutton Coldfield HC, Rectory Park, Sutton Coldfield, W. Midlands.

TOPLEY, Thomas Donald: cricketer; b. 25 February 1964, Canterbury; player Surrey 1985, Essex 1985– ; with Essex: county champs. 1986, 91, 92, Sunday League champs. 1985; Zimbabwe World Cup coach 1992. *Leisure interests*: all ball sports, photography, eating out. *Address*: Essex CCC, County Cricket Ground, New Writtle St, Chelmsford DM2 0PG.

TOPLISS, Lisa Michelle: netball player; b. 17 September 1970, Long Eaton; player Bluebells 1985–86, Moll Buzzers 86–87, Pennine 87– ; rep. Derbys. U-16 1985, U-18 86–87, U-21 87–91, snr 91– , E. Midlands U-21 87–90, snr 90– ; with Derbys.: U-21 inter-county champs. 1988, E. counties snr League champs. 1991; England U-18 debut 1986, U-21 debut 1989, tour Barbados 1990, snr debut 1992, World Games squad 1993, tour Jamaica 1993. *Leisure interests*: aerobics, running, cinema, theatre, concerts, eating out. *Address*: c/o All England Netball Assoc., Netball House, 9 Paynes Park, Hitchin, Herts. SG5 1EH.

TOPPING, Paul: Rugby League footballer; b. 18 September 1965, Wigan; player Swinton, Leigh, Oldham 1993– . *Address*: Oldham RLFC, The Pavilion, Watersheddings, Oldham OL4 2PB.

TORFASON, Gudmundor: footballer; b. 13 December 1961, Iceland; player St Mirren 1989–92, St Johnstone 92– ; Iceland int. *Address*: St Johnstone FC, McDiarmid Park, Crieff Rd, Perth PH1 2SJ.

TORRANCE, Samuel Robert: golfer; b. 24 August 1953, Largs, Ayrshire; m. Suzanne Danielle Torrance; 1 s., 1 d.; Scottish boys' champ. 1970; prof. debut 1970; Scottish prof. champ. 1978, 80, 85, 91, 93; Dunhill Cup team (Scotland) 1985–87, 89–91, 93; Ryder Cup team 1981– , winners 1985, 87; winner Zambian Open 1975, Colombian Open 1979, Irish Open 1981, Spanish Open 1982, Portuguese Open 1982, 83, Scandinavian Open 1983, Tunisian Open, Benson and Hedges Int. Open 1984, Monte Carlo Open 1985, Italian Open 1987, German Masters 1990, Jersey Open 1991, Catalan Open, Hamburg Open 1993. *Leisure interests*: snooker, tennis, fine wine. *Address*: Carnegie Sports Management, Riding Court, Riding Court Rd, Datchet, nr Windsor, Berks. SL3 9JT.

TORTOLANO, Joe: footballer; b. 6 April 1966, Stirling; player Hibernian 1985– ; Scotland U-21 int. *Address*: Hibernian FC, Easter Rd Stadium, 64 Albion Rd, Edinburgh EH7 5QG.

TORVILL, Jayne: see **CHRISTENSEN, Jayne**

TOSHACK, John: football manager; b. 22 March 1949, Cardiff; player Cardiff City 1966–70, Liverpool 70–78, player/manager Swansea City 78–84; with Liverpool: winners FA Cup 1974, European Cup 1977, UEFA Cup 1973, 76, League champs. 1972/73, 75/76, 76/77; 3 Wales U-23 caps, 40 full Wales caps; manager Real Sociedad (Spain), technical director Wales (part time) 1994. *Address*: c/o FA of Wales, Plymouth Chambers, 3 Westgate St, Cardiff, S. Glamorgan.

TOUGH, Mary Jane: netball player; b. 30 August 1967, Glasgow; player Bishopbriggs 1980–93, Bellahouston 93– ; with Bishopbriggs: winners Scottish Cup 1993, Glasgow League champs. 1992/93; rep. Glasgow District; Scotland debut and World Games squad 1989, World Champs. squad 1991. *Leisure interests*: badminton, football. *Address*: c/o Scottish Netball Assoc., Kelvin Hall, Argyle St, Glasgow G3 8AW.

TOWNSEND, Andrew: footballer; b. 23 July 1963, Maidstone; player Southampton 1985–88, Norwich City 88–90, Chelsea 90–93, Aston Villa 93– ; over 39 Ireland caps. *Address*: Aston Villa FC, Villa Park, Trinity Rd, Birmingham B6 6HE.

TOWNSEND, Gregor Peter John: Rugby Union footballer; b. 26 April 1973, Edinburgh; player Gala; Scotland B debut v. Ireland 1991, snr and Five Nations debut v. England 1993, tours Aus. 1992, Fiji/Tonga/W. Samoa 1993. *Address*: Gala RFC, Netherdale, Nether Rd, Galashiels TD1 3HE.

TRACEY, Simon: footballer; b. 9 December 1967, Woolwich; player Wimbledon 1986–88, Sheffield Utd 88– . *Address*: Sheffield Utd FC, Bramall Lane, Sheffield, S. Yorks S2 4SU.

TRAIN, Andrew John: canoeist; b. 21 September 1963, Pelsall, Staffs.; m. Alison Ann Train 1988; 2 d.; World Champs. C1 10,000m bronze medal 1991, C2 10,000m silver medal 1985, bronze 1987, 91, silver 1993, C2 marathon gold medal 1988; World Cup C2 marathon gold medals 1989, 91; Olympic squad 1984, 88, 92. *Address*: 16 Chestnut Close, Lower Moor, Pershore, Worcs. WR10 2RE.

TRAMSCHEK, Ruth Isobel: netball player; b. 17 May 1968, Glasgow; player Bishopbriggs 1986– , winners Scottish Cup 1993, Glasgow League champs. 1992/93; rep. Glasgow District 1985– , Brit. Univ., tour Aus. 1989; Scotland U-18 debut 1985, U-21 debut 1986, snr debut 1990. *Leisure interests*: running, cycling, skiing, hill-walking, travel, cooking, sewing, reading. *Address*: c/o Scottish Netball Assoc., Kelvin Hall, Argyle St, Glasgow G3 8AW.

TRANFIELD, Jennifer: squash player; b. 31 March 1975; player Queens Tower, Abbeydale Park, Worksop; rep. Yorks. 1988– ; Yorks. girls' U-14 champ. 1988, U-16 champ. 1989, U-19 champ. 1990–93; GB girls' U-14 champ. 1989, U-16 champ., U-16 open champ. 1991, U-19 open champ. 1994; Swedish jnr open champ. 1993; England U-16 debut 1990, U-19 debut 1992; European Jnr Champs. team gold and individ. bronze medals 1992, 93; World Jnr Champs. squad 1991, 93. *Leisure interests*: hockey, rounders, tennis, netball, cross-country running, swimming, surfing, walking. *Address*: 62 Rackford Rd, N. Anston, Sheffield S31 7DF.

TRUMP, Harvey Russell John: cricketer; b. 11 October 1968, Taunton; m. Nicola Trump 1992; player Somerset 1986– ; England YC tours Sri Lanka 1987, Aus. (Youth World Cup) 1988; rep. Somerset U-19 and U-21 hockey. *Leisure interests*: hockey, reading, theatre, cinema, walking. *Address*: Somerset CCC, The County Ground, Taunton, Somerset TA1 1JT.

TUCKER, Andrew St George: rifle shooter; b. 17 July 1937, Edinburgh; m. Catherine Agnes Tucker 1964; rep. Essex 1954–69 (small-bore capt. 1964–69), Surrey 1969– (full-bore capt. 1981–83); Surrey full-bore champ. 1972, 77, 79; English small-bore long-range champ. 1975, 77; Scottish full-bore champ. 1987; GB small-bore long-range champ. 1975; England debut 1963; Commonwealth Games full-bore pairs gold, individ. silver medals 1990; GB debut 1962, Kolapore Match team (winners) 1993; winner Grand Aggregate, Bisley (small-bore) 1964, 75, (full-bore) 1986, Queen's Prize, Bisley 1979, 87; only shooter to have won both small-bore and full-bore Grand Aggregate. *Publications*: *Teach Yourself Shooting*, 1964. *Address*: 58 Portsmouth Rd, Cobham, Surrey KT11 1HY.

TUCKWELL, Melanie: netball player; b. 11 March 1972, Panteg, Gwent; player Spartans 1989–91, Cardiff Institute of Higher Education 91– ; with Cardiff Institute: GB univ. champs. 1991/92, 92/93; rep. Gwent; Wales U-16 debut 1987, U-18 debut 1988, U-21 debut 1990, World Youth Champs. squad 1992, snr debut 1992, World Games squad 1993. *Leisure interests*: basketball, football, athletics, life-saving. *Address*: 27 Usk Rd, Pontypool, Gwent NP4 8AG.

TUDOR, Richard: yachtsman; b. 26 July 1959, Llandrindod, Powys; 1 s., 1 d.; skipper *British Steel II*, winner leg 1, Brit. Steel Challenge 1992/93. *Leisure interests*: rugby, football. *Address*: Pen Morfa, Golf Rd, Pwllhelli, Gwynedd.

TUFNELL, Philip Clive Roderick: cricketer; b. 29 April 1966, Barnet; 1 d.; player Middx 1986– , county champs. 1990, 93, Sunday League champs. 1992; England U-19 tour WI 1985, Test debut 1990, tours Aus. 1990/91, NZ/Aus. (World Cup) 1991/92, India/Sri Lanka 1992/93, WI 1994; MCC Young Cricketer of the Year 1984. *Leisure interests*: going to the pub, all sport, sleeping, going to clubs, playing with my daughter. *Address*: Middx CCC, Lord's Cricket Ground, London NW8 8QN.

TUNNINGLEY, Andrew: Rugby Union footballer; b. 29 March 1967, Harrogate; player Sandal, Headingley, Cambridge Univ. (Blue 1989), Saracens 1990– ; rep. E. Counties. *Address*: Saracens FC, Bramley Rd Sports Ground, Chaseside, Southgate, London N14 4AB.

TUNSTALL, Steven Robert: athlete (cross-country); b. 9 May 1964, Preston; m. Lorraine Tunstall 1989; 2 s., 1 d.; UK champ. 1993; England debut 1988; GB debut 1989, World Champs. squad 1991, 93. *Leisure interests*: guitar, photography, art, my children. *Address*: 14 Studholme Crescent, Penwortham, Preston PR1 9ND.

TURNBULL, Debra: squash player; b. 3 March 1966, St Asaph; rep. N. Wales U-19 1980–85; N. Wales girls' U-16 and U-19 champ. 1981, ladies' champ. 1982–93; Welsh girls' U-16 and U-19 champ. 1982, ladies' champ. 1983; GB girls' U-19 champ. 1983; Wales U-19 debut 1981, snr debut 1983; European Champs. squad 1992; World Champs. squad 1983. *Leisure interests*: swimming, aerobics, travel. *Address*: Strings, Colwyn Ave, Rhos-on-Sea, Colwyn Bay, Clwyd.

TURNBULL, Derek James: Rugby Union footballer; b. 2 October 1961, Hawick; m. Angie Turnbull; player Hawick 1978– ; rep. S. of Scotland; Scotland debut v. NZ (World Cup) 1987, Five Nations debut v. France 1988, Grand Slam champs. 1990, tours N. America 1985, France/Spain 1986, Aus./NZ (World Cup) 1987, Zimbabwe 1988, Japan 1989, NZ 1990. *Address*: Hawick RFC, Mansfield Park, Mansfield Rd, Hawick.

TURNELL, Andrew: racehorse trainer; b. 27 August 1948; m. Louise Turnell 1981; 2 s., 3 d.; prof. jockey 1963–82; 1st trainer's licence 1982; winner Grand National 1987 (Maori Venture), Hennessy Gold Cup 1993 (Cogent). *Address*: c/o BHB, 42 Portman Square, London W1H 0EN.

TURNER, Graham: football manager; b. 5 October 1947, Ellesmere Port; player Wrexham 1965–68, Chester City 68–73, Shrewsbury Town 73–84 (player/manager 78–84); manager Aston Villa 1984–86, Wolverhampton Wanderers 86–94; with Shrewsbury Town: 3rd Div. champs. 1978/79; with Wolverhampton Wanderers: 4th Div. champs. 1987/88, 3rd Div. champs. 1988/89. *Address*: Wolverhampton Wanderers FC, Molineux Stadium, Waterloo Rd, Wolverhampton WV1 4QR.

TURNER, Ian John: cricketer; b. 18 July 1968, Denmead; player Hants. 1989–93. *Address*: Hants. CCC, County Cricket Ground, Northlands Rd, Southampton SO9 2TY.

TURNER, Kevin Paul: powerboat racer; b. 3 April 1974, Blundeston; GB Yamato hydroplane champ. 1993; world OSY 400 hydroplane champ. 1993 (1st Brit. and youngest champ.). *Leisure interests*: motorcycling and maintenance, football, reading. *Address*: 14 The Street, Blundeston, Lowestoft, Suffolk NR32 5AQ.

TURNER, Philip: footballer; b. 12 February 1962, Sheffield; player Lincoln City 1980–86, Grimsby Town 86–88, Leicester City 88–89, Notts County 89– . *Address*: Notts County FC, Meadow Lane Ground, Nottingham NG2 3HJ.

TURNER, Robert Julian: cricketer; b. 25 November 1967, Worcs.; player Cambridge Univ. (Blue 1991), Somerset 1991– ; Combined Univ. tour Barbados 1989. *Address*: Somerset CCC, The County Ground, Taunton, Somerset TA1 1JT.

TURVEY, Joanne Sarah: oarswoman; b. 6 July 1969, Isleworth; rep. Tideway Scullers School, Putney Town RC, Upper Thames RC; GB debut 1991, Olympic squad 1992; jnr women's Devizes–Westminster canoe race record-holder. *Leisure interests*: eating out, cinema, cooking, backpacking. *Address*: 51 Waverley Ave, Twickenham, Middx TW2 6DQ.

TUTTLE, David: footballer; b. 6 February 1972, Reading; player Tottenham Hotspur 1990–93, Sheffield Utd 93– . *Address*: Sheffield Utd FC, Bramall Lane, Sheffield, S. Yorks. S2 4SU.

TUUTA, Brendon: Rugby League footballer; b. 29 April 1965, Rotarua, NZ; player Rotarua (NZ), W. Suburbs (Aus.), Featherstone Rovers 1990– ; NZ int. *Address*: Featherstone Rovers RLFC, The Croft, Batley Rd, W. Ardsley, Wakefield WF3 1DX.

TWEED, Steven: footballer; b. 8 August 1972, Edinburgh; player Hibernian 1991– ; Scotland U-21 int. *Address*: Hibernian FC, Easter Rd Stadium, 64 Albion Rd, Edinburgh EH7 5QG.

TWISTON-DAVIES, Nigel: racehorse trainer; b. 16 May 1957; m. Catherine Twiston-Davies 1988; 1 s.; 1st licence 1981; winner Scottish National 1992 (Captain Dibble), Mackeson Gold Cup 1992 (Tipping Tim). *Address*: c/o BHB, 42 Portman Square, London W1H 0EN.

TWOSE, Roger Graham: cricketer; b. 17 April 1968, Torquay; player Warks. 1989– , winners NatWest Trophy 1993. *Address*: Warks. CCC, County Ground, Edgbaston, Birmingham B5 7QU.

TYLER, Penny: windsurfer; b. 1 August 1962, Bristol; m. Philip Tyler 1988; GB ladies' funboard champ. 1989–91, nat. series champ. 1990, 91; UK ladies' nat. series champ. 1991, 92; European Champs.

raceboard silver medal 1991; World Champs. raceboard bronze medals 1991, 92. *Leisure interests*: mountain biking, eating out, spending time with my husband. *Address*: Lambourne House, Milton Keynes Village, Bucks. MK10 9AF.

TYRER, Christian: Rugby League footballer; b. 19 December 1973; player Widnes 1990– . *Address*: Widnes RLFC, Naughton Park, Lowerhouse Lane, Widnes WA8 7DZ.

UBOGU, Victor Eriakpo: Rugby Union footballer; b. 8 September 1964, Lagos, Nigeria; player Bath, winners Pilkington Cup 1990, League champs. 1992/93; rep. S.W. Div.; England B debut v. Aus. 1990, snr debut v. Canada 1992, England A tour Canada 1993, Five Nations debut v. Scotland 1994. *Address*: Bath RFC, Recreation Ground, Bath BA2 6PW.

UDAL, Shaun David: cricketer; b. 18 March 1969, Farnborough; m. Emma Jane Udal 1991; 1 d.; player Hants. 1989– . *Address*: Hants. CCC, County Cricket Ground, Northlands Rd, Southampton SO9 2TY.

UNDERWOOD, Rory: Rugby Union footballer; b. 19 June 1963, Middlesbrough; m. Wendy Underwood; 2 d.; player Middlesbrough, Leicester; with Leicester: winners Pilkington Cup 1993; rep. N. Div.; England and Five Nations debut v. Ireland 1984, Grand Slam champs. 1991, 92, tour NZ (World Cup) 1987; Brit. Lions tours Aus. 1989, NZ 1993; most-capped English player, 1st to win 50 caps. *Address*: Leicester FC, Welford Rd, Leicester LE2 7LF.

UNDERWOOD, Tony: Rugby Union footballer; b. 17 February 1969, Ipoh, Malaysia; player Leicester 1988– , Cambridge Univ. 1990–92 (Blue 1990, 91); with Leicester: winners Pilkington Cup 1993; rep. N. Div.

1988–93, London Div. 93– ; England B debut v. Fiji 1989, tour NZ 1992, snr tour Argentina 1990; Brit. Lions tour NZ 1993. *Leisure interests*: tenor saxophone, golf, squash, tennis, music, reading. *Address*: Lehman Bros Int., 1 Broadgate, London EC2M 7HA.

VAKIL, Laila: synchronized swimmer; b. 21 March 1974, Farnham; GB jnr solo and figures champ. 1990, snr duet champ. 1989, 91, 92; GB jnr debut 1988, snr debut 1989; European Jnr Champs. team bronze medal 1988, duet and team silver 1990; World Jnr Champs. figures gold and solo silver medals 1991; European Champs. duet bronze medal 1993; Olympic squad 1992 (youngest-ever Brit. synchronized swimming competitor). *Leisure interests*: all sport, dance, music, socializing. *Address*: c/o ASA, Harold Fern House, Derby Square, Loughborough, Leics. LE11 0AL.

VAN DEN HAUWE, Patrick: footballer; b. 16 December 1960, Dendermonde, Belgium; player Birmingham City 1978–84, Everton 84–89, Tottenham Hotspur 89–93, Millwall 93– ; with Everton: winners European Cup Winners' Cup 1985, League champs. 1984/85, 86/87; with Tottenham Hotspur: winners FA Cup 1991; 13 Wales caps. *Address*: Millwall FC, The Den, Zampa Rd, Bermondsey, London SE16 3LH.

VAN TROOST, Adrianus Pelrus (André): cricketer; b. 2 October 1972, Schiedam, The Netherlands; player Somerset 1991– ; Holland tours Zimbabwe 1989, Namibia 1990, Dubai 1991, Canada/NZ/SA 1992. *Address*: Somerset CCC, The County Ground, Taunton, Somerset TA1 1JT.

VATA, Rudi: footballer; b. 13 February 1969, Shkoder, Albania; player Dinamo Tirana (Albania), Celtic 1992– . *Address*: Celtic FC, Celtic Park, 95 Kerrydale St, Glasgow G40 3RE.

VAUGHAN, Alan Andrew: boxer; b. 18 June 1972, Whiston; ABA jnr champ. 1987, 88; World Jnr Champs. featherweight gold medal 1990; Olympic squad (lightweight) 1992. *Leisure interests*: all sport. *Address*: Huyton Amateur Boxing Club, Huyton, Merseyside.

VAUGHAN, John: footballer; b. 26 June 1964, Isleworth; player Fulham 1986–88, Cambridge Utd 88–93, Charlton Athletic 93– . *Address*: Charlton Athletic FC, The Valley, Floyd Rd, London SE7 8BL.

VAUGHAN, Michael: cricketer; b. 29 October 1974, Manchester; player Yorks. 1993– ; England U-19 tour India 1993. *Address*: Yorks. CCC, Headingley Cricket Ground, Leeds LS6 3BU.

VEIVERS, Philip James: Rugby League footballer; b. 25 May 1964, Beaudesert, Aus.; player Brisbane S. (Aus.), St Helens 1984– ; with St Helens: winners Premiership 1985, John Player Special Trophy 1988. *Address*: St Helens RLFC, Dunriding Lane, St Helens, Merseyside WA10 4AD.

VENABLES, Terence Frederick: football manager; b. 6 January 1943, Dagenham; m. Yvette Venables; 2 d.; player Chelsea 1960–66, Tottenham Hotspur 66–69, Queens Park Rangers 69–74, Crystal Palace 1974; manager Crystal Palace 1976–80, Queens Park Rangers 80–84, Barcelona (Spain) 84–87, Tottenham Hotspur 1987–91; as player: winner League Cup 1965 (Chelsea), FA Cup 1967 (Tottenham Hotspur), 4 England U-21 caps, snr debut v. Belgium 1964, 2 full caps; as manager: winner FA Cup 1991 (Tottenham Hotspur), 2nd Div. champs. 1978/79 (Crystal Palace), 1982/83 (Queens Park Rangers), Spanish League champs. 1984/85 (Barcelona); chief executive Tottenham Hotspur 1991–93; England coach 1994– . *Address*: c/o The FA, 16 Lancaster Gate, London W2 3LW.

VENISON, Barry: footballer; b. 16 August 1964, Consett; player Sunderland 1982–86, Liverpool 86–92, Newcastle Utd 92– ; with Liverpool: winners FA Cup 1989, League champs. 89/90; 10 England U-21 caps. *Address*: Newcastle Utd FC, St James' Park, Newcastle-upon-Tyne, Tyne & Wear NE1 4ST.

VENUS, Mark: footballer; b. 6 April 1967, Hartlepool; m. Margaret Anne Johnson 1989; 1 s.; player Hartlepool Utd 1985, Leicester City 1985–88, Wolverhampton Wanderers 88– ; with Wolverhampton Wanderers: 3rd Div. champs. 1988/89. *Address*: Wolverhampton Wanderers FC, Molineux Stadium, Waterloo Rd, Wolverhampton WV1 4QR.

VERVEER, Etienne: footballer; b. 22 September 1967, Surinam; player Ajax (The Netherlands), Chur (Switzerland), Millwall 1991– . *Address*: Millwall FC, The Den, Zampa Rd, Bermondsey, London SE16 3LH.

VEYSEY, Kenneth: footballer; b. 8 June 1967, Hackney; player Torquay Utd 1987–90, Oxford Utd 90– . *Address*: Oxford Utd FC, Manor Ground, London Rd, Headington, Oxford OX3 7RS.

VICKERS, Ian Andrew: rock climber; b. 10 May 1974, Blackburn; Yorks. and N.E. League champ. 1992; GB open champ. 1991, indoor champ. 1992; GB debut, World Cup and World Youth Champs. squads 1992. *Leisure interests*: walking, canoeing, swimming, mountain biking. *Address*: 22 Coniston Drive, Darwen, Lancs. BB3 3BJ.

VICKERS, Stephen: footballer; b. 13 October 1967, Bishop Auckland; player Tranmere Rovers 1985–93, Middlesbrough 93– . *Address*: Middlesbrough FC, Ayresome Park, Middlesbrough, Cleveland TS1 4PB.

VINNICOMBE, Christopher: footballer; b. 20 October 1970, Exeter; player Exeter City 1989–90, Rangers 90– ; 12 England U-21 caps. *Address*: Glasgow Rangers FC, Ibrox Stadium, 150 Edmiston Drive, Glasgow G51 2XD.

VIVEASH, Adrian: footballer; b. 30 September 1969, Swindon; player Swindon Town 1988– . *Address*: Swindon Town FC, The County Ground, Swindon, Wilts. SN1 2ED.

VONK, Michel: footballer; b. 28 October 1968, Alkmar, The Netherlands; player SVV Dordrecht (The Netherlands), Manchester City 1992– . *Address*: Manchester City FC, Maine Rd, Moss Side, Manchester M14 7WN.

VRTO, Dusan: footballer; b. 29 October 1965, Banksa Stiavnica, Czechoslovakia; player Banik Ostrava (Czechoslovakia), Dundee 1992– . *Address*: Dundee FC, Dens Park, Dundee DD3 7JY.

WADDELL, Hugh: Rugby League footballer; b. 1 September 1959, Ayrshire; player Blackpool, Oldham, Leeds, Sheffield Eagles 1990–93, Wakefield Trinity 93– ; GB debut v. France 1988, Brit. Lions tour Aus./NZ/Papua New Guinea 1988. *Address*: Wakefield Trinity RLFC, 171 Doncaster Rd, Belle Vue, Wakefield WF1 5EZ.

WADDLE, Christopher: footballer; b. 14 December 1960, Felling; player Newcastle Utd 1980–85, Tottenham Hotspur 85–89, Marseilles (France) 89–92, Sheffield Wednesday 92– ; 1 England U-21 cap, 62 full England caps; Football Writers' Assoc. Footballer of the Year 1993. *Address*: Sheffield Wednesday FC, Hillsborough, Sheffield, S. Yorks. S6 1SW.

WADDOCK, Gary: footballer; b. 17 March 1962, Kingsbury; player Queens Park Rangers 1979–87, Charleroi (Belgium), Millwall 1989–91, Queens Park Rangers

91– ; with Queens Park Rangers: 2nd Div. champs. 1982/83; 1 Ireland U-21 cap, 20 full Ireland caps. *Address*: Queens Park Rangers FC, Rangers Stadium, South Africa Rd, London W12 7PA.

WADSWORTH, Helen Elizabeth: golfer; b. 7 April 1964, The Gower; Welsh ladies' open amateur strokeplay champ. 1986; world fourball champ. 1987; Wales debut 1985; Curtis Cup team 1990; prof. debut 1991. *Publications*: assistant editor *Golf World* 1988–89. *Leisure interests*: hill-walking, running, skiing, piano, painting. *Address*: Int. Sports Management, Mere Golf and Country Club, Knutsford, Cheshire.

WAGHORN, Graham: ice hockey player; b. 31 December 1972, Newmarket, Ontario, Canada; player Streatham Redskins 1988–89, Solihull Barons 89–90, Moose Jaw Warriors (Canada) 1990, Nottingham Panthers 90– ; with Nottingham Panthers: winners Autumn Cup 1992; GB U-16 debut 1984, U-19 debut 1988, U-21 and snr debuts 1991, World Champs. gold medal (Pool B) 1993. *Leisure interests*: golf, cricket, baseball. *Address*: The Ice Stadium, Lower Parliament St, Nottingham, Notts.

WAINWRIGHT, Robert Iain: Rugby Union footballer; b. 22 March 1965, Perth; player Edinburgh Academicals; Scotland and Five Nations debut v. Ireland 1992, tours Japan 1989, Aus. 1992. *Address*: Edinburgh Academicals RFC, Raeburn Place, Stockbridge, Edinburgh EH4 1HQ.

WAKE, Stephen: Rugby Union footballer; b. 22 November 1968; player Llanelli 1991– . *Address*: Llanelli RFC, Stradey Park, Llanelli, Dyfed.

WAKEFORD, John Donald Marshall: Rugby Union footballer; b. 29 September 1966; player S. Wales Police, Cardiff 1993– ; Wales debut v. W. Samoa 1988. *Address*: Cardiff RFC, Cardiff Arms Park, Westgate St, Cardiff CF1 1JA.

WALKER, Alan: cricketer; b. 7 July 1962, Emley; player Northants. 1983–93, Durham 94– . *Address*: Durham CCC, County Ground, Riverside, Chester-le-Street, Co. Durham DH3 3QR.

WALKER, Andrew: footballer; b. 6 April 1965, Glasgow; player Motherwell 1984–87, Celtic 87–92, Bolton Wanderers 92– ; with Celtic: winners Scottish Cup 1988, Scottish League champs. 1987/88; 1 Scotland U-21 cap, 1 full Scotland cap. *Address*: Bolton Wanderers FC, Burnden Park, Manchester Rd, Bolton, Lancs. BL3 2QR.

WALKER, Chris Ian: squash player; b. 11 June 1967; player Lambs; GB U-23 champ. 1989; England U-14 debut 1981, U-16 debut 1983, snr debut 1989; winner Jamaican Open 1989. *Address*: c/o SRA, Westpoint, 33–34 Warple Way, London W3 0RQ.

WALKER, Desmond: footballer; b. 26 November 1965, Enfield; player Nottingham Forest 1983–92, Sampdoria (Italy) 92–93, Sheffield Wednesday 93– ; 7 England U-21 caps, over 58 full England caps. *Address*: Sheffield Wednesday FC, Hillsborough, Sheffield, S. Yorks S6 1SW.

WALKER, Fraser: swimmer; b. 10 October 1973, Dunfermline; Scottish 200m and 400m individ. medley champ. 1991, 92, 93; GB 200m individ. medley champ. 1993; Scotland debut 1991; GB debut 1993; World Student Games 200m individ. medley gold medal 1993; World Short-Course Champs. 200m individ. medley silver medal 1993. *Leisure interests*: weight training, Dunfermline Athletic FC, computer games, cycling, electronic music. *Address*: 9 Whitelaw Crescent, Dunfermline, Fife KY11 4RP.

WALKER, Graham Edwards: yachtsman; b. 6 July 1939, Wallasey; m. Annabel Hope 1963; Olympic squad (Star class) 1980, 84, 88; Admiral's Cup team 1983, 85, 87, 89, 93 (capt. 1983, 85, 93, winners 1989); Southern Cross team 1983 (capt.); winner Three-Quarter Ton Cup (*Indulgence V*) 1986; chairman UK America's Cup Challenge 1986/87. *Leisure interests*: motor racing, shooting. *Address*: Crusade Yacht Club, 14 Lincoln St, London SW3 2TP.

WALKER, Ian: footballer; b. 31 October 1971, Watford; player Tottenham Hotspur 1989– ; 4 England U-21 caps. *Address*: Tottenham Hotspur FC, 748 High Rd, Tottenham, London N17 0AP.

WALKER, James David Campbell: oarsman; b. 25 August 1968, Chester; rep. Imperial College BC 1986–88, Univ. of London BC 88–90, Molesey BC 90–91, Leander Club 91–92, Molesey BC 92– ; GB jnr debut 1985, World Jnr Champs. coxless fours silver medal 1986, U-23 debut 1987, snr debut and World Champs. eights bronze medal 1989, Olympic squad 1992. *Leisure interests*: electric and acoustic guitar, Native American history, natural history and biology. *Address*: c/o ARA, The Priory, 6 Lower Mall, London W6 9DJ.

WALKER, Joanne: gymnast (rhythmic); b. 8 March 1971, Paisley; GB ribbon and rope champ. 1990, hoop, clubs and ribbon champ. 1993; European Champs. squad 1990, World Champs. squad 1989, 91, Olympic reserve 1992. *Leisure interests*: socializing, eating, drinking. *Address*: Hillingdon School of Gymnastics, Victoria Rd, S. Ruislip, Middx.

WALKER, Michael: football manager; b. 28 November 1945, Colwyn Bay; player Shrewsbury Town 1964–66, York City 66–68, Watford 68–73, Colchester Utd 73–82; 4 Wales U-23 caps; manager Colchester Utd 1986–87, Norwich City 92–94, Everton 94– . *Address*: Everton FC, Goodison Park, Liverpool L4 4EL.

WALKER, Nicholas: footballer; b. 29 September 1962, Aberdeen; player

Leicester City 1980–82, Motherwell 82–83, Rangers 83–89, Heart of Midlothian 89– ; with Rangers: winners Scottish League Cup 1988; 1 Scotland cap. *Address*: Heart of Midlothian FC, Tynecastle Park, Gorgie Rd, Edinburgh EH11 2NL.

WALKER, Nigel Keith: Rugby Union footballer; b. 15 June 1963, Cardiff; m. Mary Walker; player Cardiff; Wales and Five Nations debut v. Ireland 1993; Olympic 110m hurdles semi-finalist 1984. *Address*: Cardiff RFC, Cardiff Arms Park, Westgate St, Cardiff CF1 1JA.

WALKER, Pamela: netball player; b. 3 September 1963, Neath; player Barry 1984– ; Wales U-18 debut 1979, U-21 and snr debuts 1982, World Champs. squad 1983, 91; rep. Wales basketball 1979–91; Welsh women's high jump champ. 1976. *Leisure interests*: aerobics, weight training, music, cinema, travel, Black history. *Address*: 351 Newport Rd, Roath, Cardiff CF1 2RN.

WALKER, Russ: Rugby League footballer; b. 1 September 1962, Barrow; player Barrow, Hull 1990– ; with Hull: winners Premiership 1991. *Address*: Hull RLFC, The Boulevard Ground, Airlie St, Hull HU3 3JD.

WALLACE, David (Danny): footballer; b. 21 January 1964, Greenwich; player Southampton 1982–89, Manchester Utd 89–93, Birmingham City 93– ; with Manchester Utd: winners European Cup Winners' Cup 1991, League champs. 1992/93; 14 England U-21 caps, 1 full England cap. *Address*: Birmingham City FC, St Andrews Ground, Birmingham B9 4NH.

WALLACE, Raymond: footballer; b. 2 October 1969, Greenwich; player Southampton 1988–91, Leeds Utd 91– ; 4 England U-21 caps. *Address*: Leeds Utd FC, Elland Rd, Leeds, W. Yorks. LS11 0ES.

WALLACE, Rodney: footballer; b. 2 October 1969, Greenwich; player Southampton 1988–91, Leeds Utd 91– ; with Leeds Utd: League champs. 1991/92; 11 England U-21 caps. *Address*: Leeds Utd FC, Elland Rd, Leeds, W. Yorks. LS11 0ES.

WALLACE, Shaun Patrick: cyclist; b. 20 November 1961, Christchurch; Commonwealth Games 4000m pursuit silver, team pursuit bronze medals 1982; World Champs. 5000m prof. pursuit silver medals 1991, 92; Olympic squad 1984; prof. debut 1986. *Leisure interests*: bicycle development, chess, sports and racing car design. *Address*: 3 Forest Rd, Chandler's Ford, Eastleigh, Hants. SO5 1NA.

WALSH, Colin: footballer; b. 22 July 1962, Hamilton; player Nottingham Forest 1979–86, Charlton Athletic 86– ; over 4 Scotland U-21 caps. *Address*: Charlton Athletic FC, The Valley, Floyd Rd, London SE7 8BL.

WALSH, Courtney Andrew: cricketer; b. 30 October 1962, Kingston, Jamaica; player Glos. 1984– (capt. 93–); Test debut 1984, WI tours England 1984, Aus. 1984/85, Pakistan/Aus./NZ 1986/87, India (World Cup) 1987/88, England 1988, Aus. 1988/89, Pakistan 1990/91, England 1991, Aus./SA 1992/93. *Address*: Glos. CCC, Phoenix County Ground, Nevil Rd, Bristol BS6 9EJ.

WALSH, Paul: footballer; b. 1 October 1962, Plumstead; player Charlton Athletic 1979– 82, Luton Town 82–84, Liverpool 84–88, Tottenham Hotspur 88–92, Portsmouth 92– ; with Liverpool: League champs. 1985/86; with Tottenham Hotspur: winners FA Cup 1991; 4 England U-21 caps, 2 full England caps. *Address*: Portsmouth FC, Fratton Park, Frogmore Rd, Portsmouth PO4 8RA.

WALSH, Steven: footballer; b. 3 November 1964, Preston; player Wigan Athletic 1982–86, Leicester City 86– . *Address*: Leicester City FC, City Stadium, Filbert St, Leicester LE2 7FL.

WALTERS, Mark: footballer; b. 2 June 1964, Birmingham; player Aston Villa 1982–88, Rangers 88–91, Liverpool 91– ; with Rangers: winners Scottish League Cup 1989, 91, Scottish League champs. 1988/89, 89/90, 90/91; 9 England U-21 caps, 1 full England cap. *Address*: Liverpool FC, Anfield Rd, Liverpool L4 0TH.

WALTON, Lisa Jane: golfer; b. 16 June 1972, Alperton; rep. Berks. 1986– ; Berks. ladies' champ. 1989 (youngest ever); England debut 1991, European ladies amateur team champs. 1993; GB debut 1993. *Leisure interests*: music. *Address*: 6 St Mary's Rd, Sindlesham, Berks. RG11 5DA.

WALTON, Peter: Rugby Union footballer; b. 3 June 1969, Alnwick; m. Diana Walton 1993; player Alnwich 1987–91, Newcastle Gosforth 91–92, Northampton 92– ; rep. Northumberland; Scotland and Five Nations debut v. England 1994. *Leisure interests*: cricket, squash, horseracing, eventing. *Address*: Northampton RUFC, Franklins Gardens, Weedon Rd, Northampton NN5 5BG.

WALWYN, Peter Tyndall: racehorse trainer; b. 1 July 1933; m. Virginia Walwyn 1960; 1 s., 1 d.; 1st licence 1960; winner 1000 Guineas 1970 (Humble Duty), Irish Derby 1974 (English Prince), 1975 (Grundy), Oaks 1974 (Polygamy), Derby, King George VI and Queen Elizabeth Diamond Stakes 1975 (Grundy). *Address*: c/o BHB, 42 Portman Square, London W1H 0EN.

WANE, Shaun David: Rugby League footballer; b. 14 September 1964, Wigan; player Wigan, Leeds 1990–93, Workington Town 93– ; GB U-21 and snr int. *Address*: Workington Town RLFC, Derwent Park, Workington, Cumbria.

WARD, Benjamin Matthew: Rugby Union footballer; b. 15 July 1965, Northampton; player Northampton 1985– , 2nd Div. champs. 1989/90. *Leisure interests*: horse-riding, golf, fitness training. *Address*: Northampton FC, Franklins Gardens, Weedon Rd, Northampton NN5 5BG.

WARD, David Mark: cricketer; b. 10 February 1961, Croydon; player Surrey 1985– , tours Barbados 1984, 89, 91; scored 2000 1st-class runs in season 1990. *Address*: Surrey CCC, The Oval, Kennington, London SE11 5SS.

WARD, Gavin: footballer; b. 30 June 1970, Sutton Coldfield; player Cardiff City 1989–93, Leicester City 93– . *Address*: Leicester City FC, City Stadium, Filbert St, Leicester LE2 7FL.

WARD, Kevin: Rugby League footballer; b. 5 August 1957, Wakefield; player Castleford, St Helens 1990– ; GB debut v. France 1984, Brit. Lions tour Aus./NZ/Papua New Guinea 1988. *Address*: St Helens RLFC, Dunriding Lane, St Helens, Merseyside WA10 4AD.

WARD, Mark: footballer; b. 10 October 1962, Huyton; player Oldham Athletic 1983–85, W. Ham Utd 85–89, Manchester City 89–91, Everton 91– . *Address*: Everton FC, Goodison Park, Liverpool L4 4EL.

WARD, Trevor Robert: cricketer; b. 18 January 1968, Farningham; m. Sarah Ann Ward 1990; player Kent 1986– ; England YC tours Sri Lanka 1987, Aus. (Youth World Cup) 1988. *Address*: Kent CCC, St Lawrence Ground, Canterbury CT1 3NZ.

WARDEN-OWEN, Edward: yachtsman; b. 25 June 1949, Holyhead; m. Susan Virginia Warden-Owen 1989; 1 s.; Olympic squad (470 class) 1980; America's Cup team 1987 (navigator *White Crusader*); Admiral's Cup team 1985 (helmsman *Phoenix*), 1989 (winners) (skipper *Indulgence VII*), 1993 (skipper *Indulgence*, winners Fastnet Race); skipper *Indulgence V*, winners Three-Quarter Ton Cup 1986. *Leisure interests*: squash, tennis, skiing, golf, horseriding. *Address*: Bruce Bank Sails Ltd, 372 Brook Lane, Warsash, Hants.

WARHURST, Paul: footballer; b. 26 September 1969, Stockport; player Oldham Athletic 1988–91, Sheffield Wednesday 91–93, Blackburn Rovers 93– ; 8 England U-21 caps. *Address*: Blackburn Rovers FC, Ewood Park, Blackburn, Lancs. BB2 4JF.

WARK, John: footballer; b. 4 August 1957, Glasgow; player Ipswich Town 1974–84, Liverpool 84–88, Ipswich Town 88–90, Middlesbrough 90–91, Ipswich Town 91– ; 8 Scotland U-21 caps, 29 full Scotland caps. *Address*: Ipswich Town FC, Portman Rd, Ipswich, Suffolk IP1 2DA.

WARMINGTON, Emma: figure skater; b. 9 July 1976, Newcastle; GB jnr ladies' champ. 1992, 93; GB jnr debut 1991, snr debut 1992. *Leisure interests*: embroidery, aerobics, cycling. *Address*: Crowtree Leisure Centre, Crowtree Rd, Sunderland SR1 3EL.

WARNER, Allan Esmond: cricketer; b. 12 May 1959, Birmingham; 1 s.; player Worcs. 1982–84, Derbys. 1985– ; with Derbys.: winners Benson and Hedges Cup 1993, Sunday League champs. 1990. *Address*: Derbys. CCC, County Cricket Ground, Nottingham Rd, Derby DE2 6DA.

WARREN, Mark: footballer; b. 12 November 1974, Clapton; player Leyton Orient 1991–93, Nottingham Forest 93– . *Address*: Nottingham Forest FC, City Ground, Nottingham NG2 5FJ.

WARRINER, Alan: darts player; b. 24 March 1962, Lancaster; m. Tracy Kim Shield 1992; England debut 1988, winners European Cup 1991, World Cup 1989, 91; winner Isle of Man Open 1986, 92, Malta Open 1988, Denmark Open 1989, Dutch Open 1989, 93, Belgian Open 1989, 90, Brit. Matchplay, Brit. Open 1990, N. American Open 1992, Finland Open 1993. *Leisure interests*: boxing, Manchester Utd FC, cricket, rugby, travel, marriage. *Address*: c/o Tommy Cox, Red House Farm, 27 Berrishill Grove, Whitby Bay, Tyne & Wear NE25 9XU.

WARWICK, Derek: F1 driver; b. 27 August 1954; m. Rhonda Warwick; 2 d.; F3 debut 1977, Vandervell F3 champ., runner-up BP F3 Champs. 1978; F2 debut 1979, rep. Theodore 1979–80, Toleman 1980, runner-up European F2 Champs. 1980; F1 debut 1981, rep. Toleman 1981–84, Renault 84–86, Brabham 1986, Arrows 1987–90, Lotus 1990, Footwork 1993, 2nd place Belgian, Brit. and SA GP 1984; world sportscar debut 1986, rep. Jaguar 1986, 91, Peugeot 1992, world champ. 1992, runner-up 1986, 91, winner Le Mans 24-hour race 1992. *Leisure interests*: golf, squash, running, weight training, tennis. *Address*: Footwork GP Int. Ltd, 39 Barton Rd, Water Eaton Industrial Estate, Bletchley, Milton Keynes, Bucks. MK2 3HW.

WARZYCHA, Robert: footballer; b. 20 August 1963, Wielun, Poland; player Gornik Zabrze (Poland), Everton 1991– ; over 20 Poland caps. *Address*: Everton FC, Goodison Park, Liverpool L4 4EL.

WASIM AKRAM: cricketer; b. 3 June 1966, Lahore, Pakistan; player Lancs. 1988– ; Test debut 1984, Pakistan tours NZ 1984/85, Sri Lanka 1985/86, India 1986/87, England 1987, WI 1987/88, Aus. 1989/90, Aus./NZ (World Cup) 1991/92, England 1992, NZ/Aus./SA/WI 1992/93 (capt.). *Address*: Lancs. CCC, Old Trafford, Manchester M16 0PX.

WATKIN, Steven Llewellyn: cricketer; b. 13 September 1964, Port Talbot; player Glamorgan 1986– , Sunday League champs. 1993; England A tours Kenya/Zimbabwe 1989/90, Pakistan/Sri Lanka 1990/91, WI 1991/92, Test debut 1991, tour WI 1994. *Address*: Glamorgan CCC, Sophia Gardens, Cardiff CF1 9XR.

WATKINSON, Michael: cricketer; b. 1 August 1961, Westhoughton; m. Susan Watkinson 1986; 1 s., 1 d.; player Lancs. 1982– (capt. 94–), winners Benson and Hedges Cup 1990 (Man of the Match).

Address: Lancs. CCC, Old Trafford, Manchester M16 0PX.

WATSON, Chris: Rugby League footballer; b. 9 September 1967; player Cutsyke ARLFC, Castleford 1991– . *Address*: Castleford RLFC, Wheldon Rd, Castleford WF10 2SD.

WATSON, David: footballer; b. 20 November 1961, Liverpool; player Norwich City 1980–86, Everton 86– (capt.); with Norwich City: 2nd Div. champs. 1985/86; with Everton: League champs. 1986/87; 7 England U-21 caps, 12 full England caps. *Address*: Everton FC, Goodison Park, Liverpool L4 4EL.

WATSON, David Thomas: Rugby League footballer; b. 24 May 1967, Waitara Taranaki (NZ); player Hull Kingston Rovers, Halifax, Bradford Northern 1992– ; NZ debut v. France 1989. *Address*: Bradford Northern RLFC, Odsal Stadium, Bradford BD6 1BS.

WATSON, Melissa: triathlete; b. 24 November 1964; GB women's champ. 1991, women's duathlon champ. 1991, 92; European Champs. duathlon individ. bronze medals 1991, 93, team silver 1991, bronze 1992, 93; UK women's 3000m champ. 1988. *Address*: c/o Brit. Triathlon Assoc., 4 Tynemouth Terrace, Tynemouth NE30 4BH.

WATSON, Michael: Rugby Union footballer; b. 2 August 1965, Sunderland; player W. Hartlepool 1992– ; rep. Combined Services. *Address*: W. Hartlepool RFC, Brierton Lane, Hartlepool, Cleveland TS25 5DR.

WATSON, Stephen: footballer; b. 1 April 1974, N. Shields; player Newcastle Utd 1991– . *Address*: Newcastle Utd FC, St James' Park, Newcastle-upon-Tyne, Tyne & Wear NE1 4ST.

WATSON, Thomas: footballer; b. 29 September 1969, Liverpool; player Grimsby Town 1988– . *Address*: Grimsby Town FC, Blundell Park, Cleethorpes, S. Humberside DN35 7PY.

WATT, Alan Gordon James: Rugby Union footballer; b. 10 July 1967, Glasgow; player Glasgow High/Kelvinside; Scotland B debut v. France 1991, snr debut v. Zimbabwe 1991, tours N. America 1991, Aus. 1992. *Address*: Glasgow High/Kelvinside RFC, Old Anniesland, Crow Rd, Glasgow.

WATT, Michael: footballer; b. 27 November 1970, Aberdeen; player Aberdeen 1989– ; Scotland U-21 int. *Address*: Aberdeen FC, Pittodrie Stadium, Pittodrie St, Aberdeen AB2 1QH.

WAUGH, Keith: footballer; b. 27 October 1956, Sunderland; player Peterborough Utd 1976–81, Sheffield Utd 81–85, Bristol City 85–89, Coventry City 89–91, Watford 91– ; with Sheffield Utd: 4th Div. champs. 1981/82. *Address*: Watford FC, Vicarage Rd Stadium, Watford, Herts. WD1 8ER.

WAY, Paul: golfer; b. 12 March 1963, Kingsbury, Middx; English open amateur strokeplay champ. 1981; Walker Cup team 1981; prof. debut 1981; Dunhill Cup team 1985; Ryder Cup team 1983, 85, winners 1985; winner Dutch Open 1982, European Open 1987. *Address*: c/o PGA European Tour, Wentworth Club, Wentworth Drive, Virginia Water, Surrey GU25 4LS.

WAY, Penny: windsurfer; b. 3 April 1962, Bristol; m. Rob Andrews 1986; UK ladies' champ. 1981–85, Olympic-class champ. 1993; Aus. ladies' champ. 1981, 82; European Champs. silver medal 1981, gold 1984, 88; World Champs. bronze medals 1982, 87, 88, gold 1986, silver 1989, Olympic-class gold 1990, 91; Olympic squad 1992; winner Silk Cut Helmsman of the Year Award 1990, Sports Aid

Foundation Sir John Cohen Memorial Award 1991, Yachtsperson of the Year 1991, Windsurfing Personality of the Year 1989–92. *Publications*: *The Usborne Book of Windsurfing*, 1988, *Competitive Windsurfing*, 1990. *Leisure interests*: mountain biking, current affairs publications, fresh air. *Address*: 10 Gladstone Close, Christchurch, Dorset BH23 3TL.

WDOWCZYK, Dariusz: footballer; b. 21 September 1962, Warsaw, Poland; player Legia Warsaw (Poland), Celtic 1989– ; Poland int. *Address*: Celtic FC, Celtic Park, 95 Kerrydale St, Glasgow G40 3RE.

WEBB, David: football manager; b. 9 April 1946, Stratford; player Leyton Orient 1964–66, Southampton 66–68, Chelsea 68–74, Queens Park Rangers 74–77, Leicester City 77–78, Derby County 78–80, Bournemouth 80–82, Torquay Utd 1984; manager Bournemouth 1980–82, Torquay Utd 84–85, Southend Utd 86–87, 88–92, Chelsea 1993, Brentford 93– . *Address*: Brentford FC, Griffin Park, Braemar Rd, Brentford, Middx TW8 0NT.

WEBB, Neil: footballer; b. 30 July 1963, Reading; m. Shelley Alexander 1985; 2 s.; player Reading 1980–82, Portsmouth 82–85, Nottingham Forest 85–89, Manchester Utd 89–92, Nottingham Forest 92– ; with Portsmouth: 3rd Div. champs. 1982/83; with Nottingham Forest: winners League Cup 1989; with Manchester Utd: winners FA Cup 1990, European Cup Winners' Cup 1991, League Cup 1992; 3 England U-21 caps, 26 full England caps. *Leisure interests*: golf, theatre, environmental issues. *Address*: Park Associates Ltd, 6 George St, Nottingham NG1 3BE.

WEBSTER, Richard Edward: Rugby League footballer; b. 9 July 1967, Morriston; 1 d.; RU: player Bonymaen, Swansea; Wales debut v. Aus. (World Cup) 1987, Five Nations debut v. Ireland 1992, tour Aus. 1991; Brit. Lions tour NZ 1993;

RL: player Salford 1993– . *Address*: Salford RLFC, The Willows, Willows Rd, Weaste, Salford M5 2ST.

WEBSTER, Simon: footballer; b. 20 January 1964, Hinckley; player Tottenham Hotspur 1982–84, Huddersfield Town 85–88, Sheffield Utd 88–90, Charlton Athletic 90–93, W. Ham Utd 93– . *Address*: W. Ham Utd FC, Boleyn Ground, Green St, Upton Park, London E13 9AZ.

WEBSTER, Stephen, MBE: motorcyclist (sidecar); b. 7 January 1960, York; m. Karen Webster 1987; 1 s., 1 d.; GB clubman's champ. 1982, GB champ. 1985–88, Supercup champ. 1989, 92; world champ. 1987–89, 91, runner-up 1992, 93, 3rd place 1986, 90; winner Seagrave Trophy 1992. *Leisure interests*: keep-fit, moto-cross, 5-a-side football. *Address*: Flawith Service Station, Flawith, Alne, Yorks.

WEEKES, Paul Nicholas: cricketer; b. 8 July 1969, Hackney; player Middx 1990– , county champs. 1993, Sunday League champs. 1992. *Address*: Middx CCC, Lord's Cricket Ground, London NW8 8QN.

WEGERLE, Roy: footballer; b. 19 March 1964, Johannesburg, SA; player Tampa Bay (USA), Chelsea 1986–88, Luton Town 88–89, Queens Park Rangers 89–92, Blackburn Rovers 92–93, Coventry City 93– ; US int. *Address*: Coventry City FC, Highfield Rd Stadium, King Richard St, Coventry CV2 4FW.

WEIR, George Wilson (Doddie): Rugby Union footballer; b. 4 July 1970, Edinburgh; player Melrose, Scottish League champs. 1991/92; rep. S. of Scotland; Scotland U-21 debut v. Wales 1990, snr debut v. Argentina 1990, Five Nations debut v. England 1992, tours NZ 1990, Aus. 1992, Fiji/Tonga/W. Samoa 1993. *Address*: Melrose RFC, The Greenyards, Melrose TD6 9SA.

WEIR, John Paul: boxer; b. 16 September 1967, Glasgow; Scottish ABA light-fly-weight champ. 1991; Scotland debut 1988, Commonwealth Games squad 1990; European Champs. light-flyweight bronze medal 1991; prof. debut 1992; titles won: WBO mini-flyweight 1993; over 6 prof. wins. *Leisure interests*: swimming, running. *Address*: St Andrew's Sporting Club, Forte Crest Hotel, Bothwell St, Glasgow G2 7EN.

WEIR, Michael: footballer; b. 16 January 1966, Edinburgh; player Hibernian 1982–87, Luton Town 87–88, Hibernian 88– ; with Hibernian: winners Scottish League Cup 1992. *Address*: Hibernian FC, Easter Rd Stadium, 64 Albion Rd, Edinburgh EH7 5QG.

WEIR, Robert Boyd: athlete (hammer and discus); b. 4 February 1961, Solihull; m. Kym Ann Weir 1989; 1 s., 1 d.; AAA hammer and discus jnr champ. 1980, snr discus champ. 1993; World Student Games hammer silver medal 1983; Commonwealth Games hammer gold medal 1982; prof. American and Canadian footballer 1985–92; 1st black hammer-thrower to rep-resent GB. *Leisure interests*: chess, backgammon, water polo, developing per-sonal training programmes, socializing. *Address*: 20 Amherst Ave, Menlow Park, California CA 94025, USA.

WELCH, Michael Leslie: golfer; b. 27 October 1972, Shrewsbury; English boys' amateur open strokeplay champ., GB boys' amateur champ., European boys' champ., world boys' champ, Wilson PGA jnr champ. 1990. *Address*: Parkside, Weston-under-Redcastle, nr Shrewsbury, Shropshire SY4 5UX.

WELLS, Alan Peter: cricketer; b. 2 October 1961, Newhaven; m. Melanie Elizabeth Wells 1987; 1 s.; player Sussex 1981– (capt.); rep. England YC v. India 1981; England A tour SA 1993/94 (vice-capt.). *Address*: Sussex CCC, County Ground, Eaton Rd, Hove, E. Sussex BN3 3AN.

WELLS, Colin Mark: cricketer; b. 3 March 1960, Newhaven; m. Celia Wells 1982; 1 d.; player Sussex 1979–93 (vice-capt. 88–90), Derbys. 94– ; England tour Sharjah (UAE) 1985, 2 1-day ints. *Address*: Derbys. CCC, County Cricket Ground, Nottingham Rd, Derby DE2 6DA.

WELLS, Martyn David: glider pilot; b. 9 September 1949, Shipston on Stour; m. Mary Wells 1977; 2 s., 2 d.; GB 15m-class champ. 1982, 87, standard-class champ. 1986, 89; GB debut 1983; UK 15m- and standard-class 500km triangular speed record-holder. *Leisure interests*: reading, travel. *Address*: The Lenticulars, Ascott Lane, Whichford, Shipston on Stour, Warks.

WELLS, Vincent John: cricketer; b. 6 August 1965, Dartford; m. Deborah Louise Wells 1989; player Kent 1987–91, Leics. 92– . *Address*: Leics. CCC, County Ground, Grace Rd, Leicester LE2 8AD.

WELSH, Brian: footballer; b. 23 February 1969, Edinburgh; player Dundee Utd 1986– . *Address*: Dundee Utd FC, Tannadice Park, Dundee DD3 7JW.

WELSH, Stephen: footballer; b. 19 April 1968, Glasgow; player Cambridge Utd 1990–91, Peterborough Utd 91– . *Address*: Peterborough Utd FC, London Rd Ground, Peterborough, Cambs. PE2 8AL.

WEMMS, Matthew Gregory: windsurfer; b. 30 September 1972, Welwyn Garden City; UK nat. series raceboard champ. 1992; World Youth Champs. bronze medal 1989, gold 1990 (1st Brit. winner); World Champs. raceboard gold medal 1993. *Leisure interests*: squash, surfing, mountain biking, roller skating, skateboarding, canoeing, water skiing. *Address*: 10 New Rd, Digswell, Welwyn, Herts. AL6 0AG.

WEST, Colin: footballer; b. 19 September 1967, Middlesbrough; player Chelsea 1985–90, Dundee 90– . *Address*: Dundee FC, Dens Park, Dundee DD3 7JY.

WEST, Richard John: Rugby Union footballer; b. 20 March 1971, Hereford; player Moseley, Gloucester 1992– ; rep. S.W. Div., Div. champs. 1993/94; England U-21 debut v. The Netherlands 1991. *Leisure interests*: squash, motocross, weight training. *Address*: Gloucester RUFC, Kingsholm, Worcester St, Gloucester GL3 3AX.

WESTGARTH, Kevin: Rugby Union footballer; b. 6 May 1961, Crowcrook, Co. Durham; player Tynedale, Gosforth, W. Hartlepool 1991– ; rep. Northumberland, N..Div. *Address*: W. Hartlepool RFC, Brierton Lane, Hartlepool, Cleveland TS25 5DR.

WESTLEY, Shane: footballer; b. 16 June 1965, Canterbury; player Charlton Athletic 1983–85, Southend Utd 85–89, Wolverhampton Wanderers 89– . *Address*: Wolverhampton Wanderers FC, Molineux Stadium, Waterloo Rd, Wolverhampton WV1 4QR.

WESTON, Martin John: cricketer; b. 8 April 1959, Worcester; m. Angela Karen Weston 1992; player Worcs. 1979–93, winners Benson and Hedges Cup 1991, county champs. 1988, 89, Sunday League champs. 1987, 88. *Leisure interests*: horseracing, golf, food and drink. *Address*: Worcs. CCC, County Ground, New Rd, Worcester WR2 4QQ.

WESTON, William Philip Christopher: cricketer; b. 16 June 1973, Durham; player Worcs. 1991– ; England U-19 tours Canada/NZ 1990/91, Pakistan 1991/92 (capt.). *Address*: Worcs. CCC, County Ground, New Rd, Worcester WR2 4QQ.

WETHERALL, David: footballer; b. 14 March 1971, Sheffield; player Leeds Utd 1991– . *Address*: Leeds Utd FC, Elland Rd, Leeds, W. Yorks. LS11 0ES.

WHARTON, Henry: boxer; b. 23 November 1967; England debut 1987; prof. debut 1989; titles won: Commonwealth super-middleweight 1991, GB super-middleweight 1992; over 14 prof. wins. *Address*: Nat. Promotions, Nat. House, 60–66 Wardour St, London W1V 3HP.

WHELAN, Philip: footballer; b. 7 March 1972, Stockport; player Ipswich Town 1990– . *Address*: Ipswich Town FC, Portman Rd, Ipswich, Suffolk IP1 2DA.

WHELAN, Ronald: footballer; b. 25 September 1961, Dublin, Ireland; player Liverpool 1979– , winners FA Cup 1986, 89, 92, European Cup 1984, League Cup 1982, 83, 84, League champs. 1981/82, 83/83, 83/84, 85/86, 87/88, 89/90; 1 Ireland U-21 cap, over 45 full Ireland caps. *Address*: Liverpool FC, Anfield Rd, Liverpool L4 0TH.

WHITAKER, John, MBE: equestrianist (show jumping); b. 5 August 1955, Huddersfield; m. Claire Barr; 1 s., 2 d.; GB champ. 1992, 93; European Champs. team and individ. silver medals 1983 (Ryan's Son), team gold and individ. bronze 1985 (Hopscotch), team gold and individ. silver 1987 (Milton), individ. and team gold 1989 (Milton), team silver 1991, 93; World Champs. team bronze medal 1982 (Ryan's Son), team silver 1986 (Hopscotch); World Cup gold medals 1990, 91 (Milton), silver (Grannusch/Milton) 1993; Olympic individ. and team silver medals 1980 (Ryan's Son), team silver 1984 (Ryan's Son); winner Derby 1983 (Ryan's Son), King George V Gold Cup 1986 (Ryan's Son), 1990 (Milton). *Address*: c/o Brit. Horse Soc., Brit. Equestrian Centre, Stoneleigh Park, Kenilworth, Warks. CV8 2LR.

WHITAKER, John James: cricketer; b. 5 May 1962, Skipton; player Leics. 1983– ; 1 Test, debut 1986, 2 1-day ints, tours Aus. 1986/87, Zimbabwe/Kenya (England A) 1990/91. *Address*: Leics. CCC, County Ground, Grace Rd, Leicester LE2 8AD.

WHITAKER, Michael: equestrianist (show jumping); b. 17 March 1960; m. Véronique Whitaker 1980; European Jnr Champs. team gold medal 1978; GB snr debut 1982; European Champs. team gold medal 1985 (Warren Point), team gold 1987 (Amanda), team gold and individ. silver 1989 (Monsanta), team silver 1991, team silver and individ. bronze 1993 (Midnight Madness); World Champs. team silver medal 1986 (Warren Point); Olympic team silver medal 1984 (Amanda), reserve 1988, squad 1992; winner Derby 1980 (Owen Gregory), 1991 92 (Monsanta), 1993 (My Messieur), King George V Gold Cup 1982 (Disney Way), 1989 (Didi), 1992 (Midnight Madness). *Address*: c/o Brit. Horse Soc., Brit. Equestrian Centre, Stoneleigh Park, Kenilworth, Warks. CV8 2LR.

WHITAKER, Véronique: equestrianist (show jumping); b. 15 January 1959, Ville, Belgium; m. Michael Whitaker 1980; GB champ. 1991 (Flarepath), ladies' champ. 1993 (Fol Amour); Belgium jnr debut 1975; European Jnr Champs. team gold medal 1975, individ. silver 1976, 77; GB debut 1982, winners Nations Cup 1991; winner Queen Elizabeth II Cup 1984 (Jingo). *Address*: Whatton Fields Farm, Whatton, Nottingham NG13 9FJ.

WHITBREAD, Adrian: footballer; b. 22 October 1971, Epping; player Leyton Orient 1989–93, Swindon Town 93– . *Address*: Swindon Town FC, The County Ground, Swindon, Wilts. SN1 2ED.

WHITE, Christopher: footballer; b. 11 December 1970, Chatham; player Peterborough Utd 1991– . *Address*: Peterborough Utd FC, London Rd Ground, Peterborough, Cambs. PE2 8AL.

WHITE, Craig: cricketer; b. 16 December 1969, Morley; m. Elizabeth Anne White 1992; player Yorks. 1990– ; Aus. YC tour WI 1990. *Address*: Yorks. CCC, Headingley Cricket Ground, Leeds LS6 3BU.

WHITE, David: footballer; b. 30 October 1967, Manchester; player Manchester City 1985–93, Leeds Utd 93– ; 6 England U-21 caps. *Address*: Leeds Utd FC, Elland Rd, Leeds, W. Yorks. LS11 0ES.

WHITE, James Warren: snooker player; b. 2 May 1962, Tooting; English amateur champ. 1979, world amateur champ. 1980; prof. debut 1980, UK champ. 1992, winner Scottish Masters 1981, Masters 1984, Irish Masters 1985, 86, Pot Black 1986, Rothmans Grand Prix 1986, 92, Mercantile Credit Classic 1986, 91, Brit. Open 1987, 92, World Matchplay Champs. 1989, 90, World Masters 1991, European Open 1992. *Address*: Cue International Leisure Ltd, 1 Regent Rd, Salford, Manchester M5 4SX.

WHITE, Stephen: footballer; b. 2 January 1959, Chipping Sodbury; player Bristol Rovers 1977–79, Luton Town 79–82, Charlton Athletic 82–83, Bristol Rovers 83–86, Swindon Town 86– ; with Luton Town: 2nd Div. champs. 1981/82. *Address*: Swindon Town FC, The County Ground, Swindon, Wilts. SN1 2ED.

WHITE, Winston: footballer; b. 26 October 1958, Leicester; player Leicester City 1976–79, Hereford Utd 79–82, Bury 83–87, Colchester Utd 87–88, Burnley 88–91, W. Bromwich Albion 91– . *Address*: W. Bromwich Albion FC, The Hawthorns, W. Bromwich B71 4LF.

WHITEHOUSE, Dane: footballer; b. 14 October 1970, Sheffield; player Sheffield Utd 1989– . *Address*: Sheffield Utd FC, Bramall Lane, Sheffield, S. Yorks S2 4SU.

WHITELOCK, Paul: Rugby Union footballer; b. 16 March 1963, Hartlepool; player W. Hartlepool 1983– ; rep. Durham U-16 and snr squad. *Address*: W. Hartlepool RFC, Brierton Lane, Hartlepool, Cleveland TS25 5DR.

WHITESIDE, Scott Peter: motorcyclist (sidecar passenger); b. 4 November 1969, Brighton; GB champ. 1991, 92. *Leisure interests*: motor sport, football, basketball. *Address*: c/o ACU, ACU House, Wood St, Rugby CV21 2YX.

WHITLOW, Michael: footballer; b. 13 January 1968, Northwich; player Leeds Utd 1988–92, Leicester City 92– ; with Leeds Utd: 2nd Div. champs. 1989/90. *Address*: Leicester City FC, City Stadium, Filbert St, Leicester LE2 7FL.

WHITTALL, Robert: hang glider/paraglider pilot; b. 21 April 1969, Leeds; GB hang gliding champ. 1988; GB debut (hang gliding) 1987, (paragliding) 1991; World Hang Gliding Champs. gold medal 1989; World Paragliding Champs. gold medal 1991; youngest-ever world champ. in both disciplines. *Leisure interests*: surfing, snowboarding, water skiing. *Address*: Pine Tree, Layton Lane, Rawdon, Leeds LS19 6RQ.

WHITTINGHAM, Guy: footballer; b. 11 November 1964, Evesham; player Portsmouth 1989–93, Aston Villa 93– . *Address*: Aston Villa FC, Villa Park, Trinity Rd, Birmingham B6 6HE.

WHITTON, Stephen: footballer; b. 4 December 1960, E. Ham; player Coventry City 1978–83, W. Ham Utd 83–86, Birmingham City 86–89, Sheffield Wednesday 89–91, Ipswich Town 91– . *Address*: Ipswich Town FC, Portman Rd, Ipswich, Suffolk IP1 2DA.

WHYMAN, Claire Louise: synchronized swimmer; b. 6 February 1975, Reading; England and GB jnr debuts 1991 (capt. 1992), snr debuts 1993. *Leisure interests*: contemporary dance, karate, keep-fit, art and photography. *Address*: c/o ASA, Harold Fern House, Derby Square, Loughborough, Leics. LE11 0AL.

WHYTE, Christopher: footballer; b. 2 September 1961, Islington; player Arsenal 1979–85, Los Angeles (USA), W. Bromwich Albion 1988–90, Leeds Utd 90–93, Birmingham City 93– ; with Leeds Utd: League champs. 1991/92; 4 England U-21 caps. *Address*: Birmingham City FC, St Andrews Ground, Birmingham B9 4NH.

WHYTE, Derek: footballer; b. 31 August 1968, Glasgow; player Celtic 1985–82, Middlesbrough 92– ; with Celtic: winners Scottish Cup 1988, 89; 6 Scotland caps. *Address*: Middlesbrough FC, Ayresome Park, Middlesbrough, Cleveland TS1 4PB.

WHYTE, Frances: flat green bowler; b. 22 September 1930, Neilston, Renfrewshire; m. Allan Whyte 1953; 2 s.; Scotland debut (outdoor) 1973; Commonwealth Games squad 1986, 90; World Champs. women's fours gold medal 1985, triples, fours and team gold 1992. *Leisure interests*: gardening, grandchildren. *Address*: 62 Houstonfield Quadrant, Houston, Renfrewshire.

WICKHAM, John Arthur: flat green bowler; b. 25 March 1951, Westminster; m. Eileen Anne Wickham 1973; 4 d.; rep. Devon 1987– (skip 89–), winners Liberty Trophy 1993; Devon singles champ. 1989, singles, pairs and fours champ. 1993; English singles champ. 1993. *Leisure interests*: walking on Dartmoor. *Address*: 97 Coombe Vale Rd, Teignmouth TQ14 9EN.

WIEGHORST, Morten: footballer; b. 25 February 1971, Glostrup, Denmark; player Dundee 1992– . *Address*: Dundee FC, Dens Park, Dundee DD3 7JY.

WIGG, Simon Antony: motorcyclist (speedway); b. 15 October 1960, Aylesbury; GB champ. 1988, 89, grass-track champ. 1981–83, 85, 89; Aus. long-track GP champ. 1989, 94; NZ long-track GP champ. 1994;

world long-track champ. 1985, 89, 90, 93. *Leisure interests*: skiing, water skiing, motocross, squash, gym training. *Address:* The Mine, 32B Gold St, Northampton NN1 1RS.

WIGHT, Robert Marcus: cricketer; b. 12 September 1969, London; player Glos. 1993– , MCC tour Kenya 1993. *Address*: Glos. CCC, Phoenix County Ground, Nevil Rd, Bristol BS6 9EJ.

WIGLEY, Steven: footballer; b. 15 October 1961, Ashton-under-Lyne; player Nottingham Forest 1981–85, Sheffield Utd 85–87, Birmingham City 87–89, Portsmouth 89–93, Exeter City 93– . *Address*: Exeter City FC, St James Park, Well St, Exeter EX4 6PX.

WILCOX, Jason: footballer; b. 15 March 1971, Farnworth; player Blackburn Rovers 1989– . *Address*: Blackburn Rovers FC, Ewood Park, Blackburn, Lancs. BB2 4JF.

WILDER, Christopher: footballer; b. 23 September 1967, Stocksbridge; player Sheffield Utd 1986– . *Address*: Sheffield Utd FC, Bramall Lane, Sheffield, S. Yorks S2 4SU.

WILKIE, Lydia Jane Mallean: lacrosse player; b. 18 May 1966, Glasgow; player Chelsea College 1984–88, Berks. Wanderers 90– ; rep. Sussex 1984–89, Berks. 90– , South 86– ; with South: territorial champs. 1993; Scotland debut 1988, World Cup squad 1989, 93. *Leisure interests*: skiing, painting, golf, bridge, crosswords. *Address*: 1 Southview Ave, Caversham, Reading RG4 0AB.

WILKINS, Raymond, MBE: footballer; b. 14 September 1956, Hillingdon; player Chelsea 1973–79, Manchester Utd 79–84, AC Milan (Italy) 84–87, Paris St Germain (France) 87–88, Rangers 88–89, Queens Park Rangers 1989– ; with Manchester Utd: winners FA Cup 1983; 1 England U-21 cap, 2 England U-23 caps, 84 full England

caps. *Address*: Queens Park Rangers FC, Rangers Stadium, S. Africa Rd, London W12 7PA.

WILKINS, Richard John: footballer; b. 28 May 1965, Streatham; m. Dawn Wilkins 1992; player Colchester Utd 1986–90, Cambridge Utd 90– . *Leisure interests*: golf, fishing, cricket. *Address*: Cambridge Utd FC, Abbey Stadium, Newmarket Rd, Cambridge CB5 8LL.

WILKINSON, Chris: tennis player; b. 5 January 1970; rep. Hants.; GB doubles champ. 1992; GB debut 1990, European Cup team 1990, 92, Davis Cup team 1991– , Olympic squad 1992; winner Kuala Lumpur Challenger 1992. *Address*: c/o LTA, The Queen's Club, W. Kensington, London W14 9EG.

WILKINSON, Gary: snooker player; b. 7 April 1966; prof. debut 1987, winner World Matchplay Champs. 1991. *Address*: c/o Cuemasters Ltd, Kerse Rd, Stirling, Scotland FK7 7SG.

WILKINSON, Howard: football manager; b. 13 November 1943, Sheffield; player Sheffield Wednesday 1962–66, Brighton and Hove Albion 66–80; manager Notts County 1982–83, Sheffield Wednesday 83–88, Leeds Utd 88– ; with Leeds Utd: 2nd Div. champs. 1989/90, League champs. 1991/92. *Address*: Leeds Utd FC, Elland Rd, Leeds, W. Yorks. LS11 0ES.

WILKINSON, Jacqueline Louise: target archer; b. 26 June 1964, Ilkley; m. Garry Wilkinson 1989; rep. Berks. 1984–86, Cumbria 87– , county indoor champ. 1987, outdoor champ. 1990, field champ. 1989–92; UAU indoor and outdoor champ. 1986; attained Grand Master Bowman status 1992; GB open champ. 1993; GB debut 1991. *Leisure interests*: singing, knitting, embroidery. *Address*: 37 Pinewoods, Gilgarran, Workington, Cumbria CA14 4RE.

WILKINSON, Paul: footballer; b. 30 October 1964, Louth; player Grimsby Town 1982–85, Everton 85–87, Nottingham Forest 87–88, Watford 88–91, Middlesbrough 91– ; with Everton: League champs. 1986/87; 4 England U-21 caps. *Address:* Middlesbrough FC, Ayresome Park, Middlesbrough, Cleveland TS1 4PB.

WILLCOCK, Dave: powerboat racer; b. 15 November 1955, Penzance; m. Deb Willcock; 1 s., 1 d.; GB offshore circuit racing B class champ. 1991–93, world champ. 1993. *Leisure interests:* squash, running, fishing, family, raising money for charity. *Address:* 3 Tofrek Terrace, Reading, Berks.

WILLEY, Neil Edward: swimmer; b. 11 September 1976, Enfield; England debut 1993; GB debut 1993; European Jnr Champs. 100m backstroke gold medal 1993; European jnr 100m backstroke, GB jnr 50m backstroke record-holder. *Leisure interests:* football, rugby. *Address:* 10 Hawkshead Lane, N. Mymms, Herts. AL9 7TB.

WILLIAMS, Andrew: footballer; b. 29 July 1962, Birmingham; player Coventry City 1985–86, Rotherham Utd 86–88, Leeds Utd 88–92, Notts County 92–   ; with Leeds Utd: 2nd Div. champs. 1989/90. *Address:* Notts County FC, Meadow Lane Ground, Nottingham NG2 3HJ.

WILLIAMS, Andrew: Rugby Union footballer; b. 31 March 1971; player Maesteg; Wales U-21 debut v. Ireland 1991, snr tour Zimbabwe/Namibia 1993. *Address:* Maesteg RFC, The Old Parish Ground, Llynfi Rd, Maesteg, Mid Glamorgan.

WILLIAMS, Brett: footballer; b. 19 March 1968, Dudley; player Nottingham Forest 1984– . *Address:* Nottingham Forest FC, City Ground, Nottingham NG2 5FJ.

WILLIAMS, Donald Scott: hockey player; b. 11 September 1966, Altrincham; player Guildford 1984–89, Havant 90– ; with

Havant: winners League Cup 1990, club champs. 1990, League champs. 1991, 92, European Cup Winners' Cup silver medallist 1991; rep. Surrey U-18 1983–84, U-21 1986–87; England debut and tour Oman/Pakistan 1989, European Cup bronze medallist 1991; GB debut 1990, Champions Trophy squad 1990, 91, Olympic squad 1992. *Leisure interests:* all sport, reading, cinema, theatre, opera, music, travel, good food and wine. *Address:* Havant HC, Havant Park, Havant, Hants.

WILLIAMS, Huw: Rugby Union footballer; b. 29 May 1964; player Llanelli 1990– , winners Welsh Cup 1991, 92, 93, Welsh League champs. 1992/93. *Address:* Llanelli RFC, Stradey Park, Llanelli, Dyfed.

WILLIAMS, Ian James: fencer (sabre); b. 26 October 1967, Bexley Heath; GB U-16 champ. 1982, 83, U-18 champ. 1984, 85, U-20 champ. 1986, 87, snr champ. 1989 (youngest ever), 91, 92; Commonwealth Champs. team bronze medal 1986, individ. silver, team bronze 1990; GB jnr debut 1985, snr debut 1989, European Champs. squad 1991, World Champs. squad 1989–91, Olympic squad 1992. *Leisure interests:* golf, tennis, guitar. *Address:* 127B Sugden Rd, London SW11 5ED.

WILLIAMS, John: footballer; b. 11 May 1968, Birmingham; player Swansea City 1991–92, Coventry City 92– . *Address:* Coventry City FC, Highfield Rd Stadium, King Richard St, Coventry CV2 4FW.

WILLIAMS, Martin: footballer; b. 12 July 1973, Luton; player Luton Town 1991– . *Address:* Luton Town FC, Kenilworth Stadium, 1 Maple Rd, Luton, Beds. LU4 8AW.

WILLIAMS, Neil Fitzgerald: cricketer; b. 2 July 1962, Hopewell, St Vincent, WI; player Middx 1982– , county champs. 1985, 90, 93, Sunday League champs. 1992; English

Counties tour Zimbabwe 1985, MCC tour Leeward Islands 1992; 1 Test, debut 1990. *Address*: Middx CCC, Lord's Cricket Ground, London NW8 8QN.

WILLIAMS, Owain Llewelyn: Rugby Union footballer; b. 10 October 1964, Bridgend; m. Angela Williams 1993; player Bridgend 1987–92, Cardiff 92– ; Wales debut and tour Namibia 1990. *Address*: Cardiff RFC, Cardiff Arms Park, Westgate St, Cardiff CF1 1JA.

WILLIAMS, Paul: footballer; b. 16 August 1965, Stratford; player Charlton Athletic 1987–90, Sheffield Wednesday 90–92, Crystal Palace 92– ; with Sheffield Wednesday: winners League Cup 1991; 4 England U-21 caps. *Address*: Crystal Palace FC, Selhurst Park Stadium, London SE25 6PU.

WILLIAMS, Peter: Rugby League footballer; b. 14 December 1960, Wigan; player Orrell (RU), Salford 1988– ; GB debut v. France 1989. *Address*: Salford RLFC, The Willows, Willows Rd, Weaste, Salford M5 2ST.

WILLIAMS, Rhodri ap Watcyn: croquet player; b. 31 December 1941, Glasgow; 4 ch.; Scotland debut 1986; Scottish open champ. 1982; winner Edinburgh Open 1980, 82, 84, 85, 88, 91, Scottish Chairman's Rosebowl 1984, 90, 91, 92. *Leisure interests*: bridge, hill-walking. *Address*: 103 Cartvale Rd, Glasgow G42 9RW.

WILLIAMS, Ricardo Cecil: cricketer; b. 7 February 1968, Camberwell; player Glos. 1991– . *Address*: Glos. CCC, Phoenix County Ground, Nevil Rd, Bristol BS6 9EJ.

WILLIAMS, Steven Michael: Rugby Union footballer; b. 3 October 1970, Neath; player Swansea, Neath 1991– ; Wales U-21 debut v. Scotland U-21 1990, Wales B debut v. The Netherlands 1990, snr tour

Namibia 1990. *Address*: Neath RFC, The Gnoll, Gnoll Park Rd, Neath, W. Glamorgan.

WILLIAMS, Tonia Lewis: oarswoman; b. 27 May 1966, Plymouth; NZ women's lightweight coxless fours champ. 1989, 90, lightweight double sculls champ. 1989, single sculls champ. 1990; GB women's double sculls champ. 1991; GB debut 1991; World Champs. lightweight women's coxless fours silver medal 1992, gold 1993. *Leisure interests*: water sports, skiing, flying kites, bicycle touring, travel, good food and wine, architecture and design, graphics. *Address*: c/o Nottinghamshire County Rowing Assoc., Nat. Watersports Centre, Holme Pierrepoint, Adbolton Lane, Nottingham.

WILLIAMS-JONES, Hugh: Rugby Union footballer; b. 10 January 1963, Bryncethin; m. Karyn Williams-Jones; 1 s., 1 d.; player Bridgend, Llanelli, Pontypridd, S. Wales Police, Llanelli; Wales B tours Italy 1986, Canada 1989, snr and Five Nations debut v. Scotland 1989, tours Aus. 1991, Zimbabwe/Namibia 1993. *Address*: Llanelli RFC, Stradey Park, Llanelli, Dyfed.

WILLIAMSON, Paul: Rugby League footballer; b. 27 November 1969, Warrington; player Woolston ARLFC, Warrington 1987– ; GB youth int. *Address*: Warrington RLFC, Wilderspool Stadium, Wilderspool Causeway, Warrington WA4 6PY.

WILLIAMSON, Robert: footballer; b. 13 August 1961, Glasgow; player Clydebank 1980–83, Rangers 83–86, W. Bromwich Albion 86–88, Rotherham Utd 88–90, Kilmarnock 90– . *Address*: Kilmarnock FC, Rugby Park, Kilmarnock KA1 2DP.

WILLIAMSON, Trevor: footballer; b. 7 November 1971, Portadown, NI; player Raith Rovers 1991– . *Address*: Raith Rovers FC, Stark's Park, Pratt St, Kirkcaldy, Fife KY1 1SA.

WILLISON, Ricky Brian: golfer; b. 30 July 1959, Ruislip; m. Alexandra Willison 1991; Middx matchplay champ. 1978, 79, 82, 83, 84, 86, amateur champ. 1984, 85, 87, 89, open champ. 1990, 91; English amateur champ. 1991; England debut 1988; Walker Cup team 1991; prof. debut 1991. *Leisure interests*: football, cricket, rugby, collecting old golf instructional books and Ben Hogan memorabilia. *Address*: 21 Wicket Rd, Perivale, Middx UB6 8YH.

WILLMORE, Tracy: hockey player; b. 26 January 1971, Clacton; player Clacton 1981–90, Chelmsford 91– ; rep. Essex U-16 1987, U-18 1988–89, U-21 1990–92 (county U-21 champs. 1990, 91, 92), snr 1990– ; England U-21 debut and U-21 home countries champs. 1992, snr training squad 1992– . *Leisure interests*: all sport, reading, meeting people. *Address*: Chelmsford HC, Chelmer Park, Beehive Lane, Chelmsford, Essex.

WILMOT, Rhys: footballer; b. 21 February 1962, Newport; player Arsenal 1980–89, Plymouth Argyle 89–92, Grimsby Town 92– ; 6 Wales U-21 caps. *Address*: Grimsby Town FC, Blundell Park, Cleethorpes, S. Humberside DN35 7PY.

WILSHIRE, Spencer Lloyd: flat green bowler; b. 7 May 1945, Rhondda; m. Ann Wilshire; 1 s., 1 d.; rep. Mid Glamorgan (outdoor) 1975– ; Welsh singles champ. (outdoor) 1978, pairs champ. (outdoor) 1975, 78, 80; GB pairs champ. (outdoor) 1976, 79, 81; Wales debut (outdoor and indoor) 1977, Commonwealth Games squad 1982, 86, World Champs. squad 1980, 84, 92. *Leisure interests*: snooker, DIY. *Address*: Plot 61, Dinan Park, Ton-Pentre, Rhondda, Mid Glamorgan CF41 7AT.

WILSON, Andrew: Rugby League footballer; b. 15 October 1963, Leeds; player Sheffield Eagles, Wakefield Trinity 1988– ; rep. Yorks. *Address*: Wakefield Trinity RLFC, 171 Doncaster Rd, Belle Vue, Wakefield WF1 5EZ.

WILSON, Christine: netball player; b. 23 December 1973, Kendal; rep. Cumbria 1986– ; Scotland U-18 debut 1992, U-21 and snr debuts 1993. *Leisure interests*: experimenting in the kitchen, reading, music. *Address*: c/o Scottish Netball Assoc., Kelvin Hall, Argyle St, Glasgow G3 8AW.

WILSON, Clive: footballer; b. 13 November 1961, Manchester; player Manchester City 1979–87, Chelsea 87–90, Queens Park Rangers 90– ; with Chelsea: 2nd Div. champs. 1988/89. *Address*: Queens Park Rangers FC, Rangers Stadium, S. Africa Rd, London W12 7PA.

WILSON, Daniel: footballer; b. 1 January 1960, Wigan; player Bury 1977–80, Chesterfield 80–83, Nottingham Forest 1983, Brighton and Hove Albion 83–87, Luton Town 87–90, Sheffield Wednesday 90–93, player/coach Barnsley 93– ; with Luton Town: winners League Cup 1988; with Sheffield Wednesday: winners League Cup 1991; 24 NI caps. *Address*: Barnsley FC, Oakwell Ground, Grove St, Barnsley, Yorks. S71 1ET.

WILSON, Grant Douglas: Rugby Union footballer; b. 10 November 1966, Edinburgh; player Preston Lodge, Boroughmuir; Scotland B debut v. Ireland 1989, snr tour Fiji/Tonga/W. Samoa 1993. *Address*: Boroughmuir RFC, Meggetland, Colinton Rd, Edinburgh EH14 1AS.

WILSON, Ian: swimmer; b. 19 December 1970, Sunderland; England youth debut 1985, intermediate debut 1987, snr debut 1989; GB youth debut 1985, snr debut 1989; World Student Games 1500m freestyle gold medal 1991; European Champs. 1500m freestyle silver medals 1991, 93; Olympic squad 1992 (1500m freestyle). *Leisure interests*: TV, music. *Address*: c/o ASA, Harold Fern House, Derby Square, Loughborough, Leics. LE11 0AL.

WILSON, Jocky: darts player; b. 22 March 1950, Kirkcaldy; GB prof. champ. 1981, 83, 86, 88; world prof. champ. 1982, 89, pairs champ. 1988; winner Brit. Matchplay 1980, 81, Brit. Open 1982. *Address*: c/o World Prof. Darts Players Assoc., 5 Hayfield Close, Wingerworth, Chesterfield, Derbys. S42 6QF.

WILSON, Kevin: footballer; b. 18 April 1961, Banbury; player Derby County 1979–85, Ipswich Town 85–87, Chelsea 87–92, Notts County 92– ; with Chelsea: 2nd Div. champs. 1988/89; over 32 NI caps. *Address*: Notts County FC, Meadow Lane Ground, Nottingham NG2 3HJ.

WILSON, Malcolm: rally driver; b. 17 February 1956, Cockermouth, Cumbria; m. Elaine Wilson 1982; 1 s.; debut 1974, rep. Ford 1980–85, Austin Rover 86–87, Vauxhall 88–89, Ford 90– ; GB champ. 1978, 79; winner Mobil Rally Challenge 1990. *Leisure interests*: skiing, cycling. *Address*: Threlkeld Leys, Brandlingill, Cockermouth, Cumbria CA13 0RD.

WILSON, Stuart: Rugby Union footballer; b. 27 March 1964, London; player Cheshunt, Saracens 1991– ; rep. Middx U-19 and U-21, Herts. *Address*: Saracens FC, Bramley Rd Sports Ground, Chaseside, Southgate, London N14 4AB.

WILSON, Tommy: footballer; b. 2 August 1961, Paisley; player Queen's Park 1979–82, St Mirren 82–89, Dunfermline Athletic 89–92, Kilmarnock 92– ; with St Mirren: winners Scottish Cup 1987; Scotland U-21 int. *Address*: Kilmarnock FC, Rugby Park, Kilmarnock KA1 2DP.

WILSON, Warren: Rugby League footballer; b. 30 May 1963, Leeds; player Hunslet, Leeds, Halifax 1990– . *Address*: Halifax RLFC, The Pavilion, Thrum Hall, Gibbet St, Halifax, W. Yorks HX1 4TL.

WINDO, Tony: Rugby Union footballer; b. 30 April 1969; player Longlevens, Gloucester; England U-21 int. *Address*: Gloucester RUFC, Kingsholm, Worcester St, Gloucester GL3 3AX.

WINSTANLEY, Mark: footballer; b. 22 January 1968, St Helens; player Bolton Wanderers 1986– . *Address*: Bolton Wanderers FC, Burnden Park, Manchester Rd, Bolton, Lancs. BL3 2QR.

WINTER, Craig David: boxer; b. 10 September 1971, Aylesbury; Welsh ABA light-middleweight champ. 1993; Wales debut 1990. *Leisure interests*: fishing. *Address*: Tan-y-Graig, Llandyrnog, Denbigh, Clwyd LL16 4NA.

WINTER, Russell James: surfer; b. 9 December 1975, Hammersmith; English cadet champ. 1989, 91, jnr champ. 1989, 91, 92, open champ. 1991; GB cadet champ. 1987–89, 91, jnr champ. 1990, 91, 93, open champ. 1993; European champ. 1989, 92; World Champs. squad 1990, 92. *Leisure interests*: squash, pool, cycling. *Address*: Bilbo Surf Shop, 6 Station Parade, Cliff Rd, Newquay, Cornwall.

WINTERBURN, Nigel: footballer; b. 11 December 1963, Nuneaton; player Wimbledon 1983–87, Arsenal 87– ; with Arsenal: League champs. 1988/89, 90/91, winners League Cup, FA Cup 1993; 1 England U-21 cap, over 2 full England caps. *Address*: Arsenal FC, Arsenal Stadium, Highbury, London N5 1BU.

WISE, Dennis: footballer; b. 16 December 1966, Kensington; player Wimbledon 1985–90, Chelsea 90– (capt.); with Wimbledon: winners FA Cup 1988; 1 England U-21 cap, 3 England B caps, over 5 full England caps. *Address*: Chelsea FC, Stamford Bridge, Fulham Rd, London SW6 1HS.

WISHART, Fraser: footballer; b. 1 March 1965, Johnstone; player Motherwell 1983–89, St Mirren 89–92, Falkirk 92–93, Rangers 93– . *Address*: Glasgow Rangers FC, Ibrox Stadium, 150 Edmiston Drive, Glasgow G51 2XD.

WOAN, Ian: footballer; b. 14 December 1967, Heswall; player Nottingham Forest 1990– . *Address*: Nottingham Forest FC, City Ground, Nottingham NG2 5FJ.

WOOD, Clare: tennis player; b. 8 March 1968; rep. Sussex; GB girls' U-16 grass court champ. 1984, ladies' champ. 1989, 93, doubles champ. 1991, 92; GB debut 1987, Wightman Cup team 1987–89, European Cup team 1988– (winners 1992), Federation Cup team 1989– . *Address*: c/o LTA, The Queen's Club, W. Kensington, London W14 9EG.

WOOD, Jason David: ice hockey player; b. 11 November 1971, Mitcham; player Medway Bears 1986–88, Peterborough Pirates 88–89, Cardiff Devils 89– ; with Cardiff Devils: winners Autumn Cup 1993, League champs., GB champs. 1989/90, 92/93; GB U-16 debut 1986, U-19 debut 1987, U-21 debut 1989, snr debut 1992. *Leisure interests*: playing soccer, jet skiing, roller hockey, working out, travel. *Address*: Wales Nat. Ice Rink, Hayes Bridge Rd, Cardiff CF1 2GH.

WOOD, John: cricketer; b. 22 July 1970, Wakefield; player Durham 1992– . *Address*: Durham CCC, County Ground, Riverside, Chester-le-Street, Co. Durham DH3 3QR.

WOOD, Julian Ross: cricketer; b. 21 November 1968, Winchester; player Hants. 1989–93, tour Barbados 1990; MCC YC tour Hong Kong 1988. *Address*: Hants. CCC, County Cricket Ground, Northlands Rd, Southampton SO9 2TY.

WOOD, Robin: canoe sailor; b. 9 December 1954; m. Linda Jayne Wood 1984; 1 s., 1 d.; GB canoe sailing champ. 1993; World Champs. canoe sailing gold medals 1987, 93. *Address*: c/o Brit. Canoe Union, John Dudderidge House, Adbolton Lane, W. Bridgford, Nottingham NG2 5AS.

WOOD, Stephen: footballer; b. 2 February 1963, Bracknell; player Reading 1981–87, Millwall 87–91, Southampton 91– ; with Reading: 3rd Div. champs. 1985/86; with Millwall: 2nd Div. champs. 1987/88. *Address*: Southampton FC, The Dell, Milton Rd, Southampton SO9 4XX.

WOOD, William Walker, MBE: flat green bowler; b. 26 April 1938, Haddington, Lothian; m. Morag Christie Wood 1967; 1 s., 1 d.; Scottish int. debut 1966; SA Games singles gold medal 1973; Commonwealth Games singles bronze medal 1974, gold 1982, pairs silver 1978, fours gold 1990; World Champs. fours silver medal 1980, singles silver and team gold 1984, singles and triples silver 1988, triples bronze, fours and team gold 1992; winner Mazda Jack High singles 1983, Hong Kong Classic pairs 1985, 86; Scotland's most-capped player (outdoor); only bowler in the world to have won a medal on 5 continents. *Leisure interests*: watching Heart of Midlothian FC. *Address*: Gifford Bowling Club, Gifford, E. Lothian.

WOODHALL, Richie: boxer; b. 19 April 1968; England debut 1987, Commonwealth Games light-middleweight gold medal 1990; Olympic light-middleweight bronze medal 1988; prof. debut 1990; titles won: Commonwealth middleweight 1992; over 13 prof. wins. *Address*: Nat. Promotions, Nat. House, 60–66 Wardour St, London W1V 3HP.

WOODLAND, Edward Huw: Rugby Union footballer; b. 23 June 1966, Tonyrefail, Mid Glamorgan; player Tonyrefail 1985–86, Pontypridd 86–88,

Maesteg 88–91, Neath 92– ; rep.
Glamorgan; Wales tour Zimbabwe/
Namibia 1993. *Leisure interests*: keeping fit,
relaxing at home. *Address*: Neath RFC,
The Gnoll, Gnoll Park Rd, Neath,
W. Glamorgan.

WOODS, Christopher: footballer; b. 14
November 1959, Boston; player Queens
Park Rangers 1979–81, Norwich City 81–86,
Rangers 86–91, Sheffield Wednesday
91– ; with Norwich City: winners League
Cup 1985, 2nd Div. champs. 1985/86; with
Rangers: winners Scottish League Cup
1987, 89, 91; 6 England U-21 caps, over 40
full England caps. *Address*: Sheffield
Wednesday FC, Hillsborough, Sheffield, S.
Yorks. S6 1SW.

WOODS, Ian: biathlete; b. 7 June 1966,
Liverpool; m. Nicky Woods 1993; GB
sprint champ. 1991, Nordic/biathlon com-
bination champ. 1993; GB debut 1988,
World Champs. squad 1989–91, 93,
Olympic squad 1992. *Leisure interests*: Bible
study. *Address*: Millyard Flat, Stock
Terrace, N. Rd, Ambleside, Cumbria
LA22 9DT.

WOODS, Neil: footballer; b. 30 July 1966,
Bradford; player Doncaster Rovers
1982–86, Rangers 86–87, Ipswich Town
87–90, Bradford City 1990, Grimsby Town
1990– . *Address*: Grimsby Town FC,
Blundell Park, Cleethorpes, S. Humberside
DN35 7PY.

WOOSNAM, Ian Harold, MBE: golfer; b. 2
March 1958, Oswestry; m. Glendryth
Mervyn Pugh 1983; 1 s., 2 d.; prof. debut
1976; world U-23 matchplay champ. 1979,
snr matchplay champ. 1987 (1st Brit.
winner), 1990; Wales debut 1980, Dunhill
Cup team 1985, 86, 88–91, 93, winners
World Cup 1987; Ryder Cup team 1983– ,
winners 1985, 87; winner Swiss Open 1982,
Brit. Masters 1983, Scandinavian Open

1984, Zambian Open 1985, Kenya Open
1986, Hong Kong Open, Jersey Open,
Madrid Open 1987, Scottish Open 1987, 90,
Irish Open 1988, 89, European Open 1988,
Mediterranean Open 1990, 91, Monte Carlo
Open 1990, 91, 92, US Masters 1991,
English Open 1993; 1st player in 36 years
to win title 3 years in a row (Monte Carlo
Open). *Publications*: Ian Woosnam's Golf
Masterpieces, 1988, *Powergolf*, 1989, 91.
Leisure interests: snooker, water skiing,
shooting. *Address*: Int. Management Group,
Pier House, Strand on the Green, London
W4 3NN.

WORRALL, Mick: Rugby League foot-
baller; b. 22 March 1962; player Oldham,
Salford, Leeds 1992– ; GB debut v. France
1984, Brit. Lions tour Aus./NZ/Papua
New Guinea 1984. *Address*: Leeds RLFC,
Bass Headingley, St Michael's Lane, Leeds
LS6 3BR.

WORTHINGTON, Nigel: footballer; b. 4
November 1961, Ballymena, NI; player
Ballymena Utd (NI), Notts County
1981–84, Sheffield Wednesday 84– ; with
Sheffield Wednesday: winners League Cup
1991; over 44 NI caps. *Address*: Sheffield
Wednesday FC, Hillsborough, Sheffield, S.
Yorks. S6 1SW.

WRAGG, Geoffrey: racehorse trainer; b. 9
January 1930; m. Patricia Wragg 1956; 1st
licence 1983; winner Derby 1983 (Teenoso),
King George VI and Queen Elizabeth
Diamond Stakes 1984 (Teenoso). *Address*:
c/o BHB, 42 Portman Square, London
W1H 0EN.

WRAY, Jonathan: Rugby League footballer; b. 14 May 1970, Leeds; player
Morley (RU), Castleford 1990– ; England
colt. *Address*: Castleford RLFC, Wheldon
Rd, Castleford WF10 2SD.

WREN, Elizabeth Marshall: flat green
bowler; b. 4 September 1953, Falkirk; m.

John Gordon Wren 1973; 1 s., 1 d.; rep. Stirling (outdoor); Scottish women's singles champ. (outdoor) 1989, (indoor) 1988, 90; GB women's singles champ. (outdoor) 1990; Scotland debut (outdoor) 1985, (indoor) 1989; 1st woman to hold both Scottish indoor and outdoor titles at same time. *Leisure interests*: swimming, walking the dogs, antique fairs. *Address*: 15 Laxdale Drive, Head of Muir, Denny, Stirlingshire FK6 5PL.

WRIGHT, Alan: footballer; b. 28 September 1971, Ashton-under-Lyne; player Blackpool 1987–91, Blackburn Rovers 91– . *Address*: Blackburn Rovers FC, Ewood Park, Blackburn, Lancs. BB2 4JF.

WRIGHT, Andrew: cyclist (mountain bike); b. 23 June 1974, Aberdeen; Scottish jnr champ. 1990, 91, N. of England jnr champ. 1991, 92, GB jnr cross-country champ. 1992; N. of Scotland champ. 1992; GB debut 1991, World Champs. squad 1991, 92. *Leisure interests*: pool, reading. *Address*: 11 Culloden Rd, Balloch, Inverness IV1 2HQ.

WRIGHT, Anthony John: cricketer; b. 27 July 1962, Stevenage; m. Rachel Wright 1986; 1 d.; player Glos. 1982– (capt. 90–93). *Address*: Glos. CCC, Phoenix County Ground, Nevil Rd, Bristol BS6 9EJ.

WRIGHT, Darren: Rugby League footballer; b. 17 January 1968, Leigh; player Leigh Miners ARLFC, Widnes 1985– ; with Widnes: winners Premiership 1988–90, Regal Trophy 1992; rep. Lancs.; GB debut v. Aus. 1988. *Address*: Widnes RLFC, Naughton Park, Lowerhouse Lane, Widnes WA8 7DZ.

WRIGHT, George: footballer; b. 22 December 1969, SA; player Heart of Midlothian 1987– . *Address*: Heart of Midlothian FC, Tynecastle Park, Gorgie Rd, Edinburgh EH11 2NL.

WRIGHT, Ian: footballer; b. 3 November 1963, Woolwich; player Crystal Palace 1985–91, Arsenal 91– ; with Arsenal: winners League Cup, FA Cup 1993; over 13 full England caps. *Address*: Arsenal FC, Arsenal Stadium, Highbury, London N5 1BU.

WRIGHT, Keith: footballer; b. 17 May 1965, Edinburgh; player Raith Rovers 1983–86, Dundee 86–91, Hibernian 91– ; with Hibernian: winners Scottish League Cup 1992; 1 Scotland cap. *Address*: Hibernian FC, Easter Rd Stadium, 64 Albion Rd, Edinburgh EH7 5QG.

WRIGHT, Mark: footballer; b. 1 August 1963, Dorchester; player Oxford Utd 1980–82, Southampton 82–87, Derby County 87–91, Liverpool 91– ; with Liverpool: winners FA Cup 1992; 4 England U-21 caps, 42 full England caps. *Address*: Liverpool FC, Anfield Rd, Liverpool L4 0TH.

WRIGHT, Nigel: Rugby League footballer; b. 8 November 1973, Wakefield; player Wakefield Trinity 1990–93, Wigan 93– ; rep. Yorks., England Schools U-16. *Address*: Wigan RLFC, The Pavilion, Central Park, Wigan WN1 1XF.

WRIGHT, Paul: footballer; b. 17 August 1967, E. Kilbride; player Aberdeen 1983–89, Queens Park Rangers 1989, Hibernian 1989–91, St Johnstone 91– ; 3 Scotland U-21 caps. *Address*: St Johnstone FC, McDiarmid Park, Crieff Rd, Perth PH1 2SJ.

WRIGHT, Peter Hugh: Rugby Union footballer; b. 30 December 1967, Bonnyrigg; m. Audrey Wright; player Lasswade, Boroughmuir; Scotland debut v. Aus. 1992, Five Nations debut v. France 1993, tours Japan 1989, Aus. 1992; Brit. Lions tour NZ 1993. *Address*: Boroughmuir RFC, Meggetland, Colinton Rd, Edinburgh EH14 1AS.

WRIGHT, Samantha: hockey player; b. 1 September 1966; player Slough; England U-18 debut 1984, snr debut 1990; England indoor debut 1986, European Indoor Cup silver medallist 1993; GB debut 1990. *Address*: Slough HC, Slough Sports Club, Chalvey Rd, Slough, Berks.

WRIGHT, Stephen: footballer; b. 27 August 1971, Bellshill; player Aberdeen 1987– ; Scotland U-21 and snr int. *Address*: Aberdeen FC, Pittodrie Stadium, Pittodrie St, Aberdeen AB2 1QH.

WRIGHT, Stephen Andrew: oarsman; b. 20 December 1967, Bromley; rep. Dover RC 1985–86, Nottingham and Union RC 86–87, Canterbury Pilgrims BC 86– , Nottinghamshire County Rowing Assoc. 87– ; GB lightweight coxless fours champ. 1988, open coxless fours champ. 1989, lightweight and open coxless fours champ. 1990, open eights champ. 1992; England jnr debut 1985, snr debut 1990; GB debut and World Champs. lightweight eights bronze medal 1990, silver 1992. *Leisure interests*: cycling, bass guitar, electronic percussion, reading. *Address*: Nottinghamshire County Rowing Assoc., Nat. Watersports Centre, Holme Pierrepoint, Adbolton Lane, Nottingham.

WRIGHT, Thomas: footballer; b. 29 August 1963, Belfast, NI; player Newcastle Utd 1988–93, Nottingham Forest 93– ; 1 NI U-21 cap, over 15 full NI caps. *Address*: Nottingham Forest FC, City Ground, Nottingham NG2 5FJ.

WRIGHT, Thomas: footballer; b. 10 January 1966, Dunfermline; player Leeds Utd 1983–86, Oldham Athletic 86–89, Leicester City 89–92, Middlesbrough 92– ; 1 Scotland U-21 cap. *Address*: Middlesbrough FC, Ayresome Park, Middlesbrough, Cleveland TS1 4PB.

WRIGLEY, Jonathon: Rugby Union footballer; b. 10 December 1966, Hartlepool; player Hartlepool Rovers, W. Hartlepool 1990– ; rep. Durham and England colts. *Address*: W. Hartlepool RFC, Brierton Lane, Hartlepool, Cleveland TS25 5DR.

WRING, Dean Stuart: Rugby Union footballer; b. 1 March 1970, Bristol; player Bristol 1988– . *Leisure interests*: golf, driving, eating out, drinking. *Address*: Bristol FC, Memorial Ground, Filton Ave, Horfield, Bristol BS7 0AQ.

WROE, Michael John: Alpine skier; b. 9 January 1972, Bangor; GB schoolboy champ. 1988, dry-slope champ. 1991; Wales debut 1987; GB debut 1992. *Leisure interests*: all mountain sports, golf, tennis, football, music, the arts, writing children's stories. *Address*: Bryn Siriol, Waunfawr, Gwynedd LL54 7AX.

WYETH, Alison: athlete; b. 26 May 1964, Southampton; AAA women's 3000m champ. 1989, 1500m champ. 1993; UK women's 1500m champ. 1990, 91; Commonwealth Games squad 1990; European Cup women's 3000m bronze medal 1993; World Champs. squad (3000m) 1991, 93; Olympic squad (3000m) 1992. *Leisure interests*: sewing, gardening, reading. *Address*: 2 Algar Close, Isleworth, Middx TW7 7AQ.

WYLLIE, Douglas Stewart: Rugby Union footballer; b. 20 May 1963, Edinburgh; m. Jennifer Wyllie; player Stewart's Melville FP, winners Middx Sevens 1982; Scotland debut v. Aus. 1984, Five Nations debut v. Wales 1985, tours NZ 1990, N. America 1991 (capt.), Fiji/Tonga/W. Samoa 1993. *Address*: Stewart's Melville FP, Inverleith, Ferry Rd, Edinburgh.

YALLOP, Frank: footballer; b. 4 April 1964, Watford; player Ipswich Town 1982– ; Canada int. *Address*: Ipswich Town FC, Portman Rd, Ipswich, Suffolk IP1 2DA.

YATES, Dean: footballer; b. 26 October 1967, Leicester; player Notts County 1985– . *Address*: Notts County FC, Meadow Lane Ground, Nottingham NG2 3HJ.

YATES, Gary: cricketer; b. 20 September 1967, Ashton-under-Lyne; player Lancs. 1990– , tours Tasmania/W. Aus. 1990, W. Aus. 1991, Johannesburg (SA) 1992, Barbados/St Lucia 1992. *Address*: Lancs. CCC, Old Trafford, Manchester M16 0PX.

YATES, Matthew: athlete; b. 4 February 1969, Rochford, Essex; AAA 1500m champ. 1991, 93; Commonwealth Games 800m bronze medal 1990; European Indoor Champs. 1500m gold medal 1992; winner NY 5th Avenue road mile 1991, Madrid road mile 1992; UK 1000m indoor record-holder. *Leisure interests*: cinema, art, modern music, current affairs, cycling, W. Ham FC. *Address*: c/o Brit. Athletics Fed., 225A Bristol Rd, Edgbaston, Birmingham B5 7UB.

YORKE, Dwight: footballer; b. 3 November 1971, Tobago; player Signal Hill (Tobago), Aston Villa 1989– ; Trinidad int. *Address*: Aston Villa FC, Villa Park, Trinity Rd, Birmingham B6 6HE.

YOUNG, David: Rugby League footballer; b. 26 July 1968, Aberdare; player Cardiff (RU), Leeds, Salford 1991– ; Wales int. and Brit. Lion (RU); Wales RL debut v. Papua New Guinea 1991. *Address*: Salford RLFC, The Willows, Willows Rd, Weaste, Salford M5 2ST.

YOUNG, Eric: footballer; b. 25 March 1960, Singapore; player Brighton and Hove Albion 1982–87, Wimbledon 87–90, Crystal Palace 90– ; with Wimbledon: winners FA Cup 1988; over 16 Wales caps. *Address*: Crystal Palace FC, Selhurst Park Stadium, London SE25 6PU.

YOUNGER, Adam Campbell: powerboat racer; b. 11 September 1963, Bournemouth; m. Sue Younger 1990 (d 1992); European offshore circuit racing class III 2-litre champ. 1993; winner Round the Island race 1980. *Leisure interests*: motor sport, tennis, badminton, motorcycling. *Address*: Golden Hill Farm, 80 Ashley Lane, Hordle, Lymington, Hants. SO41 0GA.

YOUNGS, Lucy Jane: hockey player; b. 8 February 1971, Norwich; player Harleston Magpies, Ipswich Ladies; with Ipswich: League champs. 1993; England U-18 debut and U-18 home countries champs. 1988, European Cup U-18 silver medallist 1988, U-21 debut 1991, U-21 home countries champs. 1991, 92 (vice-capt. 1992), snr debut 1992, home countries champs. and tours Barcelona (Spain) and The Netherlands 1992; Norfolk U-14 tennis champ. 1983, U-16 champ. 1984. *Leisure interests*: all sport, cooking, dancing, children. *Address*: Ipswich Ladies HC, Tuddenham Rd, Ipswich, Suffolk IP4 3QJ.

ZAHIR, Amin: fencer (sabre); b. 17 September 1970, Chelmsford; GB U-20 champ. 1990, snr champ. 1993; England debut and Commonwealth Champs. team bronze medal 1990; GB U-20 and snr debuts 1990, Olympic squad 1992; winner Cole Cup, Bristol Open 1992. *Leisure interests*: politics, parachuting, skiing, water skiing, chess, travel. *Address*: 72 Onslow Gardens, London N10 3JX.

ZAVIEH, Kirkham: fencer (sabre); b. 1 April 1968, Trinidad, WI; GB schoolboy champ. 1984; GB debut 1989, World Student Games squad 1989, 91, World Champs. squad 1991, 93, Olympic squad 1992; winner Welsh Open 1993. *Leisure interests*: music, scuba diving. *Address*: Flat 6, 8 Mercer St, London WC2.

RETIREES AND REFUGEES

(The following announced their retirement, or, in the case of managers, relinquished or lost their jobs, in 1993/94)

AKABUSI, Kriss Kezie Uche Chukwu Duru, MBE: athlete; b. 28 November 1958, Paddington; m. Monika Akabusi 1982; 2 d.; GB debut v. USSR 1983; Commonwealth Games 4 x 400m relay gold medal 1986, 400m hurdles gold 1990; European Champs. 4 x 400m relay gold medal 1986, 400m hurdles gold and 4 x 400m relay gold 1990; European Cup 4 x 400m relay gold medals 1983, 93, bronze 1985, 400m hurdles gold 1989, 91; World Champs. 4 x 400m relay bronze medal 1983, 4 x 400m relay silver 1987, 400m hurdles bronze and 4 x 400m relay gold 1991; World Cup 400m hurdles bronze medal 1989; Olympic 4 x 400m relay silver medal 1984, 4 x 400m relay and 400m hurdles bronze 1992; England team capt. 1985; UK 400m hurdles record-holder; Sports Writers' Sportsman of the Year 1991. *Leisure interests*: reading. *Address*: c/o Brit. Athletic Fed., 225A Bristol Rd, Edgbaston, Birmingham B5 7UB.

BINGHAM, William Laurie, MBE: football manager; b. 5 August 1931, Belfast, NI; m. Eunice Bingham 1955, Rebecca Bingham 1987; 1 s., 1 d.; player Glentoran (NI), Sunderland 1950–58, Luton Town 58–60, Everton 60–63, Port Vale 63–64; with Everton: League champs. 1962/63; 56 NI caps; manager Southport 1963–65, Plymouth Argyle 65–67, NI 67–71, Greece 71–73, Everton 73–77, PAOK Salonika (Greece) 78–79, NI 80–93, Al Nasir (Saudia Arabia) 86–87. *Publications: Soccer with the Stars*, 1961, *Billy*, 1987. *Leisure interests*: book-collecting, royal commemorative ware. *Address*: c/o Irish FA, 20 Windsor Ave, Belfast BT9 6EE.

BOTHAM, Ian Terence, OBE: cricketer; b. 24 November 1955, Heswall; m. Kathryn Waller 1976; 1 s., 2 d.; player Somerset 1974–86 (capt. 1984–85), Worcs. 87–91, Durham 92–93 (retired); 102 Tests, debut 1977, 116 1-day ints, tours Pakistan/NZ 1977/78, Aus. 1978/79, Aus./India 1979/80, WI 1980/81, India 1981/82, Aus./NZ 1982/83, WI 1985/86, Aus. 1986/87, NZ 1991/92, Aus. (World Cup) 1992; England capt. 1980/81; 1st player to score 100 runs and take 8 wickets, Test v. Pakistan 1978; took 100th Test wicket 1979; achieved Test double of 1000 runs and 100 wickets 1979; 1st player to score 3000 runs and take 250 wickets in Tests 1982; BBC Sports Personality of the Year 1981. *Publications: It Sort of Clicks*, 1986, *Cricket My Way*, 1989. *Address*: c/o Durham CCC, County Ground, Riverside, Chester-le-Street, Co. Durham DH3 3QR.

CAUTHEN, Steve: jockey (Flat); b. 1 May 1960; m. Amy Cauthen; winner 2000 Guineas 1979 (Tap on Wood), Derby 1985 (Slip Anchor), 1987 (Reference Point), Oaks 1985 (Oh So Sharp), 1988 (Diminuendo), 1989 (Snow Bride), 1000 Guineas, St Leger 1985 (Oh So Sharp), King George VI and Queen Elizabeth Diamond Stakes 1987 (Reference Point), Irish Derby 1989 (Old Vic), Irish 1000 Guineas 1990 (In the Groove); champ. jockey 1984, 85, 87; rode 197 winners in season 1987; winner of 4 Classics 1985. *Address*: c/o BHB, 42 Portman Square, London W1H 0EN.

COPPELL, Steve: football manager; b. 9 July 1955, Liverpool; player Tranmere Rovers 1973–75, Manchester Utd 75–83; 1 England U-23 cap, 42 full England caps; with Manchester Utd: winners FA Cup 1977; manager Crystal Palace 1984–93 (resigned). *Address*: c/o The FA, 16 Lancaster Gate, London W2 3LW.

DOOLEY, Wade Anthony: Rugby Union footballer; b. 2 October 1957, Warrington; m. Sharon Diane Dooley 1982; 2 d.; player Preston Grasshoppers; rep. Lancs. and N. Div.; England debut v. Romania 1985, Five Nations debut v. France 1985, Grand Slam champs. 1991, 92, tours NZ 1985, Aus./NZ (World Cup) 1987, Aus. 1988, Romania 1989, Argentina 1990, Aus./Fiji 1991; Brit. Lions tours Aus. 1989, NZ 1993; most-capped England lock (55 caps). *Publications: The Tower and the Glory:* The Wade Dooley Story, 1992. *Leisure interests:* relaxing with family, eating out, fell-walking, gardening, listening to music. *Address:* Preston Grasshoppers RFC, Lightfoot Green, Fulwood, Preston, Lancs. PR4 0AP.

FOSTER, Neil Alan: cricketer; b. 6 May 1962, Colchester; m. Romany Foster 1985; player Essex 1980–93 (retired), county champs. 1991, 92, Sunday League champs. 1984, 85; England YC tour WI 1980, 28 Tests, debut 1983, 48 1-day ints, tours NZ/Pakistan 1983/84, India/Aus. 1984/85, WI 1985/86, Aus. 1986/87, Pakistan/Aus./NZ 1987/88; Britannic Assurance/*Sunday Express* Cricketer of the Year 1991. *Address:* c/o Essex CCC, County Cricket Ground, New Writtle St, Chelmsford DM2 0PG.

GOULD, Robert: football manager; b. 12 June 1946, Coventry; player Coventry City 1964–68, Arsenal 68–70, Wolverhampton Wanderers 70–71, W. Bromwich Albion 71–72, Bristol City 72–73, W. Ham Utd 73–75, Wolverhampton Wanderers 75–77, Bristol Rovers 77–78, Hereford Utd 78–79; assistant manager Chelsea 1979–81, manager Coventry City 1983–84, Bristol Rovers 85–87, Wimbledon 87–90, W. Bromwich Albion 90–92, Coventry City 1992–93 (resigned); as player: winner 2nd Div. champs. 1967 (Coventry), 1977 (Wolverhampton Wanderers), FA Cup 1975 (W. Ham); as manager: winner FA Cup 1988 (Wimbledon). *Address:* c/o The FA, 16 Lancaster Gate, London W2 3LW.

GOWER, David Ivon, OBE: cricketer; b. 1 April 1957, Tunbridge Wells; m. Thorunn Gower 1992; player Leics. 1975–89 (capt. 84–86, 88–89), Hants. 1990–93 (retired); with Leics.: winners Benson and Hedges Cup 1985; 117 Tests, debut 1978, 114 1-day ints, tours Aus. 1978/79, Aus./India 1979/80, WI 1980/81, India/Sri Lanka 1981/82, Aus./NZ 1982/83, NZ/Pakistan 1983/84, India/Aus. 1984/85, WI 1985/86, Aus. 1986/87, Aus. 1990/91; England capt. 1984–86, 89. *Publications: Anyone for Cricket,* 1979, *With Time to Spare,* 1980, *Heroes and Contemporaries,* 1983, *A Right Ambition,* 1986, *Gower:* The Autobiography, 1992. *Address:* c/o Hants. CCC, County Cricket Ground, Northlands Rd, Southampton SO9 2TY.

KENDALL, Howard: football manager; b. 22 May 1946, Ryton-on-Tyne, Co. Durham; player Preston N. End 1962–66, Everton 66–73, Birmingham City 73–77, Stoke City 77–79, Blackburn Rovers 79–81, Everton 1981; manager Blackburn Rovers 1979–81, Everton 81–87, Bilbao 87–89, Manchester City 89–90, Everton 90–93 (resigned); with Everton: winners FA Cup 1984, European Cup Winners' Cup 1985, League champs. 1984/85, 86/87. *Address:* c/o The FA, 16 Lancaster Gate, London W2 3LW.

MOORHOUSE, Adrian David, MBE: swimmer (breaststroke); b. 24 May 1964, Bradford; GB 100m champ. 1981–83, 85–87, 89–91, 200m champ. 1981–83, 85, 86; Commonwealth Games 100m gold, 4 x 100m medley relay silver and 200m bronze medals 1982, 200m gold, 100m and 4 x 100m medley relay silver 1986, 100m gold and 4 x 100m medley relay silver 1990; European Champs. 200m bronze medal 1981, 200m gold and 100m silver 1983, 100m gold 1985, 100m gold, 4 x 100m medley relay silver and 200m bronze 1987, 100m gold 1989, 100m silver 1991; World Champs. 100m silver medal 1991; Olympic 100m gold medal 1988, squad 1984, 92. *Leisure interests:* backgammon, music, literature, skiing, motor bikes, eating chocolate sundaes. *Address*: c/o ASA, Harold Fern House, Derby Square, Loughborough, Leics. LE11 0AL.

MURPHY, Sean: boxer; b. 1 December 1964; ABA bantamweight champ. 1985, 86; England debut 1984; Commonwealth Games bantamweight gold medal 1986; GB debut 1984; prof. debut 1986; titles won: GB featherweight 1990; over 20 prof. wins. *Address*: c/o Frank Warren Productions, Centurion House, Bircherley Green, Hertford, Herts. SG14 1HP.

OLVER, Christopher John: Rugby Union footballer; b. 23 April 1962, Manchester; m. Susan Olver; 1 d.; player Sandbach, Harlequins, Northampton; with Harlequins: winners John Player Cup 1988; rep. Midland Div.; England debut v. Argentina 1990, tours Argentina 1990, Aus./Fiji 1991, Canada (England A) 1993 (capt.). *Address*: Northampton FC, Franklins Gardens, Weedon Rd, Northampton NN5 5BG.

PRINGLE, Derek Raymond: cricketer; b. 18 September 1958, Nairobi, Kenya; player Cambridge Univ. 1979–82 (Blue 79, 80, 81, 82), Essex 1978–93 (retired); with Essex: county champs. 1979, 83, 84, 86, 91, 92, Sunday League champs. 1984, 85; England Schools tour India 1978/79, England B tour Sri Lanka 1985/86, England A tour Zimbabwe/Kenya 1990/91, 30 Tests, debut 1982, 42 1-day ints, snr tours Aus./NZ 1982/83, NZ/Aus. (World Cup) 1991/92. *Address*: c/o Essex CCC, County Cricket Ground, New Writtle St, Chelmsford DM2 0PG.

RANDALL, Derek William: cricketer; b. 24 February 1951, Retford; m. Elizabeth Randall 1973; 1 s.; player Notts. 1972–93 (retired), county champs. 1981, 87, Sunday League champs. 1991; 47 Tests, debut 1976, 49 1-day ints, tours India/Sri Lanka/Aus. 1976/77, Pakistan/NZ 1977/78, Aus.

1978/79, Aus./India 1979/80, Aus./NZ 1982/83, NZ/Pakistan 1983/84, Sri Lanka (England B) 1985/86. *Address*: c/o Notts. CCC, Trent Bridge, Nottingham NG2 6AG.

SNELL, Julia: freestyle skier; b. 6 October 1963, Farnborough; 6 times GB ladies' ballet ski champ.; GB jnr debut 1980, snr debut 1982; European Champs. bronze medal 1990; World Cup bronze medals 1989, 92, 93, silver 1990, 91, 93, gold 1992; Olympic squad 1992; 1st Brit. woman to win World Cup skiing medal in specialist discipline. *Leisure interests*: windsurfing, tennis, in-line skating, mountain biking, photography, dressmaking. *Address*: c/o 149 Kerkdijk, 3615 Bd Westbroek, The Netherlands.

SOUNESS, Graeme James: football manager; b. 6 May 1953, Edinburgh; player Middlesbrough 1973–78, Liverpool 78–84, Sampdoria (Italy) 84–86, Rangers (player/manager) 86–91; manager Liverpool 1991–94 (resigned); as player: winner European Cup 1978, 81, 84, League Cup 1981–84, League champs. 1978/79, 79/80, 81/82, 82/83, 83/84 (Liverpool), Scottish League champs. 1986/87, 88/89, 89/90 (Rangers), 2 Scotland U-23 caps, snr debut 1975, 54 full Scotland caps; as manager: winner FA Cup 1992 (Liverpool). *Address*: c/o The FA, 16 Lancaster Gate, London W2 3LW.

STERLAND, Melvyn: footballer; b. 1 October 1961, Sheffield; player Sheffield Wednesday 1979–88, Rangers 88–89, Leeds Utd 89–94 (retired); with Leeds Utd: 2nd Div. champs. 1989/90, League champs. 1991/92; 7 England U-21 caps, 1 full England cap. *Address*: c/o Leeds Utd FC, Elland Rd, Leeds, W. Yorks. LS11 0ES.

TAVARE, Christopher James: cricketer; b. 27 October 1954, Orpington, Kent; m. Vanessa Tavaré 1980; 1 s.; player Oxford Univ. (Blue 1975–77), Kent 1974–88 (capt. 83–84), Somerset 89–93 (retired) (capt.

90–93); England debut 1980, 31 Tests, 29 1-day ints., tours India/Sri Lanka 1981/82, Aus./NZ 1982/83, Fiji/NZ/Pakistan 1983/84. *Leisure interests*: golf, music, gardening, natural history. *Address*: c/o Somerset CCC, The County Ground, Taunton, Somerset TA1 1JT.

TAYLOR, Graham: football manager; b. 15 September 1944, Worksop; m. Rita Julia Taylor 1965; 2 d.; player Grimsby Town 1962–68, Lincoln City 68–72; manager Lincoln City 1972–77, Watford 77–87, Aston Villa 87–90, England 90–93 (resigned); with Lincoln City: 4th Div. champs. 1975/76; with Watford: 4th Div. champs. 1977/78. *Publications*: *The Football Handbook* (consultant), 1979/80, *Football Today* (contributor), 1988–90, *When England Called*, 1991. *Leisure interests*: theatre, reading, 50s and 60s popular music. *Address*: c/o The FA, 16 Lancaster Gate, London W2 3LW.

WEBB, Jonathan Mark: Rugby Union footballer; b. 24 August 1963, London; m. Amanda Webb; 2 d.; player Bristol Univ., Northern, Bristol, Bath 1990–93 (retired); with Bath: winners Pilkington Cup 1992, League champs. 1990/91, 91/92, 92/93; England B debut 1987, snr debut v. Aus. 1987, Five Nations debut v. France 1988, 32 caps, tours Aus. 1988, Aus./Fiji 1991. *Address*: c/o Bath RFC, Recreation Ground, Bath BA2 6PW.

WILSON, Terence: footballer; b. 8 February 1969, Broxburn; player Nottingham Forest 1985–94 (retired), winners League Cup 1989; 3 Scotland U-21 caps. *Address*: c/o Nottingham Forest FC, City Ground, Nottingham NG2 5FJ.

WINTERBOTTOM, Peter James, MBE: Rugby Union footballer; b. 31 May 1960, Leeds; player Fleetwood, Headingley, Exeter, Harlequins; with Harlequins: winners Pilkington Cup 1991; England debut v. Aus. 1982, Five Nations debut v. Scotland 1982, Grand Slam champs. 1991, 92, 58 caps, tours SA 1984, Aus. (World Cup) 1987, Argentina 1990, Aus./Fiji 1991; Brit. Lions tours NZ 1983, 93. *Address*: c/o Harlequins FC, Stoop Memorial Ground, Craneford Way, Twickenham, Middx.

WHO SPONSORED WHOM

(Selected Sponsors of British Sport at National Level)

AUTO TRADER
★ Motor Racing's British Touring Car Championship

AXA EQUITY AND LAW
★ Cricket's Sunday League

B & Q DIY
★ Scottish League Football

**BENSON & HEDGES
(Gallaher Tobacco Ltd)**
★ Snooker's Masters Tournament
★ Cricket's Benson & Hedges Cup
★ Ice Hockey's Autumn Cup

BNB HEAD-HUNTERS
★ Real Tennis

BRITANNIC ASSURANCE
★ Cricket's Britannic Assurance Championship

BRITISH LAND
★ British Skiing Championships

**BUDWEISER
(Courage Ltd, qv)**
★ League Basketball

**CARLING
(Bass Brewers Ltd)**
★ Football's Premiership

**CHAMPAGNE MUMM
(Seagram UK Ltd)**
★ Yachting's Admiral's Cup

CHURCHILL INSURANCE
★ Bowls' World Indoor Championships

CIS INSURANCE
★ English Rugby League's Charity Shield
★ English Rugby Union's Divisional and County Championships

COCA-COLA
★ Football's Coca-Cola (League) Cup

CORNHILL INSURANCE
★ English Test Cricket

COURAGE
★ English Rugby Union

ALFRED DUNHILL
★ Golf's British Masters

**EMBASSY
(Imperial Tobacco Ltd)**
★ Darts' World Championship

ENDSLEIGH INSURANCE
★ League Football

EVER READY
★ Horseracing's Derby

EVEREST
★ Showjumping
★ Tennis's National Club League

**FAMOUS GROUSE
(Highland Distilleries Co. plc)**
★ Rugby Union's World Cup Sevens

GEC-MARCONI
★ Gliding's National Championships

**HEINEKEN
(Whitbread plc, qv)**
★ Welsh Rugby Union

**HENNESSY
(Grand Metropolitan plc)**
★ Horseracing's Hennessy Gold Cup

HI-TEC
★ Squash's British Open Championships

HOMEPRIDE
(Dalgety plc)
★ Showjumping's British Grand Prix

JOHN SMITH
(Courage Ltd, qv)
★ British International Rugby League

JOHNNIE WALKER
(Guinness plc)
★ Golf's Ryder Cup and World
Championship

KELLOGG
★ Cycling's Tour of Britain

LACOSTE SPORTSWEAR
★ Rackets

LAND ROVER
(Rover Group plc)
★ Men's Open Point-to-Point Championship

McDONALD'S RESTAURANTS
★ Athletics

McEWAN'S
(Scottish and Newcastle Breweries plc)
★ Scottish Rugby Union

MARTELL
(Seagram UK Ltd)
★ Horseracing's Grand National

MIDLAND BANK
★ Indoor Bowls

MURPHY
(Whitbread plc, qv)
★ Golf's English Open

MYCIL
(Crookes Healthcare)
★ Swimming's ASA National Championships

NATIONAL GRID
★ Cricket Umpiring

NATWEST
★ Cricket's NatWest Trophy

NETWORK Q
★ Motor Racing's RAC Rally

NORWICH UNION
★ Hockey's County Championship, Indoor
League

NUTRASWEET
★ The London Marathon

PILKINGTON
★ English Rugby Union's Pilkington Cup

PROVINCIAL INSURANCE
★ English Rugby Union's Provincial
Insurance Cup

ROYAL BANK OF SCOTLAND
★ The Hockey Association Cup
★ League Volleyball
★ Badminton's Inter-County Championship

ROYAL LIVER ASSURANCE
★ Snooker's UK Championship

ROTHMANS
★ Cricket's Village Championship

SANATOGEN
(Fisons plc)
★ English Bowls Association National
Singles Championships

SCOTSMAN PUBLICATIONS
★ Scottish Hockey's Men's Cup Finals

SILK CUT
(Gallaher Tobacco Ltd)
★ English Rugby League's Challenge Cup

SKODA
★ Snooker's New Skoda Grand Prix

SKOL
(Allied Breweries Ltd)
★ Scottish Football's Skol (League) Cup
★ World Darts Council's World
Championship

STONES
(Bass Brewers Ltd)
★ English Rugby League

SWALEC
(South Wales Electricity)
★ Rugby Union's Welsh Cup

TENNENTS
(Bass Brewers Ltd)
★ Scottish Football's Tennents Cup

TEXACO
★ Cricket's Texaco Trophy

TORRIE STOCKBROKERS
★ Scottish League Hockey

TOYOTA
★ Showjumping

TSB
★ Athletics

WEETABIX
★ Golf's Ladies' British Open

WHITBREAD
★ Yachting's Whitbread Round the World
Race
★ Horseracing's Whitbread Gold Cup

WICKES BUILDING SUPPLIES
★ Snooker's British Open

GEORGE WIMPEY
★ Real Tennis's British Open
Championship

INDEX OF ENTRANTS BY SPORT

SMYTH, William
STEELE, Mavis
THOMAS, William
THOMSON, Andrew
WHYTE, Frances
WICKHAM, John
WILSHIRE, Spencer
WOOD, William
WREN, Elizabeth

★ BOXING
AKINWANDE, Henry
AMPOFO, Francis
ARMOUR, John
AYERS, Michael
BENN, Nigel
BROWN, Neville
BROWN, Timothy
BRUNO, Frank
BURKE, Paul
CALZAGHE, Joseph
CLINTON, Patrick
COOK, James
CORE, Maurice
CROOK, Carl
DAVISON, John
DOCHERTY, Drew
DYER, Darren
EUBANK, Christopher
FIFIELD, Darren
FOSTER, Frankie
FRENCH, Terence
GRANT, Frank
HADDOCK, Neil
HARDY, Billy
HIDE, Herbie
HODKINSON, Paul
HOLLIGAN, Andy
HONEYGHAN, Lloyd
HUGHES, Mickey
JACOBS, Gary
LEWIS, Lennox
LOUGHRAN, Eamonn
McCRACKEN, Robert
McKENZIE, Duke
McMILLAN, Colin
MURPHY, Sean
NELSON, Johnny
PYATT, Christopher

REGAN, Robbie
ROBINSON, Steve
SCHWER, Billy
SMYTH, Michael
THOMAS, Karl
THOMPSON, Adrian (Carl)
TILL, Andy
VAUGHAN, Alan
WEIR, John Paul
WHARTON, Henry
WINTER, Craig
WOODHALL, Richie

★ CANOEING
BARRETT, Christopher
BOURNE, Grayson
FOX, Richard
GOODCHILD, Mark
JONES, Melvyn
LAWLER, Ivan
MARRIOTT, Gareth
MILLAR, Michael
PEARCE, Shaun
PITT, Stewart
SIMPSON, Lynn
TRAIN, Andrew
WOOD, Robin

★ CRICKET
ADAMS, Christopher
AFFORD, John
ALLEYNE, Mark
AMBROSE, Curtly
ANDREW, Stephen
ARCHER, Graeme
ASIF DIN
ATHERTON, Michael
ATHEY, Charles (Bill)
AUSTIN, Ian
AYLING, Jonathan
AYMES, Adrian
BAILEY, Robert
BAINBRIDGE, Philip
BAKKER, Paul-Jan
BALL, Martyn
BARNETT, Alex
BARNETT, Kim
BARWICK, Stephen
BASTIEN, Steven
BATTY, Jeremy

BELL, Michael
BENJAMIN, Joseph
BENJAMIN, Winston
BENSON, Justin
BENSON, Mark
BERRY, Philip
BICKNELL, Darren
BICKNELL, Martin
BISHOP, Ian
BLAKEY, Richard
BOILING, James
BOON, Timothy
BOWEN, Mark
BOWLER, Peter
BRIERS, Nigel
BRITTIN, Janette
BROAD, Brian Christopher
BROWN, Alistair
BROWN, Keith
BROWN, Simon
BURNS, Michael
BURNS, Neil
BUTCHER, Mark
BYAS, David
CADDICK, Andrew
CAIRNS, Christopher
CAPEL, David
CARR, John
CARRICK, Phillip
CHAMBERLAIN, Joanna
CHAPPLE, Glen
CHILDS, John
CONNOR, Cardigan
COOK, Nichoias
CORK, Dominic
COTTAM, Andrew
COTTEY, Phillip
COWANS, Norman
COWDREY, Graham
COX, Rupert
CRAWLEY, John
CRAWLEY, Mark
CROFT, Robert
CUMMINS, Anderson
CURRAN, Kevin
CURTIS, Timothy
DALE, Adrian
DALEY, James
DANIELS, Barbara

DAVIES, Mark
DAVIS, Richard
DAWSON, Robert
DE FREITAS, Phillip
DESSAUR, Wayne
D'OLIVEIRA, Damian
DONALD, Allan
DOWMAN, Matthew
EALHAM, Mark
EMBUREY, John
EVANS, Kevin
FAIRBROTHER, Neil
FELTHAM, Mark
FELTON, Nigel
FIELD-BUSS, Michael
FLEMING, Matthew
FLETCHER, Ian
FLINT, Darren
FOLLAND, Nicholas
FORDHAM, Alan
FOSTER, Michael
FOTHERGILL, Andrew
FOWLER, Graeme
FRASER, Alastair
FRASER, Angus
FROST, Mark
FULTON, David
GARNHAM, Michael
GATTING, Michael
GIDDINS, Edward
GOOCH, Graham
GOUGH, Darren
GRAVENEY, David
GRAYSON, Adrian
GREENFIELD, Keith
GRIFFITH, Frank
HANCOCK, Timothy
HARDEN, Richard
HARTLEY, Peter
HAYHURST, Andrew
HAYNES, Desmond
HAYNES, Gavin
HEADLEY, Dean
HEGG, Warren
HEMMINGS, Edward
HEMP, David
HEPWORTH, Peter
HICK, Graeme
HINDSON, James

HINKS, Simon
HODGES, Carole
HODGSON, Geoffrey
HOLLIOAKE, Adam
HOLLOWAY, Piran
   Christopher
HOOPER, Carl
HUGHES, Simon
HUSSAIN, Nasser
HUTTON, Stewart
IGGLESDEN, Alan
ILLINGWORTH, Richard
ILOTT, Mark
JAMES, Kevan
JAMES, Stephen
JARVIS, Paul
JOHNSON, Paul
JOHNSON, Richard
KEECH, Matthew
KELLETT, Simon
KENDRICK, Neil
KERR, Jason
KERSEY, Graham
KITSON, Suzie
KNIGHT, Nicholas
KRIKKEN, Karl
LAMB, Allan
LAMPITT, Stuart
LARKINS, Wayne
LATHWELL, Mark
LAW, Danny
LEATHERDALE, David
LEFEBVRE, Roland
LENHAM, Neil
LEWIS, Christopher
LEWIS, Jonathan
LLONG, Nigel
LLOYD, Graham
LLOYD, Timothy
LONGLEY, Jonathan
LOYE, Malachy
LYNCH, Monte
McCAGUE, Martin
MALCOLM, Devon
MALLENDER, Neil
MARSH, Steven
MARTIN, Peter
MARU, Rajesh
MAYBURY, Debra

MAYNARD, Matthew
METSON, Colin
MIDDLETON, Tony
MILLNS, David
MOLES, Andrew
MOODY, Thomas
MOORES, Peter
MORRIS, Hugh
MORRIS, John
MORTENSEN, Ole
MOXON, Martyn
MULALLY, Alan
MUNTON, Timothy
MURPHY, Anthony
MUSHTAQ AHMED
NEWPORT, Philip
NICHOLAS, Mark
NIXON, Paul
O'GORMAN, Timothy
OSTLER, Dominic
PARKER, Paul
PARKS, Robert
PARSONS, Gordon
PAYNE, Andrew
PENBERTHY, Anthony
PENNETT, David
PENNEY, Trevor
PIGOTT, Anthony
PIPER, Keith
PLIMMER, Helen
POLLARD, Paul
POOLEY, Jason
POTTER, Laurie
PRICHARD, Paul
RADFORD, Neal
RAMPRAKASH, Mark
RATCLIFFE, Jason
REEVE, Dermot
RHODES, Steven
RICHARDSON, Richard
RIPLEY, David
ROBINSON, Darren
ROBINSON, Mark
ROBINSON, Phillip
ROBINSON, Robert
ROLLINS, Robert
ROSE, Graham
ROSEBERRY, Michael
RUSSELL, Robert (Jack)

SALISBURY, Ian
SAXELBY, Mark
SCOTT, Christopher
SCOTT, Richard
SEYMOUR, Adam
SHAHID, Nadeem
SHINE, Kevin
SIMS, Robin
SMALL, Gladstone
SMIT, Jane
SMITH, Andrew
  (Gloucestershire)
SMITH, Andrew (Surrey)
SMITH, Benjamin
SMITH, David
SMITH, Ian
SMITH, Neil
SMITH, Paul
SMITH, Robin
SMITHIES, Karen
SPEAK, Nicholas
SPEIGHT, Martin
STEMP, Richard
STEPHENSON, Franklyn
STEPHENSON, John
STEWART, Alec
STOCK, Debra
SUCH, Peter
TAYLOR, Charles
TAYLOR, Clare
TAYLOR, Jonathan
TAYLOR, Neil
TERRY, Vivian
THOMAS, Stuart
THORPE, Graham
TITCHARD, Stephen
TOLLEY, Christopher
TOPLEY, Thomas
TRUMP, Harvey
TUFNELL, Philip
TURNER, Ian
TURNER, Robert
TWOSE, Roger
UDAL, Shaun
VAN TROOST, Adrianus
  (André)
VAUGHAN, Michael
WALKER, Alan
WALSH, Courtney

WARD, David
WARD, Trevor
WARNER, Allan
WASIM AKRAM
WATKIN, Steven
WATKINSON, Michael
WEEKES, Paul
WELLS, Alan
WELLS, Colin
WELLS, Vincent
WESTON, Martin
WESTON, William
WHITAKER, John
WHITE, Craig
WIGHT, Robert
WILLIAMS, Neil
WILLIAMS, Ricardo
WOOD, John
WOOD, Julian
WRIGHT, Anthony
YATES, Gary

★ CROQUET
APPLETON, David
BAMFORD, Reginald
FULFORD, Robert
OPENSHAW, David
WILLIAMS, Rhodri

★ CYCLING/ CYCLO-CROSS
ALLCOCK, Christopher
BAKER, David
BOARDMAN, Christopher
CAMMISH, Ian
COLTMAN, Gary
DANGERFIELD, Stuart
DIGHTON, Gary
DOUCE, Steve
DOYLE, Anthony
ELLIOTT, Malcolm
HAMMOND, Roger
HEMSLEY, David
ILLINGWORTH, Matthew
IVES, Michael
LILLYWHITE, Christopher
LONGBOTTOM, Peter
NORFOLK, James
OBREE, Douglas Graeme

PHILLIPS, Sarah
SALMON, Fred
STEVENSON, Peter
THACKRAY, Richard
THACKRAY, Robert
WALLACE, Shaun
WRIGHT, Andrew

★ DARTS
ANDERSON, Robert
BEATON, Stephen
BRISTOW, Eric
LOWE, John
PRIESTLEY, Dennis
WARRINER, Alan
WILSON, Jocky

★ DIVING
ALLEN, Hayley
MORGAN, Robert
MORRIS, Graham

★ EQUESTRIANISM
ARMSTRONG, Mark
BOWMAN, George
BRADLEY, Alison
BROOME, David
BROWN, Emma-Jane
DAVISON, Richard
DIXON, Karen
EDGAR, Marie
ELLIOT, Virginia
FLETCHER, Graham
FRY, Laura
GREEN, Lucinda
HESTER, Carl
JACKSON, Joanna
LENG, Virginia: see ELLIOT,
  Virginia
NOLAN, Philippa (Pippa)
PARSONS, Carol
SKELTON, Nick
STARK, Ian
THOMSON, Mary
WHITAKER, John
WHITAKER, Michael
WHITAKER, Véronique

BRACEWELL, Paul
BRADLEY, Darren
BRADSHAW, Carl
BRADY, Kieron
BRADY, William (Liam)
BRANAGAN, Keith
BRANNAN, Gerard (Ged)
BREACKER, Timothy
BREITKREUTZ, Matthias
BRESSINGTON, Graham
BREVETT, Rufus
BREWSTER, Craig
BRIGHTWELL, David
BRIGHTWELL, Ian
BRITTON, Gerard
BROCK, Kevin
BRODDLE, Julian
BROWN, John
BROWN, Kenneth
BROWN, Michael
BROWN, Philip
BRUCE, Stephen
BRYCE, Steven
BRYSON, Ian
BUCKLEY, Alan
BULL, Stephen
BUNN, Frank
BURGESS, Daryl
BURKE, David
BURKE, Mark
BURKINSHAW, Keith
BURNS, Christopher
BURNS, Hugh
BURNS, Tommy
BURRIDGE, John
BURROWS, David
BUTLER, Peter
BUTLER, Stephen
BUTTERS, Guy
BUTTERWORTH, Ian
BYRNE, David
BYRNE, John
CALDERWOOD, Colin
CAME, Mark
CAMERON, Ian
CAMPBELL, Calum
CAMPBELL, Duncan
CAMPBELL, Kevin
CAMPBELL, Stephen

CAMPBELL, Sulzeer (Sol)
CANTONA, Eric
CARR, Franz
CARRUTHERS, Martin
CARSON, Thomas
CARTER, James
CARTWRIGHT, Neil
CASCARINO, Anthony
CHAMBERLAIN, Alec
CHAMBERLAIN, Mark
CHANNING, Justin
CHAPMAN, Lee
CHAPPLE, Philip
CHARLERY, Kenneth
CHARLES, Gary
CHARLTON, Simon
CHERRY, Steven
CHETTLE, Stephen
CHILDS, Gary
CHISHOLM, Gordon
CHRISTIE, Max
CLARIDGE, Stephen
CLARK, Frank
CLARK, John
CLARK, Lee
CLARK, Martin
CLARKE, Andrew
CLARKE, Colin
CLARKE, Stephen
CLAYTON, Gary
CLELAND, Alec
CLOSE, Shaun
CLOUGH, Nigel
COCKERILL, Glenn
COLE, Andrew
COLEMAN, Christopher
COLLINS, John
COLLYMORE, Stanley
COLQUHOUN, John
CONNOLLY, Patrick
CONNOR, Robert
COOK, Paul
COOPER, Colin
COOPER, Davie
COOPER, Gary
CORK, Alan
CORNWELL, John
COSTELLO, Peter
COTON, Anthony

COTTEE, Anthony
COWAN, Thomas
COWANS, Gordon
COX, Neil
COYLE, Owen
COYLE, Ronald
COYNE, Thomas
CRABBE, Scott
CRAWFORD, Stephen
CREANEY, Gerard
CRICHTON, Paul
CROOK, Ian
CROSBY, Gary
CROSSLEY, Mark
CULVERHOUSE, Ian
CUNDY, Jason
CUNNINGHAM, Kenneth
CUNNINGTON, Shaun
CURBISHLEY, Llewellyn
   (Alan)
CURLE, Keith
CURRAN, Henry
DAILLY, Christian
DAIR, Jason
DALGLISH, Kenneth
DALZIEL, Gordon
DANIEL, Raymond
DARBY, Julian
DAVENPORT, Peter
DAVIS, Paul
DAVISON, Aidan
DAWES, Ian
DEANE, Brian
DEAS, Paul
DENNIS, Shaun
DENNISON, Robert
DEVLIN, Paul
DICKS, Julian
DIGBY, Fraser
DINNIE, Alan
DIXON, Kerry
DIXON, Lee
DOBBIN, James
DOBSON, Anthony
DODD, Jason
DODDS, William
DOLAN, Jim
DOLING, Stuart
DONAGHY, Malachy

HENDRY, John
HENRY, Nicholas
HERRERA, Roberto
HESSENTHALER, Andrew
HETHERSTON, Peter
HIGGINS, David
HIGNETT, Craig
HILEY, Scott
HILL, Colin
HILLIER, David
HILTON, Paul
HINCHCLIFFE, Andrew
HINDMARCH, Robert
HIRST, David
HIRST, Lee
HITCHCOCK, Kevin
HODDLE, Glenn
HODGE, Stephen
HODGES, Glyn
HODSON, Simeon
HOLDEN, Andrew
HOLDEN, Richard
HOLDSWORTH, David
HOLDSWORTH, Dean
HOLLOWAY, Ian
HORNE, Barry
HORNE, Brian
HORTON, Brian
HOUGHTON, Raymond
HOWELL, David
HOWELLS, David
HOWEY, Stephen
HOYLAND, Jamie
HUGHES, Ceri
HUGHES, Mark (Manchester
    Utd)
HUGHES, Mark (Tranmere
    Rovers)
HUGHES, Michael
HUGHTON, Chris
HUISTRA, Pieter
HUMPHREY, John
HUNT, Paul
HUNTER, Gordon
HURLOCK, Terence
HURST, Lee
HUTCHISON, Donald
HYSLOP, Christian
IMPEY, Andrew

INCE, Paul
INGLIS, John
IRONS, David
IRONS, Kenneth
IRONSIDE, Ian
IRVINE, Brian
IRWIN, Dennis
JACKSON, Darren
    (Hibernian)
JACKSON, Darren (Oxford
    Utd)
JACKSON, Matthew
JAMES, David
JAMES, Julian
JEMSON, Nigel
JENKINSON, Leigh
JENSEN, John
JESS, Eoin
JOBLING, Kevin
JOBSON, Richard
JOHNSEN, Erland
JOHNSON, Andrew
JOHNSON, Gavin
JOHNSON, Grant
JOHNSON, Marvin
JOHNSON, Thomas
JOHNSTON, Maurice (Mo)
JOHNSTON, Sammy
JONES, Keith
JONES, Robert
JONES, Vincent
JORDAN, Joseph
JOSEPH, Roger
KAMARA, Christopher
KANCHELSKIS, Andrei
KANE, Paul
KAY, John
KEANE, Roy
KEARTON, Jason
KEE, Paul
KEEGAN, Kevin
KEEN, Kevin
KELLY, Alan
KELLY, Anthony
KELLY, David
KELLY, Garry
KELLY, Mark
KENNA, Jeffrey
KENNEDY, Andrew

KEOWN, Martin
KERNAGHAN, Alan
KERR, Dylan
KERSLAKE, David
KHARINE, Dmitri
KILCLINE, Brian
KIMBLE, Alan
KING, John
KING, Philip
KINNAIRD, Paul
KINNEAR, Joseph
KIRK, Stephen
KITSON, Paul
KIWOMYA, Andrew
KIWOMYA, Christopher
KNIGHT, Alan
KRIVOKAPIC, Miodrag
KROMHEER, Elroy
KUBICKI, Dariusz
KUHL, Martin
KUZNETSOV, Oleg
LAKE, Michael
LAW, Bobby
LAW, Brian
LAWRENCE, Lennie
LAWS, Brian
LE SAUX, Graeme
LE TISSIER, Matthew
LEADBITTER, Christopher
LEE, David (Bolton
    Wanderers)
LEE, David (Chelsea)
LEE, Jason
LEE, Robert
LEGG, Andrew
LEIGHTON, James
LENNON, Daniel
LEVEIN, Craig
LEVER, Mark
LEWIS, Michael
LIMPAR, Anders
LING, Martin
LINIGHAN, Andrew
LINIGHAN, David
LITTLE, Brian
LITTLEJOHN, Adrian
LIVINGSTONE, Stephen
LOCKE, Adam
LOUGHLAN, Anthony

LOWE, Kenneth
LUKE, Noel
LUKIC, John
LUND, Gary
LUSCOMBE, Lee
McALLISTER, Brian
McALLISTER, Gary
McALLISTER, Kevin
McATEER, Jason
McAVENNIE, Frank
McCALL, Stuart
McCARRISON, Dugald
McCART, Chris
McCARTHY, Alan
McCARTHY, Michael
McCLAIR, Brian
McCLUSKEY, George
McCOIST, Alistair
McDERMOTT, John
McDONALD, Alan
McDONALD, Neil
McDONOUGH, Darron
McFARLAND, Roy
McGEACHIE, George
McGEE, Paul
McGINLAY, Patrick
McGINNIS, Gary
McGIVEN, Michael
McGLASHAN, Colin
McGLASHAN, John
McGOLDRICK, Edward
McGOWAN, Jamie
McGOWNE, Kevin
McGRATH, Lloyd
McGRATH, Paul
McGRAW, Mark
McGRILLEN, Paul
McINALLY, James
McINTYRE, Tom
MacKENZIE, Alan
McKEOWN, Gary
McKIMMIE, Stuart
McKINLAY, Tosh
McKINLAY, William
McKINNON, Ray
McKINNON, Rob
McLAREN, Alan
McLAREN, Andrew
McLAREN, Ross

McLAREN, Stephen
McLAUGHLIN, Joseph
McLAUGHLIN, Paul
McLEARY, Alan
McLEISH, Alex
MacLEOD, Ian
McLEOD, Joe
MacLEOD, Murdo
McLOUGHLIN, Alan
McMAHON, Stephen
McMANAMAN, Steven
McMARTIN, Grant
McMINN, Kevin (Ted)
McNALLY, Bernard
McNALLY, Mark
MacPHERSON, Angus
McPHERSON, David
McQUILLAN, John
McSKIMMING, Shaun
McSTAY, John
McSTAY, Paul
McSTAY, William
McVICAR, Donald
McWALTER, Mark
MABBUTT, Gary
MACARI, Luigi (Lou)
MACKAY, Gary
MADDEN, Lawrence
MADDISON, Neil
MADDIX, Daniel
MAGILTON, James
MAGUIRE, Gavin
MAIN, Alan
MALKIN, Christopher
MALPAS, Maurice
MANUEL, William
MARKER, Nicholas
MARRIOTT, Andrew
MARSH, Michael
MARSHALL, Gordon
MARSHALL, Ian
MARTIN, Brian
MARTIN, David
MARTIN, Lee
MARTINDALE, David
MARTYN, Nigel
MARWOOD, Brian
MASKELL, Craig
MASON, Paul

MATHERS, Paul
MATHIE, Alex
MATTHEW, Damian
MAXWELL, Alistair
MAY, Andrew
MAY, David
MEAKER, Michael
MEGSON, Gary
MELVILLE, Andrew
MENDONCA, Clive
MERSON, Paul
MIKHAILICHENKO, Alexei
MIKLOSKO, Ludek
MILLEN, Keith
MILLER, Joe
MILLER, Kevin
MILLER, Paul
MILLER, William
MILLIGAN, Michael
MILLS, Gary
MILNE, Callum
MIMMS, Robert
MINTO, Scott
MITCHELL, Alistair
MITCHELL, Graham
MITCHELL, Paul
MOHAN, Nicholas
MONCUR, John
MONTGOMERIE, Ray
MOODY, Paul
MOONEY, Brian
MOONEY, Thomas
MORAN, Kevin
MORAN, Paul
MORGAN, Stephen
MORLEY, Trevor
MORRIS, Christopher
MORRISON, Andrew
MORRISSEY, John
MORROW, Stephen
MOULDEN, Paul
MOUNTFIELD, Derek
MOWBRAY, Anthony
MUIR, Ian
MUNGALL, Steven
MURDOCH, Andrew
MURRAY, Neil
MURRAY, Shaun
MUSTOE, Robert

MUTCH, Andrew
MYERS, Andrew
NARBETT, Jonathan
NAREY, David
NAYLOR, Stuart
NDLOVU, Peter
NEAL, Philip
NEILL, Warren
NEILSON, Alan
NELSON, Craig
NEVIN, Patrick
NEWELL, Michael
NEWHOUSE, Aidan
NEWMAN, Robert
NEWSOME, Jonathan
NICHOLAS, Charles
NICHOLL, James
NICOL, Stephen
NIJHOLT, Luc
NIXON, Eric
NOGAN, Lee
NOLAN, Ian
NORMAN, Anthony
O'BRIEN, William (Liam)
O'CALLAGHAN, Kevin
O'DONNELL, Phillip
O'LEARY, David
O'NEIL, Brian
O'NEIL, John
O'NEILL, Michael
O'REGAN, Kieran
O'RIORDAN, Donal
O'SHEA, Daniel
OAKES, Scott
OGRIZOVIC, Steven
OLDFIELD, David
OLNEY, Ian
ORD, Richard
ORLYGSSON, Thorvaldur
  (Toddy)
ORMONDROYD, Ian
ORR, Neil
OSBORN, Simon
OSMAN, Russell
OTTO, Ricky
OWERS, Gary
PAATELAINEN, Mixu
PALLISTER, Gary
PALMER, Carlton

PALMER, Charles
PALMER, Roger
PARDEW, Alan
PARIS, Alan
PARKER, Garry
PARKER, Paul
PARKINSON, Gary
PARLOUR, Ray
PARRIS, George
PASCOE, Colin
PATERSON, Craig
PATERSON, Garry
PATTERSON, Mark
PAYNE, Derek
PAYTON, Andrew
PEACOCK, Darren
PEACOCK, Gavin
PEAKE, Andrew
PEAKE, Trevor
PEARCE, Andrew
PEARCE, Stuart
PEARS, Stephen
PEARSON, Nigel
PEEBLES, Gary
PEMBERTON, John
PEMBRIDGE, Mark
PENNEY, David
PENRICE, Gary
PERRY, Jason
PERRY, Mark
PERRYMAN, Stephen
PESCHISOLIDO, Paul
PEYTON, Gerald
PHELAN, Michael
PHELAN, Terence
PHILLIBEN, John
PHILLIPS, David
PHILLIPS, James
PHILLISKIRK, Anthony
PITTMAN, Stephen
PLATT, David
PLEAT, David
POINTON, Neil
POLLOCK, Jamie
POLSTON, Jonathan
POOLE, Kevin
PORTEOUS, Ian
PORTER, Gary
POTTS, Steven

POWELL, Christopher
POWELL, Darryl
POWELL, Lee
POWER, Lee
PREECE, David
PRESSLEY, Steven
PRESSMAN, Kevin
PRESTON, Allan
PRIOR, Spencer
PROCTOR, Mark
PRUDHOE, Mark
QUINN, James
QUINN, Michael
QUINN, Niall
RAE, Alexander
RAESIDE, Robert
RAMMELL, Andrew
RANKINE, Mark
RAVEN, Paul
RAYNOR, Paul
REDFEARN, Neil
REDKNAPP, Jamie
REDMOND, Stephen
REES, Anthony
REES, Jason
REES, Melvyn
REEVES, David
REGIS, Cyrille
REID, Chris
REID, Peter
REILLY, Mark
RENNIE, David
RHODES, Andrew
RICHARDSON, Kevin
RICHARDSON, Lee
RILEY, David
RIOCH, Bruce
RIPLEY, Stuart
RITCHIE, Andrew
RITCHIE, Paul
RIX, Graham
ROBERTS, Andrew
ROBERTS, Anthony
ROBERTSON, David
ROBERTSON, John
ROBINS, Mark
ROBINSON, David
ROBINSON, Leslie
ROBINSON, Liam

ROBINSON, Mark
ROBINSON, Philip
ROBINSON, Ronald
ROBSON, Bryan
ROCASTLE, David
ROCHE, David
RODGER, Graham
RODGER, Simon
RODGERSON, Ian
ROEDER, Glenn
ROGAN, Anton
ROGERS, Paul
ROSARIO, Robert
ROSENTHAL, Ronny
ROWLAND, Keith
ROYLE, Joseph
RUDDOCK, Neil
RUSH, David
RUSH, Ian
RUSH, Matthew
RUSSELL, Lee
RYAN, Vaughan
SALAKO, John
SAMWAYS, Vincent
SANCHEZ, Lawrence
SANSOM, Kenny
SANSOME, Paul
SAUNDERS, Dean
SCALES, John
SCHMEICHEL, Peter
SCOTT, Kevin
SCULLY, Patrick
SEAGRAVES, Mark
SEAMAN, David
SEDGLEY, Stephen
SEGERS, Johannes (Hans)
SELLARS, Scott
SHAKESPEARE, Craig
SHARP, Graeme
SHARPE, Lee
SHAW, George
SHAW, Richard
SHEARER, Alan
SHEARER, Duncan
SHEPHERD, Anthony
SHEPSTONE, Paul
SHERIDAN, John
SHERINGHAM, Edward
SHERON, Michael

SHERWOOD, Stephen
SHERWOOD, Timothy
SHIRTLIFF, Peter
SHORT, Christian
SHORT, Craig
SHUTT, Carl
SIMPSON, Fitzroy
SIMPSON, Neil
SIMPSON, Paul
SINCLAIR, David
SINCLAIR, Frank
SINCLAIR, Trevor
SINNOTT, Lee
SINTON, Andrew
SKILLING, Mark
SLATER, Stuart
SLAVEN, Bernard
SMALL, Bryan
SMALL, Michael
SMART, Gary
SMILLIE, Neil
SMITH, Alan
SMITH, Barry
SMITH, David
SMITH, Gary
SMITH, James
SMITH, Michael
SMITH, Paul
SMITH, Richard
SNEDDON, Alan
SNELDERS, Theo
SNODIN, Glynn
SNODIN, Ian
SOLOMAN, Jason
SOUTHALL, Neville
SOUTHGATE, Gareth
SPACKMAN, Nigel
SPEED, Gary
SPEEDIE, David
SPENCER, John
SPINK, Nigel
SPOONER, Nicholas
SRNICEK, Pavel
STARK, William
STAUNTON, Stephen
STEELE, Timothy
STEIN, Mark
STEJSKAL, Jan
STEPHENSON, Paul

STERLING, Worrell
STEVEN, Trevor
STEVENS, Gary
STEVENS, Keith
STIMSON, Mark
STOCKWELL, Michael
STORER, Stuart
STOWELL, Michael
STRACHAN, Gordon
STRODDER, Gary
STUART, Graham
STUBBS, Alan
SUCKLING, Perry
SUMMERBEE, Nicholas
SUSSEX, Andrew
SUTCH, Daryl
SUTTON, Christopher
SYMONS, Christopher (Kit)
TAGGART, Gerald
TANNER, Nicholas
TAYLOR, Colin
TAYLOR, Robert
TAYLOR, Shaun
TEALE, Shaun
TELFER, Paul
THOMAS, Dean
THOMAS, Geoffrey
THOMAS, Michael
THOMAS, Mitchell
THOMAS, Roderick
THOMAS, Tony
THOMPSON, Alan
THOMPSON, Andrew
THOMPSON, Neil
THOMPSON, Stephen
THOMSON, Ian
THOMSON, William
THORN, Andrew
THORSTVEDT, Erik
TIERNEY, Grant
TILER, Carl
TILLSON, Andrew
TILSON, Stephen
TOLSON, Neil
TORFASON, Gudmundor
TORTOLANO, Joe
TOSHACK, John
TOWNSEND, Andrew
TRACEY, Simon

TURNER, Graham
TURNER, Philip
TUTTLE, David
TWEED, Steven
VAN DEN HAUWE, Patrick
VATA, Rudi
VAUGHAN, John
VENABLES, Terence
VENISON, Barry
VENUS, Mark
VERVEER, Etienne
VEYSEY, Kenneth
VICKERS, Stephen
VINNICOMBE, Christopher
VIVEASH, Adrian
VONK, Michel
VRTO, Dusan
WADDLE, Christopher
WADDOCK, Gary
WALKER, Andrew
WALKER, Desmond
WALKER, Ian
WALKER, Michael
WALKER, Nicholas
WALLACE, David (Danny)
WALLACE, Raymond
WALLACE, Rodney
WALSH, Colin
WALSH, Paul
WALSH, Steven
WALTERS, Mark
WARD, Gavin
WARD, Mark
WARHURST, Paul
WARK, John
WARREN, Mark
WARZYCHA, Robert
WATSON, David
WATSON, Stephen
WATSON, Thomas
WATT, Michael
WAUGH, Keith
WDOWCZYK, Dariusz
WEBB, David
WEBB, Neil
WEBSTER, Simon
WEGERLE, Roy
WEIR, Michael
WELSH, Brian

WELSH, Stephen
WEST, Colin
WESTLEY, Shane
WETHERALL, David
WHELAN, Philip
WHELAN, Ronald
WHITBREAD, Adrian
WHITE, Christopher
WHITE, David
WHITE, Stephen
WHITE, Winston
WHITEHOUSE, Dane
WHITLOW, Michael
WHITTINGHAM, Guy
WHITTON, Stephen
WHYTE, Christopher
WHYTE, Derek
WIEGHORST, Morten
WILCOX, Jason
WILDER, Christopher
WILKINS, Raymond
WILKINS, Richard
WILKINSON, Howard
WILKINSON, Paul
WILLIAMS, Andrew
WILLIAMS, Brett
WILLIAMS, John
WILLIAMS, Martin
WILLIAMS, Paul
WILLIAMSON, Robert
WILLIAMSON, Trevor
WILMOT, Rhys
WILSON, Clive
WILSON, Daniel
WILSON, Kevin
WILSON, Terence
WILSON, Tommy
WINSTANLEY, Mark
WINTERBURN, Nigel
WISE, Dennis
WISHART, Fraser
WOAN, Ian
WOOD, Stephen
WOODS, Christopher
WOODS, Neil
WORTHINGTON, Nigel
WRIGHT, Alan
WRIGHT, George
WRIGHT, Ian

WRIGHT, Keith
WRIGHT, Mark
WRIGHT, Paul
WRIGHT, Stephen
WRIGHT, Thomas
   (Middlesbrough)
WRIGHT, Thomas
   (Nottingham Forest)
YALLOP, Frank
YATES, Dean
YORKE, Dwight
YOUNG, Eric

★ GLIDING
DAVIS, Andrew
EDYVEAN, Jeremy (Jed)
GORRINGE, John
MAY, Robin
ROLLINGS, Christopher
SPRECKLEY, Brian
WELLS, Martyn

★ GOLF
BAKER, Peter
BENNETT, Stephen
BRAND, Gordon
BROADHURST, Paul
BUXTON, Nicola
CALDWELL, Carole
CHAPMAN, Roger
CLARK, Howard
CLAYDON, Russell
DAVIES, Laura
DOBSON, Helen
DOUGLAS, Kitrina
DOWLING, Deborah
DUNDAS, Stephen
FALDO, Nicholas
FEHERTY, David
GALLACHER, Bernard
GILFORD, David
HALL, Julie
HOCKLEY, Joanne
JAMES, Mark
JOHNSON, Patricia (Trish)
LAMBERT, Catriona
LANE, Barry
LYLE, Alexander (Sandy)
McEVOY, Peter

McGIMPSEY, Garth
MacGREGOR, George
McKAY, Mhairi
MARSHALL, Kathryn
MAYO, Paul
MONTGOMERIE, Colin
MOODIE, Janice
MORLEY, Joanne
MOULAND, Mark
NEW, Beverley
NICHOLAS, Alison
PANTON-LEWIS, Catherine
PAYNE, James
PYMAN, Iain
RAFFERTY, Ronan
REID, Dale
RICHARDSON, Steven
STANFORD, Matthew
STEWART, Gillian
TORRANCE, Sam
WADSWORTH, Helen
WALTON, Lisa
WAY, Paul
WELCH, Michael
WILLISON, Ricky
WOOSNAM, Ian

★ GYMNASTICS
BOWLER, Paul
CAMPBELL, Marvin
CROCKER, Emily
DA CRUZ, Natalia
MUSIKANT, Philippa
THOMAS, Neil
WALKER, Joanne

★ HANG GLIDING/
PARAGLIDING
CARTER, Richard
CROSBY, Dean
FENWICK, Sarah
GOLDSMITH, Bruce
HARVEY, Peter
LEDEN, Judy
PENDRY, John
RIGG, Gordon
SANDERSON, Jocky
WHITTALL, Robert

★ HOCKEY
ASHCROFT, Christopher
ATKINS, Jill
BARROW, Jason
BAYLISS, Lisa
BONAR, Kirsty
BRIMBLE, Sue
BURTON, Louise
CLAXTON, Aileen
COOK, Christine
COPE, Lucy
COX, James
CRUTCHLEY, Robert
CULLEN, Christina
CUNLIFFE, Derek
DAVIES, Mandy
DONALD, Nicola
ELLIS, Louise
EYRE, Sally
FOWLER, David
FRASER, Susan
FRASER, Wendy
FREELAND, Richard
GIBSON, Sally
GREEN, Joanne
GULBRANDSEN, Laura
HAZLITT, Simon
HILL, Robert
JOHNSON, Kathryn
JONES, Zachary
LASLETT, Jason
LEE, Fiona
LISTER, Sandra
LOTHIAN, Jackie
LUCKES, David
McCULLOUGH, Heather
MacDONALD, Susan
MacINNES, Fiona
MILLER, Tammy
NICHOLLS, Mandy
O'BRYAN, Rachel
OTLEY, Suzanne
RAMSAY, Alison
REID, Carolyn
ROBERTSON, Michelle
ROBERTSON, Pauline
ROSE, Hilary
SAMWAYS, Claire
SHEPHERD, Gordon

SIXSMITH, Jane
SMITH, Jane
SPENCER, Kirsten
STEWART, Julie
STRONGE, Tamara
SWINDLEHURST, Alison
THOMPSON, Joanne
TOON, Joanna
WILLIAMS, Donald
WILLMORE, Tracy
WRIGHT, Samantha
YOUNGS, Lucy

★ HORSERACING
BALDING, Ian
BARONS, David
BEAUMONT, Peter
BERRY, Jack
BRITTAIN, Clive
CARSON, William
CECIL, Henry
CHANNON, Michael
CHAPPLE-HYAM, Peter
CHARLTON, Roger
COCHRANE, Raymond
COLE, Paul
DUNLOP, John
DUNWOODY, Thomas
  Richard
DWYER, Mark
EARNSHAW, Robert
EDDERY, Patrick
ELSWORTH, David
FANSHAWE, James
FITZGERALD, James
FROST, James
GASELEE, Nicholas
GIFFORD, Joshua
HANBURY, Benjamin
HANNON, Richard
HARWOOD, Guy
HENDERSON, Nicholas
HERN, William
HILLS, Barrington
HILLS, Michael
HOBBS, Peter
JONES, Isobel Diana
KINANE, Michael
KNIGHT, Henrietta

LEWIS, Geoffrey
LLEWELLYN, Carl
MAGUIRE, Adrian
MELLOR, Stanley
MUNRO, Alan
NICHOLSON, David
O'GORMAN, William
OSBORNE, Jamie
PERRATT, Linda
PIGGOTT, Lester
PIPE, Martin
PITMAN, Jennifer
REID, John
ROBERTS, Michael
ROBINSON, Philip
SIMPSON, Rodney
STOUTE, Michael
SWAN, Charles
SWINBURN, Walter
TURNELL, Andrew
TWISTON-DAVIES, Nigel
WALWYN, Peter
WRAGG, Geoffrey

★ ICE HOCKEY
BIDNER, Todd
BREBANT, Rick
CHINN, Nicky
CONWAY, Kevin
COOPER, Ian
COOPER, Stephen
CRANSTON, Tim
FERA, Rick
HAND, Tony
HANSON, Moray
HOPE, Shannon
HUNT, Simon
IREDALE, John
JOHNSON, Anthony
JOHNSON, Shaun
JOHNSON, Stephen
KELLAND, Chris
LONGSTAFFE, David
LOVELL, Lindsay
McCRONE, John
McEWEN, Doug
McKAY, Martin
MALO, André
MASON, Brian

MORRIS, Frank
MORRISON, Scott
NEIL, Scott
O'CONNOR, Mike
O'CONNOR, Scott
PENTLAND, Paul
ROBERTSON, Iain
SMITH, Damian
WAGHORN, Graham
WOOD, Jason

★ ICE SKATING
ASKEW, Philip
BELL, Stuart
CHRISTENSEN, Jayne
DEAN, Christopher
GOOCH, Nicholas
HUMPHREYS, Marika
INGS, David
JAMES, Marie
LANNING, Justin
MAIN, Stephanie
MARTIN, John
MEDNICK, Dana
TORVILL, Jayne: see
    CHRISTENSEN, Jayne
WARMINGTON, Emma

★ JUDO
BIRCH, Ryan
BRIGGS, Karen
CUSACK, William
CUSACK, Loretta
DEAN, Darren
DONOHUE, Nigel
FAIRBROTHER, Nicola
HORTON, Josephine
HOWEY, Kate
PRESTON, Luke
PRICE, Violet
RENDLE, Sharon
SARGENT, Daniel
SOUTHBY, David

★ KARATE
DUGGIN, Patricia
FLEMING, Gerard
FRANCIS, Janice
McCULLOUGH, Robert

OTTO, Wayne
SAMUEL, Mollie

★ LACROSSE
BURNS, Charlotte
COX, Ailsa
DUCKETT, Jayne
GOMM, Sarah
GRAHAM, Helena
HOUSTON, Valerie
JONES, Vivien
LAWRENCE, Sarah
McKNIGHT, Margaret
MARSHALL, Georgina
O'NEILL, Janet
SALVESEN, Emily
WILKIE, Lydia

★ MODERN
PENTATHLON
PHELPS, Richard
ROWE, Elizabeth Victoria
    (Vicky)

★ MOTORCYCLING
BIRCH, Jason
BUTTLE, Michael
COOPER, Gavin
CUDDY, Tom
DEACON, John
EDMONDSON, Paul
EDWARDS, Mark Sydney
    (Cedric)
ETHERIDGE, Christopher
FAIRBROTHER, Paul
FOGARTY, Carl
GRESSWELL, Charles
HODGSON, Neil
KNIGHT, Gary
LEASK, Perry
LUSCOMBE, Robin
MacKENZIE, Niall
NELSON, Richard
NICOLL, Kurt
PAGET, Leonard
PLATFOOT, Calvin
PRICE, Katrina
SAUNDERS, Steve
SAWFORD, Steve

SELBY, Howard
SIMMONS, Gavin
SIMPSON, Ian
SMAILES, Anthony
THOMAS, Graham
WEBSTER, Stephen
WHITESIDE, Scott
WIGG, Simon Anthony

★ MOTOR RACING
BLUNDELL, Mark
BRUNDLE, Martin
HERBERT, John
HILL, Damon
WARWICK, Derek

★ MOUNTAINEERING
BONINGTON, Christian
PAYNE, Roger
SAUNDERS, Anthony Victor
SCOTT, Douglas
STEPHENS, Rebecca

★ NETBALL
CAW, Lorraine
FAIRIE, Michele
HART, Karen
HORRELL, Janet
JACKETT, Yvonne
LOWE, Kendra
LYON, Sharyn
McCANDLISH, Lynne
McELVEEN, Karen
McLEAN, Fiona
McLOUGHLIN, Theresa
MALCOLM, Lindsay
SWANN, Angela
TOPLISS, Lisa
TOUGH, Mary
TRAMSCHEK, Ruth
TUCKWELL, Melanie
WALKER, Pamela
WILSON, Christine

★ POINT-TO-POINT
CROW, Alastair
DARE, Alison

★ POWERBOAT RACING
ABBOTT, Julien
ALLENBY, David
AUGER, Christian
BARSCH, Nicholas
DE GRAAFF, Daniel
EDWARDS, Nicholas
GREEN, Alan
HEBBARD, Steven
HORE, Stephen
KENT, Steven
LOCOCK, Jeffery
NOONE, James
TURNER, Kevin
WILLCOCK, Dave
YOUNGER, Adam

★ RACE WALKING
BROWN, Carolyn
LARBY, Verity
LUPTON, Victoria
MADDOCKS, Christopher
MORTON, Les
PARTINGTON, Steve
PENN, Andrew
SHILLABEER, Edmund
STONE, Darrell

★ RACKETS
BOONE, William
COCKROFT, Timothy
HAZEL, Shannon
PRENN, John
SMITH, Neil

★ RALLY DRIVING
BURNS, Richard
HEAD, Robbie
WILSON, Malcolm

★ REAL TENNIS
ALLEN, Katrina
CORNWALLIS, Charlotte
GARSIDE, Alexandra
JONES, Sally
LUMLEY, Penelope
McMURRUGH, Michael
RONALDSON, Christopher
SNOW, Julian

★ ROCK CLIMBING
BUTLER, Felicity
MOON, Ben
VICKERS, Ian

★ ROWING
BATTEN, Guin
BATTEN, Miriam
BEHRENS, James
BENNETT, Tracy
BRIDGE, Peter
BROWNLESS, Alison
BROWNLOW, Katharine
CORLESS, Patricia
DAVIES, Claire
DILLON, Terence
DRYDEN, Anna Marie
ELLISON, Adrian
FILSELL, Vikki
HALL, Alison
HALL, Jane
HALL-CRAGGS, Wade
HERBERT, Garry
HUNT-DAVIS, Francis
MacLENNAN, Calman
McNIVEN, James
PARISH, Matthew
PARTRIDGE, Mark
PHELPS, Richard
PINSENT, Matthew
POOLEY, Guy
REDGRAVE, Steven
ROOKS, Teawen
SEARLE, Greg
SEARLE, Jonathan
SMITH, Carl
SMITH, Claire
STANHOPE, Richard
STEWART, Gavin
STRANGE, Nicholas
TURVEY, Joanne
WALKER, James
WILLIAMS, Tonia
WRIGHT, Stephen

★ RUGBY FIVES
HEBDEN, David
NEWMAN, Peter
ROBERTS, Neil

★ **RUGBY LEAGUE**
ANDERSON, Grant
ANDERSON, Paul
ANDERSON, Tony
ASTON, Mark
ATCHESON, Paul
BAGNALL, Geoff
BAILEY, Mark
BALDWIN, Simon
BARKWORTH, Julian
BATEMAN, Allan
BELL, Nigel
BENTLEY, John
BETTS, Denis
BIRKETT, Martin
BISHOP, Paul
BLACKMORE, Richard
BLAKELEY, Steve
BOOTH, Simon
BOTICA, Frano
BROWN, Shaun
BURGESS, Andy
BUSBY, Dean
BUTT, Ikram
CALLAND, Matt
CARR, Paul
CASEY, Leo
CHAMBERLAIN, Richard
CHAMBERS, Gary
CHATFIELD, Gary
CHRISTIE, Gary
CLARK, Trevor
CLARKE, Philip
CLARKE, Troy
COLLIER, Andrew
CONNOLLY, Gary
CONWAY, Billy
COOPER, David
COOPER, Shane
CORDLE, Gerald
COSTELLO, John
COWIE, Neil
COYNE, Peter
CRITCHLEY, Jason
CROMPTON, Martin
CROOKS, Lee
CULLEN, Paul
CURRIER, Andrew
DANBY, Rob

DANIEL, Alan
DANNATT, Andrew
DARBYSHIRE, Paul
DAUNT, Brett
DAVIDSON, Paul
DAVIES, Jonathan
DERMOTT, Martin
DEVEREUX, John
DIVET, Daniel
DIVORTY, Gary
DIXON, Mike
DIXON, Paul
DONOHUE, Jason
DWYER, Bernard
EASTWOOD, Paul
EDWARDS, Shaun
ELLIS, Kevin
ELLIS, St John
ENGLAND, Keith
EYRES, Richard
FAIMALO, Esene
FAIRBANK, Karl
FALLON, James
FARRELL, Andrew
FARRELL, Anthony
FAWCETT, Vince
FIELDHOUSE, John
FISHER, Andy
FLETCHER, Michael
FLETCHER, Paul (Hull
    Kingston Rovers)
FLETCHER, Paul (Oldham)
FLYNN, Adrian
FOGERTY, Adam
FOGERTY, Jason
FORBER, Paul
FORD, Mike
FORD, Philip
FORSHAW, Mike
FORSTER, Mark
FOX, Deryck
GAMSON, Mark
GAY, Richard
GIBSON, Carl
GIBSON, Walter
GILDART, Ian
GODDARD, Richard
GOODWAY, Andrew
GOULDING, Robert

GRANT, James
GREGORY, Andy
GREGORY, Michael
GRIFFITHS, Jonathan
GRIMOLDY, Nic
GROVES, Paul
GUNN, Richard
GUNNING, John
HADLEY, Adrian
HALL, Martin
HALLAS, Graham
HAMER, Jonathan
HAMMOND, Karl
HAMPSON, Steve
HANGER, Dean
HANLAN, Lee
HANLEY, Ellery
HARLAND, Lee
HARMON, Neil
HARRISON, Chris
HARRISON, John
HARRISON, Karl
HAY, Andy
HERON, David
HESLOP, Nigel
HOLDING, Neil
HOLROYD, Graham
HOWARD, Harvey
HUGHES, Ian
HULME, David
HULME, Paul
HUNTE, Alan
HUTCHINSON, Rob
INNES, Craig
IRELAND, Andy
IRO, Kevin
IRVING, Simon
IRWIN, Shaun
JACKSON, Anthony
JACKSON, Lee
JACKSON, Michael
JACKSON, Robert
JACKSON, Wayne
JONES, David
JONES, Mark
JOYNT, Christopher
KEBBIE, Brimah
KENYON, Neil
KETTERIDGE, Martin

KOLOTO, Emosi
KUITI, Michael
LAUGHTON, Dale
LAY, Stephen
LEE, Mark
LORD, Gary
LOUGHLIN, Paul
LOWES, James
LYDON, Joseph
LYON, David
McCURRIE, Steve
McGINTY, William
McGOWAN, Stephen
McGUIRE, Bruce
McNAMARA, Steve
MACKEY, Greg
MALONEY, Francis
MANN, George
MANNING, Terry
MARCHANT, Tony
MARLOW, Ian
MARTIN, Scott
MARTYN, Tommy
MASON, Andrew
MATHER, Barrie-Jon
MEDLEY, Paul
MERCER, Gary
MIDDLETON, Graham
MIDDLETON, Simon
MOLLOY, Stephen
MORIARTY, Paul
MORRISON, Anthony
MUMBY, Keith
MYERS, David
MYLER, Robert
NAYLOR, Scott
NEILL, Jonathan
NELSON, David
NEWLOVE, Paul
NICKLE, Sonny
NIKAU, Tawera
NOLAN, Gary
NOLAN, Robert
O'BRIEN, Craig
O'DONNELL, Augustine
O'NEILL, Michael
OFFIAH, Martin
PANAPA, Sam
PARKER, Wayne

PEARSON, Martin
PENDLEBURY, John
PENNY, Lee
PERRETT, Mark
PHILLIPS, Rowland
PICKAVANCE, Ian
PLANGE, David
POWELL, Daio
POWELL, Daryl
POWELL, Roy
PRATT, Gareth
PRESTON, Mark
PRICE, Gary
PRICE, Richard
PUGSLEY, Stuart
QUIRK, Les
RAW, Andrew
RILEY, Michael
ROBINSON, Jason
ROEBUCK, Neil
ROUND, Paul
ROWLEY, Paul
RUSSELL, Richard
SAMPSON, Dean
SANDERSON, Gary
SCHOFIELD, Garry
SCOTT, Ian
SHARP, Jon
SHEALS, Mark
SHELFORD, Darrall
SHELFORD, Kelly
SHERIDAN, Ryan
SIMPSON, Owen
SIMPSON, Roger
SKERRETT, Kelvin
SLATER, Richard
SMALES, Ian
SMITH, David
SMITH, Tony
SODJE, Bright
SOUTHERNWOOD, Graham
SOUTHERNWOOD, Roy
SPENCER, Gary
SPRUCE, Stuart
STEADMAN, Graham
STEPHENS, Gareth
STOTT, Lynton
STREET, Tim
SULLIVAN, Anthony

SUMMERS, Neil
SYKES, Nathan
TAIT, Alan
THOMPSON, Andrew
THORNILEY, Anthony
THURSFIELD, John
TOPPING, Paul
TUUTA, Brendon
TYRER, Christian
VEIVERS, Philip
WADDELL, Hugh
WALKER, Russ
WARD, Kevin
WATSON, Chris
WATSON, David
WEBSTER, Richard
WILLIAMS, Peter
WILLIAMSON, Paul
WILSON, Andrew
WILSON, Warren
WORRALL, Mick
WRAY, Jonathan
WRIGHT, Darren
WRIGHT, Nigel
YOUNG, David

★ RUGBY UNION
ADAMSON, Lee
ADEBAYO, Adedayo
AINSCOUGH, Gerry
AITKEN, Scott
ALLEN, Kevin
AMOS, John
ANDREW, Christopher
  (Rob)
ANDREWS, Richard
ARMSTRONG, Gary
ARNOLD, Paul
ASHMEAD, Paul
BACK, Neil
BAIRD, Roger
BALDWIN, Gavin
BARCLAY, Stephen
BARNES, Stuart
BATES, Steven
BAYFIELD, Martin
BECK, Laurie
BEECH, Paul
BIDGOOD, Roger

BLACKMORE, Andrew
BLYTH, David
BOOBYER, Neil
BOTTERMAN, Gregg
BRACKEN, Kyran
BRIDGES, Christopher
BROWN, Alan
BROWN, Barrie
BUCKETT, Ian
BUCKTON, John
BURNELL, Andrew Paul
BURROW, Mark
BUZZA, Alan
CALLARD, Jonathan
CAMPBELL, Colin
CARLING, William
CASKIE, Don
CASS, Martin
CASSELL, Justyn
CHALLINOR, Andrew Paul
CHALMERS, Craig
CHILDS, Graham
CLARK, Gary
CLARKE, Benjamin
CLEMENT, Anthony
COCKERILL, Richard
COOKE, David
COPSEY, Anthony
CORCORAN, Ian
COWAN, Richard
CRAWLEY, Barry
CRONIN, Damian
CUMMINS, Damian
DALLAGLIO, Laurence
DAVIES, Adrian
DAVIES, Brian
DAVIES, Geraint
DAVIES, John
DAVIES, Nigel
DAVIES, Philip
DAVIES, Stuart
DAVIES, William
DAVIS, Mark
DAWE, Richard
DE GLANVILLE, Philip
DEACON, Andrew
DELANEY, Laurance
DICKSON, Roderick
DIXON, John

DODS, Michael
EDWARDS, Neil
EVANS, Ieuan
EVANS, Owen
EVANS, Paul
EVANS, Richard
FORD, Stephen
FOWKE, Robert
FOX, David
GARFORTH, Darren
GEOGHEGAN, Simon
GIBBS, Ian Scott
GRAY, Christopher
GREENWOOD, Matthew
GREGORY, Martin
GRIFFITHS, Michael
GUSCOTT, Jeremy
HACKNEY, Stephen
HALL, Jonathan
HALL, Michael
HALPIN, Garrett
HANNAFORD, Marcus
HARRIMAN, Andrew
HASTINGS, Andrew Gavin
HASTINGS, Scott
HAVERY, Steve
HENDERSON, Fergus
HICKEY, Daryl
HILL, Richard
HODDER, Paul
HOGG, Carl
HOLFORD, Paul
HOPKINS, Kevin
HOPLEY, Damian
HOWLEY, Robert
HUGHES, Gareth
HUGHES, Paul
HULL, Paul
HUNTER, Ian
HYNES, Martin
ISAAC, Gary
JARDINE, Ian
JENKINS, Garin
JENKINS, Neil
JOHNSON, Martin
JONES, Gary
JONES, Ian Wyn
JONES, Paul
JONES, Peter

JONES, Rhodri
JONES, Richard
JONES, Robert
JOSEPH, David
KARDOONI, Aadel
KEARSEY, David
KIMBERLEY, Scott
LAMERTON, Andrew
LANCASTER, Philip
LANGLEY, Mark
LEE, Andrew
LEE, Craig
LEONARD, Jason
LEWIS, Emyr
LILEY, John
LINEEN, Sean
LLEWELLYN, Gareth
LLEWELLYN, Glyn
LLOYD, Owain
LOGAN, Kenneth
McBRYDE, Robin
McCARTHY, Matthew
MacDONALD, Andrew
McINTOSH, Dale
McIVOR, David
McKINNON, Darren
MacNAUGHTON, Robert
McPHERSON, Andrew
McVIE, Malcolm
MALONE, Niall
MATTHEWS, Neil
MAY, Philip
MILES, Peter
MILLARD, David
MILLIGAN, Kenneth
MILNE, Kenneth
MITCHELL, David
MITCHELL, Simon
MONCRIEFF, Mark
MOON, Rupert
MOORE, Alexander
MOORE, Brian
MORGAN, Kevin
MORIARTY, Richard
MORRIS, Colin Dewi
MORRIS, Martyn
MORRIS, Simon
MORRISON, Iain
MULLINS, Andrew

LEE, Stephen
McMANUS, Alan
MEO, Anthony
MORGAN, Darren
MOUNTJOY, Douglas
O'SULLIVAN, Ronnie
PARROTT, John
TAYLOR, Dennis
THORNE, William
WHITE, James
WILKINSON, Gary

★ SPEEDWAY
HAVELOCK, Robert Gary
SMITH, Andrew
WIGG, Simon

★ SQUASH
ALLEN, Mark
BEESON, Bryan
BOWIE, Alison
BROWN, Shirley
CHARMAN, Linda
DAVIES, Adrian
FELTON, Sally
FURY, Sarah
GARNER, Tim
GEAVES, Fiona
HEATH, Martin
JACKMAN, Cassandra
JOHNSON, Sian
LE MOIGNAN, Martine
LEEVES, Donia
MACREE, Rebecca
MALIK, Farhana Tegwen
NICHOLL, Pauline
NICOL, Peter
OPIE, Lisa
TRANFIELD, Jennifer
TURNBULL, Debra
WALKER, Chris

★ SURFING
BURBERRY, Eden
HARGRAVES, Spencer
LOUGHRIDGE, Christopher
ROBINSON, Grant
WINTER, Russell

★ SWIMMING
AKERS, Stephen
BENNETT, Alexandra
CARL, Martin
CLAPPER, Alexander
CLAYTON, Andrew
CROSBY, Kevin
DAVIES, Sharron
DEAKINS, Joanne
FIBBENS, Michael
FOGGO, Samantha
FOSTER, Mark
GILLINGHAM, Nicholas
GOODWIN, Nicola
HARDCASTLE, Sarah
HARDIMAN, Marie
HARRIS, Martin
HENDER, Jason
HICKMAN, James
HORNER, Victoria
KING, Jaime
MADEN, Jonathon Richard
MOORHOUSE, Adrian
OSHER, Katharine
PALMER, Paul
PARRACK, James
PICKERING, Karen
ROBINS, Grant
RUCKWOOD, Adam
SHEPPARD, Alison
WALKER, Fraser
WILLEY, Neil
WILSON, Ian

★ SYNCHRONIZED
SWIMMING
CARLSEN, Adäle
DAVENPORT, Angela
ERRAUGHT, Maria
MOREAU, Jemma
SHACKLOCK, Kerry
SHORTMAN, Penny
THOMPSON, Karen
VAKIL, Laila
WHYMAN, Claire

★ TABLE TENNIS
CHEN, Xinhua
COOKE, Alan

COWAN, Jonathan
DILL, James
GLOVER, Andrea
GOODALL, Katherine
HOLT, Andrea
LOMAS, Lisa
PREAN, Carl
SYED, Matthew

★ TENNIS
BAILEY, Christopher
BAILY, James
BATES, Jeremy
COLE, Sean
CROSS, Karen
DAVIES, William
DELGADO-CORREDOR,
  Jamie
DURIE, Joanna
FOSTER, Andrew
GOMER, Sara
GRUNFELD, Amanda
HAND, Paul
HUNT, Caroline
JAVER, Monique
LOOSEMORE, Sarah
MOORE, Joanne
PETCHEY, Mark
SAPSFORD, Danny
SIDDALL, Shirli-Ann
WILKINSON, Chris
WOOD, Clare

★ TENPIN BOWLING
SMITH, Pauline

★ TRIATHLON
BREW, Robin
CAWTHORNE, Helen
COOK, Glenn
HOBSON, Richard
JENKINSON, Julian
LESSING, Simon
SMITH, Spencer
SPRINGMAN, Sarah
WATSON, Melissa

STOP PRESS

(Retirements announced, honours gained, and inter-club transfers
March – May 1994)

ADAMS, Anthony (football): with Arsenal: winners European Cup Winners' Cup

ADAMS, Michael (football): joined Stoke City from Southampton

ADEBAYO, Adedayo (RU): with Bath: winners Pilkington Cup; England tour SA

ALLEN, Clive (football): joined Millwall from W. Ham Utd

ALLON, Joseph (football): joined Port Vale from Brentford

ANDERSON, Grant (RL): with Castleford: winners Regal Trophy

ANDERTON, Darren (football): made snr England debut v. Denmark

ANDREW, Christopher Robert (RU): England tour SA

ANGELL, Brett (football): joined Everton from Southend

ARCHER, Simon (badminton): European Champs. doubles gold medal

ARMSTRONG, Christopher (football): with Crystal Palace: 1st Div. champs.

ARNOLD, Paul (RU): with Swansea: Welsh League champs.; Wales tour Canada/S. Seas

ASPINALL, Warren (football): joined Bournemouth from Portsmouth

ATCHESON, Paul (RL): with Wigan: winners Premiership

ATKINSON, Dalian (football): with Aston Villa: winners League Cup

ATKINSON, Ronald (football): with Aston Villa: winners League Cup

BABB, Philip (football): made Ireland debut v. Russia

BAKER, Peter (golf): European four-ball champ.

BARCLAY, Stephen (RU): with Swansea: Welsh League champs.

BARNES, David (football): joined Watford from Sheffield Utd

BARNES, David (Bobby) (football): joined Partick Thistle from Peterborough

BARNES, Stuart (RU): with Bath: winners Pilkington Cup, League champs.; England tour SA

BARRETT, Earl (football): with Aston Villa: winners League Cup

BATES, Jeremy (tennis): winner Korean Open

BATES, Steven (RU): England tour SA

BAYFIELD, Martin (RU): England tour SA

BEAGRIE, Peter (football): joined Manchester City from Everton

BETTS, Denis (RL): with Wigan: winners Challenge Cup, Premiership

BIGGINS, Wayne (football): joined Celtic 1993, Stoke City March 1994

BIRCH, Ryan (judo): GB U-78kg open champ.; European Champs. gold medal

BLACKMORE, Richard (RL): with Castleford: winners Regal Trophy

BLAKE, Mark (football): joined Leicester City from Portsmouth

BLUNDELL, Mark (F1): 3rd place Spanish GP

BOOBYER, Neil (RU): Wales tour Canada/S. Seas

BOONE, William (rackets): GB amateur doubles champ., open doubles champ

BOSNICH, Mark (football): with Aston Villa: winners League Cup

BOTICA, Frano (RL): with Wigan: winners Challenge Cup, Premiership

BOULD, Stephen (football): with Arsenal: winners European Cup Winners' Cup; made England debut v. Greece

BOWMAN, David (football): with Dundee Utd: winners Scottish Cup

BRADBURY, Julie (badminton): European Champs. ladies' doubles bronze medal

BREBANT, Rick (ice hockey): with Cardiff Devils: League champs., GB champs.

BREWSTER, Craig (football): with Dundee Utd: winners Scottish Cup

BROOME, David (equestrianism): announced retirement from int. competition

BRUCE, Stephen (football): with Manchester Utd: winners FA Cup, Premiership champs.

BRUNDLE, Martin (F1): joined McLaren and achieved 2nd place Monaco GP

BUCKETT, Ian (RU): with Swansea: Welsh League champs.; Wales tour Canada/S. Seas

BURNELL, Andrew Paul (RU): Scotland tour Argentina

BYRNE, John (football): joined Oxford Utd from Millwall

CALLARD, Jonathan (RU): with Bath: winners Pilkington Cup, Middx Sevens; England tour SA (replacement)

CAMPBELL, Kevin (football): with Arsenal: winners European Cup Winners' Cup

CANTONA, Eric (football): with Manchester Utd: winners FA Cup, Premiership champs.; PFA Player of the Year

CARLING, William (RU): England tour SA

CARSON, William (horseracing): winner Irish 1000 Guineas (Mehthaaf)

CAWTHORNE, Helen (triathlon): GB women's sprint champ.

CHAPPLE-HYAM, Peter (horse-racing): winner Irish 2000 Guineas (Turtle Island)

CHEN, Xinhua (table tennis): English champ.

CHINN, Nicky (ice hockey): with Cardiff Devils: League champs.

CHRISTENSEN, Jayne (ice dance): announced (re-)retirement from competition

CLARK, Gillian (badminton): European Champs. ladies' doubles bronze medal

CLARKE, Benjamin (RU): with Bath: winners Pilkington Cup; England tour SA

CLARKE, Philip (RL): with Wigan: winners Challenge Cup, Premiership

CLAXTON, Aileen (hockey): with Leicester: League champs., European Cup Winners' Cup bronze medallist

CLAYTON, Gary (football): joined Huddersfield Town from Cambridge Utd

CLELAND, Alec (football): with Dundee Utd: winners Scottish Cup

CLEMENT, Anthony (RU): with Swansea: Welsh League champs.; Wales tour Canada/S. Seas

COCKROFT, Timothy (rackets): GB amateur doubles champ., open doubles champ.

COLE, Andrew (football): PFA Young Player of the Year

COLEMAN, Christopher (foot-ball): with Crystal Palace: 1st Div. champs.

CONNOLLY, Gary (RL): with Wigan: winners Challenge Cup, Premiership

COOPER, Ian (ice hockey): with Cardiff Devils: League champs., GB champs.

COPE, Lucy (hockey): with Leicester: League champs., European Cup Winners' Cup bronze medallist

COPSEY, Anthony (RU): Wales tour Canada/S. Seas

COWANS, Gordon (football): joined Derby County from Aston Villa

COWIE, Neil (RL): with Wigan: winners Premiership

COX, Neil (football): with Aston Villa: winners League Cup

CROOKS, Lee (RL): with Castleford: winners Regal Trophy

DAILLY, Christian (football): with Dundee Utd: winners Scottish Cup

DALLAGLIO, Laurence (RU): England tour SA

DAVIES, Adrian (RU): with Cardiff: winners Welsh Cup; Wales tour Canada/S. Seas

DAVIES, John (RU): Wales tour Canada/S. Seas

DAVIES, Jonathan (RL): winner Man of Steel award

DAVIES, Laura (golf): LPGA champ.

DAVIES, Philip (RU): Wales tour Canada/S. Seas

DAVIES, Stuart (RU): with Swansea: Welsh League champs.

DAVIS, Paul (football): with Arsenal: winners European Cup Winners' Cup

DAVIS, Steve (snooker): winner Irish Masters

DAWE, Richard Graham (RU): with Bath: winners Pilkington Cup; England tour SA

DE GLANVILLE, Philip (RU): with Bath: winners Pilkington Cup; England tour SA

DEAN, Christopher (ice dance): announced (re-)retirement from competition

DERMOTT, Martin (RL): with Wigan: winners Challenge Cup

DIXON, Lee (football): with Arsenal: winners European Cup Winners' Cup

DODDS, William (football): joined St Johnstone from Dundee

DODS, Michael (RU): Scotland tour Argentina

DUNLOP, John (horseracing): winner Irish 1000 Guineas (Mehthaaf)

DUNWOODY, Thomas Richard (horseracing): winner Grand National (Miinnehoma)

DWYER, Mark (horseracing): winner Champion Hurdle (Flakey Dove)

EDWARDS, Shaun (RL): with Wigan: winners Challenge Cup, Premiership, League champs.

ELLIS, St John (RL): with Castleford: winners Regal Trophy

EVANS, Richard (RU): Wales tour Canada/S. Seas

FAIRBROTHER, Nicola (judo): European Champs. silver medal

FALCONER, William (football): joined Celtic from Sheffield Utd

FARRELL, Andrew (RL): with Wigan: winners Challenge Cup, Premiership

FERGUSON, Alexander (football): with Manchester Utd: winners FA Cup, Premiership champs.

FISHER, Allison (snooker): world women's champ.

FORD, Mike (RL): with Castleford: winners Regal Trophy

FORD, Stephen (RU): with Cardiff: winners Welsh Cup

FOSTER, Colin (football): joined Watford from W. Ham Utd

FULTON, David (cricket): maiden 1st-class 100 v. Cambridge Univ.

FURLONG, Paul (football): joined Chelsea from Watford

GARSIDE, Alexandra (real tennis): GB ladies' open champ.

GAYLE, Marcus (football): joined Wimbledon from Brentford

GEOGHEGAN, Simon (RU): Ireland tour Aus.

GIBBS, Ian Scott (RU): joined St Helens (RL)

GIGGS, Ryan (football): with Manchester Utd: winners FA Cup, Premiership champs.

GOLDING, Michael (yachting): established new record for east–west non-stop solo circum-navigation of the world (*Group 4 Securitas*)

GOODALL, Katherine (table tennis): English women's U-21 champ.

GOUGH, Darren (cricket): made England 1-day debut v NZ

GRAHAM, George (football): with Arsenal: winners European Cup Winners' Cup

GRIFFITHS, Michael (RU): with Cardiff: winners Welsh Cup

GRANT, Dalton (athletics): European Indoor Champs. gold medal

GUNNELL, Sally (athletics): UK women's 400m record-holder

HALL, Jonathan (RU): with Bath: winners Pilkington Cup

HALL, Julie (golf): English ladies' amateur champ.

HALL, Martin (RL): with Wigan: winners Premiership

HALL, Michael (RU): with Cardiff: winners Welsh Cup; Wales tour Canada/S. Seas

HALPIN, Garret (RU): Ireland tour Aus.

HARDY, Billy (boxing): won GB featherweight title

HATELEY, Mark (football): Scottish Football Writers' Assoc. Player of the Year

HAY, Andy (RL): with Castleford: winners Regal Trophy

HEATH, Martin (squash): European champs. team bronze medal

HIDE, Herbie (boxing): won WBO heavyweight title

HILL, Damon (F1): 2nd place Brazilian GP, winner Spanish GP

HILL, Richard (RU): with Bath: winners Pilkington Cup, League champs.; announced retirement

HILL, Robert (hockey): announced retirement

HOGG, Carl (RU): Scotland tour Argentina

HOLT, Andrea (table tennis): European Champs. team bronze medal

HOPLEY, Damian (RU): England tour SA

HUGHES, Mark (football): with Manchester Utd: winners FA Cup, Premiership champs.

HULL, Paul (RU): England tour SA

HUMPHREY, John (football): with Crystal Palace: 1st Div. champs.

HUNT, Christopher (badminton): European Champs. doubles gold medal

HURLOCK, Terence (football): joined Millwall from Southampton

HYSLOP, Christian (football): joined Colchester Utd from Southend

INCE, Paul (football): with Manchester Utd: winners FA Cup, Premiership champs.

IRWIN, Dennis (football): with Manchester Utd: winners FA Cup, Premiership champs.

JACKMAN, Cassandra (squash): European Champs. team gold medal

JACKSON, Colin (athletics): European Indoor Champs. 60m and 60m hurdles gold medals and world 60m hurdles indoor record

JARDINE, Ian (RU): Scotland tour Argentina

JENKINS, Garin (RU): with Swansea: Welsh League champs.

JENKINS, Neil (RU): Wales tour Canada/S. Seas

JOHNSON, Kathryn (hockey): with Leicester: League champs., European Cup Winners' Cup bronze medallist

JOHNSON, Martin (RU): England tour SA (aborted)

JONES, Robert (RU): with Swansea: Welsh League champs.

KANCHELSKIS, Andrei (football): with Manchester Utd: winners FA Cup, Premiership champs.

KEANE, Roy (football): with Manchester Utd: winners FA Cup, Premiership champs.

KELLY, Garry (football): made snr Ireland debut v. Russia

KENDALL, Howard (football; retiree): appointed manager Xanthia (Greece)

KETTERIDGE. Martin (RL): with Castleford: winners Regal Trophy

LANE, Barry (golf): winner Balearic Open

LASLETT, Jason (hockey): with Teddington: club champs., European Cup Winners' Cup bronze medallist

LAWRENCE, Lennie (football): appointed manager Bradford City

LE SAUX, Graeme (football): made England debut v. Denmark

LE TISSIER, Matthew (football): made England debut v. Denmark

LEE, Jason (football): joined Nottingham Forest from Southend Utd

LEEVES, Donia (squash): European girls' champ.

LEONARD, Jason (RU): England tour SA

LEWIS, Emyr (RU): Wales tour Canada/S. Seas

LIMPAR, Anders (football): joined Everton from Arsenal

LISTER, Sandra (hockey): with Ipswich: European Cup bronze medallist

LLEWELLYN, Gareth (RU): Wales tour Canada/S. Seas

LOGAN, Kenneth (RU): Scotland tour Argentina

LOWE, Kenneth (football): joined Birmingham City from Stoke City

McATEER, Jason (football): made Ireland debut v. Russia

McBRYDE, Robin (RU): with Swansea: Welsh League champs.; Wales tour Canada/S. Seas

McCLAIR, Brian (football): with Manchester Utd: winners FA Cup, Premiership champs.

McEWEN, Doug (ice hockey): with Cardiff Devils: League champs., GB champs.

McGINTY, William (RL): joined Workington Town from Wigan

McGIVEN, Michael (football): appointed football development manager of Ipswich Town

McGOLDRICK, Edward (football): with Arsenal: winners European Cup Winners' Cup

McGRATH, Paul (football): with Aston Villa: winners League Cup

McGUIRE, Bruce (RL): joined Warrington from Sheffield Eagles

McINALLY, James (football): with Dundee Utd: winners Scottish Cup

McIVOR, David (RU): Scotland tour Argentina

McLAREN, Andrew (football): with Dundee Utd: winners Scottish Cup

McMINN, Kevin (Ted) (football): joined Burnley from Birmingham City

McMURRUGH, Michael (real tennis): GB over-40, over-50 amateur doubles champ.

MAGUIRE, Gavin (football): joined Millwall from Portsmouth

MALONEY, Francis (RL): joined Warrington from Featherstone Rovers

MALPAS, Maurice (football): with Dundee Utd: winners Scottish Cup

MANN, George (RL): joined Leeds from St Helens

MARTYN, Nigel (football): with Crystal Palace: 1st Div. champs.

MATHER, Barrie-Jon (RL): with Wigan: winners Challenge Cup

MAY, David (football): joined Manchester Utd from Blackburn Rovers

MERSON, Paul (football): with Arsenal: winners European Cup Winners's Cup

MIDDLETON, Simon (RL): with Castleford: winners Regal Trophy

MILLEN, Keith (football): joined Watford from Brentford

MINTO, Scott (football): joined Chelsea from Charlton Athletic

MONTGOMERIE, Colin (golf): winner Spanish Open

MOODY, Paul (football): joined Oxford Utd from Southampton

MOON, Rupert (RU): Wales tour Canada/S. Seas

MOORE, Brian (RU): England tour SA

MORGAN, Kevin (RU): joined Northampton from Bristol

MORRIS, Colin Dewi (RU): England tour SA

MORRISON, Anthony (RL): with Castleford: winners Regal Trophy

MORROW, Stephen (football): with Arsenal: winners European Cup Winners' Cup

MUNRO, Donald Shade (RU): Scotland tour Argentina

MUSTOE, Lyndon (RU): with Cardiff: winners Welsh Cup

NICHOLSON, David (horseracing): saddled 1000th winner (Ramstar) at Southwell

NICOL, Andrew (RU): joined Bath from Dundee High School FP

NICOL, Peter (squash): European Champs. team bronze medal

NIKAU, Tawera (RL): with Castleford: winners Regal Trophy

O'SULLIVAN, Ronnie (snooker): winner Brit. Open

OBREE, Douglas Graeme (cycling): regained world 1-hour unpaced record

OJOMOH, Stephen (RU): with Bath: winners Pilkington Cup; England tour SA

OPIE, Lisa (squash): announced retirement

PALLISTER, Gary (football): with Manchester Utd: winners FA Cup, Premiership champs.

PANAPA, Sam (RL): with Wigan: winners Challenge Cup, Premiership; joined Salford

PARISH, Matthew (rowing): Cambridge crew, winners Univ. Boat Race

PARKER, Paul (football): with Manchester Utd: winners FA Cup, Premiership champs.

PEACOCK, Darren (football): joined Newcastle Utd from Queens Park Rangers

PEARS, David (RU): England tour SA (aborted)

PEREGO, Mark (RU): Wales tour Canada/S. Seas

PERRETT, Mark (RL): made Wales debut v. France

PERRY, Jason (football): made Wales debut v. Norway

PHILLISKIRK, Anthony (football): joined Burnley from Peterborough

PIPE, Martin (horseracing): winner Grand National (Miinnehoma)

PLATT, David (football): appointed England captain

PONTING, Nicholas (badminton): All England mixed doubles champ.

POTTER, Stuart (RU): England tour SA

POWER, Lee (football): joined Bradford City from Norwich City

PRICE, John (bowls): Welsh singles and fours champ. (indoor); GB pairs champ. (indoor)

PRICE, Mary (bowls): English women's singles champ. (indoor); GB women's pairs champ. (indoor)

PROCTOR, Wayne (RU): Wales tour Canada/S. Seas

QUINNELL, Scott (RU): Wales tour Canada/S. Seas

RADCLIFFE, Paula (athletics): English women's cross-country champ.

RAYER, Michael (RU): with Cardiff: winners Welsh Cup; Wales tour Canada/S. Seas

REDMAN, Nigel (RU): with Bath: winners Pilkington Cup, League champs.; England tour SA

REDPATH, Bryan (RU): made snr Scotland debut v. NZ 1993

REED, Andrew (RU): with Bath: winners Pilkington Cup; Scotland tour Argentina (capt.)

REID, John (horseracing): winner 1000 Guineas (Las Meninas), Irish 2000 Guineas (Turtle Island)

RICHARDS, Dean (RU): England tour SA

RICHARDSON, Kevin (football): with Aston Villa: winners League Cup; made England debut v. Greece

ROBINSON, Jason (RL): with Wigan: winners Premiership

ROBSON, Bryan (football): made last full appearance for Manchester Utd (340th) v. Coventry City; appointed player/manager Middlesbrough

RODBER, Timothy (RU): England tour SA

RODGER, Simon (football): with Crystal Palace: 1st Div. champs.

ROWNTREE, Graham (RU): England tour SA

RUSSELL, Richard (RL): with Castleford: winners Regal Trophy

RYAN, Dean (RU): England tour SA

SALAKO, John (football): with Crystal Palace: 1st Div. champs.

SAMPSON, Dean (RL): with Castleford: winners Regal Trophy

SANCHEZ, Lawrence (football): joined Swindon Town from Wimbledon

SAUNDERS, Dean (football): with Aston Villa: winners League Cup

SAXELBY, Mark (cricket): joined Durham; maiden 1st-class 100 v. Derbys.

SCHMEICHEL, Peter (football): with Manchester Utd: winners FA Cup, Premiership champs.

SEAMAN, David (football): with Arsenal: winners European Cup Winners' Cup

SHARP, Alan (RU): Scotland tour Argentina

SHARPE, Lee (football): with Manchester Utd: winners FA Cup, Premiership champs.

SHEARER, Alan (football): Football Writers' Assoc. Player of the Year

SHEARER, Duncan (football): made Scotland debut v. Austria (sub.)

SHEPHERD, Rowen (RU): Scotland tour Argentina

SHIEL, Andrew Graham (RU): Scotland tour Argentina

SKERRETT, Kelvin (RL): with Wigan: winners Challenge Cup, Premiership

SKLENAR, Jason (biathlon): GB champ.

SLAVEN, Bernard (football): joined Port Vale 1993, Darlington 1994

SMALES, Ian (RL): with Castleford: winners Regal Trophy

SMITH, Alan (football): with Arsenal: winners European Cup Winners' Cup

SMITH, David (football): joined W. Bromwich Albion from Birmingham City

SMITH, Gary (bowls): English pairs champ. (indoor)

SMITH, Ian (RU): Scotland tour Argentina

SOUTHGATE, Gareth (football): with Crystal Palace: 1st Div. champs.

STAPLES, James (RU): Ireland tour Aus.

STAUNTON, Stephen (football): with Aston Villa: winners League Cup

STEADMAN, Graham (RL): with Castleford: winners Regal Trophy

STEELE, Timothy (football): joined Hereford Utd from Bradford City

SWAN, Charles (horseracing): winner Whitbread Gold Cup (Ushers Island)

TANNER, Nicholas (football): announced retirement

TAYLOR, Graham (football; retiree): appointed manager Wolverhampton Wanderers

TEALE, Shaun (football): with Aston Villa: winners League Cup

THOMAS, Neil (gymnastics): World Champs. floor silver medal

THOMSON, Andrew (bowls): World Indoor Champs. singles gold medal; winner Mazda Jack High singles

TORVILL, Jayne see CHRISTENSEN, Jayne

TOSHACK, John (football): resigned as technical director Wales

TOWNSEND, Andrew (football): with Aston Villa: winners League Cup

TOWNSEND, Gregor (RU): Scotland tour Argentina

TURNER, Graham (football): resigned as manager Wolverhampton Wanderers

TURNER, Philip (football): joined Exeter from Notts County

UBOGU, Victor (RU): with Bath: winners Pilkington Cup, League champs.; England tour SA

UDAL, Shaun (cricket): made England 1-day debut v. NZ

UNDERWOOD, Rory (RU): England tour SA

UNDERWOOD, Tony (RU): England tour SA

WAINWRIGHT, Robert (RU): joining W. Hartlepool from Edinburgh Academicals

WALKER, Nigel (RU): with Cardiff: winners Welsh Cup

WALSH, Paul (football): joined Manchester City from Portsmouth

WALTON, Peter (RU): Scotland tour Argentina

WARK, John (football): appointed player/coach Ipswich Town

WATT, Alan (RU): Scotland tour Argentina

WEBSTER, Richard (RL): made Wales debut v. France

WELSH, Brian (football): with Dundee Utd: winners Scottish Cup

WHITTON, Stephen (football): joined Colchester Utd from Ipswich Town

WILKINS, Raymond (football): joined Crystal Palace from Queens Park Rangers as player/coach

WILLIAMS, Owain (RU): with Cardiff: winners Welsh Cup

WILLIAMS, Steven (RU): Wales tour Canada/S. Seas

WILLIAMS-JONES, Hugh (RU): Wales tour Canada/S. Seas

WINTERBURN, Nigel (football): with Arsenal: winners European Cup Winners' Cup

WOOSNAM, Ian (golf): winner Cannes Open

WYLLIE, Douglas (RU): Scotland tour Argentina

YOUNG, Eric (football): with Crystal Palace: 1st Div. champs.